646.79
Fm930

WHERE TO RETIRE IN
FLORIDA

Edited by Karen Northridge, Elizabeth Armstrong and Alan Fox

Art Direction and Cover Design: Fred W. Salzmann

Editorial Assistants: Trisha Haugh, Susan Maloney and Sara Melton

Back cover photo by Dean Chavis

Publisher's Note: This book contains information from many sources. Every effort has been made to verify the accuracy and authenticity of the information contained in this book. Although care and diligence have been used in preparation and review, the material is subject to change. It is published for general reference and not as a substitute for independent verification by readers. The publisher does not guarantee the accuracy of the information.

Published by Vacation Publications, Inc.
1502 Augusta Drive, Suite 415
Houston, TX 77057

Library of Congress Catalog Card Number: 98-61539
ISBN 0-9644216-6-6

Printed in the United States of America

VACATION
PUBLICATIONS

For Amy and Terry

ACKNOWLEDGEMENTS

We gratefully acknowledge the contributions of countless chamber of commerce executives and staff members, the staffs of county property appraisers, hospital personnel, information officers of police, sheriffs' and fire departments, senior center staff and members, and retirees. We acknowledge and thank George Gaston, Wanda Coley, Sherry Stein, Josette Butera, John Lee, Linda Thompson, Douglas Mann, Mayme S. Burdin, Christie Holliday, Art & Gracie Morgan, Mike Arts, Rosie Piliego, Dorothy Pencar, Robert Couch, Doris Pastl, Robert Bartz, James Daigle, Hal Robinson, Peter Woodham, Mary Ann Robinson, Stephen Tirey, Joe & Ruby Hydrick, Bob & Betty Schrader, Howard & Louise Stockton, Sue Munsey, Sandy Cugno, Lucille Shulklapper, Fred Willis, Ron Robison, Sheree Monroe, Art & Becky Fleming, Paul & Estelle DeGuardi, Phyllis Smith, Harriet Colucci, George Mirabal, George & Carol Craig, Jack & Grace Lake, Donna DeFronzo, Jendia Blake-Goodwin, Paul & Ginny Cate, Diane Pickett, Dal Ritchey, Vic & Muriel Laumark, Al & Jean Reeves, Norman & Kay Laws, William Wood, Kathy Aguirre, Ray Navitsky, Jim & Patsy Bagdanov, Bill & Nancy Maxson, Marshall & Annie Laurie Barton, Patricia McGarr, Linda Rust, Richard Clark, Francine Mason, Sam & Lois Ginsberg, Jack & Debby Smookler, Bill & Margaret Bauman, Marietta Mudgett, D.J. Petruccelli, Bruce Abernethy, Lorraine Antony, Roger Peters, Robert Douglass Jr., Cory Adler, Luis A. Gomez-Dominguez, Arthur Neville, Nicki Grossman, Laverne Roth, Kitty Barnes, Monique Bowen, Nicholas & Carmen Colantino, Wayne & Joyce Beck, Walter Lee III, John Meserve, Alice Klimas, Johanne Plourde, Bob & Katie Miller, Clarke & Dolly Egeler, Jane Yarnell, Gloria Chapman, Susan Krupnick-Gregorie, Ginna Thomas, Ray & Lucille Warner, Virginia Panico, Bob & Flo Cornell, Rogers & Betty Hamel, Les Haskem, Delbert & Ethel Brightman, Joan Cavanagh, Jim Poole, Kathleen Sperry, Steven Scruggs, Linda Adey, William & Doreen Redman, Vicki Yawnick, Mary Heaston, Doug Hart, Philip Lovelett, Edwin McCook, Betty Wortham, Dick & Sandy Pascoe, Hal & Virginia Palmer, Robert Neiman, Ross Thomson, Mr. & Mrs. Ken Kaatz, Judith Nadeau-McConnel, Kellie Smith, Larry Malta, Susan Berry, Charles & Mary Malta, Carolyn Karpel, Bruce Singer, Yvonne Lee, Dick Pinkerton, Jack & Sally Daniels, Bill & Eleanore Johnson, Richard & Patricia Myren, Edward Oates Jr., Conrad Fox, Joe Librandi, Steve Dennis, Carol Miller, Sarah Branan, Thomas Knapko, Pat & Ruth Sherman, Paul & Shirley Reitmeier, Jack Peake, Kathy Saxon, Jacob Stuart, Frank Billingsley, John Connors, Bill & Brenda Dougherty, John & Nancy Goss, Ed & Mary Panny, Jerome Schuler, Connie Davis, Frank Bacen Jr., Debi Parish, Bertie Reynolds, John Griffing, Ed & Gloria Maddock, Bill & Carol Ross, Jim & Janet Hess, Cherry Goodman, Norman & Gilda Gutlove, Brad Shamburger, Jack & Ann Gaddy, Tedd & Beverly Lincoln, Sally McConnell, Mr. & Mrs. Raymond Farr, Laila Haddad, Susan Evans, Marcus Johnson, Dom & Connie Ierfino, Clyde & Mary Ann Eckhart, Les Hargrave, David Farr, Ken Meeker, David May, James Burke, Ron & Gwenne Heiser, Ed & Carol Cheek, Michael Lee, Diane Spencer, Bob & June Wood, Don & Jan Metzler, Jerry & Kathy Groom, Susan McCranie, Norman & Jane Baker, Bob & Louise Ebbinghaus, Ron & Dot Firster, Paul Getting, Penny Mathes, Joseph Catrambone, Amber Ferris, Bob & Mary Alice Carroll, Jim Waters, Chris Ward, Jim Ashlock, Susanna Patterson, Harvey Schmitt, Carolyn Curtis, Charles Phillips, Susan Martin, John Hobbs, JoAnne Richards, Ellen Chmaj, JoAnne Worthington, J.B. Norton Jr., Lori Burns, Howard & Joyce Brand, George & Jean Armstrong, Herman "Reck" & Judith Niebuhr, Ron Lilly, Patricia Smith, Joyce Davis, Bob & Lillie Price, John & Barbara Riegler, John & Catherine Petre, Don Dalton, Joe & Pat Terranova, Bruce Coxe, Kenneth & Gwen Howell, Chet & Glendine Hamilton, Susan Burgess, Don & Aledia Sloan, Tom & Elizabeth Fisher, Mary Ann Robinson, Norman & Marie Phillips, Jim Hunsanger, Jim & Marion McGuffey, Harold & Pat Manning, Tony & Karen Vaina, John & Betty Moody, Larry & Gay McCarthy, Barney & Jan Rac, Bob & Eileen Dowling, Ivan & Ann Johns, Jim Lee, Deb Kaplan, Frank Topping & Christine Heaton, Charlie & Liz Clayton.

There were several chamber directors who worked overtime on short notice to arrange interviews with retirees. One special note of thanks to retired Col. Wendell Taylor, former executive director of the chamber of commerce in Marianna, who stayed at his post long after closing time one Friday evening to tout his town as a retirement haven.

Our thanks also to a myriad of helpful realtors, with a special note of gratitude to Key West's Victoria Taylor. Real estate agents answered our questions, helped us check and recheck prices and offered insightful tours of their towns.

Thanks to Louise Engle, senior management analyst in the office of Volunteer and Community Services of the Florida Department of Elder Affairs for providing information on the licensed continuing-care facilities, senior centers and state agencies available to assist in relocation and quality of life enhancement for older residents.

We would be remiss if we did not recognize the civic leaders of Pensacola, who understand that the important contributions retirees make to the economic stability and talent pool of any community far outweigh the cost of recruitment.

C O N T E N T S

C O N T E N T S

INTRODUCTION

RESEARCH — ON THE ROAD

While travelogues have no doubt been made without the producer having stepped foot on the subject soil, that is not how this book came into being. From the very first discussion of *Where to Retire in Florida*, we began to think about travel arrangements, reservations, appointments, interviews and activities that would bring us in contact with retirees where they live and play throughout the state. It was our goal to find the places best suited to retiree living — from the retiree's perspective.

Initial preparations included a questionnaire to chamber of commerce offices in more than 100 Florida towns and cities seeking information on retiree programs and services, residential communities, recreational facilities and amenities, and the names of retired couples we could interview while in the area. Some offices ignored the requests, exhibiting the same disdain with which they treat resident retirees. But most respondents were cooperative. In a few exceptional cases, they followed up with an offer to assist us in any way possible, demonstrating an understanding that migrating retirees bring a lot more to the table than they will ever take away.

Armed with camera, recorder, open minds and a flexible itinerary, we departed on the first of several monthlong sojourns. We looked deeply into 125 communities, from which we selected 99 to profile. After starting in the Keys, we traveled from Biscayne Bay all the way to Amelia Island on the east coast, from Pensacola to Marco Island on the gulf, through the large and small towns of the Panhandle and into the lake country of central and south-central Florida. This is a state with a thousand small hamlets, villages and towns. We have included all of the most popular retirement towns of past and present and have added a great many lesser known or as yet undiscovered possibilities. Several of the unfamiliar towns are among our personal favorites.

In our travels, we talked to chamber of commerce directors and staffs, senior center directors and members, newspaper editors, waiters and waitresses, merchants and shoppers, property appraisers and tax collectors, fire and police chiefs, realtors and developers, and retirees. In each town, we availed ourselves of all written material apropos of retirement. Only once, in Hialeah, were we unable to read the material. It was in Spanish. We obtained telephone books with yellow pages, local newspapers and other publications. These alone give any researcher a great head start on getting to know and understand a place.

While in town we visited residential developments and adult retirement communities. We spent time in senior centers and other facilities popular with retirees, asking questions and working to gain a sense of what life would be like as a resident. We stopped by hospitals, medical centers, colleges and universities. We noted the availability and convenience of shopping centers and malls, supermarkets, restaurants, theaters, galleries, auditoriums and other social and cultural amenities. We took a good look at the diversity and accessibility of recreational facilities, including golf courses, tennis courts, boating and fishing waters, equestrian centers and local, state and national parks and forests.

We had more than ample opportunity to measure traffic volumes and sources of congestion, especially on streets and roads frequented by retirees.

Recognizing that retirees want to feel — and be — safe and secure, we obtained statistical and comparative information on incidence of crime in Florida cities and towns from the Florida Department of Law Enforcement. On the local level, we talked to police and fire safety personnel to determine the commitment of human resources to public safety and crime control.

We made a point of interviewing only retirees who had relocated to Florida from another state. This allowed us to see Florida through the eyes of "outsiders." It came as no surprise that most retirees we interviewed were more than satisfied with their new homes. They were, after all, handpicked by chamber of commerce officials or other local organizations and tended to be active and civic-minded individuals. It was rare to find anyone to confess that the decision to retire to Florida, or the choice of a community, was a mistake.

But mistakes are made in the retirement relocation process. Some poorly planned moves fail altogether, and the retirees move to another new locale or return to their original hometown. Even some of those we interviewed had moved to Florida and later relocated within the state. Personal experiences with crime and violence, unexpected highway construction or neighborhood changes caused them to seek a safer, more tranquil environment. From these twice-relocated retirees it became clear that it is important to review long-range construction plans of the planning board and department of transportation before selecting a retirement site.

We heard over and over from retirees that it was easy to make friends because so many people were from out of state. Those who had experienced the process of moving in retirement just naturally reached out to newcomers and welcomed them to the fellowship. "We're all in the same boat," was an oft-used phrase. It's a good analogy in a peninsular state, crisscrossed with rivers and canals and dotted with lakes.

But if relocated retirees are all in the same boat once they arrive, they didn't come via the same route or on the same timetable. When we asked retirees to tell us how many times they had visited their new hometown before moving, we heard:

"We visited friends one time and bought on the next trip."

"We traveled all over Florida for eight months in a fifth-wheel."

"We visited every summer for 30 years."

"Three times over 30 years."

"Every year at Christmas for 18 years."

"We came on Tuesday, signed a contract on Friday."

As these responses indicate, there is no standard process for locating a retirement dream home. Florida has the depth, breadth and diversity to appeal to many appetites — but on-the-road research is time-consuming and expensive. Hopefully this book will help you narrow the choices and make the most of your visits to the towns that interest you.

Happy reading and happy hunting. Write to tell us where you settle.

COST OF LIVING

Any relocation means a change in the way you live and therefore a change in how you allocate and spend your money. You might be able to anticipate some of the differences, but others may come as a big surprise. When you move to Florida you may look forward to the joys of reduced heating bills. Don't forget you will likely encounter increased cooling bills as well. In the end you'll probably find that most changes in your living expenses cannot be compared directly — they involve trade-offs.

Nationally, the price index most widely used to compare living costs among cities is produced by ACCRA, a research group. Unfortunately, this index only includes a few Florida cities. We chose, instead, the Florida Price Level Index, produced by the Florida Department of Education's Office of Education Budget and Management.

The Florida Price Level Index measures cost differences from county to county within the state. We've used the most recent index, taken in 1997, to illustrate the relative cost of each of the counties of our 99 profiled towns. It covers a variety of goods and services in five major categories: food; housing; transportation; apparel; and health, recreation and personal services.

The index is based on a Florida average of 100.

Our 99 profiled cities and towns are located in 42 of Florida's 67 counties. Of these, there are nine counties above the Florida average cost of living: Monroe, Dade, Palm Beach, Broward, Collier, Pinellas, Orange, Sarasota and Martin. Monroe County, where the Florida Keys are located, is the most expensive county. Its index of 110.47 means that the cost of living there is 10.47 percent higher than the statewide average.

There are two counties with an average cost of living — Manatee and Indian River — and 31 counties listed with a cost of living below the Florida average. DeSoto County, with an index of 91.65, is the least expensive Florida county containing a profiled city. Arcadia is in DeSoto County.

In the chart on page 10, we list all cities profiled, from least expensive to most expensive, along with the county, county index and county rank among all Florida counties. A ranking of 1 denotes the most expensive county.

HE SAID/SHE SAID

Finding consistent and comparable information on each city was one of our goals. Wherever possible we give statistical data that allows you to compare prices, temperatures, population size, etc. From that information, you can judge if the town is affordable, climatically suitable and about the right size.

However, it is not possible to remove the subjective from all evaluative information. Scenic beauty and quality of life mean different things to different people. No two persons react alike to the sights, sounds, smells and indeed the total sensory experience associated with a visit to a new place.

When planning this book, we faced the issue of how to most accurately reflect our overall reaction to each town. Rather than provide a watered-down, compromised version of our impressions, we've given you two opinions — with no punches pulled. We tell you upfront our individual perspectives, how each of us views the town, in the HE SAID/SHE SAID summaries. It goes without saying that these remarks are not intended to substitute for a careful review of the profiled materials. They represent a sound-bite summarization of our personal views of each town's worthiness for retirement living.

Predictably, we didn't always see eye to eye. Agreements and disagreements are an important part of the process of searching for your ideal retirement locale. We found that we don't necessarily look for the same things in a town. Often we liked the same place for completely different reasons. We repeatedly heard the same thing from retired couples we interviewed. They told us that their choice of retirement location was favored by one spouse more than the other. Or that one spouse made a much easier adjustment to the new hometown. Those individuals who each expressed enjoyment and contentment in their new surroundings often found completely separate sources of interest. We've given you our responses based on our own likes and dislikes, needs and desires for a well-rounded lifestyle.

RATINGS

It would have been easy to find the one and only place to retire in Florida based on statistically measurable factors. Such a rating would have pinpointed a spot on the map that offers the best combination of per capita hospital beds, tennis courts and golf holes, plus the lowest property taxes, housing costs and overall cost of living. But that would have left out the flora and fauna, the sunrises and sunsets, and all the other intangibles that help paint a total picture of quality of life.

We wanted to express what we saw, read, heard and felt as well as those things that could be measured. We wanted to capture the form and essence of each locale in the ratings. The star ratings are our individual opinions based on everything we encountered throughout Florida. Every town is rated from one to five stars, with five stars being the best.

As we assigned ratings, we wrestled with all sorts of questions about what makes a city livable. Particularly difficult was the task of rating some of the extraordinary cities and towns of southeast Florida, which seem to offer the best and worst of urban living. Places that have more people, more crime, more traffic and a higher cost of living also tend to have more cultural amenities, more health-care providers, more colleges and more recreational facilities.

Coral Gables is an example of a five-star city in a one-star environment. Taken out of the Metro-Dade area, it would certainly top our list. But crime, traffic and the general congestion of everything outside the Coral Gables city limits reduced its livability in our estimation. We recognize that some people prefer urban settings. For you, Coral Gables or other metropolitan areas may provide a delightful-

COST OF LIVING — FLORIDA PRICE LEVEL INDEX

Cities Profiled	County	FPLI	Rank	Cities Profiled	County	FPLI	Rank
Arcadia	DeSoto	91.65	64	Englewood (part)	Charlotte	97.74	15
Marianna	Jackson	91.76	62	Port Charlotte	Charlotte	97.74	15
Lake City	Columbia	92.26	58	Punta Gorda	Charlotte	97.74	15
DeFuniak Springs	Walton	92.41	55	Jacksonville	Duval	97.98	14
Live Oak	Suwannee	92.64	53	Altamonte Springs	Seminole	98.38	13
Crystal River	Citrus	92.66	52	Sanford	Seminole	98.38	13
Homosassa Springs	Citrus	92.66	52	Winter Springs	Seminole	98.38	13
Inverness	Citrus	92.66	52	Brandon	Hillsborough	99.21	12
Dade City	Pasco	93.13	48	Sun City Center	Hillsborough	99.21	12
New Port Richey	Pasco	93.13	48	Tampa	Hillsborough	99.21	12
Zephyrhills	Pasco	93.13	48	Vero Beach	Indian River	100.05	11
Ocala	Marion	93.15	47	Bradenton	Manatee	100.29	10
Perry	Taylor	93.57	39	Longboat Key (part)	Manatee	100.29	10
Sebring	Highlands	93.67	38	Stuart	Martin	101.22	9
Amelia Island/Fernandina Beach	Nassau	93.69	37	Englewood(part)	Sarasota	101.26	8
Clermont	Lake	94.21	35	Longboat Key (part)	Sarasota	101.26	8
Leesburg	Lake	94.21	35	Sarasota	Sarasota	101.26	8
Mount Dora	Lake	94.21	35	Siesta Key	Sarasota	101.26	8
The Villages	Lake	94.21	35	Venice	Sarasota	101.26	8
Pensacola	Escambia	94.86	34	Orlando	Orange	101.88	7
Brooksville	Hernando	95.04	32	Winter Garden	Orange	101.88	7
Panama City	Bay	95.39	30	Winter Park	Orange	101.88	7
Apalachicola	Franklin	95.52	29	Clearwater	Pinellas	101.91	6
Bartow	Polk	95.64	27	Dunedin	Pinellas	101.91	6
Lakeland	Polk	95.64	27	Largo	Pinellas	101.91	6
Lake Wales	Polk	95.64	27	Palm Harbor	Pinellas	101.91	6
Winter Haven	Polk	95.64	27	St. Petersburg	Pinellas	101.91	6
Gainesville	Alachua	95.72	26	St. Petersburg Beach	Pinellas	101.91	6
Kissimmee	Osceola	95.77	25	Tarpon Springs	Pinellas	101.91	6
Tallahassee	Leon	96.18	24	Marco Island	Collier	102.25	5
Palm Coast	Flagler	96.25	23	Naples	Collier	102.25	5
Daytona Beach	Volusia	96.38	21	Coral Springs	Broward	103.42	4
DeLand	Volusia	96.38	21	Deerfield Beach	Broward	103.42	4
New Smyrna Beach	Volusia	96.38	21	Fort Lauderdale	Broward	103.42	4
Ormond Beach	Volusia	96.38	21	Hollywood	Broward	103.42	4
Destin	Okaloosa	96.38	21	Pompano Beach	Broward	103.42	4
Fort Walton Beach	Okaloosa	96.38	21	Boca Raton	Palm Beach	103.45	3
St. Augustine	St. Johns	96.92	19	Boynton Beach	Palm Beach	103.45	3
Bonita Springs	Lee	97.15	18	Delray Beach	Palm Beach	103.45	3
Cape Coral	Lee	97.15	18	Jupiter & Tequesta	Palm Beach	103.45	3
Fort Myers	Lee	97.15	18	Lake Worth	Palm Beach	103.45	3
Fort Myers Beach	Lee	97.15	18	West Palm Beach	Palm Beach	103.45	3
North Fort Myers Beach	Lee	97.15	18	Coral Gables	Dade	107.23	2
Pine Island	Lee	97.15	18	Hialeah	Dade	107.23	2
Sanibel-Captiva	Lee	97.15	18	Key Biscayne	Dade	107.23	2
Fort Pierce	St. Lucie	97.36	17	Miami Beach	Dade	107.23	2
Port St. Lucie	St. Lucie	97.36	17	Big Pine Key	Monroe	110.47	1
Cocoa Beach	Brevard	97.65	16	Key Largo	Monroe	110.47	1
Melbourne	Brevard	97.65	16	Key West	Monroe	110.47	1
Palm Bay	Brevard	97.65	16	Marathon	Monroe	110.47	1
Titusville	Brevard	97.65	16				

ly fulfilling lifestyle.

Additionally, the urban centers of southeast Florida have more cultural, racial and ethnic diversity than many less developed areas. In southeast Florida there are well-established enclaves of Cubans, Haitians, South Americans and Central Americans. Wandering the streets of Hialeah we found it easy to imagine we had been transported out of the United States to enjoy the sights, sounds and fragrances of one of our Latin neighbors. Quirky Key West has its own unique mix of Caribbean, Latin and American influences.

The ratings are consistent with our commitment to honesty and fairness about everything we saw, read, felt and encountered. We didn't always reach consensus. But the profiles should contain enough information for you to determine the extent to which each town measures up to your dreams and expectations, so you can affix your own star ratings. Those that we both rated as five-star towns are marked with this symbol so you'll be able to spot them easily. The following list shows our personal picks.

Florida's Five-Star Retirement Towns

He Said		She Said
✔	Boca Raton	✔
✔	Dade City	✔
✔	Longboat Key	✔
✔	Mount Dora	✔
✔	Sarasota	✔
✔	Sun City Center	✔
✔	Venice	✔
	Bradenton	✔
	Coral Springs	✔
✔	Fort Myers	
✔	Gainesville	
	Jupiter & Tequesta	✔
✔	Lakeland	
✔	Naples	
	Ormond Beach	✔
✔	Pensacola	
✔	Sanibel-Captiva Islands	
	Siesta Key	✔
	Tallahassee	✔
✔	Vero Beach	
	Winter Park	✔

WEATHER

The statistical weather information included in each profile is taken from reports of the National Oceanic and Atmospheric Administration. There are 97 weather stations in Florida which have been tracking weather information for more than 30 years. Using data from the weather station closest to each town, we show the normal average daily high and low temperatures in degrees Fahrenheit and the normal average precipitation.

Beyond the statistics, on the subject of Florida's weather, there are as many opinions as there are retirees. We found disagreement from person to person, city to city and region to region.

We posed the question to two locals we met on a golf course in Key West. One said that summers there were ideal, weatherwise, never getting too warm for comfort. The other explained that he spends his summers in New England to escape the unbearable heat and humidity.

Some retirees explained their adjustment to Florida's summertime heat in terms of the aging body's presumed physiological need for warmer temperatures. Others told us that some individuals seemed to acclimatize more quickly than others.

Irrespective of these sentiments, it is our shared opinion that neither tradewinds, offshore breezes, nor the shade of the old oak tree can produce a comfortable outdoor summer environment, no matter where you are in Florida. This is an opinion shared by thousands of retired Floridians who regularly spend their summers in the elevated environs of western North Carolina or another cool spot.

On the other hand, the wonderfully mild Florida winter was most often mentioned to us as the strongest magnet drawing retirees to the state — outranking all other reasons 10 to one.

Winter temperatures are significantly impacted by location in the state. As far south as Orlando, citrus growers have lost entire orchards to deep freezes. But unlike Buffalo and Minneapolis, where hard freezes last for weeks and even months, there are spots like Crystal River or Mount Dora where a rare, 25-degree reading at 5 a.m. may give way to a 70-degree temperature by noon.

For many retirees, winter's gray, overcast skies bring on deep depression. To these retirees the clear skies that most often accompany winter's lower temperatures in Florida may be of greater import than the temperature itself. Residents everywhere were quick to tell us that cloudy conditions rarely last more than a day during the winter.

Hurricanes are generally associated with Florida's weather patterns, but most Florida residents are only peripherally affected by the winds and heavy rains these storms produce. More retirees cite the frequency and severity of summer thunderstorms as the most bothersome weather phenomenon. In fact, the National Weather Service Bureau in Miami notes that Florida leads the nation in deaths by lightning.

There also are financial factors to consider. Heavy rains, possible flooding and high winds are common and can have an impact on the condition of your home, neighborhood and ability to get around town. Along some portions of the coastline, erosion is, or can become, a problem. Before purchasing property, you can contact the National Flood Insurance Program, P.O. Box 6468, Rockville, MD 20849-6468, (800) 427-5583, to order flood insurance rate maps. The maps are available by city, town and county and cost $5 for 10 maps, plus $2.50 for shipping and handling. The maps indicate flood hazard boundaries and can help you determine whether you could be hit with extra property-owners insurance costs or if you should consider purchasing flood insurance to protect your investment.

The bottom-line on Florida's weather is simply this: If you plan to live in your home year-round, visit during each season of the year to know what you are getting into. Florida is almost guaranteed to offer a better winter than the weather you leave behind. And on those few days each year when the weather keeps you indoors, it becomes a good topic of conversation.

TAXES

Many retirees are initially delighted when they learn that Florida has no state or local income tax. But that is not to say the state is tax-free. Florida collects an intangibles tax, estate tax and sales tax. It is noteworthy for property owners that the burden of financing the public school systems is shifted from the state to local governments, which generally pay the school district bills with revenues from property tax assessments.

Each profile notes the local sales tax, which includes the state sales tax of 6 percent and any additional tax added by local governments. Prescription drugs, groceries and medical services are exempt from sales tax.

We've included the 1997 property tax rates as provided by the county property appraisers' offices. New property tax rates are proposed at the end of August each year but are retroactive for the entire calendar year.

Homes are assessed at 100 percent of market value, less exemptions. Florida allows permanent residents a $25,000 homestead exemption off the assessed value of their home. It is available to all homeowners if the home (1) was purchased before December 15, (2) became the permanent residence before January 1 of the previous tax year, (3) is not rented out and (4) is not claimed under any other exemption. Homestead exemptions can be filed during the months of January and February at the county property appraiser's office. The state also allows a $500 widow's or widower's exemption.

Florida expresses its property tax rates as a millage rate per dollar of valuation. We converted the millage rate to dollars per $1,000 of valuation in our tax examples. We found rates ranging from less than $14 in sections of Naples to $29 in some parts of Tampa. The sample property tax calculations are for homes valued at $100,000, $150,000 and $250,000. We have taken the $25,000 homestead exemption in these examples.

Many cities and towns have a variety of rates depending on the location of the home. In cities where there were several different rates, we've given a range from lowest to highest. In one city we were told there were 200 rates. We examined their tax rate book and found seven different tax rates but 200 different taxing districts. In a few towns where we were not able to obtain all the potentially applicable rates, we identified one or more rates that applied to locations where retirees live.

Use the sample tax calculations as rough guidelines only. Property tax millage rates are the purview of the property appraiser's office in the county in which the town is located. The easiest way to determine your own tax burden is to call that office and provide the address of a specific property.

Though the profiles of individual towns do not include information on Florida's intangibles tax, it is an important tax to evaluate in your plans for a Florida relocation. A special report published by *Where to Retire* magazine,

"Intangibles Taxes," shows that Florida is one of only four states with such a tax. There are two types of intangibles taxes in Florida: the annual tax and the non-recurring tax. Intangibles taxes are assessed on stocks, bonds, loans, notes and other specified personal property and must be filed each year between January 1 and June 30. The annual intangibles tax rate is $1 per $1,000 of taxable value on the first $100,000 if filing singly or $200,000 if married, filing jointly. The tax rate rises to $2 per $1,000 for all intangible personal property in excess of $100,000 if filing singly, or in excess of $200,000 if married filing jointly. There is a $20,000 exemption from the total intangible property value for single filers or $40,000 for married couples filing jointly.

The non-recurring tax applies to any note, bond or other obligation for payment of money only to the extent it is secured by mortgage, deed of trust or other lien upon real property situated in Florida. The non-recurring tax rate is $2 per $1,000 with no exemptions allowed. The tax is due and payable at the time the financial instrument is presented for recording or within 30 days following the creation of the obligation. For more information on intangibles taxes in Florida, contact the Division of Taxpayer Assistance, (800) 352-3671.

The estate tax is a pick-up tax on the federal estate tax and applies only on estates valued at $600,000 or more.

REAL ESTATE

Florida's residential real estate portfolio reflects diverse architectural styles and innovative land uses. There are waterfront, water-view and water-access developments; high-rise condominiums on the beach; country clubs with golf villas and patio homes; established urban and suburban neighborhoods; manufactured-home developments; and mobile home parks. With so many choices, where do you begin a search for your own special retreat?

We began by trying to track down a means of comparing housing costs from place to place. Statistics regarding median home costs and median rent are from the *1997 Florida Statistical Abstract*. The census bureau's median value data are based on the respondent's estimate of the current worth of the property including the house and land. The data exclude properties of more than 10 acres, those with businesses on the property and mobile homes.

Under the heading "Communities Popular With Retirees," we have attempted to mention a cross section of housing available to retirees. Our intent was to note those residential areas that typify what you can expect to find in an area. We personally explored all types of housing and believe anyone serious about buying a home in Florida should see as many options as possible. Here are a few of the offerings we found among the most appealing.

On Top of the World is a gated, 29-year-old community northeast of Clearwater where the preferred minimum age is 55. It features condominiums with a complete amenities package that includes free golf privileges for residents. Condominiums are priced from the high $60s to $110s.

Tuscawilla, an established country club community at Winter Springs, northeast of Orlando, has 11 neighborhoods of outstanding homes priced from the $80s to more than $600,000.

Sun City Center, just 25 minutes from downtown Tampa, is a 5,000-acre, self-contained community of single-family homes and villas priced from the $70s to more than $300,000.

The canal-front homes at Punta Gorda Isles are upscale, shining examples of a sailor's paradise ashore.

Of course, one of the most popular retiree housing options is a manufactured home. They are beautifully displayed in communities such as St. Lucie Falls in Stuart, The Falls at Ormond in Ormond Beach and throughout Lake County.

Still another option is the mobile home. In and around Zephyrhills, tens of thousands of mobile homes dot the landscape.

Just in case you're concerned that the state may run out of space for new homes before you select your private garden spot, let us assure you, that is not likely to happen. Many areas are just beginning to be settled, while others are in transition. For example, the hill country just 30 minutes west of Orlando International Airport was occupied by citrus groves until a hard freeze destroyed more than 90 percent of the trees 15 years ago. Now thousands of acres are being converted to residential development. There are still huge areas of central and Panhandle Florida that have barely been discovered. And unbelievable though it may seem, many coastal areas such as Pine Island off Fort Myers and the Cape Haze Peninsula just to the north are underdeveloped.

We found several small communities, like Pine Island, where retirees did not want us to extol the virtues of their locale in our book. They do not wish to open their doors to a rush of development for fear of changing the nature of the place. When you become a resident in Florida you may become acutely aware of the tensions between developers, environmentalists, conservationists, newcomers and those who have lived in Florida long enough to be considered natives. As in many areas favored for outdoor recreation, there are battles among those who use the land, those who wish to preserve it, and those who wish to change the use of the land. Newcomers may get caught in the battle in the form of impact fees for new construction, taxes and assessments on utilities, moratoriums on development, changing uses of waterways and legislation that redirects access to public lands and waters. These elements can have a variety of effects on the property owner, some positive, some negative. Explore the forces at work in any neighborhood you are considering to see how your lifestyle could be effected.

In our profiles we have noted continuing-care retirement communities (CCRCs) licensed by the state as of June 1996, according to the Florida Department of Health and Rehabilitative Services. This represents only a fraction of the total assisted-living units available to retirees. For those retirees who prefer a community offering some level of assistance, there are thousands of adult congregate-living facilities, adult foster homes and CCRCs in Florida.

CRIME & SAFETY

Retirement relocation can be the most satisfying move you ever make. For most people, it is the first time to freely choose where to live, unhampered by job constraints. Often this decision means leaving a major urban center for a less developed, less hurried, less peopled place. Many retirees report that they hope to get away from crime and violence when they relocate. And many equate the reduced threat of crime with smaller towns. Indeed, many small towns do enjoy a much lower crime rate. But not all. We found some that suffer as much as their urban counterparts.

Crime rate data used in the profiles was provided by the Florida Department of Law Enforcement's Uniform Crime Reports Section. The data is for 1996. Our intent in providing the number of crimes per 1,000 persons in a city is to give you a method of comparing the number of crimes among towns large and small.

Some of the profiled towns are not incorporated cities and therefore do not have their own municipal police departments to compile local crime reports. In the profiles of these towns, we give the county crime rate as reported for the county sheriff's jurisdiction.

There are some factors that are not reflected in the crime rates. For example, the rates do not include seasonal increases in population, but are based on the year-round population. A resort city such as Key West, which is host to nearly one million visitors each year, but home to just about 28,000, has a crime rate that is higher than it would be if the population figure was adjusted to include visitors. Further, the crime rate shown in our profiles does not differentiate between violent crimes and property crimes. If crime is high on your list of concerns, check the crime rate, talk to residents and gather more information about the relative safety of different areas of town. Local law enforcement offices can provide additional information about the prevalence of various types of crime.

Each profile includes emergency and non-emergency telephone numbers for your reference.

HOMELESS & BLIGHT

Statistical data on homelessness comes from the U.S. Census.

Virtually all cities and towns have unattractive areas that could stand some sprucing up. We sought to identify and report on those areas that are truly blighted, using Webster's definition, "anything that destroys, prevents growth or causes devaluation." We found housing slums, large industrial complexes in or near residential neighborhoods, proliferations of billboards and signs, uncontrolled concentrations of trailer parks and unkempt and unpainted public buildings.

But the sun always returns to the sunshine state. Cities and towns throughout the state are busy at work cleaning up and restoring their older sections. Many are taking advantage of federal and state sponsored programs to help with their efforts. Overall we discovered that there are many more renovations and restorations than blighted areas. We saw federally and state sponsored Main Street restorations, Tree City USA designations and entire downtown regions listed on the National Register of Historic Places. There are many Florida communities where the involved citizenry will not permit blighted conditions to materialize or exist for long. Don't get stuck in a place that does!

HEALTH CARE

By one account, in 1882 a very ill early settler, a doctor, moved to an area near Clermont, FL, to die. He soon made a miraculous recovery that he attributed to the "healthful climate." It is not surprising that a state which has long received new residents on doctors' recommendations should develop one of the finest health care systems in the nation. When retirees are asked to compare local facilities with those available before their move, they almost always rate them equal to or better than those in the towns they left.

Even retirees who moved from large urban centers that boast some of the premier hospitals in the world are reluctant to give lower marks to much smaller, regional facilities in their corner of Florida. People we talked to cited the excellent quality of care they felt they had received since relocating and higher levels of personal concern shown by doctors, nurses and other medical personnel.

Clearly the quality and accessibility of full service medical care varies in Florida as it does in other states. But even in the most remote places, such as Marco Island, a fast route to advanced medical care almost always is available. For emergencies, Marco Island has an urgent care center with a helipad so patients can be flown to Naples or Fort Myers.

If you happen to settle in Broward County, you'll find more than 3,240 firms involved in health services, roughly one out of every 10 businesses.

Our conclusion: quality health care is readily available throughout the state of Florida.

GETTING SMART

Motivated to learn new skills, earn a degree, meet like-minded people with a common interest and expand personal-growth horizons? Retirees are going back to the classroom in record numbers. Some told us they are back in school to keep up with children and grandchildren. Some said they feel life is different and better in a college town. Still others are merely continuing patterns of the pursuit of education that they have maintained throughout their lives.

Whatever the motivation, many people we talked to surprised us by saying that they chose a town because of the educational opportunities. More frequently, they said they only found their niche in the society of a new community after getting involved with local learning institutions.

Community colleges, a comprehensive state university system and an extensive network of private colleges and universities put high-quality education in almost every community in the state. Lifelong learning opportunities abound. At community colleges, continuing-education courses are popular with retirees seeking to expand their general knowledge. Many courses of study are created specifically to appeal to the interests of students of retirement age.

Another learning lab, accessible and widely used by retirees to satisfy a thirst for education, is the senior center. There are literally hundreds of senior centers throughout the state that offer a great variety of courses. Foreign languages, basic computer skills and arts and crafts are professionally taught, often by retired college professors, business executives and artists. These classrooms are filled with eager-to-learn, third-age students. Both the learned and the learner find a creative outlet in such classes.

Elderhostel, a non-profit educational organization, offers short-term academic programs (usually one week) hosted by educational institutions throughout the country. It has a strong presence in Florida, where individuals 60 years and older vie for admission to programs with far more applicants than accommodations. Elderhostel was started to offer learning vacations, but it also takes registrants who already live in the area. A recent count found 13 Elderhostel programs in Florida.

The Elderhostel Institute Network is a national association of learning-in-retirement institutes, also known as LRIs. Lynn University, Florida Atlantic University, the University of Miami, Nova University, the University of Central Florida, Palm Beach Community College, the University of West Florida and Eckerd College are among the campuses in Florida that have developed special programs dedicated to older learners. Some are created by the universities and staffed by university personnel. Others are market-driven memberships where courses are developed and taught or led by members. Often these programs are structured to take advantage of the accumulated wisdom and experience of the members. Courses rely more on group interaction than typical lecture sessions. Many LRIs offer intergenerational and mentoring programs that allow students to learn about and contribute to the community.

Fees and tuition change each year. If you choose to attend a state supported or public school it is important to establish permanent residency. Tuition for non-Florida residents generally costs twice as much.

JUST FOR SENIORS

The local senior center is one of the most prized facilities in every town we visited. Usually organized and partially funded by the state agency on aging, these facilities are known by a variety of names — multipurpose senior center, senior services center, senior citizens center or simply the senior place. But whatever the name, the basic purpose is the same: to provide a facility where seniors come together to eat, learn, play, exercise, find companionship and receive assistance for a multitude of needs. Some centers are strictly needs-oriented, serving meals to those who need assistance. But more often, centers offer a wide range of activities, services and resources.

To dispel any stereotypical image you may be harboring, just spend some time in one of these centers. You'll soon realize that the zest for life and learning is going strong.

Group meals; arts and crafts; chess, bridge and pinochle games; piano, organ and dance lessons; Spanish, French, German and Italian language classes; Medicare and income tax assistance; blood pressure screening; and job placement services are regularly scheduled on the monthly calendar of activities. Adult day care, art exhibits and sales of members' arts and crafts, organized tours and outings and even theatrical productions by center members are offered.

We chatted with members in centers across the state.

Many spoke lovingly of the directors, staffs and the friendships developed through long years of association. One retiree said, "The Port Charlotte Cultural Center is a major, important aspect of our retirement experience. There's always something to do and someone to help to get your mind off your troubles." It is crystal clear that these centers are performing a vital and life-enhancing role in the daily routine of thousands of retired Floridians.

There is a significant duality in the essential functions of the centers. They provide a source of assistance for those who are troubled, alone or simply in need of a meal. But senior centers also serve as a therapeutic outlet for those who feel a need to help others. Volunteerism plays an important role in the lives of retirees, most of whom are leaving a life of steady, productive employment and looking for ways to spend the long, sometimes empty hours of newfound freedom. In our profiles we've listed senior centers under the heading "Just for Seniors," but they could have been listed under "Getting Involved," too. Just about wherever you find them, these centers are a real resource for the community.

GETTING INVOLVED

The Florida Department of Elder Affairs cites as a priority "the organization of a corps of volunteers in every local community to give input of life experiences and expertise to the enhancement of the quality of life for all Floridians."

Through volunteerism, retirees are helping to make their communities safer, more caring and more enduring. And what could be better than making new friends and acquaintances through an immediate bond of common interest? Throughout our journeys, retirees reported to us that getting involved in a new community has given them a sense of well-being, belonging and the pride of accomplishment.

We've listed a variety of not-for-profit organizations that rely on the services of volunteers. There are chapters of AARP led by volunteers in almost every community. If you find no listing for AARP, the chamber of commerce usually can provide the name and contact information for the current president or another officer.

Many cities and towns also have chapters of RSVP (Retired Senior Volunteer Program) and SCORE (Service Corps of Retired Executives). Volunteer counselors with RSVP and SCORE provide pro bono services and professional assistance to thousands of small businesses and not-for-profit organizations.

Chambers of commerce, visitor centers, parks and recreation facilities, museums, health-care and educational institutions as well as hundreds of social service and cultural organizations depend heavily on volunteers. If we haven't listed the type of organization you're interested in, check with the chamber of commerce, the local public library or the local telephone directory for additional possibilities.

Volunteerism is often thought of as the most popular form of employment for retirees. The money isn't so good, but it offers a greater degree of personal satisfaction than many occupations. If you're looking for work on a "thanks for a job well done" basis, chances are excellent you'll find it in Florida.

RECREATION, ENTERTAINMENT & AMENITIES

Retirees' leisure interests run the gamut. Any town worth your consideration should offer the activities, amenities and opportunities of your retirement dreams. Further, a community should have enough depth to permit exploration of new possibilities. Each city profile lists activities and facilities, from sport complexes to public libraries, so that you can see if the towns you're considering are equipped to offer the lifestyle you seek.

We have been accused of bias, leaning toward golf as the ultimate form of recreation and sporting entertainment.

Of course, it is just one of many pastimes enjoyed by retirees in Florida. But the fact that there are no less than 1,000 golf courses in the state attests to the above-average popularity of the game. We haven't listed every golf course, though it seems as if we've covered most. Whenever possible, we included the number of holes and the course's par. We've noted that many courses are semiprivate, meaning members get first choice of tee times, but anyone can play — for a fee.

Tennis is just about as popular as golf and somewhat more accessible. In addition to the public and private courts we list, many small communities and developments have resident-only courts that have not been listed.

Water sports are another of Florida's main attractions. It seems that half of the cities and towns in Florida are situated on a chain of lakes and the other half are located on the gulf, ocean or a river. In fact, there are 30,000 lakes and 166 rivers, so this perception is not too far off base. The chains of lakes and rivers produce long stretches of navigable waters in many parts of the state, even permitting residents of interior regions to traverse waterways all the way to the gulf or Atlantic. One county has so many lakes — roughly 1,400 with names — that they named it Lake County. Boating, sailing, canoeing and fishing naturally are the focal points of recreational activity in many parts of the state, particularly in Lake County.

Parks, greenbelts and nature preserves add interest, beauty and a full realm of outdoor activities to a place. Retirees told us they love to visit parks for communing with nature, visiting with friendly passers-by, exercise and sports. For all these reasons, state parks are high on the priority list for Florida, which maintains more than 100 of them. Because of environmental concerns, large areas of the state have been set aside as national forests, parks and preserves. In central Florida, where mining operations have ruled the land for decades, former mining sites have been turned into parklands, making a noticeable improvement.

Among the newest public greens are linear parks. These are mostly abandoned railroad corridors, bought by state, county and non-profit organizations as part of the nationwide Rails-to-Trails program. The converted trails are populated by walkers, bicyclers, joggers and skaters. Some linear parks even have an adjacent trail for equestrians.

Florida's cultural possibilities rival those of some of the largest metropolitan areas, both in grandeur of the facilities and quality of presentation and programming. Art and history museums, performing arts centers and college and university forums bring world-class artistic talent and productions to appreciative audiences. We heard many transplanted northerners confide that they attend more plays, shows and cultural events now than when the same renowned productions were showcased in their former hometowns. They cited lower ticket prices, less concern about nighttime safety, increased ease of driving and parking and more time for leisure as reasons for increased attendance.

Depending on your destination in the state, chances are you will have greater exposure to more diverse recreational and cultural resources than before your relocation. Use this section of the profiles to see if a town has the basic elements of your ideal location.

WHO LIVES HERE

In a survey of subscribers to *Where to Retire* magazine, a majority of readers said they wanted to settle in a small town or suburban area, a place with a population of less than 50,000. We heard much the same thing in our interviews and conversations with retirees throughout the state. Their reasons for relocating included a search for safety, reduced traffic congestion and, for many, the chance to feel that they know their neighbors.

We've used population information from the U.S. Census and the *1997 Florida Statistical Abstract* produced by the Bureau of Economic and Business Research of the University of Florida. The two sources provide the statistical background on population size, growth rate, age, and household and per capita incomes.

Use this information in conjunction with comments throughout the text about growth rates, the seeming adequacy of the infrastructure and the ability of government officials to provide the necessary leadership to maintain and enhance the quality of life. Be alert to towns with shrinking populations. It could be that the local economy is faltering or that residents are fleeing the city's taxes, traffic congestion or crime for nearby unincorporated areas. Beware of towns with rapidly rising populations. Retirees in smaller towns expressed both delight and dismay that their new-found haven might be discovered by others. Some fear growth will change the things they love in their new hometown. Many small cities and towns lose the essential qualities that drive population growth when they grow too rapidly.

Several of the areas we chose to profile are not incorporated entities, but have well-defined characteristics and sometimes even boundaries. Some are suburban areas that are growing beyond bedroom community status. Eventually, they may be incorporated or annexed. Others are defined by their natural or man-made resources rather than by a municipal government. Population information for unincorporated areas was provided by the local chambers of commerce.

NUMBERS TO KNOW

The chamber of commerce thrives in even the smallest villages and hamlets, serving as the best source of newcomer information. Sometimes several adjoining small towns band together to support a joint chamber, sharing the cost of rent, staff salaries and operating expenses. The Greater Pine Island Chamber of Commerce, for example, has responsibility for the entire island, including the communities of Matlacha, St. James City and Bokeelia.

Chamber staffs are almost invariably augmented by volunteers, often retirees, who provide invaluable service to their communities through their insightful assistance to prospective residents. As researchers seeking to learn about a town's compatibility with retirees, we found retiree volunteers a significant source of information.

After the chamber of commerce number, we've listed a few of the most commonly requested telephone numbers. These may be of help once you've begun the relocation process. At that time, you may want to call the local chamber of commerce for an extended list of sources and resources, or request local telephone directories so you can find the numbers yourself.

WHAT TO READ

Local newspapers are the best source of current information on what's really going on. The papers provide a reflection of the community itself in the advertisements, classifieds and editorials.

Newcomer's guides produced by the chambers of commerce are another valuable source once you've narrowed your selection of towns. Many of the relocation guides are available free of charge. Other magazine-type annual or semiannual guides cost as much as $6.

GETTING AROUND

While most Floridians rely on their cars, the availability of other means of transportation can be important. We repeatedly heard from retirees that proximity to an airport with commercial service is high on the list of requirements for an ideal hometown. Each profile describes the major public transportation services, if any, including buses, taxis, trains and airports. We have listed city tours where we found them. Although almost every town has someone giving a tour of something, where no particular tours came to our attention, the listing shows "none."

Under the public transportation category, we occasionally found free or reduced fare senior services. Requirements for use of the services vary and change frequently. Contact the transportation provider for their current offerings.

No discussion of getting around could possibly be complete without mentioning traffic volumes. In the section on traffic we have given our general observations of traffic volumes and/or problems. We admit the frequent references to heavy traffic are, at least partially, a product of our sheltered past. Keep in mind as you read our comments that for us, having spent our lives in small to medium-sized towns, more than two cars at a traffic signal constitutes a traffic jam.

However, it was our observation that traffic on I-95 along the southeast coast from Jupiter to Key Largo was uncomfortably heavy. This stretch of highway is one of only four — and by far the worst — that we traversed in the state that we deem totally unacceptable for frequent travel. The other areas to avoid are I-95 in the Jacksonville area, I-4 from Orlando to Tampa and U.S. 19, particularly from Crystal River to St. Petersburg. This is not an all-inclusive list. There are other highways that develop formidably hazardous driving conditions from time to time.

Many retirees manage to avoid rush-hour driving, or at least morning drive-time. It's more difficult to miss evening rush hour if you dine out frequently. Traffic congestion is greatly magnified from the winter holidays until April in popular vacation areas. The lesson is, you should be sure to test the traffic of your potential new locale, especially in peak season.

We heard a few horror stories from retirees who failed to look into this important aspect of homesite selection. They found it difficult just to get out of their neighborhood to go to the grocery store. Another couple was planning to move because the street their home was on had so much traffic at night that it kept them awake. Still, most traffic-related problems can be discovered prior to buying with a little investigative work such as a personal inspection or a call to the local planning board or department of transportation.

JOBS

Retirees aren't the only ones who find Florida attractive. Some of the largest manufacturing and non-manufacturing companies in the country are headquartered here. Many major international corporations have significant regional representation throughout the state. High-tech and biomedical companies, agribusiness, service organizations and, of course, tourism, provide employment. To give you an indication of the overall economic status of each county, we've noted the unemployment rates by county as published by the Bureau of Economic and Business Research in the *1997 Florida Statistical Abstract*. The Abstract reported information from the U.S. Department of Labor's Bureau of Labor Statistics and the State of Florida's Department of Labor and Employment Security.

We've also included telephone numbers for state and local employment programs. Florida Jobs and Benefits provides a statewide computerized network of employment opportunities and aptitude testing for more than 400 occupations.

UTILITIES

Utility services are provided by state-regulated monopolies throughout most of Florida. In some areas, utility services are provided by a combination of major suppliers and local or regional co-operatives. We heard very few complaints from retirees about their utilities — either pricing or availability.

It is difficult to estimate your initial utilities expenditures prior to moving. Most utilities costs depend on the exact address and status of your new home. In areas where there are building moratoriums or where new construction required new infrastructure, new homeowners may pay substantial service initiation fees. Once initial installation and service set-up costs have been covered, utilities providers should be able to quote specific service rates for specific new addresses.

Florida Power & Light is the largest provider of electric-ity. There are several electric co-ops scattered throughout the state servicing both urban and rural areas. In some cases, counties and municipalities have formed local utility companies to buy and resell electricity, natural gas, water and sewer services to their captive customers.

GTE, United Telephone, Bell South, Sprint and Sprint-United are the major telephone service providers within the state.

Peoples Gas, Central Florida Gas Co. and West Florida Natural Gas provide pipeline gas to most of Florida. Areas not yet reached by pipeline rely on local propane dealers.

Water and sewer services are provided by local, government-run utilities in almost every incorporated area. Private wells and septic tank systems still are in use in just a few areas. The Florida Keys Aqueduct Authority provides water for all the Keys from deep-well sources in Florida City.

All the major cable television operators and several smaller regional companies have franchises in the state. We've noted the company or companies that serve each of the towns profiled.

PLACES OF WORSHIP

We discovered through our interviews that the No. 1 source of new friendships for many relocating retirees is a church or synagogue. They also are the organizations of choice for social activities and volunteerism.

Florida is indeed a melting pot for retirees from all ethnic, cultural, socioeconomic and religious backgrounds. Nothing proves this fact better than the diversity of houses of worship located conveniently in population centers across the state. Space constraints prevented us from listing all churches and all denominations represented. Yet knowing the importance of the church to a large portion of retirees, we've given a summation of the number of Catholic, Protestant and Jewish houses of worship.

THE ENVIRONMENT

"Not in my back yard" takes on new importance when selecting a home for the leisure years in a new and unfamiliar place. Landfills, airports and toxic waste sites are generally pretty obvious. Not quite so easily identified are the hidden problems: polluted canals, rivers and lakes. We used several federal and state reports to compile information about each town's unique environmental status.

EPA-listed Superfund Sites

Information regarding Superfund sites comes from the U.S. Environmental Protection Agency's (EPA) Florida sites fact sheets, updated in 1996. The term Superfund refers to a national program that was created by legislation in 1980 to uncover and clean up hazardous materials spills and contaminated sites. We've noted the general location of EPA-Superfund sites that are within the same county as the town profiled.

Drinking Water

Using reports from the EPA's national study of lead levels in the drinking water of public water systems, we've noted problem areas in the profiles of affected cities. Nationally, the EPA found 819 cities that exceeded the lead "action level" of 15 parts per billion (ppb) in drinking water. The action level was established under the EPA's 1992 "Lead and Copper Rule" of the Safe Drinking Water Act.

The EPA's release explains that "elevated lead levels are rarely found in ground water or in surface water, such as rivers and lakes, that serve as the sources of drinking water. Instead, lead enters drinking water primarily after the water leaves the treatment plant. The water may be sufficiently corrosive to cause lead to leach from household plumbing pipes and fixtures, and from lead service lines used in some water distribution systems."

The EPA adds, "These monitoring results do not represent average drinking water lead levels in these communitites. Systems are required to test the tap water in high-risk residences where higher lead levels are expected to be found."

High-risk residences are described as those served by lead service lines or containing lead interior piping or copper piping with lead solder installed after 1982. The law states that a drinking water system exceeds the lead action level if more than 10 percent of the monitored high-risk residences have drinking water lead levels of more than 15 ppb. For more information the EPA suggests contacting the local drinking water supplier or the EPA's Safe Drinking Water Hotline, (800) 426-4791.

Surface Water

Due to the prominence of water sports and activities in the lives of Floridians, and because surface waters and wetlands cover more than one third of the state, we give an overview of the water quality of local rivers, lakes, streams, estuaries, harbors, bays, bayous and canals in each profile. The information we provide is a very brief distillation of the "1996 Florida Water Quality Assessment 305(b) Technical Appendix" from the Basin Planning and Management Section of the Florida Department of Environmental Protection.

The report describes sources of pollution, efforts underway to reduce pollution and protect the water quality, and rating information that describes each body of water as good, fair or poor. Water quality ratings are based on a classification system that describes the range of uses for each body of water. For example a Class I stream (the most pristine) is designated for drinking water, whereas a Class V stream (the most polluted) is designated for navigation, utility and industrial use. When the quality of the water supports its designated uses, it is generally referred to as good water quality. Fair quality generally means it partially meets its designated use, and poor quality means that the water quality does not meet its designated use.

We've also noted which bodies of water are designated for protection and/or improvement. Status as an Outstanding Florida Water, or OFW, means that the Florida Department of Environmental Regulation grants an added degree of protection to prevent the lowering of existing water quality. In practice, the designation limits the types of permits that can be issued to interested parties (e.g. builders, industry and business) for practices such as waste discharge into the water or into an upstream tributary.

Another special designation is SWIM or Surface Water Improvement and Management status, which calls for de-velopment and implementation of plans to improve and manage the quality of the water. Many OFW waters also have the SWIM designation.

One other important designation, that which provides the greatest degree of protection, is the Outstanding National Resource Water. This status is granted only to select water-bodies. Waters with this status are Biscayne Bay National Monument, Big Cypress National Preserve and Everglades National Park.

Air Quality

We reviewed reports from the Florida Department of Environmental Protection's Division of Air Resources. Generally, the reports track the levels of six pollutants: ozone, nitrogen oxide, sulphur dioxide, particulate matter, lead and carbon monoxide. There are 97 monitoring sites in the state that monitor some or all of these pollutants. Cities with populations of 200,000 have the facilities and equipment to routinely test the air quality for the six pollutants. Additionally, some locations have special purpose monitors because there are known problems or pollutant sources in the area that must be checked. Other than that, towns generally only monitor pollutants when they have the money, expertise and a reason to watch a particular local source. In our profiles, we noted the few instances when a particular city's air quality did not meet one of the standards.

Water quality, preservation of wildlife habitats and the loss of natural resources to development, industry or other causes come under the jurisdiction of the Florida Department of Environmental Protection. Its stated mission is "to protect, conserve, and restore the air, water and natural resources of the state." If you are interested in a reader-friendly guide to Florida's environmental programs, the Florida Department of Environmental Protection publishes "Florida: State of the Environment" (see page 220 for address). It provides an overview of the concerns, problems, actions and possible solutions to maintaining and improving the great outdoors.

We've included information on the environment to help you make informed decisions regarding your relocation. It is possible to buy a home only to find out too late that an EPA Superfund site is just down the road or that the lake you planned to fish in every day has periodic closures due to pollutants. You may find an ideal waterfront location where you can tie up your boat at your back door, only to learn that boat traffic is restricted to protect wildlife habitats.

In a state that attracts people because of its enormous wealth of natural resources, it is best to know in advance the status of those resources: polluted, protected, restored or off-limits to development.

EVENTS AND FESTIVALS

City profiles address the issue of when to visit from the perspective of the chamber of commerce, i.e. with a listing of special activities, festivals, shows, races, athletic events, regattas and fishing tournaments. These events tend to attract large numbers of visitors and are noted by the chambers as highlights of the entertainment calendar.

You'll quickly realize that most of these events are scheduled to coincide with the peak season — fall, winter and spring — when the weather is at its zenith, snowbird platoons are at full strength, vacationers are present and accounted for, and streets and highways are filled to capacity.

Contrary to this point of view, retirees almost unanimously endorse off-season visits — when the real Florida emerges and the carnival atmosphere disappears. Their theory: if you can tolerate Florida in the summer — when high heat and humidity are accompanied by afternoon thunderstorms, hordes of biting insects (aka no-see-ums) and a generally sedentary atmosphere — then you'll love it during the winter. Of course, to get a more complete picture, you really should make protracted visits during each of the four seasons over a multiyear span.

WHERE TO EAT

Much of Florida is developed for and by tourists, and the most populous and popular areas have every imaginable type of dining. Several cities claim titles such as the highest per capita restaurant count.

We have not personally sampled all of the restaurants listed. Instead, we supplemented our own dining experiences with recommendations from travel writers, chambers of commerce and local residents. Wherever possible, we list a range of options, from inexpensive to very expensive, from barbecue to haute cuisine. There are areas where Cuban menus predominate, and others that are known for down-home cooking or seafood.

Some restaurants close down or operate on a reduced schedule during the summer season when their business slows with the flight of the snowbirds.

Many of the towns profiled are far off the typical tourist track. They have few restaurants that are known beyond their city limits. In a few towns, finding no consensus of opinion about which local eateries to recommend, and where we had no personal favorites, we offer no recommendations. Our advice to you is to do what we do: Look for parking lots filled with cars bearing Florida license plates. Then you'll know where the locals eat.

WHERE TO STAY

Lodging comes in every shape and variety in Florida. There are fabulous destination resorts, historic bed-and-breakfast inns, beach-front cottages, well-known chain motels and hotels, and vacation condos that rent by the day, week, month or year. We note our favorites, generally in the moderate price category, as well as those recommended to us.

Despite Florida's obvious reliance on tourists, not all areas have the tourist volume to support a variety of hotels. Where we found no consensus to support mentioning one or more establishments, we suggest that you ask for recommendations from the chamber of commerce or a real estate agent, or perhaps just see what looks good when you arrive. We confess that there were a few towns where we chose to press on into the night rather than stay in what we saw as the available lodging.

ISSUES

Every city and town has its issues. This section is intended to reflect the concerns that were grabbing headlines or simply on the minds of resident retirees during our visits. In just a few towns we observed less-than-ideal conditions or situations and have mentioned these as issues.

Most of what we heard sounded familiar — they're the same concerns Americans are dealing with across the country. There were questions and controversies about street-widening, construction of six-lane interstate highways through residential neighborhoods, less than satisfactory water quality and rising crime. Less common were the worries over pesky insects and the size of a deer herd.

One theme running through most of the comments we heard was the concern about future growth, overcrowding and traffic congestion of once sparsely populated areas of Florida. Most retirees are willing and even proud to talk about the splendors of their own little Garden of Eden. But they were only half joking when they admonished us not to tell anyone else about their town for fear that newcomers would descend and spoil its beauty.

Retirees told us of other concerns that did not make it into the profiles. We heard that health-care costs are an immediate concern. Local politics and politicians also are the source of many complaints. For the most part, retirees told us that they want to live quiet, orderly lives, shielded from the strident bombast sometimes associated with small-town politics.

Clearly, it is best to investigate the issues of a town before relocating. A subscription to the local newspaper can reveal a lot about the nature of such problems as well as how the town's leaders deal with problems — real and manufactured.

RELOCATION TIPS

Scattered throughout the book we've included advice on a variety of relocation topics. These tips touch on everything from the wisdom of renting before buying a home in a new town to money-saving tips when hiring a moving company.

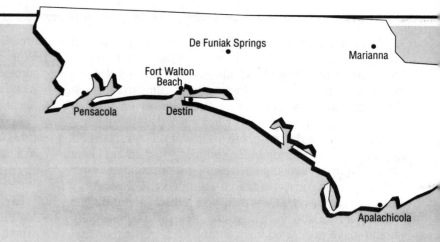

WHERE TO RETIRE IN
FLORIDA

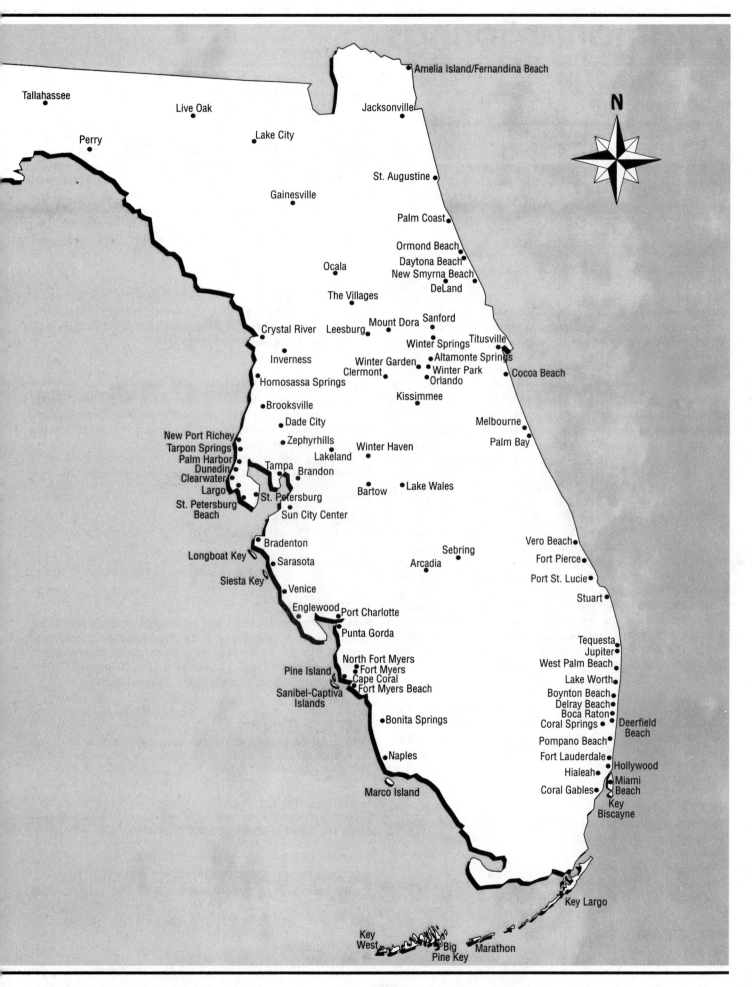

Tallahassee

Live Oak

Perry

Lake City

Gainesville

Ocala

The Villages

Crystal River   Leesburg   Mount Dora   Sanford

Inverness   Winter Garden   Altamonte Springs

Homosassa Springs   Clermont   Winter Park
Orlando

Brooksville   Kissimmee

Dade City

New Port Richey   Zephyrhills   Winter Haven

Tarpon Springs

Palm Harbor   Lakeland

Dunedin   Tampa   Brandon

Clearwater

Largo   Bartow   Lake Wales

St. Petersburg   St. Petersburg

Beach   Sun City Center

Bradenton

Longboat Key   Sebring

Sarasota   Arcadia

Siesta Key

Venice

Englewood   Port Charlotte

Punta Gorda

North Fort Myers

Pine Island   Fort Myers

Cape Coral

Sanibel-Captiva   Fort Myers Beach

Islands

Bonita Springs

Naples

Marco Island

Amelia Island/Fernandina Beach

Jacksonville

St. Augustine

Palm Coast

Ormond Beach
Daytona Beach
New Smyrna Beach
DeLand

Winter Springs   Titusville

Cocoa Beach

Melbourne

Palm Bay

Vero Beach

Fort Pierce

Port St. Lucie

Stuart

Tequesta
Jupiter
West Palm Beach

Lake Worth

Boynton Beach
Delray Beach
Boca Raton
Coral Springs   Deerfield
Beach

Pompano Beach

Fort Lauderdale   Hollywood

Hialeah   Miami
Beach
Coral Gables

Key
Biscayne

Key Largo

Key
West   Big   Marathon
Pine Key

N

21

Altamonte Springs

HE SAID: ✭ ✭ ✭
I like the pace and ambiance of Altamonte Springs. The town is clean and visually attractive, and there's a sense of safety. A nice place to get away from the excesses of Greater Orlando.

SHE SAID: ✭ ✭ ✭ ✭
A pretty town, it's clean and well-planned. There are upscale neighborhoods, restaurants and shops and good medical care. I would look here for a place to retire.

In central Florida, it's easy to be overwhelmed by tourists and tourist attractions. Even the tiny town of Zellwood has its "All-You-Can-Eat Sweet Corn Festival," bringing flocks of visitors. But not Altamonte Springs. Its "attraction" for out-of-towners is the Altamonte Mall, once billed as the largest regional mall in central Florida. It lost that honor in 1995 when the new and larger Seminole Towne Center opened only a few miles away in Sanford.

Altamonte Springs is at the heart of the northern metro Orlando area, surrounded by smallish municipalities in the 10,000 to 50,000 population range. The town is predominately a shopping mecca, regional health-care center, major employment base and drive-through town for those on the way to nearby suburbs. Besides the Altamonte Mall, the town boasts the Florida Hospital and the headquarters for Kirchman Corporation, a large computer software company.

Few recreational, cultural and social activities are available in Altamonte but can be found in neighboring towns. The finer residential developments — The Springs, Sweetwater Oaks and Sabal Point — are north of the city limits and have a Longwood address. Altamonte Springs has some good residential neighborhoods, but the best are in outlying areas.

Altamonte Springs doesn't have a golf course, but there are many :thin a five-mile radius. Water sports are limited in the city, but ere are numerous lakes and rivers in the broader area that beckon shermen, boaters and other water enthusiasts. Orlando is 25 minutes south, offering lots of entertainment and dining possibilities. So while Altamonte probably won't score high on most charts, it is worth checking out if you're in the area.

WEATHER

	Winter	Spring	Summer	Fall
Normal daily high/low	72/49	86/64	91/71	77/57
Normal precipitation	10 in.	12 in.	19 in.	8 in.

Disaster watch: Northeast Florida has not been hit by a major hurricane since 1900.

TAXES
Sales tax: 7%. **Property tax:** $20.63 per $1,000 valuation. Sample tax calculations include a $25,000 homestead exemption.

Home value	Tax
$100,000	$1,547
$150,000	$2,579
$250,000	$4,642

REAL ESTATE
Median home value: $92,108 (Seminole County). **Median rent:** $661/month (Seminole County). **Communities popular with re-**

tirees: Oak Harbor, in Altamonte Springs just three minutes from the mall, has lake-access condominiums priced from the $80s. According to ReMax Realty, (407) 682-1200, Sabal Point Country Club has resales of golf villas, duplexes and single-family homes priced from the $120s to $300s. Sweetwater Oaks has homes priced from the mid-$120s to $250s and up. The Springs offers apartments as well as villas and single-family homes priced from the low $100s and up. With the exception of Oak Harbor, these communities are not actually within the city limits, but are the communities that area retirees choose. **Licensed continuing-care retirement communities:** None. The Sanford Center is an adult congregate living facility with 110 units and a full activities program, (407) 260-2433.

CRIME & SAFETY
Crimes per 1,000 population: 81. **Non-emergency police:** (407) 830-3816. **Non-emergency fire department:** (407) 830-3844. **Police, fire, ambulance emergencies:** 911.

HOMELESS & BLIGHT
The city generally is nice in both commercial and residential areas. There's a municipal division responsible for urban beautification. Route 436, which bisects the city east to west, is essentially a strip shopping center, but not as garish as some.

The U.S. Census reported 53 homeless persons in shelters and 18 visible in street locations in Seminole County, population 287,529.

HEALTH CARE
Hospitals: Florida Hospital, 220 beds, full service, (407) 830-4321.
Physicians: 58. **Specialties:** 37.

GETTING SMART
Webster University, (407) 869-8111, offers graduate and under-graduate degrees. Schools in the Orlando area include **University of Central Florida**, (407) 823-2000, which grants undergraduate, graduate and professional degrees, and **Rollins College**, (407) 646-2000, which offers undergraduate and graduate degrees.

JUST FOR SENIORS
George D. Perkins Civic Center hosts senior citizen activities, (407) 830-3971.

GETTING INVOLVED
Citizen Volunteer Programs, (407) 834-2677. **Library Volunteers**, (407) 830-3895. **RSVP**, (407) 323-4440.

RECREATION, ENTERTAINMENT & AMENITIES
Public golf: None within the city limits, and no space to build any. Sabal Point Country Club, semiprivate, is just north of the city. **Private golf:** Rolling Hills in Longwood is only two miles away. **Public tennis courts:** Eastmonte Park, three lighted courts, and Westmonte Park, four lighted courts. **Private tennis courts:** Sabal Point Country Club. **Parks:** Eastmonte, 21 acres;

Westmonte, 14 acres; and Merrill Park, 28 acres. All have recreation centers with a variety of cultural and sporting facilities. Lake Lotus is an 88-acre multiple-use park. **Public swimming pools:** Westmonte Park. **Water sports:** Boating, canoeing and water-skiing. **River/gulf/ocean:** Numerous lakes and the Wekiva River, which meanders through the heart of the city. **Running/walking/biking:** Merrill Park has a half-mile jogging/nature trail. Wekiva Springs State Park, a few miles northwest of the city, has a 13-mile hiking trail. **Horses/riding:** The Equestrian Center is a riding academy. Wekiva Springs State Park has eight miles of trails. **Hunting:** Hunting and fishing licenses and information, (407) 321-1130, ext. 7605. **Movie theaters:** 16 screens. **Art museums:** None. Residents go to Orlando and Winter Park. **History museums:** None. **Theaters:** Altamonte Springs Amphitheatre. Performing arts and cultural enterprises are scattered throughout Greater Orlando. **Library:** Altamonte Springs Library and Cultural Center. **Attractions:** None. **Necessities:** All here.

   Smart Shopper Tip: Altamonte Mall has four major department stores — Burdine's, J.C. Penney, Gayfer's and Sears — and more than 175 specialty shops. It's centrally located and easy to access.

WHO LIVES HERE
Population: 39,153 year-round residents, an increase of 3,986 since 1990. **Age 65+=**11.0% in Seminole County. **Median household income:** $37,495 (Seminole County). **Per capita income:** $23,400 (Seminole County).

NUMBERS TO KNOW
Chamber of commerce: In Casselberry, (407) 834-4404. **Voter registration:** (407) 321-1130, ext. 7701. **Vehicle registration, tags & title:** (407) 330-4600. **Driver's license:** (407) 330-6720.

WHAT TO READ
Orlando Sentinel, daily newspaper, (407) 420-5000.

GETTING AROUND
Bus: LYNX Transit Authority, (407) 841-8240. **Taxi:** Yellow Cab, (407) 425-3111. **Tours:** None. **Airport:** Orlando International. **Traffic:** North-south traffic flows smoothly due to I-4, which diverts a heavy volume of vehicles around the city. But Altamonte Road (Route 436), the main east-west thoroughfare and the site of Altamonte Mall, Florida Hospital, city hall and a dozen shopping centers, is heavily trafficked and somewhat slow.

JOBS
County unemployment rate: 3.0%. **Florida Jobs and Benefits:** In Sanford, (407) 330-6700.

UTILITIES
Electricity: Florida Power, (407) 629-1010. **Gas:** Peoples Gas, (407) 425-4662. **Water & sewer:** Altamonte Springs Utilities, (407) 830-3874. **Telephone:** Sprint-United, (407) 339-1811. **Cable TV:** TCI of Central Florida, (407) 869-6600.

PLACES OF WORSHIP
Two Catholic and 25 Protestant churches.

THE ENVIRONMENT
The Wekiva River and Little Wekiva River have been rated as having fair to good water quality. Both have protected status with the designation of Outstanding Florida Waters. However, the Wekiva River is considered threatened and has shown a declining quality trend. Lake Monroe has poor water quality but is improving. Lake Jessup and Lake Howell also show poor quality. Lake Apopka has poor water quality, but has been designated as a SWIM water body for surface water improvement and management. Lake Kathryn has fair to good quality, and Lake Maitland shows good quality.

EVENTS AND FESTIVALS
No recurring annual events.

WHERE TO EAT
Maison & Jardin, 430 S. Wymore Road, American/continental, expensive to very expensive, (407) 862-4410. **Straub's,** 512 E. Altamonte Drive, seafood, moderate, (407) 831-2250.

WHERE TO STAY
Orlando North Hilton, (407) 830-1985. **Holiday Inn Altamonte Springs,** (407) 862-4455. **Residence Inn by Marriott,** (407) 788-7991.

ISSUES
There were no significant issues under discussion when we visited.

RELOCATION TIPS

Certain household items cannot be handled by a professional moving company because they are either too dangerous or illegal to carry. Ask the moving company for a list of items they will not carry before you begin packing. Usually banned:
- Paints, turpentine and varnish.
- Flammable liquids, including nail polish remover and lighter fluid.
- Bleach.
- Firearms and ammunition.
- Matches.
- Some plants and animals.

Note: If you pack such items without the knowledge of the mover, you are liable for any fires or other damage they cause.

Amelia Island/Fernandina Beach

HE SAID: ★ ★ ★
Much potential has been lost to bulldozers and fast-buck transactions devoid of aesthetic sensitivity. I suppose that can be said for much of Florida and the earth. "There's still a place," as the area's boosters remind us, but it's getting a little frayed around the edges.

SHE SAID: ★ ★ ★
Not too far from Jacksonville, Amelia Island attracts lots of tourist and weekend traffic. The small downtown area is very quaint with small shops and a few restaurants. You might want to stay at one of the bed-and-breakfast inns. I would visit, but would not relocate here.

The town of Fernandina Beach, at the north end of Amelia Island, is small and charming. The 50-block downtown historic district, called Old Town, has earned a spot on the National Register of Historic Places, showcasing late Victorian architecture. Amelia Island Plantation and Summer Beach, both upscale resort developments, are lush, tropical and impressive. But the beach-front strip of small cottages and typical beach motels along the northeast coast of the island is unimaginative and unimpressive, as is much of the inland residential and commercial development.

Near the Georgia border, Amelia Island boasts 13 miles of sandy, quiet beaches, golf and tennis, and docks and marinas. The 82 civic, social and fraternal organizations keep permanent residents busy, despite a dearth of cultural resources and entertainment to provide real escape from routine. Of course, the malls and amenities of Jacksonville are just a 40-minute commute away.

Yet not everyone will find Amelia Island's solitude and remoteness attractive. Not even vacationers who come here to rest and relax are prepared for the isolation one finds along the northeast beaches.

It is obvious that public planning and aesthetic preservation were not foremost in the minds and actions of officials and developers in many parts of the island. Retirees here note that while building codes are carefully observed in Fernandina Beach, zoning enforcement is weak in unincorporated Nassau County. One retiree warns that it's a "buyer beware" market.

Another unhappy resident blames the "buddy system at work on the Fernandina Beach Zoning Commission" for unequal and unfair enforcement of zoning ordinances. Such complaints seem endemic to some communities. If you decide to retire here, prepare yourself for the frustrations and vagaries of small-town politics.

WEATHER
	Winter	Spring	Summer	Fall
Normal daily high/low	66/46	83/64	88/72	72/54
Normal precipitation	11 in.	11 in.	19 in.	9 in.

Disaster watch: Northeast Florida has not been hit by a major hurricane since 1900.

TAXES
Sales tax: 6%. **Property tax:** $23.97 (Fernandina Beach) and $17.14 (unincorporated Amelia Island) per $1,000 valuation. Sample taxes are calculated at the rate of $23.97 and include a $25,000 homestead exemption.

Home value	Tax
$100,000	$1,798
$150,000	$2,996
$250,000	$5,393

REAL ESTATE
Median home value: $86,992 (Nassau County). **Median rent:** $632/month (Nassau County). **Communities popular with retirees:** Amelia Island Plantation offers homes priced from $200,000 and homesites from $45,000, (800) 874-6878 or (904) 277-5980. Lakewood subdivision has 200 single-family homes priced from the $100s to $150s. Summer Beach, a 450-acre development, has the following offerings, according to Marcy Mock, (800) 322-7448: Sailmaker Condominiums, oceanfront and poolside, $123,900 to $299,900; Sea Watch and Outrigger Townhomes, oceanfront homes from $599,000 to $650,000; Seaside and Oceanside Homes, patio homes from $199,900 to $289,000; Ocean Place Condos, mid-rise condos from $329,900 to $549,000; Ocean Village Homes, single-family homes from $299,000 to $465,000; Sea Chase Condos, luxurious oceanfront condos from $475,000 to $850,000; and Carlton Dunes Condos, mid-rise luxury condos starting at $650,000. **Licensed continuing-care retirement communities:** None.

CRIME & SAFETY
Crimes per 1,000 population: 67 (Fernandina Beach). **Non-emergency police:** Fernandina Beach Police, (904) 277-7342. Nassau County Sheriff, (904) 225-0331. **Non-emergency fire department:** Fernandina Beach, (904) 277-7331. Nassau County, (904) 321-5732. **Police, fire, ambulance emergencies:** 911.

HOMELESS & BLIGHT
We saw no homeless persons and no blighted areas. There are some small, run-down houses as you approach the beach.

The U.S. Census reported finding no homeless persons in shelters or visible on the streets of Nassau County, population 43,941.

HEALTH CARE
Hospitals: Baptist Medical Center, 54 beds, 24-hour emergency, full service, (904) 202-2000.
Physicians: 39. **Specialties:** 20.

GETTING SMART
Florida Community College, Fernandina Beach campus, (904) 225-0506. **Offerings:** Classes for college credit are taught evenings at the local high school. Most credits are transferable to a 4-year institution. **Nassau County Adult and Continuing Education Office**, (904) 321-5826. **Offerings:** Introduction to computers, landscaping, interior design, languages and WordPerfect are among the courses.

JUST FOR SENIORS
Council on Aging, (904) 261-0701.

GETTING INVOLVED
Nassau County Volunteer Center provides services to 42 non-profit agencies, (904) 261-2771. Other clubs include: Arts

Alliance of Nassau County, Newcomers Club and Retired, But Not Tired, Club.

RECREATION, ENTERTAINMENT & AMENITIES

Public golf: Fernandina Beach Municipal, 27 holes. **Private golf:** Amelia Island Plantation, 45 holes, and Golf Club of Amelia Island (Summer Beach), 18 holes. **Public tennis courts:** Atlantic Avenue Park. **Private tennis courts:** Amelia Island Plantation, ranked among America's top 50 tennis resorts. **Parks:** Fort Clinch State Park has 1,119 acres at the northern tip of Amelia Island. **Public swimming pools:** Recreation department pools at Atlantic Avenue and Elm Street. **Water sports:** Sailing, scuba diving, surfing and fishing. **River/gulf/ocean:** The Amelia River (Intracoastal Waterway) separates the island from the Mainland. Egans Creek bisects the northern half of the island before entering the harbor at Old Town. The Atlantic provides fishing and water sports. **Running/walking/biking:** Try the nature trails in Fort Clinch State Park and the fitness trail at Ybor Alvarez Complex. Residents can join the Fernandina Beach Running Group. **Horses/riding:** You can ride horseback on the beach at Seahorse Stables. Wild horses roam Cumberland Island, just north of Amelia Island, accessible by ferry. **Hunting:** Hunting and fishing licenses, (904) 261-5566. **Movie theaters:** Two screens. **Art museums:** Island Art Association Gallery. **History museums:** Amelia Island Museum of History. **Theaters:** Amelia Community Theatre, Amelia Fine Arts Series and Fernandina Little Theatre. **Library:** One. **Attractions:** Amelia Island Lighthouse, Old Town, Amelia Island Plantation and Historic Fernandina Beach. **Necessities:** If it's not here, it is available in Jacksonville, 40 minutes away.

   Smart Shopper Tip: There are at least seven shopping areas on the island, including the Centre Street Historic District, C House Colony, Amelia Plaza, Island Walk, Sadler Square, Palmetto Walk and the Village Shops. For serious shopping, plan a trip to Regency Square in Jacksonville.

WHO LIVES HERE

Population: 10,438 year-round residents in Fernandina Beach, an increase of 1,673 since 1990. **Age 65+ = 11.6%** in Nassau County. **Median household income:** $33,586 (Nassau County). **Per capita income:** $21,488 (Nassau County).

NUMBERS TO KNOW

Chamber of commerce: (800) 226-3542 and (904) 261-3248. **Voter registration:** (904) 321-5735. **Vehicle registration, tags & title:** (904) 261-5566. **Driver's license:** (904) 225-8947.

WHAT TO READ

Newsleader, weekly newspaper, (904) 261-3696. **Nassau County Record**, weekly newspaper, (904) 879-2727.

GETTING AROUND

Bus: Care-A-Van provides transportation to doctors, other appointments, etc. for seniors, (904) 261-0700. **Taxi:** Benjamin's Taxi, (904) 261-7278, or Sandlin Cab, (904) 261-3037. **Tours:** Emerald Princess Day Cruises, (800) 842-0115. **Airport:** Jacksonville International is 29 miles away. **Traffic:** Light.

JOBS

County unemployment rate: 3.7%. **Florida Jobs and Benefits:** (904) 277-7272.

UTILITIES

Electricity: Florida Public Utilities, (904) 261-3663. **Gas:** None. **Water & sewer:** Florida Public Utilities, (904) 261-3663, or Southern States Utilities for southern part of Amelia Island, (800) 432-4501. **Telephone:** Bell South, (800) 789-9025 in Florida, or (800) 753-2909 out-of-state. **Cable TV:** Media One Cable Service, (904) 261-3624.

PLACES OF WORSHIP

More than 60 churches in the county, representing Catholic and 16 Protestant denominations.

THE ENVIRONMENT

Both the Okefenokee National Wildlife Refuge and Fort Clinch State Aquatic Preserve have been given protected status as Outstanding Florida Waters. St. Marys River generally has an excellent water quality rating except in three areas: the South prong near Lake City, Little St. Marys and the Amelia River Estuary. These sections generally have fair water quality. The Amelia River Estuary is affected by the Fernandina Wastewater Treatment Plant, several pulp and paper mills and urban runoff. Fort George River and Sisters Creek show good water quality. Mills Creek shows poor water quality.

EVENTS AND FESTIVALS

Senior PGA Golf Tournament - March. **Bausch & Lomb Tennis Championship** - April. **Eight Flags Shrimp Festival** - May. **Tour of Historic District Homes** - December. **Victorian Seaside Christmas** - November-January 1.

WHERE TO EAT

Brett's Waterway Cafe, 1 S. Front St., seafood, continental, expensive, (904) 261-2660. **The Grill**, 4750 Amelia Island Parkway at the Ritz-Carlton, American, expensive to very expensive, (904) 277-1100.

WHERE TO STAY

Amelia Island Plantation, (904) 261-6161 or (800) 874-6878. **Bailey House Bed & Breakfast Inn**, (904) 261-5390. **Ritz-Carlton**, (904) 277-1100.

ISSUES

There is a quiet struggle taking place between old-line Georgia families who own much of the old, settled properties on the island and who want to retain its rusticity, and resort developers who are building upscale hotels such as the Ritz-Carlton and golf-course-centered communities such as the Plantation and Summer Beach. Newcomers are likely to hear a lot of squabbling about zoning law changes and may witness an increasing rate of growth and change.

Apalachicola

Many current retirees first heard of Apalachicola in 1947 when Bing Crosby and Bob Hope immortalized the town in the movie "The Road to Rio." If you haven't paid a visit during the intervening years, don't worry. You haven't missed a thing. The only change is the addition of Franklin County's one traffic light, in the heart of town.

We made a fortuitous wrong turn on our way to the chamber of commerce and found ourselves in front of the *Apalachicola Times* building. Going inside to pick up a copy of the paper, we met manager John Lee, a transplanted midwesterner who launched into a 20-minute dissertation — tongue-in-cheek — on the reasons people should not retire to Apalachicola. In a nutshell, he reasoned that retirement there is a health hazard. Here's the scenario he painted: After spending a year or two in a totally relaxed, unhurried, idyllic environment, you begin to feel like a youngster again and decide to start a second career, feeling so good you work day and night until the ol' ticker can't stand it anymore and finally gives out.

Despite this, John provided us with two publications that certainly made Apalachicola look tempting. "52 Great Ways to Enjoy Franklin County," published by the *Times*, and the chamber's "Walking and Driving Tour" brochure list the area's recreational amenities. Among the suggestions: sail the Gulf Intracoastal Waterway, which starts in the eastern Apalachicola Bay and terminates in Texas; take a 45-minute ferry ride across St. George Sound to Dog Island and soak up some sun; drive over to St. George Island to spend the day snorkeling and collecting seashells; and visit Fort Gadsden State Historic Site. Or, as John Lee says, "Get a copy of the *Times,* go to your favorite spot, put up your feet and read the latest news."

Apalachicola was officially established in 1831. Its roots in the cotton business still can be seen in historic district homes that once were the mansions of the cotton magnates. Many early 1840s-era antebellum homes now are being restored by retirees who were attracted to the town by its sense of history, quaintness and tranquillity. Others are discovering the unspoiled beauty of St. George Island, accessible by bridge from Eastpoint, just east of town.

For those who grew up in a small town and went to the big city to earn a living and raise a family, but have yearned for the day when they could return to a slower-paced, simpler time, Apalachicola is the town that time forgot.

WEATHER

	Winter	Spring	Summer	Fall
Normal daily high/low	64/48	82/66	88/73	71/54
Normal precipitation	12 in.	10 in.	22 in.	11 in.

Disaster watch: Northwest Florida has been hit by six major hurricanes since 1900.

TAXES
Sales tax: 6%. **Property tax:** $25.25 per $1,000 valuation. Sample tax calculations include a $25,000 homestead exemption.

Home value	Tax
$100,000	$1,894
$150,000	$3,156
$250,000	$5,681

REAL ESTATE
Median home value: $81,769 (Franklin County). **Median rent:** $206/month (Franklin County). **Communities popular with retirees:** East Point, West St. George Island and the historic neighborhoods of Apalachicola are attracting retirees, according to Marilyn Hogan of the chamber of commerce. Lots on west St. George Island are priced from $12,000 to $300,000. Single-family homes sell for $80,000 to $1 million. In historic Apalachicola many older homes have been renovated. For example, one home in need of total rehabilitation was available for $39,000. **Licensed continuing-care retirement communities:** None.

CRIME & SAFETY
Crimes per 1,000 population: 36. **Non-emergency police:** (850) 653-9432. **Non-emergency fire department:** (850) 653-9319. **Police, fire, ambulance emergencies:** 911.

HOMELESS & BLIGHT
Apalachicola is a town forgotten by time. Much of it looks the same as it might have 50 years ago — just more weathered. Some might call it blighted, others would say the town is graced with vestiges of an honorable past. There was no evidence of homeless persons.

The U.S. Census recorded the county's population as 8,967, with 17 homeless persons counted in shelters.

HEALTH CARE
Hospitals: George E. Weems Memorial Hospital, 22 beds, 24-hour emergency care, minor surgery, (850) 653-8853. **Physicians:** 12. **Specialties:** General surgery, family practice.

GETTING SMART
There are no college or university campuses in Apalachicola.

JUST FOR SENIORS
Senior Citizens of Franklin County, (850) 653-8910. **Franklin County Senior Center** is 15 miles away in Carrabelle, (850) 697-3760.

GETTING INVOLVED
Apalachicola Area Historical Society, (850) 653-9524. **Economic Development Council**, (850) 222-3000.

RECREATION, ENTERTAINMENT & AMENITIES
Public and private golf: None. **Semiprivate golf:** St. Joseph Bay Country Club (30 minute drive). Wildwood Country Club (45 minute drive). Environmental approval is holding up construction of a 9-hole public course along Island Drive leading to St. George Island. **Public tennis courts:** None. **Private tennis courts:** None. **Parks:** St. George Island State Park lies just off the coast. Two city parks, Waterfront-Lafayette and Battery, have fishing piers and picnic facilities. Also, Apalachicola National Forest. **Public swim-**

ming pools: None. **Water sports:** More than 180 species of fish are spawned here, so fishing is a primary pastime in the waters around town. Also, canoeing, sailing, scuba diving and snorkeling. **River/gulf/ocean:** Apalachicola Bay is one of the most productive bays in the country, supporting major fisheries for oysters, shrimp and crab. Two rivers, the bay, bayous, tidal creeks, marshes and barrier islands all play a part in the ecology of the area. **Running/walking/biking:** Apalachicola National Forest provides miles of forest hiking trails. This entire area is so sparsely populated that it is ideal for running, walking and cycling. St. George Island State Park has hiking and nature studies. **Horses/riding:** No stables, but good horse country for those who own horses. **Hunting:** Plenty of hunting sites for fox, deer, bear and turkey. For licenses and information, contact the Florida Game and Freshwater Fish Commission, (850) 265-3676. **Movie theaters:** None. **Art museums:** None. **History museums:** Historic district homes dating to the 1830s; Gorrie Museum, a tribute to inventor of the ice maker; and Apalachicola Maritime Museum. **Theaters:** The Dixie Theater has summer stock. **Library:** Municipal Library. **Attractions:** Fort Gadsden State Historic Site, St. George Island State Park and Cape St. George Lighthouse. **Necessities:** A post office, three banks, five groceries (but no supermarkets), eleven restaurants, two gas stations, one new car dealership, hardware store, two funeral homes and seven motels and inns.

Smart Shopper Tip: Shoppers will have to make regularly scheduled trips to Panama City or Tallahassee. Retail establishments here are easy to find, clustered near Franklin County's only traffic signal at Market Street and Avenue E (U.S. Highway 98).

WHO LIVES HERE
Population: 2,815 year-round residents, an increase of 213 since 1990. **Age 65+** = 17.3% in Franklin County. **Median household income:** $19,803 (Franklin County). **Per capita income:** $15,431 (Franklin County).

NUMBERS TO KNOW
Chamber of commerce: (850) 653-9419. **Voter registration:** (850) 653-9520. **Vehicle registration, tags & title:** (850) 653-9323. **Driver's license:** (850) 670-8061.

WHAT TO READ
Apalachicola Times, weekly newspaper, (850) 653-8868. **A Guide to Florida's Forgotten Coast**, (850) 653-9419.

GETTING AROUND
Bus: Commuter bus transportation between Apalachicola, East Point and St. George Island. **Taxi:** None. **Tours:** Historic district carriage tours. **Airport:** Tallahassee Regional is 85 miles away; Panama City Regional is 65 miles away. **Traffic:** None.

JOBS
County unemployment rate: 4.6%. **Florida Jobs and Benefits:** (850) 653-9790.

UTILITIES
Electricity: Florida Power Corp., (800) 700-8744. **Gas:** AmeriGas Corp., (850) 653-9531. **Water & sewer:** Apalachicola City Hall, (850) 653-9319. **Telephone:** G. T. Comm., (850) 229-7231. **Cable**

TV: Media Comm., (800) 239-8411.

PLACES OF WORSHIP
One Catholic and 11 Protestant churches.

THE ENVIRONMENT
Water quality has been rated as generally fair to good throughout the bay. Concerns have been raised about the rapid development of St. George Island and also about the impact of the fisheries on the area.

EVENTS AND FESTIVALS
St. George Island Chili Cookoff & Auction - March. **Florida Seafood Festival** - November.

WHERE TO EAT
Apalachicola Seafood Grill and Steak House, 100 Market Street, seafood and steaks, moderate to expensive, (850) 653-9510. **The Gibson Inn**, Market Street, seafood, steaks and specialty dishes, moderate, (850) 653-2191. **Oyster Cove Seafood Bar & Grill**, 200 Gunn St., expensive, (850) 927-2600. **That Place In Apalach**, 15 Avenue D, crab cakes, light seafood dishes, pasta, moderate to expensive, (850) 653-9888.

WHERE TO STAY
Gibson Inn, (850) 653-2191. **St. George Inn**, (850) 670-2903. **Buccaneer Inn** (St. George Island), (800) 847-2091.

ISSUES
Expect the new to confront the old, and the old to oppose the new. Most residents of this town like it just the way it is. High-energy newcomers who want to add a few entertainment opportunities do not find many local supporters.

RELOCATION TIPS

Many moving companies offer additional services that can run up the total cost of the move. Decide in advance if you want to handle them yourself or pay to have the mover handle them for you. Generally, the following services are not free:
- Disconnecting/reconnecting appliances.
- Disconnecting/reconnecting light fixtures.
- Removing drapes, curtains and other window coverings.
- Disassembling, crating a grand piano.
- Packing a grandfather clock.
- Disassembling, crating a pool table with a slate.

Arcadia

In the 1890s, Arcadia was in the middle of the cattle wars as
immortalized by famous cowboy painter Frederic Remington. As
you approach Arcadia today, you get the impression that some of the
100-year-old makeshift buildings are still in use, squatting by the
roadside, housing flea markets, junkyards and cheap motels.

Fortunately, as you enter the downtown area the appearance
improves and begins to reflect the efforts of the Florida Main Street
Program. Since 1985, $3.5 million has been invested in 100-plus
projects. More than 370 buildings now are listed on the National
Register of Historic Places. The downtown is quiet and clean —
good and bad for merchants. Downtown offers a secure environment for shoppers, but with only 38 persons per square mile in the
DeSoto County market, there aren't enough shoppers.

Cattle ranching, citrus growing and agriculture drive the economy,
but not strongly enough as more than 7 percent of the available work
force was unemployed at the time we visited.

Positives in Arcadia include a number of attractive manufactured
housing developments. Among them, Arcadia Village Country
Club is a gated, beautifully landscaped adult community with a
nine-hole golf course, clubhouse, a host of recreational facilities,
fishing lakes and nature preserves. It should make everybody's top
10. Manufactured-home developments are so highly valued that
when the chamber of commerce was asked to name the five most
important attributes the community has to attract retirees, they
named only three — all manufactured-home and mobile home
parks.

But they do have another asset — the Peace River — which flows
for 47 miles through the pastoral countryside of DeSoto County. It
is designated as a National Canoe Trail, bringing canoeists, campers, fishermen and sightseers from far and wide.

One final asset is its location: Arcadia is only 49 miles from
Sarasota and 47 miles from Fort Myers.

WEATHER

	Winter	Spring	Summer	Fall
Normal daily high/low	77/56	89/71	91/76	80/57
Normal precipitation	8 in.	14 in.	21 in.	7 in.

Disaster watch: Southwest Florida has been hit by five major
hurricanes since 1900.

TAXES

Sales tax: 7%. **Property tax:** $25.94 per $1,000 valuation. Sample
tax calculations include a $25,000 homestead exemption.

Home value	Tax
$100,000	$1,946
$150,000	$3,243
$250,000	$5,837

REAL ESTATE

Median home value: $74,401 (DeSoto County). **Median rent:**
$442/month (DeSoto County). **Communities popular with
retirees:** There are a lot of real estate listings for manufactured
homes priced from the $20s to $40s and site-built, single-family
homes priced from the $40s to mid-$60s. DeSoto Village Mobile Home Park offers homes priced from the high $20s, (941)
494-2900. Arcadia Village has manufactured homes priced
from the mid-$30s to mid-$60s, (941) 494-5669. Arcadia City
Mobile Home Community features homes priced to the $30s,
(941) 494-3939. The Habitat at Sunnybreeze, on the Peace
River, 12 miles southwest of Arcadia, is a new, 89-acre, deed-
restricted community. Oversized lots are from 1/2 acre to 6
acres. Single-family homes with a minimum of 1,850 square
feet and a 2-car garage are priced from $125,000-$250,000.
Licensed continuing-care retirement communities: None.

CRIME & SAFETY

Crimes per 1,000 population: 129. **Non-emergency police:** (941)
993-4660. **Non-emergency fire department:** (941) 494-3229.
Police, fire, ambulance emergencies: 911.

HOMELESS & BLIGHT

There are 374 buildings within a 58-block historic district that
are listed on the National Register of Historic Places. It was
selected as a Florida Main Street City in 1985 and several
million dollars have been spent on rehabilitation and restoration. There are some excellent building restorations including
the Depot and Koch buildings, but despite this effort, the
downtown and surrounding areas still lack distinction. Not
blighted but not really attractive.

The U.S. Census reported 170 homeless persons in shelters and 67
visible in street locations in DeSoto County, population 23,865.

HEALTH CARE

Hospitals: DeSoto Memorial Hospital, 82 private rooms, 34-bed
surgery, eight-bed intensive care unit, 24-hour emergency, specialties, full service, (941) 494-3535.
Physicians: 48 in DeSoto County. **Specialties:** 22.

GETTING SMART

South Florida Community College, (941) 993-1757. **Offerings:**
Two-year associate's degrees, general studies and student development services. **Florida Southern College**, (941) 494-7373. **Offerings:** Bachelor's degree in liberal arts studies for people over 40.

JUST FOR SENIORS

Margaret Way Senior Friendship Center, (941) 494-3378.

GETTING INVOLVED

There are 53 clubs and organizations. Call the chamber for information about **AARP**, **Arcadia Tourist Club** (organizes activities for
seniors), **DeSoto County Historical Society** and **Fine Arts Association**.

RECREATION, ENTERTAINMENT & AMENITIES

Public golf: Arcadia Municipal, nine holes/par 36; Live Oak
Golf Club, semiprivate, nine holes/par 27; and Sunnybreeze

Golf Club, 27 holes/par 108. **Private golf:** Arcadia Village Country Club, nine holes/par 27. **Public tennis courts:** Multiple courts available at four municipal recreation centers. **Private tennis courts:** None. **Parks:** DeSoto County, Morgan City and Myakka River State Park. **Public swimming pools:** None. **Water sports:** Canoe outpost of the 67-mile National Canoe Trail on the Peace River. **River/gulf/ocean:** The Peace River flows by Arcadia on its 47-mile trip through DeSoto County, bringing canoeists, campers, fishermen and sightseers to the area. **Running/walking/biking:** A bike path runs from Arcadia Village to Wal-Mart Plaza. There are walking paths in DeSoto Park and Morgan Park. **Horses/riding:** All-Florida Saddle Club. The Royal Lipizzaner Stallions of Austria train in nearby Myakka City from January through March. **Hunting:** None. **Movie theaters:** Twin. **Art museums:** None. **History museums:** The Depot, DeSoto County Historical Society and Peace River Valley Historical Society. **Theaters:** DeSoto Little Theater. **Library:** DeSoto County. **Attractions:** Arcadia Village Country Club, Peace River and the absence of traffic jams, hustle and bustle. **Necessities:** Four banks, two savings and loan associations, supermarkets and discount general merchandise stores.

Smart Shopper Tip: Three shopping plazas downtown will accommodate your basic needs. Drive to Sarasota or Fort Myers in less than an hour for extras.

WHO LIVES HERE
Population: 6,577 year-round residents, an increase of 89 since 1990. **Age 65+** = 20.1% in DeSoto County. **Median household income:** $20,443 (DeSoto County). **Per capita income:** $17,625 (DeSoto County).

NUMBERS TO KNOW
Chamber of commerce: (941) 494-4033. **Voter registration:** (941) 993-4871. **Vehicle registration, tags & title:** (941) 993-4861. **Driver's license:** (941) 993-4861.

WHAT TO READ
The Arcadian, weekly newspaper, (941) 494-2434. **DeSoto Sun Herald**, daily newspaper, (941) 494-7600. **Tampa Tribune**, daily newspaper, (941) 993-1700.

GETTING AROUND
Bus: Margaret Way Senior Friendship Center, for seniors, (941) 494-5965. **Taxi:** Arcadia Cab, (941) 993-1711. **Tours:** Self-guided tour of 20 restored, historic buildings. **Airport:** Sarasota/Bradenton International and Southwest Florida International are both within an hour's drive. **Traffic:** A strong road network, including U.S. Highway 17, serves Arcadia. Traffic is light even during peak hours.

JOBS
County unemployment rate: 7.4%. **Florida Jobs and Benefits:** (941) 575-5770.

UTILITIES
Electricity: Florida Power & Light, (941) 334-7754. **Gas:** None. **Water & sewer:** City of Arcadia, (941) 494-4114. **Telephone:** United Telephone, (800) 282-7229. **Cable TV:** ComCast Cable, (800) 363-4037.

PLACES OF WORSHIP
One Catholic and 48 Protestant churches.

THE ENVIRONMENT
Surface water quality in the area is affected by agriculture, Arcadia's waste-water treatment plant and range land. There have been fish kills due to spills from a phosphate dam. Though some index measurements put the Peace River's rating in the fair water quality category, it has relatively good water quality in this area and has shown an improving trend.

EVENTS AND FESTIVALS
DeSoto County Fair - March. **Arcadia All-Florida Championship Rodeo** - March and July. **Watermelon Festival** - May. **Christmas Card Lane** - December. **Arcadia Main Street Block Party and Historic Homes Tour** - December.

WHERE TO EAT
Wheeler's Goody Cafe, 13 S. Monroe Ave., home-style country cooking, inexpensive, (941) 494-3909. **Paradise**, 903 N. Brevard Ave., steak, seafood, chicken, inexpensive, (941) 494-2061.

WHERE TO STAY
Best Western Arcadia Inn, (941) 494-4884. **Historic Parker House**, a bed and breakfast, (941) 494-2499 or (800) 969-2499.

ISSUES
Attracting jobs and residents and reducing the crime rate. The town has done a lot to improve its appeal. It spent millions on downtown revitalization. It has a good road network, a good location and historical assets. Still, Arcadia needs people and a strong economic base to fulfill its potential.

RELOCATION TIPS

If you'll be moving a pet, have it bathed, groomed and dipped before you move to ensure that your pet will be clean and free of fleas and other insects when it arrives at your new home. Use your pet's regular water bowl and food bowls and set up familiar bedding and toys. These things signal the animal that this new place is home. Let your dog or cat explore your new home and outside surroundings gradually, allowing at least a week or two for acclimatization.

Bartow

HE SAID: ✮ ✮ ✮
It doesn't have the same hometown qualities of Dade City, the beauty of Mount Dora or the seaside village charm of Dunedin, but it does have a secure feel about it that holds some attraction in these violent times. That and the sparseness of traffic are enticing, but not enough to bring my moving van to its doors.

SHE SAID: ✮ ✮
There are no frills or fanfare, just simple and slowed-down living. Very little to do and very limited shopping. I would not retire here.

The drive into Bartow on Route 60 from the west reveals miles of phosphate mining and fertilizer manufacturing operations interspersed with miles of citrus groves. This is the phosphate mining capital of the world and the largest citrus-producing region in Florida.

Bartow, the county seat, takes a back seat to its larger and better known neighbors, Lakeland and Winter Haven, a few miles north. A city with few frills, it has some nice features. The Civic Plaza provides a cool resting place for downtown shoppers and workers. The Civic Center has courts for tennis, handball and racquetball and a swimming pool large enough to accommodate the entire citizenry — or at least all those who want to swim. The county courthouses, both old and new, stand with majesty downtown. For recreation, the appropriately named Peace River offers fishing, boating and a venue for exploratory excursions along its southerly course to Charlotte Harbor and the Gulf of Mexico.

There are eight parks and wildlife management areas and five golf courses within a few miles of Bartow. These occupy land reclaimed from phosphate mining operations, donated or dedicated for public use by the phosphate companies "as proof that mining does not permanently scar the environment," according to a phosphate industry official. That, of course, does not change the polluted status of the Peace and Alafia rivers.

An in-town Health Walk course is an unexpected symbol of progressiveness in a town that shows little interest in making giant strides into the 21st century. In fact, a great deal of the 19th century still is apparent in Bartow's public buildings and houses. If the town has any appeal for retirees, it is probably its obvious reluctance to change.

Bartow is proudly described in chamber of commerce literature as "one of those rare communities where people can still enjoy late afternoon strolls and the secluded privacy of their own back yard." That pretty well sums up the charm of Bartow.

WEATHER

	Winter	Spring	Summer	Fall
Normal daily high/low	76/52	89/65	92/72	80/58
Normal precipitation	9 in.	13 in.	21 in.	7 in.

Disaster watch: Southwest Florida has been hit by five major hurricanes since 1900.

TAXES
Sales tax: 6%. **Property tax:** $17.72 per $1,000 valuation. Sample tax calculations include a $25,000 homestead exemption.

Home value	Tax
$100,000	$1,329
$150,000	$2,215
$250,000	$3,986

REAL ESTATE
Median home value: $89,109 (Polk County). **Median rent:** $542/month (Polk County). **Communities popular with retirees:** There are seven mobile home parks, none upscale. Floral Lakes is the nicest. There are several nice, old homes that with a few restorative touches could appeal to those with a bent for historical preservation. Oak Hammock offers manufactured homes priced from the high $10s to high $30s, excluding the cost of the land lease, (800) 423-6814. **Licensed continuing-care retirement communities:** None.

CRIME & SAFETY
Crimes per 1,000 population: 101. **Non-emergency police:** (941) 534-5034. **Non-emergency fire department:** (941) 534-5044. **Police, fire, ambulance emergencies:** 911.

HOMELESS & BLIGHT
Bartow is in the heart of a phosphate mining and fertilizer manufacturing district, thus much of the suburban landscape is marred by these operations. The town itself is clean, open-spaced and seems fairly prosperous. We did not see any homeless persons.

The U.S. Census reported 172 homeless persons in shelters and 33 visible in street locations in Polk County, population 405,382.

HEALTH CARE
Hospitals: Columbia Bartow Memorial Hospital, 56 beds, 24-hour emergency, full service, (941) 533-8111. Ground breaking for a new $30 million replacement facility took place in the spring of 1998.
Physicians: 57. **Specialties:** 29.

GETTING SMART
There are no college or university campuses in Bartow. **Warner Southern College** in Lake Wales, (941) 638-1426. **Offerings:** Four-year Christian college offers liberal arts degrees. **Webber College** in Lake Wales, (941) 638-1431. **Offerings:** Two- and four-year degrees in business administration with a concentration in travel and tourism. **Florida Southern College** in Lakeland, (941) 680-4111. **Offerings:** Four-year and MBA degree programs.

JUST FOR SENIORS
Bartow Multipurpose Senior Center, (941) 534-0393. **Golden Age Club**, (941) 534-0121. **VISTE** (Volunteers In Service To the Elderly), (941) 284-0828. A senior citizen hunting and fishing certificate is free.

GETTING INVOLVED
There are 26 civic organizations. **Downtown Bartow, Inc.**, (941) 534-4030.

RECREATION, ENTERTAINMENT & AMENITIES
Public golf: Bartow Municipal Golf Course. **Private golf:** None.

Florida Price Level Index: 95.64 (Polk County). **Rank:** 27th most expensive county.

Public tennis courts: Civic Center Complex. Private tennis courts: None. Parks: Mary Holland Park has 26 acres. There are many parks in the area on reclaimed phosphate lands. Public swimming pools: Civic Center Complex. Water sports: Boating and water-skiing. River/gulf/ocean: The IMC Corporation Wildlife Management Area has a 310-acre man-made lake. Also, Peace River and Lake Hancock, the largest lake in west-central Florida. Running/walking/biking: Mary Holland Park has a trail primarily used for jogging. The in-town Health Walk course uses city sidewalks. The rural environment offers many opportunities. Horses/riding: There are horse farms and stables in the area and plenty of room for riding. Hunting: Duck hunting during season, contact the Florida Game and Freshwater Fish Commission, (941) 648-3206. Movie theaters: Bartow Drive-In. Art museums: None. History museums: The restored 1908 courthouse now houses the Polk County Historical Museum. Theaters: None. Library: Polk County Historical and Genealogical Library is located in the 1908 courthouse. Bartow Public is in a new building. Attractions: None that bring tourists. Peace River is popular for recreation. Necessities: Seven banks and the usual array of small-town goods and services.

Smart Shopper Tip: For serious shopping, drive 20 miles to Lakeland Square Mall and browse through its five anchors and 130 stores.

WHO LIVES HERE
Population: 14,925 year-round residents, an increase of 209 since 1990. **Age 65+** = 19.6% in Polk County. **Median household income:** $26,191 (Polk County). **Per capita income:** $19,126 (Polk County).

NUMBERS TO KNOW
Chamber of commerce: (941) 533-7125. **Voter registration:** (941) 534-7380. **Vehicle registration, tags & title:** (941) 534-4711. **Driver's license:** (941) 678-4160. **Visitors bureau:** (800) 828-7655.

WHAT TO READ
The Ledger, daily newspaper, (941) 802-7000. **Polk County Democrat,** biweekly newspaper, (941) 533-4183.

GETTING AROUND
Bus: No public intra-city transportation. **Taxi:** None. **Tours:** None. **Airport:** Tampa International and Orlando International are both about an hour away. **Traffic:** Though Bartow is dissected by several major highways, traffic generally is light and congestion avoidable.

JOBS
County unemployment rate: 6.6%. **Florida Jobs and Benefits:** In Lakeland, (941) 499-2340.

UTILITIES
Electricity: City of Bartow, (941) 534-0100. **Gas:** Central Florida Gas Corp., (941) 293-2125. **Water & sewer:** City of Bartow, (941) 534-0100. **Telephone:** GTE Florida, (941) 687-2937. **Cable TV:** ComCast Cable, (941) 533-9029.

PLACES OF WORSHIP
37 Protestant churches.

THE ENVIRONMENT
The Peace River suffers from pollutants from mining operations and discharge from waste-water treatment plants (WWTP). It has been rated as having generally poor water quality but is improving. Lake Hancock and other nearby lakes are affected by mining operations and past discharge from a WWTP and have generally poor water quality.

The lower Alafia River exhibits poor water quality. A phosphate processing facility at the mouth of the river contributes to the degradation of the lower Alafia. Radium levels in this river are higher than any other stream on Florida's west coast, also thought to be due to phosphate mining residues.

There is one EPA-listed Superfund site in Polk County. The Alpha Chemical Corporation site is located in Kathleen, three miles north of Lakeland.

EVENTS AND FESTIVALS
Bloomin' Arts Festival - April.

WHERE TO EAT
Contact the chamber of commerce for suggestions, (941) 533-7125.

WHERE TO STAY
Stanford Inn, (941) 533-2393.

ISSUES
With a new hospital building under construction, a recent ribbon-cutting ceremony for the new Bartow Public Library and the conversion of the old courthouse to a new historical museum, Bartow seems to be taking care of its building infrastructure. Now it needs to concentrate on its elevated juvenile crime rate with the same intensity.

RELOCATION TIPS

If you've purchased a used home, have all the locks re-keyed since it is not at all unusual for real estate agents and friends of the previous residents to have keys to your new house. Rather than try to account for and collect all the keys, arrange to have a locksmith come out immediately so you can rest comfortably at night. While the locksmith is at your home, make sure you have keys for everything, including outdoor utility, storage and tool rooms.

Big Pine Key

HE SAID: ★ ★
> *There is a need for places like this. Individualists seeking a life without excessive peer influence, avid fishermen, water enthusiasts and those who yearn for a secluded, rural environment should take a look. All others need not apply!*

SHE SAID: ★ ★
> *You are in the center of Big Pine Key before you realize it. A very laid-back community with few shopping facilities and little entertainment. Most houses are set back in wooded areas, away from the main stream of traffic. I got a very desolate feeling while driving around Big Pine Key. It's not for me.*

In July 1992, Monroe County adopted an ordinance severely limiting the number of building permits that can be issued each year for the construction of new dwelling units. As a result, the development rate in the unincorporated county dropped from an average of 552 dwelling units each year since 1972 to 255 units per year for the next 10 years.

Slowing the rate of growth was essential for the following reasons: timely hurricane evacuation; limited traffic capacity of the only through artery, U.S. 1; protection of sensitive onshore and offshore natural resources; the capacity to pipe in potable water from the mainland; and prevention of further degradation of onshore water quality by limiting construction of new septic tank systems and eliminating cesspits.

Sparsely inhabited and encompassing more acreage than any of the other Keys, Big Pine's chief attractions are water and solitude. Almost all residential development is either on the waterfront or has canal access to the seas. For those fed up with life in the fast lane and cold climates, Big Pine Key provides plenty of peace and quiet with unending opportunities for boating, fishing and water sports.

Interior lands are used by commerce, government and churches. Other non-waterfront land is reserved for parks and wildlife refuges. This is the home of the Key deer, a small white-tail deer on the endangered species list.

To learn the personality of this Key through the residents themselves, we talked to several before we began to see its appeal. Art and Gracie Morgan retired to Big Pine Key in 1984 from Superior, WI. They own a double-wide manufactured home in an adult community and spend their time boating, fishing, swimming, sunbathing and biking. They say, "If you don't do those things, there is nothing to do — day or night — on Big Pine Key." They weren't complaining. They chose Big Pine Key for its weather, water and relaxed atmosphere. It's not for everyone, but for some it just may be a perfect retirement fit.

Note: You'll commonly see addresses and directions in the Keys based on U.S. Highway 1 Mile Markers, abbreviated as MM.

WEATHER

	Winter	Spring	Summer	Fall
Normal daily high/low	76/67	85/76	89/79	80/71
Normal precipitation	6 in.	10 in.	15 in.	9 in.

Disaster watch: The Keys have been hit by three major hurricanes since 1900.

TAXES

Sales tax: 7%. **Property tax:** $16.12 per $1,000 valuation. Sample tax calculations include a $25,000 homestead exemption.

Home value	Tax
$100,000	$1,209
$150,000	$2,015
$250,000	$3,627

REAL ESTATE

Median home value: $141,640 (Monroe County). **Median rent:** $888/month (Monroe County). **Communities popular with retirees:** Almost all residential properties are resales, and all are expensive. A "fixer-upper" selling for $100,000 in 1993 now sells for $150,000. Homes priced under $200,000 are very limited and move fast. In Whispering Pines, a three-bedroom, 2,100-square-foot stucco house on a 75-by-137-foot lot is priced at $309,000. Prices range from $200,000 to $495,000 for similar models with comparable space. Cudjoe Gardens, a deed-restricted community of $200,000 canal-front homes, has open-water homes priced at $450,000 and up. Cahill Pines and Palms, Cudjoe Harbor Estates and Pine Channel Estates have single-family homes from $175,000 to $350,000. For information, contact ERA Lower Keys, (305) 872-2822. Residential real estate prices are high due to restricted land use. Two factors keep prices up: a land-use ordinance limiting new construction permits in the Keys to 255 per year, and the Key Deer National Wildlife Refuge, which encompasses approximately 8,000 acres and is dedicated to the preservation of the Key deer. **Licensed continuing-care retirement communities:** None.

CRIME & SAFETY

Crimes per 1,000 population: 68 (Monroe County sheriff's jurisdiction). **Non-emergency police:** (305) 872-3311. **Non-emergency fire department:** (305) 872-2844. **Police, fire, ambulance emergencies:** 911.

HOMELESS & BLIGHT

No homeless persons were visible. According to the U.S. Census, Monroe County's population of 78,024 includes 15 homeless persons in shelters and 126 visible in street locations.

HEALTH CARE

Hospitals: Fishermen's Hospital, 18 miles away in Marathon, 58 beds, full service, (305) 743-5533. Big Pine Professional Plaza, Big Pine Medical Complex and Big Pine Medical and Minor Emergency Center all offer health-care services. **Physicians:** 25. **Specialties:** 16.

GETTING SMART

There are no schools on Big Pine Key. Adults can enroll in classes at **Florida Keys Community College** in Key West, (305) 296-9081, or Marathon, (305) 743-2133. **Offerings:** Two-year degree programs, various workshops, courses and seminars.

JUST FOR SENIORS

AARP, (305) 872-3990. **Monroe County Nutrition Program**, (305) 872-3617. **Senior Center**, (305) 872-3990. **Monroe County Social Services** in Marathon, (305) 289-6016.

GETTING INVOLVED
Lions, (305) 872-9357. Big Pine Friends of Animals, (305) 872-2374.

RECREATION, ENTERTAINMENT & AMENITIES
Public golf: None here, nearest is Key West Resort. Private golf: None. Public tennis courts: None. Private tennis courts: None. Parks: Bahia Honda State Park between Marathon and Big Pine Key; Key Deer National Wildlife Refuge; Watson's Hammock, with hardwood trees and subtropical foliage; and Big Pine Nature Trail. Public swimming pools: None. Water sports: Scuba diving at the Looe Key National Marine Sanctuary, five miles south of Big Pine, offers a spectacular living coral reef. There's fishing for sailfish, dolphin, marlin, shark, wahoo, mackerel, tuna, barracuda, grouper, snapper, tarpon and other varieties. Sea kayaking, water-skiing, snorkeling and windsurfing are also popular. River/gulf/ocean: Gulf of Mexico and the Atlantic Ocean. Running/walking/biking: Limited vehicular traffic means there are many running, walking and biking opportunities. Try the trail at the Blue Hole rock quarry pond to see deer, alligators and exotic birds. Horses/riding: Yes. Hunting: None. Movie theaters: None here, though there are two in Key West and two in Marathon. Art museums: None. History museums: None. Theaters: None. Library: Monroe County Library branch. Attractions: Blue Hole. Necessities: Banks, limited retail shopping, a supermarket, real estate agencies and a post office.

Smart Shopper Tip: You can go 20 miles to Marathon or 31 miles to Key West, but to do any serious shopping, you should make the 128-mile trip to Miami and the Mainland. Big Pine shopping is of the tourist variety where, as one ad read, "You can purchase tropical handmade clothing and a fresh-baked loaf of bread right at the same location." From October through May you can spend weekends at the Big Pine Key International Flea Market.

WHO LIVES HERE
Population: 4,820 year-round residents, an increase of 614 since 1990. Age 65+ = 17.5% in Monroe County. Median household income: $30,720 (Monroe County). Per capita income: $27,210 (Monroe County).

NUMBERS TO KNOW
Chamber of commerce: (305) 872-2411 for newcomer information. Voter registration: Any bank or library in Monroe County, (305) 289-6017. Vehicle registration, tags & title: Mobile unit makes scheduled stops, (305) 743-5585. Driver's license: (305) 289-2306. Visitors information center: (800) 872-3722.

WHAT TO READ
Managing Growth in the Florida Keys: Environmental and Economic Stress in the Conch Republic, written by John E. Fernsler, 191 Giralda Avenue, Penthouse, Coral Gables, FL 33134. Key West Citizen, daily newspaper, (305) 294-6641. Lower Keys Barometer, weekly, (305) 872-0106.

GETTING AROUND
Bus: No local public transportation. Taxi: Island Taxi, (305) 664-8181. Tours: Go Tours, (305) 743-9876. Airport: Key West International (30 miles). Marathon Airport (21 miles) has a new passenger terminal. Traffic: Very light; heavier during the tourist season.

JOBS
County unemployment rate: 2.5%. Florida Jobs and Benefits: In Key West, (305) 292-6775. In Marathon, (305) 289-2475.

UTILITIES
Electricity: Coastal Electric Service, (305) 872-4133. Gas: National Propane, (305) 294-3527. Water & sewer: Florida Keys Aqueduct Authority, (305) 296-2454. Telephone: Bell South, (800) 789-9025 in Florida, or (800) 753-0710 out-of-state. Cable TV: TCI Cablevision of Florida, (305) 743-5776.

PLACES OF WORSHIP
One Catholic and six Protestant churches.

THE ENVIRONMENT
The island waters that open to the Atlantic Ocean or Gulf of Mexico are rated as having good water quality and are all designated as Outstanding Florida Waters, granting them legal protection against any significant change in water quality. There are pollution problems in many of the man-made canals and marinas. Along the east coast lies the only living coral reef in the continental United States The delicate reefs are easily damaged by careless divers, boat anchors and commercial ship grindings and/or spills. The Florida Keys National Marine Sanctuary Plan has not delivered the death blow to local water sports — boating, diving, snorkeling and fishing — that some feared. On the contrary, its protective covenants should enhance the quiet Lower Keys lifestyle for decades to come.

EVENTS AND FESTIVALS
Island Food Festival - March. Underwater Music Festival - July. Annual Island Art Fair - December.

WHERE TO EAT
K. D's Big Pine Steaks & Seafood at MM 30.5, Overseas Highway (U.S. 1), steak, seafood, moderate, (305) 872-2314. Big Pine Coffee Shop at MM 30, Overseas Highway, home-style, inexpensive, (305) 872-2790.

WHERE TO STAY
There are no rated hotels or motels in Big Pine Key. Check on vacation rental homes with ERA Lower Keys Realty, (305) 872-2258, or Big Pine Vacation Rentals, (305) 872-9863.

ISSUES
The Building Permit Allocation System could mean a long wait and severe restrictions on where your new home can be built. Before you make the trip to pick out your lot or select a builder, contact the Monroe County Growth Management Division, 2798 Overseas Highway, Suite 400, Marathon, FL 33050-2227, and ask for information. Restricted growth may turn out to be a blessing for those with the patience and perseverance to work it out.

Boca Raton

HE SAID: ★ ★ ★ ★ ☆
> *As far as I'm concerned, a prerequisite for any retirement locale is a golf course. So I'm naturally attracted to Boca, which has more than its fair share. If the cost of living wasn't so darn high, I'd move here right now.*

SHE SAID: ★ ★ ★ ★ ☆
> *I wouldn't have any trouble retiring in Boca Raton if I could afford the area between Route A1A and South Federal Highway. This is a magnificent area. Busy streets lined with interesting shopping centers and businesses give way to a tree-lined residential area. A cut above.*

Boca Raton excels in beauty and amenities. It has more greenery and open space than most cities have in their best sections. A sense of serenity emanates from the surroundings; orderly streets, a surprising spaciousness and lush landscaping are prominent here.

Much of the housing in the Boca Raton area is centered around club developments. In fact, a map reveals no less than 26 country club communities, most with at least one golf course.

Beyond golf courses, the diversity of the city's resources and assets defies comparison. It has beaches, canals, lakes, residential neighborhoods, parks, recreational facilities, hospitals, museums, cultural facilities and civic organizations. And, it has people who care about the quality of life.

The Mae Volen Senior Center speaks to the caring and giving nature of this city. With almost 1,000 members, the center provides a wide range of services, including the usual arts and crafts and shopping excursions. You'll also find income tax assistance, nutrition programs, a day-care program and a Wednesday bingo game. The cheerful demeanor of its members, beautifully landscaped grounds and well-maintained facility speak volumes about the relationship between the city and its older citizens.

Florida Atlantic University is another example of Boca's resources. The university of 13,000 students occupies an 850-acre campus in the heart of the city. In addition to providing intellectual stimulus, it is a popular forum for concerts, dance and theater. Best of all, the university is senior-friendly, offering the Lifelong Learning Society to encourage the pursuit of education, regardless of age.

Though the city has a strong business community, emphasizing high-tech companies and corporate headquarters, its downtown is a low-key business center, designed to be peopled. The industrial corridor adjacent to I-95 acts as a buffer zone, protecting the aesthetics of the residential areas and keeping some traffic out of the city.

Unincorporated areas west of the city are benefiting from Boca's popularity and offer lower-cost housing. More than 75,000 people now live in Boca West, Mission Bay, Town Center and other areas where real estate is somewhat less expensive.

If you have the wherewithal to afford life in Boca Raton, life here could afford you ample opportunity for enjoyment.

WEATHER

	Winter	Spring	Summer	Fall
Normal daily high/low	77/59	86/69	91/74	82/65
Normal precipitation	8 in.	18 in.	20 in.	13 in.

Disaster watch: Nine major hurricanes have hit southeast Florida since 1900.

TAXES
Sales tax: 6%. **Property tax:** $21.09 per $1,000 valuation. Sample tax calculations include a $25,000 homestead exemption.

Home value	Tax
$100,000	$1,582
$150,000	$2,636
$250,000	$4,745

REAL ESTATE
Median home value: $101,611 (Palm Beach County). **Median rent:** $773/month (Palm Beach County). **Communities popular with retirees:** Bonnie Goldstein with Arvida Realty Sales, Ltd., (561) 347-3431, or (800) 443-8182 says the following properties are drawing retirees: Boca Century Village, condos and garden apartments from $30,000-$80,000; Boca Tecca Country Club, golf course homes from $55,000-$130,000; Whisper Walk, condos and villas from $60,000-$140,000; Boca West, gated with villas, condos and townhouses from $90,000-$280,000; and Polo Club, with condos, villas and townhouses from $160,000-$320,000 and single-family homes from $260,000-$1,000,000. **Licensed continuing-care retirement communities:** Edgewater Pointe Estates, 414 independent living units, 60 sheltered nursing beds and 41 community beds, (561) 391-6305; St. Andrews Estates, 635 independent living units and 120 community beds, (561) 487-5500. Several adult congregate living facilities are located here, including The Fountains, (561) 395-7510, and Avante at Boca Raton, (561) 394-6282.

CRIME & SAFETY
Crimes per 1,000 population: 42. **Non-emergency police:** (561) 338-1234. **Non-emergency fire department:** (561) 367-6700. **Police, fire, ambulance emergencies:** 911.

HOMELESS & BLIGHT
Every community has a low-income area, even Boca Raton. But here it is neither run-down nor ramshackle. We saw no evidence of blight or homeless persons. The county's U.S. Census population figure of 863,000 includes 416 homeless persons.

HEALTH CARE
Hospitals: Boca Raton Community Hospital, 394 beds, full service, (561) 395-7100. **West Boca Medical Center**, 185 beds, full service, (561) 488-8000. **Boca Raton Outpatient Surgery and Laser Center**, 151 physicians, 11 specialties, (561) 362-4400. **Physicians:** 500+. **Specialties:** 45+.

GETTING SMART
Palm Beach Community College, South Campus, (561) 367-4500. Associate degrees and university transfer credits. **Florida Atlantic University**, (561) 297-3000. FAU's Lifelong Learning Society, (561) 297-3171. **Offerings:** Lifelong Learning Society members can enroll in regular course offerings or special LIFEcourse programs for degree credit, non-credit or audit. **Lynn University**, (561) 994-0770, offers the Institute for Learning in Retirement (ILIR), (561) 883-0999. **Offerings:** Bachelor's degree programs in accounting, business administration, marketing, behavioral science, history, political science and liberal arts. Through ILIR, members can take up to three non-credit, eight-week courses in psychology, music, poetry, literature, movies and humanities. ILIR courses are peer-directed.

JUST FOR SENIORS
Mae Volen Senior Center offers many services to members, including telephone reassurance checkups, (561) 395-8920. **Ruth**

Rales Jewish Family Service, (561) 852-3333. **AARP,** (561) 479-4154.

GETTING INVOLVED
More than 100 organizations, supported by thousands of local volunteers, provide a variety of services to groups and individuals of all ages and circumstances. **United Way of South Palm Beach County,** (561) 547-1000. **Boca Raton Historical Society,** (561) 395-6766. **Elder Hotline,** (561) 547-8677.

RECREATION, ENTERTAINMENT & AMENITIES
There are 25 golf courses in Boca Raton. **Public golf:** Municipal Golf Course, Red Reef Executive Course and seven other public or semiprivate courses. **Private golf:** Boca Woods Country Club, Camino Del Mar Country Club, Wood Field Country Club, Wycliff Golf and Country Club, to name a few. **Public tennis courts:** Memorial Park Municipal Tennis Center has nine lighted courts, Patch Reef Park has 17 courts, plus courts at many public parks. **Private tennis courts:** Athletic Center at Boca Pointe Country Club, Boca Raton Bath & Tennis Club, and Racquet Club of Boca Raton. **Parks:** An extensive park system offers more than 30 recreation sites, including 93-acre Spanish River Park, 67-acre Gumbo Limbo Nature Center and 55-acre Patch Reef Park. **Public swimming pools:** Meadows Park Pool and Mission Bay Olympic Aquatic Training Facility. **Water sports:** Water-skiing, surfing, snorkeling, scuba diving, windsurfing and fishing are all popular. **River/gulf/ocean:** The Atlantic Ocean, Intracoastal Waterway and several canals offer lots of water access for sports and fishing. **Running/walking/biking:** Many parks have jogging/fitness trails and exercise courses. Call the Boca Raton Road Runners and Walkers Club for information, (561) 395-4433. The Boca Raton Bicycle Club offers a tour of Boca on the third Sunday of each month with police escort. Or, call Boca Schwinn, (561) 391-0800, to join the weekly 38-mile group ride to Lake Worth and back. **Horses/riding:** An equestrian center, stable and riding academy are in the area. **Hunting:** Not allowed within city limits. Licenses and information, (561) 355-2622 in Florida only. **Movie theaters:** 28 screens at three theaters. **Art museums:** Boca Raton Museum of Art, Ritter Art Gallery at Florida Atlantic University and the International Museum of Cartoon Art. **History museums:** Boca Raton Historical Society, Singing Pines Children's Museum and F.E.C. Railroad Station. **Theaters:** Harid Conservatory, Caldwell Theatre Company, Florida Atlantic University Theater, Florida Academy of Dramatic Art, Little Palm Theatre (children's programs) and Royal Palm Dinner Theatre. **Library:** Boca Raton Public Library and Southwest County Regional Library. **Attractions:** The Sporting Club of Boca, Gumbo Limbo Nature Center, Royal Palm Polo Sports Club, Boca Raton Resort & Club. **Necessities:** Retail, financial and other services abound.

Smart Shopper Tip: Town Center at Boca Raton is the largest and busiest shopping mall, with almost 200 stores in 1.3 million square feet. There are at least 25 other shopping centers in the area, so careful shoppers compare prices around town. All of the most elite names in retail as well as the discount giants compete in this market, where nearly half of the households have annual income in excess of $52,000.

WHO LIVES HERE
Population: 68,432 year-round residents, an increase of 6,946 since 1990. **Age 65+** = 25.0% in Palm Beach County. **Median household income:** $33,094 (Palm Beach County). **Per capita income:** $36,057 (Palm Beach County).

NUMBERS TO KNOW
Chamber of commerce: (561) 395-4433. **Voter registration:** (561) 355-2650. **Vehicle registration, tags & title:** (561) 355-2622. **Driver's license:** (561) 681-6333.

WHAT TO READ
Boca Raton News, daily newspaper, (561) 395-8300. **Palm Beach Post,** daily newspaper, (561) 820-4100. **Boca Raton Annual,** a chamber of commerce publication, (561) 395-4433.

GETTING AROUND
Bus: PalmTran, (561) 233-1166. **Taxi:** Yellow Cab, (561) 395-3221. **Tours:** Historical Society schedules guided tours, (561) 395-6766. **Airport:** Palm Beach International, 25 miles north, or Fort Lauderdale International, 20 miles south. **Traffic:** There's a good road network. Avoid Glades Road during rush hour.

JOBS
County unemployment rate: 6.4%. **Work Force Development Center:** In Delray, (561) 737-4925.

UTILITIES
Electricity: Florida Power & Light, (561) 994-8227. **Gas:** Florida Public Utilities Co., (561) 278-2636. **Water & sewer:** City of Boca Raton, (561) 393-7750. **Telephone:** Bell South, (561) 994-8227 in Florida, or (800) 753-0710 out-of-state. **Cable TV:** ComCast Cablevision, (561) 391-7550.

PLACES OF WORSHIP
Six Catholic and 58 Protestant churches, nine Jewish synagogues.

THE ENVIRONMENT
Sections of the West Palm Beach and Hillsboro canals have been rated as having poor water quality. Fish kills have periodically occurred in the West Palm Beach Canal after heavy rains that drain from the Chemair Spray hazardous waste site. There is one EPA-listed Superfund site in Palm Beach County. It is BMI-Textron in Lake Park.

EVENTS AND FESTIVALS
Royal Palm Polo Arts & Crafts Festival - January. **International Gold Cup Polo Tournament** - March. **Meet Me Downtown** - March. **Mizner Festival** - April/May. **Boca Festival Days** - August.

WHERE TO EAT
La Vielle Maison, 770 E. Palmetto Park Road, French, expensive to very expensive, (561) 391-6701. **Nick's Italian Fishery,** 1 Boca Place, Italian-American, moderate to expensive, (561) 994-2201. **Maxaluna,** 5050 Town Center Circle, Italian, moderate to expensive, (561) 391-7177.

WHERE TO STAY
Boca Raton Resort & Club, (561) 395-3000. **Boca Raton Marriott,** (561) 392-4600. **Radisson Bridge Resort,** (561) 368-9500. **Best Western University Inn,** (561) 395-5225.

ISSUES
Like other cities, there are conflicts here about the pace and progress of development and growth. Unlike other cities, Boca Raton seems to be able to resolve such issues with a single goal in mind — the preservation and enhancement of quality of life.

Bonita Springs

HE SAID: ★ ★ ★
> *I had trouble getting in, around and through this community of 26,000 people. It will be interesting to watch how Bonita Springs deals with accelerating growth.*

SHE SAID: ★ ★ ★
> *Located between Fort Myers and Naples, this fast-growing area offers affordable living in many housing styles. Some areas are not so upbeat, but others are beautiful. I might consider Bonita Springs as a place to retire.*

A large, unincorporated area straddling the Lee/Collier county line, it is shown on the chamber of commerce map as bordering both Fort Myers and Naples. All in all, it's a rather impressive chunk of real estate attached to an erstwhile fishing village.

It has the misfortune of attracting both retirees and other new residents at a faster clip than roads and basic infrastructure can accommodate them. When we visited, traffic was at a standstill on both U.S. Highway 41 north and south and Bonita Beach Road, the only "in town" east-west corridor to the beach.

This area has a lot of catching up to do before it is a well-rounded community in the tradition of its northern and southern neighbors. This poses problems and opportunities for new residents moving in during the next few years. Uncrowded restaurants are nice, but the food quality and dining choices don't compare with Naples. The layers of bureaucracy that control every aspect of life in incorporated cities are not here, but neither are many of the services and amenities that accompany these taxing authorities. Fortunately, many of the social and cultural amenities are accessible in Naples and Fort Myers in less time than it takes to cross town in a large city.

Housing options are plentiful. Residents choose from lake, beach, canal and bay-front condominiums and townhomes, gated golf communities, upscale manufactured housing developments, established single-family neighborhoods and quiet, rural areas.

Bonita Beach is a very popular place. Private condominiums mix with resort lodgings along the wide, white sand beach leading to the pretty, blue-green Gulf waters. It's scenic and apparently free of erosion problems.

There are some pretty places in Bonita Springs, but frankly, the overall mix is not one of great scenic beauty. Helter-skelter unplanned growth without the controls of a local planning-zoning authority could produce more problems than solutions.

WEATHER

	Winter	Spring	Summer	Fall
Normal daily high/low	76/55	88/68	91/75	81/62
Normal precipitation	7 in.	14 in.	26 in.	6 in.

Disaster watch: Southwest Florida has been hit by five major hurricanes since 1900.

TAXES
Sales tax: 6%. **Property tax:** $19.11 per $1,000 valuation. Sample tax calculations include a $25,000 homestead exemption.

Home value	Tax
$100,000	$1,433
$150,000	$2,389
$250,000	$4,300

REAL ESTATE
Median home value: $101,528 (Lee County). **Median rent:** $641/month (Lee County). **Communities popular with retirees:** Bonita Bay offers single-family homes, villas and condominiums priced from the $170s to more than $2 million, (800) 277-4119. Hunters Ridge Country Club has coach homes from the $110s, villas from the $140s and single-family homes from the $180s, (941) 992-4242. Pelican Landing has coach homes from the $140s, golf course villas from the $200s and single-family homes from the $250s, (941) 992-9020. Southern Pines is an adult manufactured-home community, (941) 947-1515. **Licensed continuing-care retirement communities:** None.

CRIME & SAFETY
Crimes per 1,000 population: 36 (Lee County sheriff's jurisdiction). **Non-emergency police:** (941) 495-4800. **Non-emergency fire department:** (941) 992-3320. **Police, fire, ambulance emergencies:** 911.

HOMELESS & BLIGHT
The Bonita Springs Community Redevelopment Agency has been involved in downtown improvements. The area is clean and orderly. There was no evidence of homeless persons.

The U.S. Census reported 97 homeless persons in shelters and 203 visible in street locations in Lee County, population 335,113.

HEALTH CARE
Hospitals: Bonita Springs Medical Center, minor emergencies, family medical care facility, outpatient surgery, (941) 992-7000. **North Collier Hospital**, 50 beds, acute care, 24-hour emergency, general care and obstetrics, (941) 597-1417. **Physicians:** 16. **Specialties:** 9.

GETTING SMART
Florida Gulf Coast University opened its doors in 1997. It is located just 15 minutes from the heart of Bonita Springs. Offerings: 16 undergraduate and 10 graduate degree programs, (941) 590-1000. Other college and university campuses are located in Fort Myers and Naples.

JUST FOR SENIORS
Bonita Springs Recreation Center is a multipurpose center used by seniors for a variety of scheduled activities, (941) 992-2556. A Senior Citizens Association is here also.

GETTING INVOLVED
Friends of the Library can be contacted through the Bonita Springs Public Library, (941) 992-0101. **Meals on Wheels**, (941) 498-5251. The chamber can provide phone numbers for **AARP**, **Bonita Improvement Group** and the **Newcomers Club**.

RECREATION, ENTERTAINMENT & AMENITIES
Public golf: Bonita Fairways Country Club, 9 holes/par 29. Bonita Golf Club, 18 holes/par 72; Country Creek, semiprivate, 18 holes/par 60; Hunters Ridge Country Club, semiprivate, 18 holes/par 72; and Pelican's Nest, 36 holes/par 144. **Private golf:** Bonita Bay Club, 54 holes/par 216; Spanish Wells Country Club, 18 holes/par 72; Wildcat Run, 18 holes/par 72; and Worthington Country Club, 18 holes/par 72. **Public tennis**

courts: The Tennis Experience, Bonita Fairways and Bonita Springs Recreation Complex. **Private tennis courts:** Breckenridge Bath & Tennis Club. **Parks:** Barefoot Beach State Preserve, Big Cypress Swamp, Bonita Springs Community Park, Corkscrew Swamp Sanctuary, Delnor-Wiggins Pass State Recreation Area, Koreshan State Historic Park and Lovers Key State Recreation Area. **Public swimming pools:** Bonita Springs Recreation Complex. **Water sports:** Boating, canoeing and sailing. **River/gulf/ocean:** Estero Bay, Gulf of Mexico and the Imperial River. **Running/walking/biking:** Bonita Beach Road has a separate bike lane. There are a number of venues for these activities including the beaches and several area parks. **Horses/riding:** Palm Stables offers a variety of services and there are plenty of rural lands for riding. **Hunting:** Big Cypress Wildlife Management area permits seasonal hunting of deer and wild hogs. Contact the Florida Game and Freshwater Fish Commission, (941) 648-3206. **Movie theaters:** None. **Art museums:** No museums, but there is the Art League of Bonita Springs. **History museums:** None. **Theaters:** Bonita Springs Community Center. **Library:** Bonita Springs Public. **Attractions:** Everglades Wonder Gardens offers a large display of Florida Wildlife. The Naples/Fort Myers Greyhound Track is in Bonita Springs. **Necessities:** All here.

Smart Shopper Tip: Bonita Springs Plaza and Bonita Springs Center are OK for necessities. The Coastland Center, about 20 minutes south on U.S. 41, has four anchors and more than 100 shops.

WHO LIVES HERE
Population: 26,300 year-round residents increases to about 45,000 during high season, November to May. **Age 65+** = 25.7% in Lee County. **Median household income:** $29,174 (Lee County). **Per capita income:** $23,664 (Lee County).

NUMBERS TO KNOW
Chamber of commerce: (941) 992-2943. **Voter registration:** In Lee County, (941) 339-6300, or in Collier County, (941) 774-8451. **Vehicle registration, tags & title:** (941) 339-6000. **Driver's license:** (941) 278-7194.

WHAT TO READ
Bonita Banner, semiweekly newspaper, (941) 992-2110. **Fort Myers News-Press**, daily newspaper, (941) 992-1900. **Naples Daily News**, daily newspaper, (941) 332-2572.

GETTING AROUND
Bus: No public intra-city transportation, but a trolley runs from Bonita Springs to Fort Myers Beach, (941) 275-8726. **Taxi:** Yellow Cab, (941) 495-3200. **Tours:** Seminole Gulf Railway provides narrated round trips between Fort Myers and Bonita Springs. **Airport:** Southwest Florida International is 30 minutes away. **Traffic:** Bonita Beach Road, the only east-west through-street, is heavily congested. Some developments lack good access to north-south arteries.

JOBS
County unemployment rate: 3.3%. **Florida Jobs and Benefits:** (941) 939-8704.

UTILITIES
Electricity: Florida Power & Light, (941) 262-1322. **Gas:** None. **Water & sewer:** Bonita Springs Utilities, (941) 992-0711. **Telephone:** Sprint-United Telephone, (941) 262-2161. **Cable TV:** Media One, (941) 432-9277.

PLACES OF WORSHIP
Two Catholic and 20 Protestant churches.

THE ENVIRONMENT
The Imperial River and Estero River have been rated as having generally good water quality. The Imperial River shows a stable trend. Its quality and trend may be adversely affected by the rapid urbanization of the area. Estero Bay has good overall water quality based on an index of biological species diversity, but has poor to fair index measurements of other characteristics. The Cocohatchee River has a fair water quality rating.

Areas with the designation of Outstanding Florida Waters are the Big Cypress National Preserve, Cape Romano State Aquatic Preserve, Rookery Bay State Aquatic Preserve & National Estuarine Research Reserve, Everglades National Park and the Fakahatchee Strand State Preserve. Everglades National Park/Florida Bay also has been designated for improvement and management.

One of the biggest problems in the area is an unnatural oscillation of salinity, which damages sea grasses and lowers the productivity and fish yields in the estuary. This is due to the severe alteration of water flow by the construction of drainage canals.

Health advisories recommending no consumption and limited consumption of largemouth bass have been issued for portions of Everglades National Park due to high mercury content.

EVENTS AND FESTIVALS
Koreshan Unity Lunar Festival - April. **Watermelon Festival** - May.

WHERE TO EAT
Cafe Margaux, 3405 Pelican Landing Parkway, French, moderate, (941) 992-6588. **McCully's Rooftop**, 25999 Hickory Blvd., continental, moderate to expensive, (941) 992-0033.

WHERE TO STAY
Comfort Inn, (941) 992-5001. **Hampton Inn**, (941) 947-9393.

ISSUES
How will fast growth impact real estate investments and quality of life?

One risk of moving into a rapidly developing community is the uncertainty about which way the area will grow, and what that growth will do to your real property investment. To the extent possible, check this out because it can be all-important in an area with the booming growth of Bonita Springs — about 1,000 new homes each year.

Lee and Collier counties already are under fire from the Southwest Florida Regional Planning Council for inadequate road planning in the Bonita Springs area. New developments are being approved without regard to how residents will access their homes from north-south arteries.

Boynton Beach

There have been some very real problems here despite the fact that the city possesses some of the qualities that appeal to retirees. For example, it boasts more than 20 golf courses within a five-mile radius, excellent shopping and a good hospital. Boynton Beach also has some very attractive country club-style housing developments.

According to Bill McGowan, a reporter for the Palm Beach Post, recent municipal elections have produced more effective leadership. City officials are focusing on redevelopment of substandard housing areas, reducing the crime rate and improving race relations. A new private-initiative waterfront project, aided by city incentives, has brought shops, restaurants and marina improvements to a previously neglected downtown area. In some blighted neighborhoods, buildings have been razed and new linear parks constructed.

Boynton Beach does not have much right to the term "beach" since its beach front can be measured in feet rather than miles. The outstanding feature of the shoreline is the absence of tall buildings or commercial development. The biggest drawback is the lack of good ocean access. Only two small parks offer public entry to the beach — one with a daily parking fee and very limited parking space.

It appears that the city recognizes its problems, and is finally committed to dealing with them.

WEATHER

	Winter	Spring	Summer	Fall
Normal daily high/low	76/58	85/69	90/75	80/65
Normal precipitation	9 in.	17 in.	21 in.	14 in.

Disaster watch: Nine major hurricanes have hit southeast Florida since 1900.

TAXES
Sales tax: 6%. **Property tax:** $25.18 per $1,000 valuation. Sample taxes include a $25,000 homestead exemption.

Home value	Tax
$100,000	$1,888
$150,000	$3,147
$250,000	$5,665

REAL ESTATE
Median home value: $101,611 (Palm Beach County). **Median rent:** $773/month (Palm Beach County). **Communities popular with retirees:** Aberdeen Golf & Country Club offers single-family homes priced from around $170,000 to more than $300,000 and villas from $116,900 to $150,000. The Lakes of Westchester Golf & Country Club offers single-family homes from $130,000-$160,000. Colonial Club condominiums on the Intracoastal waterway have one- and two-bedroom units from $47,000 to $105,000. Grande Palms has single-family homes from $124,900 to $159,900. **Licensed continuing-care retirement communities:** None.

CRIME & SAFETY
Crimes per 1,000 population: 115. **Non-emergency police:** (561) 375-6100. **Non-emergency fire department:** (561) 375-6325. **Police, fire, ambulance emergencies:** 911.

HOMELESS & BLIGHT
We saw both homeless persons and blighted areas.

The U.S. Census counted 219 homeless persons in shelters and 197 visible in street locations in Palm Beach County, population 863,518.

HEALTH CARE
Hospitals: Bethesda Memorial Hospital, 362 beds, full service, (561) 737-7733.
Physicians: 200+. **Specialties:** 36+.

GETTING SMART
Barry University, (561) 364-8220. **Offerings:** Bachelor's Degrees in five fields of study. **Florida Atlantic University** in Boca Raton, (561) 297-3000, offers the Lifelong Learning Society, (561) 297-3171. **Offerings:** The university has nine colleges, offering programs in more than 61 four-year degree fields as well as advanced degrees. Lifelong Learning Society members can enroll in regular course offerings or special LIFE-course programs for degree credit, non-credit or audit. **Palm Beach Atlantic College** in West Palm Beach, (561) 803-2000. **Offerings:** Four-year liberal arts degrees and MBA program. There is a continuing-education program offering courses for credit and non-credit.

JUST FOR SENIORS
Bethesda 55 Plus is a free-membership program sponsored by Bethesda Memorial Hospital for adults age 55 and over, providing a variety of free and discounted health services, (561) 737-7733. **Ezell Hester Community Center** offers "Seniors' Drop-In" Monday-Thursday, (561) 732-5545. Recently, a Senior Advisory Board chairperson, speaking in support of a proposed new senior center, was quoted as saying, "There aren't many activities in our community and there are many lonely people."

GETTING INVOLVED
Soup Kitchen, (561) 732-7595. **SCORE,** (561) 278-7752.

RECREATION, ENTERTAINMENT & AMENITIES

Public golf: There are 20 golf courses within a five-mile radius, including Cypress Creek Country Club, Boynton Beach Municipal Golf Course and Westchester Golf & Country Club. **Private golf:** Aberdeen Golf & Country Club, Delray Dunes Golf & Country Club, Pine Tree Golf Course, The Village of Golf and Hunters Run Golf & Racquet Club. **Public tennis courts:** Boynton Beach Municipal Racquet Center, Sara Sims Park and Caloosa Park. **Private tennis courts:** Aberdeen Golf & Country Club and Rainberry Bay Tennis Club. **Parks:** At the Loxahatchee National Wildlife Refuge one can observe wildlife and enjoy hiking, fishing, boating, canoeing and airboating. **Public swimming pools:** Wilson Municipal. **Water sports:** Swimming, snorkeling, scuba diving, sailing, water-skiing and others. **River/gulf/ocean:** Boynton Beach is one mile from the Gulf Stream. Sailfish, kingfish, mackerel, dolphin, grouper and red snapper are just a few of the catches possible offshore. Lakes and canals throughout the city provide freshwater angling. Lake Worth and the Intracoastal Waterway add waterfront housing opportunities. **Running/walking/biking:** Caloosa Park has bicycle paths and a 1.8-mile trail with exercise stations. **Horses/riding:** Sea Ridge Farms offers boarding, lessons, training and sales. **Hunting:** Call the Florida Game and Freshwater Fish Commission, (561) 355-2622. **Movie theaters:** Two theaters with nine screens. **Art museums:** Boynton Beach Art Center and Freedom Hall Community Center are venues for limited cultural fare. Go north to Palm Beach or south to Boca Raton for a wider range. **Theaters:** Theatre Club of the Palm Beaches in Manalapan. **Library:** Boynton Beach Public Library. **Attractions:** None. **Necessities:** All the basics are here.

Smart Shopper Tip: There are 16 shopping centers, but look no farther than the Boynton Beach Mall, which has five major anchors, more than 150 shops and a food court.

WHO LIVES HERE

Population: 52,311 year-round residents, an increase of 6,027 since 1990. **Age 65+** = 25.0% in Palm Beach County. **Median household income:** $33,094 (Palm Beach County). **Per capita income:** $36,057 (Palm Beach County).

NUMBERS TO KNOW

Chamber of commerce: (561) 732-9501. **Voter registration:** (561) 355-2650. **Vehicle registration, tags & title:** (561) 355-2622. **Driver's license:** (561) 681-6333.

WHAT TO READ

Sun-Sentinel, daily newspaper, (561) 736-9700. **Boynton Times,** weekly newspaper, (800) 275-8820. **Gold Coast Shopper,** weekly publication, (561) 736-1996.

GETTING AROUND

Bus: BBTA, (561) 375-6200. **Taxi:** Metro Taxi, (561) 276-2230. **Tours:** None. **Airport:** Palm Beach International is 15 minutes north. **Traffic:** No significant bottlenecks.

JOBS

County unemployment rate: 6.4%. **Work Force Development Center:** In Delray, (561) 637-7000.

UTILITIES

Electricity: Florida Power & Light, (561) 697-8000. **Gas:** Florida Public Utilities, (561) 278-2636. **Water & sewer:** City of Boynton Beach, (561) 375-6300. **Telephone:** Bell South, (800) 789-9025 in Florida, or (800) 753-0710 out-of-state. **Cable TV:** COMCAST, (561) 478-8300, or Adelphia Cable, (561) 930-2225, depending on location of residence.

PLACES OF WORSHIP

Two Catholic and 34 Protestant churches, plus one Jewish synagogue.

THE ENVIRONMENT

Sections of surrounding canals, notably the West Palm Beach Canal, have been rated as having poor surface water quality. Boynton Beach Canal shows fair water quality and an improving ten-year trend. There is one EPA-listed Superfund site in the county. It's located in Lake Park.

EVENTS AND FESTIVALS

G.A.L.A., Boynton's Great American Love Affair - March. **Holiday Parade** - December. **Holiday Boat Parade** - December.

WHERE TO EAT

Banana Boat Restaurant, 739 E. Ocean Ave., seafood, American, moderate, (561) 732-9400. **Lucille & Otley's,** 1021 S. Federal Hwy., American, inexpensive to moderate, (561) 732-5930.

WHERE TO STAY

Holiday Inn Catalina, (561) 737-4600. **Comfort Lodge,** (561) 732-4446.

ISSUES

This is a city that started late and slowly on redevelopment of its substandard housing and resolution of human issues problems. Will progress continue or get sidetracked by the same leadership malaise that once gripped the city?

Bradenton

Bradenton is a quaint and charming city-town. This term is used
because even though the population puts it in the city category, it has
many of the characteristics of a small riverside town.

Downtown is busy but uncongested. It's a place where city and
county bureaucrats, white collar workers and health professionals
spend their working hours. They work in neat, clean buildings and
skyscrapers that share space with tropical palms, huge oaks and
colorful bougainvillea. Then at the close of the work day, many walk
to their homes along the nearby Manatee River.

To find out why downtown is so quiet, just head out along Cortez
Road. There, a mall and 17 shopping centers vie for retail trade from
endless streams of shoppers, browsers and sightseers. When not
shopping, these same hordes clog six traffic lanes in a determined
effort to be somewhere else.

Bradenton has the Braden and Manatee Rivers, Terra Ceia and
Palma Sola bays and the Gulf of Mexico. Residents fish, swim,
participate in a variety of water sports and most importantly, live in
an assortment of homes on or near the water. There are condominiums, villas, canal homes and houseboats, many of which are within
walking distance of downtown.

Bradenton Beach, with its own town hall, shares Anna Maria
Island with the towns of Anna Maria and Holmes Beach. In some
places the island is so narrow that spray from the Gulf and bay might
simultaneously put a damper on social activities. But who's complaining? With hundreds of miles of waterfront all around, residents
have no shortage of water-related options and activities to occupy
their leisure hours.

If all the water resources are not enough, golf enthusiasts have a
crack at more than 30 public and private golf courses in the county
— one of the highest per capita concentrations in the state. Tennis
courts, lawn bowling greens, shuffleboard and other outdoor game
venues are plentiful as well.

Life can be good in Bradenton.

WEATHER

	Winter	Spring	Summer	Fall
Normal daily high/low	74/52	86/64	90/72	79/58
Normal precipitation	9 in.	12 in.	26 in.	7 in.

Disaster watch: Southwest Florida has been hit by five major
hurricanes since 1900.

TAXES
Sales tax: 7%. **Property tax:** $19.76 per $1,000 valuation. Sample
tax calculations include a $25,000 homestead exemption.

Home value	Tax
$100,000	$1,482
$150,000	$2,469
$250,000	$4,445

REAL ESTATE
Median home value: $90,527 (Manatee County). **Median rent:**
$536/month (Manatee County). **Communities popular with retir-
ees:** Mount Vernon, a 434-condominium complex on Sarasota Bay
with homes priced from the high $50s to low $90s, (941) 366-7360.
Lakewood Ranch, a master-planned community with lakes and golf
course, offers single-family homes from the $80s to $130s, (800)
30-RANCH. University Park Country Club, a luxury golf course
community, has prices from the $200s to $1,000,000, (941) 351-
7777. **Licensed continuing-care retirement communities:** Freedom Village, 654 independent living units, 120 sheltered beds,
(941) 798-8190. Westminster Asbury, 277 independent living units,
18 sheltered nursing beds, 75 community beds, (941) 748-4161.

CRIME & SAFETY
Crimes per 1,000 population: 78 (Bradenton); 81 (Bradenton
Beach). **Non-emergency police:** (941) 746-4111. **Non-emergency
fire department:** (941) 747-1161. **Police, fire, ambulance emergencies:** 911.

HOMELESS & BLIGHT
Bradenton has a clean, modern downtown with some small-town
characteristics. It has some areas of substandard housing, but you
have to look for them. They are not obvious. We did not see any
homeless people.

The U.S. Census reported 62 homeless persons in shelters and two
visible in street locations in Manatee County, population 211,707.

HEALTH CARE
Hospitals: Columbia Blake Medical Center, 383 beds, 24-hour
emergency, acute care, full service, (941) 792-6611. **Manatee
Memorial Hospital,** 512 beds, 24-hour emergency, acute care, full
service, (941) 746-5111.
Physicians: 300. **Specialties:** 37.

GETTING SMART
Manatee Community College, (941) 755-1511. **Offerings:** Two-
year associate degrees, continuing-education classes for one-year
certificates and a variety of non-degree courses.

JUST FOR SENIORS
AARP, (941) 755-1773. **Elder Help Line/Better Living For
Seniors,** (941) 749-7127. **Neighborly Senior Centers,** (941) 748-
6974. **Rogers Garden Multipurpose Senior Center,** (941) 747-
2337. **Woodwind Senior Center,** (941) 748-2641.

GETTING INVOLVED
Volunteer Services, (941) 746-7117. **Volunteer Voices** and **RSVP,**
(941) 748-6974. **United Way First Call for Help,** (941) 748-3645.

RECREATION, ENTERTAINMENT & AMENITIES
Public golf: Heather Hills Golf Club, 18 holes/par 61; Manatee
County Golf Club, 18 holes/par 71; Palma Sola Golf Club, 18
holes/par 69; River Run Golf Links, 18 holes/par 70; Peridia
Golf & Country Club, semiprivate, 18 holes/par 55; Pinebrook/
Ironwood, semiprivate, 18 holes/par 56; Rosedale Golf and
Country Club, semiprivate, 18 holes/par 72; River Club, semi-
private, 18 holes/par 72; Tara Golf and Country Club, semipri-
vate, 18 holes/par 72; and Village Green Golf Club, semipri-
vate, 18 holes/par 58. **Private golf:** Bradenton Country Club,

18 holes/par 71, and El Conquistador Country Club, 18 holes/par 72. **Public tennis courts:** Bayshore, Blackburn, Braden River, C.V. Walton Racquet Center and Jessie P. Miller. **Private tennis courts:** Nick Bollettieri Tennis Center has 75 courts. Others are available at the Racquet Club of El Conquistador. **Parks:** Six city recreation parks, plus DeSoto National Park and 556-acre Lake Manatee State Park. **Public swimming pools:** East Bradenton Recreation Complex and G.T. Bray Municipal Park Aquatic Center. **Water sports:** Boating, parasailing, sailboarding, sailing, snorkeling and water-skiing. **River/gulf/ocean:** Braden River, Manatee River, Palma Sola Bay, Sarasota Bay and the Gulf of Mexico. **Running/walking/biking:** Myakka River State Park has a 7,500-acre wilderness preserve with self-guided trails for hikers and bikers. G.T. Bray Municipal Park's 140 acres include jogging and bike paths. **Horses/riding:** There are several farms, stables and riding academies in Manatee County and plenty of open land east of Bradenton for riding. **Hunting:** None. **Movie theaters:** 24 screens. **Art museums:** Art League of Manatee County. **History museums:** South Florida Museum. **Theaters:** Bradenton Municipal Auditorium, Manatee Civic Center, Manatee Players Riverfront Theatre and Neel Auditorium at Manatee Community College. **Library:** Central, plus five branches in Manatee County. **Attractions:** Bishop Planetarium, Bradenton Lawn Bowling Club, DeSoto National Memorial, Gamble Mansion Plantation, Manatee Village Historical Park, Myakka River State Park and the Pittsburgh Pirates spring training camp. **Necessities:** All here.

Smart Shopper Tip: The DeSoto Square Mall, with more than 100 stores, combined with 17 shopping centers along a six-mile strip of Cortez Road should offer more than adequate shopping options. If you can't find it here, it hasn't been invented.

WHO LIVES HERE
Population: 48,011 year-round residents, an increase of 4,242 since 1990. **Age 65+** = 27.1% in Manatee County. **Median household income:** $27,441 (Manatee County). **Per capita income:** $24,758 (Manatee County).

NUMBERS TO KNOW
Chamber of commerce: (941) 748-3411. **Voter registration:** (941) 749-7181. **Vehicle registration, tags & title:** (941) 748-8000. **Driver's license:** (941) 741-3010. **Visitors bureau:** (941) 729-9177.

WHAT TO READ
Bradenton Herald, daily newspaper, (941) 748-0411. **Sarasota Herald-Tribune**, daily newspaper, (941) 742-6150.

GETTING AROUND
Bus: Manatee County Area Transit, (941) 749-7116. **Taxi:** Checker Cab, (941) 755-9339. **Tours:** Myakka Wildlife Tours, (941) 365-0100. **Airport:** Sarasota/Bradenton International. **Traffic:** Downtown streets are uncongested and a pleasure to navigate. Route 684 (also known as 44th Avenue, Cortez Road and Beach Road) is a nightmare, especially in the mall and shopping district.

JOBS
County unemployment rate: 2.5%. **Florida Jobs and Benefits:** (941) 741-3030.

UTILITIES
Electricity: Florida Power & Light, (941) 639-1106, or Peace River Electric Co-op, (941) 722-2729, depending on location of residence. **Gas:** Peoples Gas, (941) 366-4277. **Water & sewer:** Bradenton Water Dept., (941) 748-0800. **Telephone:** GTE Florida, (800) 483-4200. **Cable TV:** Time-Warner Communications, (941) 748-1822.

PLACES OF WORSHIP
Four Catholic and 131 Protestant churches and one Jewish synagogue.

THE ENVIRONMENT
The Braden River has been rated as having fair water quality and may improve with the upgrade of Bradenton's waste-water treatment plant (WWTP). The Manatee River and estuary have generally good water quality, but show problem areas. Lake Manatee State Recreation Area has received status as an Outstanding Florida Water (OFW). Efforts are underway to purchase land for preservation along the Manatee River. Other similarly located areas are being converted from agricultural use to residential use.

Sarasota Bay is designated as an OFW and is part of the EPA's National Estuary Program. Sarasota Bay, between Bradenton and Sarasota, and Longboat Key Estuary have generally fair water quality. They are negatively affected by urban runoff and discharge from the Sarasota WWTP. Anna Maria Key Estuary and the St. Armands Key Estuary have generally good water quality. Whitaker Bayou has poor water quality and receives effluent from the Sarasota WWTP. There have been occasional closings of the shellfish harvesting areas in Whitaker Bayou.

EVENTS AND FESTIVALS
Cortez Fishing Festival - February. **Bradenton Beach Festival** - March. **Manatee County Heritage Week** - March. **Florida Heritage Festival** - April. **Taste of Manatee** - November.

WHERE TO EAT
Beach Bistro, 6600 Gulf Drive at Holmes Beach, continental, moderate to expensive, (941) 778-6444. **Lee's Crab Trap**, 4815 Memphis Road, crab and seafood, inexpensive to expensive, (941) 729-7777. **Sandbar**, 100 Spring Avenue in Anna Maria, seafood, inexpensive to moderate, (941) 778-0444. **Seafood Shack**, 4110 127th St. W. at Cortez, moderate, (941) 794-1235.

WHERE TO STAY
Five Oaks Inn Bed and Breakfast, (941) 723-1236. **Holiday Inn-Riverfront**, (941) 747-3727. **Park Inn Club**, (941) 795-4633. **Catalina Beach Resort**, (941) 778-6611.

ISSUES
Retirees cite "petty little taxes" and the "snowbird season"– when it sometimes takes 20 minutes to go three blocks – as their principal beefs. Can it retain its small-town charm in the face of big-city challenges? This seems to be the larger question. At this time it appears to have the answer.

Brandon

HE SAID: ★★★
There is no single, unique feature that leaps to mind when thinking about Brandon. I was put off at first by what seemed like an endless strip of commercial activity before I found my way into the real Brandon. It gets better with familiarity.

SHE SAID: ★★★
A well-planned community, it offers residential areas in a variety of price ranges. The few billboards it has are below the treetops. People are friendly in this area next door to Tampa. I would look here for a place to retire.

Why live with the trials and tribulations, frustrations and congestion of Tampa when you can reside in Brandon? You can enjoy the quiet, uncomplicated, rural lifestyle and still be in downtown Tampa in less than 30 minutes for the price of a small toll.

Once you get away from the main commercial corridor along Brandon Boulevard, you'll find a collection of small, unpretentious villages. In these neighborhoods, which may be settled around a lake, a church, a school or country club, simple pleasures are close at hand. You might wake up to the singing of birds or a view of deer grazing in a nearby meadow.

The area has experienced rapid population growth in the past decade, the result of a burgeoning local economy and an increase in the number of residents who commute to work in Tampa. Less than nine percent of Greater Brandon's population is retired. There are a few retirement homes in Brandon, but you won't find a lot of old folks sitting around on park benches bemoaning the lack of activity in their lives. Canoeing on the Alafia River, participating in a program at the Center Place Fine Arts & Civic Association or driving a golf ball down the fairway at one of four outstanding courses are just a few of the possibilities.

Residential communities in the area offer a variety of high quality, active lifestyles. Strawberry Ridge is an inexpensive, adult manufactured-home community. River Hills Country Club is a beautiful and spacious championship golf-course community.

It seems that the more you see of Brandon the better it gets. Brandon will continue to grow on you long after you choose to sink your retirement roots in this fertile ground.

WEATHER

	Winter	Spring	Summer	Fall
Normal daily high/low	73/53	86/67	90/74	78/58
Normal precipitation	8 in.	10 in.	20 in.	6 in.

Disaster watch: Since 1900, northwest Florida has been hit by six major hurricanes and southwest Florida has been hit by five.

TAXES
Sales tax: 6.75%. **Property tax:** $25.27 per $1,000 valuation. Sample taxes include a $25,000 homestead exemption.

Home value	Tax
$100,000	$1,895
$150,000	$3,159
$250,000	$5,686

REAL ESTATE
Median home value: $100,951 (Hillsborough County). **Median rent:** $607/month (Hillsborough County). **Communities popular** with retirees: River Hills Country Club offers homes from the high $90s to $700s, (813) 681-3555. Strawberry Ridge is an adult manufactured-home community with prices starting in the low $50s, (813) 689-9423 or (800) 344-8995. **Licensed continuing-care retirement communities:** None.

CRIME & SAFETY
Crimes per 1,000 population: 66 (Hillsborough County sheriff's jurisdiction). **Non-emergency police:** (813) 247-8000. **Non-emergency fire department:** (813) 272-6600. **Police, fire, ambulance emergencies:** 911.

HOMELESS & BLIGHT
This is a clean, open area. No blighted areas or homeless persons noted. Route 60, one of the three main business corridors through the area, is virtually a five-mile strip shopping center, but even so it has fewer signs and is less cluttered than most.

The U.S. Census reported 434 homeless persons in shelters and 327 visible in street locations in Hillsborough County, population 834,054.

HEALTH CARE
Hospitals: Columbia Brandon Regional Medical Center, 255 beds, 24-hour emergency, acute care, full service, (813) 681-0520. **Physicians:** 385 on staff at hospital. **Specialties:** 30.

GETTING SMART
Hillsborough Community College, Brandon campus, (813) 253-7802. **Offerings:** Two-year degrees in arts and sciences plus continuing-education courses.

JUST FOR SENIORS
Elder Help Line, (813) 273-3779. There is an active AARP chapter in Brandon. Call the chamber of commerce for contact information.

GETTING INVOLVED
There are 91 clubs and organizations in the area, including the Brandon League of Fine Arts, Brandon Newcomers Club and Citizens for Alafia River Preservation. **Library Literacy Volunteers**, (813) 273-3650. **Meals on Wheels**, (813) 689-0458.

RECREATION, ENTERTAINMENT & AMENITIES
Public golf: Bloomingdale Golfers Club, semiprivate, 18 holes/par 72, and Diamond Hill Golf Course, semiprivate, 18 holes/par 72. **Private golf:** Buckhorn Springs Golf and Country Club, 18 holes/par 72, and River Hills Country Club, 18 holes/par 72. **Public tennis courts:** Brandon Recreation Center. **Private tennis courts:** Brandon Swim & Tennis Club and River Hills Country Club. **Parks:** Lithia Springs County Park is a 160-acre park with a natural spring for year-round swimming in 72-degree water. Also, ten public parks. **Public swimming pools:** None. **Water sports:** Boating and canoeing. **River/gulf/ocean:** Alafia River, Lithia Springs and Valrico Lake. **Running/walking/biking:** Brandon Running Association. Several parks have nature, exercise and jogging trails. **Horses/riding:** Plenty of open pasture and lightly traveled backroads. **Hunting:** Hunting and fishing licenses, (813) 272-6040. **Movie**

theaters: 14 screens. **Art museums:** Center Place Fine Arts & Civic Association. **History museums:** None. **Theaters:** Valrico Civic Center. **Library:** Brandon Public. **Attractions:** None of a man-made variety. Lithia Springs, undeveloped stretches of the Alafia River, Valrico Lake and the unspoiled landscape south of Bloomingdale. **Necessities:** Most are here.

Smart Shopper Tip: Brandon Town Center Mall and the commercial sector of Brandon Boulevard will fill all your basic needs.

WHO LIVES HERE
Population: 123,000 year-round residents in 89-square-mile Greater Brandon. **Age 65+** = 12.9% in Hillsborough County. **Median household income:** $30,296 (Hillsborough County). **Per capita income:** $21,509 (Hillsborough County).

NUMBERS TO KNOW
Chamber of commerce: (813) 689-1221. **Voter registration:** (813) 272-5850. **Vehicle registration, tags & title:** (813) 272-6020. **Driver's license:** (813) 272-2714.

WHAT TO READ
Brandon News, free weekly newspaper, (813) 689-7764. **Tampa Tribune**, Brandon/South Bay edition, daily newspaper, (813) 685-4581. **St. Petersburg Times**, daily newspaper, (727) 893-8111.

GETTING AROUND
Bus: Hillsborough Area Regional Transit (HART), (813) 254-4278. **Taxi:** United Cab Co., (813) 661-9100. **Tours:** None. **Airport:** Tampa International is 30 minutes away. **Traffic:** As long as you stay off Route 60 as much as possible, you can move freely through the eight communities of Greater Brandon.

JOBS
County unemployment rate: 3.1%. **Job Service of Florida:** (813) 744-6000.

UTILITIES
Electricity: Tampa Electric Co., (813) 223-0800. **Gas:** Peoples Gas, (813) 272-1501. **Water & sewer:** Hillsborough County Water Department, (813) 272-6680. **Telephone:** GTE Florida, (800) 483-4200. **Cable TV:** Time Warner Cable, (813) 684-6400.

PLACES OF WORSHIP
Three Catholic and 81 Protestant churches, one Jewish synagogue and three others.

THE ENVIRONMENT
Water quality throughout Tampa Bay generally has been rated as fair to poor. The best water quality in the bay is in lower Tampa Bay. The worst water quality in the area is in Hillsborough and McKay bays, although Hillsborough Bay has shown some recovery recently.

A report by the Florida Department of Environmental Regulation states, "Due to the ecological, economic and aesthetic importance of this water body, Tampa Bay has become a major focus of local, regional and state actions to reverse the negative trends." It has been legislatively designated as a priority SWIM (Surface Water Improvement and Management) water body.

Lithia Springs has good water quality. The north prong of the Alafia River shows generally fair water quality while the south prong shows generally good water quality. Alafia River State Park has protected status as a designated Outstanding Florida Water.

There are nine EPA-listed Superfund sites in Hillsborough County, including the Sydney Mine Sludge Ponds in Brandon.

EVENTS AND FESTIVALS
Florida State Fair - February. **Brandon Balloon Classic** - April. **Independence Day Parade** - July.

WHERE TO EAT
Romano's Macaroni Grill, 132 Brandon Town Center Drive, Italian, moderate, (813) 685-6530.

WHERE TO STAY
Budgetel Inn, (813) 684-4007. **Homestead Village**, (813) 643-5900.

ISSUES
Brandon is the fastest-growing community in the Tampa Bay area. In the past decade, it has attracted major corporate and industrial giants, retail establishments and land developers at a record clip. Much of this activity has been good, but it is beginning to create problems. Lagging new road construction, inadequate school classrooms and intrusion of commercial activity into previously quiet residential neighborhoods have some residents uneasy about the future. Before settling on a site for your retirement home, find out as much as you can about pending new road construction and zoning changes that might impact your neighborhood.

RELOCATION TIPS

As soon as you arrive in your new home, take some time to check for problems. Is the electricity on? Is the telephone working? Do you have hot water? Before the sun gets too low in the sky on moving day, check your lights, phone, water heater and plumbing. It's best to find problems as early in the day as possible so they can be taken care of before you are stuck in the dark without any idea where to find a flashlight — or in the shower without hot water.

Brooksville

HE SAID: ✭ ✭ ✭
I wouldn't choose to live in Brooksville, but I could sure look long and hard at the golfing communities around nearby Weeki Wachee and Spring Hill.

SHE SAID: ✭ ✭ ✭
This small town with rolling, green hills is situated away from busy interstates and city life. It is probably a good place to raise a family, but it's too remote for me.

Brooksville, the seat and heart of Hernando County, is ideally situated at the juncture of highways 50, 41 and 98, 11 miles west of I-75 and 12 miles east of U.S. Highway 19. Ideal because it has been spared the brunt of the 127 percent population growth that the county experienced during the 1980s, yet its roads can carry you — in a matter of minutes — to the multifaceted natural resources and attractions that propelled this growth.

Ridge Manor and Spring Lake to the east, and Spring Hill, Weeki Wachee and Hernando Beach to the west have all experienced rapid growth in housing and societal infrastructure and should be visited while in the area.

The town of Brooksville is not outstanding, serving principally to dispense municipal and county services to its residents and acting as a commercial hub in a county short on shopping facilities and retail service outlets. But, it is old enough to have acquired some of the trappings of a historic district, having been named the county seat in 1856. Highlights include a number of old brick streets downtown, the Hernando Historical Museum in a beautifully restored antebellum house, a white-pillared county courthouse and neighborhoods of fine, old homes, several on the National Register of Historic Places.

The real strengths of this area, though, are in the number of golf and country club housing developments and the diversity of recreational opportunities offered by the Gulf, the lakes, forests and wildlife refuges so prominent in the rural landscape. It is a veritable paradise for fishing, golfing, hiking, bicycling and horseback riding.

WEATHER

	Winter	Spring	Summer	Fall
Normal daily high/low	74/51	87/65	90/71	78/57
Normal precipitation	11 in.	13 in.	23 in.	7 in.

Disaster watch: Northwest Florida has been hit by six major hurricanes since 1900.

TAXES
Sales tax: 6%. **Property tax:** $28.47 or $28.53 per $1,000 valuation, depending on location. Sample taxes were calculated at the rate of $28.53 and include a $25,000 homestead exemption.

Home value	Tax
$100,000	$2,140
$150,000	$3,566
$250,000	$6,419

REAL ESTATE
Median home value: $84,611 (Hernando County). **Median rent:** $440/month (Hernando County). **Communities popular with retirees:** Brookridge West features manufactured homes priced from $30,000 to $100,000, (800) 780-9378. Glen Lakes is a country club community of single-family homes priced from the $100s to $400s, (800) 222-9003. Sylvan Grove offers manufactured homes priced from the $50s to the $90s, (352) 799-5399. Silverthorn, a golf-club community, has villas from the $90s and single-family homes from the $130s to $500s. **Licensed continuing-care retirement communities:** None.

CRIME & SAFETY
Crimes per 1,000 population: 97. **Non-emergency police:** (352) 754-6800. **Non-emergency fire department:** (352) 544-5445. **Police, fire, ambulance emergencies:** 911.

HOMELESS & BLIGHT
We saw no homeless persons during our visit. For a town more than 140 years old, we saw surprisingly few neighborhoods of substandard housing.

The U.S. Census reported 19 homeless persons in shelters among Hernando County's population of 101,115.

HEALTH CARE
Hospitals: Brooksville Regional Hospital, 91 beds, full service, 24-hour emergency, (352) 796-5111. There are four additional hospitals within a short driving distance of Brooksville, including Oak Hill, which has 150 beds and 125 physicians. **Physicians:** 30. **Specialties:** 15.

GETTING SMART
University of South Florida Conference Center at Chinsegut Hill, located four miles north of Brooksville, (352) 796-2242. **Offerings:** Two Elderhostel programs are offered in February and March; they're held in an 1842 manor house that sits on a hilltop in a secluded forest. **Brooksville Adult Education Center**, (352) 544-6410. **Offerings:** Art classes. **Pasco-Hernando Community College**, (352) 796-6726. **Offerings:** Two-year degree programs in arts and sciences, as well as non-credit continuing-education courses.

JUST FOR SENIORS
Lykes Enrichment Center at Brooksville Regional Hospital, (352) 796-5111. **Senior Citizens Club of Hernando County**, (352) 596-1095.

GETTING INVOLVED
Community Service Organizations, (352) 796-1425. **United Way** in Spring Hill, (352) 688-2026.

RECREATION, ENTERTAINMENT & AMENITIES
Public golf: There are 15 courses within 25 miles, including The Quarry in Brooksville. **Private golf:** Brookridge Country Club, Brooksville Golf & Country Club and Glen Lakes Country Club. **Public tennis courts:** Tom Varn Park and Hernando Park. **Private tennis courts:** Brooksville Golf & Country Club. **Parks:** Chinsegut National Wildlife Refuge, Withlacoochee State Forest, Tom Varn Park, Kennedy Park and Hernando Park. **Public swimming pools:**

None. **Water sports:** Boating, canoeing, sailing, water-skiing, scuba diving, windsurfing and jet-skiing. **River/gulf/ocean:** Numerous freshwater lakes, Weeki Wachee River, Withlacoochee River and the Gulf of Mexico are within a 30-minute drive. **Running/walking/biking:** Colonel Robins Nature Trail, 2.5 miles; Croom Hiking Trail, 29.1 miles; McKethan Lake Nature Trail, 2 miles; Richloam Hiking Trail, 30.9 miles; and Withlacoochee State Trail, 47 miles. There are 120 miles of bike paths in the Withlacoochee State Forest. **Horses/riding:** Whispering Meadows is an equestrian center, (352) 799-9505. **Hunting:** The area is teeming with wildlife. Contact the Florida Game and Freshwater Fish Commission, (352) 754-6720, for seasons and approved locations. **Movie theaters:** Two screens at the Brooksville Twin. **Art museums:** None. **History museums:** Chinsegut Manor House, Hernando Historical Museum and the Heritage Museum. **Theaters:** Civic Auditorium, Performing Arts Center at Hernando High School and Performance Place, 11 miles east in Ridge Manor. **Library:** Lykes Memorial County, plus three branches within the county. **Attractions:** Boyett Groves, Chinsegut Manor House, Buccaneer Bay and adjacent Weeki Wachee Spring, and the Heritage Museum. **Necessities:** All are here or nearby.

Smart Shopper Tip: Highways 41 and 50, south and west, are loaded with plazas and shopping centers, but Gulf View Square Mall, some 30 miles away in Port Richey, has it all.

WHO LIVES HERE
Population: 7,798 year-round residents, an increase of 209 since 1990. **Age 65+** = 32.2% in Hernando County. **Median household income:** $23,095 (Hernando County). **Per capita income:** $18,190 (Hernando County).

NUMBERS TO KNOW
Chamber of commerce: (352) 796-0697. **Voter registration:** (352) 754-4125. **Vehicle registration, tags & title:** (352) 754-4180. **Driver's license:** (352) 754-6762.

WHAT TO READ
Hernando Today, newspaper, three days a week, (352) 796-1949. **St. Petersburg Times**, daily newspaper, (727) 893-8111. **Tampa Tribune**, daily newspaper, (352) 796-6715.

GETTING AROUND
Bus: Trans-Hernando is a paratransit system for the disadvantaged and disabled, (352) 799-1510. **Taxi:** Diamond Taxi, (352) 799-6225. **Tours:** None. **Airport:** Tampa International is 50 miles away. **Traffic:** Light. An excellent network of roads handles traffic well. The new Suncoast Parkway will put you in Tampa in about 45 minutes.

JOBS
County unemployment rate: 4.3%. **Florida Jobs and Benefits:** (352) 754-6730. **Job Line:** (352) 754-4418.

UTILITIES
Electricity: Florida Power Corp., (800) 700-8744, or Withlacoochee River Electric Co-op, (352) 596-4000, depending on location of residence. **Gas:** Southern State Utilities, available only in Spring Hill, (352) 382-1930. **Water & sewer:** City of Brooksville, (352) 544-5400. **Telephone:** Bell South, (800) 789-9025 in Florida, or (800) 753-2909 out-of-state. **Cable TV:** Time-Warner Cable, (800) 892-0805.

PLACES OF WORSHIP
One Catholic and 51 Protestant churches. One Jewish synagogue in Spring Hill.

THE ENVIRONMENT
The spring-fed rivers in the area, including the Weeki Wachee, generally have been rated as having very good water quality. The Weeki Wachee has some bacteria problems from unknown sources. Rodgers Park on the river was temporarily closed to swimming due to high coliform bacteria counts, but has since reopened.

EVENTS AND FESTIVALS
Brooksville Raid Festival - January. **Downtown Springtime Crafts Fair** - March. **Spring Bluegrass Festival** - April. **Under the Spreading Oaks Fine Arts Show** - November.

WHERE TO EAT
Bayport Inn, 4835 Cortez Blvd., American, Gulf seafood, moderate, (352) 596-1088. **Blueberry Patch Tea Room**, 414 E. Liberty St., American, inexpensive to moderate, (352) 796-6005.

WHERE TO STAY
Holiday Inn, (352) 796-9481.

ISSUES
Housing west of Brooksville could be affected by the routing of the Suncoast Parkway. Newcomers should determine the route before buying in the area; call Suncoast Parkway, (813) 856-4488, for information.

RELOCATION TIPS

Cut the costs of your move by avoiding the moving industry's busiest days and season. Pick midweek and midmonth move dates. Peak times to avoid are May 15 through September 15, the first two days of any month, the last five days of any month and weekends. Another good reason to avoid moving during the summer months: The physical aspects of moving are much less taxing during cooler weather.

Cape Coral

Based on its size, location and enormous water resources, you could easily expect Cape Coral to outshine many of its more famous sister cities in Florida. It is the city with the second largest land area in the state, located at a midpoint on the southwest Gulf coast. Because it is bordered by the Caloosahatchee River, Matlacha Pass and Pine Island Sound, with 400 miles of saltwater and freshwater canals and 11 miles of river frontage, more than two-thirds of its homes sit at the water's edge. But the truth about Cape Coral is that there are dozens of cities that are better known, more easily identifiable and in fact more remarkable.

You could chalk it up to a lack of longevity. Cape Coral wasn't even populated until 1958. It cannot be expected to compete with the 400-plus-year history of St. Augustine. Daytona Beach was host to the Daytona 500 before Cape Coral even existed. Fort Lauderdale's spring break phenomenon was in full swing while turkey, deer and wild hogs still roamed the wetlands now occupied by the Cape Coral City Hall.

Some might cite the absence of a legendary figure in the town's development as the difference between Cape Coral and other more renowned spots. Fort Myers had both Thomas Edison and Henry Ford. Ponce de Leon searched for the fountain of youth in St. Augustine. Addison Mizner's touch is indelibly laid in the architecture and beauty of Boca Raton. Henry Flagler left his imprint on the Palm Beaches and southeast Florida, while John Ringling brought art and the circus to Sarasota.

Cape Coral's failure to attract or build any institutions of note might be the cause of its anonymity. It has no nationally acclaimed university, medical center, performing arts center, planetarium, zoological park or natural history museum.

And while all these factors might have played a role in shaping Cape Coral, the central determinant is probably that early developers were more intent on selling real estate than building a community. Since much of the area was marshlands, construction consisted of dredging canals and filling low places to improve habitability. This pattern, repeated throughout the 114-square-mile area, produced one of the largest continuous residential neighborhoods in the state. There is practically a boat dock in every back yard. Trouble is, if you don't have a boat, there's little else to do.

Much of the area is short on vegetation and landscaping, which is probably due to the type of soil of this former marshland. But the dearth of greenery gives an unsettling impression of unfinished work and a too-open vista to the entire city.

WEATHER

	Winter	Spring	Summer	Fall
Normal daily high/low	76/55	88/68	91/75	81/62
Normal precipitation	7 in.	14 in.	26 in.	6 in.

Disaster watch: Southwest Florida has been hit by five major hurricanes since 1900.

TAXES

Sales tax: 6%. **Property tax:** $22.05 per $1,000 valuation. Sample tax calculations include a $25,000 homestead exemption.

Home value	Tax
$100,000	$1,654
$150,000	$2,756
$250,000	$4,961

REAL ESTATE

Median home value: $101,528 (Lee County). **Median rent:** $641/month (Lee County). **Communities popular with retirees:** Maureen Haag with Douglas Realty, (941) 542-6906, reports these price ranges: Canal homes range from the low $100s to $500,000. Duplex units are priced from the mid-$70s to $110s. Condominiums that are not on the water are priced from $45,000, and waterfront condos from $100,000. Custom, lakefront homes in the Eight-Lakes area are priced from $300,000. **Licensed continuing-care retirement communities:** Gulf Coast Village has 237 independent living units, 31 sheltered nursing beds and 29 community beds, (941) 772-1333.

CRIME & SAFETY

Crimes per 1,000 population: 42. **Non-emergency fire department:** (941) 574-0506. **Police, fire, ambulance emergencies:** 911.

HOMELESS & BLIGHT

Cape Coral is a wide-open area with dispersed governmental and commercial activities. Buildings are low to the ground; there are few signs, and landscaping is low-density. There is no downtown in the classic sense. This planned city was not settled until 1958, so there are no pronounced run-down areas. We saw no evidence of homeless persons.

The U.S. Census reported 97 homeless persons in shelters and 203 visible in street locations in Lee County, population 335,113.

HEALTH CARE

Hospitals: Cape Coral Hospital, 309 beds, acute care, 24-hour emergency, full service, (941) 574-2323.
Physicians: 193. **Specialties:** 32.

GETTING SMART

There are no college or university campuses in Cape Coral. The following are in Fort Myers. **Adult and Community Education**, Lee County School District, (941) 334-7172. **Offerings:** Courses are designed to broaden general knowledge and introduce new subjects. **Barry University**, (941) 278-3041. **Offerings:** Adult and continuing education. **Edison Community College**, (941) 489-9300; continuing education, (941) 489-9235. **Offerings:** Two-year degrees and continuing-education programs. **Florida Gulf Coast University**, (941) 590-1000. **Offerings:** 16 undergraduate and 10 graduate degree programs.

JUST FOR SENIORS

Tony Rotino Senior Center, (941) 574-0807. **Lake Kennedy Senior Center**, (941) 574-0575. **Cape Coral Retired Citizens**, (941) 549-3661.

GETTING INVOLVED

There are 170 clubs and organizations including **AARP, Cape Coral Beautification Association, Cape Coral Civic Association, Cape Coral Historical Society, Citizens for Good Government of Cape Coral, New Resident Club** and **RSVP**. Call the chamber for contact information.

RECREATION, ENTERTAINMENT & AMENITIES

Public golf: Coral Oaks Golf Course, 18 holes/par 72. **Semiprivate golf:** Cape Coral Executive Golf Course, nine holes/par 30; Cape Coral Golf & Tennis Resort, 18 holes/par 72; and Royal Tee Country Club, 18 holes/par 72. **Public tennis courts:** J. Chandler Burton Memorial Park and the Yacht Club. **Private tennis courts:** Cape Coral Golf & Tennis Resort. **Parks:** Ecology Park is a 365-acre nature park and wildlife refuge. Others include Four Freedoms Park, Guiffrida Park, Jason Verdow Memorial Park, Jaycee Park, Lake Kennedy Park and Veterans Memorial Park. **Public swimming pools:** Yacht Club. **Water sports:** Boating and sailing. **River/gulf/ocean:** Caloosahatchee River, Matlacha Pass, Pine Island Sound, the Gulf of Mexico and 400 miles of canals. **Running/walking/biking:** Ecology Park Nature Trail and Jaycee Park track and exercise stations. There are several designated bike paths and trails. **Horses/riding:** Stables and the 4-H Equestrian Center provide boarding, lessons and riding opportunities. **Hunting:** None. **Movie theaters:** 10 screens. **Art museums:** Arts Studio and the Norman Rockwell Collection at the Cape Coral Historical Museum. **History museums:** Cape Coral Historical Museum. **Theaters:** Cultural Park Theatre. **Library:** Cape Coral Public. **Attractions:** Sun Splash Family Water Park. **Necessities:** All here.

Smart Shopper Tip: Coralwood and Del Prado Malls and Santa Barbara Center will fulfill most of your shopping needs.

WHO LIVES HERE

Population: 90,026 year-round residents, an increase of 15,035 since 1990. **Age 65+** = 25.7% in Lee County. **Median household income:** $29,174 (Lee County). **Per capita income:** $23,664 (Lee County).

NUMBERS TO KNOW

Chamber of commerce: (941) 549-6900. **Chamber of Southwest Florida Welcome Center:** (941) 278-7194. **Voter registration:** (941) 458-7020. **Vehicle registration, tags & title:** (941) 339-6000. **Driver's license:** (941) 574-1991. **Visitors Bureau,** (941) 338-3800,

WHAT TO READ

Cape Coral Breeze, daily newspaper, except Sunday, (941) 574-1110. **Fort Myers News-Press**, daily newspaper, (941) 945-7300.

GETTING AROUND

Bus: Lee TRAN, (941) 275-8726. **Taxi:** Lou's Taxi, (941) 549-5272. **Tours:** None. **Airport:** Southwest Florida International Airport. **Traffic:** There are no major highways bisecting Cape Coral, and there is no central downtown — thus no heavily traveled roadways. Del Prado Boulevard has some congestion at peak hours. A new bridge linking Cape Coral with Fort Myers is the shortest route possible between these two cities.

JOBS

County unemployment rate: 3.3%. **Job Line:** (941) 574-0535. **Florida Jobs and Benefits:** In Fort Myers, (941) 278-7140.

UTILITIES

Electricity: Lee County Electric Co-op, (941) 549-1131. **Gas:** None. **Water & sewer:** City of Cape Coral, (941) 574-7722. **Telephone:** Sprint-United Telephone, (941) 335-3111. **Cable TV:** Time Warner, (941) 574-2020.

PLACES OF WORSHIP

Three Catholic and 36 Protestant churches, two Jewish synagogues and two other faiths.

THE ENVIRONMENT

The Caloosahatchee River State Recreation Area has protected status as an Outstanding Florida Water. The Caloosahatchee Estuary has been rated as having fair to poor water quality. It is affected by channelization and urban and agricultural runoff. Polluted tributaries flow into the river. The river's water quality ranges from good at and above Orange River, to fair in the Cape Coral/Fort Myers area, to poor just upstream.

EVENTS AND FESTIVALS

Riverview Art Festival - January. **Cape Coral Winter Festival** - February. **Best Southwest Festival** - April. **Taste of the Cape** - September. **Tree-Lighting Ceremony** - December. **Christmas Boat-A-Long** - December.

WHERE TO EAT

Ariani, 1529 S. E. 15th Terrace, Italian, moderate, (941) 772-8000. **Brigands**, 1708 Cape Coral Parkway, steaks, seafood, pasta, moderate, (941) 540-4665.

WHERE TO STAY

Cape Coral Golf & Tennis Resort, (941) 542-3191. **Quality Inn**, (941) 542-2121. **Casa Loma Motel**, (941) 549-6000.

ISSUES

The city is experiencing rapid growth and trying to play catch-up with new water and sewer line construction.

Clearwater

HE SAID: ☆ ☆ ☆
Clearwater seems to have fewer problems,
more advantages and better natural and man-made features
than the other municipalities on the bay.

SHE SAID: ☆ ☆ ☆ ☆
This large, spacious town offers lots to retirees.
I think Clearwater is worth a look, but I would stay away
from the overly congested beach area.

It has big city amenities with lots of small-town charm. In fact, despite its urban character, Clearwater still has elements that are pleasantly reminiscent of earlier times.

Old meets new where palms and moss-draped oaks line streets that are home to new and attractive municipal and county government buildings. Within those structures, progressive city and county officials keep close tabs on infrastructure needs and act to maintain the way of life that keeps Clearwater ahead of its urban neighbors in the Tampa Bay area.

In Clearwater, the amenities are numerous. Fabulous Gulf beaches give it appeal. A wide assortment of housing alternatives offer residents a choice of waterfront views: bay, Gulf, lake, canal, harbor or island. And while the beach areas can get crowded, there are still some quieter places. There are private country clubs and the 10,000-resident On Top of the World development from which to choose a home and neighborhood.

In a matter of minutes the Courtney Campbell Causeway can take you across Old Tampa Bay to the restaurants, malls, historical sites, theme parks, sports arenas and cultural or social events of Tampa. Or, you can stay close to home and attend performances at Ruth Eckerd Hall at the Baumgardner Center for the Performing Arts. In local circles, this is considered "the premier performing arts center of the south" with its year-round schedule of dramas, ballets and classical, pop and jazz concerts.

Clearwater has a large retiree population, and in the words of one retiree, "everything a retiree could ever want" is here.

It seems clear that retirees have been good for Clearwater. Local economists have credited retirees' spending with creating a nearly recession-free economy. In fact, nearly one third of all personal income in Pinellas County comes in the form of retirees' investment dividends, interest income, rent and social security payments.

WEATHER

	Winter	Spring	Summer	Fall
Normal daily high/low	72/52	85/66	90/73	78/58
Normal precipitation	10 in.	10 in.	23 in.	8 in.

Disaster watch: Since 1900, northwest Florida has been hit by six major hurricanes, and southwest Florida has been hit by five major hurricanes.

TAXES
Sales tax: 7%. **Property tax:** $22.83 per $1,000 valuation. Sample tax calculations include a $25,000 homestead exemption.

Home value	Tax
$100,000	$1,712
$150,000	$2,854
$250,000	$5,137

REAL ESTATE
Median home value: $103,808 (Pinellas County). **Median rent:** $614/month (Pinellas County). **Communities popular with retir-**

ees: On Top of the World is an adult condominium development with prices from the high $60s to $110s, (800) 733-3417. **Licensed continuing-care retirement communities:** Bayview Gardens, 340 rental units and off-site health care, (813) 797-7400. Regency Oaks, 401 independent living units in Phase I, 60 sheltered nursing beds, (813) 791-3381.

CRIME & SAFETY
Crimes per 1,000 population: 74. **Non-emergency police:** (813) 562-4242. **Non-emergency fire department:** (813) 562-4334. **Police, fire, ambulance emergencies:** 911.

HOMELESS & BLIGHT
There was no evidence of homeless persons. Downtown Clearwater and Clearwater Beach are very nice areas, as are most of the residential and commercial districts. Zoning and sign ordinances seem to work effectively. There are pockets of substandard housing, as in any large city.

The U.S. Census reported 1,105 homeless persons in shelters and 75 visible on the streets of Pinellas County, population 851,659.

HEALTH CARE
Hospitals: Clearwater Community Hospital, 133 beds, 24-hour emergency, full service, (813) 447-4571. It offers a free-benefits club for seniors, **Senior Friends Club**, (813) 588-5788. **Morton Plant Hospital**, 740 acute-care beds, cancer center, cardiac center, chest pain emergency center, (813) 462-7000.
Physicians: 492. **Specialties:** 49.

GETTING SMART
Tampa College, Clearwater campus, (813) 530-9495. **Offerings:** Associate's, bachelor's and master's degree programs. **St. Petersburg Junior College**, Clearwater campus, (813) 341-3600. **Offerings:** Two-year degree programs in 70 fields. **Eckerd College** in St. Petersburg, (813) 867-1166, and Palm Harbor, (813) 784-7566. **Offerings:** Bachelor's degree programs, evening/weekend independent study and college credit courses. It also offers the Academy of Senior Professionals, (813) 864-8834, with classes in life enrichment and liberal arts subjects as well as intergenerational, mentoring and community service programs.

JUST FOR SENIORS
Clearwater Senior Citizens Center, (727) 444-4999. **Levison-Clearwater Senior Center**, (813) 461-5777. **Senior Citizens Services, Inc.**, (813) 442-8104.

GETTING INVOLVED
AARP, (813) 576-1155. **SCORE**, (813) 532-6800. **Senior Citizen Community Service Employment Opportunities**, (727) 441-9925.

RECREATION, ENTERTAINMENT & AMENITIES
Public golf: There are 26 courses available to the public, including Airco Golf Club, 18 holes/par 72; Clearwater Country Club, 18 holes/par 72; Clearwater Golf Park, 18 holes/par 63; and Glen Oaks Country Club municipal course, 18 holes/par 54. **Private golf:** Cove Cay Country Club, 18 holes/par 70; Feather

Sound Country Club; 18 holes/par 72; and On Top of the World, 18 holes/par 65. **Public tennis courts:** Royal Racquet Club. **Private tennis courts:** Sheraton Sand Key Resort and Presti Tennis Center. **Parks:** More than 1,000 acres at 56 parks. The chamber of commerce touts Sand Key Park as one of the top 20 beaches in the world. Coachman Park, downtown, features stage productions for the entire family. **Public swimming pools:** Long Center. **Water sports:** Sailing, scuba diving, jet-skiing, parasailing, windsurfing and water-skiing. **River/gulf/ocean:** Clearwater Harbor, Old Tampa Bay, Lake Chataugua, Little Pass, Mandalay Channel, Stevenson Creek and the Gulf of Mexico. **Running/walking/biking:** 47-mile Pinellas Trail comes through downtown for walkers, joggers, bicyclists and skaters. **Horses/riding:** There are stables and riding academies in northeast Clearwater and unincorporated areas. **Hunting:** None. **Movie theaters:** 20 screens. **Art museums:** None. **History museums:** Dorothy Thompson African American Museum and Florida Military Aviation Museum. **Theaters:** Ruth Eckerd Hall, Octagon Arts Center, Francis Wilson Playhouse, Royalty Theater Company and three dinner theaters. **Library:** Clearwater Public and four branches. **Attractions:** Clearwater Marine Science Center Aquarium/Museum, Clearwater Beach, Philadelphia Phillies winter training camp and Suncoast Seabird Sanctuary. **Necessities:** All here.

Smart Shopper Tip: No matter where you live in Clearwater, there's an enclosed mall nearby. Countryside Mall to the north is the best in the bay area, with four major anchors and 166 stores. Clearwater Mall, with four anchors and about 100 stores, is more centrally located. Bay Area Outlet mall has 127 factory stores.

WHO LIVES HERE
Population: 104,472 year-round residents, an increase of 5,803 since 1990. **Age 65+** = 24.6% in Pinellas County. **Median household income:** $29,009 (Pinellas County). **Per capita income:** $25,765 (Pinellas County).

NUMBERS TO KNOW
Chamber of commerce: (813) 461-0011. **Voter registration:** (813) 464-3551. **Vehicle registration, tags & title:** (813) 464-5560. **Driver's license:** (813) 725-7943. **Visitors bureau:** (727) 464-7200.

WHAT TO READ
Clearwater Times, daily newspaper, (813) 895-1181. **Clearwater Leader**, weekly newspaper, (727) 397-5563. **Right Downtown**, monthly newsletter, (813) 461-0011. **Tampa Tribune**, daily newspaper, (813) 799-7400.

GETTING AROUND
Bus: Jolly Trolley offers rides seven days a week throughout Clearwater Beach. PSTA (Pinellas Suncoast Transit Authority) runs buses on a scheduled route through downtown, (813) 530-9911. **Taxi:** Yellow Cab, (813) 799-2222. **Tours:** Self-guided tour of downtown with maps from historical society. **Airport:** St. Petersburg/Clearwater International and Tampa International. **Traffic:** Avoid Gulf to Bay Boulevard, which becomes the Courtney Campbell Causeway, during rush hours. North-south traffic moves well considering that the main route is the infamous U.S. Highway 19.

JOBS
County unemployment rate: 3.4%. **Florida Jobs and Benefits:** (813) 725-7920.

UTILITIES
Electricity: Florida Power Corp., (813) 443-2641. **Gas:** Clearwater Gas System, (813) 462-6340. **Water & sewer:** Pinellas County Public Utilities, (813) 464-4714. **Telephone:** GTE Florida, (800) 483-4200. **Cable TV:** Time Warner Cable, (727) 797-1818.

PLACES OF WORSHIP
Four Catholic and 104 Protestant churches, plus three Jewish synagogues.

THE ENVIRONMENT
Water quality in the area has been rated as mostly fair to poor. According to the Florida Department of Environmental Regulation, the degradation of the bay has prompted intensive efforts over the last 10 years to reverse the trend. Protective management policies, legislation and regulation have been adopted. Some improvement has been seen, especially in Hillsborough Bay. The Pinellas County portion of Tampa Bay has received protected status with the designation as an Outstanding Florida Water.

There is one EPA-listed Superfund site in Pinellas County. It is the Stauffer Chemical Co. plant in Tarpon Springs.

EVENTS AND FESTIVALS
Philadelphia Phillies Spring Training - March/April. **Fun 'N' Sun** - April. **Octoberfest** - October. **Kahlua Cup Regatta** - November.

WHERE TO EAT
There are more than 500 restaurants in Clearwater and Clearwater Beach. **Julie's Seafood & Sunsets**, 351 Gulfview Blvd., seafood and sandwiches, moderate, (813) 441-2548. **Heilman's Beachcomber**, 447 Mandalay Ave., diverse menu, southern-style fried chicken, moderate to expensive, (813) 442-4144.

WHERE TO STAY
Belleview Biltmore Resort & Spa, (813) 442-6171. **Courtyard by Marriott**, (813) 572-8484. **Sheraton Sand Key Resort**, (813) 595-1611.

ISSUES
A beautiful city requires constant attention to maintain its good looks. That is exactly what keeps Clearwater in the forefront of Florida's visually attractive population centers. Peak-season tourism brings traffic congestion and steep competition for access to beaches, restaurants and other amenities.

Clermont

Clermont is a town in transition. Ten years ago, its citrus-fueled economy was devastated by a hard freeze that destroyed more than 90 percent of its groves. The town is now beginning to focus on retirees to provide a new source of growth and revenue for the area.

A quiet, unhurried atmosphere, a chain of lakes and some beautiful lake-side homes are its principal offerings. Retirees listed the hilly setting, cleanliness and friendly people as other factors in its favor.

Negative comments about the area focused on the inconvenience of limited shopping facilities and restaurants. One retiree mentioned the "awful lightning in the summer," and another cited the profusion of insects in lake-front neighborhoods at certain times of the year.

To add perspective, none of these drawbacks have slowed the migration of both retirees and wage-earners to the area. In fact, builders and developers are having a hard time keeping up with demand. Affordable, low-maintenance, outdoor-oriented subdivisions are springing up in former orange groves, across the hills and valleys around Clermont, and to a lesser extent, on the much pricier real estate around the popular Chain of Lakes.

Life in Clermont offers lakes, hills, recreational opportunities, friendly neighbors and a progressive, people-driven local government. For entertainment, shopping, dining and cultural pursuits, residents often go to nearby Orlando and Leesburg. Proximity to urban amenities, coupled with Clermont's own best features, is producing a lifestyle many retirees find irresistible.

With its land being converted from citrus groves to residential development, Clermont is experiencing population growth that may test its ability to protect and retain its best qualities. Fortunately, it seems to have the government infrastructure and enlightened citizenry necessary for the task. It's easy to see a bright future for those who choose to spend the next 25 years or so in this "gem of the hills."

WEATHER

	Winter	Spring	Summer	Fall
Normal daily high/low	74/51	88/65	91/72	77/58
Normal precipitation	10 in.	13 in.	21 in.	7 in.

Disaster watch: Northwest Florida has been hit by six major hurricanes since 1900.

TAXES
Sales tax: 7%. **Property tax:** $19.68 per $1,000 valuation. Sample tax calculations include a $25,000 homestead exemption.

Home value	Tax
$100,000	$1,476
$150,000	$2,460
$250,000	$4,428

REAL ESTATE
Median home value: $90,181 (Lake County). **Median rent:** $438/month (Lake County). **Communities popular with retirees:** There are 10 mobile-home parks and manufactured-home communities with prices ranging from the high $30s to mid-$80s. Lakeshore Drive around Lake Minnehaha has single-family homes from the $180s to more than $1 million, (352) 394-7777. Palisade Country Club has golf cottages and custom homes from the low $100s to $400s, (352) 394-3933. Kings Ridge is an adult, gated golf-course community with single-family homes from the $70s to mid-$100s, (352) 242-1192. **Licensed continuing-care retirement communities:** None.

CRIME & SAFETY
Crimes per 1,000 population: 59. **Non-emergency police:** (352) 394-5588. **Non-emergency fire department:** (352) 394-7662. **Police, fire, ambulance emergencies:** 911.

HOMELESS & BLIGHT
We saw no homeless persons and no blighted areas. Clermont does not have a pronounced downtown. In fact, city hall is on the edge of the incorporated area and somewhat isolated from the general populace. A pedestrian/bicycle trail that starts downtown and follows the old Seaboard Railroad right-of-way is helping efforts to bring more people to the town center. The town is clean, but not particularly attractive. There is no historic district. Lake housing areas are very pretty.

The U.S. Census reported 68 homeless persons in shelters and one visible on the streets of Lake County, population 152,104.

HEALTH CARE
Hospitals: South Lake Memorial Hospital, 68 beds, full service, 24-hour emergency, (352) 394-4071.
Physicians: 37. **Specialties:** 14.

GETTING SMART
Lake-Sumter Community College holds classes at South Lake High School, (352) 365-3573. **Offerings:** Extension course study toward a two-year associate's degree, continuing-education courses and non-credit courses.

JUST FOR SENIORS
There is no senior center here, but Jenkins Auditorium hosts many activities for seniors.

GETTING INVOLVED
There are about 50 fraternal and civic organizations and clubs.

AARP, (352) 624-9529. **Meals on Wheels,** (352) 394-3349.

RECREATION, ENTERTAINMENT & AMENITIES

Public golf: Clerbrook Resort, Green Valley Golf Course and Palisades Golf & Country Club, semiprivate. **Private golf:** Swiss Fairways, nine holes. **Public tennis courts:** Carroll Street Park, East Avenue Park and Kehlor Park. **Private tennis courts:** None. **Parks:** Jaycee Beach on Lake Minneola is Florida's longest inland white-sand beach. Others: Kehlor, Peter Pool, and Palatlakaha municipal parks, plus 1,790-acre Lake Louisa State Park. **Public swimming pools:** None. **Water sports:** Boating, canoeing, sailplaning, scuba diving, swimming and water-skiing. **River/gulf/ocean:** Palatlakaha River and 15 lakes, including lakes Minneola, Minnehaha and Louisa. **Running/walking/biking:** Fitness trail/jogging path circles Lake Center. Lake Louisa State Park has walking/nature study areas. Triathlon participants cycle 112 miles through the uncrowded hills of south Lake County. A recently completed 3.5 mile sector of the Florida Rails to Trails through Clermont will eventually connect to the east with the 17-mile West Orange Trail in Oakland and to the west with the Van Fleet Trail. **Horses/riding:** There are stables and plenty of places to ride in the hills. **Hunting:** In season, in rural areas of south Lake County, (352) 343-9622. **Movie theaters:** None. Two were under construction at press time. **Art museums:** South Lakes Art League. **History museums:** House of Presidents Wax Museum. **Theaters:** Jenkins Auditorium and South Lake High School Auditorium. **Library:** Cooper Memorial. **Attractions:** Citrus Tower, Lakeridge Winery & Vineyards, Seminole-Lake Gliderport and Sky World Paraplanes. **Necessities:** Most necessities are here, but little else.

Smart Shopper Tip: The local Kmart can only get you so far. Plan to make regular trips to Orlando or Leesburg, both less than an hour away.

WHO LIVES HERE

Population: 7,582 year-round residents, an increase of 672 since 1990. **Age 65+ =** 27.9% in Lake County. **Median household income:** $24,804 (Lake County). **Per capita income:** $19,459 (Lake County).

NUMBERS TO KNOW

Chamber of commerce: (352) 394-4191. **Voter registration:** (352) 343-9734. **Vehicle registration, tags & title:** (352) 343-9602. **Driver's license:** In Tavares, (352) 742-6167.

WHAT TO READ

Orlando Sentinel, daily newspaper, (800) 359-5353. **The Daily Commercial,** Leesburg daily newspaper, (352) 365-8200. **South Lake Press,** weekly newspaper, (352) 394-2183. **The News Leader,** weekly newspaper, (352) 242-9818.

GETTING AROUND

Bus: No public intra-city transportation. **Taxi:** South Lake Taxi, (352) 242-0220. **Tours:** None. **Airport:** Orlando International is 30 minutes away. **Traffic:** Traffic within the city is very light. Good highways for through-traffic — Route 50 and U.S. Highway 27 — skirt the town. Florida's Turnpike, a few miles northeast, carries most of the long-distance traffic.

JOBS

County unemployment rate: 3.8%. **Florida Jobs and Benefits:** In Leesburg, (352) 360-6518. **Job Line:** For Lake County, (352) 343-5627.

UTILITIES

Electricity: Florida Power Corp., (800) 700-8744, or Sumter Electric Co-op, (352) 429-2195, depending on residence location. **Gas:** Lake Apopka Natural Gas Co., (352) 394-3480. **Water & sewer:** Clermont Utility Dept., (352) 394-3350. **Telephone:** United Telephone, (352) 381-5600. **Cable TV:** Time-Warner, (352) 394-5541.

PLACES OF WORSHIP

One Catholic and 28 Protestant churches.

THE ENVIRONMENT

Lakes Louisa, Minnehaha and Minneola have been rated as having good water quality. The Palatlakaha River near the area has generally good water quality. Lake Apopka has generally poor water quality and has been designated for improvement and management.

The Tower Chemical Co. in Clermont is an EPA-listed Superfund site now undergoing cleanup.

EVENTS AND FESTIVALS

Labor Day Festival on the Lake - September. **The Great Floridian Triathlon** - October. **Octoberfest. Light Up Clermont Festival** - December.

WHERE TO EAT

Colony Cove Theatre & Grille, 528 Eighth St., steaks, seafood, salads, inexpensive, (352) 242-4569. **Crown Restaurant,** 1340 E. Highway (Route) 50, beef and seafood, moderate to expensive, (352) 394-3887. **The Rusty Fox,** 649 12th St., steaks, seafood, pastas, moderate, (352) 394-3333. **On the Corner Seafood Grill,** 801 W. Montrose St., seafood, moderate, (352) 394-6911.

WHERE TO STAY

Best Western Highpoint Inn, (352) 429-9033.

ISSUES

Clermont has some deficiencies, but its proximity to Orlando helps alleviate much of the deprivation. It also is blessed with many natural resources — lakes, hills, wildlife, open spaces — that endear it to those looking for a quiet, peaceful place in the sun.

It is on the verge of an increased growth rate that could test its ability to retain the best it has to offer while accommodating new residents. It seems to be up to the task.

Cocoa Beach

HE SAID: ✮ ✮
> *As much as I enjoy Space Center activities,
> the beaches and the diversity of Greater Cocoa Beach, this
> is what it must be like to live in a beehive. There's too much
> buzz and busyness.*

SHE SAID: ✮ ✮
> *This is more of a tourist town than a residential community.
> It has lots of souvenir shops and there's very little foliage.
> Drive through, but don't stop. It's not for me.*

There are two common bonds holding the seven varying communities of the Space Coast together: water and the John F. Kennedy Space Center. Other than these shared elements, each of the communities offers just a piece of the pie.

Cocoa Beach mostly is a small resort/residential community. Cocoa, slightly larger, is primarily commercial and industrial. It also is the site of Olde Cocoa Village, where a $1 million rejuvenation program created a pedestrian mall with cobblestone streets, oak-shaded brick sidewalks, period street lamps and restored turn-of-the-century buildings. It attracts major art shows and shoppers. Merritt Island, sitting squarely between Cocoa and Cocoa Beach, has numerous residential neighborhoods and the Kennedy Space Center. Cape Canaveral is primarily residential with many small businesses, while Rockledge is residential and industrial. Port Canaveral is a shipping and cruise port, and Patrick Air Force Base is home to 2,296 military personnel and their families.

For residents, the specialization of the towns means traversing the area to meet various needs. Retiring to Cocoa Beach would be fine until it was time to shop or go to the doctor. For these necessities, residents must go to Merritt Island or Rockledge. For a riveting cultural experience, or to stimulate the mind, residents must cross the causeway to Cocoa.

Causeways spanning the Indian River, Sykes Creek, New Found Harbor and the Banana River are as essential as breathing for those living on the Space Coast. Therein lies one of the major deterrents to a stress-free retirement here — traffic jams spawned by too many cars and too few viable routes.

The Kennedy Space Center is the primary attraction for more than 3 million visitors annually. No doubt it served as the magnet that first attracted most of the area's retirees. Once here as tourists, they were captivated by its natural tropical beauty, won over by its 25 miles of broad, sandy beaches and sold by the location's easy access to the Gold Coast, Orlando, Disney World and even the Gulf Coast communities.

The Cocoa Beach area is busy. This may be the thing that attracts some retirees. The diversity and variety of the area create a fulfilling environment. The trick is to know when to venture forth and when to stay home and let the tourists and daily commuters have the right-of-way.

WEATHER

	Winter	Spring	Summer	Fall
Normal daily high/low	73/50	86/64	90/71	78/57
Normal precipitation	9 in.	13 in.	23 in.	10 in.

Disaster watch: Northeast Florida has not been hit by a major hurricane since 1900.

TAXES

Sales tax: 6%. **Property tax:** $20.89 per $1,000 valuation in Cocoa Beach. Of the local communities, Rockledge assesses the highest property tax, $21.66 per $1,000 valuation, and Cape Canaveral the lowest, $17.33. Sample tax calculations are for Cocoa Beach and include a $25,000 homestead exemption.

Home value	Tax
$100,000	$1,567
$150,000	$2,611
$250,000	$4,700

REAL ESTATE

Median home value: $84,370 (Brevard County). **Median rent:** $548/month (Brevard County). **Communities popular with retirees:** Coldwell Banker, (407) 784-5796, provided the following: Cocoa Beach Country Club has 2,000-square-foot single-family homes starting at around $200,000; Emerald Seas has ocean-front condos averaging 1,800 square feet for $186,500 to the mid-$200,000s; Harbor Isles has 1,400-square-foot riverfront condos starting at around $100,000; Cape Shores Condominiums in Cape Canaveral are priced from the $60s; and canal homes in the Cocoa Beach area start at around $125,000. **Licensed continuing-care retirement communities:** None.

CRIME & SAFETY

Information is for Cocoa Beach. **Crimes per 1,000 population:** 78. **Non-emergency police:** (407) 868-3333. **Non-emergency fire department:** (407) 868-3330. **Police, fire, ambulance emergencies:** 911.

HOMELESS & BLIGHT

We saw no homeless persons or blighted areas, unless you consider the high density of billboards and neon lights as blight. In Brevard County, population 398,978, the U.S. Census reported 196 homeless persons in shelters and 18 on the streets.

HEALTH CARE

Hospitals: Cape Canaveral Hospital, 225 beds, full service, (407) 799-7111. **Wuesthoff Hospital**, 308 beds, general acute care, (407) 636-2211.
Physicians: 205. **Specialties:** 40.

GETTING SMART

Brevard Community College in Cocoa, (407) 632-1111. **Offerings:** Five primary programs: University Parallel, technical, vocational, adult education and continuing education for personal enrichment or toward a two-year degree. **University of Central Florida** in Cocoa, (407) 632-6476. **Offerings:** Twenty fields of study including business administration, education, engineering and public administration leading to bachelor's and master's degrees. **Rollins College** in Rockledge, (407) 646-2161, and in Melbourne, (407) 726-0432. **Offerings:** Five fields of study (arts and communication, business, computer science, education and social science) leading to associate's, bachelor's or master's degrees.

JUST FOR SENIORS

Area Agency on Aging, (407) 228-1800. **AARP,** (407) 267-6190. **Freedom 7 Senior Citizens Center,** Cocoa Beach, (407) 784-2313. **Martin Andersen Senior Center,** Rockledge, (407) 631-7549. **Senior Employment Program,** (407) 254-7517. **Senior Helpline,** (407) 631-2747.

GETTING INVOLVED

The Cocoa Beach area has dozens of social service and community service organizations. **American Red Cross,** (407) 494-2402. **Meals on Wheels,** (407) 639-8770, ext.

222. **RSVP,** (407) 631-2749.

RECREATION, ENTERTAINMENT & AMENITIES

Public golf: Cocoa Beach Country Club, 27 holes; Savannahs at Sykes Creek, 18 holes/par 72; and Turtle Creek Golf Club. **Private golf:** Rockledge Country Club, 18 holes. **Public tennis courts:** There are 55 tennis courts in the area including those at the Cocoa Beach Recreation Complex, Cocoa Beach Country Club, Rockledge Park and Cape Canaveral Recreation Center. **Private tennis courts:** Rockledge Country Club. **Parks:** There are 61 public parks. Kiwanis Island Park & Community Center is centrally located off the Merritt Island Causeway. To the north is Merritt Island National Wildlife Refuge and farther still, just east of Titusville, is the Canaveral National Seashore. **Public swimming pools:** Cocoa Beach Recreation Complex, McLarty Park and Pineda Park. **Water sports:** Scuba diving, surfing, windsurfing, sailing, yachting, canoeing and fishing. **River/gulf/ocean:** St. Johns River and Lake Poinsett to the west, plus Indian and Banana Rivers, Sykes Creek, New Found Harbor, Barge Canal and Atlantic Ocean all make this area a water fanatic's paradise. **Running/walking/biking:** Merritt Island National Wildlife Refuge has 22 acres of nature trails. There's also Kiwanis Island Park Exercise Trail and Rockledge Park jogging/exercise trails. **Horses/riding:** Numerous stables offer training, boarding, trails and sales. **Hunting:** Florida Game and Freshwater Fish Commission, (352) 732-1225. Florida Marine Patrol, (800) 342-5367. South Brevard Service Complex for hunting, (407) 255-4410. **Movie theaters:** Four theaters with 14 screens. **Art museums:** Central Brevard Art Association in Cocoa. **History museums:** Astronaut Memorial Hall & Planetarium in Cocoa and Brevard Museum of History & Natural Science. **Theaters:** Cocoa Village Playhouse, Children's Community Theater & Fine Arts Auditorium. Performing arts groups include the Florida Space Coast Philharmonic, Surfside Players, Lyceum Series and Brevard Chorale Society. **Library:** In Cocoa, Cape Canaveral, Cocoa Beach and Merritt Island. **Attractions:** Kennedy Space Center, Spaceport USA, Astronaut Hall of Fame, Brevard Community College Planetarium, Florida Solar Energy Center, Canaveral National Seashore, Merritt Island National Wildlife Refuge, Cocoa Beach Expo Center and Cocoa Beach Pier. **Necessities:** All within the seven communities that make up Greater Cocoa Beach.

Smart Shopper Tip: Retail stores are plentiful. Go in any direction and you'll find a major shopping area. The biggest and best is Merritt Square Mall with 120-plus stores.

WHO LIVES HERE

Population: 12,818 year-round residents in Cocoa Beach, an increase of 695 since 1990. **Age 65+** = 18.3% in Brevard County. **Median household income:** $33,061 (Brevard County). **Per capita income:** $20,747 (Brevard County).

NUMBERS TO KNOW

Chamber of commerce: (407) 459-2200. **Voter registration:** (407) 455-1404. **Vehicle registration, tags & title:** (407) 455-1412. **Driver's license:** (407) 449-5002. **Visitors bureau:** (407) 452-4390.

WHAT TO READ

Orlando Sentinel, daily newspaper, (407) 420-5000. **Florida Today,** daily newspaper, (407) 259-5000. **Space Coast Press,** weekly newspaper, (407) 454-6300. **The Tribune,** weekly newspaper, (407) 259-5555.

GETTING AROUND

Bus: Space Coast Area Transit System, (407) 633-1878. **Taxi:** Canaveral Cab Co., (407) 783-8294; Always Ready Cab Co., (407) 459-0107. **Tours:** Europa Cruise Line offers half-day cruises. Both Carnival and Premier cruise lines offer cruises from here. **Airport:** Melbourne International is 20 miles away. Orlando International is 40 miles away. **Traffic:** It can be a nightmare, especially when the peak tourist season coincides with a major launch from Cape Canaveral. More than 50,000 cars have been clocked in a 24-hour period on one of the two causeways connecting Cocoa, Merritt Island and Cocoa Beach.

JOBS

County unemployment rate: 4.8%. **Florida Jobs and Benefits:** (407) 690-3220.

UTILITIES

Electricity: Florida Power & Light, (407) 723-7795. **Gas:** City Gas Co. of Florida, (407) 636-4644. **Water & sewer:** City of Cocoa, Utilities Dept., (407) 639-7500. **Telephone:** Bell South, (800) 789-9025 in Florida, or (800) 753-2909 out-of-state. **Cable TV:** Time-Warner Cable, (407) 254-3300.

PLACES OF WORSHIP

Four Catholic and 103 Protestant churches as well as one Jewish synagogue.

THE ENVIRONMENT

Urban development has taken its toll around the Sykes Creek portion of the Banana River and the middle western section of Indian River from Titusville to Cocoa; these areas are rated as having poor water quality.

In 1993, the EPA found lead measuring 132 parts per billion (ppb) in the drinking water of the Kennedy Space Center System. The EPA action level is 15 ppb.

There is one EPA-listed Superfund site in Brevard County, located in Palm Bay.

EVENTS AND FESTIVALS

Seafest - March. **Cocoa Village Spring Art Show** - April. **Space Congress** - April. **Cocoa Beach Fest** - May. **International Food, Craft and Cultural Festival** - June. **Port Weekend** - September. **Cocoa Village Autumn Art Festival** - October. **Seminole Indian & Florida Pioneer Festival** - October. **Space Coast Art Festival** - November.

WHERE TO EAT

Bernard's Surf, 2 S. Atlantic Ave., seafood, prime rib, steaks, moderate, (407) 783-2401. **Mango Tree,** 118 N. Atlantic Ave., continental, moderate to expensive, (407) 799-0513. **Heidelberg,** 7 N. Orlando Ave., German-American, moderate, (407) 783-6806. **Yen Yen,** 2 N. Atlantic Ave., Chinese, moderate, (407) 783-9512.

WHERE TO STAY

Howard Johnson Plaza-Hotel, (407) 783-9222. **Ocean Suite Hotel,** (407) 784-4343. **Wakulla Motel,** (407) 783-2230. **Cocoa Beach Hilton,** (407) 799-0003.

ISSUES

Budgeting for the space program is always a concern since the area's economy is so heavily dependent on it.

Coral Gables

HE SAID: ★ ★ ★ ★
*Coral Gables is an oasis of beauty, serenity,
law and order in the midst of rough-and-tough Dade County.
I felt perfectly safe here. However, outside the town limits,
high urban crime rates prevail. I cannot recommend
anything this far southeast.*

SHE SAID: ★ ★ ★ ★
*It's a beautiful city. It has all the amenities, a variety
of residential areas and a lot to recommend it. But it is too
busy, too big and too crowded for me. I would never
consider retiring here.*

Coral Gables is different. The town — really a small city — was planned and created by George Merrick in the early 1900s. Planning and zoning laws help distinguish Coral Gables from the rest of Florida. Strict rules, rigidly enforced, regulate everything from architecture — which is almost entirely Spanish — to landscaping and grounds maintenance.

Local government and civic leaders maintain such tight control over Coral Gables that things which become issues for other cities — aesthetics, services, the homeless, commercial development, zoning, education, quality of life—never seem to be a problem here. It is a city that prides itself on architectural beauty, arts, international business and fine educational and medical facilities. Driving around the city, you both see and sense the stability, beauty and harmony of the place.

Residents here are among the economically privileged. Almost one quarter of the Gables' 16,000 households earns $75,000.

The University of Miami, with its main campus sitting squarely in the middle of the city, employs more than 5,000 people. The three major hospitals in Coral Gables employ more than 1,600.

Although Coral Gables is home to more than 120 multinational corporations, only 5 percent of the land area is occupied by commercial properties, and 1 percent is industrial. Single-family homes occupy 54 percent.

It has the warm and sunny climate, idyllic seaside character, subtropical vegetation and wide spectrum of cultural amenities that most dream about for retirement. It also has a price tag that proves dreams are not cheap. So if you seek an urban environment and can tolerate the threat of increased lawlessness that brews outside the city limits, then visit Coral Gables and bring your wallet.

WEATHER

	Winter	Spring	Summer	Fall
Normal daily high/low	77/61	85/72	89/76	80/66
Normal precipitation	6 in.	19 in.	21 in.	12 in.

Disaster watch: Southeast Florida has been hit by nine major hurricanes since 1900.

TAXES

Sales tax: 6.5%. **Property tax:** $24.45 per $1,000 valuation. Sample tax calculations include a $25,000 homestead exemption.

Home value	Tax
$100,000	$1,834
$150,000	$3,056
$250,000	$5,501

REAL ESTATE

Median home value: $117,429 (Dade County), $275,000 (Coral Gables). **Median rent:** $764/month (Dade County). **Communities**

popular with retirees: There are no planned retirement communities but plenty of single-family neighborhoods ideal for retirees. Merrick's original design included several residential villages of the world: Chinese Village, French Country Village, French City Village and Dutch South African Village.

At $165,000, Coral Gables has the highest average home price in Dade County, according to the chamber of commerce. Approximately 1,500 condominium units have been built here and range from $120,000 to $700,000. Waterfront or canal-front homes start at $300,000. The Riviera Country Club offers golf course homes that should come with the warning, "You can't join on the city's average household income of $54,000." If you are lucky, you might find a 1,200-square-foot house for $85,000. Or you could pay up to $8.5 million for a larger property. **Licensed continuing-care retirement communities:** None.

CRIME & SAFETY

Crimes per 1,000 population: 117. **Non-emergency police:** (305) 442-1600. **Non-emergency fire department:** (305) 460-5560. **Police, fire, ambulance emergencies:** 911.

HOMELESS & BLIGHT

During our visits, the homeless population was not visible within the city limits of Coral Gables. According to the Census, Dade County's 1.9 million population included 1,235 homeless people in shelters and another 495 visible on the streets.

HEALTH CARE

One of the brightest aspects of retirement living here is the quality and availability of medical service. **Hospitals: Coral Gables Hospital**, 285 beds, full service, (305) 445-8461. **Doctors' Hospital of Coral Gables**, 285 beds, full service, (305) 666-2111. **Vencor Hospital**, 53 beds, acute care only, (305) 448-1585. **Physicians:** 300+. **Specialties:** 40.

GETTING SMART

University of Miami, Institute for Retired Professionals, (305) 284-5072. **Offerings:** Retirees can audit graduate or undergraduate lecture courses on the Coral Gables campus (on a space-available basis). Monthly Distinguished Faculty Luncheon Lecture Series and peer-led study/discussion groups are held on campus at the Wesley Center. Subjects include philosophy, art, music, history, languages, psychology, religion, drama, archaeology, literature, geography and others. **The Adult Education Center** is part of the Dade County Public Schools system, with courses held at Coral Gables Senior High School, (305) 443-4871. **Offerings:** Courses include a wide range of general studies such as foreign languages, aerobics, business, computers and art.

JUST FOR SENIORS

There are no services or facilities offered by the city just for seniors; however, Dade County and Miami provide many, including transportation and homemakers' services. **Senior Employment** is an AARP program that provides transitional minimum wage employment for seniors in the job market, (305) 643-9697.

GETTING INVOLVED

Residents have extraordinary opportunities for involvement in the community. Clubs and organizations too numerous to detail are open to those willing to serve. More than a dozen historical landmarks, museums and arts organizations use docents. Contact the chamber of commerce to find out how to get involved.

RECREATION, ENTERTAINMENT & AMENITIES

Public golf: The Biltmore Golf Course, 18 holes/par 71; Granada, nine holes. **Private golf:** Riviera Country Club. **Public tennis courts:** 33. **Private tennis courts:** 19. **Parks:** There are 30 in all. Fairchild Tropical Garden is the largest tropical botanical garden in the continental United States. Matheson Hammock Park has a pool formed by a tropical atoll and a sandy beach. **Public swimming pools:** Yes. **Water sports:** Biscayne Bay and Biscayne National Park offer plenty of water-related activities. **River/gulf/ocean:** Six miles of Atlantic shoreline. **Running/walking/biking:** Parks, recreation areas and stretches of the Coral Gables Canal and Waterway System. **Horses/riding:** Yes. **Hunting:** No. **Movie theaters:** Lots; scattered throughout the city. **Art museums:** The Lowe Art Museum at the University of Miami has more than 8,000 pieces in its collection, including works by El Greco, Goya and Rembrandt. **History museums:** Coral Gables House is the 1906 boyhood home of the city's founder, George Merrick. **Theaters:** Miracle Theatre. Minorca Playhouse is home to the Florida Shakespeare Theatre and also hosts dance and theater companies. At the university, Ring Theatre offers musicals, dramas and comedies by professionals, students and faculty. New Theatre stages both experimental and traditional works. **Library:** Coral Gables Public. **Attractions:** Football (University of Miami Hurricanes). Also, the Venetian Pool, a giant coral quarry made into an elaborate swimming pool with grottoes, rock cliffs, an arched bridge, shaded porticos and Spanish towers. **Necessities:** It's all here.

Smart Shopper Tip: For entertainment and shopping, walk the Miracle Mile, an illustrious string of elegant and smart shops along Coral Way between Douglas and Le Jeune roads. Try Miracle Center, a 27-store mall with a fanciful, futuristic design. Excellent shopping centers lace the city on South Dixie Highway, Coral Way, Bird Road and Ponce de Leon Boulevard.

WHO LIVES HERE

Population: 42,238 year-round residents, an increase of 2,147 since 1990. **Age 65+** = 14.4% in Dade County. **Median household income:** $26,743 (Dade County). **Per capita income:** $21,058 (Dade County).

NUMBERS TO KNOW

Chamber of commerce: (305) 446-1657. **Voter registration:** (305) 375-4600. **Vehicle registration, tags & title:** (305) 375-5678. **Driver's license:** (305) 229-6333. **Visitors bureau:** (305) 539-3063.

WHAT TO READ

Coral Gables News, semiweekly newspaper, (305) 669-7355. **Miami Herald,** daily newspaper, (305) 350-2111.

GETTING AROUND

Bus: Metrobus, Maps-by-Mail from Metrobus, (305) 654-6586. Ask for "First Time Rider's Kit." **Taxi:** Yellow Cab, (305) 444-4444; Central Cab, (305) 532-5555. **Tours:** Old Town Trolley, (305) 296-6688. **Airport:** Miami International. **Traffic:** Good highway access. Population density of surrounding areas combined with influx of tourists and seasonal residents cause urban congestion.

JOBS

County unemployment rate: 7.2%. **Florida Jobs and Benefits:** (305) 252-4440.

UTILITIES

Electricity: Florida Power & Light, (305) 442-8770. **Gas:** City Gas, (305) 691-0313. **Water & sewer:** Miami-Dade Water & Sewer Authority, (305) 665-7488. **Telephone:** Bell South, (800) 789-9025 in Florida, or (800) 753-0710 out-of-state. **Cable TV:** Miami TCI, (305) 326-1574.

PLACES OF WORSHIP

One Catholic and 29 Protestant churches, plus two Jewish synagogues.

THE ENVIRONMENT

The Miami River has been rated as having poor water quality due to urban and agricultural runoff, boat discharges and sewage overflows. It also has high levels of metals contamination in its sediment. The Miami River negatively impacts Biscayne Bay, which is a protected water body. Efforts to improve the Miami River are underway, but slowed by conflicting authorities and controversy.

There are 12 EPA-listed Superfund sites in Dade County; none are in Coral Gables.

EVENTS AND FESTIVALS

Beaux Arts Festival-January. **The Merrick Fest**-February. **Junior Orange Bowl Festival**-November/December. **Gallery Hop on the Trolley**-First Friday of each month.

WHERE TO EAT

With more than 120 restaurants, the Gables claims the title of restaurant capital of south Florida. **Aragon Cafe**, first floor of Colonnade Hotel, 180 Aragon Ave., seafood, elegant and expensive, (305) 441-2600.

WHERE TO STAY

Omni Colonnade Hotel, 305) 441-2600. **Holiday Inn**, University of Miami, (305) 667-5611. **Hotel Place St. Michel**, (305) 444-1666. **The Biltmore**, (305) 445-1926.

ISSUES

There is one issue that galvanizes residents and city leaders: rampant crime in the cities surrounding the Gables. Crime threatens to cut off the flow of European and American tourists as well as the in-migration of retirees. Pronouncements from business and civic leaders condemn the lawlessness of the rest of south Florida, while touting Coral Gables as an oasis of beauty, peace and tranquillity. But, this city is not an island. There is cause for concern about sharing Dade County's reputation — earned or not. As beautiful and progressive as the city is, we would think twice about retiring here until measures are in place to restore law and order to all of Dade County's municipalities.

Coral Springs

HE SAID: ✶ ✶ ✶ ✶
Coral Springs has earned acclaim as the "best place to raise a family in south Florida," and to the extent that these same qualities are attractive to retirees, it also has to be one of the best places to retire in south Florida.

SHE SAID: ✶ ✶ ✶ ✶ ✶
It seems like a country club. On arriving, I noticed the residential neighborhoods, surrounding golf courses, clean and wide streets and the absence of neon and painted signs. Strip shopping centers are tasteful and set back from the street. Best of all, the people are friendly and the place seems safe. Look at Coral Springs when making a relocation decision.

This is a city we almost didn't visit because the chamber of commerce labeled it as "not noted as a retirement community." But our interest was peaked by an ad referring to Coral Springs' upscale residential, commercial and industrial aspects, so we decided to find out for ourselves.

Just a 20-minute drive from the Atlantic coast, it seemed we were hundreds of miles from the touristy, sometimes congested beach scene. The atmosphere in Coral Springs was clean and fresh, the traffic free-flowing, and the boulevards broad and lined with trees.

You won't find Coral Springs in most tour books, and that, it seems, is good for this largely residential community west of Pompano Beach. It is a master-planned community in the best sense. It was conceived about 30 years ago by Coral Ridge Properties, a Westinghouse subsidiary that still owns property here worth almost $1 billion. Planning has made a positive, visible impact here, incorporating the best features for a livable city—award-winning schools, fabulous parks, outstanding health-care facilities, abundant and convenient shopping, safe, clean, uncrowded neighborhoods and a responsive municipal structure offering countless community activities.

Sign ordinances and other restrictions help give Coral Springs a refreshingly uncluttered horizon. No mammoth signs marking fast-food joints and gas stations obtrude on the landscape. In fact, relatively little business is allowed here. The city has allocated 800 acres for business and industry; currently about 600 acres are in use.

We spoke with two couples who had retired here, one from New Jersey and the other from New York. When discussing their reasons for moving to Coral Springs, they mentioned many of the same qualities we noticed, also pointing out the city's proximity to three major airports and its nearness to the urban amenities of Boca Raton, Fort Lauderdale, Miami, Naples and Key West, minus the frenetic pace of living in those communities. Lucille Shulklapper, formerly of New Rochelle, NY, added the "sincerity of its people" to the list. "When clerks in the grocery store ask, 'May I help you?' they really mean it," Lucille said.

WEATHER

	Winter	Spring	Summer	Fall
Normal daily high/low	77/59	86/69	91/74	82/65
Normal precipitation	8 in.	18 in.	20 in.	13 in.

Disaster watch: Southeast Florida has been hit by nine major hurricanes since 1900.

TAXES
Sales tax: 6%. **Property tax:** $25.04 per $1,000 valuation. Sample tax calculations include a $25,000 homestead exemption.

Home value	Tax
$100,000	$1,878
$150,000	$3,130
$250,000	$5,634

REAL ESTATE
Median home value: $107,554 (Broward County). **Median rent:** $809/month (Broward County). **Communities popular with retirees:** Heron Bay, home of the PGA Honda Classic, offers townhouses, courtyard homes, single-family homes and large estate homes priced from the $130s to $1 million, (800) 290-8053. Wyndham Lakes offers patio and single-family homes priced from the $120s to $300s, (954) 255-0902. **Licensed continuing-care retirement communities:** None. There are assisted-living facilities such as Park Summit, (954) 752-9500.

CRIME & SAFETY
Crimes per 1,000 population: 49. **Non-emergency police:** (954) 344-1800. **Non-emergency fire department:** (954) 344-1800. **Police, fire, ambulance emergencies:** 911.

HOMELESS & BLIGHT
This is one of the cleanest, brightest, best organized cities we visited in Florida. There are no homeless evident and no blighted areas that we saw. Broad, tree-lined streets and carefully manicured landscapes are the rule. Coral Springs has been recognized as Tree City USA for several years by the National Arbor Day Foundation.

Broward County, population 1.25 million, had a homeless count of 1,023 in the Census.

HEALTH CARE
Hospitals: **Coral Springs Medical Center**, 200 beds, full service, (954) 344-3000. Nearby are **HCA Northwest Regional Hospital** in Margate, (954) 974-0400, and **University Hospital** in Tamarac, (954) 721-2200. **Physicians:** 1,000+ (North Broward). **Specialties:** 37.

GETTING SMART
Nova University, Coral Springs campus, (954) 752-3020. **Offerings:** Courses for personal and professional growth. Advanced degrees. **Broward Community College**, Coconut Creek campus, (954) 973-2240. **Offerings:** Two-year degrees in English, math, foreign languages, science, business, computer science, humanities and other fields.

JUST FOR SENIORS
Northwest Focal Point Senior Center in Margate, (954) 973-0300.

GETTING INVOLVED
Seniors Foundation, (954) 977-9505. Pick up a monthly calen-

dar of events, activities and organizations at the chamber of commerce, library, City Hall, Coral Ridge Realty and many area banks.

RECREATION, ENTERTAINMENT & AMENITIES

Public golf: Carolina Club and Broken Woods Country Club. **Private golf:** Eagle Trace and The Country Club of Coral Springs. **Public tennis courts:** Broken Woods Country Club, Mullins Park and Cypress Park. **Private tennis courts:** The Country Club of Coral Springs and Tennis Club of Eagle Trace. **Parks:** More than 38 community and neighborhood parks totaling 600 acres. Mullins Park has a sports complex, pool and activity center. Cypress Park has ball fields, pool, tennis and racquetball courts, clubhouse and trails. **Public swimming pools:** Aquatic Complex & Fitness Center, Mullins Park and Cypress Park. **Water sports:** Lakes offer fishing and swimming. Water-skiers travel alongside boaters on their way to the Intracoastal Waterway via the C-14 (Pompano) Canal. **River/gulf/ocean:** Riverside Park has the city's first boat ramp to the C-14 Canal. **Running/walking/biking:** Walkers and joggers favor University Park. Other trails run through Cypress Park, Cypress Hammock Park and Orchid Park. **Horses/riding:** Parkland Equestrian Center offers riding, horseman's association classes, clinics, dressage, competition and shows. **Hunting:** None within city limits. Regulated hunting is permitted in some unincorporated areas of Broward County and the Everglades. **Movie theaters:** 17 screens at three cinemas. **Theaters:** Opus Playhouse Community Theatre offers stage productions, and City Centre books plays, concerts, public events, the Florida Philharmonic and pops and symphony concerts. **Museums:** The Schacknow Museum of Fine Arts. **Library:** Coral Springs Library. **Attractions:** Aquatic Complex, Coral Springs City Nature Centers and Loxahatchee Everglades Tours. **Necessities:** All here.

Smart Shopper Tip: Coral Square Mall, a regional shopping mall with more than 200 stores, has everything you could ever want. Why go elsewhere? If you do, you'll find there are hundreds of well-known, high-quality retailers in the malls and shopping centers in and around Coral Springs.

WHO LIVES HERE

Population: 102,916 year-round residents, an increase of 24,052 since 1990. **Age 65+** = 19.3% in Broward County. **Median household income:** $31,289 (Broward County). **Per capita income:** $26,192 (Broward County).

NUMBERS TO KNOW

Chamber of commerce: (954) 752-4242. **Voter registration:** (954) 755-4636, ext. 213. **Vehicle registration, tags & title:** (954) 765-5050. **Driver's license:** In Margate, (954) 327-6333. **Coral Springs Citizens Service Division:** (954) 755-4636, ext. 211.

WHAT TO READ

Sun-Sentinel, daily newspaper, (954) 572-2000. **Coral Springs Forum,** weekly newspaper, (954) 752-7474. **Guide to Greater Coral Springs,** annual, and the **Coral Springs Chamber Focus,** monthly newsletter, (954) 752-4242. **Coral Springs Citizen,** 10 times a year, (954) 344-1014.

GETTING AROUND

Bus: Broward County Mass Transit, (954) 357-8400. **Taxi:** Yellow Cab, (954) 565-5400; Family Car Service, (954) 755-7751. **Tours:** None. **Airport:** Three airports are within an hour's drive: Palm Beach, Fort Lauderdale and Miami. Metro-Rail provides service to all three. **Traffic:** Plenty of it, but it flows smoothly.

JOBS

County unemployment rate: 5.0%. **Florida Jobs and Benefits:** (954) 969-3541. **Job Line:** (954) 755-4636, ext. 311.

UTILITIES

Electricity: Florida Power & Light, (954) 797-5000. **Gas:** Peoples Gas, (954) 763-8900. **Water & sewer:** City of Coral Springs Water & Sewer, (954) 344-1110. **Telephone:** Bell South, (800) 789-9025 in Florida, or (800) 753-0710 out-of-state. **Cable TV:** Cable TV of Coral Springs, (954) 344-1001.

PLACES OF WORSHIP

23 churches, temples and ministries representing Protestant, Catholic and Jewish faiths.

THE ENVIRONMENT

For information on recycling for single-family homes and duplexes, call (954) 755-4636, ext. 616.

Water quality in the Cypress Creek Canal generally is rated as fair. There are seven EPA-listed Superfund sites in Broward County, none of which are in Coral Springs.

EVENTS AND FESTIVALS

Our Town Festival - October. **Special Olympics. Top Gun Air Show. Junior Olympics Swimming Championships. Girls' Basketball Nationals. International Soccer Championships.** For specific dates of events call the chamber's "Just Ask" hot line, (954) 752-4242.

WHERE TO EAT

Outback Steakhouse, 650 Riverside Drive, American, chicken, steak, hamburgers, moderate, (954) 345-5965. **Il Porcino,** 8037 W. Sample Road, northern Italian, dinner only, moderate, (954) 344-9446.

WHERE TO STAY

La Quinta of Coral Springs, (954) 753-9000 or (800) 531-5900. **Wellesley Inn,** (954) 344-2200 or (800) 444-8888.

ISSUES

There are indications that the city's rapid population growth is causing serious shortages in a number of areas.

Neighborhood traffic problems, school overcrowding, consistent code enforcement and beefed-up police presence are current issues being addressed by city fathers.

Crystal River

HE SAID: ★ ★
I would be very reluctant to retire to Crystal River until city officials demonstrate a leadership role in removing visual eyesores — mainly excessive signage along U.S. Highway 19 and run-down areas around Kings Bay — and an understanding that an attractive town needs more than new commerce.

SHE SAID: ★ ★
This spread-out town is littered with billboards. There's very little to attract anyone who may be driving through town. Some residential areas are nice. If you like to be around nature, this is probably a good place for you. It claims fame as the home of the manatee. If you want the social life, this is not the place to be. I would not retire here.

"Crystal River is primed for growth," says Marlon Lightfoot, executive vice president of the chamber of commerce. And growing it is, but much of the growth appears to be at the expense of the natural beauty of the area. A five mile strip of small businesses and shopping centers along heavily traveled U.S. 19 is about all you see while driving through town.

It's unfortunate because the town has so much unrealized potential. Although Crystal River sits squarely in the middle of the "nature coast," you don't realize that the coast, or any body of water, is nearby unless you search for it.

Kings Bay and Crystal River (the river, not the town) are hidden from view by an unattractive, fish-camp-type environment. This western part of town should be the focal point and main tourist attraction of the region. The springs of Kings Bay produce nearly two million gallons of crystal clear, 72-degree, fresh water daily. They attract gentle, giant manatees from November through April when the waters of the Gulf are much cooler. These same springs could be a much bigger draw for tourists — if you could get to the bay area and if there were any first-class lodgings there. But it's going to take a lot of civic-minded leadership and commitment to develop this area.

A good sign ordinance, strictly enforced zoning laws and a determined effort to develop the arts and cultural resources could make this a first-class town. Despite a great location, some outstanding regional landmarks and a huge potential, it still has a long way to go.

WEATHER

	Winter	Spring	Summer	Fall
Normal daily high/low	72/47	87/64	91/71	77/54
Normal precipitation	11 in.	13 in.	23 in.	7 in.

Disaster watch: Northwest Florida has been hit by six major hurricanes since 1900.

TAXES
Sales tax: 6%. **Property tax:** $24.35 per $1,000 valuation. Sample tax calculations include a $25,000 homestead exemption.

Home value	Tax
$100,000	$1,826
$150,000	$3,044
$250,000	$5,479

REAL ESTATE
Median home value: $79,140 (Citrus County). **Median rent:** $345/month (Citrus County). **Communities popular with retirees:** Crystal River Village offers manufactured homes priced from the low $30s, excluding land lease costs, (800) 882-7161 or (352) 795-7161. Other communities include Pelican Cove, Meadow Crest, Seven Rivers Country Club and Woodland Estates. **Licensed continuing-care retirement communities:** None.

CRIME & SAFETY
Crimes per 1,000 population: 132. **Non-emergency police:** (352) 795-4241. **Non-emergency fire department:** (352) 795-1928. **Police, fire, ambulance emergencies:** 911.

HOMELESS & BLIGHT
We saw no homeless persons. The run-down houses and several unpaved streets immediately adjoining Kings Bay are a blight on what should be a tourist attraction and major drawing card for Crystal River. U.S. 19, which runs through the town, is an unregulated jungle of signs and billboards. Except for some upscale residential developments, this is not a very attractive town.

The U.S. Census reported no homeless persons among Citrus County's population of 93,515.

HEALTH CARE
Hospitals: Seven Rivers Community Hospital, 120 beds, full service, 24-hour emergency, (352) 795-6560. **Physicians:** 36. **Specialties:** 31.

GETTING SMART
Central Florida Community College in Lecanto is five miles east of Crystal River, (352) 854-2322. **Offerings:** Two-year degrees in arts and sciences.

JUST FOR SENIORS
The nearest senior center is in Lecanto, (352) 746-1842. There is an AARP group here; call the chamber of commerce for contact information.

GETTING INVOLVED
RSVP operates from the senior center in Lecanto, (352) 622-5444. **United Way of Citrus County**, (352) 795-8844. **Crystal River Woman's Club**, (352) 795-5488.

RECREATION, ENTERTAINMENT & AMENITIES
Public golf: Plantation Inn & Golf Resort. Just east of Crystal River in Beverly Hills are Pine Ridge Golf Course and Twisted Oaks Country Club. **Private golf:** Citrus Hills Golf Club, 36 holes, and Seven Rivers Golf & Country Club. In Beverly Hills, Black Diamond Club. **Public tennis courts:** Bicentennial Park. **Private tennis courts:** Citrus Hills Golf & Country Club. **Parks:** Bicentennial Park and Fort Island Beach. **Public swimming pools:** Bicentennial Park. **Water sports:** Boating, canoe-

ing, scuba diving and snorkeling. **River/gulf/ocean:** The springs of Kings Bay produce around 600 million gallons of fresh water annually, creating the six-mile-long Crystal River, which flows into the Gulf of Mexico. **Running/walking/biking:** Homosassa Springs State Wildlife Park, Withlacoochee State Forest and other public areas provide ample options. **Horses/riding:** There are no stables or riding academies in Crystal River, but plenty of back roads for riding. **Hunting:** Citrus County offers seven rivers, a game reserve and 22 miles of chain lakes for hunting and fishing. Licenses, (800) 347-4356. **Movie theaters:** None. **Art museums:** None. **History museums:** Crystal River State Archaeological Site and the Coastal Heritage Museum. **Theaters:** None. **Library:** Coastal Region Public. **Attractions:** Crystal River State Archaeological Site. Crystal River/Chassahowitzka National Wildlife Refuge, accessible by boat, is an estuarian habitat and sanctuary for manatees where divers are permitted to swim with the 2,000-pound sea cows. Homosassa Springs State Wildlife Park also is popular. **Necessities:** All available.

Smart Shopper Tip: Crystal River Mall, anchored by Belk-Lindsey, Kmart, J.C. Penney and Sears, is the best bet in the region.

WHO LIVES HERE
Population: 4,114 year-round residents, an increase of 64 since 1990. **Age 65+ =** 31.5% in Citrus County. **Median household income:** $21,458 (Citrus County). **Per capita income:** $17,189 (Citrus County).

NUMBERS TO KNOW
Chamber of commerce: (352) 795-3149. **Voter registration:** (352) 637-9910. **Vehicle registration, tags & title:** (352) 637-9480. **Driver's license:** (352) 795-4221.

WHAT TO READ
Citrus County Chronicle, daily newspaper, (352) 563-6363. **Citrus Times**, Citrus County edition of St. Petersburg Times, daily newspaper, (352) 795-5252. **Tampa Tribune**, daily newspaper, (352) 796-6715. **Beverly Hills Visitor**, weekly newspaper, (352) 746-4292.

GETTING AROUND
Bus: Citrus County Transportation System operates on a door-to-door basis, taking residents to shopping centers, parks, doctors' offices and elsewhere. One-day advance reservation required, (352) 746-4844. **Taxi:** West Coast Taxicab, (352) 563-2909. **Tours:** None. **Airport:** Tampa International is 65 miles south; Orlando International is 65 miles southeast. **Traffic:** There are no towns of significant size on U.S. 19 north of Crystal River; consequently, through-traffic is light in this area. Traffic on local roads is very light.

JOBS
County unemployment rate: 6.7%. **Florida Jobs and Benefits:**

(352) 568-1325.

UTILITIES
Electricity: Florida Power Corp., (800) 700-8744. **Gas:** None. **Water & sewer:** Citrus County Public Works, (352) 746-2694. **Telephone:** Sprint-United Telephone Co., (800) 339-1811. **Cable TV:** Time-Warner Cable, within 352 area code, (800) 892-0805.

PLACES OF WORSHIP
One Catholic and 25 Protestant churches, plus one Jewish synagogue.

THE ENVIRONMENT
The spring-fed rivers, Crystal River, Homosassa River, Chassahowitzka River and the Weeki Wachee River, have been rated as having generally very good water quality. Crystal River and Kings Bay are designated as Outstanding Florida Waters (OFW), giving them protected status. Both also have been designated for management and improvement. Citrus County is seeking OFW status for the Chassahowitzka and Homosassa/Halls rivers.

EVENTS AND FESTIVALS
Crystal River Manatee Festival - February. **Taste of Citrus** - October. **Under the Pines Art Fest** - Thanksgiving weekend. **Christmas Parade** - December.

WHERE TO EAT
Andre's of Citrus Hills, 510 E. Hartford St. at Citrus Hills Country Club, steak and seafood, moderate, (352) 746-6855. **Plantation Inn**, Route 44, east of U.S. 19/98, prime rib, seafood, moderate to expensive, (352) 795-4211. **Charlie's Fish House**, 224 U.S. Highway 19 N., seafood, inexpensive, (352) 795-3949.

WHERE TO STAY
Plantation Inn & Golf Resort, (352) 795-4211. **Comfort Inn**, (352) 563-1500. **Best Western Crystal River Resort**, (352) 795-3171.

ISSUES
Florida Power Corporation operates the Crystal River Nuclear Energy Complex on Crystal Bay, seven miles north of Crystal River. It is one of the country's largest power-producing facilities and a double-edged sword. It provides considerable tax revenues to Citrus County and creates a lot of well-paying jobs for the community. But, many people don't like living near a nuclear power plant. The plant probably has been a negative factor in terms of attracting retirees to the area. The SunCoast Parkway, an extension of Veterans Parkway under construction north from Tampa, will swing by east of town sometime in the next 10 years. Good for access, but sure to bring an accelerated growth rate.

Dade City

HE SAID: ★ ★ ★ ★ ★
> *It brought back warm memories of my childhood*
> *in a small town and of a vastly different time and age.*
> *I really believe it's possible to recapture that lifestyle here.*
> *I would sure like to give it a try.*

SHE SAID: ★ ★ ★ ★ ★
> *This small, clean town has friendly people and*
> *feels safe. It has quaint shops plus easy access to larger*
> *cities. Stop and take a look at Dade City.*
> *I certainly would.*

From the time we approached Dade City from U.S. Highway 301, we believed we had finally discovered the quintessential small Florida town for retirees — or for anyone, for that matter.

The drive in from Lakeland, through mostly open, slightly undulating countryside, is dotted with orange groves, fields of long-leaf pines and farms. The scenery is not spectacular, but simple and soothing.

The modern glass and stucco Pasco County Courthouse, on appropriately named Live Oak Avenue, is an imposing presence in this town of a little more than 6,000 residents. Somehow it blends nicely with the turn-of-the-century restored antique shops, unique restaurants, brick-paved streets and moss-hung oaks that surround downtown. Strollers move slowly along the safe, clean streets, smiling and saying hello to strangers.

Modest, tidy residential neighborhoods with parks, tennis courts and playgrounds push in on the town center from all sides, placing all who reside there within easy walking distance of downtown cafes and restaurants. Autos are a nicety but not a necessity here.

Dade City's location provides access to shopping, cultural amenities and water sports for those who desire them. It's just six miles from I-75, 35 miles from the Gulf and less than an hour from Tampa and Lakeland. Yet it sits in the midst of a sparsely developed area. Buffered on the north by the Withlacoochee State Forest, it avoids the overcommercialization and excesses of nearby densely populated areas.

Our conversations with the staffs at the chamber of commerce, hospital, county property appraiser's office, shops and real estate agency, and with our waitress at Lunch on Limoges, reinforced our early impressions of the warmth, friendliness and helpfulness of Dade City's townspeople. They're the kind of folk you want to have as neighbors, fellow church members and golfing partners.

WEATHER

	Winter	Spring	Summer	Fall
Normal daily high/low	75/51	88/65	92/71	79/57
Normal precipitation	11 in.	14 in.	22 in.	7 in.

Disaster watch: Northwest Florida has been hit by six major hurricanes since 1900.

TAXES

Sales tax: 6%. **Property tax:** $27.34 per $1,000 valuation. Sample tax calculations include a $25,000 homestead exemption.

Home value	Tax
$100,000	$2,051
$150,000	$3,418
$250,000	$6,152

REAL ESTATE

Median home value: $79,923 (Pasco County). **Median rent:** $422/month (Pasco County). **Communities popular with retirees:** There are no developments particularly for retirees; they live throughout the area. **Licensed continuing-care retirement communities:** None. The Edwinola is a licensed adult congregate living facility located downtown in a restored home, (352) 567-6500.

CRIME & SAFETY

Crimes per 1,000 population: 130. **Non-emergency police:** (352) 521-1495. **Non-emergency fire department:** (352) 357-2345. **Police, fire, ambulance emergencies:** 911.

HOMELESS & BLIGHT

This restored small town is appealing and attractive. The City-County Registries of Historic Sites includes 63 houses, churches, depots, banks, cemeteries, schools and other structures, as well as parks and even landmark palm trees.

The U.S. Census counted 43 homeless persons in shelters and nine visible in street locations in Pasco County's population of 281,131.

HEALTH CARE

Hospitals: Columbia Dade City Hospital, 120 beds, full service, 24-hour emergency, (352) 567-6726.
Physicians: 130+. **Specialties:** 34.

GETTING SMART

St. Leo College, (352) 588-8200. **Offerings:** Four-year liberal arts degree programs with traditional courses and programs for adults. **Pasco-Hernando Community College**, (352) 567-6701. **Offerings:** Two-year degrees in arts and sciences are transferable to the state university system. Many continuing-education courses are also offered.

JUST FOR SENIORS

CARES (Community Aging & Retirement Services) operates several programs including Meals on Wheels, Alzheimer's support groups and an adult day-care center, (813) 782-9396. **Senior Friends** at Dade City Hospital, (352) 521-1170.

GETTING INVOLVED

Ambassadors, (352) 567-3769. **CARES**, (813) 782-9396. **Downtown Dade City Main Street**, (352) 567-0284. **RSVP**, sponsored by the District School Board of Pasco County, (352) 567-8220.

RECREATION, ENTERTAINMENT & AMENITIES

Public golf: Saint Leo Abbey Golf Course, Sundance Golf & Country Club and Town & Country RV Resort & Golf Club. **Private golf:** Saddlebrook Resort, 15 minutes away. **Public**

tennis courts: Jim Courier, once the top-ranked men's tennis player, lived here, and the entire county has tennis fever. Most city and county parks and community colleges have courts. **Private tennis courts:** Saddlebrook Resort. **Parks:** Withlacoochee River Park is a 606-acre wilderness park with nature trails and primitive camping. Also, John S. Burks Memorial Park. **Public swimming pools:** City park. **Water sports:** Canoeing on the Withlacoochee. **River/gulf/ocean:** There are a number of small lakes, mostly shallow with little boating activity. **Running/walking/biking:** Hiking and bicycling along the nature trails and hilly terrain of east Pasco County are very popular. **Horses/riding:** An equestrian trail is being constructed on about 3,000 acres adjoining the Withlacoochee River Park. Several stables and trails are located in the county. **Hunting:** Freshwater fishing and hunting licenses and information, (352) 521-4368. Richloam Tract in the Withlacoochee State Forest is noted for good hunting. **Movie theaters:** Two screens. **Art museums:** Heritage Arts Association. **History museums:** Florida Pioneer Museum. **Theaters:** Armory Auditorium, Dan Cannon Auditorium, Pasco Middle School Auditorium and the St. Leo College Fine Arts Theater. Performing arts include the Center Stage Players, the St. Leo Dance Company and the St. Leo Fine Arts Cultural Series. **Library:** Hugh Embry branch. **Attractions:** Historic Church Street, Muscogee Indian Village and Pioneer Florida Museum. **Necessities:** All are here, including 11 banks and financial institutions, new car dealerships, several shopping centers and both city and county government offices.

Smart Shopper Tip: One of the principal attractions is the charming downtown, where you can shop for antiques, fashions and specialty items or dine in one of a half-dozen excellent restaurants. Of course, serious shopping is available in Tampa or Lakeland (Lakeland Square Mall) in less than an hour.

WHO LIVES HERE
Population: 6,136 year-round residents, an increase of 503 since 1990. **Age 65+** = 29.0% in Pasco County. **Median household income:** $22,071 (Pasco County). **Per capita income:** $18,808 (Pasco County).

NUMBERS TO CALL
Chamber of commerce: (352) 567-3769. **Voter registration:** Pasco County Courthouse, (352) 521-4302. **Vehicle registration, tags & title:** (352) 521-4368. **Driver's license:** (352) 521-1441.

WHAT TO READ
The Pasco News, weekly newspaper, (352) 567-5639. **St. Petersburg Times**, daily newspaper, (800) 888-7012. **Tampa Tribune**, (813) 788-5541.

GETTING AROUND
Bus: No intra-city public transportation. **Taxi:** Paradise Taxi, (352) 567-5311. **Tours:** None. **Airport:** Tampa International is 45 minutes away. **Train:** Amtrak, (800) 872-7245. **Traffic:** U.S. 301 brings some traffic into downtown, but I-75, only minutes away, keeps most of it out. The streets were quiet when we visited, but the sidewalks had a number of strolling pedestrians.

JOBS
County unemployment rate: 4.2%. **Florida Jobs and Benefits:** (352) 521-1485.

UTILITIES
Electricity: Tampa Electric, (352) 567-5101, or Withlacoochee River Electric Co-op, (352) 567-5133, depending on location of residence. **Gas:** None. **Water & sewer:** Dade City Utilities, (352) 523-5053. **Telephone:** Sprint, (800) 432-1111. **Cable TV:** Time-Warner Cable, (800) 892-4968.

PLACES OF WORSHIP
Three Catholic and 33 Protestant churches.

THE ENVIRONMENT
The surface water quality generally has been rated as very good, especially along the Withlacoochee River, which has been designated an Outstanding Florida Water. Problem areas include the Dade Canal, below the city, which has poor water quality, and the Little Withlacoochee River and sections of the upper Withlacoochee, which have fair to poor water quality.

EVENTS AND FESTIVALS
Kumquat Festival - January. **Spring Bluegrass Festival** - April. **Pioneer Day** - September. **Church Street Christmas** - December.

WHERE TO EAT
Lunch on Limoges, 14139 Seventh St., seafood, chicken, moderate, (352) 567-5685. **A Matter of Taste**, 14121 Seventh St., American and Cuban, inexpensive to moderate, (352) 567-5100.

WHERE TO STAY
Rainbow Fountain Motel, (352) 567-3427. **Valencia Motel**, (352) 567-5691. Saddlebrook Resort is about 20 miles away.

ISSUES
This town is healthy and thriving. Of course, it doesn't hurt that it is the county seat and repository of all of the tax revenues. Agriculture is the big economic factor. Fortunately for the residents of Dade City, western Pasco County — especially the coastal areas — has seen the most growth in the past 25 years. This is likely to change as new retirees seek the quiet and tranquillity of more rural environments in the years ahead. Dade City may be a target of that growth. Hopefully, it can retain its small-town charm and character.

Daytona Beach

HE SAID: ★ ★ ★
> *I always find something new and interesting about this city on my visits. While it is not at the top of my list, I would not dismiss the possibility of living here without a good deal of research.*

SHE SAID: ★ ★
> *Daytona Beach is a large tourist town with wall-to-wall accommodations on the beach and throughout. Lots of sea and cement. There's nothing appealing enough for a permanent stay. I would not retire here.*

It is touted as the "world's most famous beach," a claim impossible to prove, but possibly accurate. Millions of vacationers have come from around the world to enjoy the 500-foot-wide white sand beach that stretches for miles. The legendary auto races held here for the last four decades also have drawn their share of tourists to Daytona Beach.

Since 1902, when a Stanley Steamer set a record of 27 miles per hour in a race on the beach, the city has boasted of three reasons for visitors to come: sand, sun and speed. Since then, racing has taken on a new importance, beginning with the opening of NASCAR headquarters here in 1947. Now more than 100,000 race fans swarm into Daytona International Speedway for the Pepsi 400, Daytona 500 and other races.

Retirees we met cited sand and sun as positive factors in their retirement experiences, but put speedway races in a category with spring break as things they would rather avoid. In spite of the population influx, most say it is possible to maintain a fairly consistent pattern of living during major racing events. Daytona's popular retirement housing communities are located safe distances from the Speedway, and with careful planning and preparation, massive traffic tie-ups can be avoided. However, it might be a good idea to plan your own spring break away from the city during the annual episodes of vernal madness.

Greater Daytona Beach, which includes Daytona Beach Shores, Port Orange, Ponce Inlet and Ormond Beach to the north, offers a good deal of diversity in its recreational, cultural and educational opportunities. Golf, water sports, sunbathing, shopping and nightlife are noted as the favorite pastimes of many retirees. Added to that are great possibilities for dining out at a long list of restaurants, including a personal favorite, Aunt Catfish's on the west side of the Port Orange Bridge.

Many soon-to-be retirees think of Daytona as too busy and too touristy to seriously consider retiring here, but it has an exceptional combination of natural and man-made attributes attractive to many seniors. In addition, there are wonderful parks and recreation areas, historical sights and artifacts, and opportunities for volunteering one's time and talent to a variety of social service organizations.

WEATHER

	Winter	Spring	Summer	Fall
Normal daily high/low	71/50	84/65	89/72	76/57
Normal precipitation	9 in.	12 in.	18 in.	10 in.

Disaster watch: Northeast Florida has not been hit by a major hurricane since 1900.

TAXES

Sales tax: 6%. **Property tax:** Rates range from $25.41 to $26.74 per $1,000 valuation, depending on location. Sample taxes are calculated at the rate of $26.74 and include a $25,000 homestead exemption.

Home value	Tax
$100,000	$2,006
$150,000	$3,343
$250,000	$6,017

REAL ESTATE

Median home value: $85,601 (Volusia County). **Median rent:** $517/month (Volusia County). **Communities popular with retirees:** Riverwood Plantation is a community with clubhouse, pool and tennis, where 1,800-square-foot single-family homes start at $119,000. Palmas Bay Club is a gated section of Riverwood offering larger single-family homes priced from the $200s to $750s, (904) 238-3500. Towers at Ponce Inlet is an ocean-front condominium development with units priced from the $160s to $200s, (904) 322-2000. The new LPGA International golf community, (904) 274-2900, has five distinct neighborhoods: Jubilee with single-family homes from the low $100s to mid-$140s; Acclaim with Key West-style homes from the $150s to $200s; Promenade with luxury golf homes from the low $200s; Festiva with Mission-style villas from $229,000; and LionsPaw Grand with estate homes starting at $400,000. **Licensed continuing-care retirement communities:** None.

CRIME & SAFETY

Crimes per 1,000 population: 120. **Non-emergency police:** (904) 255-1431. **Non-emergency fire department:** (904) 258-3184. **Police, fire, ambulance emergencies:** 911.

HOMELESS & BLIGHT

Homeless persons and blighted areas are not obvious here. On the contrary, the city and its business community have worked hard to keep the city clean — a good idea since it depends on tourism to keep the coffers full.

The U.S. Census reported 187 homeless persons in shelters and 35 visible in street locations in Volusia County, population 370,712.

HEALTH CARE

Hospitals: Halifax Medical Center, 545 beds, full service, (904) 254-4000. **Columbia Medical Center**, 214 beds, full service, (904) 239-5000.
Physicians: 500+. **Specialties:** 53.

GETTING SMART

There are six college and university campuses in Daytona Beach. **Daytona Beach Community College,** (904) 255-8131. **Offerings:** Two-year degree programs, adult and continuing education. Also sponsors the **Elder Institute**, with classes for seniors in an array of subjects including computers, painting, dancing and "Retirement—Learning to Love It." The Institute offers seminars and workshops in addition to course study, as requested by seniors. **Bethune-Cookman College**, (904) 252-8667. **Offerings:** No courses specifically for seniors. Courses offered are for degree credit and are attended by all age levels. **University of Central Florida**, (904) 255-7423. **Offerings:** Bachelor's and master's degree programs.

JUST FOR SENIORS

Council on Aging, (904) 253-4700. **Senior Citizens' Information**, (904) 255-7543. **Senior Citizens' Law Unit**, (904) 253-4700.

GETTING INVOLVED

Citizens Information & Referral Service, (904) 253-0564. **Meals on Wheels** and **RSVP**, (904) 253-4700. **United Way**, (904) 253-0564.

RECREATION, ENTERTAINMENT & AMENITIES

Public golf: LPGA International, Cypress Knoll Golf Club, Daytona Beach Golf & Country Club, Daytona Par 3 and Indigo Lakes Hilton Golf & Tennis Resort. **Private golf:** Pelican Bay Country Club and Spruce Creek Country Club. **Public tennis courts:** City Island Recreation Area, Derbyshire Recreation Area, Cypress Courts and Daytona Beach Golf & Country Club. **Private tennis courts:** Indigo Lakes Hilton Golf & Tennis Resort, Oceans Racquet Club and Oceans Tennis Club. **Parks:** There are 37 parks, recreation areas, wildlife refuges and recreation complexes in the Greater Daytona-Halifax River area. **Public swimming pools:** Cypress State Recreation Complex. **Water sports:** Boating, sailing, surfing, diving, jet-skiing, sailboarding, windsurfing and fishing (deep-sea, surf and pier). **River/gulf/ocean:** 23 miles of Atlantic beaches and the Halifax River (Intracoastal Waterway). **Running/walking/biking:** Cypress State Recreation Complex has a fitness trail. Hard sand beaches are used by walkers and joggers. Downtown Manatee Island Park primarily is a walking trail. **Horses/riding:** Several riding academies and stables. **Hunting/fishing:** Florida Game and Freshwater Fish Commission, (904) 758-0525. **Movie theaters:** 35 screens. **Art museums:** Art League of Daytona Beach, Daytona Beach Community College Fine Arts Gallery, and Museum of Arts & Science and Planetarium. **History museums:** Halifax Historical Museum. **Theaters:** Daytona Beach Community College, Daytona Playhouse, Oceanfront Bandshell & Park, Peabody Auditorium and Seaside Music Theatre. **Library:** City Island, Dickerson Community Center and S. Cornelia Young branches. **Attractions:** Daytona Beach Kennel Club, Daytona Beach Jai Alai, Daytona Farmers Market, Daytona Flea Market & Antique Showplace, Daytona International Speedway, Museum of Arts & Science and Planetarium, and Ocean Center. **Necessities:** Everything you need and more!

Smart Shopper Tip: Volusia Mall, Daytona Mall and the Daytona Beach Outlet Mall provide more than 200 shopping opportunities — virtually all major department stores and outlets are in the city. The Antique & Collectibles Showplace at the Daytona Flea Market usually hosts more than 100 dealers.

WHO LIVES HERE

Population: 63,801 year-round residents, an increase of 1,810 since 1990. **Age 65+** = 22.6% in Volusia County. **Median household income:** $26,071 (Volusia County). **Per capita income:** $18,951 (Volusia County).

NUMBERS TO KNOW

Chamber of commerce: (904) 255-0981. **Voter registration:** (904) 254-4690. **Vehicle registration, tags & title:** (904) 254-4610. **Driver's license:** (904) 238-3142. **Visitors bureau:** (800) 854-1234. **Daytona Beach Welcome Center:** (904) 677-3308.

WHAT TO READ

Daytona Beach News-Journal, daily newspaper, (904) 252-1511. **Daytona Times**, weekly newspaper, (904) 253-0321. **Seniors Today**, biweekly, free, (904) 677-7060.

GETTING AROUND

Bus: VOTRAN, fixed-route bus service, (904) 761-7700. VOTRAN's Jolly Trolley runs along Route A1A Monday through Saturday. **Taxi:** Yellow Cab, (904) 255-8294. **Tours:** None. **Airport:** Daytona Beach International. **Traffic:** You'll have to devise alternate routes during Speedway events and leave town during spring break to avoid traffic problems.

JOBS

County unemployment rate: 3.7%. **Florida Jobs and Benefits:** (904) 254-3780. **Job Line:** (904) 254-4607.

UTILITIES

Electricity: Florida Power & Light, (904) 252-1541. **Gas:** Peoples Gas, (904) 253-5635. **Water & sewer:** Utilities Dept., City of Daytona Beach, (904) 258-3130. **Telephone:** Bell South, (800) 789-9025 in Florida, or (800) 753-0710 out-of-state. **Cable TV:** TCI Cablevision, (904) 760-9941.

PLACES OF WORSHIP

Five Catholic and more than 100 Protestant churches, plus two Jewish synagogues.

THE ENVIRONMENT

The Halifax River generally has been rated as having fair water quality, except for the section between Ormond Beach and Daytona Beach, which has poor water quality. Tomoka Marsh State Aquatic Preserve has protected status, designated as an Outstanding Florida Water.

The EPA reported that the water system of the City of South Daytona had lead levels of 48 parts per billion (ppb) in its drinking water and the City of Daytona Beach had lead levels of 20 ppb. The EPA action level is 15 ppb. Volusia County has one EPA-listed Superfund site, Sherwood Medical, located three miles north of DeLand.

EVENTS AND FESTIVALS

Daytona 500 - February. **Daytona 200 Motorcycle Classic** - March. **Daytona Beach Skyfest** - April. **Pepsi 400** - July. **Florida International Festival** - July/August. **Turkey Rod Run** - October. **Halifax Art Festival** - November.

WHERE TO EAT

Aunt Catfish's, 4009 Halifax Drive in Port Orange, catfish, seafood, beef, chicken, moderate, (904) 767-4768. **Riccardo's**, 610 Glenview Blvd., Italian, moderate, (904) 253-3035. **St. Regis Restaurant**, 509 Seabreeze Blvd., American, continental, moderate to expensive, (904) 252-8743.

WHERE TO STAY

Beach Quarters Resort, (904) 767-3119. **Daytona Beach Hilton**, (800) 525-7350. **Sun Viking Lodge**, (800) 874-4469.

ISSUES

In 1989, the Ladies Professional Golf Association (LPGA) decided to relocate its national headquarters to Daytona Beach. Local environmentalists, affordable housing advocates and other special-interest groups fought licensing permit battles for the next five years to ensure a responsible development plan.

Today, an outstanding headquarters building and 18-hole golf course are precursors of a first-class community that will feature a second 18-hole course, resort hotel and residential-commercial complex. Now everyone is happy, and without delving too deeply into the controversy, it appears that local activists have the tools and willpower to impact growth and manage the manner in which it is carried out. That can't be all bad!

Deerfield Beach

HE SAID: ☆
It's a nice place to spend a few days on the beach, but I wouldn't want to live here.

SHE SAID: ☆ ☆
A good place to vacation, but not a great deal of anything else to offer retirees. I would not retire here.

Once you've eaten at Charley's Crab and strolled the beach and pier, you've just about exhausted the charms of Deerfield Beach.

The chamber's No.1 stated objective is to attract new industrial and commercial facilities. However, employees of these enterprises may have trouble affording housing in the city. One realtor explained that there is very little new construction in Deerfield. Ocean-front condos range from a low of $150,000 to more than $500,000. Single-family, ocean-front estates are priced in the $3 million range. Condos on the Intracoastal Waterway start at $125,000. Moving inland a good distance from the ocean, retirees may find single-family homes from about $125,000 to more than $250,000. If money is no object, check the golf course homes at Deer Creek Golf and Tennis Club.

Deerfield has a one-mile public beach, a 722-foot fishing pier that never closes and an assortment of parks and recreation areas appealing to tourists and residents alike. That's about it for amenities.

The Northeast Focal Point Senior Center is an excellent facility, serving about 250 people each day. It serves hot lunches and operates both an intergenerational day-care program and an Alzheimer's care program. Additionally, it provides transportation to and from the center and to medical appointments. The center also provides medical lectures, a recreation program, arts and crafts and legal assistance.

Shopping areas west of the Intracoastal are undistinguished. Residential neighborhoods here also are uninspiring. If artistic and cultural pursuits are important to you, be prepared to travel to Deerfield's more cosmopolitan neighbors — West Palm Beach, Boca Raton or Fort Lauderdale — because there is no art in Deerfield Beach.

WEATHER

	Winter	Spring	Summer	Fall
Normal daily high/low	77/59	86/69	91/74	82/65
Normal precipitation	8 in.	18 in.	20 in.	13 in.

Disaster watch: Southeast Florida has been hit by nine major hurricanes since 1900.

TAXES

Sales tax: 6%. **Property tax:** $27.20 per $1,000 valuation. Sample taxes include a $25,000 homestead exemption.

Home value	Tax
$100,000	$2,040
$150,000	$3,400
$250,000	$6,120

REAL ESTATE

Median home value: $107,554 (Broward County). **Median rent:** $809/month (Broward County). **Communities popular with retirees:** No single area. According to some local realtors, there is no inexpensive real estate here. **Licensed continuing-care retirement communities:** None. Two assisted-living facilities to note: The Horizon Club, a Marriott Senior Living Community, (954) 481-2304, and The Forum at Deer Creek, (954) 698-6269.

CRIME & SAFETY

Law enforcement is provided by the Broward County Sheriff's Department. **Crimes per 1,000 population:** 69. **Non-emergency police:** (954) 480-4300. **Non-emergency fire department:** (954) 480-4350. **Police, fire, ambulance emergencies:** 911.

HOMELESS & BLIGHT

We saw a few homeless persons at night outside family-style restaurants. Strip shopping centers are unattractive and seem to beckon loiterers. The U.S. Census counted 1,023 homeless persons in Broward County, population 1.25 million.

HEALTH CARE

Hospitals: There are no full-service hospitals here. **Boca Baton Radiation Therapy,** (954) 481-8733. **Minor EmergiCenter,** (954) 421-8181. **Praxis Alzheimer Care Campus,** (954) 428-8544. The largest nearby hospital is **North Broward Medical Center** in Pompano Beach, 419 beds, full service, (954) 941-8300. **Physicians:** 50. **Specialties:** 18.

GETTING SMART

There are no college or university campuses in Deerfield Beach. **Broward Community College,** north campus, (954) 973-2240. **Offerings:** Two-year degree programs in English, math, foreign languages, science, business, computer science, humanities and other fields. **Florida Atlantic University** in Boca Raton, (561) 297-3000, offers the Lifelong Learning Society, (561) 297-3171. **Offerings:** The university has nine colleges, offering programs in more than 61 four-year degree fields as well as advanced degrees. Lifelong Learning Society members can enroll in regular course offerings or special LIFEcourse programs for degree credit, non-credit or audit.

JUST FOR SENIORS

National Association of Retired Federal Employees, (954) 426-1072. **Northeast Focal Point Senior Center,** (954) 480-4449.

GETTING INVOLVED

Deerfield Beach Historical Society, (954) 429-0378. **Friends of the Library,** (954) 360-1380. **Volunteer Broward,** (954) 522-6761. A list of professional, civic and social organizations is available from the chamber.

RECREATION, ENTERTAINMENT & AMENITIES

Public golf: Deer Creek Golf Club, 18 holes/par 72. **Private golf:** Century Village Golf Club. **Public tennis courts:** Pioneer Park, Deerfield Beach Tennis Center, Constitution Park, Ecidar

Park and Westside Park. **Private tennis courts:** Deer Creek Racquet Club. **Parks:** Deerfield Island Park is a wilderness nature park on the Intracoastal Waterway. Quiet Waters Park has 427 acres for swimming, fishing, canoeing, board sailing, camping and picnicking. **Public swimming pools:** Quiet Waters Park. **Water sports:** Water-skiers are pulled across a lake by cables at Quiet Waters Park. **Horses/riding:** None. **Hunting:** None. **River/gulf/ocean:** There is a 722-foot fishing pier on the one-mile public beach. The city is laced with lakes, canals and waterways. **Running/walking/biking:** Trails at Ecidar and Quiet Waters parks. **Movie theaters:** 13 screens at two theaters. **Art museums:** None. **History museums:** Historic 1920s Butler House. **Theaters:** The Drama Center presents children's theater, drama classes and professional stage shows. **Library:** Deerfield Beach Library. **Attractions:** The beach and pier. **Necessities:** All are readily available.

Smart Shopper Tip: Try the Hillsboro Shops for home improvements. Sawgrass Mills, the largest discount mall in the country, is a short drive west.

WHO LIVES HERE
Population: 49,384 year-round residents, an increase of 2,387 since 1990. **Age 65+ =** 19.3% in Broward County. **Median household income:** $31,289 (Broward County). **Per capita income:** $26,192 (Broward County).

NUMBERS TO KNOW
Chamber of commerce: (954) 427-1050. **Voter registration:** (954) 831-1225. **Vehicle registration, tags & title:** (954) 765-5050. **Driver's license:** (954) 327-6333.

WHAT TO READ
Sun-Sentinel, daily newspaper, (954) 421-1777. **Deerfield Beach Observer**, weekly newspaper, (954) 428-9045. **Deerfield Beach Thursday Times**, weekly newspaper, (954) 698-6397.

GETTING AROUND
Bus: Broward County Mass Transit, (954) 357-8400. **Taxi:** Yellow Cab, (954) 565-5400. **Tours:** Water Taxi, travels from Deerfield Beach to Pompano, (954) 467-6677. **Airport:** Fort Lauderdale and Palm Beach International are within an hour's drive. **Traffic:** The only real traffic hang-ups occur when the drawbridge across the Intracoastal is raised. Once you know the schedule, it's easy to avoid the wait.

JOBS
County unemployment rate: 5.0%. **Florida Jobs and Benefits:** In Pompano Beach, (407) 969-3541.

UTILITIES
Electricity: Florida Power & Light, (954) 797-5000. **Gas:** Peoples Gas, (954) 527-1511. **Water & sewer:** City of Deerfield Beach, (954) 480-4276. **Telephone:** Bell South, (800) 789-9025 in Florida, or (800) 753-0710 out-of-state. **Cable TV:** Media One, (954) 946-7011.

PLACES OF WORSHIP
33 Catholic, Protestant and non-denominational churches, plus two Jewish synagogues.

THE ENVIRONMENT
The Hillsboro and West Palm Beach canals running through Deerfield Beach and the vicinity have been rated as having poor water quality due to urban and agricultural runoff.

There are seven EPA-listed Superfund sites in Broward County; none are in Deerfield Beach.

EVENTS AND FESTIVALS
Deerfield Beach Art Show - January. **Deerfest** - November.

WHERE TO EAT
Brooks, 500 S. Federal Highway, French, seafood, expensive, (954) 427-9302. **Pal's/Charley's Crab**, Cove Yacht Basin, on Route 810, seafood, pasta, moderate to expensive, (954) 427-4000.

WHERE TO STAY
Comfort Inn, Oceanside, (954) 428-0650. **Embassy Suites/Deerfield Beach Resort**, (954) 426-0478. **Hilton**, (954) 427-7700.

ISSUES
When the chamber of commerce appears to focus its agenda very narrowly on business and industry — exclusive of the people who will live and work there — it is easy to believe the city is uninterested in its citizens. Perhaps the citizens are uninterested in the city as well. The result is an environment that most retirees would not choose.

RELOCATION TIPS

To establish permanent residency in Florida: Register to vote, file a notarized Declaration of Domicile at the county courthouse, file your federal income tax return in Florida, apply for a Florida driver's license and vehicle registration, or file your Florida intangibles tax return within the state. You don't need to reside in Florida for any specified length of time before establishing your residency.

DeFuniak Springs

HE SAID: ☆ ☆ ☆
*DeFuniak Springs has a classic hometown look and feel
with enough cultural, social and physical amenities to satisfy
most people. Plus, it's near larger population centers
for those who need more. I really like this town
and its genuine, down-to-earth people.*

SHE SAID: ☆ ☆
*There are very few retirees here. The nearest shopping
mall is an hour's drive away in Fort Walton Beach. There
are only strip shopping centers here and a small downtown
area. I would not retire here — the only drawing point
I see is the weather.*

When driving through the central panhandle, stop and spend several days at the Hotel DeFuniak. From this bed-and-breakfast inn you can explore the Victorian village one resident dubs "delightful DeFuniak." At the Chatauqua Auditorium office of the Chamber of Commerce and Visitor Center, pick up a copy of the Walton County Heritage Association's "Walking Tour of Historic Homes" and John Paul Jones' work "Lotus Land Revisited." Take the suggested 1.3-mile stroll around Lake DeFuniak. Surrounding the 60-foot-deep lake are 23 structures, many open to visitors, so stop as often as possible to explore the history and essence of this town. There's one magnificent magnolia tree too, which makes you wonder if you're still in Florida.

For lunch, there's Edie's Cafe or the Busy Bee Cafe, which specializes in fried green tomatoes. And, for a real history lesson on the town's past and a glowing assessment of the town's future, look up Diane Pickett, founder of the Turn Around Society (now Partners in Progress), which was started to encourage the revitalization of DeFuniak Springs.

By car, you can visit Miles' Feather Farm and Strickland's Christmas Tree Farm or drive through pastoral countryside, past dense pine forests, grazing pastures, and fields of corn, soybean, wheat and sugar cane.

Ginny and Paul Cate moved to DeFuniak from Ohio in the early 1980s. They like the mild climate with its change of seasons; friendly, energetic people; respect for local history; the small size, making it easy to walk to downtown shops, restaurants, grocery stores, churches, the post office and library; and the proximity to the white sand beaches of the Gulf and the waters of Choctawhatchee Bay.

When asked what DeFuniak Springs needs to attract retirees, Paul answers, "Not a whole lot. A good, attractive manufactured-home development would help."

DeFuniak does have many of the components of an ideal retirement town: good location, adequate transportation network, abundant natural resources, a rich historical background, nearness to water for fishing, swimming and boating, golf courses and wonderful, forward-looking residents who are excited about its future.

WEATHER

	Winter	Spring	Summer	Fall
Normal daily high/low	67/41	86/59	91/67	73/45
Normal precipitation	17 in.	15 in.	20 in.	13 in.

Disaster watch: Northwest Florida has been hit by six major hurricanes since 1900.

TAXES
Sales tax: 7%. **Property tax:** $19.85 per $1,000 valuation. Sample tax calculations include a $25,000 homestead exemption.

Home value	Tax
$100,000	$1,489
$150,000	$2,481
$250,000	$4,466

REAL ESTATE
Median home value: $80,599 (Walton County). **Median rent:** $459/month (Walton County). **Communities popular with retirees:** DeFuniak Springs does not have a subdivision or development with a concentration of retirees. Many live in the historic district around Lake DeFuniak, and others in homes with acreage, which skirt the town center. **Licensed continuing-care retirement communities:** None.

CRIME & SAFETY
Crimes per 1,000 population: 48. **Non-emergency police:** (850) 892-8513. **Non-emergency fire department:** (850) 892-8515. **Police and medical emergencies:** (850) 892-8511. **Fire emergencies:** (850) 892-8512.

HOMELESS & BLIGHT
We did not see any homeless persons. In fact, according to the U.S. Census, Walton County, population 27,760, does not have any homeless persons. We saw no blighted areas; several organizations work toward the town's historic restoration and preservation.

HEALTH CARE
Hospitals: Walton Regional Hospital, 50 beds, acute care, 24-hour emergency service, (850) 892-5171. New facility under construction. In Fort Walton Beach there's the **Fort Walton Beach Medical Center**, 247 beds, full service, (850) 862-1111. **Physicians:** 13. **Specialties:** 10.

GETTING SMART
Okaloosa-Walton Community College, DeFuniak Springs campus, (850) 892-8100. **Offerings:** Core courses toward two-year degrees. Beginning computer courses are popular with seniors. Continuing-education courses include 55-Drive Alive and Cajun cooking.

JUST FOR SENIORS
Elder Care Services, (850) 892-7030. **Northwest Florida Area Agency on Aging**, (850) 892-8168. **Better Living for Seniors**, (850) 892-8165.

GETTING INVOLVED
American Red Cross in Fort Walton Beach, (850) 243-3322. **Chautauqua Neighborhood Center**, (850) 892-8100. **RSVP**, (850) 892-7030. **Shelter House**, (850) 892-5411.

COST OF LIVING
Florida Price Level Index: 92.41 (Walton County). **Rank:** 55th most expensive county.

RECREATION, ENTERTAINMENT & AMENITIES
Public golf: None. **Semi-private golf:** DeFuniak Springs Country Club. **Public tennis courts:** Four. **Private tennis courts:** DeFuniak Springs Country Club. **Parks:** Lake Stanley Park, Pat Covell Park, Little League Ball Park and Wayside Park. Numerous state recreation areas and parks within an hour's drive. **Public swimming pools:** None. **Water sports:** Freshwater fishing is reported to be excellent at Juniper, Holley and Kings lakes, north of town, and at several rivers and streams in the county. **River/gulf/ocean:** Choctawhatchee Bay and the Gulf of Mexico are less than an hour south. **Running/walking/biking:** Lake DeFuniak — a spring-fed, sand-bottom, perfectly round lake — is circled by a 1.3-mile health path that's popular with joggers. The rural character of the area provides numerous scenic venues. **Horses/riding:** This is horse country with plenty of pasture lands, forests, farms and stables. Seyvilla Arabian Horse Farms breeds and raises horses for sale. **Hunting:** Deer, duck, wild turkey and many other types of small game. Florida Game and Freshwater Fish Commission, (850) 892-8000. **Movie theaters:** None. **Art museums:** None. **History museums:** Historic Circle Drive has examples of Victorian architecture. **Theaters:** Heritage Association. **Library:** Walton-DeFuniak Public Library. **Attractions:** Walking tour of historic homes. Community Civic Center. **Necessities:** Several financial services institutions, two new car dealerships, a post office, 11 real estate agencies, 10 gas stations, 12 beauty salons, two barber shops and 23 restaurants, as well as grocery stores and discount stores.

Smart Shopper Tip: It would be wise to plan regular shopping excursions to Fort Walton Beach (46 miles), Panama City (63 miles), Pensacola (76 miles) or Tallahassee (119 miles) if you are shopping for more than the necessities. In DeFuniak you'll find: Food World, Thrift-Way, Winn-Dixie, Wal-Mart, J.C. Penney Catalog Sales, Sears Merchant Store, TG&Y-McCrory, Top-Dollar, Wise Department Store, Shoe City and a handful of others.

WHO LIVES HERE
Population: 5,466 year-round residents, an increase of 266 since 1990. **Age 65+** = 15.7% in Walton County. **Median household income:** $23,283 (Walton County). **Per capita income:** $14,360 (Walton County).

NUMBERS TO KNOW
Chamber of commerce: (850) 892-3191. **Voter registration:** (850) 595-3900. **Vehicle registration, tags, title:** (850) 892-8121 **Driver's license:** (850) 892-8085.

WHAT TO READ
Northwest Florida Daily News, (850) 863-1111. **DeFuniak Herald-Breeze,** weekly newspaper, (850) 892-3232. **Trade Winds,** weekly advertiser, (850) 892-7078. **"Lotus Land Revisited,"** John Paul Jones, *Florida Living,* December 1991, available at the chamber of commerce.

GETTING AROUND
Bus: No public intra-city transportation. **Taxi:** City Cab Co., (850) 892-3916. **Tours:** Self-guided walking tour of historic district with brochure from chamber. **Airport:** Okaloosa Air Terminal is 30 miles away. **Traffic:** U.S. Highway 90, U.S. 331 and I-10 provide excellent highway access.

JOBS
County unemployment rate: 3.9%. **Florida Jobs and Benefits:** (850) 833-9106. **Senior Employment Program:** (850) 892-5121.

UTILITIES
Electricity: Gulf Power Co., (850) 892-2154. **Gas:** City Natural Gas Dept., (850) 892-8500. **Water & sewer:** City of DeFuniak Springs, (850) 892-8503. **Telephone:** Sprint/CENTEL, (850) 664-3200. **Cable TV:** TCI Cable, (850) 892-3155.

PLACES OF WORSHIP
One Catholic and 34 Protestant churches.

THE ENVIRONMENT
The Choctawhatchee River basin generally has a good water quality rating, with the exception of Upper Holmes Creek, east of DeFuniak, which receives pollutants from waste-water treatment facilities. West Sandy Creek has fair water quality, which is expected to improve as a result of an upgrade of DeFuniak's waste-water treatment plant.

EVENTS AND FESTIVALS
Chautauqua Festival - April. **Octoberfest. Hometown Christmas** - November.

WHERE TO EAT
Mom & Dad's, W. U.S. Highway 90, Italian, inexpensive, (850) 892-5812. **Edie's Cafe,** 301 N. Ninth St., lunch only, sandwiches, chef's salads, inexpensive, (850) 892-4847. **McClain's Family Steakhouse,** Highway 331 S., steaks , seafood, buffet, inexpensive, (850) 892-2402.

WHERE TO STAY
Best Western Crossroads Inn, (850) 892-5111. **Comfort Inn,** (850) 892-1333.**Hotel DeFuniak,** (850) 892-4383.

ISSUES
Visitor center officials report seeing an increase in interest from potential retiree newcomers. They believe this is due to the loss of benefits and facilities for retired military in other Florida areas, prompting them to look at towns near Eglin Air Force Base in Fort Walton Beach.

This town isn't going to boom, but it seems destined to grow at an above-average rate in the years ahead. A nice manufactured-home community on one of the nearby lakes would be a strong attraction for potential newcomers, as would a medium-priced golf course development of single-family custom homes.

DeLand

We have had the pleasure of visiting DeLand several times in the past 25 years, and each time we are struck by the fact that despite population growth, new buildings and major renovations, the town always seems to stay the same. This perception was reinforced by a conversation with the executive vice president of the chamber of commerce, who moved here 28 years ago. At the time, he thought of DeLand as a temporary way station while looking for a Florida home. But he could never bring himself to leave. For him, DeLand still has the same small-town quality that attracted him many years ago.

Some 20 miles from the shores of Daytona Beach and 50 miles from the excitement and entertainment of Walt Disney World, DeLand's location near the banks of the wild and scenic St. Johns River supplies diverse recreational opportunities for residents. Fishing, hunting, boating, swimming, water-skiing, canoeing, snorkeling and scuba diving in the lakes and springs that dot the rural countryside are only some of the outdoor activities that attract residents.

Stetson University, with its century-old, oak-shaded campus and impressive buildings, brings youth and vitality, education and culture, new people and new ideas to the community. A strong continuing-education program with more than 25 weeks of Elderhostel courses consistently sells out.

The qualities that you notice when exploring this community range from the concrete to the intangible. Count the health-care facilities and doctors. Add outstanding adult retirement communities, residential neighborhoods and wonderful historic district. Look at the many social service organizations and observe the caring, thoughtful nature of the volunteers and staff. Finally, notice the friendly residents. They could be your neighbors one day.

WEATHER

	Winter	Spring	Summer	Fall
Normal daily high/low	72/47	86/62	90/70	77/53
Normal precipitation	10 in.	14 in.	23 in.	9 in.

Disaster watch: Northeast Florida has not been hit by a major hurricane since 1900.

TAXES

Sales tax: 6%. **Property tax:** $26.42 per $1,000 valuation. Sample tax calculations include a $25,000 homestead exemption.

Home value	Tax
$100,000	$1,982
$150,000	$3,303
$250,000	$5,945

REAL ESTATE

Median home value: $85,601 (Volusia County). **Median rent:** $517/month (Volusia County). **Communities popular with retirees:** Long Leaf Plantation has single-family homes priced from the $100s to $200s. Bent Oaks has single-family homes priced from the low $100s to the $280s, (904) 734-7347. Cross Creek has single-family homes priced from the $100s to $170s, (904) 738-4272. The Oaks offers manufactured homes priced from the $60s, (904) 738-4272. This information is from Gardner Ruggles, Watson Realty, (800) 445-8986. **Licensed continuing-care retirement communities:** Alliance Retirement Center of DeLand has 144 independent living units and 60 community beds, (904) 734-3481. Florida Lutheran Retirement Center has 176 independent living units and assisted-living facilities, but no skilled nursing units, (904) 736-5800.

CRIME & SAFETY

Crimes per 1,000 population: 136. **Non-emergency police:** (904) 734-1711. **Non-emergency fire department:** (904) 734-3499. **Police, fire, ambulance emergencies:** 911.

HOMELESS & BLIGHT

In 1985. Deland became the first officially designated "Main Street" city in Florida. Today, the fruits of this $2,000,000 public investment, which generated $50,000,000 in private improvements, can be readily seen. DeLand is clean, well-maintained, active but uncrowded, with a pleasant atmosphere for shopping, dining or just strolling. We did not see any homeless persons.

According to the U.S. Census, Volusia County's population of 370,712 included 187 homeless persons in shelters and 35 homeless persons visible in street locations.

HEALTH CARE

Hospitals: West Volusia Memorial, 156 beds, 24-hour emergency, acute care, full service, (904) 734-3320. **Physicians:** 100+. **Specialties:** 28.

GETTING SMART

Stetson University, (904) 822-7000 for admissions, (904) 822-7500 for continuing education. **Offerings:** Graduate and undergraduate degrees in 28 disciplines. The continuing-education department offers occasional workshops and seminars that attract senior enrollees. The department introduced an Elderhostel program in 1983 and now offers more than 25 weeks of courses annually. **Daytona Beach Community College**, DeLand campus, (904) 228-3090. **Offerings:** Two-year associate degrees in arts or sciences. Continuing and adult education courses in computers, genealogy, landscaping, stained glass, psychology, etc.

JUST FOR SENIORS

County Council on Aging, (904) 736-7747. **Senior Activity Center**, (904) 740-6860. DeLand's chapter of the **National Association of Retired Federal Employees** (NARFE) helps seniors fill out insurance papers, medical claim forms and other paperwork not requiring the services of an attorney or accountant, (904) 738-4479.

GETTING INVOLVED

Florida Greeting Service, (904) 734-6031, welcomes newcomers and helps them get acquainted with the city. **RSVP**, (904) 736-7747. **SCORE**, (904) 255-6889.

RECREATION, ENTERTAINMENT & AMENITIES

Public golf: Glen Abbey Golf Club and Southridge. **Private golf:** DeLand Golf & Country Club and Deltona Country Club. **Public tennis courts:** City of DeLand Courts, Stetson University Courts. **Private tennis courts:** Brandywine Racquet Club. **Parks:** Blue Springs State Park, Hontoon Island State Park and nearby Ocala National Forest. There are 17 city or county parks and recreational facilities. **Public swimming pools:** Chisholm Park. **Water sports:** Tubing, snorkeling, scuba diving, houseboating. Fishing in the St. Johns River yields trophy-winning bass. **River/gulf/ocean:** St. Johns River; nearby lakes George, Woodruff and Monroe; Blue Springs and DeLeon Springs. **Running/walking/biking:** Lake Woodruff National Wildlife Refuge has nature trails, hiking and bird-watching. There are three fitness trails in town. **Horses/riding:** There are a few stables and riding academies, but the area is not noted for horses. **Hunting:** Bow and arrow hunting is permitted in Lake Woodruff National Wildlife Refuge. Information on freshwater fishing and hunting, Florida Game and Freshwater Fish Commission, (904) 985-7880. **Movie theaters:** Eight screens. **Art museums:** African-American Museum of the Arts, The Duncan Gallery of Art, DeLand Cultural Arts Center and Deland Museum of Art. **History museums:** Henry A. DeLand House and Stone Street Historical Museum. **Theaters:** Theater Center, Elizabeth Hall Auditoriun, Stover Theater. Also, the DeLand Little Symphony. **Library:** DeLand Public. **Attractions:** Downtown DeLand's National Historic District, Gillespie Museum of Minerals, Stetson University, DeLand Lawn Bowling Club and the arrival of the manatees to Blue Spring State Park each winter. Twenty miles south is Central Florida Zoological Park. **Necessities:** All are here, including local, county, state and federal government offices.

   Smart Shopper Tip: The Woodland Plaza, West Volusia Regional Shopping Center and downtown shops will fill most of your routine shopping needs. Numerous malls and shopping centers are just 30 minutes away in the Daytona Beach area.

WHO LIVES HERE

Population: 18,371 year-round residents, an increase of 1,749 since 1990. **Age 65+** = 22.6% in Volusia County. **Median household income:** $26,071 (Volusia County). **Per capita income:** $18,951 (Volusia County).

NUMBERS TO KNOW

Chamber of commerce: (904) 734-4331. **Voter registration:** (904) 736-5930. **Vehicle registration, tags & title:** (904) 736-5936. **Driver's license:** (904) 736-5325. **Visitors bureau:** (800) 749-4350 or (904) 734-4331.

WHAT TO READ

The DeLand Beacon, weekly newspaper, (904) 734-4622. **Daytona Beach News-Journal**, daily newspaper, (904) 734-1551. **Orlando Sentinel** (Volusia edition), daily newspaper, (800) 347-6868.

GETTING AROUND

Bus: Council on Aging, (904) 736-7747, provides transportation for medical appointments, shopping, congregate dining and social functions. **Taxi:** Tom's Taxi, (904) 734-3417. **Tours:** None. **Airport:** Daytona Beach International is 20 miles away. **Train:** Amtrak, (800) 872-7245. **Traffic:** Light.

JOBS

County unemployment rate: 3.7%. **Florida Jobs and Benefits:** (904) 736-5335.

UTILITIES

Electricity: Florida Power Corp., (904) 734-3770. **Gas:** Florida Public Utilities, (904) 734-1951. **Water & sewer:** City of DeLand, (904) 736-3900. **Telephone:** Bell South, (800) 789-9025 in Florida, or (800) 753-0710 out-of-state. **Cable TV:** Time Warner Communications, (904) 775-7300.

PLACES OF WORSHIP

One Catholic and 56 Protestant churches, plus one Jewish synagogue.

THE ENVIRONMENT

DeLand is in an area defined as the upper St. Johns River basin. The water bodies of the area have been found to be adversely affected by urban development, though several lakes and rivers, including the Wekiva River, Little Wekiva River and Blackwater Creek, have been given protected status as Outstanding Florida Waters (OFW). Others with the OFW designation include Lake Woodruff National Wildlife Refuge, St. Johns River National Wildlife Refuge, Blue Springs State Park and Tosohatchee State Reserve. Lakes Howell, Jessup and Monroe have been rated as having poor water quality. Health advisories recommending limited consumption of largemouth bass due to mercury content have been issued for Lake Sawgrass, Puzzle Lake, Lake Hellen Blazes and the St. Johns River at the Econlockhatchee River. Lake George, designated for Surface Water Improvement and Management (SWIM), has fair and improving water quality.

   The Sherwood Medical site, three miles north of DeLand, is on the EPA Superfund list.

EVENTS AND FESTIVALS

Manatee Festival - January. **DeLand Outdoor Art Festival, Central Florida Hot Air Balloon Rally** - March. **Volusia County Fair & Youth Show, Fall Festival of the Arts** - November. **Christmas Street Parade, Christmas Boat Parade, Candle Tour of Historic Homes** - December.

WHERE TO EAT

The Original Holiday House, 704 N. Woodland, buffet features roasts, lamb, seafood, salads, inexpensive to moderate, (904) 734-6319. **The Steak Place**, 1330 N. Woodland, steak, seafood, chicken, moderate, (904) 734-8070.

WHERE TO STAY

Holiday Inn, (904) 738-5200. **Orange Tree Inn**, (904) 734-0670. **University Inn**, (904) 734-5711.

ISSUES

There appear to be no significant issues impacting the future desirability of DeLand for retirees. Whether or not to approve construction of a Super Wal-Mart is the biggest item on the agenda.

Delray Beach

HE SAID: ★ ★ ★ ★
> *It is not my favorite southeast Florida beach town,*
> *but its beauty and attractions place it among my top picks.*

SHE SAID: ★ ★ ★
> *It's pretty here. Downtown, east of I-95, offers lots*
> *of antique stores, art galleries, shops and restaurants*
> *without south Florida's usual heavy traffic. If I retired here,*
> *I would live in the residential area west of I-95, where there*
> *are lots of neighborhood shopping centers and several*
> *private, gated communities with golf courses, club houses,*
> *tennis courts and beautiful lakes.*

Some would say that Delray Beach grows on you. There are, in fact, many features that seem more remarkable after leaving the area. Perhaps that's exactly the way a hometown should feel.

Ocean Boulevard — sans high-rise apartments and condominiums — is reminiscent of less settled, small-town beach fronts not often found in southern Florida. The downtown district, heralded by banners proclaiming "Stroll An Original, Stroll Atlantic Avenue," is quaint and pretty with more than 200 shops and restaurants in about 12 blocks.

Delray has the largest beach in the county. It's wide, clean and uncrowded. Better still, it has plenty of parking.

Indicative of Delray's intention to remain a lovely, liveable city was the 1988 creation of four historic districts. These have helped preserve the charm and beauty of early 20th-century architecture in designated neighborhoods.

No visit to Delray Beach is complete without a leisurely stroll through Morikami Park Museum and Japanese Gardens, a serene 200-acre pine forest. The museum contains exhibits of Japanese folk arts and culture as a tribute to the Yamato colony established here at the turn of the century.

But the real strength of Delray as a retirement community is west of I-95, where dozens of adult communities share space with golf courses, parks, excellent shopping facilities, hospitals and quick access to north-south interstates, international airports and nearby cities. Living out here, one would have easy access to the beach and downtown, yet leave behind the hassles of tourist season.

Delray Beach is definitely worth a hard look.

WEATHER

	Winter	Spring	Summer	Fall
Normal daily high/low	77/59	86/69	91/74	82/65
Normal precipitation	8 in.	18 in.	20 in.	13 in.

Disaster watch: Southeast Florida has been hit by nine major hurricanes since 1900.

TAXES

Sales tax: 6%. **Property tax:** $24.58 per $1,000 valuation. Sample tax calculations include a $25,000 homestead exemption.

Home value	Tax
$100,000	$1,844
$150,000	$3,073
$250,000	$5,530

REAL ESTATE

Median home value: $101,611 (Palm Beach County). **Median rent:** $773/month (Palm Beach County). **Communities popular with retirees:** Heritage Park includes four rental retirement communities offering independent living and multiple levels of care, (561) 499-7744. Huntington Point features condominiums and villas priced from the $100s to mid-$140s. Gleneagles offers single-family homes and condominiums with prices from the mid-$120s to $300s. Lakes of Delray has condominiums priced from the $50s to $80s. Coral Lakes, gated, outstanding amenities, villas, condos and patio homes from the $100s to $160s. Newport Cove, gated, low-maintenance community of single-family homes from $125,000 to $160,000. Floral Lakes, gated, one-story villas from $105,000 to $135,000. **Licensed continuing-care retirement communities:** Harbour's Edge, 276 independent living units, (561) 272-7979; Abbey Delray, 360 independent living units, (561) 278-3249; and Abbey Delray South, 290 independent living units, (561) 272-9600.

CRIME & SAFETY

Crimes per 1,000 population: 122. **Non-emergency police:** (561) 243-7800. **Non-emergency fire department:** (561) 243-7401. **Police, fire, ambulance emergencies:** 911.

HOMELESS & BLIGHT

Beautification and redevelopment needs have been targeted and addressed through the Decade of Excellence program, a $21.5 million initiative begun in 1990.

The U.S. Census reports that Palm Beach County, population 863,518, had 416 homeless persons. A little more than half, or 219, were counted in shelters.

HEALTH CARE

Hospitals: Bethesda Memorial Hospital, 362 beds, full service, (561) 737-7733. **Delray Medical Center**, 211 beds, acute care and cardiac center, (561) 498-4440. **Pinecrest Hospital**, 60-bed rehabilitation facility, (561) 495-0400. **Fair Oaks Hospital**, 100-bed psychiatric hospital, (561) 495-1000.
Physicians: 200+. **Specialties:** 66.

GETTING SMART

There are no college or university campuses in Delray Beach. **Florida Atlantic University** in Boca Raton, (561) 297-3000, offers the Lifelong Learning Society, (561) 297-3171. **Offerings:** The university has nine colleges, offering programs in more than 61 four-year degree fields as well as advanced degrees. Lifelong Learning Society members can enroll in regular course offerings or special LIFEcourse programs for degree credit, non-credit or audit. **Lynn University** in Boca Raton, (561) 994-0770, offers the Institute for Learning in Retirement (ILIR), (561) 883-0999. **Offerings:** Bachelor's degree programs in accounting, business administration, marketing, behavioral science, history, political science and liberal arts. ILIR offers peer-directed courses. Members can take up to three non-credit courses per eight-week semester. **Palm Beach Community College** in Lake Worth, (561) 439-8000. **Offerings:** 76 two-year associate in arts degrees, 50 two-year associate in sciences degrees plus continuing-education courses and personal enrichment seminars.

JUST FOR SENIORS
AARP, (561) 650-6100. Senior Employment, (561) 479-3914. Elder Help Line, (561) 930-5040.

GETTING INVOLVED
The chamber's annual directory lists 45 civic, fraternal and social clubs and organizations. SCORE, (561) 278-7752. United Way, (561) 375-6600. Delray Beach Art League, (561) 243-0958.

RECREATION, ENTERTAINMENT & AMENITIES
Public golf: Delray Beach Municipal Course, Kings Point Atlantic, Kings Point Flanders, Lakeview Golf Course, Sherwood Park, Villa Delray Country Club and the Villages of Oriole each offers an 18-hole course. Semi-private golf: The Links at Polo Trace. Private golf: Delaire Country Club and the Delray Dunes Golf and Country Club. Public tennis courts: Tennis Center hosts the annual Virginia Slims tournament. Also Pompey Park. Private tennis courts: Rainberry Bay Tennis Club. Parks: Loxahatchee National Wildlife Refuge is only a short drive west. Morikami Park and Museum, Pompey Park, Miller Park and Barwick Park. Public swimming pools: Pompey Park and Aqua Crest. Water sports: Windsurfing, sailing and kayaking are popular. River/gulf/ocean: There's 1.5 miles of public beach on the Atlantic and Intracoastal Waterway. Bass fishing and water-skiing at Lake Ida, a 300-acre freshwater lake. Running/walking/biking: Bike paths, exercise and fitness trails are abundant throughout the city. Morikami Park has a 1.5-mile path. Beach walkers club, (561) 243-7352. Horses/riding: None. Hunting: None in city limits. Movie theaters: Several. Art museums: Cornell Museum of Art and History at the Old School Square Cultural Arts Center. History museums: Morikami Park Museum and Japanese Gardens. Theaters: Delray Beach Playhouse and the 1925 Theatre at Old School Square. Library: Delray Beach Public Library, Palm Beach County Library. Attractions: Old School Square is a multimillion dollar cultural arts center. Morikami Museum and Japanese Gardens. Necessities: Nothing's missing.

Smart Shopper Tip: Atlantic Avenue is the central retail and shopping district that most cities and towns only dream about. There's also the Pineapple Grove shopping area, akin to New York City's Soho neighborhood, with a myriad of thrift and consignment shops. Delray Mall and other shopping centers stock more conventional items.

WHO LIVES HERE
Population: 52,920 year-round residents, an increase of 5,736 since 1990. Age 65+ = 25.0% in Palm Beach County. Median household income: $33,094 (Palm Beach County). Per capita income: $36,057 (Palm Beach County).

NUMBERS TO KNOW
Chamber of commerce: (561) 278-0424. Voter registration: (561) 276-1226. Vehicle registration, tags & title: (561) 355-2622. Driver's license: In Boca Raton, (561) 681-6333.

WHAT TO READ
Boca Raton News, daily newspaper, (561) 395-8300. Palm Beach Post, daily newspaper, (561) 279-3408.

GETTING AROUND
Bus: PalmTram, (561) 930-4BUS. Taxi: Metro Taxi, (561) 276-2230. Tours: Sightseeing lunch and dinner cruises on the Ramblin' Rose Riverboat, (561) 243-0686. Airport: Palm Beach International is 15 minutes away. Traffic: Moderate to light in downtown, but can get heavy on the major east-west thoroughfares that lie west of I-95.

JOBS
County unemployment rate: 6.4%. Florida Jobs and Benefits: (561) 637-7000.

UTILITIES
Electricity: Florida Power & Light, (561) 994-8227. Gas: Florida Public Utilities Co., (561) 278-2636. Water & sewer: City of Delray Beach, (561) 243-7100. Telephone: Bell South, (800) 753-0710. Cable TV: Adelphia Cable, (561) 272-2522.

PLACES OF WORSHIP
Four Catholic and 54 Protestant churches, plus four Jewish synagogues. Each year on Easter Sunday, hundreds attend a non-denominational sunrise service at the Pavilion overlooking the beach at Atlantic Avenue and Ocean Boulevard.

THE ENVIRONMENT
Surface water quality has been rated as fair to poor in canals. Sections of nearby canals, notably the Hillsboro and West Palm Beach canals, are known to have poor water quality due to urban, industrial and agricultural runoff.

There is one EPA-listed Superfund site in the county, BMI-Textron in Lake Park.

EVENTS AND FESTIVALS
Hatsume Fair - February. The Delray Affair - April. Roots Cultural Festival - July/August. Harvest Fest - November.

WHERE TO EAT
Boston's on the Beach, 40 South Ocean Blvd., seafood, American, moderate, (561) 278-3364. Busch's Seafood & Grill, 840 E. Atlantic Ave., seafood, beef, moderate, (561) 278-7600. Damiano's, 52 N. Swinton Ave., continental, seafood, beef, moderate to expensive, (561) 272-4706.

WHERE TO STAY
Marriott, (561) 278-0882. Seagate Hotel & Beach Club, (561) 276-2421. Wright by the Sea, (561) 278-3355.

ISSUES
If there are any unresolved issues bothering residents here, we didn't hear of them. The *Palm Beach Post* editorial board said of Delray Beach: "This city is as close to ideal as it gets."

Destin

HE SAID: ☆ ☆ ☆
I would opt for a road less traveled, more growing room, and more diverse opportunities for creative and productive involvement in society.

SHE SAID: ☆ ☆
Destin reminded me of some place we might have gone for a family vacation when our children were small. Vacation, yes. Retirement, no.

Surrounded on three sides by the waters of Choctawhatchee Bay, Joe's Bayou, Destin Harbor, East Pass and the Gulf of Mexico, Destin is destined to be overwhelmed by fishermen and boaters someday. It is a fisherman's paradise, variously called "the world's luckiest fishing village" and the "billfish capital of the world," and it is reputed to have the best fishing hole on the Emerald Coast.

But these very qualities may ultimately close Destin's doors to future retirees. The town, incorporated in 1984, is already running out of land. While most towns are measured in square miles, Destin is better explained in terms of acreage, having a total of 3,795 acres. Roughly one-third of this area is residential, another third is commercial, recreational and industrial, and the remainder is vacant. That's about 1,300 acres for all future development, since the city's limits are pretty much fixed by the surrounding water and parklands.

Destin is a bedroom community for Fort Walton Beach, a vacation magnet; the population swells from about 11,000 to 25,000 during peak tourist season. It is popular with military retirees because of the numerous service-connected perks and attractions of nearby Eglin Air Force Base. It has very little to offer non-military retirees, few cultural amenities and only a handful of clubs and associations for its residents.

Retirees we interviewed cited clean air, beautiful beaches and nice people as the foremost attractions. All predictable characteristics, given its location on the coast. While it may still have the qualities sought after by retirees, it may not have them for long. If the area's growth rate accelerates and combines with the additional traffic resulting from the new Mid-Bay Bridge, the quiet, clean character of today may soon become a thing of the past.

WEATHER

	Winter	Spring	Summer	Fall
Normal daily high/low	65/41	84/61	90/69	72/47
Normal precipitation	17 in.	14 in.	21 in.	13 in.

Disaster watch: Northwest Florida has been hit by six major hurricanes since 1900.

TAXES

Sales tax: 7%. **Property tax:** $15.62 per $1,000 valuation. Sample tax calculations include a $25,000 homestead exemption.

Home value	Tax
$100,000	$1,172
$150,000	$1,953
$250,000	$3,515

REAL ESTATE

Median home value: $84,075 (Okaloosa County). **Median rent:** $598/month (Okaloosa County). **Communities popular with retirees:** Indian Bayou Country Club and Golf Course has single-family homes priced from the $200s to $1 million. The original developer has sold all lots, but both lots and homes are available for resale by individuals. Holiday Isle has condominiums, townhomes and single-family homes priced from the low $100s to $1.5 million, (800) 837-5108 or (850) 837-0009. Destin Pointe, a new 39-acre, Gulf-front, Caribbean-style development, has lots from $77,900 to $700,000, condominium resales from $200,000 to $350,000, and single-family homes from $300,000 to $1.5 million, (800) 624-6017 or (850) 837-4800. **Licensed continuing-care retirement communities:** None.

CRIME & SAFETY

Crimes per 1,000 population: 25 (Okaloosa County sheriff's jurisdiction). **Non-emergency police:** (850) 651-7400. **Non-emergency fire department:** (850) 837-8413. **Police, fire, ambulance emergencies:** 911.

HOMELESS & BLIGHT

U.S. Highway 98, the so-called Miracle Strip Highway, would be better dubbed "Neon Highway." Almost all of the commercial district of Destin lies along this corridor, attracting more vehicles and people than it can reasonably accommodate. We saw no homeless persons.

The county, population 143,776, had 40 homeless persons in shelters and 17 on the streets, according to the U.S. Census.

HEALTH CARE

Hospitals: No hospital in Destin. Other hospitals are located in Fort Walton Beach, including **Fort Walton Beach Medical Center**, 247 beds, full service, (850) 862-1111.
Physicians: 15. **Specialties:** 10.

GETTING SMART

There are no college or university campuses in Destin. Fort Walton has campuses of the **University of West Florida**, (850) 474-2000; **Troy State University**, (850) 244-7414; and **Okaloosa-Walton Community College**, (850) 863-6501.

JUST FOR SENIORS

Activities such as trips, crafts and luncheons are scheduled for seniors at the **Destin Community Center**, (850) 654-5184.

GETTING INVOLVED

Destin has no social service organizations listed in any of its literature or yellow pages. There are chapters of the American Legion, Elks Lodge, VFW and Kiwanis.

RECREATION, ENTERTAINMENT & AMENITIES

Public golf: Seascape Resort, 18 holes/par 72; Indian Bayou, 27 holes; and The Garden, nine holes/par 27. **Semiprivate golf:** Emerald Bay and Kelly Plantation. **Public tennis courts:** Legion Park. **Private tennis courts:** Destin Racquet & Fitness Center. **Parks:** Henderson Beach State Park has more than 250 acres and all the amenities. Others: Clement E. Taylor City Park and Crystal Beach Wayside Park. **Public swimming pools:** None. **Water sports:** Diving, snorkeling, spearfishing, shelling, lobstering, parasailing and fishing—shore, pier, deep sea and offshore. **River/gulf/ocean:** Surrounded on three sides by Choctawhatchee Bay, East Pass (the only channel passage to the Gulf between Panama City and Pensacola), Destin Harbor and the Gulf of Mexico. Three bayous knife deeply into the city, creating hundreds of waterfront homesites. **Running/walking/biking:** New 3.5-mile Mid-Bay Bridge has a lane for pedestrians and bicyclers. **Horses/riding:** One local stable. **Hunting:** No hunting in the area. Fishing licenses required. Florida Game and Freshwater Fish Commission, (850) 892-8000. **Movie theaters:** 10 screens. **Art museums:** None. **History museums:** Destin Fishing Museum, Old Post Office Museum and the Museum of the Sea & Indian. **Theaters:** Destin Community Center and the Destin Theatre Youth Association. **Library:** Destin City Library. **Attractions:** Big Kahuna, the largest man-made waterfall; Destin Bridge Catwalk; and tours of Eglin Air Force Base. **Necessities:** It has just about everything, except a new-car dealership.

Smart Shopper Tip: The Miracle Strip (U.S. 98) has a few shopping centers, but any extended shopping spree will require a trip to Santa Rosa Mall at Fort Walton Beach or even Pensacola.

WHO LIVES HERE
Population: 10,690 year-round residents, an increase of 2,600 since 1990. **Age 65+ = 10.6%** in Okaloosa County. **Median household income:** $31,520 (Okaloosa County). **Per capita income:** $19,795 (Okaloosa County).

NUMBERS TO KNOW
Chamber of commerce: (850) 837-6241. **Voter registration:** (850) 837-4242. **Vehicle registration, tags & title:** (850) 651-7315. **Driver's license:** (850) 833-9122.

WHAT TO READ
Northwest Florida Daily News, daily newspaper, (850) 863-1111. **The Destin Log,** semiweekly newspaper, (850) 837-2828.

GETTING AROUND
Bus: No public intra-city transportation. **Taxi:** Destin Cab Co., (850) 837-2411. **Tours:** None. **Airport:** Okaloosa Air Terminal. **Traffic:** If you can stay off U.S. 98 you're OK, but that's hard to do when it's the only thoroughfare.

JOBS
County unemployment rate: 3.4%. **Florida Jobs and Benefits:** (850) 833-9106.

UTILITIES
Electricity: Gulf Power Co., (850) 664-6500. **Gas:** Okaloosa County Gas District, (850) 244-5197. **Water & sewer:** Destin Water Users, (850) 837-6146. **Telephone:** Sprint/CENTEL, (800) 326-2497, or 811 locally. **Cable TV:** Cox Communications, (850) 862-0175.

PLACES OF WORSHIP
Three Catholic and 11 Protestant churches.

THE ENVIRONMENT
Historically the area has been rated as having good surface water quality, due to sparse development and use. There have been fish kills reported in Joe's Bayou.

EVENTS AND FESTIVALS
Destin May Fest - May. **The Blessing of the Fleet** - Forty days after Easter. **Destin Cup Sailing Regatta** - September. **Destin Deep Sea Rodeo** - October. **Destin Seafood Festival** - October.

WHERE TO EAT
Flamingo Cafe, 414 U.S. Highway 98 E., seafood, Cajun, Caribbean, moderate to expensive, (850) 837-0961. **Louisiana Lagniappe,** 775 Gulf Shore Drive, Louisiana seafood, steaks, live Maine lobster, expensive, (850) 837-0881. **Marina Cafe,** 404 U.S. Highway 98 E., Italian, Louisiana seafood, moderate to expensive, (850) 837-7960.

WHERE TO STAY
Sandestin Beach Hilton, (850) 267-9500 or (800) HILTONS. **Sandestin Beach Resort,** (850) 267-8000 or (800) 277-0800. **Tops'l Beach & Racquet Club,** (850) 267-9222 or (800) 476-9222.

ISSUES
An already popular resort was made more accessible by the 1993 opening of Mid-Bay Bridge. The issue is whether Destin, with only one through-highway, will survive as a desirable retirement destination or be overwhelmed by vacationers and travelers passing through the small town.

RELOCATION TIPS

Important packing tips to keep in mind:

● Wrap plates individually, then again in groups of three. Do not lay them flat. Stand them on edge inside the box. Pack record albums on edge also.

● Leave clothes in dresser drawers.

● Consider shipping books by mail or through a parcel service, such as UPS. The UPS or postal book rate may be less expensive than the moving company's fee for carrying the same items.

● Label the sides of each box clearly. Include your name, moving contract number, the room where the box will go and a general description of the contents. Don't forget to write "fragile" on boxes with breakable items.

Dunedin

HE SAID: ★ ★ ★ ★
Its attractions are not theme parks, ornate buildings or even outstanding residential neighborhoods. Rather, they are more subtle things such as a quiet, unhurried atmosphere. It is close to metropolitan amenities, yet is largely unaffected by the negative aspects of big-city life. I am smitten by this town and find very little to detract from my image of an ideal retirement community. It is definitely on my short list.

SHE SAID: ★ ★ ★ ★
This pretty, small town on the west coast is one of the most inviting. It's clean and feels safe, plus there are lots of different retirement areas. I would look here for a place to retire.

This is a special small town with a surprising village atmosphere you don't expect to find in this busy corner of southwest Florida. Downtown Main Street is slow-paced, quiet and quaint, possessing many of the qualities that attract retirees to the area.

The town is particularly pedestrian-friendly, giving you many options for scenic walking. Along the popular Pinellas Trail you'll find joggers, bikers and skaters as well as walkers out for health and recreation. The trail runs through the heart of town and is guarded from the limited vehicular traffic by a stop sign. It's possible to walk Dunedin's quiet streets to almost anyplace you want to go in the city — shops, businesses or the waterfront. Beach walkers will find miles of white sand beaches on the offshore barrier islands where Honeymoon and Caladesi state parks are located.

Of course you may elect to drive to Countryside or Clearwater malls, just minutes from downtown; to Clearwater and St. Petersburg beaches a few minutes farther; or to Tampa, about 20 to 30 minutes from home. Edgewater Drive affords a delightful and picturesque view of Clearwater Harbor.

While the very popular, 10,000-resident On Top of the World adult condo development is not officially located within Dunedin's city limits, it is home to many whose lives and livelihoods are focused toward Dunedin. In addition, condos, manufactured homes, and single-family, site-built homes in well-kept, affordable communities are located throughout the town and along the bays, bayous and lagoons of northern Dunedin.

Dunedin is the winter home of the Toronto Blue Jays and within minutes of the professional sports and cultural events, theme parks and historic attractions of Tampa/St. Pete/Clearwater. Its residents have access to a glittering, glamorous lifestyle that would challenge the most avid socializer. Those who choose not to venture outside the confines of the city limits can eschew life in the fast lane and enjoy the pace of small-town America. Dunedin has the qualities of a hometown where you can choose when and how to make the most of the excitement and diversity of nearby urban centers.

WEATHER

	Winter	Spring	Summer	Fall
Normal daily high/low	72/52	85/66	90/73	78/58
Normal precipitation	10 in.	10 in.	23 in.	8 in.

Disaster watch: Since 1900, northwest Florida has been hit by six major hurricanes and southwest Florida has been hit by five.

TAXES

Sales tax: 7%. **Property tax:** $22.26 per $1,000 valuation. Sample tax calculations include a $25,000 homestead exemption.

Home value	Tax
$100,000	$1,670
$150,000	$2,783
$250,000	$5,009

REAL ESTATE

Median home value: $73,800 (Pinellas County). **Median rent:** $614/month (Pinellas County). **Communities popular with retirees:** There are 11 mobile home parks and 45 condominium complexes in Dunedin. Condominium developments include Edgewater Arms, Heather Hills, Mediterranean Manor and Patricia Oaks. Manufactured-home communities include Golden Acres, Golden Crest, Honeymoon, Lake Haven and Lake Highlander. **Licensed continuing-care retirement communities:** Mease Manor, (813) 733-1161, has 343 independent living units. Assisted living and nursing beds are part of a 36-acre campus that includes Mease Hospital, Mease Assisted Living and Mease Continuing Care.

CRIME & SAFETY

Crimes per 1,000 population: 46. **Non-emergency police:** (813) 582-6200. **Non-emergency fire department:** (813) 738-1859. **Police, fire, ambulance emergencies:** 911.

HOMELESS & BLIGHT

Interest in downtown revitalization began in 1973; current improvements are overseen by the Community Redevelopment Agency. An annual design awards program has been an effective means of involving the whole community in aesthetic enhancements. The town was awarded the prestigious White House "Take Pride in America" award in 1987 for its Adopt A Tree program. There were no homeless persons or blighted areas that we saw. In fact, it is as neat, clean and quaint as any town in Florida.

The U.S. Census reported 1,105 homeless persons in shelters and 75 visible in street locations in Pinellas County, population 851,659.

HEALTH CARE

Hospitals: Mease Hospital and Clinic, 300 beds, full service, 24-hour emergency, (813) 733-1111.
Physicians: 215+. **Specialties:** 34.

GETTING SMART

Schiller International University, (813) 736-5082. **Offerings:** Bachelor's and master's degrees, as well as certificates.

JUST FOR SENIORS

Adult Day Care includes telephone reassurance, in Clearwater (813) 443-1560. **Neighborly Senior Services**, operates Meals on

Wheels, (813) 573-9444. **Senior Citizens Center**, (813) 738-1911.

GETTING INVOLVED
Pinellas Opportunity Council, (727) 327-8690. **Dunedin Historical Society**, (813) 736-1176.

RECREATION, ENTERTAINMENT & AMENITIES
Public golf: Chi Chi Rodriguez Golf Course, 18 holes/par 69; Countryside Executive Golf Course, 18 holes/par 58; Dunedin Country Club, semiprivate, 18 holes/par 72; and St. Andrew Links, 18 holes/par 54. **Private golf:** Countryside Country Club, 18 holes/par 72, and On Top of the World Golf Course, 18 holes/par 65. **Public tennis courts:** Louis A. Vanech Recreational Complex. **Private tennis courts:** Dunedin Country Club, On Top of the World. **Parks:** There are 29 municipal parks with more than 1,400 acres. Caladesi State Park, accessible only by boat, is a popular, unspoiled beach area. A five-minute trip via a causeway takes you to Honeymoon Island for park/beach recreation. **Public swimming pools:** Highlander Municipal Park. **Water sports:** Sailing, surfing and water-skiing. **River/gulf/ocean:** Various bays, bayous, lagoons and the Gulf of Mexico. **Running/walking/biking:** Pinellas Trail, a 47-mile-long linear park, passes through the heart of downtown and is ideal for walking, jogging, bicycling or skating. **Horses/riding:** None. **Hunting:** None. **Movie theaters:** None in Dunedin, but more than 20 screens at more than a dozen theaters in adjoining Countryside and Clearwater. **Art museums:** Dunedin Fine Art Center. **History museums:** Dunedin Historical Society & Museum in the Orange Belt Railroad Depot. **Theaters:** Dunedin Community Center. The Ruth Eckerd Center for Performing Arts in Clearwater is 15 minutes away. **Library:** Dunedin Public. **Attractions:** Winter home of the Toronto Blue Jays. Almost anything in the city is within walking distance. **Necessities:** All within five miles.

Smart Shopper Tip: Countryside Mall, only minutes from downtown, has 166 stores, including Burdines, Dillards, J.C. Penney and Sears, plus an ice-skating rink.

WHO LIVES HERE
Population: 35,586 year-round residents, an increase of 1,159 since 1990. **Age 65+** = 24.6% in Pinellas County. **Median household income:** $29,009 (Pinellas County). **Per capita income:** $25,765 (Pinellas County).

NUMBERS TO KNOW
Chamber of commerce: (813) 733-3197. **Voter registration:** (813) 464-3551. **Vehicle registration, tags & title:** (813) 464-5560. **Driver's license:** (813) 725-7940.

WHAT TO READ
Clearwater Times, daily newspaper, (813) 895-1181. **St. Petersburg Times**, daily newspaper, (813) 893-8111. **Sun Coast News**, weekly newspaper, (813) 849-7500. **Tampa Tribune**, daily newspaper, (813) 799-7400.

GETTING AROUND
Bus: Pinellas Suncoast Transit Authority, (813) 530-9911. **Taxi:** Yellow Cab, (813) 799-2222. **Tours:** None. **Airport:** Tampa International is 20 miles away. Also, St. Petersburg International. **Traffic:** It's far enough off the beaten path that traffic is not a problem.

JOBS
County unemployment rate: 3.4%. **Florida Jobs and Benefits:** (813) 725-7920.

UTILITIES
Electricity: Florida Power Corp., (813) 443-2641. **Gas:** Clearwater Gas System, (813) 562-4600. **Water & sewer:** City Water Dept., (813) 733-4151. **Telephone:** GTE, (800) 483-4200. **Cable TV:** TCI Cablevision, (813) 736-1436.

PLACES OF WORSHIP
Two Catholic and 30 Protestant churches, one Jewish synagogue and one Islamic center.

THE ENVIRONMENT
The Pinellas County region is highly urbanized, leading to pollution problems in almost all the feeder creeks and lakes. St. Joseph Sound near Clearwater and some of the feeder creeks have water quality problems.

There is one EPA-listed Superfund site in Pinellas County. It is the Stauffer Chemical Co. plant in Tarpon Springs.

EVENTS AND FESTIVALS
Mardi Gras on Main Street - February. **Highland Games & Scottish Festival** - April. **Art Harvest** - November.

WHERE TO EAT
Jesse's Seafood House, 345 Causeway Blvd., seafood, moderate to expensive, (813) 736-2611. **Kelly's**, 319 Main St., seafood, steak, moderate, (813) 736-5284. **Bon Appetit**, 148 Marina Plaza, seafood, lamb, crab cakes, moderate, (813) 733-2151.

WHERE TO STAY
Best Western-Yacht Harbor Inn, (813) 733-4121. **Inn on the Bay**, (727) 734-7689.

ISSUES
Keeping "delightfully different" Dunedin from becoming a clone of all other Gulf Coast communities is the primary issue. It is fortunate that the malls and resort beaches that attract a large influx of cars and people are near — but not in — Dunedin.

Englewood

HE SAID: ☆ ☆ ☆
It has what I most desire in a retirement place: the opportunity to enjoy some peace and quiet without locking myself within four walls. But it lacks many amenities and is short on housing options. I wouldn't rule it out entirely.

SHE SAID: ☆
A laid-back community with little to do except fish and walk in the sun. I would not retire here.

It is hard to pin a label on Englewood or even to define its parameters. Greater Englewood has as much claim to the huge peninsular area formed by the Gulf, Charlotte Harbor and Myakka River as any of the smaller neighboring communities. It straddles southwest Sarasota County and northwest Charlotte County. And though this peninsula is almost the same shape and size as the Clearwater/Largo/St. Petersburg peninsula, it is vastly different in terms of population density, development, social-cultural-recreational infrastructure and economic wealth. It is probably near the same stage of development as its more advanced, northern look-alike was some 30 to 40 years ago.

This means there are still some frontiers for newcomers looking for quiet, secluded, unspoiled places. There are bargains in land and improved real estate. There are stretches of open road still uncluttered by traffic. In fact, heavily traveled U.S. Highway 41 doesn't come close to the city.

As a result of its slower-than-average development during the last 25 years, Englewood has some rough edges. The central business district is small, about four or five blocks long, and reminiscent of many other small Florida towns. The counties provide good basic services, but there is a paucity of arts and cultural organizations and facilities.

Englewood has been most successful in attracting blue collar retirees and fishermen from the Midwest. They come seeking relief from bitter winters, high population densities and rising costs of living. They find this respite in mobile home parks, manufactured-home communities, villas by the bay and small, single-family homes.

Because most of the big-spending snowbirds from the east have not discovered this part of Florida, it remains affordable. This is apparent in the wide range of modestly priced housing available here. Limited numbers of wealthy retirees have discovered the area, as evidenced by Gulf-front mansions on remote northern Manasota Key.

The lack of wide, white sand beaches precludes hordes of sun 'n' fun lovers from descending on the area. Beaches are shallow, steep and losing ground to rising tides. High waters wash threateningly around the stilts of some Gulf-front homes along Englewood Beach. Be wary of this property and opt instead for the protected shores of Lemon Bay.

Be advised that if tranquillity and solitude are what you're looking for in a retirement home, you had better hurry on down and enjoy them while you can. It is predicted that Englewood's population will double in the next 10 years. And doubtless, the quality of life will be impacted by the busy characteristics of more developed cities.

Disaster watch: Southwest Florida has been hit by five major hurricanes since 1900.

TAXES
Sales tax: 7%. **Property tax:** $16.53 per $1,000 valuation in Charlotte County; from $13.86 to $18.86 per $1,000 valuation in Sarasota County. Sample taxes are calculated at the rate of $18.86 and include a $25,000 homestead exemption.

Home value	Tax
$100,000	$1,415
$150,000	$2,358
$250,000	$4,244

REAL ESTATE
Median home value: $91,147 (Charlotte County); $101,531 (Sarasota County). **Median rent:** $329/month (Charlotte County); $714/month (Sarasota County). **Communities popular with retirees:** Englewood Beach Villas offers two-bedroom units priced from the mid-$90s to $200,000, (941) 474-7171. Lemon Bay Isles is an adult manufactured-home community with prices from the mid-$70s to $120s, (941) 474-5504. Windward at Cape Haze offers single-family and patio homes priced from the mid-$130s to mid-$220s, (941) 697-1300. Oyster Creek Golf and Country Club is a gated, deed-restricted community of maintenance-free single-family homes from the $120s, (941) 473-9226. **Licensed continuing-care retirement communities:** None.

CRIME & SAFETY
Both counties supply regular deputy patrols of Greater Englewood. Charlotte County provides a local substation, while Sarasota County has a Community Policing Unit. **Crimes per 1,000 population:** 30 (Charlotte County sheriff's jurisdiction); 45 (Sarasota County sheriff's jurisdiction). **Non-emergency police:** (941) 474-3233 for Charlotte County Sheriff or (941) 486-2374 for Sarasota County Sheriff. **Non-emergency fire department:** (941) 474-3311. **Police, fire, ambulance emergencies:** 911.

HOMELESS & BLIGHT
Englewood does have some unattractive mobile home parks and concrete block homes, but nothing particularly blighted. No evidence of homeless persons.

The U.S. Census reported eight homeless persons visible in street locations of Charlotte County, population 110,975. In Sarasota County, population 277,776, the census bureau counted 84 homeless persons in shelters and 11 visible on the streets.

HEALTH CARE
Hospitals: Columbia Englewood Community Hospital, 100 beds, acute care, 24-hour emergency, full service, (941) 475-6571. **Physicians:** 69. **Specialties:** 23.

GETTING SMART
Charlotte County Adult and Community Education, (941) 255-7430. **Offerings:** As many as 200 non-credit courses are offered in the Englewood area.

WEATHER

	Winter	Spring	Summer	Fall
Normal daily high/low	74/54	85/67	90/73	80/60
Normal precipitation	8 in.	11 in.	22 in.	7 in.

JUST FOR SENIORS

Charlotte County Senior Services, (941) 475-7149. **Tringali Community Center,** (941) 473-1018.

GETTING INVOLVED

Meals on Wheels, (941) 474-4445. **Friends of the Library,** (941)474-3515. **Lemon Bay Historical Society,** (941) 474-5837.

RECREATION, ENTERTAINMENT & AMENITIES

Public golf: None. **Semiprivate golf:** Boca Royale Golf & Country Club, 18 holes/par 72; Myakka Pines Golf Club, 27 holes/par 108; Oyster Creek Golf & Country Club, 18 holes/par 60; and Wildflower Golf Club, 18 holes/par 60. Lemon Bay Golf Club, 18 holes/par 72, is private. **Public tennis courts:** Englewood Recreation Center, Lemon Bay High School, Tringali Community Center and West Charlotte Community Center. **Private tennis courts:** Colony Don Pedro, Englewood Tennis Club, Fiddler's Green Condos, Golden Tee Condos and Palm Manor Condo. **Parks:** Englewood Beach, Englewood Recreation Center, Indian Mound Park, Lemon Bay Park, Myakka River State Park and Tringali Community Center. **Public swimming pools:** None. **Water sports:** Boating, fishing, sailing, scuba diving, snorkeling, water-skiing and windsurfing. **River/gulf/ocean:** Gottfried Creek, Rocky Creek, Lemon Bay and the Gulf of Mexico. **Running/walking/biking:** Indian Mound Park has a short nature trail. Englewood Recreation Center has a fitness/nature trail and Lemon Bay Park has a picnic area, trails and an environmental center. **Horses/riding:** There are no stables in the area, but plenty of open space in the Myakka River Valley and on Manasota Key. **Hunting:** For information and licenses, Florida Game and Freshwater Commission, (941) 648-3203. **Movie theaters:** None. **Art museums:** Englewood Fine Arts Center. **History museums:** None. **Theaters:** Back Stage Theatre, Lemon Bay High School Auditorium and Lemon Bay Playhouse. Of note is the Englewood Performing Arts Series. **Library:** Elsie Quirk County and Englewood/Charlotte Public. **Attractions:** None of note except the remote beaches. A retired couple from Ohio mentioned the quiet atmosphere and beautiful sunsets. **Necessities:** Most can be found in the area.

Smart Shopper Tip: Lemon Bay to the north and Merchants Crossing to the south are both good shopping centers for basic needs. Drive 20 miles to Port Charlotte Town Center Mall for extras.

WHO LIVES HERE

Population: 45,000-plus year-round residents in Greater Englewood. **Age 65+** = 34.3% in Charlotte County, 32.6% in Sarasota County. **Median household income:** $26,094 (Charlotte County); $30,662 (Sarasota County). **Per capita income:** $20,539 (Charlotte County); $33,445 (Sarasota County).

NUMBERS TO KNOW

Chamber of commerce: (941) 474-5511. **Voter registration:** (941) 474-8188. **Vehicle registration, tags & title:** (941) 741-4801. **Driver's license:** (941) 483-5995.

WHAT TO READ

Englewood Sun Herald, daily newspaper, (941) 474-5521. **Sara-** sota **Herald-Tribune,** daily newspaper, (941) 474-5115.

GETTING AROUND

Bus: SCAT (Sarasota County Area Transit) operates buses between Englewood and Sarasota, (941) 484-9571. **Taxi:** Mary's Taxi, (941) 475-8294. **Tours:** None. **Airport:** Sarasota/Bradenton International and Southwest Florida International in Fort Myers are both about an hour away. **Traffic:** Very light. No through-traffic. There are so few cars, you forget you're in southwest Florida.

JOBS

County unemployment rate: 3.4% (Charlotte County); 2.6% (Sarasota County). **Florida Jobs and Benefits:** In Sarasota, (941) 361-6100, or in Venice, (941) 483-5935.

UTILITIES

Electricity: Florida Power & Light, (941) 917-0708 in Florida, or (800) 226-3545 out-of-state. **Gas:** None. **Water & sewer:** Englewood Water District, (941) 474-3217. **Telephone:** GTE Florida, (800) 483-4200. **Cable TV:** ComCast Cable, (941) 474-9561.

PLACES OF WORSHIP

One Catholic and 24 Protestant churches, plus one Jewish synagogue.

THE ENVIRONMENT

The Lemon Bay Estuary System and Lemon Bay State Aquatic Preserve have protected status as Outstanding Florida Waters. The water quality of Lemon Bay is improving. The Placida Harbor/Lemon Bay area is rated as having mostly good water quality but there have been periodic bans on shellfishing. Gottfried Creek, Forked Creek and Alligator Creek have mostly fair water quality.

EVENTS AND FESTIVALS

Englewood Fine Arts Festival - March. **Celebration in Englewood** - July 4. **Pioneer Days** - September.

WHERE TO EAT

Flying Bridge II, 2080 S. McCall Road, American, moderate, (941) 474-2206.

WHERE TO STAY

Palm Island Resort in Cape Haze, (941) 697-4800. Days Inn, (941) 474-5544.

ISSUES

Beach erosion along the barrier islands needs attention and action. There's a current mind-set of "let nature take its course." Some folks think the 3 percent bed tax collected by the local tourism bureau should be diverted to beach renourishment. Stump Pass, the only feasible boat entry to Lemon Bay, is too shallow and needs dredging to accommodate larger vessels. Why not put that excess sand on the beaches?

Fort Lauderdale

HE SAID: ✭ ✭ ✭
> *If you've been fighting hordes of people and lines of traffic throughout your working years and are just looking for a quiet place in the sun, an occasional relaxed round of golf and a slow-paced and affordable lifestyle, stay out of Fort Lauderdale, Broward County and south Florida. It's expensive and congested.*

SHE SAID: ✭ ✭ ✭
> *If you are looking for a large metropolis with a warm to hot year-round climate, stop here. It offers everything in entertainment and its beaches are beautiful. However, I want a somewhat slower pace.*

It seems to have everything. There's beautiful ocean-front and canal housing, outstanding public beaches, the New River meandering through town, the arts and entertainment, a newly revitalized business district and charming Las Olas Boulevard. There is prosperity in every direction, and developers are having a field day. Renovations seem to have been thoughtfully planned and artistically executed.

But, there's also shoulder-to-shoulder people and bumper-to-bumper traffic.

Despite a population increase of only 937 people from 1980 to 1997, Fort Lauderdale is feeling the effects of too many people and too much traffic. It is the urban job center for residents of towns to the west such as Sunrise, Plantation, Davie, Cooper City, Pembroke Pines, Coral Springs, Tamarac and Parkland. These "western settlements" gained a staggering 196,533 residents from 1980 to 1990.

Every day, young, urban professionals pour into Fort Lauderdale to high-paying jobs, using major traffic routes for their commute from high-priced homes outside the city limits. Subdivision development is overwhelming Broward County's schools and traffic systems. As far west as the Everglades, there is no respite.

For the retiree looking for an active lifestyle with opportunity for involvement in civic affairs, access to first-rate cultural happenings, beaches and water sports — and who doesn't mind urban crowds — Fort Lauderdale is as good as it comes. For others, it has too many people going too many places in too much of a hurry.

WEATHER

	Winter	Spring	Summer	Fall
Normal daily high/low	78/60	86/70	90/75	82/65
Normal precipitation	8 in.	20 in.	21 in.	12 in.

Disaster watch: Southeast Florida has been hit by nine major hurricanes since 1900.

TAXES
Sales tax: 6%. **Property tax:** $26.79 per $1,000 valuation. Sample tax calculations include a $25,000 homestead exemption.

Home value	Tax
$100,000	$2,009
$150,000	$3,349
$250,000	$6,028

REAL ESTATE
Median home value: $107,554 (Broward County). **Median rent:** $809/month (Broward County). **Communities popular with retirees:** The Fort Lauderdale Area Association of Realtors reported that for 1996 the average price was $143,451 for a new single-family house and $70,126 for a condo. Coral Ridge Towers is a 25-story adult co-op on the Intracoastal Waterway. A one-bedroom condo costs $35,000 to $50,000. Two-bedroom units go for $55,000 to $65,000. Galt Ocean Drive offers oceanfront, high-rise condo living for $100,000 to $375,000. With 23 miles of coastline and 300 miles of inland waterways, retirees have their pick of water-access living. Gloria Gold with Eastside Property can provide current listings, (954) 561-2671 or (954) 565-7644. **Licensed continuing-care retirement communities:** Covenant Village of Florida, (954) 472-2860. Williamsburg Landing, (954) 566-1775 is a licensed adult congregate living facility.

CRIME & SAFETY
Crimes per 1,000 population: 169. **Non-emergency police:** (954) 761-5700. **Non-emergency fire department:** (954) 761-5320. **Police, fire, ambulance emergencies:** 911.

HOMELESS & BLIGHT
Fort Lauderdale has undergone a $670 million redesign of its downtown and beach front. It is clean, attractive and uncrowded. We did not encounter homeless persons or see any seriously blighted neighborhoods.

The U.S. Census counted 1,023 homeless persons in Broward County, population 1.25 million, with 381 of the homeless persons counted in shelters and 642 visible on the streets.

HEALTH CARE
Hospitals: Broward General Medical Center, 744 beds, full service, (954) 355-4400. **Holy Cross Hospital**, 597 beds, full service, (954) 771-8000. **Imperial Point Medical Center**, 204 beds, full service, (954) 776-8500. **Cleveland Clinic Hospital**, 150 beds, acute care, (954) 568-1000. **Florida Medical Center Hospital**, 459 beds, (954) 735-6000. **North Ridge Medical Center**, 391 beds, full service, (954) 776-6000. **Vencor Hospital**, 64 beds, acute care, (954) 764-8900.
Physicians: 1,000+. **Specialties:** 56.

GETTING SMART
Broward Community College, (954) 761-7400. **Offerings:** Two-year degrees and a variety of non-credit courses and seminars. **Florida Atlantic University**, (954) 236-1000. **Offerings:** Older adults may enroll for credit or audit the courses on a space-available basis through the Lifelong Learning Society in Boca Raton. **Florida Metropolitan University/Fort Lauderdale College**, (954) 568-1600. **Offerings:** Bachelor's degree programs in accounting, computer information systems, hospitality management, marketing and business administration. It also offers a master's degree in business administration.

JUST FOR SENIORS
Assisted Living Network, (800) 344-0599. **Holiday Park Social Senior Center**, (954) 761-5383. **N.W. Federated Women's Satellite Senior Center**, (954) 584-0093. **Senior Aides Employment Program**, (954) 563-3464.

GETTING INVOLVED
Federation of Senior Citizens, (954) 749-3802. **RSVP**, (954) 563-8991. **Senior Connection**, (954) 714-3464. **Volunteer Broward**, (954) 522-6761.

RECREATION, ENTERTAINMENT & AMENITIES
Golf: 50-plus courses, public and private. Public courses include American Golfers Club, Oak Ridge Country Club and Rolling Hills Golf Resort. **Public tennis courts:** 550 tennis

courts, including Bonaventure Racquet Club and Holiday Park. **Private tennis courts:** Widely available at private clubs. **Parks:** There are 300-plus parks in Broward County, including Secret Woods Nature Center, 37 acres; Hugh Taylor Birch State Recreation Area, 180 acres with hiking trails, picnic facilities and more; Snyder Park, 92 acres with fishing, boating and nature trails; and John U. Lloyd Beach State Recreation Area in Dania. **Public swimming pools:** Yes. **Water sports:** Name the sport and you can find it here. Three reefs along the shoreline and sunken ships create excellent diving. There's sport fishing, tournament fishing, water-skiing, sailing, etc. **River/gulf/ocean:** With 165 miles of navigable waterways, 23 miles of beach, hundreds of canals, Bahia Mar Yacht Basin, Port Everglades and the New River, Fort Lauderdale is also known as the "Venice of America." **Running/walking/biking:** Downtowners enjoy the Riverwalk. Many municipal recreation areas have trails. **Horses/riding:** Stables and riding academies offer training, boarding and trail rides. **Hunting:** None. **Movie theaters:** More than 20. **Art museums:** The Museum of Art, Broward Art Guild and Art Institute of Florida. **History museums:** Fort Lauderdale Historical Society Museum and Stranahan House. **Theaters:** Broward Center for the Performing Arts offers plays and music. Parker Playhouse does Broadway shows. **Library:** Broward County Main Library is an eight-story, 261,000-square-foot research and resource center. Branches throughout. **Attractions:** Bonnet House, International Swimming Hall of Fame, King-Cromartie House, Manatee Viewing Area, Seminole Indian Village, Esplanade Park, Discovery Center and Museum of Archaeology. **Necessities:** Urban advantage — it's all here.

Smart Shopper Tip: Ten miles west of Fort Lauderdale is Sawgrass Mills, the world's largest outlet mall. The Swap Shop is a huge flea market with entertainment. There's also the 150-store Galleria and 138-store Broward Mall. Wander down Las Olas Boulevard to enjoy an eclectic collection of chic shops and restaurants.

WHO LIVES HERE
Population: 105,175 year-round residents, an increase of 937 people since 1990. **Age 65+** = 19.3% in Broward County. **Median household income:** $31,289 (Broward County). **Per capita income:** $26,192 (Broward County).

NUMBERS TO KNOW
Chamber of commerce: (954) 462-6000. **Voter registration:** (954) 357-7050. **Vehicle registration, tags & title:** (954) 765-4560. **Driver's license:** (954) 327-6333. **Visitors bureau:** (954) 765-4466. **Arts & entertainment hotline:** (954) 357-5700.

WHAT TO READ
Sun Sentinel, daily newspaper, (954) 356-4000. **Visitor's Guide**, from the chamber of commerce, (954) 462-6000.

GETTING AROUND
Bus: Broward County Mass Transit, (954) 357-8400. **Taxi:** Friendly Checker, (954) 923-2302, and Yellow Cab, (954) 565-5400. **Tours:** Water Taxi, (954) 467-6677. **Airport:** Fort Lauderdale International, (954) 359-6100. **Traffic:** Surprisingly, traffic within the city is not that bad. But long lines form getting in and out of town at rush hour.

JOBS
County unemployment rate: 5.0%. **Florida Jobs and Benefits:** (954) 677-5400.

UTILITIES
Electricity: Florida Power & Light, (954) 797-5000. **Gas:** Peoples Gas, (954) 763-8900. **Water & sewer:** City of Fort Lauderdale, (954) 761-5150. **Telephone:** Bell South, (800) 789-9025 in Florida, or (800) 753-0710 out-of-state. **Cable TV:** Comcast Cable, (954) 527-6600.

PLACES OF WORSHIP
Thirty-six Catholic and 408 Protestant churches, plus 16 Jewish synagogues.

THE ENVIRONMENT
Surface-water quality has been rated as fair to poor. The New River has been adversely affected by urban and agricultural water runoff, illegal septic tank discharge, vessel sewage discharge and, in the past, discharge from waste-water treatment plants. Some areas have potentially high coliform bacteria counts. Canals also are frequently choked with weeds, which are mechanically removed or treated with herbicides. Metals including tin, copper, zinc and chromium have been found in sediment at all marina sites.

There are seven EPA-listed Superfund sites in Broward County, and three of them are in Fort Lauderdale.

Nearby, the City of Dania's Public Water System was found to have lead levels measuring 78 parts per billion (ppb), exceeding the EPA's action level of 15 ppb.

EVENTS AND FESTIVALS
Riverwalk Arts & Crafts Show - January. **Las Olas Art Festival** - March. **Florida Derby Day at Gulf Stream County Park**- March. **Fort Lauderdale Fall Home Show** - September. **Fort Lauderdale International Boat Show** - October/November. **Winterfest Boat Parade & Light Up Lauderdale** - December.

WHERE TO EAT
There are more than 2,500 restaurants in Greater Fort Lauderdale.

WHERE TO STAY
Pier 66 Hotel & Marina, (954) 525-6666. **Lago Mar**, (954) 523-6511. **Riverside**, (954) 467-0671.

ISSUES
Random violence in south Florida is causing a drop in tourism. Some also attribute the population flight to western suburbs to urban violence.

Contradictions in building codes and leniency in zoning cause some concern among residents. For example, homeowners are testing and contesting the regulations regarding maximum height of ocean-front homes. The city has a height limit of 35 feet, but the state's building code allows ocean-front, single-family homes to rise 35 feet from the bottom of the first inhabited floor. One homeowner built a first-floor living space 17.9 feet above sea level, presumably to allow tidal surges to wash under the home.

Longtime Fort Lauderdale real estate agent Gloria Gold feels zoning is a big issue. According to Gold, the zoning commission is too liberal in permitting non-conforming structures and uses. She urges stronger controls to protect residential areas and beaches, much the same way the downtown area has benefited from planned redevelopment.

Fort Myers

HE SAID: ★ ★ ★ ★ ★
*It is one of my favorite Gulf Coast cities even though
the Gulf is actually about 12 miles away. I would have
no qualms about spending my retirement here. The most
difficult choice would be that of location: riverfront
condominium, single-family home on a canal, golf course
villa or townhouse.*

SHE SAID: ★ ★ ★
*It truly is the "City of Palms." Beautiful residential areas
and plenty to do to keep busy. The only drawback is lots and
lots of traffic. I would not look here.*

McGregor Boulevard is one of the premier streets in Florida. The address of the Thomas Edison and Henry Ford winter estates, the Burroughs Home, Fort Myers Country Club and some of the finest residential communities in the city, it runs about 10 miles in a southwesterly direction culminating at the Sanibel-Captiva Island Causeway. Along much of the way it parallels the Caloosahatchee River enroute to the Gulf.

Looking west toward the river, a motorist can see the sparkling high-rise condominiums that are popular with many retirees, neighborhoods of upscale, canal-front homes and smaller homes. Beautifully maintained, stately mansions from an earlier time also are within view.

The river is an important focal point for housing as well as for much of the city's activity. It is the site of the Fort Myers Yacht Basin, which draws boats and tall ships from around the world, including many that cross the state via canal from the Atlantic. The Harborside Convention Hall is the rallying point for numerous conventions and trade shows. Centennial Park & Riverwalk is favored for picnicking, strolling, fishing and just quietly enjoying a breathtaking sunset over the broad expanse of the river.

Arts and cultural activities are prominent features of the Fort Myers lifestyle, sharing at least equal billing with recreational pursuits. Forty-eight golf courses, dozens of parks and recreation centers, an abundance of yacht clubs, marinas, docks and piers lure residents and tourists alike to engage in outdoor fun and games.

Health care is another noted resource. Southwest Florida Regional Medical Center's open-heart surgery program is recognized as one of the best in the state. Five hospitals and medical centers are situated within Greater Fort Myers to provide quick access to medical expertise no matter where you live.

Fort Myers has a unique combination of small-town charm and big-city sophistication. Towering royal palms and huge oaks have a way of narrowing wide boulevards and not-so-wide back streets to lend a Key West quality to many of the older areas. Elegant mansions are nestled in perfect harmony alongside fine, smaller homes, giving the casual passerby a sense of community. The Spanish Mediterranean architecture that prevails throughout the city heightens the effect. The composite impression may make you yearn to be part of it.

WEATHER

	Winter	Spring	Summer	Fall
Normal daily high/low	76/55	88/68	91/75	81/62
Normal precipitation	7 in.	14 in.	26 in.	6 in.

Disaster watch: Southwest Florida has been hit by five major hurricanes since 1900.

TAXES
Sales tax: 6%. **Property tax:** From $17.25 to $22.85 per $1,000

valuation. Sample tax calculations at $22.85 include a $25,000 homestead exemption.

Home value	Tax
$100,000	$1,714
$150,000	$2,856
$250,000	$5,141

REAL ESTATE
Median home value: $96,397 (Lee County). **Median rent:** $641/month (Lee County). **Communities popular with retirees:** The McGregor Boulevard area has resales and new single-family homes and canal homes priced from the low $100s to more than $1 million. Riverfront and off-water condos range from the mid-$60s to the $300s. Parker Lakes offers single-family homes with prices from the mid-$100s to $200s and villas from the $120s to $140s, (941) 482-8070. **Licensed continuing-care retirement communities:** Calusa Harbor, 371 independent living units, 40 sheltered nursing beds and 60 community beds, (941) 332-3333. Shell Point Village, 836 independent living units, 149 sheltered nursing beds and 31 community beds, (941) 466-1111.

CRIME & SAFETY
Crimes per 1,000 population: 152. **Non-emergency police:** (941) 338-2111. **Non-emergency fire department:** (941) 334-6222. **Police, fire, ambulance emergencies:** 911.

HOMELESS & BLIGHT
Fort Myers is a mostly beautiful city with some problem areas in the northern section. Some shopping centers have closed and stores relocated due to a combination of low sales volume and excessive crime. Steps are being taken to rejuvenate these neighborhoods and stores are beginning to reopen. We saw no homeless persons.

The U.S. Census reported 97 homeless persons in shelters and 203 visible in street locations in Lee County, population 335,113.

HEALTH CARE
Hospitals: Charter Glade Hospital, 144 beds, (941) 939-0403. **Gulf Coast Hospital**, 120 beds, full service, (941) 768-5000. **Lee Memorial Hospital**, 647 beds, full service, (941) 332-1111. **Southwest Florida Regional Medical Center**, 400 beds, full service, (941) 939-1147.
Physicians: 742. **Specialties:** 60.

GETTING SMART
Lee County School District, adult and continuing education, (941) 334-7172. **Offerings:** Courses are designed to broaden general knowledge and introduce new subjects. **Barry University**, (941) 278-3041. **Offerings:** Adult and continuing education. **Edison Community College**, (941) 489-9300; continuing education, (941) 489-9235. **Offerings:** Two-year degrees and continuing-education programs. **Florida Gulf Coast University**, (941) 590-1000, the state's 10th public school, opened in the fall of 1997. Anticipated maximum enrollment is 10,000. **The University of South Florida – Fort Myers** campus was phased into the new school. **Offerings:** Undergraduate and graduate degrees.

JUST FOR SENIORS
City of Fort Myers Senior Center, (941) 332-1288. **Dr. Ella Piper**

Center, (941) 332-5346. **Lake Kennedy Senior Center**, (941) 574-0575.

GETTING INVOLVED
Lee County Alliance of the Arts, (941) 939-2787. **Senior Friendship Centers**, (941) 275-1881. **SCORE**, (941) 489-2935.

RECREATION, ENTERTAINMENT & AMENITIES
Public golf: Eastwood Golf Course, 18 holes/par 72; Fort Myers Country Club, 18 holes/par 72; Gateway Golf & Country Club, 18 holes/par 72; River's Edge Country Club, 18 holes/par 72; Golfview, semiprivate, nine holes/par 27; Kelly Greens, semiprivate, 18 holes/par 72; Olde Hickory Golf & Country Club, semiprivate, 18 holes/par 72; and San Carlos Golf Club, semiprivate, 18 holes/par 71. **Private golf:** Cross Creek Country Club, 18 holes/par 60; Eagle Ridge Golf Club; Fiddlesticks Country Club; and The Landings. **Public tennis courts:** Bay Beach Racquet Club, Billy Bowlegs Park, The Dunes, F.M. Racquet Club, Jerry Brooks Park and Oasis Tennis Club. **Private tennis courts:** Gateway Golf & Tennis Club and Park Meadow Tennis Club. **Parks:** More than 24 parks, beaches and wildlife refuges in Lee County. Centennial Park & Riverwalk, Lovers Key State Recreation Area, Nature Center & Planetarium of Lee County, Lakes Park, Billy Bowlegs Park and a six-mile cypress swamp. **Public swimming pools:** Wes Nott Swimming Pool and Billy Bowlegs Park. **Water sports:** Boating, canoeing, sailing and water-skiing. **River/gulf/ocean:** Caloosahatchee River, Estero Bay and San Carlos Bay. **Running/ walking/biking:** Edwards Drive along the riverfront, nature trails in parks and McGregor Boulevard. **Horses/riding:** There are ranches, stables and riding academies in town. **Hunting:** None. **Movie theaters:** 46 screens. **Art museums:** William R. Frizzell Cultural Center. **History museums:** Fort Myers Historical Museum. **Theaters:** Arcade Theater, Barbara B. Mann Performing Arts Hall, Harborside Convention Hall and William R. Frizzell Cultural Center. **Library:** Fort Myers/Lee County. **Attractions:** Eden Vineyards Winery & Park, Fort Myers Yacht Basin, Nature Center & Planetarium, Burroughs Home, Thomas Edison's winter home and Mangoes (Henry Ford's winter home), Seminole Gulf Railway and the Boston Red Sox spring training camp. **Necessities:** All here.

Smart Shopper Tip: Edison Mall, Bell Tower Mall, Sanibel Factory Stores, Royal Palm Square and Metro Mall are all worthy of a visit.

WHO LIVES HERE
Population: 46,522 year-round residents, an increase of 1,575 since 1990. **Age 65+** = 25.7% in Lee County. **Median household income:** $29,174 (Lee County). **Per capita income:** $23,664 (Lee County).

NUMBERS TO KNOW
Chamber of commerce: (941) 332-3624. **Voter registration:** (941) 339-6300. **Vehicle registration, tags & title:** (941) 339-6000. **Driver's license:** (941) 278-7192. **Public Resources:** Helps residents identify and locate municipal agencies, local social service organizations, (941) 332-2737.

WHAT TO READ
Fort Myers News-Press, daily newspaper, (941) 335-0233. **Sun Coast Visitor's Guide**, (941) 481-0266.

GETTING AROUND
Bus: Lee TRAN, (941) 275-8726. **Taxi:** Bluebird Taxi, (941) 275-8294. **Tours:** Babcock Wilderness Adventures, (941) 489-3911. J.C. Sightseeing Boat Cruises, (941) 334-6652. **Airport:** Southwest Florida International. **Traffic:** Timing is important. McGregor Boulevard and the Caloosahatchee River bridges become bottlenecks during rush hour.

JOBS
County unemployment rate: 3.3%. **Florida Jobs and Benefits:** (941) 278-7140.

UTILITIES
Electricity: Florida Power & Light, (941) 334-7754. **Gas:** None. **Water & sewer:** City of Fort Myers, (941) 332-6855. **Telephone:** Sprint/United Telephone, (800) 699-0728. **Cable TV:** Adelphia Cable, (941) 334-8055, or Media One, (941) 793-3433, depending on location of residence.

PLACES OF WORSHIP
Eleven Catholic and 137 Protestant churches, plus five Jewish synagogues.

THE ENVIRONMENT
The EPA reported that the Fort Myers Water District, serving a population of 52,500, had lead levels of 43 parts per billion (ppb) in its drinking water. The EPA action level for lead is 15 ppb.

The Caloosahatchee River State Recreation Area has protected status as an Outstanding Florida Water. The Caloosahatchee Estuary has a fair to poor water quality rating. It is affected by channelization and urban and agricultural runoff. Polluted tributaries flow into the Caloosahatchee. The river's water quality ranges from good at and above Orange River, to fair in the Fort Myers area, to poor just upstream. Fort Myers uses the Caloosahatchee River above Franklin Locks and above the Orange River as its potable water source.

EVENTS AND FESTIVALS
Lee Sidewalk Arts & Crafts Show - January. **Edison Festival of Light** - February. **Hibiscus Show & Plant Sale** - June. **New Arts Festival** - August. **Taste of the Town** - November. **Christmas in Downtown** - December.

WHERE TO EAT
Peter's La Cuisine, 2224 Bay St., continental, expensive, (941) 332-2228. **The Veranda**, 2122 Second St., continental, expensive, (941) 332-2065.

WHERE TO STAY
Courtyard by Marriott, (941) 275-8600. **Radisson Inn**, (941) 936-4300. **Amtel Marina Hotel & Suites**, (941) 337-0300. **Sanibel Harbor Resort & Spa** is between Sanibel and Fort Myers, (941) 466-4000.

ISSUES
It has so much appeal that everyone wants to be a part of it. New commercial, industrial and residential developments are vying for available land. Can the "City of Palms" retain its small-town charm while growing by "leafs and fronds"?

Fort Myers Beach

HE SAID: ✮ ✮
It's strictly a resort. If I decide to retire to this part of Florida, I'll go with the area's best and retire to either Fort Myers, Sanibel or Naples.

SHE SAID: ✮ ✮
A seasonal resort area, it's too congested for comfort. I would not retire here.

The best feature of Fort Myers Beach is its location between Fort Myers and Naples. These are two outstanding cities with strong appeal for retirees.

The second-best feature is the quality of its clean, wide, white sand beaches. They often are called the world's safest beaches because the water is shallow and there is no undertow. The shallow water means erosion is not a problem either.

You can retire here on Estero Island with just over 6,000 permanent-resident neighbors, but this is not small-town living. You will have to compete for space with some 1.5 million vacationers in southwest Florida who while away a few hours on these sandy shores each year. Visitors jam the island's two-lane road, beaches and other common areas.

The entire island is only seven miles long and a half-mile wide — at its widest point. At some points it is only a stone's throw across. Its 1,600 acres are developed with more than 14 dwelling units per acre. As you can imagine, traffic is horrendous during the peak season. One resident notes, "It has been designated as a Community Redevelopment Agency blighted area because of the level of traffic congestion."

Fort Myers Beach is principally a resort. There are some privately owned and occupied residences, but not all are owner-occupied year-round. The island is finite in size, yet an ever-increasing number of people cross its causeways every year, so congestion can only worsen.

WEATHER

	Winter	Spring	Summer	Fall
Normal daily high/low	76/55	88/68	91/75	81/62
Normal precipitation	7 in.	14 in.	26 in.	6 in.

Disaster watch: Southwest Florida has been hit by five major hurricanes since 1900.

TAXES
Sales tax: 6%. **Property tax:** Rates range from $17.25 to $22.85 per $1,000 valuation. Sample taxes are calculated at the rate of $22.85 and include a $25,000 homestead exemption.

Home value	Tax
$100,000	$1,714
$150,000	$2,856
$250,000	$5,141

REAL ESTATE
Median home value: $107,660 (Lee County). **Median rent:** $641/month (Lee County). **Communities popular with retirees:** Estero Beach & Tennis Club is a high-rise condominium complex on the Gulf with prices ranging from the mid-$80s to low $100s. Resales are available through local real-estate agents. Denise Treinen with Prudential Florida Realty, (941) 463-4488, or (800) 237-2752 notes the following housing options: 500- to 600-square-foot Gulf-front efficiencies start in the $80s; upscale luxury condos are priced up to the $600s; and new bay-front construction is priced from the $200s to $400s. **Licensed continuing-care retirement communities:** None.

CRIME & SAFETY
The Lee County Sheriff's Office maintains a command station at Lynn Hall Park and another just off the island. **Crimes per 1,000 population:** 36 (Lee County sheriff's jurisdiction). **Non-emergency police:** (941) 765-2300. **Non-emergency fire department:** (941) 694-2833. **Emergency Rescue Squad:** (941) 463-6162. **Police, fire, ambulance emergencies:** 911.

HOMELESS & BLIGHT
A noticeable difference between this and many other resort areas is signage control — it is in effect and working here.

The U.S. Census reported 97 homeless persons in shelters and 203 visible in street locations in Lee County, population 335,113.

HEALTH CARE
Hospitals: There are three minor emergency centers on the island, and the beach fire department has life support ambulances to transport patients to hospitals in Fort Myers . **Lee Memorial Health Park Medical Center**, in Fort Myers, 220 beds, full service, (941) 433-7799. **Gulf Coast Hospital**, in Fort Myers, 120 beds, full service, (941) 768-5000. **Lee Memorial Hospital**, in Fort Myers, 407 beds, full service, (941) 332-1111. **Southwest Florida Regional Medical Center**, in Fort Myers, 400 beds, full service, (941) 939-1147.
Physicians: 7. **Specialties:** 3.

GETTING SMART
There are no college or university campuses in Fort Myers Beach, but there are four in Fort Myers. **Florida Gulf Coast University**, (941) 590-1000. **Offerings:** Undergraduate and graduate degree programs. **Edison Community College**, (941) 489-9300; continuing education, (941) 489-9235. **Offerings:** Two-year degrees and continuing-education programs. **Barry University**, (941) 278-3041. **Offerings:** Adult and continuing education. **Lee County School District**, adult and continuing education, (941) 334-7172. **Offerings:** Courses to broaden general knowledge and introduce new subjects.

JUST FOR SENIORS
No programs or facilities just for seniors.

GETTING INVOLVED
Fort Myers Beach Art Association, (941) 463-3909. **Friends of the Library**, (941) 463-9691. Call the chamber for informa-

tion about the **Fort Myers Beach Civic Association** and the **Fort Myers Beach Historical Society**.

RECREATION, ENTERTAINMENT & AMENITIES

Public golf: Bay Beach Golf Course, 18 holes/par 61. **Private golf:** None. **Public tennis courts:** Bay Beach Racquet Club and Bay Oaks Recreation Center. **Private tennis courts:** Estero Beach & Tennis Club. **Parks:** Lynn Hall Memorial Park and a 600-foot fishing pier are centers of activity for beach-goers. The 16-acre Bowditch Point Park is popular with nature walkers and picnickers. **Public swimming pools:** None. **Water sports:** Boating, jet-skiing, parasailing, sailing, shelling, snorkeling, water-skiing and windsurfing. **River/gulf/ocean:** Estero Bay, San Carlos Bay and the Gulf of Mexico. **Running/walking/ biking:** The beach extends the full seven-mile length of the island. Bicycle and pedestrian paths traverse the Matanzas Pass Bridge to the Mainland. **Horses/riding:** None. **Hunting:** None. **Movie theaters:** One screen. **Art museums:** Art Association Building and Red Coconut Arts and Crafts Club. **History museums:** None. **Theaters:** None. **Library:** Fort Myers Beach Public. **Attractions:** Fort Myers Beach rides the coattails of its neighbors, Sanibel Island and Fort Myers, when it comes to attractions. It has a wide, accessible public beach. **Necessities:** Post office, service stations, restaurants, resort accommodations, banks, supermarket and small boutiques.

Smart Shopper Tip: There are no major department or discount stores on the island. Plenty of resort boutiques. Travel to the Sanibel Factory Stores just off the causeway or to one of Fort Myers' four malls.

WHO LIVES HERE

Population: 6,034 year-round residents, 42,000 seasonal residents and more than 1.5 million annual visitors. **Age 65+ =** 25.7% in Lee County. **Median household income:** $29,174 (Lee County). **Per capita income:** $23,664 (Lee County).

NUMBERS TO KNOW

Chamber of commerce: (941) 454-7500 or (800) 782-9283. **Voter registration:** Through the chamber, (941) 454-7500. **Vehicle registration, tags & title:** (941) 339-6000. **Driver's license:** In Fort Myers, (941) 278-7192. **Visitors bureau:** (800) 237-6444.

WHAT TO READ

Beach Bulletin, weekly newspaper, (941) 463-4421. **Beach Observer,** weekly newspaper, (941) 482-7111. **News-Press,** Fort Myers daily newspaper, (941) 335-0200.

GETTING AROUND

Bus: Lee TRAN, (941) 275-8726. Trolley rides are free for seniors. **Taxi:** Yellow Cab, (941) 332-1055. **Tours:** Island Water Tours, (941)765-4354. Captiva Cruises, (941) 472-5300. **Airport:** Southwest Florida International is 12 miles away. **Traffic:** The only thoroughfare, two-lane Estero Boulevard (Route 865), is swamped during tourist season.

JOBS

County unemployment rate: 3.3%. **Florida Jobs and Benefits:** In Fort Myers, (941) 278-7140.

UTILITIES

Electricity: Florida Power & Light, (941) 334-7754. **Gas:** None. **Water & sewer:** Florida Cities Water Co., (941) 936-0247. **Telephone:** Sprint-United Telephone, (941) 335-3111. **Cable TV:** Media One, (941) 432-9277.

PLACES OF WORSHIP

One Catholic and five Protestant churches.

THE ENVIRONMENT

The EPA reported that the Fort Myers Water District, serving a population of 52,500, had lead levels of 43 parts per billion (ppb) in its drinking water. The EPA action level for lead is 15 ppb.

The Caloosahatchee River State Recreation Area has protected status as an Outstanding Florida Water.

The Caloosahatchee Estuary has been rated as having fair to poor water quality. It is affected by channelization and urban and agricultural runoff. Polluted tributaries flow into the Caloosahatchee. The river's quality ranges from good at and above Orange River, to fair in the Fort Myers area, and poor just upstream.

The waters of the Gulf of Mexico in the Estero Bay area are judged to be good, though no sampling has been done. Estero Bay itself has fair to poor water quality ratings on two measurements but is judged to be good overall.

EVENTS AND FESTIVALS

Shrimp Festival - February/March. **American Championship Sandsculpting Festival** - October/November.

WHERE TO EAT

The Bridge, 708 Fisherman's Wharf, seafood, moderate, (941) 765-0050. **Snug Harbor Restaurant,** 645 San Carlos Blvd., seafood, moderate to expensive, (941) 463-4343. **The Mucky Duck,** 2500 Estero Blvd., English pub-style seafood, moderate, (941) 463-5519.

WHERE TO STAY

Santa Maria, (941) 765-6700. **Best Western Pink Shell Beach & Bay Resort,** (941) 463-6181. **Outrigger Beach Resort,** (941) 463-3131.

ISSUES

An effort to stem further development of this already saturated island was the headline issue during our most recent visit.

Fort Pierce

HE SAID: ★
Unattractive and unappealing are the kindest words I can use to describe my feelings about Fort Pierce.

SHE SAID: ★ ★
Country club housing won't sell and is going on auction in this economically distressed city. Manufactured-home communities are offered on leased land without the option to purchase. This is not for me.

The Main Street program to revitalize downtown Fort Pierce was initiated about eight years ago to preserve and restore historic sites and structures. The project includes an $8 million courthouse expansion, a new city hall and an 85,000-square-foot state office building. The Fort Pierce Yacht Center has 99 new slips, and there is a new Harbour Master's building and a half-million dollar Riverwalk, complete with picnic areas and gardens.

But, there are also neighborhoods with littered curbs, shanties, storefront churches, abandoned buildings, vacant lots and rutty dirt roads. Homeless persons and addicts sleep in garbage-strewn alleys.

We saw neighborhoods where zoning either doesn't exist or is ineffective, leaving single-family homes next to trailer parks, multi-story condominiums, motels and furnished apartments. Not a very attractive mix.

We visited a golf and country club community that sounded very appealing on paper. We found there were no homes for sale as the project had been foreclosed. The properties were being disposed of at public auction.

There are some quiet, secluded stretches. Areas on Hutchinson Island and along the Indian River might merit consideration. Someday, the efforts at revitalization may pay off, but this city has a long way to go before its neighborhoods will feel safe and comfortable.

WEATHER

	Winter	Spring	Summer	Fall
Normal daily high/low	75/54	85/67	90/73	80/61
Normal precipitation	8 in.	12 in.	19 in.	11 in.

Disaster watch: Southeast Florida has been hit by nine major hurricanes since 1900.

TAXES
Sales tax: 6%. **Property tax:** $28.65 per $1,000 valuation. Sample taxes include a $25,000 homestead exemption.

Home value	Tax
$100,000	$2,149
$150,000	$3,581
$250,000	$6,446

REAL ESTATE
Median home value: $87,020 (St. Lucie County). **Median rent:** $549/month (St. Lucie County). **Communities popular with retirees:** Gator Trace offers condominiums priced from the mid-$70s, garden villas from the high $80s to high $90s and single-family homes from the $140s to $200s, (561) 464-7442. **Licensed continuing-care retirement communities:** None.

CRIME & SAFETY
Crimes per 1,000 population: 150. **Non-emergency police:** (561) 461-3820. **Non-emergency fire department:** (561) 462-2300. **Police, fire, ambulance emergencies:** 911.

HOMELESS & BLIGHT
Just about everywhere there are signs of blight, run-down homes and abandoned buildings. In fact, it seems as though more of Fort Pierce is blighted than not.

According to the U.S. Census, St. Lucie County, population 150,171, had 336 homeless persons, with 309 counted in shelters and 27 on the streets.

HEALTH CARE
Hospitals: Columbia Lawnwood Regional Medical Center, 353 beds, full service, (561) 461-4000. **Columbia Lawnwood Pavilion**, 60 beds, psychiatry, (561) 466-1500.
Physicians: 150+ (St. Lucie County). **Specialties:** 38+.

GETTING SMART
Indian River Community College, (561) 462-4722. **Offerings:** More than 100 two-year degree progams and continuing education for personal enhancement. **Barry University**, (561) 871-8000. **Offerings:** Adult and continuing education, degree programs in nursing, business and arts and sciences. **Florida Atlantic University**, (561) 785-9970. **Offerings:** Those 60 and over can audit regular courses free of charge on a space-available basis. There is a class fee for people ages 50-59. Registration is at the main campus in Boca Raton. For more information on the program for those 60 and older, (561) 297-3294.

JUST FOR SENIORS
AARP, (561) 461-9049. **Helping Hand Neighbors Senior Center**, (561) 464-7880. **St. Lucie County Council on Aging** and **St. Lucie County Senior Center**, (561) 465-5220, provide education, recreation, transportation, financial assistance, adult day care and RSVP.

GETTING INVOLVED
Approximately 150 organizations are listed in the Fort Pierce directory including **RSVP**, (561) 732-1674, and **SCORE**, (561) 489-0548.

RECREATION, ENTERTAINMENT & AMENITIES
Public golf: Gator Trace Golf & Country Club, semiprivate, 18 holes/par 70; Indian Pines, 18 holes/par 70; Indian Hills, 18 holes; and Fairwinds Golf Course, semiprivate, 18 holes/par 70.
Private golf: Spanish Lakes Fairways, 18 holes, and Meadowood Golf & Country Club, 18 holes/par 72. **Public tennis courts:** Lawnwood Recreational Complex, 10 courts; Pepper Beach Park, two courts; Jaycee Park, four courts; and Lakewood Park. **Private tennis courts:** Meadowood Golf & Country Club.
Parks: City parks are Dreamland, Fort Pierce Community Center, Jaycee Park Jetty, Pinewood, Pioneer, Rotary, Surfside, 10th Street and 29th Street. There's also the Savannas Recreation Area, Lawnwood Recreation Complex, the Fort Pierce Inlet State Recreation Area and Frederick Douglass Memorial

Park on Hutchinson Island. **Public swimming pools:** St. Lucie County Open Space Park and Paradise Park. **Water sports:** Swimming, boating, snorkeling, scuba diving, surfing, sport fishing, board sailing and water-skiing. **River/gulf/ocean:** St. Lucie County has 21 miles of ocean front and 50 miles of shoreline on the Indian River, but Fort Pierce has just 3,231 feet of ocean front. The Savannas (the last freshwater lagoon system in the state), canals and creeks provide opportunities for freshwater fishing. Fort Pierce Inlet is the Intracoastal Waterway's opening to the Atlantic. The South Beach Fishing Jetty is a renowned fisherman's paradise. **Running/walking/biking:** Lawnwood Recreation Complex Nature Trails, Rivergate Park, Savannas Recreation Area and Jack Island State Preserve, where only foot traffic is allowed. **Horses/riding:** One stable offers training and boarding facilities, (561) 468-0101. **Hunting:** Licenses required for fishing and hunting. Florida Game and Freshwater Fish Commission, (561) 625-5122. **Movie theaters:** Two theaters, more than six screens. **Art museums:** Backus Art Gallery. **History museums:** St. Lucie County Historical Museum. **Theaters:** McAlphin Fine Arts Center hosts concerts, plays, lectures and other events at the Indian River Community College campus. St. Lucie Community Theater produces theater events for adults and children. St. Lucie County Civic Center presents opera, ballet and other events. Indian River Memorial Park Amphitheater hosts musical and stage productions. **Library:** St. Lucie County Library, Lakewood Park and the Main Library. **Attractions:** Fort Pierce Jai Alai Fronton, the UDT-SEAL Museum, which displays gear used by underwater demolition teams, and the Heathcote Botanical Gardens. **Necessities:** All necessities are here.

Smart Shopper Tip: Okeechobee Road is a shopper's mecca with the Orange Blossom Mall, Wal-Mart Plaza and the Manufacturers' Outlet Center less than a mile apart.

WHO LIVES HERE
Population: 37,484 year-round residents, an increase of 654 since 1990. **Age 65+** = 22.7% in St. Lucie County. **Median household income:** $26,387 (St. Lucie County). **Per capita income:** $17,747 (St. Lucie County).

NUMBERS TO KNOW
Chamber of commerce: (561) 461-2700. **Voter registration:** (561) 462-1500. **Vehicle registration, tags & title:** (561) 462-1653. **Driver's license:** (561) 468-3956.

WHAT TO READ
The Tribune, daily newspaper, (561) 461-2050.

GETTING AROUND
Bus: Community Transit, (561) 464-7433. **Taxi:** Pronto Taxi, (561) 335-7510. **Tours:** St. Lucie River Tours, (561) 871-2817. **Airport:** Palm Beach International is the closest airport offering commercial service. St. Lucie County International Airport is for commuter and private aircraft. **Traffic:** Very light.

JOBS
County unemployment rate: 12.6%. **Florida Jobs and Benefits:**

(561) 468-4060.

UTILITIES
Electricity: Fort Pierce Utilities, (561) 466-1600. **Gas:** Fort Pierce Utilities, Natural Gas Dept., (561) 466-1600. **Water & sewer:** Fort Pierce Utilities, (561) 466-1600. **Telephone:** Bell South, (800) 789-9025 in Florida, or (800) 753-0710 out-of-state. **Cable TV:** TCI, (561) 461-5311.

PLACES OF WORSHIP
Three Catholic and 100-plus Protestant churches, plus one Jewish synagogue.

THE ENVIRONMENT
A 1992 air quality summary reported two incidents when Fort Pierce did not meet the standards for particulate matter in the air. Other air pollutants levels were not tested.

Fort Pierce generally has been rated as having fairly good surface water quality, but has other problems. Concentrations of mercury in fish tissue were high enough to warrant a no-consumption advisory for largemouth bass from the Savannas in the area between Fort Pierce and Stuart.

The EPA reported lead levels in the drinking water of St. Lucie County Utilities of 41 parts per billion (ppb). The EPA action level for lead is 15 ppb.

EVENTS AND FESTIVALS
Mardi Gras - February. **Backus Daze** - Mid-March. **Sights and Sounds of Christmas Festival** - Sunday after Thanksgiving.

WHERE TO EAT
Captain's Galley, 825 N. Indian River Drive, seafood, American, busy for breakfast, inexpensive to moderate, (561) 466-8495. **Mangrove Mattie's**, 1640 Seaway Drive, seafood, moderate to expensive, (561) 466-1044. **P.V. Martin's**, 5150 N. Route A1A, American, moderate to expensive, (561) 465-7300.

WHERE TO STAY
Harbor Light Inn-Edgewater Motel, (561) 468-3555 or (800) 286-1745. **Mellon Patch Inn**, (561) 461-5231 or (800) 656-7824.

ISSUES
The problems facing this town are numerous. The high crime and unemployment rates, high incidence of substandard housing and a growing reluctance of retirees and others to settle in this southeast quadrant of Florida are being addressed through a mostly government-sponsored building program designed to revitalize the downtown and waterfront sections.

A retiree who lives in a secured building, 12-story Seapoint Towers on Hutchinson Island, characterized the town as "a mess," with rampant drug abuse and institutionalized unemployment. This retiree likes her own "safe" environment, but noted that the ocean is trying to recapture the island. If you like Hutchinson Island, check out erosion problems before buying.

Fort Walton Beach

HE SAID: ★ ★ ★
I enjoyed visiting Fort Walton Beach. I like its small-town atmosphere and imagine it's great for military retirees who like the proximity to Eglin Air Force Base. But with water on three sides and a huge air force base on the fourth side there's no room for newcomers. Great for vacationing but I wouldn't want to retire here.

SHE SAID: ★ ★ ★
Fort Walton is a popular family beach, clean and not so heavily traveled. The town and its residential areas are separated from the beach by the Intracoastal Waterway, which is great for getting away from the beach crowd and traffic. Seems to be a great place for military retirees. I might consider retiring here.

It is more than a case of simple oversight that the Emerald Coast Newcomer's Guide describes Fort Walton Beach as a place to "begin a business, move a business to, raise a family, or just visit," but not as a place to retire.

It's a wonderful place to vacation. The people are as warm and inviting as the beaches. It offers just about every type of goods and services. But, it's a little too crowded and not in a position to do much about it. In 1940, there were about 90 people living in Fort Walton Beach. Today, the incorporated area has more than 22,000 people. That doesn't sound like much, but consider that Greater Fort Walton Beach has about 85,000 residents and add in thousands of tourists, and it becomes too crowded and busy.

Two factors may make the area unattractive to retirees. First, all east-west traffic goes squarely through the heart of town on U.S. Highway 98, creating horrendous traffic jams during tourist season. Worse, there is little possibility of rerouting traffic, since there is no viable alternate route. Second, and more important, the town cannot expand its boundaries. Eglin Air Force Base, the largest in the country, completely shuts off any chance for future expansion of the city limits. The only way for Fort Walton to grow is up.

So, while Fort Walton Beach is the largest community between Pensacola and Panama City, with more cultural amenities and shopping facilities than surrounding towns and the beautiful emerald-green waters and snow-white sands of Santa Rosa Island, it is not the premier retirement mecca in the area. Both Destin and Sandestin attract a larger percentage of older newcomers.

WEATHER

	Winter	Spring	Summer	Fall
Normal daily high/low	65/41	84/61	90/69	72/47
Normal precipitation	17 in.	14 in.	21 in.	13 in.

Disaster watch: Northwest Florida has been hit by six major hurricanes since 1900.

TAXES
Sales tax: 7%. **Property tax:** $18.12 per $1,000 valuation. Sample tax calculations include a $25,000 homestead exemption.

Home value	Tax
$100,000	$1,359
$150,000	$2,265
$250,000	$4,077

REAL ESTATE
Median home value: $85,517 (Okaloosa County). **Median rent:** $598/month (Okaloosa County). **Communities popular with retirees:** Bob Hope Village, (850) 651-5770, and Teresa Village, (850) 862-8778, have apartments, primarily occupied by widows of Air Force enlisted persons. Westwood Retirement Community offers full-service, independent-living apartments, (850) 863-5174. Bluewater Bay, near Fort Walton Beach, is a 2,000-acre planned community with prices ranging from the low $100s to more than $500,000 for patio homes, townhomes and single-family homes, (850) 897-2879. **Licensed continuing-care retirement communities:** None.

CRIME & SAFETY
Crimes per 1,000 population: 53. **Non-emergency police:** (850) 244-8111. **Non-emergency fire department:** (850) 863-1134. **Police, fire, ambulance emergencies:** 911.

HOMELESS & BLIGHT
Like most resort towns, Fort Walton Beach has an abundance of billboards and neon lights. We didn't see any homeless persons.

The U.S. Census reported a population of 143,776 for the county, with 40 homeless persons counted in shelters and 17 visible on the streets.

HEALTH CARE
Hospitals: Fort Walton Beach Medical Center, 247 beds, acute care, full service, (850) 862-1111. **Gulf Coast Treatment Center**, 79 beds, psychiatry, (850) 863-4160. **Physicians:** 145. **Specialties:** 32.

GETTING SMART
Okaloosa-Walton Community College, (850) 678-5111. **Offerings:** More than 60 associate's degrees. **University of West Florida**, (850) 863-6565. **Offerings:** Undergraduate and graduate degrees. **Troy State University**, (850) 244-7414. **Offerings:** Undergraduate and graduate degrees.

JUST FOR SENIORS
Elder Services of Okaloosa County, (850) 833-9165. **Senior Citizens Center**, (850) 244-1511, has more than 600 members, plus 250 non-resident members during the winter. **Senior Friends Association**, (850) 863-7590, is affiliated with Fort Walton Beach Medical Center.

GETTING INVOLVED
There are 16 social service organizations here. **Meals on Wheels**, (850) 833-9165. **RSVP**, (850) 833-9165.

RECREATION, ENTERTAINMENT & AMENITIES
Public golf: Fort Walton Beach Municipal Golf Course, 36 holes, and Shalimar Pointe Golf & Country Club. **Private golf:** Hurlburt Field (U.S. Air Force) Golf Course. **Public tennis courts:** Fort Walton Beach Municipal Tennis Center and Shalimar Pointe Resort Tennis Center. **Private tennis courts:** Fort Walton Racquet Club. **Parks:** Six city athletic complexes, five multipurpose community centers, 11 city parks and three county parks. **Public swimming pools:** Embry Riddle. **Water sports:** Boating, especially sailing on Choctawhatchee Bay, surfing, parasailing, scuba diving, snorkeling, water-skiing,

fishing and canoeing. **River/gulf/ocean:** Cinco Bayou forms the northern boundary of the city. Choctawhatchee Bay curves around the east. Santa Rosa Sound and The Narrows form the southern border. Santa Rosa Island lies between the city and the Gulf. **Running/walking/biking:** Besides shoreline paths, there is the Vesta Heights Park track. The Northwest Florida Track Club sponsors more than 10 races each year. **Horses/riding:** Numerous stables are located in the county. No horseback riding on beaches. **Hunting:** Eglin Reservation, (850) 882-4164, has hunting, fishing, camping and recreation facilities on 464,000 acres. **Movie theaters:** 18 screens. **Art museums:** Fort Walton Beach Art Museum and the Arts & Design Society. **History museums:** Indian Temple Mound Museum & Park. **Theaters/performing arts:** Okaloosa-Walton Community College Proscenium Playhouse & Music Theatre, Stage Crafters Community Theatre, Community Concert Association, Okaloosa Symphony Orchestra, Northwest Florida Ballet, Emerald Coast Community Band and Fort Walton Beach Community Chorus. **Library:** City of Fort Walton Beach Public Library. **Attractions:** Air Force Armament Museum, Eglin Air Force Base, Focus Center, Gulfarium and Okaloosa Island Fishing Pier. **Necessities:** All available.

   Smart Shopper Tip: Among the hundreds of stores, look to Santa Rosa Mall with more than 100 shops and four major department stores. Or, bargain shop among the Manufacturer's Outlet Center's 30 name-brand stores.

WHO LIVES HERE
Population: 22,044 year-round residents, an increase of 637 since 1990. **Age 65+ =** 10.6% in Okaloosa County. **Median household income:** $31,520 (Okaloosa County). **Per capita income:** $19,795 (Okaloosa County).

NUMBERS TO KNOW
Chamber of commerce: (850) 244-8191. **Voter registration:** (850) 651-7272. **Vehicle registration, tags & title:** (850) 651-7300. **Driver's license:** (850) 833-9121. **Visitors bureau:** (850) 651-7131.

WHAT TO READ
The Daily News, daily newspaper, (850) 863-1111. **Okaloosa News Leader,** weekly newspaper, (850) 689-1492. **Okaloosa County Reporter,** weekly newspaper, (850) 863-3549.

GETTING AROUND
Bus: No public intra-city transportation. **Taxi:** Emerald Coast Taxi, (850) 244-3242. **Tours:** None. **Airport:** Okaloosa County Air Terminal. **Traffic:** On average, 34,900 vehicles travel daily on U.S. Highway 98 through Fort Walton Beach.

JOBS
County unemployment rate: 3.4%. **Florida Jobs and Benefits:** (850) 833-9106.

UTILITIES
Electricity: Gulf Power Co., (850) 244-4770. **Gas:** Okaloosa County Gas District, (850) 968-9873. **Water & sewer:** Fort Walton Beach Utilities, (850) 243-3141. **Telephone:** Sprint-CENTEL,

(850) 664-3200, or 811 locally. **Cable TV:** Cox Communications, (850) 862-0175.

PLACES OF WORSHIP
Two Catholic and 75 Protestant churches, one Buddhist temple and one Jewish synagogue.

THE ENVIRONMENT
The area has had good water quality ratings due to sparse development and little use. In recent years, Dons Bayou has experienced a low-grade, chronic fish kill from unknown sources.

EVENTS AND FESTIVALS
Annual Fort Walton Beach Seafood Festival - April. **St. Mary's Spring Fling** - April. **Struggling Artists' Show & Sale** - May and November. **Billy Bowlegs Festival** - June. **Festival of Greece** - September. **Fiesta Italiana** - October.

WHERE TO EAT
Los Rancheros, 300 Eglin Parkway, Mexican, moderate, (850) 862-2007.

WHERE TO STAY
Holiday Inn, (850) 932-2214. **Ramada Beach Resort,** (800) 447-0010, (800) 472-1790 or (850) 243-9161.

ISSUES
It is our observation — right or wrong — that Fort Walton Beach has its hands full trying to satisfy the needs of its two major constituencies — the military and the vacationers. It has little time or space for retirees.

RELOCATION TIPS

Once you've arrived at your new home, don't sign the inventory sheet from the moving company until you've carefully surveyed each box and item as they are unloaded, no matter how tired and distracted you feel. A signed inventory sheet is your agreement that all of your belongings arrived in "apparent good condition" — unless you have added some notes to the contrary.

Beware of boxes that look like they've been crushed. They probably have been. Carefully inspect the contents of every box that appears damaged. And, while the driver is unloading the truck, check on the items in "fragile" boxes to make sure that they survived the trip intact.

Gainesville

HE SAID: ☆ ☆ ☆ ☆ ☆

The large network of active seniors — volunteering time and talent to numerous worthy causes and enjoying a plethora of social, educational and recreational activities — attests to the quality of life to be expected on retiring to Gainesville. This place certainly has a high rank on any short list of potential retirement sites I might compile.

SHE SAID: ☆ ☆ ☆ ☆

This is a clean, slow-paced college town with friendly people and a lot to offer. Entering the city, I noticed the well-maintained residential areas. I felt very safe. I could look for a place to retire here.

The Gainesville Metropolitan Statistical Area had a labor force of 114,346 persons in 1997, and all but 3,659, or 3.2 percent, were employed. It is the home of a college and a university which together employ about 14,000 and are attended by more than 46,000. The city is served by six health-care centers with more than 1,800 beds and more than 1,400 physicians and surgeons on staff.

Within a 25-mile radius of the city are municipal, county, state and national parks, wildlife preserves, lakes, springs, rivers and forests. In other words, there is easy access to outstanding recreation. The Gainesville area has enough man-made and natural resources to reward those seeking the great outdoors.

Housing options run the gamut. Take a look at Haile Plantation, a master-planned community of single-family homes; The Atrium and The Village, full-service, independent-living rental retirement communities; or Mile Run, a prestigious planned community with garden homes and single-family homes.

A great network of interstates and U.S. highways crisscross the area. Gainesville is close enough to east and west coast population centers to allow residents to participate in coastal-area activities. Better still, it is far enough removed that residents can avoid the frenzy of people and traffic that plague both coasts.

These are just a few of the superlatives that make Gainesville a special place to live. While the downtown stays busy, it is not a beehive of activity, nor is it the domicile of towering skyscrapers. It is attractive and progressive looking, with a hint of small-town ambiance.

WEATHER

	Winter	Spring	Summer	Fall
Normal daily high/low	70/46	86/63	90/71	75/53
Normal precipitation	11 in.	13 in.	20 in.	7 in.

Disaster watch: North-central Florida is primarily affected by tropical storms and thunderstorms. Northeast Florida has not been hit by a major hurricane since 1900.

TAXES

Sales tax: 6%. **Property tax:** $28.44 per $1,000 valuation. Sample taxes include a $25,000 homestead exemption.

Home value	Tax
$100,000	$2,133
$150,000	$3,555
$250,000	$6,399

REAL ESTATE

Median home value: $86,900 (Alachua County). **Median rent:** $607/month (Alachua County). **Communities popular with retir-** ees: The Atrium is a full-service rental retirement community, (352) 378-0773. Haile Plantation is a master-planned community with 20-plus neighborhoods of single-family homes and garden villas priced from the low $100s to more than $600,000, (352) 335-4999. Mile Run offers garden homes and single-family homes priced from the $90s to $150s, (352) 374-4225. The Village offers luxury apartments on 80 wooded acres, (352) 373-4032. **Licensed continuing-care retirement communities:** None.

CRIME & SAFETY

Crimes per 1,000 population: 101. **Non-emergency police:** (352) 334-2400. **Non-emergency fire department:** (352) 334-2590. **Police, fire, ambulance emergencies:** 911.

HOMELESS & BLIGHT

The city is clean, open and attractive. We did not note any homeless. According to the U.S. Census, Alachua County's population of 181,596 included 35 homeless persons in shelters and seven visible in street locations.

HEALTH CARE

Hospitals: There are six hospitals in Gainesville including the following. **Alachua General Hospital**, 424 beds, full service, (352) 372-4321. **Columbia North Florida Regional Center**, 278 beds, acute care, specialties, full service, (352) 333-4000. **Shands Hospital** at the University of Florida, 576 beds, full service, (352) 395-0111. **Veterans Administration Hospital**, 478 beds plus 120-bed nursing home, (352) 376-1611.
Physicians: 1,400+. **Specialties:** All represented.

GETTING SMART

University of Florida, (352) 392-3261. **Offerings:** 52 undergraduate degrees in 114 majors, 123 master's programs and 76 doctoral programs. **Santa Fe Community College**, (352) 395-5000. **Offerings:** The Community Education program, (352) 395-5193, features life enrichment, liberal arts, intergenerational and mentoring programs, community service activities and vocational/technical classes in seven-week sessions. Classes are held at various locations on campus and in churches, senior centers and other local facilities. **City College**, (352) 335-4000. **Offerings:** Associate of science degrees in law, medicine, business and accounting.

JUST FOR SENIORS

Area Agency on Aging, (352) 378-6649. **Senior Citizens Bus Card**, (352) 334-2600. **Senior Community Service Employment Program**, (352) 378-6750. **Thelma Bolton Center**, (352) 334-2189. **Senior Advantage**, a health benefits program for people 55 and older.

GETTING INVOLVED

Community Action Agency, (352) 373-7667. **Information and Referral Services**, (352) 728-8700. **RSVP**, (352) 622-5444, serves more than 70 different sites in Alachua County with a corps of 600 volunteers. There's also a **Newcomer's Club**; contact the chamber of commerce for information.

RECREATION, ENTERTAINMENT & AMENITIES

Public golf: Ironwood Municipal Golf Course, 18 holes; Marion Oaks Country Club, 36 holes; Meadowbrook Golf Club, 18 holes; and Villages of Westend Golf Club, 18 holes/par 60. **Private golf:** Gainesville Golf & Country Club, 18 holes, and University of Florida Golf Course. **Public tennis courts:** Westside Park has eight courts. There are about 20 other municipal courts. **Private tennis courts:** Gainesville Golf & Country Club and Woodside Racquet Club. **Parks:** There are 13 state parks, lakes and recreation areas; 30 city parks and recreation centers; San Felasco Hammock State Preserve; and Paynes Prairie State Preserve. **Public swimming pools:** Three. **Water sports:** Boating, tubing, canoeing, scuba diving, swimming and fishing. **River/gulf/ocean:** Newnans, Orange and Santa Fe lakes offer freshwater fishing and boating. It's 55 miles to the Gulf at Cedar Key; 73 miles to the Atlantic at St. Augustine and 98 miles to Daytona Beach. **Running/walking/biking:** Endless miles of rolling, back-country roads and parks are perfect for hiking and biking. Hawthorne Trail, a 17-mile section of Florida's rails-to-trails program, attracts walkers, cyclers and horseback riders. **Horses/riding:** Paynes Prairie State Preserve has several miles of trails. Boarding, breeding, training, showing and riding are popular in this horse country setting, with 20 stables and riding academies in the area. **Hunting:** Abundant hunting lands. Call (352) 374-5282 for hunting/fishing licenses and boat registration. **Movie theaters:** 30 screens. **Art museums:** Santa Fe Gallery, Thomas Center, University Gallery and Samuel P. Harn Museum of Art. **History museums:** Florida Museum of Natural History. **Theaters:** Center for the Performing Arts at the University of Florida, Hippodrome State Theatre and Gainesville Little Theater. Performing arts groups include Ballet Theatre, Florida Players, Santa Fe Players Chamber Orchestra and Dance Alive! **Library:** Alachua County, plus facilities at the University of Florida and Santa Fe Community College. **Attractions:** Devil's Millhopper State Park, Fred Bear Museum, Kanapaha Botanical Gardens, Morningside Nature Center and the Thomas Center. Call the University of Florida, (352) 375-4683 ext. 6800, for information on athletic events. **Necessities:** Everything you would expect to find in a major metropolitan area is here.

Smart Shopper Tip: Gainesville has 21 malls, shopping centers and plazas. If that's not enough, you can drive to Jacksonville in about an hour or to Tampa in two hours. Try Gainesville's Artisans' Guild if you're interested in local arts and crafts.

WHO LIVES HERE

Population: 99,870 year-round residents, an increase of 14,795 since 1990. **Age 65+ =** 9.8% in Alachua County. **Median household income:** $26,683 (Alachua County). **Per capita income:** $19,984 (Alachua County).

NUMBERS TO KNOW

Chamber of commerce: (352) 334-7100. **Voter registration:** (352) 374-5252. **Vehicle registration, tags & title:** (352) 374-5263. **Driver's license:** (352) 955-2111. **Visitors bureau:** (352) 374-5231.

WHAT TO READ

Gainesville Sun, daily newspaper, (352) 374-5000.

GETTING AROUND

Bus: Regional Transit System, (352) 334-2614. **Taxi:** Safety Cabs, (352) 372-1444. **Tours:** None listed. **Airport:** Gainesville Regional. **Train:** Amtrak stops in nearby Waldo, (800) 872-7245. **Traffic:** Traffic is surprisingly light.

JOBS

County unemployment rate: 3.1%. **Florida Jobs and Benefits:** (352) 955-2245.

UTILITIES

Electricity, gas, water & sewer: Gainesville Regional Utilities, (352) 334-3434. **Telephone:** Bell South, (800) 789-9025 in Florida, or (800) 753-0710 out-of-state. **Cable TV:** Cox Communications, (352) 377-2123.

PLACES OF WORSHIP

Four Catholic and 182 Protestant churches, plus three Jewish synagogues.

THE ENVIRONMENT

Hogtown Creek has been rated as having poor to good surface water quality. It has been affected by a nearby Superfund site and urban runoff. Newnans Lake has fair to poor water quality, and Paynes Prairie and Lochloosa lakes have good water quality. Orange Lake and Lochloosa Lake are designated as Outstanding Florida Waters.

Cabot/Koppers is a 170-acre EPA-listed Superfund site near the intersection of North 23rd Avenue and North Main Street in Gainesville.

EVENTS AND FESTIVALS

Spring Arts Festival - April. **Downtown Festival & Art Show** - November.

WHERE TO EAT

Emiliano's Cafe & Bakery, 7 S.E. First Ave., Caribbean, moderate, (352) 375-7381. **Sovereign Restaurant,** 12 S.E. Second Ave., continental, expensive, (352) 378-6307.

WHERE TO STAY

Hampton Inn, (352) 371-4171. **Cabot Lodge,** (352) 375-2400. **Radisson Hotel,** (352) 377-4000. **Residence Inn,** (352) 371-2101.

ISSUES

There seemed to be no issues of a lasting, controversial nature when we visited. As in many towns, drugs are a concern, but a comprehensive education program aimed at drug abuse prevention and elimination won the community a federal grant five years in a row.

Hialeah

HE SAID: ★
> *I could never retire to a community of nearly 200,000 inhabitants that doesn't have a golf course.*

SHE SAID: ★ ★
> *On entering Hialeah, I immediately had a feeling of overcrowding. Too many people too close together for me.*

Just north of Miami, Hialeah has two strong allures that are bringing retirees here from across the country. The first is the universal appeal of living in a community populated by persons of common ethnic and cultural backgrounds. There is a decidedly Cuban culture developing here, where 87.6 percent of the population is Hispanic, and of that, 65 percent is Cuban.

The second factor drawing retirees is the availability and quality of health care. Statistically, Hialeah leads Dade County and the state of Florida in the per capita number of doctors, dentists, hospitals and health-care facilities.

And for aficionados of thoroughbred racing, Hialeah has an additional attraction — the famed Hialeah Park & Race Course.

Unlike most other south Florida locales, Hialeah is not a resort town. It is largely a residential and industrial community. As Florida's fifth largest city, Hialeah is home to more than 700 manufacturing firms and supports a large number of small businesses as well. But much to the chagrin of local leaders, it lacks the recreational amenities of its neighbors.

According to Arthur Neville, a representative of David Jenkins Associates, which specializes in real estate for industrial development, Hialeah comes up short on the kinds of recreational and cultural diversity most retirees want. While it has a strong appeal for Cubans seeking to sustain their culture and heritage, it lacks many amenities, including golf, tennis, art and history museums, and the performing arts.

WEATHER

	Winter	Spring	Summer	Fall
Normal daily high/low	77/59	86/70	89/75	81/65
Normal precipitation	7 in.	21 in.	24 in.	11 in.

Disaster watch: Southeast Florida has been hit by nine major hurricanes since 1900.

TAXES

Sales tax: 6.5%. **Property tax:** $26.30 per $1,000 valuation. Sample tax calculations include a $25,000 homestead exemption.

Home value	Tax
$100,000	$1,973
$150,000	$3,288
$250,000	$5,918

REAL ESTATE

Median home value: $117,429 (Dade County). **Median rent:** $764/month (Dade County). **Communities popular with retirees:** None in particular. **Licensed continuing-care retirement communities:** None. There are several adult congregate living facilities offering varying degrees of care, including: Care & Love, 20 residents, opened 1985, (305) 888-0187; Epworth Village, 435 residents, opened 1980, (305) 556-3500; and Seniors Palace, 34 residents, opened 1985, (305) 885-7733.

CRIME & SAFETY

The crime rate for Hialeah is not available. Hialeah has not reported its crime statistics since 1992's Hurricane Andrew destroyed its computer system. **Non-emergency police:** (305) 687-2525. **Non-emergency fire department:** (305) 883-6900. **Crimestoppers Anonymous:** (305) 471-TIPS. **Police, fire, ambulance emergencies:** 911.

HOMELESS & BLIGHT

There are many clean and prosperous family neighborhoods, but there also are many pockets of substandard housing. City officials and civic leaders are working hard to correct the problems.

The U.S. Census Bureau counted 1,235 homeless in Dade County's shelters and an additional 495 on the streets among the county's 1.9 million population.

HEALTH CARE

Hospitals: **Hialeah Hospital**, 411 beds, full service, (305) 693-6100. **Palmetto General Hospital**, 360 beds, full service, (305) 823-5000. **Palm Springs General Hospital**, 247 beds, full service, (305) 558-2500. **Southern Winds**, 60 beds, (305) 558-9700. **Physicians:** 267. **Specialties:** 42.

GETTING SMART

Miami-Dade Community College, north campus, part of the largest community college in the nation, (305) 237-1000. **Offerings:** Two-year degree programs in 24 disciplines, plus personal enrichment courses. **Barry University**, 20 minutes east of Hialeah, (305) 899-3000. **Offerings:** Undergraduate and graduate degree programs, plus adult and special education classes.

JUST FOR SENIORS

Goodlett Adult Center, (305) 825-4947. **Hialeah Adult Center**, (305) 883-8020. **Wilde Adult Center**, (305) 556-0833.

GETTING INVOLVED

Christian Homes for Children, (305) 825-0517. **Family Counseling Services**, (305) 573-2500. **His House**, (305) 430-0085. **RSVP**, (305) 375-5335.

RECREATION, ENTERTAINMENT & AMENITIES

Public golf: Golf Club of Miami, in Miami Lakes, 54 holes. **Private golf:** Miami Lakes Country Club, located north of town, and Miami Springs Country Club to the south. **Public tennis courts:** None. **Private tennis courts.** None. **Parks:** Amelia Earhart Park offers trails and a fishing lake. Small parks in the city total more than 100 acres. **Public swimming pools:** Several. **Water sports:** There are 25 lakes in the area, but only the lake at Amelia Earhart Park has boating facilities. **River/gulf/ocean:** Twenty minutes to Biscayne Bay and Miami Beach. **Running/walking/biking:** Most public parks have paths. **Horses/riding:** Hialeah Park & Race Course, often called the world's most beautiful, also is noted for its pink flamingo colony. **Hunting:** None. **Movie theaters:** Four theaters, with multiple screens. **Library:** Dade County Public Library branch in Miami Lakes. **Art museums:** None. **History museums:** None. **Theaters:** None. **Attractions:** Bill Graham Farm Village. **Necessities:** All available.

Smart Shopper Tip: Westland Mall and Palm Springs Mile Shopping Center capture the greatest share of shoppers' dollars, though the city is laced with smaller shopping centers.

WHO LIVES HERE
Population: 207,053 year-round residents, an increase of 19,045 from 1990. **Age 65+** = 14.4% in Dade County. **Median household income:** $26,743 (Dade County). **Per capita income:** $21,058 (Dade County).

NUMBERS TO KNOW
Chamber of commerce: (305) 887-1515. **Voter registration:** (305) 375-4600. **Vehicle registration, tags & title:** (305) 375-5678. **Driver's license:** (305) 827-4043. **Visitors bureau:** (305) 539-3000.

WHAT TO READ
El Sol de Hialeah, Spanish-language newspaper, (305) 887-8324. **The Miami Herald**, daily newspaper, (305) 350-2111. **El Matancero**, Spanish-language newspaper, (305) 643-4888.

GETTING AROUND
Bus: Metro-Dade Transit System has four routes. MetroRails crosses south Hialeah, (305) 770-3131. Maps-by-Mail from Metrobus, (305) 654-6586, ask for "First Time Rider's Kit." **Taxi:** All-American Taxi, (305) 947-3333. **Tours:** None. **Airport:** Ten minutes to Miami International. **Traffic:** Moderate to heavy during rush hour.

JOBS
County unemployment rate: 7.2%. **Florida Jobs and Benefits:** (305) 375-1871.

UTILITIES
Electricity: Florida Power & Light, (305) 442-8770. **Gas:** City Gas Company of Florida, (305) 691-8710. **Water & sewer:** Miami-Dade Water & Sewer Department, (305) 665-7488. **Telephone:** Southern Bell, (305) 780-2355 in Florida, or (800) 753-0710 out-of-state. **Cable TV:** Dynamic Cablevision, (305) 827-9941.

PLACES OF WORSHIP
85 churches, including 12 Catholic churches, plus one Jewish synagogue.

THE ENVIRONMENT
Nearby Miami River is heavily polluted by urban and agricultural runoff, sewage overflow and boat discharges. The river's sediment is contaminated with metals and pesticides. The U.S. Army Corps of Engineers may dredge the sediments to improve navigation, but no acceptable site for the disposal of the sediments has been found.

Dade County has 12 EPA-listed Superfund sites, including two in Hialeah: B&B Chemical Co. and Standard Auto Bumper Corp.

EVENTS AND FESTIVALS
Flamingo Handicap - April. **River Cities Festival** - April. **Widener Handicap** - May.

WHERE TO EAT
El Segundo Viajante, 2846 Palm Ave., Cuban, inexpensive, (305) 888-5465. **Coco Palm Restaurant**, 7707 N.W. 103rd St., American favorites and continental specialties, moderate and up, (305) 825-1000.

WHERE TO STAY
Holiday Inn, (305) 362-7777. **Park Plaza Hotel**, (305) 825-1000. **Courtyard by Marriott**, (305) 556-6665.

ISSUES
Residents and civic leaders feel that Dade County ignores Hialeah when requesting and doling out federal funds. Specifically, leaders point to the lack of sufficient aid following Hurricane Andrew and little to no funding for performing and visual arts centers and the refurbishment of local auditoriums. Former Mayor Julio Martinez was quoted in a local paper as saying, "They just don't take us seriously."

RELOCATION TIPS

If you have a small budget for retirement housing, check into manufactured homes. New manufactured homes offer many features of traditional site-built homes, including cathedral ceilings, formal dining rooms, wood-burning fireplaces and deluxe master baths with built-in whirlpools. The Manufactured Housing Institute reports that the construction cost per square foot is approximately $25 for a manufactured home, while a traditional site-built home is $50 or more per square foot, excluding the cost of the land. Of course the final cost of a manufactured home can increase as buyers add basics like heating and air-conditioning, upgrade features, and pay to move into a manufactured-home community with amenities.

Hollywood

HE SAID: ★ ★ ★ ★
Hollywood is the exception to my rule that crime and crowds make south Florida too inhospitable to recommend. It may have lost some of its appeal, but it's still a great place to retire

SHE SAID: ★ ★ ★
The slower pace of Hollywood is soon felt — and appreciated. In the heart of town, the main street is attractively divided by trees, shrubs and flowers. Sidewalk cafes lend a warm and inviting aura to Hollywood. Visit this place before making a relocation decision.

They don't call it the diamond of Florida's Gold Coast without reason. Hollywood has a feeling of safety, a look of cleanliness and a sense of efficiency that gives it an upscale hometown appeal. Recent years have brought a new look to downtown, where old buildings have been refurbished as stores and restaurants. With brick sidewalks and rows of colorful canopies, downtown beckons people to spend their time and money here.

At the beach, especially on the Broadwalk, there is a lighthearted atmosphere as tourists and residents walk, jog, bike and people-watch.

If you're looking for something, chances are you'll find it on Hollywood Boulevard. This is classic Main Street, running through the heart of the city from the coast to the westernmost side of town. All types of housing, shopping, parks, gardens and government offices line the avenue. There are three landmark traffic circles along Hollywood Boulevard; from miles away you'll see the attractive seven-story twin glass towers on Presidential Circle. Unlike other parts of south Florida, there are few high-rises to block your view.

Hollywood has recreation for everyone. For outdoor activities, there's fishing, boating, golf, tennis, scuba diving, walking, biking, jogging and relaxing at the beach. Indoors, spectators can enjoy jai alai, baseball and the performing and visual arts. Racing enthusiasts will get their fill of greyhound, horse and car meets. Special events such as festivals and rodeos draw residents and tourists.

With attractive residential neighborhoods, outstanding health-care facilities, unparalleled transportation network and delightful climate, what more can a retiree want?

WEATHER

	Winter	Spring	Summer	Fall
Normal daily high/low	78/60	86/70	90/75	82/65
Normal precipitation	8 in.	20 in.	21 in.	12 in.

Disaster watch: Southeast Florida has been hit by nine major hurricanes since 1900.

TAXES
Sales tax: 6%. **Property tax:** $26.97 per $1,000 valuation. Sample taxes include a $25,000 homestead exemption.

Home value	Tax
$100,000	$2,023
$150,000	$3,371
$250,000	$6,068

REAL ESTATE
Median home value: $107,554 (Broward County). **Median rent:** $809/month (Broward County). **Communities popular with retirees:** Retirees reside in communities throughout the city. Beautiful palm-lined streets, modern and clean buildings and an abundance of parks and gardens give the city an appeal few can match. Unique to Hollywood is the Great Neighborhoods Program. The city has established a package of incentives to enhance the quality of life in the city's residential neighborhoods, including free or low-cost building permits, permit rebates and reduced-cost loans for renovations. All neighborhoods are eligible, with no income limitations. **Licensed continuing-care retirement communities:** None. There are dozens of adult congregate living facilities, including: Nova Palms, (954) 923-5057; North Lake Retirement Home, (954) 922-2643; and Northpark Retirement Community, (954) 989-8008.

CRIME & SAFETY
Crimes per 1,000 population: 99. **Non-emergency police:** (954) 967-4357. **Non-emergency fire department:** (954) 967-4248. **Police, fire, ambulance emergencies:** 911. The city has installed better lighting and security walls in all neighborhoods.

HOMELESS & BLIGHT
If there is a blighted neighborhood, we did not see it. Nor did we see any homeless persons as we toured the city. The U.S. Census recorded Broward County's total population as more than 1.25 million with a homeless population of 1,023.

HEALTH CARE
Hospitals: Vencor Hospital, 124 beds, full service, (954) 920-9000. **Hollywood Medical Center**, 334 beds, full service, (954) 966-4500. **Memorial Hospital**, 680 beds, full service, (954) 987-2000. **Hollywood Pavilion**, psychiatric hospital, (954) 962-1355. **Physicians:** 831. **Specialties:** 49.

GETTING SMART
Broward Community College, Pembroke Pines/Hollywood campus, (954) 963-8876. **Offerings:** Two-year degrees in 46 career programs. **Hollywood Hills Adult Center**, (954) 985-5236. **Offerings:** Evening classes for all ages. College credit and non-credit courses, GED classes and English as a second language. **Nova Southeastern University**, located in Davie, approximately 20 minutes from downtown Hollywood, (954) 262-7300. **Offerings:** Bachelor's degree programs in business, education, liberal arts; graduate degrees in education, computer and information sciences, psychology, oceanography, law, business and social studies. **Institute for Retired Professionals**, Nova University, (954) 262-8471. **Offerings:** Courses run October through June, three days per week, three hours a day. Topics include literature, oceanography, philosophy, psychology and foreign policy and are taught by distinguished lecturers, faculty and institute members.

JUST FOR SENIORS
Multi Purpose Adult Center, (954) 921-3408. Senior Assistance Center (a referral service), (954) 714-3464. Hollywood Beach Culture & Community Center (a favorite gathering place for seniors seeking social, cultural and educational activities), (954) 921-3600.

GETTING INVOLVED
Clubs, fraternities, social service and non-profit organizations number in the dozens. Of significance are: **SCORE**, (954) 966-8415. **Volunteer Broward**, a United Way agency that refers volunteers to approximately 400 organizations in Broward County, (954) 522-6761.

RECREATION, ENTERTAINMENT & AMENITIES

Public golf: Eco Grande Golf Course, nine holes; Hollywood Golf & Country Club, 18 holes; and Orangebrook Golf Course, 36 holes. **Private golf:** Oak Ridge Country Club; Sunset Golf Course, nine holes; and Emerald Hills Country Club. **Tennis courts:** Numerous public and private courts, lighted and unlighted. **Parks:** 20. Favorites include Topeekeegee Yugnee for freshwater swimming, fishing and boating, Hollywood North Beach Park, Brian Piccolo Park and the John U. Lloyd Beach State Park in Dania. **Public swimming pools:** Located at many public parks. **Water sports:** Fishing, boating, scuba diving and sailing are favorite pastimes of residents and visitors seeking to enjoy Hollywood's public beaches and six miles on the Intracoastal Waterway. **River/gulf/ocean:** Atlantic beaches plus hundreds of miles of shore at lakes and canals. **Running/walking/biking:** Try the trails at Brian Piccolo Park, Hollywood North Beach Park, Topeekeegee Yugnee Park and West Lake Park. Tourists and residents enjoy the two-and-a-half mile Broadwalk along the beach. There's one path for foot traffic and another for bicycles. **Horses/riding:** Stables, riding academies and trails in the neighboring communities of Coconut Creek and Davie. **Hunting:** None. **Movie theaters:** 19 screens. **Art museums:** Hollywood Art Museum and the Art & Culture Center of Hollywood. **History museums:** Hollywood Historical Society. **Theaters:** Hollywood Playhouse, Theatre Under the Stars and Young Circle Park Bandshell. The Greater Hollywood Philharmonic Orchestra offers a full season, including its Sunday Afternoon Concert Series in December. **Library:** Hollywood branch of the Broward County Public Library. **Attractions:** Seminole Indian Village and Hollywood Greyhound Track. **Necessities:** If you can't find it here, you can find it 20 minutes away in Fort Lauderdale or 45 minutes away in Miami.

Smart Shopper Tip: There are three major shopping malls here: Hollywood Fashion Center, Hollywood Mall and Oceanwalk Mall. Downtown Hollywood has an old-fashioned, small-town shopping district with unique shops. Within a short drive are three regional malls.

WHO LIVES HERE

Population: 126,522 year-round residents, an increase of 4,802 since 1990. **Age 65+** = 19.3% in Broward County. **Median household income:** $31,289 (Broward County). **Per capita income:** $26,192 (Broward County).

NUMBERS TO KNOW

Chamber of commerce: (954) 923-4000. **Voter registration:** (954) 357-7050. **Vehicle registration, tags & title:** (954) 765-5050. **Driver's license:** (954) 327-6333. **Visitors bureau:** (954) 765-4466.

WHAT TO READ

Sun Sentinel, daily newspaper, (954) 356-4000. **Hollywood Annual Relocation Guide,** from the chamber of commerce, (954) 923-4000.

GETTING AROUND

Bus: Broward County Transit, (954) 357-8400. **Taxi:** AAA Checker Cab, (954) 923-9999; Yellow Cab, (954) 565-5400. **Tours:** The Downtown Hollywood Trolley travels from downtown to the beach, (954) 921-3016. **Airport:** Fort Lauderdale/Hollywood International Airport is 15 minutes from downtown. Port Everglades is within the city limits. **Traffic:** Several highways and interstates are easily accessible.

JOBS

County unemployment rate: 5.0%. **Florida Jobs and Benefits:** (954) 967-1010. **Job Line:** (954) 921-3292.

UTILITIES

Electricity: Florida Power & Light, (954) 797-5000. **Water & sewer:** Hollywood City Water Dept., (954) 921-3241. **Telephone:** Bell South, (800) 789-9025 in Florida, or (800) 753-0710 out-of-state. **Cable TV:** TCI Digital Cable, (305) 652-9900.

PLACES OF WORSHIP

There are more than 80 churches representing 25 denominations, plus four Jewish synagogues.

THE ENVIRONMENT

Surface water quality has been rated as fair to poor in this part of the state. Both the New River and Miami River have heavily polluted sections.

There are seven EPA-listed Superfund sites in the county; none are in Hollywood.

EVENTS AND FESTIVALS

Hollywood Sun 'n' Fun Festival - January. **Seminole Indian Tribal Fair** - February. **Florida Derby Festival** - March. **Hollywood Jazz Festival** - October.

WHERE TO EAT

Bavarian Village, 1401 N. Federal Highway, varied menu with German specialties, early-bird fixed-price menu, moderate to expensive, (954) 922-7321. **Martha's on the Intracoastal,** 6024 N. Ocean Drive, continental menu, entertainment and dancing, expensive, (954) 923-5444.

WHERE TO STAY

Holiday Inn, (954) 923-8700. **Howard Johnson Hollywood Beach Resort,** (954) 925-1411. **Hollywood Beach Resort Hotel,** (954) 921-0990.

ISSUES

Fewer Canadians are coming to Hollywood's beaches, choosing Florida's west coast instead. This could be a problem, since Canadians represent about 65 percent of all tourists to Hollywood.

The Hollywood Economic Growth Corporation (HEGC) has been very successful in attracting new economic growth through incentive packages and low-interest loans. Downtown revitalization efforts are paying off and the city is becoming more attractive both for residents and businesses.

Care should be taken to ensure a balance is achieved between business growth and the resources that make the city so attractive for tourists and retirees.

Homosassa Springs

HE SAID: ✮ ✮
A good place to spend some time in the great outdoors, but it lacks the ingredients for a well-rounded lifestyle. It takes rusticity a notch too far.

SHE SAID: ✮ ✮
This is a small town located on busy U.S. Highway 19 with large communities of manufactured homes. There's limited shopping and recreation. I would not retire here.

Three settings define this piece of the "Nature Coast." These include Homosassa Springs, essentially a 5-mile unincorporated strip of commerce on U.S. 19; the springs at Homosassa Springs State Wildlife Park, a 55-foot-deep, 6 million-gallons-an-hour producer of crystal clear, 72-degree water where manatees may be observed 365 days a year; and finally, Homosassa, an old, dilapidated fishing village that offers a rustic mix of mobile homes, small frame cottages, marinas, fish camps and trailer parks, with an occasional new home development tossed in.

The latter Homosassa will appeal exclusively to old salts and new ones for whom fishing, boats and water provide all that is needed for complete happiness in life. If this description fits you, then you may want to look at the Riverhaven Village development.

Homosassa Springs is home to Stonebrook Estates, a manufactured-home community with a nice entrance, an uninspired setting and "for sale" signs everywhere.

But about six miles down U.S. 19, with a Homosassa mailing address, lies Sugarmill Woods. Here you'll find 15,000 acres of homes and villas. Streets are mostly cul-de-sacs, and each home faces a park, meadow or golf course fairway, providing an air of openness and quiet for every homesite. A 27-hole golf and racquet club is among the recreational outlets for its members.

In a nutshell, the Homosassa area offers a variety of opportunities for persons who enjoy a close-to-nature lifestyle, but very little for "joiners," concertgoers, shoppers and those who prefer the indoor activities of creative retirement.

WEATHER

	Winter	Spring	Summer	Fall
Normal daily high/low	72/47	87/64	91/71	77/54
Normal precipitation	11 in.	13 in.	23 in.	7 in.

Disaster watch: Northwest Florida has been hit by six major hurricanes since 1900.

TAXES

Sales tax: 6%. **Property tax:** $17.94 per $1,000 valuation. Sample tax calculations include a $25,000 homestead exemption.

Home value	Tax
$100,000	$1,346
$150,000	$2,243
$250,000	$4,037

REAL ESTATE

Median home value: $79,140 (Citrus County). **Median rent:** $345/month (Citrus County). **Communities popular with retirees:** Riverhaven Village is a rustic riverfront community of single-family homes and villas priced from the $100s to $500s. For information, contact Remax real-estate agent Jody Broom,

(352) 795-2441. Stonebrook Estates has manufactured homes ranging from the low $20s to the mid-$50s, excluding the cost of the lot lease, (352) 628-4304. Sugarmill Woods offers resale villas ranging from the mid-$60s to the low $80s. Single-family and estate homes, new and resales are priced from the low $100s to the $240s, (352) 382-2100. **Licensed continuing-care retirement communities:** None.

CRIME & SAFETY

Crimes per 1,000 population: 23 (Citrus County sheriff's jurisdiction). **Non-emergency police:** (352) 726-4488. **Non-emergency fire department:** (352) 628-3434. **Police, fire, ambulance emergencies:** 911.

HOMELESS & BLIGHT

Homosassa is strictly a fishing village with a mix of mobile homes (some dilapidated) and small frame houses, interspersed with an occasional new house. It's an unattractive mixture. Homosassa Springs' commercial area, with too many signs along U.S. 19, is not much better.

No homeless persons were reported in the U.S. Census population count for Citrus County.

HEALTH CARE

Hospitals: There are no hospitals in Homosassa Springs. The nearest is **Seven Rivers Hospital**, 12 miles away in Crystal River. It is a 120-bed, full-service hospital with 24-hour emergency care, (352) 795-6560.
Physicians: 16. **Specialties:** 7.

GETTING SMART

Central Florida Community College in Lecanto is nine miles away, (352) 746-6721. **Offerings:** Two-year degrees in arts and sciences.

JUST FOR SENIORS

Lecanto Senior Center, (352) 746-1842. There is an AARP group, but no official office. Ask the chamber of commerce for the name and telephone number of the current president.

GETTING INVOLVED

Friends of the Homosassa Springs State Wildlife Park, (352) 628-5343. **Homosassa Civic Club**, (352) 628-9333.

RECREATION, ENTERTAINMENT & AMENITIES

Public golf: Plantation Golf Resort in Crystal River. **Private golf:** Southern Woods Country Club and Sugarmill Woods. **Public tennis courts:** Homosassa Recreational Park has two lighted courts. **Private tennis courts:** In Sugarmill Woods, there's the Oak Village Bath & Tennis Club. **Parks:** Homosassa Area Recreation Park, Homosassa Springs State Wildlife Park and Yulee Sugar Mill Ruins State Historic Site. **Public swimming pools:** None. **Water sports:** Boating, canoeing, fishing and scuba diving. **River/gulf/ocean:** Homosassa River and the Gulf of Mexico. **Running/walking/biking:** Homosassa Area Recreation Park has a fitness trail. There are paths and trails through Chassahowitzka National Wildlife Refuge. **Horses/ riding:** There are plenty of places to ride on the back roads of this underpopulated area. Diamond K Ranch in Lecanto, (352) 628-9186. **Hunting:** Licenses and information, (352) 637-9485. In season, game includes deer, dove, quail and wild hogs. **Movie theaters:** None. **Art museums:** Riverworks Art Gallery. **History museums:** Yulee Sugar Mill Ruins State Historic Site. **Theaters:** The Curtis Peterson Auditorium in Lecanto hosts cultural and civic activities. **Library:** Homosassa Public. **Attractions:** Homosassa Springs State Wildlife Park and the Yulee Sugar Mill. **Necessities:** Banks, credit unions, car dealerships, a funeral home, gas stations, grocery stores, general merchandise stores, pharmacies, medical offices, real estate agencies and a post office.

   Smart Shopper Tip: Homosassa Regional Shopping Center, with a Wal-Mart and a Winn-Dixie supermarket, serves basic needs. Drive about 10 miles to Crystal River Mall for other shopping.

WHO LIVES HERE
Population: 39,000 residents live in and around unincorporated Homosassa Springs, according to the chamber of commerce. **Age 65+ = 31.5%** in Citrus County. **Median household income:** $21,458 (Citrus County). **Per capita income:** $17,189 (Citrus County).

NUMBERS TO KNOW
Chamber of commerce: (352) 628-2666. **Voter registration:** (352) 637-9910. **Vehicle registration, tags & title:** (352) 795-5537. **Driver's license:** In Crystal River, (352) 795-4221.

WHAT TO READ
Citrus County Chronicle, daily newspaper, (352) 563-6363. **Tampa Tribune**, daily newspaper, (813) 259-7422.

GETTING AROUND
Bus: Citrus County's Public Transportation System operates on a door-to-door basis, taking residents to shopping centers, parks, doctors' offices and elsewhere. One-day advance reservations needed, (352) 746-4844. **Taxi:** Liberty Stagecoach, (352) 628-0680. **Tours:** None. **Airport:** Tampa International is 60 miles south. **Traffic:** Traffic volume on usually hectic U.S. 19 is moderate in this area.

JOBS
County unemployment rate: 6.7%. **Florida Jobs and Benefits:** (352) 746-6721.

UTILITIES
Electricity: Withlacoochee River Electric Co-op, (352) 795-4382, or Florida Power, (800) 700-8744, depending on location. **Gas:** None. **Water & sewer:** Homosassa Special Water District, (352) 628-3740. Many residents have private wells. **Telephone:** United Telephone, (352) 726-2600. **Cable TV:** Time-Warner Cable, (800) 892-0805.

PLACES OF WORSHIP
One Catholic and 15 Protestant churches.

THE ENVIRONMENT
The spring-fed rivers of the area, including the Weeki Wachee, Chassahowitzka, Homosassa and Crystal rivers, generally have been rated as having very good water quality. Crystal River and Kings Bay have been designated as Outstanding Florida Waters (OFW). The county has applied for OFW designations for the Homosassa/Halls and Chassahowitzka rivers as well.

EVENTS AND FESTIVALS
Events: Chamber Antique Boat & Car Show - February. **Homosassa River Raft Race** - June. **Homosassa Arts, Crafts & Seafood Festival** - November. **Homosassa Christmas Boat Parade** - December.

WHERE TO EAT
K.C. Crump, 3900 Halls River Road, seafood and beef, moderate, (352) 628-1500.

WHERE TO STAY
Ramada Inn, (352) 628-4311. **Riverside Inn Resort**, (352) 628-2474.

ISSUES
A proposed new limited-access parkway out of Tampa will pass through Citrus county, bringing more traffic, people and commerce to the area. Potential buyers of residential property along its path would be well-advised to check with the Florida Highway Department for the exact route to judge its likely impact.

RELOCATION TIPS

The threat of hurricanes and tropical storms is a reality for much of coastal Florida. Hurricane season lasts from June through November. At the start of the hurricane season, make sure you have emergency supplies including flashlights, extra batteries, bottled water, a battery-operated portable radio, first-aid kit, masking tape, sheets/blankets, waterproof matches, candles, non-perishable canned food that does not require cooking and a non-electric can opener. It's wise to have an evacuation plan as well. Find out where the nearest hurricane shelter is and determine evacuation routes. If a hurricane watch is issued for your area there are some precautions you can take, such as making sure you have an adequate supply of prescription medicines on hand and filling the car's gas tank.

Inverness

This is an average town, remarkable only for the Tsala Apopka Lakes. Unfortunately, these lakes recently resembled a chain of marshes due to a long dry spell. One retiree who lives on Gospel Island, east of Inverness, expressed real concern about the continuing decline of water levels in the lakes and the Withlacoochee River, which feeds the lakes. Even the chamber of commerce has publicly lamented the "low water problems caused by a long-term rainfall deficit."

One real asset for outdoor-types who enjoy hiking and exploring is the popular 47-mile Withlacoochee State Trail. Part of Florida's Rails-to-Trails program, it runs north and south past Inverness and provides a paved hiking and biking pathway and a parallel mulched trail for horseback riding.

The town has a good — but not outstanding — historic district, an adequate hospital and access to Central Florida Community College nine miles west. There are a number of plazas and strip shopping centers, very limited sociocultural infrastructure, some very nice residential neighborhoods and some not so nice.

One retiree says she likes the slow pace of the town but admits, "It sometimes gets too slow."

Another retiree observes that "there are no budget-busting Broadway shows or fancy New York-style restaurants" — a gross understatement.

From the outside, it seems that Inverness may be best for local people who already have family, friends and an established way of life here.

WEATHER

	Winter	Spring	Summer	Fall
Normal daily high/low	72/47	87/64	91/71	77/54
Normal precipitation	11 in.	13 in.	23 in.	7 in.

Disaster watch: Northwest Florida has been hit by six major hurricanes since 1900.

TAXES
Sales tax: 6%. **Property tax:** $26.06 per $1,000 valuation. Sample tax calculations include a $25,000 homestead exemption.

Home value	Tax
$100,000	$1,955
$150,000	$3,258
$250,000	$5,864

REAL ESTATE
Median home value: $79,140 (Citrus County). **Median rent:** $345/month (Citrus County). **Communities popular with retirees:** Stoneridge Landing is a manufactured-home community where residents lease the lots. Homes range from the mid-$20s to $90s, excluding lease costs, (800) 779-1226 or (352) 637-1400. Villages of Citrus Hills is made up of several subdivisions of single-family homes. Land prices start in the $20s and up depending on acreage. Single-family homes run from the $60s to the $150s, excluding land cost, (352) 746-6121. **Licensed continuing-care retirement communities:** None.

CRIME & SAFETY
Crimes per 1,000 population: 34. **Non-emergency police:** (352) 726-2121. **Non-emergency fire department:** (352) 726-2221. **Police, fire, ambulance emergencies:** 911.

HOMELESS & BLIGHT
There are some unattractive mobile home parks in the suburban areas, as in much of Florida, but we noted no homeless persons or truly blighted areas.

The U.S. Census reported no homeless persons in Citrus County's population of 93,515.

HEALTH CARE
Hospitals: Citrus Memorial Hospital, 171 beds, full service, 24-hour emergency, (352) 726-1551.
Physicians: 60. **Specialties:** 31.

GETTING SMART
Central Florida Community College in Lecanto is nine miles west of Inverness, (352) 746-6721. **Offerings:** Two-year degrees in arts and sciences.

JUST FOR SENIORS
Inverness Multipurpose Senior Center, (352) 726-1009. **Lecanto Senior Center** is just five miles west, (352) 746-1842. **Citrus Memorial Hospital Share Club,** (352) 344-6900.

GETTING INVOLVED
Inverness Community Redevelopment Agency, (352) 726-2611. **Meals on Wheels,** (352) 726-0350. **School Volunteer Program,** (352) 726-1931. **United Way of Citrus County** in Crystal River, (352) 795-8844.

RECREATION, ENTERTAINMENT & AMENITIES
Semiprivate golf: Citrus Hills Golf Club, 36 holes; Lakeside Country Club, 18 holes; Point O'Woods Golf Club, nine holes; and Inverness Golf & Country Club, 18 holes. **Public tennis courts:** Whispering Pines Park has four lighted courts. **Private tennis courts:** Inverness Golf & Country Club. **Parks:** Fort Cooper State Park has a fresh-water beach, fishing and boating. Whispering Pines Park, with more than 300 acres, is one of the largest city-owned

parks in the state. **Public swimming pools:** Whispering Pines Park. **Water sports:** Boating, canoeing, sailing, scuba diving and water-skiing. **River/gulf/ocean:** The Withlacoochee River and Tsala Apopka Lakes are prominent on the eastern border. The Gulf waters at Crystal River and Homosassa are less than 30 minutes away. **Running/walking/biking:** Hikers, bikers and horseback riders use the Withlacoochee State Trail, a 47-mile linear state park. This corridor is one of the first railroad rights-of-way purchased under the Florida Rails-to-Trails program. Fort Cooper State Park has 10 miles of self-guided nature trails. Whispering Pines Park has more than eight miles of trails. **Horses/riding:** Fort Cooper State Park and the Withlacoochee State Trail. **Hunting:** There's 22 miles of chain lakes for hunting and fishing; residents 65 or older get a free senior citizen hunting and fishing certificate, (352) 637-9485. **Movie theaters:** Six screens. **Art museums:** Citrus County Museum. **History museums:** Citrus County Historical Society at the Old Courthouse. **Theaters:** Curtis Peterson Auditorium in Lecanto hosts cultural and civic activities. Citrus County Cultural Center has community theater performances. **Library:** Lakes Region. **Attractions:** Tsala Apopka, a 22-mile chain of lakes and marshes covering 24,000 acres; Withlacoochee State Forest; and the Crown Hotel's collection of replicated British crown jewels. **Necessities:** All the basics are available.

Smart Shopper Tip: The Inverness Regional Shopping Center and Citrus Center will meet most shopping needs. A short trip to Crystal River Mall or a 45-minute drive to Ocala will augment your shopping choices.

WHO LIVES HERE
Population: 6,801 year-round residents, an increase of 1,004 since 1990. **Age 65+** = 31.5% in Citrus County. **Median household income:** $21,458 (Citrus County). **Per capita income:** $17,189 (Citrus County).

NUMBERS TO KNOW
Chamber of commerce: (352) 726-2801. **Voter registration:** (352) 637-9910. **Vehicle registration, tags & title:** (352) 637-9400. **Driver's license:** (352) 726-6865.

WHAT TO READ
Citrus County Chronicle, daily newspaper, (352) 489-3373. **Let's Go**, weekly entertainment magazine, (352) 796-1949. **St. Petersburg Times**, daily, (352) 860-7300.

GETTING AROUND
Bus: Citrus County Transportation System provides a door-to-door service. One-day advance reservations are required. Hours and days of operation are limited, (352) 746-4844. **Taxi:** Highlands Taxi, (352) 344-0383. **Tours:** Van Go Tours, (352) 344-5353. Wild Bill's Airboat Tours, (352) 726-6060. **Airport:** Tampa International is 66 miles away. **Traffic:** Very light, even on U.S. Highway 41, the main north-south artery.

JOBS
County unemployment rate: 6.7%. **Florida Jobs and Benefits:**

(352) 746-6721. **Green Thumb** is a federally funded program designed to help people over age 55 find work to supplement social security income, (352) 726-5477.

UTILITIES
Electricity: Florida Power Corp., (800) 700-8744. **Gas:** National Propane, (352) 726-1522. **Water & sewer:** Inverness Utilities Dept., (352) 726-5016. **Telephone:** Sprint, (800) 326-2731. **Cable TV:** Time-Warner Cable, within 352 area code, (800) 892-0805. Adelphia Cable Vision, (352) 637-6666.

PLACES OF WORSHIP
One Catholic and 29 Protestant churches.

THE ENVIRONMENT
Water quality in the area generally has been rated as very good, especially the Withlacoochee River, which is designated as an Outstanding Florida Water. Spring-fed Rainbow River, near Dunellon, has excellent water quality. The Tsala Apopka Lakes have fair water quality. Though there are few water quality problems in the area, officials rate most of the water bodies as threatened.

EVENTS AND FESTIVALS
Citrus County Fair - March. **Festival of the Arts** - November. **Inverness Christmas Parade** - December.

WHERE TO EAT
Andre's of Citrus Hills, 510 E. Hartford St., international cuisine, moderate to expensive, (352) 746-6855. **Churchill's**, 109 N. Seminole Ave., in the Crown Hotel, continental, moderate to expensive, (352) 344-5555.

WHERE TO STAY
The Crown Hotel, (352) 344-5555.

ISSUES
The Tsala Apopka chain of lakes is characterized by the Florida Bureau of Surface Water Management as being more like a large grassy marsh with a series of pools of open water than a true lake. It is sometimes referred to as the Little Everglades. Water levels are determined by the flow of the Withlacoochee River, which fluctuates a great deal, having been recorded as high as 8,660 cubic feet per second in March 1960 and as low as 95 cubic feet per second in June 1985.

Both the Withlacoochee River and Tsala Apopka Lakes are popular residential areas, particularly with boat owners and country clubbers. But, residents of the area are experiencing low-water problems caused by a lengthy rainfall deficit. Many boats and docks have been left high and dry.

Before buying real estate in this area, it might be wise to consider the impact of long-term dry spells.

Jacksonville

HE SAID: ★ ★ ★
Despite its many superlatives, with almost 700,000 inhabitants and nearly that many vehicles jamming its streets and highways, the pace is too frenetic for me.

SHE SAID: ★ ★ ★
This huge metropolis has everything to offer — both good and bad. The outlying areas are beautiful. There you find a lot of military retirees, and possibly me. I would consider the area, but not Jacksonville itself and certainly not Jacksonville Beach.

Jacksonville lays claim to some pretty impressive statistics. Every major interstate highway leads to it. It is home to more than 30 retired Navy admirals. Jacksonville serves as the site of the Tournament Players Golf Championship and the NCAA Gator Bowl. It has a 25-mile stretch of wide open beaches. It even has some relatively affordable housing.

Jacksonville Naval Air Station (NAS), Cecil Field NAS, Mayport Naval Station and the Naval Aviation Depot are examples of the military presence, which impacts the city with its 45,000-plus military and civilian employees and $1.1 billion payroll.

But the "Emerald City" doesn't always glitter. All those interstates pour incessant streams of traffic in, over, around and through the city, often creating traffic jams of nightmarish proportions. It has received unwanted attention as another dangerous Florida city, resulting from snipers who fired at motorists on I-295 and I-95. The *Wall Street Journal* flagged it with a negative rating as a place for raising children.

As is the case with any major city, there are good and bad factors to be weighed and neighborhoods to be evaluated. Selection of a neighborhood is especially important in Jacksonville. Here numerous self-contained, former small municipalities, each with its own malls, restaurants, historic district, cultural opportunities and recreational amenities, offer a myriad of housing options and a diversity of lifestyles.

While the city boasts of its miles of wide-open beaches, much of Jacksonville Beach is blighted and unattractive. Anyone considering retirement in this area should visit Mayport, Atlantic Beach, Neptune Beach and Ponte Vedra Beach as possible alternatives to Jacksonville Beach.

WEATHER
	Winter	Spring	Summer	Fall
Normal daily high/low	68/44	84/62	90/71	74/51
Normal precipitation	11 in.	12 in.	21 in.	8 in.

Disaster watch: Northeast Florida has not been hit by a major hurricane since 1900.

TAXES
Sales tax: 6.5%. **Property tax:** Rates range from $19.75 to $21.42 per $1,000 valuation, depending on location. Sample taxes are calculated at the rate of $21.42 and include a $25,000 homestead exemption.

Home value	Tax
$100,000	$1,607
$150,000	$2,678
$250,000	$4,820

REAL ESTATE
Median home value: $87,014 (Duval County). **Median rent:** $594/month (Duval County). **Communities popular with re-** tirees: Cypress Village offers garden homes and detached villas priced from the $110s to mid-$160s, (904) 223-4663 or (800) 228-6163. Cimarrone Golf & Country Club has club homes priced from the mid-$140s to mid-$200s and estate homes priced from the high $180s to $400s, (904) 287-4000. Eagle Harbor has an 18-hole golf course, pool, tennis courts, nature preserve and biking-jogging trails. Homes are priced from the $120s to $400s, (904) 269-4000. Hampton Glen offers single-family homes priced from the mid-$130s to $300s, (904) 363-9077. Pace Island, a 977-acre gated community on Doctor's Lake with 10 miles of nature walks, has some homes priced from the low $100s to $1,000,000, (904) 269-7707. **Licensed continuing-care retirement communities:** Wesley Manor Retirement Village has 317 independent living units and 57 community beds, (904) 287-7300.

CRIME & SAFETY
Crimes per 1,000 population: 86 (Jacksonville); 87 (Jacksonville Beach). **Non-emergency police:** (904) 630-0500. **Non-emergency fire department:** (904) 630-0522. **Police, fire, ambulance emergencies:** 911.

HOMELESS & BLIGHT
There are pockets of blight in some communities fringing downtown and Jacksonville Beach. Despite reports in the *Jacksonville Business Journal* that the city has abandoned its 20-year effort to redevelop downtown, progress is being made.

The U.S. Census population count for Duval County was 672,971, which included 665 homeless persons in shelters and 155 visible in street locations.

HEALTH CARE
Hospitals: There are 4,605 beds in more than 20 hospitals and medical centers, including a Mayo Clinic.
Physicians: 2,300. **Specialties:** 55.

GETTING SMART
Jacksonville University, (904) 745-7000. **Offerings:** 62 undergraduate and 14 graduate degree programs, the College of Weekend Studies and Elderhostel programs. **University of North Florida,** (904) 620-1000. **Offerings:** Several undergraduate and graduate degree programs, plus a doctorate in education. **Florida Community College at Jacksonville,** four campuses, (904) 225-0506. **Offerings:** Two-year degrees and adult education. GOLD (Golden Opportunities for Lifelong Development) offers courses for people 55 and older, (904) 632-3281. **The Life Center of Shepherd's Centers of America,** (904) 356-1423. **Offerings:** Courses in life enrichment, liberal arts and wellness are held in area churches for people 55 and older.

JUST FOR SENIORS
First Call Information & Crisis Line, (904) 632-0600. **Jacksonville Senior Services,** (904) 630-0928. **Lane/Wiley Senior Center** and **Mary L. Singleton Senior Center,** (904) 630-0995. **Senior Citizen Special Events,** (904) 630-0995. **Woodland Acres Senior Center,** (904) 725-0624.

GETTING INVOLVED
RSVP, (904) 630-0998. **SCORE,** (904) 443-1900. **Volunteer Jacksonville,** (904) 398-7777.

COST OF LIVING
Florida Price Level Index: 97.98 (Duval County). **Rank:** 14th most expensive county.

RECREATION, ENTERTAINMENT & AMENITIES
Public golf: Pineview Golf & Country Club, Champions, Deerfield Lakes Golf Club, Golf Club of Jacksonville and Hyde Park are among 20 listed. **Private golf:** Cimarrone Golf & Country Club, Deer Creek Country Club and Hidden Hills Country Club are among 20 listed. **Public tennis courts:** Boone Park, Huguenot Tennis Center and Southside Courts. **Private tennis courts:** Big Tree Racquet & Fitness Club, Deerwood Club and The Woods Tennis & Swim Club. **Parks:** 120 municipal parks, plus Hanna Park, Little Talbot Island State Park and Metropolitan Park. **Public swimming pools:** 29. **Water sports:** Boating, boat shows, beach festivals, fishing tournaments, sailing regattas, etc. **River/gulf/ocean:** St. Johns River, Intracoastal Waterway, Atlantic Ocean and Trout River. **Running/walking/biking:** Theodore Roosevelt Preserve, Fort Caroline National Memorial, the Riverwalk, Big Talbot Island State Park, Little Talbot Island and the University of North Florida. **Horses/riding:** Several stables and academies. **Hunting:** Licenses, (904) 630-2005. **Movie theaters:** 100-plus screens. **Art museums:** The African Art Collection of Edward Waters College, Alexander Brest Fine Arts Museum, Cummer Gallery of Art and Jacksonville Art Museum. **History museums:** Firehouse Museum, Jacksonville Historical Center, Jacksonville Museum of Science & History, Museum of Southern History. **Theaters:** Alhambra Dinner Theatre, Civic Auditorium, Florida National Pavilion and Metropolitan Park, Jacksonville Actor's Theatre, Moran Theater, Prime Osborne Convention Center, River City Playhouse, Theatre Jacksonville, Times-Union Center and Veteran's Memorial Coliseum. Performing arts: FCCI Artist Series, Florida Ballet, Jacksonville Symphony Orchestra and St. Johns River City Band. **Library:** Main library, 13 branches and bookmobile. **Attractions:** Anheuser-Busch Brewery, Jacksonville Landing, Jacksonville Zoo, Karpelts Manuscript Library Museum, Maritime Museum and Mayport. **Necessities:** Everything a major city can offer.

Smart Shopper Tip: Eight regional malls, including Regency Square, one of the largest in the South; Jacksonville Landing, a downtown waterfront complex; and seven flea markets ensure shopping satisfaction.

WHO LIVES HERE
Population: 691,656 year-round residents, an increase of 56,426 since 1990. **Age 65+** = 10.0% in Duval County. **Median household income:** $31,892 (Duval County). **Per capita income:** $22,337 (Duval County).

NUMBERS TO KNOW
Chamber of commerce: Jacksonville, (904) 366-6600; Jacksonville Beaches, (904) 249-3868. **Voter registration:** (904) 630-1410. **Vehicle registration, tags & title:** (904) 630-1916. **Driver's license:** (904) 727-5545 or (904) 777-2121. **Visitors bureau:** (904) 798-9111.

WHAT TO READ
Florida Times-Union, daily newspaper, (904) 359-4111. **Jacksonville Business Journal**, weekly newspaper, also publishes **Discover Jacksonville**, (904) 396-3502. **Jacksonville Magazine**, (904) 396-8666.

GETTING AROUND
Bus: Jacksonville Transportation Authority, seniors ride free with proof of age, (904) 630-3181. Automated Skyway Express is a downtown monorail. **Taxi:** 15-plus companies. Yellow Cab, (904) 260-1111. **Tours:** Jacksonville Party Boats, (904) 396-2333. **Airport:** Jacksonville International. **Traffic:** Can be horrendous.

JOBS
County unemployment rate: 3.7%. **Florida Jobs and Benefits:** (904) 798-4780. **Job News Line**, (904) 630-1144.

UTILITIES
Electricity: Jacksonville Electric Authority, (904) 632-5200. **Gas:** Peoples Gas, (904) 739-1211. **Water & sewer:** Jacksonville Department of Public Works, (904) 630-1620. **Telephone:** Bell South, (800) 789-9025 in Florida, or (800) 753-2909 out-of-state. **Cable TV:** Media One, (904) 731-7700.

PLACES OF WORSHIP
More than 500 churches and six Jewish synagogues.

THE ENVIRONMENT
The lower St. Johns River basin has been designated for improvement and management, as has Lake Disston. The Duval County portion of the basin generally has been rated as having poor surface water quality. Cedar River has the worst water quality in the area and has frequent fish kills.

The Outstanding Florida Water designation has been granted to Haw Creek State Preserve, Mike Roess Gold Head Branch State Park, Nassau River, St. Johns River Aquatic Preserve, Kingsley Lake, the upper portion of North Forth Black Creek, and Ravine Gardens.

Duval County has six EPA-listed Superfund sites: Cecil Field Naval Air Station, Hipps Road Landfill, Jacksonville Naval Air Station, Pickettville Road Landfill, Whitehouse Oil Pits and Yellow Water Road Dump.

EVENTS AND FESTIVALS
The Players Championship - March. **Feast and Fest** - April. **A Taste of Jacksonville** - April. **Riverwalk Arts & Crafts Festival** - May. **Greater Jacksonville Kingfish Tournament** - July. **Riverwalk Seafest** - September. **Jacksonville Jazz Festival and Cecil Field Air Show** - October. **Jacksonville Light Parade** - November. **Gator Bowl Football Classic** - January. **The Cultural Council**, a recording of arts and entertainment events, (904) 355-1500.

WHERE TO EAT
Crawdaddy's, 1643 Prudential Drive, seafood, Cajun, moderate to expensive, (904) 396-3546. **Juliette's**, 245 Water St., in the Omni Hotel, continental, expensive, (904) 355-6664. **Sterling's Cafe**, 355 St. Johns Ave., continental, expensive, (904) 387-0700.

WHERE TO STAY
Hampton Inn, (904) 281-0443. **House on Cherry Street**, (904) 384-1999. **Omni Hotel**, (904) 355-6664. **Sea Turtle Inn**, (904) 249-7402.

ISSUES
Crime prevention in some areas, image enhancement in north Jacksonville, housing discrimination, violence and drugs were all in the news when we last visited. But, this is a great city and getting better.

Jupiter & Tequesta

HE SAID: ★ ★ ★ ★
*It didn't take us long to conclude that Jupiter
was among our favorite towns in Florida, with warm
and friendly people and a peaceful environment in
which to enjoy its amenities.*

SHE SAID: ★ ★ ★ ★ ★
*This is a place everyone should consider.
Entering the town, you can immediately see that it's a little
different. The town is spacious, with no tall office buildings
and lots of palms, shrubs and flowers. Jupiter's main street,
Indiantown Road, leads over the Intracoastal Waterway to
the Atlantic Ocean and some very pretty beaches.
I definitely recommend Jupiter.*

We spent the night in Jupiter on our way south to Key West and promised ourselves we would stop again on the return trip north. It is the last quiet outpost in southeast Florida before plunging into the faster tempos of West Palm Beach, Fort Lauderdale and Greater Miami.

Clean, unhurried and tropical, Jupiter's beautifully landscaped public areas, shopping centers and residential neighborhoods are its distinguishing hallmarks. Water everywhere provides wonderful recreation and scenic housing sites.

There are two ongoing concerns. The first is beach erosion and the potential impact a hurricane could have on low-lying Jupiter Island, which sits just north of Jupiter. Shortly before our visit, an ocean-front cottage slid into the sea due to high tides.

Secondly, the raising and lowering of drawbridges in the area cause long traffic delays, up to 20 minutes. When you arrive, study local maps and learn the drawbridge schedules.

We spoke with retirees who said they like having everything at their fingertips in Jupiter. Beaches, shopping, supermarkets, restaurants and the Jupiter Dinner Theatre were mentioned. Several celebrities have homes in the area, including Perry Como and Greg Norman. Burt Reynolds has lent his name to many local landmarks.

Upon completion, the 2,300-acre community of ABACOA will have 4,000 residences, a winter-training facility for the St. Louis Cardinals and Montreal Expos, a Florida Atlantic University campus, parks, golf course and retail-industrial complexes.

The area includes the town of Jupiter, Jupiter Inlet Colony, the Village of Tequesta and upscale Juno Beach. Jupiter Island in neighboring Martin County is a small but lovely spot. Despite Jupiter's rapid growth during the past decade, it has retained its quiet and friendly ways and continues to protect its scenic beauty.

WEATHER

	Winter	Spring	Summer	Fall
Normal daily high/low	76/58	85/69	90/75	80/65
Normal precipitation	9 in.	17 in.	21 in.	14 in.

Disaster watch: Southeast Florida has been hit by nine major hurricanes since 1900.

TAXES
Sales tax: 6%. **Property tax:** $21.98 (Jupiter), $23.68 (Tequesta) per $1,000 valuation. Sample taxes are calculated at the rate of $23.68 and include a $25,000 homestead exemption.

Home value	Tax
$100,000	$1,776
$150,000	$2,960
$250,000	$5,328

REAL ESTATE
Median home value: $101,611 (Palm Beach County). **Median rent:** $773/month (Palm Beach County). **Communities popular with retirees:** Indian Creek Golf Club has condominiums, duplex villas and single-family homes that range in price from $80,000 to $150,000. With about 1,000 housing units, the 18-hole golf course gets a lot of play. Little Club in Tequesta has condominiums starting at $50,000, single-family homes from $125,000 and a nine-hole golf course. North Passage, bordered by the Riverbend Golf Course, the pine forest of Jonathan Dickinson State Park and the Loxahatchee River, offers waterfront custom homes from the $300s, townhomes from the high $120s and non-waterfront single-family homes from the $170s. J.T. Brokers Realty, (561) 746-4848, provided information and price ranges. **Licensed continuing-care communities:** The Waterford (Juno Beach), has 289 independent living units and 60 community beds, (561) 627-3800.

CRIME & SAFETY
Crimes per 1,000 population: 51 (Jupiter); 32 (Tequesta). **Non-emergency police:** (561) 746-6201. **Non-emergency fire department:** (561) 575-6250. **Police, fire, ambulance emergencies:** 911.

HOMELESS & BLIGHT
We saw no evidence of homeless people or blighted areas. We were impressed by the beauty of the whole area, especially the shopping centers and residential neighborhoods.

The U.S. Census counted 219 homeless persons in shelters and 197 on the streets in Palm Beach County, population 863,518.

HEALTH CARE
Hospital: Jupiter Medical Center, 156 beds, full service, (561) 747-2234.
Physicians: More than 200 in the area. **Specialties:** 31.

GETTING SMART
Palm Beach Community College, (561) 625-2500, offers courses at Palm Beach Gardens (15 minutes from Jupiter). **Offerings:** Two-year degrees in arts and sciences as well as continuing studies, credit and non-credit, for personal enrichment. Retirees can join the school's Institute of New Dimensions, (561) 439-8186, for eight-week classes in life enrichment, liberal arts and wellness. **Florida Atlantic University** north campus, (561) 297-3000, is scheduled to move to Jupiter in about two years. **Offerings:** Graduate and undergraduate degrees in arts and humanities, business, education, engineering, nursing, science, urban studies and public affairs.

JUST FOR SENIORS
Area Agency on Aging, (561) 694-7601. **Palm Beach County Senior Services,** (561) 627-5765.

GETTING INVOLVED
Jupiter and Tequesta have all the clubs and professional, fraternal and religious organizations you would expect to find. **Habitat for Humanity,** (561) 743-3660. **Jupiter-Tequesta Athletic Associa-**

tion is a group of volunteers who organize athletic programs for more than 2,500 children, (561) 288-5690.

RECREATION, ENTERTAINMENT & AMENITIES
Public golf: Indian Creek Golf Course, 18 holes/par 72, and Jupiter Dunes Golf Course. **Private golf:** Admiral's Cove Golf Course, 45 holes; Cypress Links; Loxahatchee Club; Old Trail Golf Club, 36 holes/par 72 and par 71; and Tequesta Country Club. **Public tennis courts:** Carlin Park, Jupiter Bay Racquet Club and Loggerhead Park. **Private tennis courts:** Jonathan's Landing, Jupiter Ocean & Racquet Club and River Edge Bath & Tennis Club. **Parks:** Carlin Park offers a 110-acre beach; J.W. Corbett Wildlife Management Area has 56,000 acres for camping and fishing. Jonathan Dickinson State Park offers guided walks, fishing, camping, boating, horse paths and bicycle trails within its 10,248 acres. There's also Jupiter Beach, Dubois, Burt Reynolds, Jupiter Lighthouse and Riverside Drive parks. **Public swimming pools:** North County Aquatic Complex. **Water sports:** Boating, sailing, fishing, swimming, snorkeling and scuba diving. **River/gulf/ocean:** Three miles of Atlantic coastline. The Loxahatchee River and Intracoastal Waterway flow into the ocean through Jupiter Inlet. **Running/walking/biking:** Carlin Park Heart Trail, Coral Cove Park Nature Trail, Loggerhead Park Nature Trail. **Horses/riding:** Jonathan Dickinson State Park. There are several riding academies and stables in the area. **Hunting:** J.W. Corbett Wildlife Management Area has deer, wild hog, squirrel and quail in season, (561) 624-6989. Florida Game and Freshwater Fish Commission, (561) 625-5122. **Movie theaters:** 14 screens. **Art museums:** Lighthouse Gallery & School of Art. **History museums:** Dubois Pioneer House, Florida History Center and Museum, and Jupiter Inlet Lighthouse. **Theaters:** The Carousel Jupiter Theatre, Coastal Playhouse and Carlin Park Amphitheater. In Tequesta, the Burt Reynolds Institute for Theatre Training presents comedies, dramas and musicals. **Library:** County Library in Jupiter and North County Branch Library in Tequesta. **Attractions:** Blowing Rocks Preserve, Marinelife Center of Juno Beach, Burt Reynolds Ranch and Film Studio, and Jupiter Inlet Lighthouse. **Necessities:** Everything's available.

Smart Shopper Tip: The best bet is Indiantown Road, between I-95 and U.S. Highway 1, and the shops along U.S. 1 in the Village at Tequesta. There are 23 plazas and shopping centers with national chains and local boutiques. The Gardens Mall, about six miles south in Palm Beach Gardens, is a 1.2 million-square-foot complex with five major department stores.

WHO LIVES HERE
Population: 30,992 year-round residents in Jupiter, an increase of 6,085 since 1990. 4,686 year-round residents in Tequesta, an increase of 187 since 1990. **Age 65+** = 25.0 % in Palm Beach County. **Median household income:** $33,094 (Palm Beach County). **Per capita income:** $36,057 (Palm Beach County).

NUMBERS TO KNOW
Chamber of commerce: (561) 746-7111. **Voter registration:** (561) 746-5134 in Jupiter; in Tequesta, (561) 288-5637 (Martin County) or (561) 355-2650 (Palm Beach County). **Vehicle registration, tags & title:** (561) 355-2622. **Driver's license:** (561) 681-6333. **Visitors bureau:** (800) 554-PALM or (561) 471-3995.

WHAT TO READ
The Courier Journal, weekly newspaper, (561) 746-5111. **Palm Beach Post,** daily newspaper, (561) 820-4100. **50 Plus**, weekly tabloid, (561) 778-9800.

GETTING AROUND
Bus: PalmTran, (561) 233-1111. **Taxi:** Jupiter Taxi, (561) 743-7323. **Tours:** Manatee Queen, sightseeing boat tours, (561) 744-2191. **Airport:** Palm Beach International is 18 miles away. **Traffic:** Watch out for drawbridge tie-ups.

JOBS
County unemployment rate: 6.4%. **Florida Jobs and Benefits:** (561) 221-4071.

UTILITIES
Electricity: Florida Power & Light, (561) 287-5400. **Gas:** Peoples Gas, (561) 694-1103. **Water & sewer:** Town of Jupiter, (561) 746-5134. **Telephone:** Bell South, (800) 789-9025 in Florida, or (800) 753-0710 out-of-state. **Cable TV:** Adelphia Cable, (561) 627-3600, or ComCast, (561) 478-5866.

PLACES OF WORSHIP
Four Catholic and 36 Protestant churches, plus one Jewish synagogue.

THE ENVIRONMENT
The same restrictions on development that have preserved Jupiter's peaceful atmosphere also have protected its waters. Jupiter Sound has been rated as having good water quality.

There is one EPA-listed Superfund site in Palm Beach County, located in Lake Park. The EPA reported that the Hobe Sound Water Co., serving a population of 4,000, had lead in its drinking water measuring 19 parts per billion (ppb). The EPA action level is 15 ppb.

EVENTS AND FESTIVALS
Artfest by the Sea - March. **Seafare** - May. **Indian Summer Arts & Crafts Festival** - October.

WHERE TO EAT
Charley's Crab,1000 N. U.S. Highway 1, fresh seafood, menu changes daily, moderate to expensive, (561) 744-4710. **The Crab House,**1065 A1A Service Road, tropical atmosphere, seafood, expensive, (561) 744-1300. **O'Brians**, 12860 U.S. Highway 1, steaks, expensive, (561) 626-5880.

WHERE TO STAY
Best Western Intracoastal Inn, (561) 575-2936. **Jupiter Waterfront Inn,** (561) 747-9085. **Jupiter Beach Resort,** (561) 746-2511.

ISSUES
Retirees we spoke with have nothing but praise for Jupiter. They love to indulge in the arts and entertainment in West Palm Beach, Fort Lauderdale and Miami, then return home to the charm and tranquillity of Jupiter.

Key Biscayne

HE SAID: ★ ★
While pricey Key Biscayne has rebounded from the destruction and trauma of 1992's Hurricane Andrew, it is not now, nor is it ever likely to be, a viable retirement alternative for the average, middle-class American.

SHE SAID: ★ ★ ★
It's a true island paradise, but there's not enough shopping or variety of entertainment and amenities to keep me here. Taking the toll bridge to Miami just to run errands is too much trouble.

Key Biscayne, incorporated in 1991 as the Village of Key Biscayne, is a community in transition. It is no longer a bedroom community of Miami, and it is not yet an independent small town.

In the recent past, Key Biscayne was a very expensive haven for those who sought the sophistication, opportunities and eliteness of Miami's arts and entertainment without its over-crowding, over-commercialization and excessive traffic. Local sources estimate that approximately one-third of Key Biscayne's residents are retirees, one-third are investors and part-time occupants and the remaining third are younger couples who commute to jobs in Miami. The current trend seems to be toward absentee owners and investors. Would-be residents are being priced out of the market by speculators, many of them from Europe, South and Central America and the Far East.

The island's tropical beauty and provincial charm were devastated by Hurricane Andrew, which caused extensive property damage. The lush vegetation that gave the area the appearance of a subtropical paradise was virtually wiped out.

Properties damaged by the hurricane were quickly repaired and housing rebuilt. The Village received funds from the Department of Transportation and the Federal Emergency Management Agency to replace trees on public rights-of-way and in other public areas. Nevertheless, it will be some time before the subtropical flora that distinguished the island can match its former beauty.

Key Biscayne is experiencing all the attendant challenges and opportunities of change. Between the loss of its distinctive foliage and the rapid escalation of housing prices, Key Biscayne is losing its remaining promise for middle-class retirees.

WEATHER

	Winter	Spring	Summer	Fall
Normal daily high/low	75/64	82/74	87/78	79/69
Normal precipitation	6 in.	15 in.	15 in.	9 in.

Disaster watch: Southeast Florida has been hit by nine major hurricanes since 1900.

TAXES
Sales tax: 6.5%. **Property tax:** $22.08 per $1,000 valuation. Sample tax calculations include a $25,000 homestead exemption.

Home value	Tax
$100,000	$1,656
$150,000	$2,760
$250,000	$4,968

REAL ESTATE
Median home value: $312,500. **Median rent:** $764/month (Dade County). **Communities popular with retirees:** No area in particular. With a land area only a mile long and 1.25 miles wide, any spot is water-accessible, and that is a key factor in real estate pricing. The island is completely built-out, so land is expensive and new construction entails demolition of existing structures. Key Biscayne Realty, (305) 361-8800, provided these general price ranges: Small one-bedroom condos and townhouses, not on the beach, start at around $125,000. A 1,800-square-foot single-family fixer-upper, not on the water, will cost $250,000 — minimum. Two-bedroom townhomes near the beach, with a pool, cost around $275,000. One-bedroom waterfront condos start at $210,000. Two-bedroom waterfront condos start at $260,000. Penthouses and single-family, waterfront homes start at more than $1.5 million. **Licensed continuing-care retirement communities:** None.

CRIME & SAFETY
Crimes per 1,000 population: 47. **Non-emergency police:** (305) 365-5505. **Non-emergency fire department:** (305) 365-8989. **Police, fire, ambulance emergencies:** 911.

HOMELESS & BLIGHT
There is no room here for blight — everything and every place is too expensive. The homeless were not visible on the streets during our visit.

The U.S. Census counted 1,730 homeless among Dade County's 1.9 million population, with 1,235 in shelters and 495 visible on Dade County streets.

HEALTH CARE
There are no hospitals on the island. Highly regarded Baptist Hospital and many others are located in Miami. **Hospitals: Mercy Hospital** is the closest full-service facility. It's located about 15 minutes away on the Mainland and has 512 beds, (305) 854-4400.
Physicians: 9. **Specialties:** 4.

GETTING SMART
You have to go to the Mainland for educational pursuits beyond high school. The University of Miami and Barry University are the closest and the largest. **Barry University**, (305) 899-3000, in Miami Springs is a private Catholic university. **Offerings:** Undergraduate and graduate degree programs. **University of Miami**, Institute for Retired Professionals, (305) 284-5072. **Offerings:** Graduate or undergraduate lecture courses, monthly Distinguished Faculty Luncheon Lecture Series and peer-led study/discussion groups. Sample subjects: archaeology, art, drama, geography, history, languages, music and philosophy.

JUST FOR SENIORS
There are no services or facilities available on the island just for seniors.

GETTING INVOLVED

There are plenty of opportunities for volunteerism and civic involvement here. In 1991, residents voted to incorporate the island as the Village of Key Biscayne, and the new Village offices are exploding with activity. **Library Foundation and Village Beautification Foundation**, (305) 361-3493. Contact the Village Manager, (305) 365-5511, or chamber of commerce, (305) 361-5207, for further information.

RECREATION, ENTERTAINMENT & AMENITIES

Public golf: Crandon Park Golf Course. **Private golf:** None. **Public tennis courts:** Calusa Park and International Tennis Center. **Private tennis courts:** Grand Bay Club and Key Biscayne Yacht Club. **Public swimming pools:** None. **Parks:** Bill Baggs Cape Florida State Recreation Area, Calusa Park, Crandon Park Beach and Virginia Key Beach. **Water sports:** Boating, fishing, diving, snorkeling and more. Try Crandon, Rickenbacker and Virginia Key marinas. Biscayne Bay and the Gulf Stream currents off the Atlantic provide excellent fishing grounds. **River/gulf/ocean:** The island enjoys the benefits of crystal clear Biscayne Bay and the Atlantic Ocean. **Running/walking/biking:** Trails wind through Bill Baggs park, Crandon Park and the Village Green. Call Dade County Bicycle and Pedestrian Program for routes, (305) 375-4507. **Movie theaters:** None. **Art museums:** None. **History museums:** Cape Florida Lighthouse Keeper's Home. **Theaters:** Calusa Playhouse. **Library:** Key Biscayne Public. **Attractions:** Crandon Park and Cape Florida Lighthouse at Bill Baggs park. **Necessities:** Most are here, but for variety, go to the Mainland.

Smart Shopper Tip: Key Biscayne doesn't have the population base to support major chains, so even though it boasts six shopping centers, malls and arcades, the establishments are along the lines of small boutiques, ice cream parlors and barber shops. To do real shopping you must make the eight-mile drive across the causeway to the Mainland.

WHO LIVES HERE

Population: 8,937 year-round residents, an increase of 83 since 1990. **Age 65+** = 14.4% in Dade County. **Median household income:** $26,743 (Dade County). **Per capita income:** $21,058 (Dade County).

NUMBERS TO KNOW

Chamber of commerce: (305) 361-5207. **Voter registration, vehicle registration, tags & title:** (305) 365-5511. **Driver's license:** (305) 229-6333.

WHAT TO READ

Islander News, weekly newspaper, (305) 361-3333.

GETTING AROUND

Bus: Metrobus, (305) 770-3131, offers Maps-by-Mail; ask for the "First Time Rider's Kit." **Taxi:** Rickenbacker, (305) 365-0000. **Tours:** None. **Airport:** Miami International. **Traffic:** Crandon Boulevard is the main thoroughfare and gets congested at peak times — especially during tourist season when 250,000 visitors come through town.

JOBS

County unemployment rate: 7.2%. **Florida Jobs and Benefits:** In Coral Gables, (305) 289-2475.

UTILITIES

Electricity: Florida Power & Light, (305) 442-8770. **Gas:** None. **Water & sewer:** Miami-Dade Water & Sewer, (305) 665-7488. **Telephone:** Bell South, (800) 789-9025 in Florida, or (800) 753-0710 out-of-state. **Cable TV:** Adelphia Cable, (305) 255-3770.

PLACES OF WORSHIP

One Catholic and three Protestant churches on the island.

THE ENVIRONMENT

Preventing the pollution and destruction of Biscayne Bay has long been a concern. The bay has gained status as a protected water and now maintains good water quality ratings. It is still threatened by the heavily polluted Miami River, which empties into the bay.

There are 12 EPA-listed Superfund sites in Dade County; none are in Key Biscayne.

EVENTS AND FESTIVALS

Key Biscayne Art Festival - January. **Royal Caribbean Senior PGA Tournament** - February. **Lipton International Tennis Players Championships** - March. **Parade and Kiwanis Picnic** - July 4. **Winterfest** - December.

WHERE TO EAT

Stefano's, 24 Crandon Blvd., Italian cuisine, moderate to expensive, (305) 361-7007. **La Carreta**, 12 Crandon Blvd., Cuban and Latin American, moderate to expensive, (305) 365-1177. **Linda B. Steakhouse**, 320 Crandon Blvd., steak, lobster, moderate to expensive, (305) 361-1111.

WHERE TO STAY

Key Colony, (305) 361-2170. **Sonesta Beach Resort**, (305) 361-2021.

ISSUES

Key Biscayne is now incorporated as a self-sufficient village, but it still has work to do to provide its citizens a full range of amenities, facilities, goods and services. Slogans for the island, such as "Buy Key Biscayne" and "Key It on the Key," urge residents to spend their money at home. Residents say that the island still does not offer everything they need at competitive prices.

Key Largo

HE SAID: ★ ★
This is a playground for Miamians and a stopover for vacationers on their way to the Lower Keys. It boasts some areas of historic interest, but the claims are largely artificial and Hollywoodish. Key Largo is more appealing to me as a vacation resort than a place to retire.

SHE SAID: ★ ★
Water lovers will relish Key Largo. Retirees who enjoy a hot climate and ample water sports could enjoy this life. But, nightlife is quiet, and shopping is limited. This is not a place where I would want to retire.

Looking at the never-ceasing lines of traffic on Overseas Highway (U.S. Highway 1) in Key Largo, waiting for a table at crowded restaurants and seaside attractions, or searching in vain for a vacancy sign at one of the hotels, motels, lodges or campgrounds makes the published population figure of nearly 15,600 seem "fishy."

While it is a haven for fishermen, Key Largo is not the sleepy little village that this statistic implies. Hundreds of thousands of American and foreign tourists, south Florida weekenders and snowbirds swell the real wintertime population. Some are on one-night stopovers enroute to the Lower Keys and Key West. Others arrive by boat, spending their nights aboard ship while dining and sightseeing ashore during the day. Still others — literally thousands — spend a few months here each year before returning to their permanent residences in the north.

Hidden behind tree-lined U.S. Highway 1 are a variety of neighborhoods. Communities of manufactured homes, single-family houses and condominiums — some with clubhouses — dot the area. Access to the water is easy. Many homesites are on canals, and there is plenty of docking in the local marina.

Whatever their reasons for being here, residents all seem to be enjoying themselves. Lucille and Ray Warner, who moved to Key Largo from Ohio many years ago, call it paradise and say they'll never leave. Ray is so proud of his hometown that he and his neighbors spend time picking up trash left by tourists.

It seems as if the local authorities require residents to use "paradise" to describe the Keys since it comes up so often in conversation. A close-knit and friendly community, residents say they "visit one another, attend club meetings, walk around the neighborhood, play bingo and have dinner together."

Not a bad way to spend your life in paradise!

Note: You'll commonly see addresses and direction in the Keys based on U.S. Highway 1 Mile Markers, abbreviated as MM.

WEATHER

	Winter	Spring	Summer	Fall
Normal daily high/low	78/64	86/73	90/78	81/69
Normal precipitation	6 in.	14 in.	15 in.	10 in.

Disaster watch: The Keys have been hit by three major hurricanes since 1900.

TAXES
Sales tax: 7%. **Property tax:** $14.65 per $1,000 valuation. Sample tax calculations include a $25,000 homestead exemption.

Home value	Tax
$100,000	$1,099
$150,000	$1,831
$250,000	$3,296

REAL ESTATE
Median home value: $145,610 (Monroe County). **Median rent:** $888/month (Monroe County). **Communities popular with retirees:** Lillian Brown at Century 21- Keysearch Realty, (305) 451-4321, suggested Silver Shores, manufactured and site-built homes with resales generally priced from the mid-$30s to the mid-$70s and higher; Ocean Reef, a golf and tennis club that offers homes priced from $250,000 to more than $1 million; and Holiday Plantation Villas with condominiums under $100,000. **Licensed continuing-care retirement communities:** None.

CRIME & SAFETY
Crimes per 1,000 population: 68 (Monroe County sheriff's jurisdiction). **Non-emergency police:** (305) 853-3211. **Non-emergency fire department:** (305) 460-5560. **Police, fire, ambulance emergencies:** 911.

HOMELESS & BLIGHT
There were no homeless persons visible. There are some unattractive areas with substandard housing.

The U.S. Census counted 126 homeless persons visible on the streets and 15 in shelters in Monroe County, population 78,024.

HEALTH CARE
Hospitals: Mariner's Hospital, at MM 88.5 in Tavernier, 42 beds, full service, (305) 852-4418.
Physicians: 28. **Specialties:** 20.

GETTING SMART
Florida Keys Community College in Tavernier, (305) 852-8007. **Offerings:** Two-year degree programs in arts and sciences, plus continuing-education courses, seminars and workshops.

JUST FOR SENIORS
Monroe County Social Services, (305) 852-7125. **Plantation Key Convalescent Center,** (305) 852-3021. **Veterans Affairs,** (305) 451-0164.

GETTING INVOLVED
There are many clubs, civic associations and organizations here. Check the Relocation Guide, available from the chamber of commerce. **Key Largo Volunteer Ambulance Corp.,** (305) 451-2766. **Friends of the Library,** (305) 451-2396. **Habitat for Humanity,** (305) 367-3662. **Nature Conservancy,** (305) 296-3880.

RECREATION, ENTERTAINMENT & AMENITIES
Public golf: Ocean Reef Country Club. **Private golf:** None. **Public tennis courts:** None. **Private tennis courts:** Ocean Pointe, Plantation Yacht Harbor Resort, Key Largo Inn, Kona Kai, Marina Del Mar, Sheraton. **Parks:** John Pennekamp Coral Reef State Park at MM 102.5 is famous for its 120 square miles of living coral reefs, sea-grass beds and mangrove swamps. Much is accessible only by boat. Harry Harris Park, at MM 92.5 in Tavernier, is a family park and beach. Everglades National Park, about 25 miles north across Blackwater Sound, encompasses 1.4 million acres. Visitors may see bald eagles among 300 species of birds, plus alligators, bobcats and deer. **Public swimming pools:** None. **Water sports:** Key Largo claims the

title of sport diving capital of the world. Charter boats, backcountry guides and party boat rentals offer opportunities for boating, canoeing, sailing, diving, snorkeling, windsurfing, parasailing and fishing. **River/gulf/ocean:** Florida Bay and the Atlantic, plus canals around every corner. **Running/walking/biking:** A bike path runs along Overseas Highway from MM 106 to MM 86 in Islamorada. There are many trails in the Everglades area. **Horses/riding:** None. **Hunting:** None. **Movie theaters:** Two screens in Tavernier. **Art museums:** The Gallery. **History museums:** Maritime Museum of the Florida Keys at MM 102.6. **Theaters:** None. **Library:** Monroe County Public and Helen Wadley Public. **Attractions:** The original African Queen used in the movie. Also, Dolphins Plus, a research center. **Necessities:** Banks, retail stores, supermarkets, real estate agencies, post office, gas station.

  Smart Shopper Tip: Drive 26 miles to Florida City for major purchases. Since Key Largo is essentially a tourist town, merchants price their wares accordingly.

WHO LIVES HERE
Population: About 15,600 year-round residents, according to the chamber of commerce. **Age 65+ =** 17.5% in Monroe County. **Median household income:** $30,720 (Monroe County). **Per capita income:** $27,210 (Monroe County).

NUMBERS TO KNOW
Chamber of commerce: (305) 451-1414 or (800) 822-1088. **Voter registration:** (305) 852-7106. **Vehicle registration, tags & title:** (305) 852-7150. **Driver's license:** (305) 853-3562. **Visitors bureau:** (800) 352-5397.

WHAT TO READ
Florida Keys Keynoter, biweekly newspaper, (305) 451-4960. **The Reporter**, weekly newspaper, (305) 852-3216. **Free Press**, free weekly publication, (305) 664-2266.

GETTING AROUND
Bus: No public intra-city transportation. **Taxi:** Island Taxi, (305) 664-8181. **Tours:** Go Tours, (305) 743-9876. **Airport:** Miami International. **Traffic:** Moderate on weekdays; heavy on weekends.

JOBS
County unemployment rate: 2.5%. **Florida Jobs and Benefits:** In Marathon, (305) 289-2475.

UTILITIES
Electricity: Florida Keys Electric Co-op, (305) 852-2431. **Gas:** National Propane, (305) 852-3229. **Water & sewer:** Florida Keys Aqueduct Authority, (305) 852-8068. **Telephone:** Bell South, (800) 789-9025 in Florida, or (800) 753-0710 out-of-state. **Cable TV:** TCI Cablevision of Florida, (305) 852-2288.

PLACES OF WORSHIP
Two Catholic and 17 Protestant churches, plus one Jewish synagogue.

THE ENVIRONMENT
The island waters that open to the Atlantic Ocean and Gulf of Mexico are rated as having good water quality and are all designated as Outstanding Florida Waters, granting them legal protection against any significant change in water quality. There are pollution problems in many of the man-made canals and marinas. Along the east coast lies the only living coral reef in the continental United States. The delicate reefs are easily damaged by careless divers, boat anchors and commercial ship grindings and/or spills.

EVENTS AND FESTIVALS
Seafood Festival - January. **Sportfishing Festival Tournaments** - February. **Rain Barrel Arts Festival** - March. **July Fourth Parade. Island Jubilee** - November. **Christmas Boat Parade** - December.

WHERE TO EAT
Treetops at the Washington Beach Resort Key Largo at MM 97, seafood, steaks, Caribbean, expensive, (305) 852-5553. **Italian Fisherman** at MM 104, seafood, Italian, moderate, (305) 451-4471.

WHERE TO STAY
Jules' Undersea Lodge, (305) 451-2353. **Marina Del Mar Resort & Marina**, (305) 451-4107. **Washington Beach Resort Key Largo**, (305) 852-5553 or (800) 826-1006.

ISSUES
There are no burning issues troubling the residents we contacted nor making headlines in the newspapers. In Key Largo, land-use restrictions on development have been accepted and are being eased into place to protect the environment from destructive forces. As the *Free Press* put it, "Life goes on in a busy paradise. Hopefully the wind will slow down and the fishing will pick up."

RELOCATION TIPS

Before you pack up and move 30 years of accumulated possessions, consider how much of your household you really should take with you. One of the most common mistakes made during a relocation is taking too much. Here are three reasons to reduce before you move.

1) A majority of relocating retirees move to smaller homes and find that they do not have room for everything that fit in their former residence.

2) Some people find that the heavy, dark wood furniture of their former homes does not suit their new Florida lifestyle or home decor.

3) It costs more to move more.

Key West

HE SAID: ☆ ☆ ☆

*Key West is about 25 years past its prime.
It could have been a wonderful place to retire during the
1960s or '70s, but I wouldn't want to begin
that odyssey here today.*

SHE SAID: ☆ ☆ ☆

*Key West is a great place for active retirees. You can get
involved with the community through historic preservation,
theater productions or volunteering your time. The calm
waters offer great boating. But non-tourist shopping and
nightlife are limited. Traffic on U.S. Highway 1 is very heavy
during tourist season, which lasts from October through
May. I would not retire here.*

The only way to reach Key West by car is on a narrow two-lane highway. While traveling only as fast as the slowest driver in south Florida, you can enjoy the wonders of the 113-mile Overseas Highway (U.S. 1), the Seven-Mile Bridge and some of the most beautiful emerald-green waters imaginable. Just don't try to do it in a hurry.

The newer sections of Key West could be suburbs of any small tourist town. They're filled with strip shopping centers, fast-food restaurants and second-class motels. In town, small wooden houses clutter narrow streets. Sidewalks are lined with slow-moving, window-shopping tourists. Aromas from dozens of open-air cafes mingle in the air.

After wandering the streets, touring the restored historic district and visiting with longtime residents, one senses something special about this end-of-the-line town. Only 90 miles from Cuba, Key West swings to a Latin beat and has the feel of a tropical island with its lush vegetation, brightly colored, often ramshackle buildings and slow pace of life. Long known as a community of creative writers and artists, it has been home to Ernest Hemingway, Tennessee Williams, John James Audubon and other notables. In more recent years, many seeking a gay lifestyle have settled here. Residents describe Key West as a paradise peopled by thoughtful, unpretentious, intelligent and artistic creatures.

Residents also say it is a great place for active, young retirees. It invites involvement with the community. Water sports and recreation are abundant, and the calm waters offer great cruising around the island and in nearby coves.

Inhabitants describe Key West as a democratic society, where a $600,000 home shares a block with a $100,000 shack, and occupants of both get along beautifully. Low availability has made housing costs skyrocket. There is no unused land in Key West.

The crowds of tourists and the festive air they bring to the streets day and night lend an aura of security to those who may not be accustomed to seeing homeless persons sleeping in darkened recesses. Locals seem to feel safe here, too, telling us that crime is almost nonexistent. Unfortunately, FBI crime reports do not support this sense of safety.

Visit Key West. Enjoy it as a tourist. But, take time to gauge your expectations to the Key West lifestyle.

Note: You'll commonly see addresses and directions in the Keys based on U.S. Highway 1 Mile Markers, abbreviated as MM.

WEATHER

	Winter	Spring	Summer	Fall
Normal daily high/low	76/67	85/76	89/79	80/71
Normal precipitation	6 in.	10 in.	15 in.	9 in.

Disaster watch: The Keys have been hit by three major hurricanes since 1900.

TAXES

Sales tax: 7%. **Property tax:** $17.64 per $1,000 valuation. Sample tax calculations include a $25,000 homestead exemption.

Home value	Tax
$100,000	$1,323
$150,000	$2,205
$250,000	$3,969

REAL ESTATE

Median home value: $145,610 (Monroe County). **Median rent:** $888/month (Monroe County). **Communities popular with retirees:** No particular area. It is estimated that Key West's median home cost is about twice the county average due to the costs of necessary renovations on most resales. **Licensed continuing-care retirement communities:** None.

CRIME & SAFETY

Crimes per 1,000 population: 101. **Non-emergency police:** (305) 294-2511. **Non-emergency fire department:** (305) 292-8145. **Police, fire, ambulance emergencies:** 911.

HOMELESS & BLIGHT

The homeless are undeniably present. The homeless and general uncleanliness of popular tourist areas near the waterfront are among the most pressing issues here.

The U.S. Census counted 15 homeless persons in shelters and 126 visible in street locations in Monroe County, population 78,024.

HEALTH CARE

Hospitals: Florida Keys Memorial Hospital, Stock Island at MM 5.5, is not full service, (305) 294-5531. **Physicians:** 42. **Specialties:** 17.

GETTING SMART

Florida Keys Community College, (305) 296-9081. **Offerings:** Associated with the Tennessee Williams Fine Arts Center, continuing education courses include photography, creative writing, jewelry-making, sculpture, arts and crafts. Classes are open to winter residents as well as year-round residents. **St. Leo College**, (305) 293-2847. **Offerings:** Two and four-year liberal arts degree programs with studies in criminology, human resources administration, business administration and management. **Troy State University**, (305) 293-2987. **Offerings:** Graduate programs in educational leadership management.

JUST FOR SENIORS

AARP, (305) 292-3565. **Monroe County Social Services**, (305) 292-4573, offers meals, transportation, in-home services, job training and employment. **Senior Citizens Center**, (305) 374-6099.

GETTING INVOLVED

Key West Neighborhood Improvement Association, (305) 293-8898. Old Island Restoration Foundation, (305) 294-9501. Red Barn Theatre, (305) 296-9911. Tennessee Williams Fine Arts Center, (305) 296-1520.

RECREATION, ENTERTAINMENT & AMENITIES

Public golf: Key West Golf Course. Private golf: None. Public tennis courts: Higgs County Beach. Private tennis courts: Holiday Inn, Atlantic Breeze Condos and Key Wester Resort. Parks: Higgs Beach, Fort Zachary Taylor State Park, Mallory Square and Smathers Beach. Public swimming pools: One. Water sports: Several marinas and yacht clubs; offshore fishing is reputed to be some of the best; water-skiing, especially on the Gulf side; many reefs for interesting scuba diving and snorkeling. River/gulf/ocean: Atlantic Ocean and the Gulf of Mexico. Running/walking/biking: Get a "Walking and Biking Guide to Key West," by Sharon Wells, Key West Publications, (305) 294-8380. Horses/riding: None. Hunting: None. Movie theaters: Two. Art museums: The Audubon House, East Martellow Museum & Gallery, Haitian Art Company and Little White House Museum. History museums: Hemingway Home & Museum, Heritage House Museum. Key West Lighthouse Museum, Mel Fisher Maritime Heritage Society Museum and the Wrecker's Museum. Theaters: Red Barn Theatre, Tennessee Williams Fine Arts Center and the Waterfront Playhouse. Library: Bookmobile makes frequent stops. Attractions: Berenson's Key West Greyhound Track, Key West Aquarium, sunsets on Mallory Dock, Turtle Kraals and the Wharf Dolphin Show. Necessities: Banks, retail stores (no mall), supermarkets, real estate agencies, post office, gas stations.

Smart Shopper Tip: Go to the Mainland for serious shopping. You'll save money and increase your chances of finding what you want.

WHO LIVES HERE

Population: 27,305 year-round residents, an increase of 2,473 since 1990. Age 65+=17.5% in Monroe County. Median household income: $30,720 (Monroe County). Per capita income: $27,210 (Monroe County).

NUMBERS TO KNOW

Chamber of commerce: (305) 294-2587. Voter registration: (305) 292-3416. Vehicle registration, tags & title: (305) 294-8403. Driver's license: (305) 292-6747. Visitors bureau: (800) 352-5397. Hospitality House: (305) 294-9501.

WHAT TO READ

Key West Citizen, daily newspaper, (305) 294-6641. Solares Hill, monthly newspaper, (305) 294-3602. "Portraits: Wooden Houses of Key West," by Sharon Wells and Lawson Little, Key West Publications, (305) 294-8380.

GETTING AROUND

Bus: City of Key West Port and Transit Authority, (305) 292-8160. Taxi: All cabs operate from a central dispatcher, (305) 294-4444 or (305) 296-7777. Tours: Old Town Trolley and the Conch Tour Train. Airport: Key West International. Traffic: One lane in and one lane out. It can be slow going during peak tourist season. If you can adopt a laid-back "Keys attitude," it will help when trying to get somewhere.

JOBS

County unemployment rate: 2.5%. Florida Jobs and Benefits: (305) 292-6775.

UTILITIES

Electricity: City Electric System, (305) 294-5272. Gas: National Propane, (305) 294-3527. Water & sewer: Florida Keys Aqueduct Authority, (305) 296-2454. Telephone: Bell South, (800) 789-9025 in Florida, or (800) 753-0710 out-of-state. Cable TV: TCI Cablevision of Florida, (305) 296-6572.

PLACES OF WORSHIP

One Catholic and 32 Protestant churches, plus two Jewish synagogues.

THE ENVIRONMENT

The island waters that open to the Atlantic Ocean or Gulf of Mexico have good water quality ratings and are designated as Outstanding Florida Waters, granting them legal protection against any significant change in water quality. There are pollution problems in many of the man-made canals and marinas. Along the east coast lies the only living coral reef in the continental United States. The delicate reefs are easily damaged by careless divers, boat anchors and commercial ship grindings and/or spills. Erosion along Key West's shoreline is a concern.

EVENTS AND FESTIVALS

Old Island Days - Mid-January to mid-March. Conch Republic Independence Celebration - April. Songwriters Festival - May. Key West Theatre Festival - October. World Championship Offshore Powerboat Race Week - November.

WHERE TO EAT

Kelly's, 301 Whitehead St.,"We will cook your catch," Caribbean, moderate, (305) 293-8484. Pier House Restaurant, 1 Duval St., local seafood, expensive, (305) 296-4600.

WHERE TO STAY

Holiday Inn Beachside, (305) 294-2571. Marquesa Hotel, (305) 292-1919. Pier House Resort & Spa, (305) 296-4600.

ISSUES

Civic leaders are concerned that Duval Street, Key West's most famous avenue, is being taken over by T-shirt shops, electronics stores and worse. Gerry Tinlin, president of the hotel/motel association, was quoted as saying, "We've got to take it back... now."

Civic leaders and retirees want tougher building codes and stricter enforcement of existing codes to protect the historic district.

"Unbecoming an Art Colony" was the headline of an article by Gordon Lacy for the Solares Hill newspaper. He lamented the disappearance of artists, saying that the light hasn't changed, but prices have. He claimed that rising rents and a lack of city funding are forcing artists to flee.

Kissimmee

Kissimmee would still be a sleepy, central Florida town if Walt Disney World had not arrived on the scene in 1971, "ushering in a new period of dynamic development and prosperity," as the chamber of commerce guide puts it. However, it's debatable whether Disney did the town a favor by choosing an adjoining wilderness tract to build the world's largest entertainment complex.

Today there are two Kissimmees. The old Kissimmee, laid out near the northwest shore of Lake Tohopekaliga, still has the architectural remnants and peaceful atmosphere of an earlier time. However, the wealth brought by the hordes of overnight guests has transformed the skyline with new construction. A striking civic center, library, courthouse and hospital are among the buildings erected in recent years.

The new Kissimmee features miles and miles of motels, restaurants, amusement parks and attractions built in the last 30 years. The new section is both a blessing and a curse to the area. It has stimulated the development of new retirement communities, golf courses, organizations and cultural and recreational resources that are attractive to retirees. But there's been a corresponding increase in traffic, pollution, crime, substandard housing and low-paying jobs.

The Kissimmee-St. Cloud Chain of Lakes area, south of U.S. Highway 192, does offer lifestyle opportunities that few retirees could resist. It is geared to outdoor activities and recreational pursuits with the social and cultural amenities of Orlando nearby. But there are some ominous clouds behind this silver lining. Prospective retiree residents should look at all the ramifications of living near the world's most popular tourist attraction before making the move to this area.

WEATHER

	Winter	Spring	Summer	Fall
Normal daily high/low	76/51	88/65	91/72	80/58
Normal precipitation	8 in.	11 in.	20 in.	17 in.

Disaster watch: Central Florida is primarily subject to tropical storms and thunderstorms.

TAXES

Sales tax: 7%. **Property tax:** $21.26 per $1,000 valuation. Sample tax calculations include a $25,000 homestead exemption.

Home value	Tax
$100,000	$1,595
$150,000	$2,658
$250,000	$4,784

REAL ESTATE

Median home value: $92,383 (Osceola County). **Median rent:** $583/month (Osceola County). **Communities popular with retirees:** If you are interested in a turn-key community, don't leave the area without visiting Celebration, Florida's newest and finest small town, (407) 566-3448. Christine Endicott of Ramada Properties, (407) 847-8100, provided real estate information for the area. Buenaventura Lakes offers single-family homes, condos and villas priced from the $70s to the $180s. Hunters Creek has homes priced from the $100s to $400s and up. Orange Gardens has single-family homes priced from the $80s to the $100s. Good Samaritan Retirement Village has 425 acres for its 2,000 residents living in garden/patio apartments and mobile homes. Whispering Pines has manufactured homes from the $40s, (407) 847-8119. **Licensed continuing-care retirement communities:** None.

CRIME & SAFETY

Crimes per 1,000 population: 102. **Non-emergency police:** (407) 847-0176. **Non-emergency fire department:** (407) 518-2222. **Police, fire, ambulance emergencies:** 911.

HOMELESS & BLIGHT

Old Kissimmee is quaint yet progressive, with new municipal and county buildings springing up everywhere. New Kissimmee, along U.S. highways 17 and 192 and Route 535 (all roads leading to Walt Disney World), is inundated with motels, restaurants, shopping centers and signs advertising motels, restaurants and shopping centers. Not a very pretty sight. We did not see any homeless.

The U.S. Census reported 32 homeless persons in shelters in Osceola County, population 107,728.

HEALTH CARE

Hospitals: Columbia Kissimmee Surgical Center (407) 870-0573. **Osceola Regional Medical Center**, 169 beds, full service, (407) 846-2266. **Florida Hospital-Kissimmee**, 120 beds, full service, (407) 846-4343.
Physicians: 200. **Specialties:** All within the county.

GETTING SMART

Valencia Community College, Osceola campus, (407) 847-9496. **Offerings:** Two-year degrees in arts and sciences.

JUST FOR SENIORS

Osceola County Senior Citizen Center/Council on Aging, (407) 846-8532 or (407) 847-4357.

GETTING INVOLVED

There are about 100 social, fraternal, civic and service organizations. **Osceola Opportunity Center**, (407) 847-6016. **RSVP**, (407) 846-8532. **United Way**, (407) 846-3271. **Volunteer Center**, in Orlando, (407) 896-0945. **American Red Cross**, (407) 847-2780.

RECREATION, ENTERTAINMENT & AMENITIES

Public golf: Buenaventura Lakes Golf Club West, Crystalbrook Golf Club, Falcon's Fire Golf Club and Orange Lake Country Club. **Private golf:** Kissimmee Bay Country Club and Kissimmee Golf Club. **Public tennis courts:** Kissimmee Parks & Recreation Center, Oak Street Park, Orange Lake Country Club and Partin Triangle Park are among many locations of public courts in the area. **Private tennis courts:** Private courts at hotels and resorts. **Parks:** Lake Shore Recreation Center and Park are the most popular of numerous municipal and county parks. **Public swimming pools:** Civic Center. **Water sports:** The

Kissimmee Chain of Lakes is touted as one of the most beautiful and exciting recreation regions in the state, with endless opportunities for fishing, boating, sailing and canoeing. **River/gulf/ocean:** Kissimmee Waterway is a 50-mile series of lakes connecting Lake Tohopekaliga with Lake Okeechobee. **Running/walking/biking:** Bike paths and nature walks are available in many public parks. Campbell-Kissimmee Lakefront Park has a jogging track along the lake. **Horses/riding:** East Lake Park in St. Cloud has a horse trail. Poinciana Riding Stables has 750 acres with miles of trails. **Hunting:** Hunting and fishing licenses are required. Those 65 or older can obtain a no-cost certificate through the county tax collector's office, (407) 847-1525. **Movie theaters:** 13 screens. **Art museums:** Osceola Center for the Arts. **History museums:** Elvis Presley Museum and the Tupperware Museum of Historic Containers. The Osceola County Historical Society hosts exhibitions in the Center for the Arts. **Theaters:** Osceola Center for the Arts and the Tupperware Center. **Library:** Buenaventura Lakes Public and Kissimmee Public, plus Osceola County Law Library. **Attractions:** Gatorland, Monument of States, Osceola County Stadium & Sports Complex, Houston Astros spring training, Tupperware World Headquarters (with 1,500 acres of gardens and lakes), Water Mania and Xanadu, a prototype of the house of the future. **Necessities:** All available.

Smart Shopper Tip: Osceola Square Mall, Manufacturer's Mall, Osceola Flea & Farmers Market and Old Town are all worthy shopping experiences. None compare to the Florida Mall, which is 20 minutes north and features six major department stores and more than 200 specialty shops.

WHO LIVES HERE
Population: 38,787 year-round residents, an increase of 8,450 since 1990. **Age 65+ =** 13.8% in Osceola County. **Median household income:** $27,921 (Osceola County). **Per capita income:** $16,317 (Osceola County).

NUMBERS TO KNOW
Chamber of commerce: (407) 847-3174. **Voter registration:** (407) 847-1220. **Vehicle registration, tags & title:** (407) 847-1525. **Driver's license:** (407) 846-5232. **Visitors bureau:** (407) 847-5000.

WHAT TO READ
Orlando Sentinel, daily newspaper, (407) 420-5000. **Osceola News-Gazette**, weekly newspaper, (407) 425-8809. **Osceola Star**, weekly Spanish/English-language newspaper, (407) 933-0174.

GETTING AROUND
Bus: No public intra-city transportation. **Taxi:** Yellow Cab, (407) 846-2222. **Tours:** None. **Airport:** Orlando International is 15 miles away. **Train:** Amtrak Passenger Service, (800) 872-7245. **Traffic:** There is a lot of traffic in and around Kissimmee, but you can avoid major problems by staying off the heavily traveled Disney tourist routes, especially U.S. highways 441 and 192.

JOBS
County unemployment rate: 3.7%. **Florida Jobs and Benefits:** (407) 897-2880.

UTILITIES
Electricity, water & sewer: Kissimmee Utility Authority, (407) 933-7777. **Gas:** None. **Telephone:** Sprint, (407) 339-1811. **Cable TV:** Time Warner Communications, (407) 892-8466.

PLACES OF WORSHIP
One Catholic and 39 Protestant churches.

THE ENVIRONMENT
Lake Tohopekaliga, also known as Lake Toho, generally has been rated as having poor to fair water quality, the worst in the area. However, since a governmental task force identified the sources of the lake's problems in 1980, the lake has shown noteworthy improvements. Water quality is also improving in Canoe Creek, which now rates good in places, and Lake Kissimmee, which generally has fair ratings. Health advisories recommending limited consumption of largemouth bass due to mercury content have been issued for Lake Kissimmee, Lake Toho, East Lake Toho and Lake Istokpoga. Lake Okeechobee and the Kissimmee River have been designated for surface water improvement and management. Crooked Lake and the Butler Chain of Lakes have been designated as Outstanding Florida Waters. Other water bodies in the region have generally good water quality, including most of East Lake Toho, Lake Ajay, Boggy Creek, Reedy Canal, Lake Butler, Lake Conway, Alligator Lake, Lake Russell and Canoe Creek.

EVENTS AND FESTIVALS
Silver Spurs Rodeo - February. **Kissimmee Bluegrass Festival** - March. **Kissimmee Boat-A-Cade** - June. **Silver Spurs Rodeo** - July. **Osceola Art Festival** - September. **Florida State Air Fair** - October.

WHERE TO EAT
Kissimmee Steak Company, 2047 E. Space Coast Parkway, steaks, seafood, moderate, (407) 847-8050. **The Black-Eyed Pea,** 5305 W. Irlo Bronson Memorial Highway, American, inexpensive, (407) 397-1500.

WHERE TO STAY
Casa Rosa Inn, (407) 396-2020. **Radisson Inn Maingate,** (407) 396-1400. **Ramada Resort-Maingate East at the Parkway,** (407) 396-7000.

ISSUES
With its proximity to Walt Disney World, Kissimmee's principal function appears to be providing hotel/motel/restaurant space for tourists. Since these service businesses generally pay minimum wage, they attract a disproportionate number of unskilled/low-skilled workers to Kissimmee. Lots of inexpensive apartment complexes have been built. New road construction projects and commercial developments are competing with residential builders who need to house a growing work force and retiree population. Potential new residents must consider whether such a booming area is ideal for retirement.

Lake City

HE SAID: ☆

I can't describe Lake City with words like quaint, charming or friendly. While it has a road network that makes it easy to get to, the same network also makes it easy to get out. I believe retirees looking for a place to settle down will soon find themselves on the road again. I did.

SHE SAID: ☆

Located at the crossroads of I-10 and I-75, Lake City has a lot of traffic, billboards and fast-food restaurants. The "gateway to Florida" may be a stop, but not a stay. I would not retire here.

They call their city the gateway to Florida. From almost any place in Lake City you can be on I-10 heading east or west, or I-75 heading north or south, in about five minutes. If you need to leave town even faster, the city is served by U.S. highways 90, 41 and 441, as well as routes 250, 47, 100 and 247.

Lake City has three hospitals that provide excellent health care for residents. The city is well-served by government and private institutions, transportation facilities and a diversified industrial-commercial business base that provides good, stable employment. But this is not enough. The city itself lacks any unique, distinguishing characteristic that stamps it as special or causes one to want to hang around for a longer look.

The web of interstates, highways, roads and streets, lined with neon-lighted fast-food restaurants, gas stations and tire stores, is an eyesore, creating an unsettling atmosphere on entering or leaving the city. Such sights leave little room for quiet neighborhoods or historic preservation. In fact, in spite of its history, dating to the 1840s, the town center looks old rather than historic.

A 1991 brochure for Lake City states that more than a million visitors spend the night in Columbia County each year. It's our guess that less than 1,000 spend a second night.

It's too bad that the town's name does not more aptly describe its personality and features. Set in a land of forests, lakes and rivers, Lake City's natural ambiance has been destroyed by too many 20th-century trappings. The rural charm and rusticity you would hope to find in a town of 10,000 people has been overpowered and lost in a flash of neon and plastic.

WEATHER

	Winter	Spring	Summer	Fall
Normal daily high/low	68/44	85/61	90/69	74/50
Normal precipitation	13 in.	14 in.	20 in.	8 in.

Disaster watch: No major hurricanes have hit this area directly.

TAXES

Sales tax: 6%. **Property tax:** $23.66 per $1,000 valuation. Sample tax calculations include a $25,000 homestead exemption.

Home value	Tax
$100,000	$1,775
$150,000	$2,958
$250,000	$5,324

REAL ESTATE

Median home value: $75,198 (Columbia County). **Median rent:** $432/month (Columbia County). **Communities popular with retirees:** Eastside Village offers single-family homes priced from the $60s, (800) 842-7100 or (904) 752-8267. Quail Heights Country Club has single-family homes priced from the $70s to $120s, (904) 752-3339. **Licensed continuing-care retirement communities:** None.

CRIME & SAFETY

Crimes per 1,000 population: 150. **Non-emergency police:** (904) 752-4344. **Non-emergency fire department:** (904) 758-5442. **Police, fire, ambulance emergencies:** 911.

HOMELESS & BLIGHT

We saw no homeless persons. Many of the streets leading into downtown are cluttered with fast-food restaurants, gas stations and other businesses catering to through-traffic.

The U.S. Census reported 175 homeless in shelters and 41 visible on the streets in Columbia County, population 42,613.

HEALTH CARE

Hospitals: Lake City Medical Center, 75 beds, full service, acute care, 24-hour emergency, (904) 752-2922. **Lake Shore Hospital**, 128 beds, acute care, 24-hour emergency, outpatient surgery, (904) 755-3200. **Veterans Administration Medical Center**, 362 beds, full service, (904) 755-3016.

Physicians: 45. **Specialties:** 22.

GETTING SMART

Lake City Community College, (904) 752-1822. **Offerings:** Two-year associate degree programs.

JUST FOR SENIORS

Better Living for Seniors, (904) 755-0235, provides meals, transportation and recreation. **Golden Age Senior Center**, (904) 755-0264.

GETTING INVOLVED

Red Cross, (904) 752-0650. **United Way**, (904) 752-5604. **Woman's Club**, (904) 755-0347.

RECREATION, ENTERTAINMENT & AMENITIES

Semiprivate golf: Quail Heights Country Club, 18 holes. **Private golf:** Lake City Country Club, 18 holes, welcomes tourists. **Public tennis courts:** Cannon Creek Tennis has five courts. **Private tennis courts:** None. **Parks:** Olustee Battlefield State Historic Site, Stephen Foster State Park, Osceola National Forest, O'Leno State Park and Ichetucknee Springs State Park, which is south of town between Branford and Fort White. **Public swimming pools:** Lake City Municipal. **Water sports:** Canoeing, boating and rafting. **River/gulf/ocean:** The Suwannee and Santa Fe rivers and Olustee Beach at Ocean Pond Lake provide freshwater recreation. Cedar Key, about 85 miles south on the Gulf, is a popular resort. **Running/walking/biking:** All are popular in the area. O'Leno State Park is ranked among the best hiking and jogging parks in Florida. Osceola National Forest offers trails and paths. **Horses/riding:** O'Leno State Park has excellent trails. **Hunting:** Hunting and fishing licenses and information, (904) 758-1077. **Movie theaters:** Six screens. **Art museums:** None. **History museums:** Columbia County Historical Museum, Civil War Museum at Olustee Battlefield State Historic Site and the Stephen Foster State Park Museum. **Theaters:** Tison Auditorium hosts Community Concert and Little Theatre productions. **Library:** Columbia County Public. **Attractions:** Florida Sports Hall of Fame, Osceola National Forest, Ocean Pond Lake and the Suwannee Valley Zoo. **Necessities:** Post office, six banks, city and county offices, retail stores, supermarkets, restaurants, hardware and department stores, hotels, motels and real estate agencies.

 Smart Shopper Tip: Gleason Mall, with 23 stores anchored by J.C. Penney and Goody's Family Clothing, will satisfy most shoppers' needs. Plan periodic trips to Gainesville or even Jacksonville for bigger shopping sprees.

WHO LIVES HERE
Population: 10,052 year-round residents, an increase of 426 people since 1990. **Age 65+** = 14.5% in Columbia County. **Median household income:** $25,343 (Columbia County). **Per capita income:** $16,414 (Columbia County).

NUMBERS TO KNOW
Chamber of commerce: (904) 752-3690. **Voter registration:** (904) 758-1026. **Vehicle registration, tags & title:** (904) 758-1077. **Driver's license:** (904) 758-0511.

WHAT TO READ
Lake City Reporter, daily newspaper, (904) 752-1293.

GETTING AROUND
Bus: No public intra-city transportation. **Taxi:** Express Cab Co., (904) 755-9994. **Tours:** None. **Airport:** Gainesville Regional is about 45 miles away. **Traffic:** Very heavy for a small town; most of it is just passing through.

JOBS
County unemployment rate: 5.1%. **Florida Jobs and Benefits:** (904) 758-0433.

UTILITIES
Electricity: Clay Electric, (904) 752-7447. **Gas:** City of Lake City, (904) 752-2031 ext. 243. **Water & sewer:** Lake City Utilities, (904) 752-2031. **Telephone:** Bell South, (800) 789-9025 in Florida, or (800) 753-0710 out-of-state. **Cable TV:** Time Warner Cable, (904) 752-6161.

PLACES OF WORSHIP
One Catholic and 80 Protestant churches.

THE ENVIRONMENT
The Santa Fe River has been given protected status as an Outstanding Florida Water. Alligator Lake has a poor water quality rating. Until 1987, it received discharges from the Lake City waste-water treatment plant. An elevated mercury content has been found in largemouth bass; a reduced consumption advisory has been issued for parts of the river basin.

EVENTS AND FESTIVALS
Olustee Battle Festival & Re-enactment - February. **Garden Club Antiques Show** - March. **Alligator Fest** - May. **Festival of Lights** - November/December.

WHERE TO EAT
There are 59 restaurants. The chamber of commerce provides lists, (904) 752-3690.

WHERE TO STAY
Comfort Inn, (904) 755-1344. **Hampton Inn**, (904) 752-3419.

ISSUES
Lieutenant Laxton, public information officer for the Lake City police department, says that the extensive interstate and federal highway network serving Lake City makes it a strategic location for drug distribution throughout the Southeast. But recent law enforcement efforts, including creation of a joint city-county drug interdiction task force, have resulted in a significant scale-back in drug dealing. Almost 400 kids participate in activities at a neighborhood resource center built by federal and state anti-drug-abuse grants in what was once termed "drug-ridden northeast Lake City."

 If the city could exert the same intense focus on correcting some of its esthetics problems, it might someday live up to the image its name implies.

RELOCATION TIPS

When preparing to relocate, take a complete inventory of your belongings. Keep photographs, videotapes, sales receipts and serial numbers with your inventory. Though taking inventory can be time consuming, it may save you money and problems later. You can use your inventory when negotiating with moving companies or when arranging for new homeowners' insurance. In case of a claim for loss, most insurance companies will require an inventory with proof of the cost.

Lakeland

HE SAID: ★ ★ ★ ★ ☆

Don't take my word for it. You really have to experience Lakeland — up close and personal — to gain a significant appreciation for all it has to offer.

SHE SAID: ★ ★ ★

This sprawling city has it all — good and bad. There are colleges, good location, Florida climate and, worst of all, lots of traffic. Too much hustle and bustle — it's not for me.

Lakeland has one of the most beautiful downtowns in Florida. Here you'll find parks, museums, libraries and college campuses. Paths for jogging and walking wind around lakes, and palm and oak trees grace the landscape. Lakeland boasts a pleasant mix of old and new architecture, including Mediterranean Revival, Spanish Mission, Georgian and Frank Lloyd Wright designs.

Phosphate mining, citrus growing and tourism are the big revenue producers here, and Publix supermarket headquarters, Lakeland Regional Medical Center and Watson Clinic are the big employers. But Lakeland is by no means exclusively about business and industry. It is about people, housing, leisure and recreation; it meets the requirements for visually pleasing places and vistas, arts and culture, education and quality of life. It is probably the most complete town of its size in Florida.

You can't describe Lakeland without mentioning lakes Hollingsworth and Morton, two of the 13 notable lakes in the area (both are downtown) and the newly restored Lake Mirror Promenade in the Munn Park Historic District. The beauty and accessibility of these popular public areas are important aspects of the pride and enjoyment residents take in their city.

Retiree housing is abundant, located in the inner city around the lakes and in dozens of newer developments on the outskirts. While in the area, look at the communities of Highland Fairways, Sandpiper Golf and Country Club, Silver Lakes, Palm Springs, Steeple Chase, Imperial Lakes, The Grasslands at Oakbridge and Scandinavia USA.

Unlike many other towns, you don't have to live in the suburbs to have an attractive, secure environment. The established neighborhoods around Lake Morton and Lake Hollingsworth, close to the center of town, offer quality homes in a wide range of prices. The settings here feature manicured lawns, towering oaks, old brick roads and sidewalks.

If you're looking for a progressive, civic-minded, people-oriented city with lots of public amenities, great location and outstanding housing, look no further.

WEATHER

	Winter	Spring	Summer	Fall
Normal daily high/low	75/53	88/66	91/73	79/59
Normal precipitation	9 in.	12 in.	20 in.	6 in.

Disaster watch: Since 1900, northwest Florida has been hit by six major hurricanes and southwest Florida has been hit by five.

TAXES

Sales tax: 6%. **Property tax:** Rates range from $20.92 to $23.37 per $1,000 valuation, depending on location. Sample taxes are calculated at the rate of $23.37 and include a $25,000 homestead exemption.

Home value	Tax
$100,000	$1,753
$150,000	$2,921
$250,000	$5,258

REAL ESTATE

Median home value: $89,190 (Polk County). **Median rent:** $542/month (Polk County). **Communities popular with retirees:** Highland Homes has two-, three-, and four-bedroom single-family homes from the $50s to $100s, (941) 619-7103. Paradise Lakes, an adult community, has single-family homes from the $40s, (941) 425-5175. Eagle Brooke, a gated golf-course community, has single-family homes from the mid-$140s, (941) 701-0501. Silver Lakes, a gated adult community, has custom-built single-family homes from the mid-$80s, (941) 859-0206. **Licensed continuing-care retirement communities:** Carpenter's Home Estates, 387 independent living units and 60 sheltered nursing beds, (941) 858-3847. Florida Presbyterian Homes, 194 independent living units, (941) 682-7787.

CRIME & SAFETY

Crimes per 1,000 population: 125. **Non-emergency police:** (941) 499-6900. **Non-emergency fire department:** (941) 499-8200. **Police, fire, ambulance emergencies:** 911.

HOMELESS & BLIGHT

We saw no homeless persons. There are pockets of substandard housing in the northern sections. Lakeland is a beautiful city with a totally revitalized downtown benefiting from an infusion of more than $100 million in public and private investments during the past 10 years.

The U.S. Census counted 172 homeless persons in shelters and 33 visible on the streets of Polk County, population 405,382.

HEALTH CARE

Hospitals: Lakeland Regional Medical Center, 897 beds, full service, 24-hour emergency, acute care, (941) 687-1100. **The Watson Clinic** lays claim to being the largest medical group practice in Florida with 170 physicians in 38 medical specialties, (941) 680-7000. **Palm View Hospital**, private psychiatric hospital, (941) 682-6105.

Physicians: 300+. **Specialties:** 48.

GETTING SMART

Florida Southern College, (941) 680-4111. **Offerings:** Full undergraduate curriculum and MBA degree program at this private, four-year college. **University of South Florida**, (941) 667-7000. **Offerings:** 89 degrees, including 19 doctoral degrees at this graduate research university. **Polk Community College**, (941) 297-1000. **Offerings:** Two-year degrees in arts and sciences with all credits transferable to the University of South Florida. It also has an active continuing-education program, offering a wide range of classes.

JUST FOR SENIORS

Multipurpose Senior Center, (941) 499-2606.

GETTING INVOLVED

The Lakeland Newcomer's Guide lists 90 clubs and organizations. **Lakeland Greeters**, (941) 858-3623. **RSVP**, (941) 688-2501. **SCORE**, (941) 687-4403.

RECREATION, ENTERTAINMENT & AMENITIES

Public golf: Bramble Ridge Golf Course. **Private golf:** Cleveland Heights Golf & Country Club, 27 holes; Sandpiper Golf &

Country Club; Schalamar Creek; Grasslands Golf & Country Club; and Lone Palm Golf Club. **Public tennis courts:** Scott Kelly Recreation Complex, eight courts; Simpson Park, two courts; and Veterans Park, 16 courts. **Private tennis courts:** There are numerous courts at private clubs, schools and housing developments. **Parks:** There are 24 parks and recreation areas in and around town. **Public swimming pools:** Adair Park, Scott Kelly Recreation Complex and Simpson Park. **Water sports:** Airboating, canoeing, sail plane flights and water-skiing. **River/ gulf/ocean:** There are a dozen lakes in the city limits, including Lake Parker, Lake Hollingsworth and Lake Morton. **Running/ walking/biking:** There are paths and walkways around lakes Hollingsworth, Morton and Mirror that are good for both jogging and walking. Lakes Hollingsworth, Parker and Hunter also have bicycle trails. Polk County has produced a bicycle map with color coded travel routes in and around Lakeland. **Horses/ riding:** The Polk County Rails-to-Trails program has acquired a 29-mile railroad right-of-way, which is being developed for horseback riders, bicyclists and hikers. **Hunting:** Florida Game and Freshwater Fish Commission, (941) 648-3203, for information on fishing in Lakeland and hunting in unincorporated, rural county areas. **Movie theaters:** 35 screens. **Art museums:** Polk Museum of Art, Harrison Center for the Arts and Melvin Art Gallery. **History museums:** Sun 'N' Fun Aviation Museum. **Theaters:** Lakeland Center has the 2,186-seat Youkey Theater, plus an arena and a conference hall. Other venues: Florida Southern College, Polk Community College and Lake Mirror Theatre. Performing groups include the Imperial Symphony Orchestra and the Pied Piper Players. **Library:** Two public libraries. **Attractions:** Detroit Tigers hold spring training here. Florida Southern College provides maps for self-guided tours of the 12 buildings on campus designed by Frank Lloyd Wright, the largest collection of his architecture in the world. Munn Park Historic District. **Necessities:** All are available.

Smart Shopper Tip: Lakeland Square Mall, anchored by Dillard's, Belk-Lindsey, Sears, Burdines and J.C. Penney Co., is the area's finest.

WHO LIVES HERE
Population: 75,193 year-round residents, an increase of 4,617 since 1990. **Age 65+** = 19.6% in Polk County. **Median household income:** $26,191 (Polk County). **Per capita income:** $19,126 (Polk County).

NUMBERS TO KNOW
Chamber of commerce: (941) 688-8551. **Voter registration:** (941) 499-2764. **Vehicle registration, tags & title:** (941) 603-6421. **Driver's license:** (941) 499-2320. **Visitors bureau:** (800) 828-7655.

WHAT TO READ
The Ledger, daily newspaper, (941) 802-7000. **Tampa Tribune,** daily newspaper, (941) 683-6531. **Senior Times,** monthly magazine, (941) 353-0444.

GETTING AROUND
Bus: Lakeland Area Mass Transit, (941) 688-7433, operates Handy Bus, providing door-to-door service for the elderly and handicapped. **Taxi:** Checker, (941) 665-8151. **Tours:** Munn

Park Historic District Walking Tour brochure available at the chamber of commerce. **Airport:** Tampa International is 38 miles away. **Traffic:** Florida Avenue, Lakeland's main north-south street, is a challenge to the uninitiated motorist. But the city has a good network of streets and boulevards for those who know how to get around.

JOBS
County unemployment rate: 6.6%. **Florida Jobs and Benefits:** (941) 499-2340.

UTILITIES
Electricity: Lakeland Electric, (941) 688-9535. **Gas:** People's Gas, (941) 686-3153. **Water & sewer:** Lakeland Water, (941) 688-9535. **Telephone:** GTE, (800) 483-4200. **Cable TV:** Time-Warner Cable, (941) 965-7766.

PLACES OF WORSHIP
There are 176 churches, including three Catholic, 153 Protestant, and one Jewish synagogue.

THE ENVIRONMENT
Lake Parker, Banana Lake, Lake Hancock and their tributaries have been rated as having some of the poorest water quality in the state.

There is one EPA-listed Superfund site located three miles north of Lakeland in Kathleen. Cleanup activities at the Alpha Chemical Corporation site have been completed. Monitoring of the site will continue until 1995.

EVENTS AND FESTIVALS
Detroit Tigers spring training - March/April. **Orange Cup Regatta Hydroplane Races** - Week after Easter. **Sun-N-Fun EAA Fly-In** - April. **Mayfaire-by-the-Lake** - May. **Fall Festival** - September. **Snowfest** - December.

WHERE TO EAT
Steak and prime rib places are all around town. **Red Fox Grill,** 1239 E. Memorial, steak, seafood, moderate to expensive, (941) 683-5500. **Texas Cattle Company,** 735 E. Main St., steak, lobster, seafood, moderate to expensive, (941) 686-1434.

WHERE TO STAY
There are the usual motel chains. **Sheraton Four Points Hotel,** (941) 647-3000. **Holiday Inn-South,** (941) 646-5731.

ISSUES
Lakeland is one of Florida's oldest cities, but local leaders have used selective demolition, renovation, restoration and new construction in the ongoing revitalization of the community. Some of its oldest neighborhoods are still its finest, while its public- and private-sector buildings are bright, modern symbols of extensive diversification and renewal.

It is highly unlikely that anything can stand in the way of Lakeland's growth and determination to remain one of the premier places to live and work in Florida.

Lake Wales

HE SAID: ☆ ☆
I formed somewhat contradictory opinions of Lake Wales. It has its good points, including downtown rehabilitation and the Lake Wales Country Club Village. It also has some not-so-good points like the blighted, unattractive areas on the outskirts of town and an overall dearth of amenities and resources. Lake Wales leaves room for improvement.

SHE SAID: ☆
This small, rural town is too far off the beaten path for me. I saw little to attract retirees other than the climate, which is not unique. I would not retire here.

Lake Wales occupies a spot along Florida's geographical ridge. As such, one of the highlights of the town is Bok Tower Gardens, created in 1928. At an elevation of 298 feet, this attraction is located at one of the highest points in the state. The tower rises 200 feet and houses a carillon with bells that ring every half hour. The surrounding gardens offer a 128-acre sanctuary.

Downtown Lake Wales has undergone significant rehabilitation since it became a Main Street USA city. A number of buildings are listed on the National Register of Historic Places; renovations include a pedestrian mall. There are some popular cultural opportunities offered through the Lake Wales Museum and Cultural Center, better known as The Depot. The Black Hills Passion Play and the Nativity Play are annual events enjoyed by residents and tourists alike.

There are a lot of retirees here. Walden Shores is a popular waterfront retirement community on Lake Weohyakapka (also known as Lake Walk-in-Water). Two rental communities east of town, Nalcrest and Fedhaven, were originally built for retired letter carriers and other federal employees, but now welcome all retirees. They offer air-conditioned garden apartments priced from $282 per month. But the *crème de la crème* in retiree housing is Lake Wales Country Club Village, which offers custom designed single-family homes, condos and villas in a golf and tennis community with a grand clubhouse and glorious view. It is a truly first-class place to spend your retirement years.

Unfortunately, civic leaders have permitted the approaches to the city to reflect poorly on its appearance. At one point on Route 60, badly run-down houses share space with paint and body shops and dilapidated, burned-out mobile homes.

The chamber of commerce cites a modest cost of living, a picturesque, warm, close-knit community, events and cultural center activities as the things that attract retirees. The ease of getting to either coast via Route 60 is another plus. In about an hour and a half, residents can reach Clearwater to the west or Vero Beach to the east and still have enough time to enjoy a full day's activities.

Lake Wales has the location, natural resources, scenic vistas and some of the attractions needed to become a much-favored retiree mecca. But the crown jewel is somewhat tarnished. It needs to do a better job on overall aesthetics. It needs more golf courses and retiree housing. And, it should expand its cultural amenities. Lake Wales has a lot of potential — but it hasn't yet arrived.

WEATHER

	Winter	Spring	Summer	Fall
Normal daily high/low	77/51	89/64	92/71	81/56
Normal precipitation	9 in.	13 in.	20 in.	6 in.

Disaster watch: Southeast Florida has been hit by nine major hurricanes since 1900.

TAXES
Sales tax: 6%. **Property tax:** $25.77 per $1,000 valuation. Sample tax calculations include a $25,000 homestead exemption.

Home value	Tax
$100,000	$1,933
$150,000	$3,221
$250,000	$5,798

REAL ESTATE
Median home value: $89,362 (Polk County). **Median rent:** $542/month (Polk County). **Communities popular with retirees:** North Pointe has single-family homes priced from the low $80s. Lake Wales Country Club Village features custom homes, villas and condominiums, from $175,000 to $300,000. Country Oaks has single-family homes from the $80s to the $250s, and Oakwood homes run from $125,000 to $200,000. Contact Bill Cousins, Westlake Real Estate Company, (941) 676-8058 or (800) 397-8051. Towerwood is an adult manufactured-home community with prices from the high $30s to low $60s, excluding the cost of the lot lease, (941) 676-6068. Walden Shores has manufactured homes priced from the high $20s to the high $50s, excluding cost of land lease, (941) 696-7100 or (800) 654-9715. **Licensed continuing-care retirement communities:** None.

CRIME & SAFETY
Crimes per 1,000 population: 90. **Non-emergency police:** (941) 678-4223. **Non-emergency fire department:** (941) 678-4203. **Police, fire, ambulance emergencies:** 911.

HOMELESS & BLIGHT
We saw no homeless persons. This is a clean town with a pedestrian mall and restored downtown area. Some storefronts could stand renovation but the overall appearance is OK. The outskirts, especially along Route 60 west, are trashy looking. Some bulldozing appears to be in order.

The U.S. Census reported 172 homeless persons in shelters and 33 visible in street locations in Polk County, population 405,382.

HEALTH CARE
Hospitals: Lake Wales Medical Center, 177 beds, acute care, 24-hour emergency, (941) 676-1433.
Physicians: 30. **Specialties:** 13.

GETTING SMART
Warner Southern College, (941) 638-7250. **Offerings:** Four-year Christian college in the liberal arts tradition. **Webber College**, (941) 638-1431. **Offerings:** Two- and four-year degrees in business administration with concentrations in accounting, finance and management.

JUST FOR SENIORS
Community Center, (941) 678-4003.

GETTING INVOLVED

Lake Wales Arts Council, (941) 676-8426. **Lake Wales Care Center** operates the Lake Wales Literacy Council and Meals on Wheels, (941) 676-6678. **Lake Wales Hospital Volunteers**, (941) 676-1433.

RECREATION, ENTERTAINMENT & AMENITIES

Public golf: Golf Course at Highland Park, semiprivate, 18 holes/par 72; Oakwood Golf Club, 18 holes/par 72; and River Ranch Resort Golf Course, nine holes. **Private golf:** Lake Wales Country Club, 18 holes/par 72. **Public tennis courts:** Lake Wales City Courts. **Private tennis courts:** Lakes Wales Country Club and Walden Shores. **Parks:** The city has 125 acres for leisure activities. Tiger Creek Nature Preserve is a 4,400-acre treasure owned by the Nature Conservancy. **Public swimming pools:** None. **Water sports:** Boating, canoeing and water-skiing. **River/gulf/ocean:** Lake Wales, about one square mile in size, sits in the heart of the town. A number of larger lakes just five to 10 miles from the city serve as sites for housing developments. **Running/walking/biking:** Babson Park Audubon Center has the Caloosa Nature Trail. A bike path around Lake Wales is popular with walkers and joggers. **Horses/riding:** Plenty of stables, riding academies and open spaces for horseback riding. East of town, the River Ranch Resort has a weekly rodeo, hayrides and horseback riding. **Hunting:** Deer, duck and alligator. Call Florida Game and Freshwater Fish Commission, (941) 648-3206 for information. **Movie theaters:** Two screens. **Art museums:** Lake Wales Arts Center. **History museums:** Lake Wales Museum and Cultural Center (The Depot). **Theaters:** Lake Wales Little Theatre. Also, Lake Wales Amphitheater is the set of the Black Hills Passion Play and the Nativity Play. **Library:** Lake Wales Public. **Attractions:** Black Hills Passion Play, Bok Tower Gardens and Spook Hill. **Necessities:** Most.

Smart Shopper Tip: The shops in downtown Lake Wales and Eagle Ridge Mall will quench your shopping thirst.

WHO LIVES HERE

Population: 10,027 year-round residents, an increase of 357 people since 1990. **Age 65+** = 19.6% in Polk County. **Median household income:** $26,191 (Polk County). **Per capita income:** $19,126 (Polk County).

NUMBERS TO KNOW

Chamber of commerce: (941) 676-3445. **Voter registration:** (941) 534-7380. **Vehicle registration, tags & title:** (941) 774-8177. **Driver's license:** (941) 678-4163.

WHAT TO READ

Lake Wales News, weekly newspaper, (941) 676-3467.

GETTING AROUND

Bus: No public intra-city transportation. **Taxi:** Lake Wales Cab Co., (941) 676-1089. **Tours:** None. **Airport:** Orlando International is 60 miles away. **Traffic:** Very little traffic in Lake Wales, which has no major thoroughfares downtown.

JOBS

County unemployment rate: 6.6%. **Florida Jobs and Benefits:** (941) 678-4155.

UTILITIES

Electricity: Florida Power Corp., (800) 700-8744. **Gas:** Central Florida Gas Co., (941) 293-2125. **Water & sewer:** Lake Wales Water Dept., (941) 678-4196. **Telephone:** GTE Florida, (800) 483-4200. **Cable TV:** ComCast Cable, (941) 676-8514.

PLACES OF WORSHIP

One Catholic and 45 Protestant churches.

THE ENVIRONMENT

Nearby lakes, including Crooked Lake, Lake Weohyakapka, Lake Rosalie and Lake Buffum, have been rated as having mostly good water quality. Lake Kissimmee has generally fair and improving water quality. Crooked Lake is designated as an Outstanding Florida Water and is thus protected, but it has experienced serious water level decreases over the past 20 years. Health advisories recommending limited consumption of largemouth bass due to mercury content have been issued for Lake Kissimmee.

Polk County has one EPA-listed Superfund site located in Kathleen, three miles north of Lakeland.

EVENTS AND FESTIVALS

Black Hills Passion Play - February through Easter Sunday. **Mardi Gras** - February. **Lake Wales Art Show** - March or April. **Pioneer Days** - October. **Christmas Parade** - December.

WHERE TO EAT

Black Forest Buffet Restaurant, U.S. Highway 27, four miles south of Route 60, American and German, inexpensive, (941) 638-3036. **Chalet Suzanne Restaurant**, Chalet Suzanne Road, continental, very expensive, (941) 676-6011. **Vinton's**, 229 E. Stuart Ave., French and Creole, expensive, (941) 676-8242.

WHERE TO STAY

Chalet Suzanne Country Inn, (941) 676-6011. **River Ranch**, (941) 692-1321.

ISSUES

Some downtown merchants were concerned about the potential loss of business resulting from the new Eagle Ridge Regional Mall, but there appears to be no negative impact. Parking still is a problem.

Retirees mentioned an increase in drug-related crime and heavy lightning as concerns. But, they added that they love the slow pace, neighborliness and community spirit of Lake Wales.

Lake Worth

HE SAID: ☆
I like the slower pace, the municipal beach complex and the numerous water sports possible here. But that's about it. The taxes are high and expectations low.

SHE SAID: ☆ ☆
This is not an attractive place. There are some new planned residential areas and shopping centers west of I-95. But, I would not retire here.

The key in defining your viewpoint of Lake Worth as a potential retirement town is location — both the town's location and your home's location.

Town boosters talk of Lake Worth's ideal location in the heart of the Palm Beaches. It is true that Lake Worth is well-situated to access the amenities of the other cities and towns along the coast. And while Lake Worth has a beautiful, white sand beach and plenty of opportunities for water enthusiasts and golfers, it lacks the cultural, recreational, shopping and social opportunities that many retirees find necessary for a fulfilled, well-rounded life.

The neighborhoods to the east of I-95, near the downtown area, consist of small, run-down houses, many of which are abandoned. There are some beautiful $200,000-plus homes surrounding the town's namesake, Lake Worth. And, three or four miles west of I-95, retiree housing is dominant in attractive new golf and country club developments.

Overall, the city relies too much on neighboring cities and towns for many amenities and lacks a cohesive community spirit and the determination to provide improved services for its residents. A $21,000,000 urban renewal project has just been completed, bringing sorely needed visual improvements to a blighted downtown.

WEATHER

	Winter	Spring	Summer	Fall
Normal daily high/low	76/58	85/69	90/75	80/65
Normal precipitation	9 in.	17 in.	21 in.	14 in.

Disaster watch: Southeast Florida has been hit by nine major hurricanes since 1900.

TAXES
Sales tax: 6%. **Property tax:** $27.98 per $1,000 valuation. Sample tax calculations include a $25,000 homestead exemption.

Home value	Tax
$100,000	$2,099
$150,000	$3,498
$250,000	$6,296

REAL ESTATE
Median home value: $104,167 (Palm Beach County). **Median rent:** $773/month (Palm Beach County). **Communities popular with retirees:** Herv Hugel with Neighborhood Realty, (561) 533-6072, cites two popular condominium projects: Lake Clark Gardens has units priced from the mid-$20s to $50s. Murray Hills has units from the $30s to $50s. "Nothing new is being built in Lake Worth," he says. **Licensed continuing-care retirement communities:** Bishop Gray Inn, 66 independent living units, 27 sheltered nursing beds, 60 community beds, (561) 965-5954.

CRIME & SAFETY
Crimes per 1,000 population: 152. **Non-emergency police:** (561) 586-1611. **Non-emergency fire department:** (561) 586-1711. **Police, fire, ambulance emergencies:** 911.

HOMELESS & BLIGHT
We did not see any homeless people. Some older parts of Lake Worth, east of I-95, have pockets of substandard housing.

The U.S. Census reported 219 homeless persons in shelters and 197 on the streets in Palm Beach County, population 863,518.

HEALTH CARE
Hospitals: While there are no hospitals in Lake Worth, Palm Beach County has 12 with more than 2,770 beds. **JFK Medical Center**, a few miles south in Atlantis, is the nearest full-service facility, 369 beds, (561) 965-7300. **Palm Beach Regional Hospital**, to the north, 200 beds, full service, (561) 967-7800. **Physicians:** 93+. **Specialties:** 29.

GETTING SMART
Palm Beach Community College, (561) 967-7222. **Offerings:** The Institute of New Dimensions, (561) 439-8186, is a membership program for retired persons, offering eight-week courses in life enrichment, liberal arts and wellness. The college also offers non-credit continuing-education courses.

JUST FOR SENIORS
Crisis Line, (561) 547-1000. **Senior Citizen's Center**, (561) 586-6102. **AARP** and **Lake Worth Senior Activities** are two other organizations for seniors.

GETTING INVOLVED
Lake Worth has more than 150 civic, fraternal, social, tourism and youth organizations. **Friends Assisting Seniors**, (561) 967-5859. Call the chamber of commerce for more information about **RSVP**, **Project Lake Worth** and other organizations.

RECREATION, ENTERTAINMENT & AMENITIES
Public golf: Lucerne Lakes Golf Club, Lake Worth Golf Club and Atlantis Country Club. **Private golf:** Lacuna Golf & Country Club, Palm Beach National Golf & Country Club, Poinciana Country Club and Sherbrooke Golf & Country Club. **Public tennis courts:** Sunset Ridge Park and John Prince Memorial Park. **Private tennis courts:** Lake Worth Racquet & Swim Club. **Parks:** John Prince Park is a 665-acre regional park with a 338-acre lake. Others are Bryant Park and Barton Park. **Public swimming pools:** Lake Worth Municipal Beach. **Water sports:** Swimming, snorkeling, scuba diving, windsurfing, water-skiing, freshwater and saltwater fishing, and boating. **River/gulf/ocean:** Lake Osborne and the lakes of John Prince Park offer excellent freshwater fishing. Lake Worth, a very large segment of the Intracoastal Waterway, provides recreational boating and fishing. The Atlantic offers quick access to Gulf Stream deep-sea fishing. **Running/walking/biking:** John

Prince Park offers nature trails and a 5-mile bike path along the shores of Lake Osborne. Bryant Park has a lake-side path. **Horses/riding:** There are stables and riding academies offering lessons, boarding, training and rentals. **Hunting:** Licenses, required for freshwater fishing and hunting, are available from the tax collector's office, (561) 355-2622. **Movie theaters:** One theater. **Art museums:** Lannan Foundation Museum and Palm Beach Community College Museum of Art. **History museums:** Museum of the City of Lake Worth. **Theaters:** Lake Worth Playhouse offers year-round theatrical productions; Palm Beach Community College Theatre hosts guest artists and student productions. **Library:** City of Lake Worth Public Library. **Attractions:** Gulfstream Polo Grounds hosts matches November through April. **Necessities:** All here.

   Smart Shopper Tip: Smart shoppers will browse through the Worth Avenue Palm Beach shops but buy at one of the many plazas and shopping centers in Lake Worth. There also are big, new regional malls in the area.

WHO LIVES HERE
Population: 30,181 year-round residents, an increase of 1,617 from 1990. **Age 65+ =** 25.0% in Palm Beach County. **Median household income:** $33,094 (Palm Beach County). **Per capita income:** $36,057 (Palm Beach County).

NUMBERS TO KNOW
Chamber of commerce: (561) 582-4401. **Voter registration:** (561) 355-2650. **Vehicle registration, tags & title:** (561) 355-2622. **Driver's license:** In West Palm Beach, (561) 433-3635.

WHAT TO READ
Sun Sentinel, daily newspaper, (561) 736-1777. **Lake Worth Herald**, weekly newspaper, (561) 585-9387. **Condo News**, weekly newspaper, (561) 471-0329.

GETTING AROUND
Bus: CoTran, (561) 233-1111. The Lolly the Trolley line, three San Francisco-style buses, covers three primary routes between shopping areas, downtown and beaches, (561) 586-1600. **Taxi:** Yellow Cab, (561) 689-2222. **Tours:** None. **Airport:** Palm Beach International is 10 minutes away. **Traffic:** Very light traffic. This is not a dynamic, on-the-go city.

JOBS
County unemployment rate: 6.4%. **Florida Jobs and Benefits:** (561) 357-6301.

UTILITIES
Electricity: Lake Worth Utilities, (561) 533-7300. **Gas:** Florida Public Utilities, (561) 832-2461. **Water & sewer:** Lake Worth Utilities, (561) 533-7300. **Telephone:** Bell South, (800) 789-9025 in Florida, or (800) 753-0710 out-of-state. **Cable TV:** ComCast Cable, (561) 478-5866.

PLACES OF WORSHIP
Three Catholic and 51 Protestant churches, plus two Jewish synagogues.

THE ENVIRONMENT
The Lake Worth area has been rated as having mostly good surface water quality, except south of the inlet where the West Palm Beach Canal enters. There is one EPA-listed Superfund site in Palm Beach County; it is BMI-Textron in Lake Park.

EVENTS AND FESTIVALS
Festival by the Lake - January. **Finlandia Days** - March.

WHERE TO EAT
Bohemian Garden, 5450 Lake Worth Road, continental, moderate, (561) 968-4111. **John G's**, 10 S. Ocean Blvd., seafood, inexpensive to moderate prices, (561) 585-9860.

WHERE TO STAY
You don't have to spend a lot to stay in Lake Worth; there are several budget motels. **Holiday Inn West Palm Beach Turnpike**, (561) 968-5000. **Martinique Motor Lodge**, (561) 585-2502. **Sea Wulf Inn**, (561) 586-5550.

ISSUES
High utility bills, high crime rates and absentee landlords are pinpointed by locals as the biggest problems in Lake Worth. High property taxes are a concern, since the Lake Worth millage rate is among the highest in the county.

RELOCATION TIPS
If you plan to bring your boat to Florida, you can get information by mail before you set out. The Department of Environmental Protection will provide boating regulations and safety information. Write or call the Department of Environmental Protection, Division of Law Enforcement, 3900 Commonwealth Blvd., Mail Station 665, Tallahassee, FL 32399, (850) 488-5757. You can obtain regional chart packets and a copy of Florida Fishing and Boating from the Florida Sports Foundation, 2964 Wellington Circle N., Tallahassee, FL 32308, (850) 488-8347.

Largo

HE SAID: ★ ★
It lacks many of the natural and man-made attractions that help to define the quality and character of neighboring towns and cities. I do not find Largo attractive as a tourist destination or retirement community.

SHE SAID: ★ ★
It offers a more affordable place in the sun than many of the neighboring communities. Largo has lots of mobile and manufactured-home parks. But, it's a sprawling town of strip shopping centers, some occupied, some vacant. I would not retire here.

Largo sits squarely in the middle of the Greater Tampa Bay peninsula between better-known sister cities Clearwater and St. Petersburg. Surprisingly, it lacks many of the cards you would expect to find in the hands of such a prominently placed player. It has nothing to match the museums, performing arts, sports or shopping of its larger neighbors. Somehow, it failed by less than a mile to gain entry to Old Tampa Bay, and though it has some limited frontage on the Gulf's Intracoastal Waterway, the smaller municipalities of Belleair and Indian Rocks Beach claim all of the adjoining, top-dollar real estate fronting the Gulf. Even the Cross Bayou Canal passes just out of sight of the city's southern limits. Thus, Largo must rely primarily on small lakes and creeks for water sports — a poor second choice in a land surrounded by Gulf waters.

What it does have is a lot of manufactured homes. While site-built single-family homes occupy more residential acreage, attached homes and manufactured housing units are more numerous. At last count, there were 12,000 manufactured homes in Largo, constituting 31 percent of total housing units.

A combination of a relatively low property tax millage rate and low value housing has kept the city coffers less full than those of its more affluent neighbors. Property taxes provide less than 8 percent of total government revenues. Retiree income, credited with making Pinellas County's economy almost recession-free, doesn't seem to be working as well in Largo. Boarded-up, vacant shops in a mall, areas of lagging commercial activity and substandard housing in parts of the city indicate that Largo has a less vigorous economy.

But don't get the idea that the town is bankrupt. There are some bright spots. There is a new downtown city hall complex with much-vaunted, state-of-the-art computers and a $200 million resource recovery facility to dispose of refuse. The city has acquired a $1.5 million parcel of land for an expansion of Largo Central Park, including a new entranceway. Largo has good medical facilities, some nice golf courses and some upscale residential neighborhoods. But it still falls short when tallying amenities and features.

WEATHER

	Winter	Spring	Summer	Fall
Normal daily high/low	72/52	85/66	90/73	78/58
Normal precipitation	10 in.	10 in.	23 in.	8 in.

Disaster watch: Since 1900, northwest Florida has been hit by six major hurricanes and southwest Florida has been hit by five.

TAXES
Sales tax: 7%. Property tax: $21.11 per $1,000 valuation. Sample tax calculations include a $25,000 homestead exemption.

Home value	Tax
$100,000	$1,583
$150,000	$2,639
$250,000	$4,750

REAL ESTATE
Median home value: $105,780 (Pinellas County). Median rent: $614/month (Pinellas County). Communities popular with retirees: Hidden Springs offers single-family homes priced from the $130s to $200s, (813) 586-2040. Seabrooke has single-family homes priced from the $260s and up, (813) 586-2040. Palm Hill Country Club is an adult community of manufactured homes with prices from the high $20s to the high $50s, (813) 581-8731. Twenty-four percent of housing is manufactured homes. Licensed continuing-care retirement communities: None.

CRIME & SAFETY
Crimes per 1,000 population: 52. Non-emergency police: (813) 587-6717. Non-emergency fire department: (813) 587-6714. Police, fire, ambulance emergencies: 911.

HOMELESS & BLIGHT
The city has several substandard areas — both residential and commercial — and generally lacks aesthetic appeal, despite seven housing improvement programs.

The U.S. Census reported 1,105 homeless persons in shelters and 75 visible in street locations in Pinellas County, population 851,659.

HEALTH CARE
Hospitals: Columbia Largo Medical Center, 256 beds, 24-hour emergency, full service, (813) 588-5200. Sun Coast Hospital, 300 beds, full service, (813) 586-7193.
Physicians: 250+. Specialties: 38.

GETTING SMART
There are no college or university campuses offering general interest studies in Largo. There are several in surrounding communities. Eckerd College in St. Petersburg, (813) 867-1166. Offerings: Bachelor's degree programs, evening/weekend independent study. It offers the Academy of Senior Professionals, (813) 864-8834, with classes in life enrichment and liberal arts subjects, as well as intergenerational, mentoring and community service programs. St. Petersburg Junior College, (813) 341-3600. Offerings: Two-year degrees in arts and sciences. Florida Metropolitan University, Pinellas campus, (813) 530-9495. Offerings: Associate's, bachelor's and master's degrees. University of South Florida at St. Petersburg, (727) 553-1536. Offerings: 26 undergraduate degree programs, four master's degree programs and a doctorate in marine biology.

JUST FOR SENIORS
Largo Community Center, (813) 587-6722. Largo Senior Center, (727) 588-5788. North County Adult Day Care, (727) 443-1560.

GETTING INVOLVED
Hospice of the Florida Suncoast, (813) 586-4432. SCORE, (813) 532-6800.

RECREATION, ENTERTAINMENT & AMENITIES
Public golf: Bardmoor North Golf Course, 18 holes/par 72; East Bay Golf Club, semiprivate, 18 holes/par 72; Largo Municipal, 18 holes/par 62; Palm Hill Country Club, semiprivate, nine holes/par 30; and Pinecrest Golf Club, semiprivate, 18 holes/par 55. Private golf: Bayou Golf Club, 18 holes/par 72. Public tennis courts: Bayhead Tennis & Shuffleboard Complex, Horseshoe Center and Southwest Complex. Private tennis courts: Bardmoor Tennis & Fitness Club and Largo Tennis Club. Parks: Largo has 12 recreational facilities and 670 acres of leisure space. Heritage Park & Museum, Southwest Complex and Highland Avenue Complex are outstanding examples of municipal facilities. Public swimming pools: Highland Avenue Complex and Southwest Complex. Water sports: Boating, canoeing and sailing. River/gulf/ocean: Allen's Creek, Mackay Creek, Taylor Reservoir, the headwaters of Lake Seminole, a number of small lakes and about one mile of frontage on the Gulf's Intracoastal Waterway. Running/walking/biking: The Pinellas Trail, a 47-mile linear park for walking, jogging, bicycling and skating, runs through Largo. Also Largo Narrows Nature Park, Bonner Park and Northeast Park. Horses/riding: None. Hunting: None. Movie theaters: 25 screens. Art museums: No museums. Gesner Fine Art Gallery. History museums: Pinellas Historical Museum. Theaters: Largo Cultural Center has a 333-seat theater. Eight O'Clock Theatre. Library: Largo Public. Attractions: Heritage Park. Necessities: Most are here.

Smart Shopper Tip: The Largo Mall and Bay Area Outlet Mall provide good shopping diversity. If you need more, Ulmerton Road, running east-west through the city, is loaded with shopping centers.

WHO LIVES HERE
Population: 68,038 year-round residents, an increase of 2,128 since 1990. Age 65+ = 24.6% in Pinellas County. Median household income: $29,009 (Pinellas County). Per capita income: $25,765 (Pinellas County).

NUMBERS TO KNOW
Chamber of commerce: (813) 584-2321. Voter registration: (813) 464-3551. Vehicle registration, tags & title: (813) 464-5560. Driver's license: (813) 725-7940.

WHAT TO READ
Clearwater Times, daily newspaper, (813) 895-1181. Largo Leader, weekly newspaper, (727) 397-5563. St. Petersburg Times, daily newspaper, (813) 893-8111. Tampa Tribune, daily newspaper, (813) 799-7400.

GETTING AROUND
Bus: Pinellas Suncoast Transit Authority, (813) 530-9911. Taxi: Yellow Cab, (727) 585-8294. Tours: None. Airport: St. Petersburg/Clearwater International is 2.5 miles outside Largo's city limits. Traffic: U.S. 19 and 19A running north-south, and Ulmerton Road going east-west are heavily traveled and should be avoided when possible. Otherwise, traffic flows smoothly on a good street network.

JOBS
County unemployment rate: 3.4%. Florida Jobs and Benefits: (813) 725-7920. AARP Senior Employment: (813) 441-9925. Job Line: (813) 587-6716.

UTILITIES
Electricity: Florida Power Corp., (813) 895-8711. Gas: Peoples Gas, (813) 826-3333. Water & sewer: Pinellas County Water System, (813) 464-4714. Telephone: GTE Florida, (800) 483-1000. Cable TV: Time Warner, (813) 562-5015.

PLACES OF WORSHIP
Four Catholic and 32 Protestant churches.

THE ENVIRONMENT
High population density and shoreline development has led to a gradual degradation of the Tampa Bay estuary. As a result, surface water quality throughout the area has been rated as generally fair to poor. Efforts are underway to reverse the trend and improve water quality. The Pinellas County portion of Tampa Bay has received protected status as an Outstanding Florida Water.

There is one EPA-listed Superfund site in Pinellas County. It is the Stauffer Chemical Co. plant in Tarpon Springs.

EVENTS AND FESTIVALS
Renaissance Festival - March/April. Country Jubilee - October. Fall Food Festival - November.

WHERE TO EAT
Contact the chamber of commerce for suggestions.

WHERE TO STAY
The chamber of commerce lists Belleair Village Motel/Apartments, (813) 584-7131. There are no other listings offered by the chamber.

ISSUES
Largo has run out of space, a situation with both negative and positive implications. Older, less attractive areas of the city are more likely to be rehabilitated in a tight land market. But the city is becoming increasingly congested. Once a farming, cattle and citrus town, Largo now focuses on high-tech commerce, retail sales, diversified housing and a considerable transportation network.

Leesburg

HE SAID: ★ ★ ★
The lure of the lakes is not a strong draw for me since I am not a boater. But if you like both boating and golfing, don't settle anywhere until you've checked out Leesburg.

SHE SAID: ★ ★ ★
It attracts lots of retirees to its manufactured-home communities, where there are ample activities available in the neighborhoods. But the downtown area has little to offer. I would not retire here.

Leesburg is Lake County's largest city, with a population of about 15,000 within the incorporated area and more than 50,000 in the greater area. It has the ambiance and feel of a larger-than-average small town and a diversity of amenities and housing uncommon to a small city.

An excellent medical center, community college, impressive community center, modern sports complex, museum, theater, library and enclosed mall are among the features that attract retirees to the area. A 95 percent occupancy rate on Main Street draws a good flow of vehicular and foot traffic through an attractive, rehabilitated downtown. There's plenty of parking, a sense of security and good rapport between merchants and shoppers. And, in this town settled in 1857, there are plentiful projects for historians, restorationists and antiquaries.

Three principal features account for Leesburg's popularity with retirees: lakes, housing and location. The presence and navigability of the Oklawaha Chain of Lakes is a real thrill for both fishermen and boaters who cherish this connection with the Atlantic.

A variety of housing options await newcomers. There are site-built and manufactured homes, villas and condos in settings that range from established urban neighborhoods to more rural surroundings, and from secluded, wooded spots to locations on the water or on a fairway. There are dozens of adult retirement communities, country clubs and marina-based developments.

Finally, Leesburg's central location allows quick, easy access to both east and west coasts, as well as day trips to Disney World.

Greater Leesburg offers such a wide variety of retirement housing and lifestyle opportunities that would-be residents should allow plenty of time to select their neighborhood and home. If Leesburg sounds like a good spot to you, try to spend several weeks during summer and winter seasons exploring the area and inspecting the various communities.

WEATHER

	Winter	Spring	Summer	Fall
Normal daily high/low	71/48	86/64	90/71	76/55
Normal precipitation	10 in.	12 in.	17 in.	7 in.

Disaster watch: Northeast Florida has not been hit by a major hurricane since 1900.

TAXES
Sales tax: 7%. **Property tax:** $21.19 per $1,000 valuation. Sample tax calculations include a $25,000 homestead exemption.

Home value	Tax
$100,000	$1,589
$150,000	$2,649
$250,000	$4,768

REAL ESTATE
Median home value: $90,181 (Lake County). **Median rent:** $438/month (Lake County). **Communities popular with retirees:** Hawthorne at Leesburg, a gated community of manufactured homes priced from the $30s to $70s, (800) 525-8077. Lake Griffin Harbor offers manufactured homes priced from the $30s, (352) 326-5106. Highland Lakes, a gated adult community with a 10-acre recreation complex, has site-built homes and villas priced from the $80s, (800) 533-5940 The Plantation at Leesburg is a gated golf and country club with two- and three-bedroom site-built homes from the $80s to mid-$100s, (800) 233-8536. Pennbrooke Fairways has single-family homes priced from the mid-$70s, (800) 828-9699 or (352) 326-5600. **Licensed continuing-care retirement communities:** Lake Port Square has 400 independent living units, 10 sheltered nursing beds and 50 community beds, (352) 728-8525.

CRIME & SAFETY
Crimes per 1,000 population: 87. **Non-emergency police:** (352) 787-2121. **Non-emergency fire department:** (352) 728-9780. **Police, fire, ambulance emergencies:** 911.

HOMELESS & BLIGHT
Downtown is clean and orderly with no homeless persons visible. Neighborhoods near the urban center are established enclaves of modest homes, centered around churches, community parks and facilities. Retirees live in outlying areas around lakes and golf courses.

The U.S. Census reported 68 homeless persons in shelters and one visible on the streets of Lake County, population 177,000.

HEALTH CARE
Hospitals: Leesburg Regional Medical Center, 294 beds in the acute care facility and 120 beds in the hospital-based skilled nursing facility, 24-hour emergency, full service, (352) 323-5762.
Physicians: 100+. **Specialties:** 30.

GETTING SMART
Lake-Sumter Community College, (352) 787-3747. **Offerings:** Two-year associate degrees in arts and sciences, and a variety of personal enrichment courses.

JUST FOR SENIORS
Senior Center, (352) 326-3644. **Senior Services**, meals and in-home services (352) 326-3540.

GETTING INVOLVED
Cultural Arts Society of Leesburg, (352) 787-0000. **Habitat for Humanity,** (352) 728-5655. **RSVP,** (352) 365-1995. **United Way of Lake County,** (352) 787-7530.

RECREATION, ENTERTAINMENT & AMENITIES

Public golf: Plantation at Leesburg, 18 holes; Pennbrooke, nine holes; and Water Oak, 18 holes. There are 17 courses within 30 minutes. **Private golf:** Silver Lake Golf & Country Club, 18 holes. **Public tennis courts:** Susan Street Complex and Venetian Gardens Public Park. **Private tennis courts:** Harbor Hills, Har-Tru Courts and Hawthorne. **Parks:** The 100-acre Venetian Gardens on Lake Harris is the largest of 10 municipal parks. **Public swimming pools:** Dabney Recreation Complex and Venetian Gardens Public Park. **Water sports:** Boating, canoeing, fishing, sailing and water-skiing. **River/gulf/ocean:** Lake Harris (the largest lake in the county) and Lake Griffin both have access to the chain of lakes leading to St. Johns River and ultimately to the Atlantic Ocean. Both are heavily used for boating, fishing, recreation and exploring. **Running/walking/biking:** Lake-side parks and hundreds of miles of lightly traveled streets and rural roads accommodate the most avid walkers, runners and cyclists. **Horses/riding:** Only a short distance from the famous horse breeding area of Ocala, there are several riding academies and stables and plenty of open pastures. **Hunting:** Fishing and hunting licenses and information, (352) 343-9622. **Movie theaters:** 10 screens. **Art museums:** Cultural Arts Building at Venetian Gardens. **History museums:** Leesburg Heritage Society Museum. **Theaters:** Melon Patch Theater, Fine Arts Center at Lake Sumter Community College. **Library:** Leesburg Public. **Attractions:** Lakes Harris and Griffin and the Lake Griffin State Recreation Area. **Necessities:** All are available.

Smart Shopper Tip: Lake Square Mall is Lake County's premier shopping mall with three major department stores and more than 75 shops. There are nine other shopping centers in the county.

WHO LIVES HERE

Population: 15,409 year-round residents, an increase of 626 since 1990. **Age 65+** = 27.9% in Lake County. **Median household income:** $24,804 (Lake County). **Per capita income:** $19,459 (Lake County).

NUMBERS TO KNOW

Chamber of commerce: (352) 787-2131. **Voter registration:** (352) 343-9734. **Vehicle registration, tags & title:** (352) 754-4180. **Driver's license:** (352) 360-6508.

WHAT TO READ

Daily Commercial, daily newspaper, (352) 787-0600. **The Lake News**, weekly newspaper, (352) 787-6277.

GETTING AROUND

Bus: Transportation for seniors, (352) 360-6618. **Taxi:** City Cab, (352) 787-5550. **Tours:** Florida Water Safari, (352) 360-8130. **Airport:** Orlando International is 50 miles away. **Traffic:** Florida's Turnpike, accessible from U.S. Highway 27, gets you to Orlando in less than an hour. U.S. highways 27 and 441 bring a lot of traffic through Leesburg's suburbs. Downtown is busy but congestion-free.

JOBS

County unemployment rate: 3.8%. **Florida Jobs and Benefits:** (352) 360-6518. **Job Line:** For Lake County, (352) 343-5627.

UTILITIES

Electricity: Florida Power Corp., (800) 700-8744. **Gas, water & sewer:** City of Leesburg, (352) 728-9800. **Telephone:** Sprint United Telephone, (352) 326-3535. **Cable TV:** ComCast Cable, (352) 787-7875.

PLACES OF WORSHIP

One Catholic and 57 Protestant churches, plus one Jewish synagogue.

THE ENVIRONMENT

Lake Harris has been rated as having fair water quality. Lake Griffin is negatively affected by upstream pollution from Lake Apopka and waste-water treatment plants (WWTP); it has poor water quality. Lake Apopka has been designated for improvement and management, as has the Upper Oklawaha River Basin. Additionally, Lake County has eliminated further WWTP discharge to the lakes. The water district is working to acquire farms along the chain of lakes and the Oklawaha River to restore the flood plain wetlands. These actions are expected to help improve water quality in the lakes. Lake Griffin State Recreation Area and the Clermont Chain of Lakes have protected status as Outstanding Florida Waters.

There is one EPA-listed Superfund site in Lake County, Tower Chemical in Clermont.

EVENTS AND FESTIVALS

Fun and Art Festival - March. **Fourth of July Parade. Mainstreet Holiday Craft Bazaar** - November. **Tree Lighting Ceremony & Parade** - December.

WHERE TO EAT

Redhouse Saloon, 1350 W. North Blvd., fajitas, ribs and steaks, inexpensive to moderate, (352) 323-9222. **Takis Restaurant**, 1234 W. North Blvd., Greek and Italian, moderate, (352) 787-2344. **Vic's Embers Supper Club**, 7940 U.S. Highway 441, steaks, seafood and lobster, moderate, (352) 728-8989.

WHERE TO STAY

There are 17 hotels/motels in the area, including several of the budget chains.

ISSUES

With a restored downtown, beautiful suburbs and lakes, and pretty countryside, Leesburg's civic boosters feel the town is ideally situated to gain a lion's share of relocating retirees well into the next century. There appear to be no issues or obstacles standing in the way.

Live Oak

HE SAID: ★ ★ ★ ★
*This is near the top of the list of my favorite small towns
in Florida. It has a genuine "Mayberry" quality few towns
can duplicate.*

SHE SAID: ★ ★ ★
*A lovely, spacious small town, it's clean and inviting.
It's bordered on three sides by the Suwannee River with lots
of agriculture, yet only minutes from I-10, I-75 and easy
access to larger cities. I would look at this
place for retirement.*

The Suwannee River, memorialized by Stephen Foster, winds lazily in a huge arc around three sides of Live Oak before settling on a southerly course to the Gulf of Mexico. The river, the largely agrarian economy, an obsession with bicycling and the quiet, clean, warm and friendly town itself all combine to define Live Oak.

Writer Marjorie Kinnan Rawlings wrote in 1942, "We need above all, I think, a certain remoteness from urban confusion." She may have been thinking of her home in Cross Creek, FL, when she penned those words, but they are prophetically descriptive of Live Oak today. For those who find that the thrill of concerts, symphonies and professional sporting events pales by comparison to the quiet joy and camaraderie of a bicycling journey along clean, flowing rivers and springs, Live Oak is the place to be. Indeed, the sense of being separated from the hustle and bustle, congestion, crime and violence of much of America extends to most pastimes pursued by those living in Live Oak.

Live Oak isn't paradise. It isn't all things to all people. For one thing, a nine-hole golf course isn't nearly enough. But there are other courses within a 30-minute drive. The absence of institutions of higher learning may be a problem for some folks, while others won't want to live more than 15 minutes from a 200-store megamall.

What it does have are dozens of events and activities revolving around the numerous springs of Suwannee County. These create a thriving market for scuba diving outfitters. And then there's bicycling. The Suwannee Bicycle Association, a non-profit group dedicated to promoting environmental awareness, education and personal fitness through bicycling, canoeing and hiking, has developed more than 20 tours. Many active seniors take part in these tours. In fact, 30 percent of the riders in a past Bicycle Festival were over age 50, and 20 percent were over 60.

What does Live Oak offer? A brochure from the town of Live Oak and the region ended with these words: "Indian villages thrived in this area thousands of years ago for the same reasons that people visit or live here today — good water, a pleasant climate, a good growing season and a pleasant place to live."

When you think about it, these are four pretty important factors in our search for Camelot. If you're looking for these things in your third age, look no further. You've found them.

Disaster watch: No major hurricanes have hit this area directly.

TAXES
Sales tax: 7%. **Property tax:** $23.53 per $1,000 valuation. Sample tax calculations include a $25,000 homestead exemption.

Home value	Tax
$100,000	$1,765
$150,000	$2,941
$250,000	$5,294

REAL ESTATE
Median home value: $74,901 (Suwannee County). **Median rent:** $370/month (Suwannee County). **Communities popular with retirees:** Advent Christian Village has manufactured and mobile home sites, garden apartments, midrise apartments, land-lease homes, intermediate care center and skilled nursing, (800) 647-3353. **Licensed continuing-care retirement communities:** None.

CRIME & SAFETY
Crimes per 1,000 population: 35. **Non-emergency police:** (904) 364-3445. **Non-emergency fire department:** (904) 362-1313. **Police, fire, ambulance emergencies:** 911.

HOMELESS & BLIGHT
We saw no homeless nor blighted areas. The U.S. Census reported 11 homeless persons in shelters and none on the streets in Suwannee County, population 26,780.

HEALTH CARE
Hospitals: Shands at Live Oak, 60 beds, 24-hour emergency, (904) 362-1413.
Physicians: 12. **Specialties:** 5.

GETTING SMART
There are no college or university campuses in the Live Oak area. The **Stephen Foster State Folk Culture Center** offers Elderhostel programs. Call (904) 397-2733 for details.

JUST FOR SENIORS
Better Living for Seniors, (904) 364-5673. **Suwannee County Senior Center**, (904) 362-1164.

GETTING INVOLVED
Florida Sheriff's Youth Ranches, (904) 842-5501.

WEATHER

	Winter	Spring	Summer	Fall
Normal daily high/low	71/44	87/61	91/70	76/50
Normal precipitation	13 in.	13 in.	19 in.	8 in.

RECREATION, ENTERTAINMENT & AMENITIES
Public golf: Suwannee Country Club, nine holes. Suwannee

River Valley Golf & Country Club is 10 miles north in Jasper and has 18 holes. **Private golf:** None. **Public tennis courts:** Live Oak Recreation Center, 12 courts. **Private tennis courts:** Suwannee Country Club. **Parks:** Suwannee River State Park has nature trails, a boat ramp and springs. Hart Springs Park, a hard-to-find county park, offers swimming in cold, clear spring water. Also, Live Oak Recreation Center. **Public swimming pools:** City/county pool. **Water sports:** Canoeing, boating, snorkeling, scuba diving and tubing, mostly on the Suwannee River. **River/gulf/ocean:** Much outdoor recreation revolves around the Suwannee River. Steinhatchee, a scenic fishing village on the Gulf, is 53 miles southwest. **Running/walking/biking:** Suwannee Bicycle Association has developed 22 routes ranging from 10.3 miles to more than 100 miles throughout the region. Suwannee River State Park also has trails. **Horses/riding:** Breeders, dealers and outfitters attest to the popularity of equestrian activity here. **Hunting:** There are several hunting and fishing preserves in the area; call (904) 364-3428 for seasons. Thousands of acres are leased to hunt clubs. **Movie theaters:** None. **Art museums:** None. **History museums:** Suwannee County Museum. **Theaters:** None. **Library:** Suwannee River Regional Library. **Attractions:** Florida Sheriff's Boys Ranch, Suwannee River State Park, Stephen Foster State Folk Culture Center, Suwannee County Coliseum & Fairgrounds, and Langford Stadium. **Necessities:** Four banks, three savings and loan associations, a post office, pharmacies, real estate agencies, insurance agents, car dealers, supermarkets, discount stores, department stores, hardware and general merchandise.

Smart Shopper Tip: Live Oak has a small mall and three shopping plazas. An attractive, revitalized downtown supports retail and professional businesses. Plan to travel an hour or two on major shopping trips.

WHO LIVES HERE
Population: 6,578 year-round residents, an increase of 246 since 1990. **Age 65+** = 18.0% in Suwannee County. **Median household income:** $21,767 (Suwannee County). **Per capita income:** $16,621 (Suwannee County).

NUMBERS TO KNOW
Chamber of commerce: (904) 362-3071. **Voter registration:** (904) 362-2616. **Vehicle registration, tags & title:** (904) 362-2816. **Driver's license:** (904) 362-5550.

WHAT TO READ
Suwannee Democrat, semiweekly newspaper, (904) 362-1734. **Gainesville Sun**, daily newspaper, (800) 443-9493. **Branford News**, weekly newspaper, (904) 935-1427.

GETTING AROUND
Bus: Suwannee Valley Transit Authority provides bus transportation to Gainesville medical facilities, (904) 362-7433. **Taxi:** City Cab, (904) 364-1902. **Tours:** None. **Airport:** Gainesville Regional is 60 miles away. **Train:** Seaboard Coastline (CSX) provides daily east-west service, (800) 327-5405. **Traffic:** Very light.

JOBS
County unemployment rate: 4.9%. **Florida Jobs and Benefits:** (904) 254-3780.

UTILITIES
Electricity: Suwannee Valley Electric Co-op, (904) 362-2226. **Gas, water & sewer:** City of Live Oak, (904) 362-2276. **Telephone:** ALLTEL Florida, (904) 362-4222. **Cable TV:** Time Warner Cable, (904) 362-3535.

PLACES OF WORSHIP
One Catholic and 55 Protestant churches.

THE ENVIRONMENT
The Suwannee River has been designated as an Outstanding Florida Water and is considered to be one of the state's treasures. Water quality generally has been rated as good, though there are pollution sources: mining in the upper river basin; a poultry processing plant; and in Georgia, waste-water treatment plant discharges to the Withlacoochee and effluent from a pulp mill, also to the Withlacoochee. The Withlacoochee and Suwannee rivers connect.

The EPA lists Brown Wood Preserving, located two miles west of Live Oak, as a Superfund site that has been cleaned up. Deletion from the Superfund list occured Sept. 22, 1995.

EVENTS AND FESTIVALS
Stephen Foster Day - January. **Community Arts Festival** - March. **Suwannee Bicycle Festival** - May. **Florida Folk Festival** - May. **Blue Grass Festival** - October. **Christmas on the Square** - December.

WHERE TO EAT
There are 42 restaurants in Suwannee County, including **Dixie Grill & Steer Room**, at Howard Street and Dowling Avenue, Southern, seafood, inexpensive to moderate, (904) 364-2810.

WHERE TO STAY
Best Western Suwannee River Inn, (904) 362-6000. **Econo-Lodge**, (904) 362-7459. **Parker Motel & Restaurant**, (904) 362-2790.

ISSUES
We learned of no unique, front-burner issues while checking into Live Oak. The townspeople appear to be happily engaged in enjoying life, while the politically active among them rhetorically address real and perceived community concerns. In the newspaper's "Mayor's Corner," the concern was finding a place for youngsters to hang out during the summer, besides the Hardee's parking lot.

Longboat Key

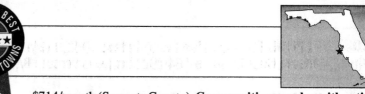

HE SAID: ★ ★ ★ ★ ☆
It is appropriately called the "island paradise." I would not hesitate to spend my golden years looking out across these white sand beaches at glorious sunsets.

SHE SAID: ★ ★ ★ ★ ☆
Golf, tennis, bike trails and a beautiful beach mean there's plenty to do. And there are several different residential areas from which to choose. With no billboards in sight, it's beautiful here — but expensive. I could retire here.

Through the years, consistently high standards and strict enforcement of zoning laws and ordinances protecting the island's flora and fauna have resulted in a garden environment. From the island's only north-south thoroughfare, Gulf of Mexico Drive, much of the town is partially or totally obscured from view by lush tropical growth.

The island was originally zoned to accommodate up to 60,000 persons. Over the years, wise stewards have scaled back its growth potential to current levels of approximately 7,500 full-time residents — 20,000 during tourist season. Oddly enough, tiny Longboat Key is shared by two counties, with about 2,647 people living in Manatee County, while 3,957 live in Sarasota County.

It is an upscale resort with few public access routes to the beaches and even fewer public parking facilities. So if you want a convenient way to reach Longboat Key's beaches, you can check into a resort or purchase a residence here. But real estate is expensive, almost unattainable for the retiree with average resources. Gulf-front lots are scarce but available for $595,000 and up. As it is now, almost all of the island is built-out so that any new construction requires tearing down the old.

One real treat of living on Longboat Key is its nearness to St. Armands Circle, an enchanting visitor destination for dining, shopping, sightseeing and people-watching. Another particularly special aspect is the key's accessibility to the outstanding cultural, social and recreational amenities of Bradenton and the Sarasota area. For exceptional beauty and location, Longboat Key is unbeatable.

WEATHER

	Winter	Spring	Summer	Fall
Normal daily high/low	74/52	86/64	90/72	79/58
Normal precipitation	9 in.	12 in.	26 in.	7 in.

Disaster watch: Southwest Florida has been hit by five major hurricanes since 1900.

TAXES

Sales tax: 7%. **Property tax:** There are four rates, depending on location and county: Manatee County (beach side) $21.80, (bayside) $20.78, Sarasota County (beach side) $17.77, (bayside) $16.75, per $1,000 valuation. Sample taxes are calculated at the rate of $21.80 and include a $25,000 homestead exemption.

Home value	Tax
$100,000	$1,635
$150,000	$2,725
$250,000	$4,905

REAL ESTATE

Median home value: $103,662 (Manatee County); $107,053 (Sarasota County). **Median rent:** $536/month (Manatee County);

$714/month (Sarasota County). **Communities popular with retirees:** In the Sunset Beach area, two- or three-bedroom condominiums overlooking the Gulf start at $225,000. Townhome units on the bay side at Fairway Bay, a midrise building, are priced from the high $190s to high $540s. Village homes are priced from the $110s to upper $360s. Lots start in the high $80s in the village, the low to mid-$110s on a canal and the mid-$590s on the Gulf, according to Wagner Realty, (941) 383-5577. **Licensed continuing-care retirement communities:** None.

CRIME & SAFETY

Crimes per 1,000 population: 18. **Non-emergency police:** (941) 316-1977. **Non-emergency fire department:** (941) 316-1944. **Police, fire, ambulance emergencies:** 911.

HOMELESS & BLIGHT

This is one of the most beautiful places in Florida. There is not an inch of blighted space on the key. We saw no homeless persons.

The U.S. Census reported 62 homeless persons in shelters and two visible in street locations in Manatee County, population 211,707. For Sarasota County's population of 277,776, the 1990 census counted 84 homeless persons in shelters and 11 visible in street locations.

HEALTH CARE

Hospitals: There is no hospital on Longboat Key. **Manatee Memorial Hospital** in Bradenton, 512 beds, acute care, 24-hour emergency, full service, (941) 746-5111. **Bay Isles Medical Center** for immediate care, (941) 383-8843.
Physicians: 3. **Specialties:** 2.

GETTING SMART

There are no college or university campuses on Longboat Key. **Longboat Key Art Center**, art classes in a variety of media, (941) 383-2345. **The Education Center**, continuing education, (941) 383-8811. **Manatee Community College** in Bradenton, (941) 755-1511. **Offerings:** Two-year associate's degrees, continuing-education classes for one-year certificates, and a variety of non-degree courses.

JUST FOR SENIORS

The only references to seniors in any literature from Longboat Key are the Senior Men's Tennis Association and the Senior Men's Softball League.

GETTING INVOLVED

There are not many clubs or organizations here. Longboat Key has Kiwanis, Lions, Garden Club, Democratic Club and the Historical Society.

RECREATION, ENTERTAINMENT & AMENITIES

Public golf: None. **Private golf:** There are three, including Longboat Key Club, 45 holes. **Public tennis courts:** Two.

Private tennis courts: Longboat Bay Club; Hilton Beach Resort; Veranda Beach Club; and Longboat Key Club, 38 courts. **Parks:** Bayfront Park Recreation Center. **Public swimming pools:** None. **Water sports:** Boating, sailing and snorkeling. **River/gulf/ocean:** Sarasota Bay and the Gulf of Mexico. **Running/walking/biking:** You can tour the island's back streets or take the 10-mile bicycle path along Gulf of Mexico Drive. **Horses/riding:** None. **Hunting:** None. **Movie theaters:** None. **Art museums:** Longboat Key Art Center. **History museums:** None. **Theaters:** Community Center. **Library:** Longboat Public. **Attractions:** Mote Marine Aquarium. **Necessities:** Three banks, a post office, supermarkets, hardware store, physicians, dentists and dry cleaners.

Smart Shopper Tip: Shops at the Chart House, the Centre Shops and Avenue of the Flowers are beautifully landscaped shopping areas in town, but you haven't seen beautiful until you shop St. Armands Circle on St. Armands Key.

WHO LIVES HERE
Population: 6,604 year-round residents, an increase of 667 since 1990. **Age 65+** = 27.1% in Manatee County and 32.6% in Sarasota County. **Median household income:** $27,441 (Manatee County); $30,662 (Sarasota County). **Per capita income:** $24,758 (Manatee County); $33,445 (Sarasota County).

NUMBERS TO KNOW
Chamber of commerce: (941) 383-2466. **Voter registration:** (941) 749-7181. **Vehicle registration, tags & title:** (941) 748-8000. **Driver's license:** In Bradenton, (941) 741-3017 or (941) 741-3015.

WHAT TO READ
Longboat Observer, weekly newspaper, (941) 383-5509. **Bradenton Herald**, daily newspaper, (800) 748-6666. **Sarasota Herald-Tribune**, daily newspaper, (941) 365-6060.

GETTING AROUND
Bus: Manatee County Area Transit, (941) 749-7116. **Taxi:** Suncoast Sedans, (800) 525-4661 or (941) 383-1235. **Tours:** None. **Airport:** Sarasota/Bradenton International, 30 minutes. **Traffic:** With limited accommodations and an out-of-the-way location, Longboat Key does not draw heavy volumes of tourist traffic. Local traffic is light to moderate.

JOBS
County unemployment rate: 2.5% (Manatee County); 2.5% (Sarasota County). **Florida Jobs and Benefits:** In Sarasota, (941) 361-6100.

UTILITIES
Electricity: Florida Power & Light, (941) 334-7754. **Gas:** Peoples Gas, (941) 366-4277. **Water & sewer:** Town Hall, (941) 383-3721, or Manatee County Public Utilities, (941) 795-3410, depending on location of residence. **Telephone:** GTE, (800) 483-4200. **Cable TV:** Time Warner Communications, (941) 748-1822.

PLACES OF WORSHIP
Three churches (Catholic, Episcopal and non-denominational) and one Jewish synagogue.

THE ENVIRONMENT
Sarasota Bay is designated as an Outstanding Florida Water, which protects its status. It also is part of the EPA's National Estuary Program. Sarasota Bay, between Bradenton and Sarasota, and Longboat Key Estuary have been rated as having generally fair water quality. Both are negatively affected by urban runoff and discharge from the Sarasota Wastewater Treatment Plant (WWTP). Anna Maria Key Estuary and the St. Armands Key Estuary have generally good water quality. Whitaker Bayou has poor water quality; it receives effluent from the Sarasota WWTP. There have been occasional closings of the shellfish harvesting areas.

EVENTS AND FESTIVALS
Call (941) 383-2466 for dates and details. **Arts Festival & Fair** - March or April. **Island Fest** - March or April. **Suncoast Offshore Grand Prix** - July or August. **Tacky Tourist Summertime Fun** - July or August. **Art on the Avenue** - October or November. **St. Jude Fundraiser** - October or November. **Longboat Key Amateur Golf Tournament** - November.

WHERE TO EAT
Euphema Haye, 5540 Gulf of Mexico Drive, steak, duck, seafood, moderate to expensive, (941) 383-3633. **Lynches Landing Bar and Grill**, 4000 Gulf of Mexico Drive, Irish, moderate, (941) 383-0791. **Poseidon**, 3454 Gulf of Mexico Drive, seafood, moderate to expensive, (941) 383-2500.

WHERE TO STAY
Colony Beach & Tennis Resort, (941) 383-6464. **Longboat Key Hilton Beach Resort**, (941) 383-2451. **The Resort at Longboat Key Club**, (941) 383-8821.

ISSUES
The only issue on the public agenda at this time is whether or not the town should build more public tennis courts — they have two at Bayfront Park & Recreation Center — and where they should be built. The arguments for and against on both points are hot and heavy—just what one would expect on an issue of such magnitude, in paradise.

Some previously emotional issues for the island included raccoons, peacocks, beach renourishment (adding sand to counteract erosion) and amendments to the island's comprehensive plan for development.

Marathon

It doesn't look like a small town in the classic sense — a community with a convenient blend of housing, commerce and social interaction — until you look behind the five-mile shopping strip extending along Overseas Highway (U.S. Highway 1) from Mile Markers 53 to 48. Hidden from view you will find the houses, schools, churches, parks and marinas that complete the community picture.

Marathon High School, the Natural History Museum, Marathon Public Library, Fishermen's Hospital, numerous churches and dozens of community organizations are among the landmarks and amenities noted by Marathon's boosters. Local residents and public officials supply the pride you can expect from those who live here and enthusiastically market its attributes.

In 1992 Monroe County adopted an ordinance limiting the number of building permits that can be issued each year for the construction of new dwelling units. Ostensibly to facilitate the "safe and timely evacuation of the Keys prior to a hurricane," the real reasons for the permit allocation system have more to do with environmental and public health concerns. Cesspool elimination is a key provision of the ordinance.

Karen Farley-Wilkinson, with ReMax Key to the Keys Realty, provided a not-so-subtle clue about real estate and who lives here when she said, "We have a saying down here: Paradise don't come cheap." She means it too. Like the other Florida Keys, Marathon is in Florida's most expensive county, with housing being the priciest item. But there is plenty of vacation rental property available. If you think you might be interested, rent a place, spend a month or two and get to know Marathon before you buy.

Note: You'll commonly see addresses and directions in the Keys based on U.S. Highway 1 Mile Markers, abbreviated as MM.

WEATHER

	Winter	Spring	Summer	Fall
Normal daily high/low	76/67	85/76	89/79	80/71
Normal precipitation	6 in.	10 in.	15 in.	9 in.

Disaster watch: The Keys have been hit by three major hurricanes since 1900.

TAXES

Sales tax: 7%. **Property tax:** $15.22 per $1,000 valuation. Sample tax calculations include a $25,000 homestead exemption.

Home value	Tax
$100,000	$1,142
$150,000	$1,903
$250,000	$3,425

REAL ESTATE

Median home value: $141,640 (Monroe County). **Median rent:** $888/month (Monroe County). **Communities popular with retirees:** Key Colony Beach, population 1,049, now an incorporated town within Greater Marathon, was established in the 1950s as a retirement community. It offers a nine-hole/par-3 golf course, beaches, boating facilities and some fabulous homes. Duck Key, about 10 miles away, has beautiful but expensive homes. Marathon's 60 islands and islets provide access to waterfront housing — for a price. According to realtor Karen Farley-Wilkinson, (305) 743-2300, low-end housing is pricier here than high-end homes on the mainland. Non-waterfront manufactured housing starts at $80,000 for older models, $120,000 for homes with water access. Waterfront condos range from $95,000 to $560,000. Medium-sized single-family homes sell for $200,000 plus on a canal. Waterfront homes on Sombrero Isle start at $550,000. **Licensed continuing-care retirement communities:** None.

CRIME & SAFETY

Crimes per 1,000 population: 68. **Non-emergency police:** (305) 289-2430. **Non-emergency fire department:** (305) 289-6010. **Police, fire, ambulance emergencies:** 911.

HOMELESS & BLIGHT

There were no homeless persons visible during our time here. Everything was clean and orderly. The U.S. Census reported 15 homeless persons in shelters and 126 visible in the streets of Monroe County, population 78,024.

HEALTH CARE

Hospitals: Fishermen's Hospital, 58 beds, full service, 24-hour emergency, (305) 743-5533. **Physicians:** 35. **Specialties:** 13.

GETTING SMART

Florida Keys Community College, (305) 743-2133. **Offerings:** Two-year degrees in arts and sciences as well as a variety of continuing-education workshops, courses and seminars.

JUST FOR SENIORS

AARP, (305) 743-4008. **Monroe County Social Services**, (305) 289-6016. **Senior Center**, (305) 743-4008.

GETTING INVOLVED

There are 55 organizations noted in the chamber's guide, offering many opportunities to get involved in the community. **United Way**, (305) 296-3464.

RECREATION, ENTERTAINMENT & AMENITIES

Public golf: Key Colony Beach, nine holes/par 3. **Private golf:** Sombrero Country Club, 18 holes/par 72. **Public tennis courts:** Two. **Private tennis courts:** Sombrero Country Club. **Parks:**

Crane Point Hammock is a 63-acre nature preserve with two museums on site. Sombrero Beach Park is popular with families. Bahia Honda State Recreation Area at MM 37 is one of the most popular beaches in the Keys. **Public swimming pools:** None. **Water sports:** Florida Keys National Marine Sanctuary and Marathon Marine Sanctuary provide spectacular snorkeling and scuba diving. There's also fishing and boating. **River/gulf/ocean:** The Atlantic Ocean, Gulf of Mexico and canals everywhere. **Running/walking/biking:** A much-used path runs along U.S. 1 from MM 45 through Marathon to MM 54 at Key Colony Beach Causeway. Another path runs from U.S. 1 along Sombrero Beach Boulevard to Sombrero Beach. Parts of the Seven-Mile Bridge, just west of Marathon, are popular with cyclists and pedestrians. **Horses/riding:** Some residents own horses, but there are none for hire. **Hunting:** None. **Movie theaters:** Two. **Art museums:** There is an art guild that holds exhibits. **History museums:** Children's Museum of the Florida Keys and the Museum of Natural History of the Keys are located in Crane Point Hammock. **Theaters:** Marathon Community Theatre. **Library:** Marathon Public. **Attractions:** Captain Hook's Seaquarium and the Dolphin Research Center. **Necessities:** Banks, supermarkets and grocery stores, real estate agencies, post office, gas stations, restaurants, hotels and motels.

Smart Shopper Tip: Marathon has a number of shopping centers. There's Gulfside Village, Townsquare Mall, Whaler's Plaza and the Kmart Shopping Plaza. Still, it's wise to shop the Mainland for the best prices.

WHO LIVES HERE
Population: 9,338. **Age 65+** = 17.5% in Monroe County. **Median household income:** $30,720 (Monroe County). **Per capita income:** $27,210 (Monroe County).

NUMBERS TO KNOW
Chamber of commerce: (305) 743-5417 or (800) 842-9580. **Voter registration:** (305) 289-6017. **Vehicle registration, tags & title:** (305) 743-5585. **Driver's license:** (305) 289-2306. **Visitors bureau:** (800) 352-5397.

WHAT TO READ
Florida Keys Keynoter, semiweekly newspaper, (305) 743-5551. **Keys Advertiser**, free weekly publication, (305) 743-8766. **Managing Growth in the Florida Keys: Environmental and Economic Stress in the Conch Republic**, written by John E. Fernsler, 191 Giralda Ave., Penthouse, Coral Gables, FL 33134.

GETTING AROUND
Bus: No public intra-city transportation; residents rely on cars, boats and bicycles. **Taxi:** Action Express, (305) 289-9418. **Tours:** Go Tours, (305) 743-9876. **Airport:** Marathon Airfield at MM 52. No picture of Marathon would be complete without mention of the 8,000-foot airstrip, which brings jet and commuter air service from Miami, Fort Lauderdale and other major Florida cities. Key West International Airport is 50 miles away. **Traffic:** Residents complain of the lack of a turning lane. Heavy tourist traffic inevitably runs through town.

JOBS
County unemployment rate: 2.5%. **Florida Jobs and Benefits:** (305) 289-2475.

UTILITIES
Electricity: Florida Keys Electric Co-op, (305)743-5344. **Gas:** None. **Water & sewer:** Florida Keys Aqueduct Authority, (305) 743-5409. **Telephone:** Bell South, (800) 789-9025 in Florida, or (800) 753-0710 out-of-state. **Cable TV:** TCI Digital Cable, (305) 743-5776.

PLACES OF WORSHIP
One Catholic and 12 Protestant churches.

THE ENVIRONMENT
The island waters that open to the Atlantic Ocean or Gulf of Mexico are rated as having good water quality and are all designated as Outstanding Florida Waters, granting them legal protection against any significant change in water quality. There are pollution problems in many of the man-made canals and marinas. Along the east coast lies the only living coral reef in the continental United States. The delicate reefs are easily damaged by careless divers, boat anchors and commercial ship grindings and/or spills. Beach erosion is a problem throughout the Keys, particularly at Bahia Honda's 0.9-mile beach.

EVENTS AND FESTIVALS
The Renaissance Faire - January. **Seven-Mile Bridge Run** - April. **Marathon Offshore Challenge Powerboat Race** - September. **Sombrero Cup Regatta** - November.

WHERE TO EAT
Anthony's Ristorante, 97630 Overseas Highway, Italian, seafood, steak, moderate, (305) 853-1177. **Kelsey's** at MM 48.5, continental, expensive, (305) 743-9018. **Castaway**, 1406 Oceanview Ave., seafood, moderate, (305) 743-6247.

WHERE TO STAY
Hawk's Cay Resort and Marina, (305) 743-7000. **Key Colony Beach Motel**, (305) 289-0411. **Sombrero Resort and Lighthouse Marina**, (305) 743-2250.

ISSUES
Before you get serious about retiring to Marathon or any other part of the Florida Keys, contact the Monroe County Growth Management Division, 2798 Overseas Highway, Suite 400, Marathon, FL 33050-2227, for a copy of the "Building Permit Allocation System Questions and Answers." Be prepared for a lot of red tape and a long, costly application process.

Marco Island

HE SAID: ★ ★ ★
*Those who take shore leave on Marco Island find
little to do. It's a great place to visit, but I wouldn't want
to be stranded here.*

SHE SAID: ★ ★ ★ ★
*Beautiful, lush and expensive. There are lots of high-rise
condos and single-family homes. Life would be easy here.
I could retire here.*

Marco is an island of canals. Literally hundreds of two- and three-block streets end at water's edge. One recent, unofficial survey discovered 6,134 dead-end sidewalks. Only the eastern and western shorelines, interior golf courses and the area around Mackle Park are unbroken by canals.

Obviously water plays a dominant role in the lives of residents and visitors alike. Whether for the sheer pleasure and therapeutic benefit it brings to those who love sand and sea breezes, or for the boating, fishing and water sports, water is ever-present and ever-important.

What does Marco have for the retiree who enjoys the island setting and excellent weather cited by the chamber, but who doesn't want to spend every day on a boat or strolling the beach? The *Marco Island Eagle* listed 72 happenings during a 30-day period, but only 10 actually took place on Marco. Most were in Naples and Fort Myers. So while there is plenty to do in southwest Florida, Marco Island is not the center of these activities.

We asked the chamber to name the five most important attractions for retirees. In addition to the good weather and island environment, they listed the retiree population, the ease of getting around and the size of the community. Unfortunately, uncontrolled growth and over-commercialization are the most significant threats to the current lifestyle.

After turning down incorporation five times since 1980, voters finally approved city status in 1997. County zoning, land-use ordinances and deed restrictions, generally unenforceable before, should fare better under the watchful eye of a municipal bureaucracy.

Almost all of Marco Island's Gulf shoreline and much of the bay front is beautifully adorned with multistory resort properties and private residence condominiums. Most of the privately owned condos are owner-occupied only part of the time and rented as resort property for the remainder. Marco Island is a wonderful, expensive vacation destination and a wonderful, expensive locale for part-time residency.

WEATHER

	Winter	Spring	Summer	Fall
Normal daily high/low	78/55	88/66	91/72	83/61
Normal precipitation	6 in.	14 in.	24 in.	6 in.

Disaster watch: Southwest Florida has been hit by five major hurricanes since 1900.

TAXES

Sales tax: 6%. **Property tax:** $15.00 per $1,000 valuation. Sample taxes include a $25,000 homestead exemption.

Home value	Tax
$100,000	$1,125
$150,000	$1,875
$250,000	$3,375

REAL ESTATE

Median home value: $121,400 (Collier County). **Median rent:** $644/month (Collier County). **Communities popular with retirees:** Phyllis Gentile with Prudential Florida Realty, (800) 423-0289, reports these general price ranges. One-bedroom, inland condominiums start in the mid-$60s. Waterfront condominiums throughout the island are priced from the $150s and beachfront units from the $250s. Inland single-family homes start in the $120s and a typical three-bedroom canal home with boat dock runs from the low-$300s and up. The Riviera is a condominium complex in Hideaway Beach with homes priced from the $600s to more than $1.5 million, (941) 394-8121. **Licensed continuing-care retirement communities:** None.

CRIME & SAFETY

Crimes per 1,000 population: 60 (Collier County sheriff's jurisdiction). **Non-emergency police:** (941) 793-9300. **Non-emergency fire department:** (941) 394-2108. **Police, fire, ambulance emergencies:** 911.

HOMELESS & BLIGHT

We saw no blighted areas and no homeless persons on the island. The U.S. Census reported 137 homeless persons in shelters and 218 visible in street locations in Collier County, population 152,099.

HEALTH CARE

Hospitals: Health Care Center, 24-hour emergency, EMS ambulance, helicopter ambulance landing site, Lifeline Emergency medical response, (941) 394-8234.
Physicians: 18. **Specialties:** 8.

GETTING SMART

There are no college or university campuses on Marco Island. The following are in Naples. **Edison Community College**, (941) 732-3700. **Offerings:** Two-year associate's degrees. **International College of Naples**, (941) 774-4700. **Offerings:** Two- and four-year degrees.

JUST FOR SENIORS

AARP/55 Alive, (941) 729-7742. **YMCA Adult Program** includes aerobics classes, "aqua slimnastics," fitness training, bridge, chess, arts and crafts, dance, plays, concerts, educational programs, a senior's club and meeting facilities for up to 675 people, (941) 394-3144.

GETTING INVOLVED

Art League of Marco Island, (941) 394-4221. **Historical Society**, (941) 394-7921. **Marco Island Civic Association** (MICA) is the island's oldest and largest organization with 2,800 members, (941) 642-7778.

RECREATION, ENTERTAINMENT & AMENITIES
Public golf: Marco Shores Country Club, 18 holes/par 72. **Private golf:** Hideaway Beach, nine holes, and Marriott's Marco Island Resort and Golf Club, 18 holes/par 72. **Public tennis courts:** Tommie Barfield Elementary School. **Private tennis courts:** Collier Racquet Club and Radisson Suite Beach Resort. **Parks:** Collier-Seminole State Park, The Conservancy's Briggs Nature Center and Frank E. Mackle Jr. Park. **Public swimming pools:** None. **Water sports:** Boating, canoeing, parasailing, sailing and water-skiing. **River/gulf/ocean:** Barfield Bay, Collier Bay, Marco Bay, Marco River, Roberts Bay and the Gulf of Mexico. **Running/walking/biking:** Mackle Park has a walking/biking path. Wide streets and sidewalks with cul-de-sacs throughout the island provide opportunities. **Horses/riding:** None. **Hunting:** None. **Movie theaters:** Three screens. **Art museums:** Art League of Marco Island. **History museums:** None. The Calusa Indian shell mounds are rich in history. **Theaters:** Marco Players perform community theater. **Library:** Marco Island Public. **Attractions:** Trolley tour to the Calusa Indian shell mounds and Indian Hill, Goodland, Cedar Bay Marina and Tigertail Beach. **Necessities:** A post office, financial institutions, pharmacies, small retail shops and three supermarkets.

Smart Shopper Tip: Town Center, Marco's biggest mall with 40 shops and restaurants, is OK, but the Coral Isle Factory Stores just off the island offer better bargains.

WHO LIVES HERE
Population: 12,700 year-round residents. Seasonal residents add another 15,000 to the population. **Age 65+** = 25.6% in Collier County. **Median household income:** $33,598 (Collier County). **Per capita income:** $32,878 (Collier County).

NUMBERS TO KNOW
Chamber of commerce: (941) 394-7549. **Collier County Information:** (941) 774-8999. **Voter registration:** (941) 774-8450. Through the chamber, (941) 394-7549. **Vehicle registration, tags & title:** (941) 394-6986. **Driver's license:** In Naples, (941) 417-6385.

WHAT TO READ
Marco Island Eagle, semiweekly newspaper, (941) 394-7592. **Marco Review**, magazine published five times per year, (941) 642-0251. **Naples Daily News**, daily newspaper, (941) 642-6566.

GETTING AROUND
Bus: Marco Trolley, (941) 394-1600. **Taxi:** Classic Taxi, (941) 394-1888. **Tours:** Sunshine Tours, (941) 642-5415. **Airport:** Southwest Florida International and Naples Municipal. **Traffic:** Major roads around the island are congested in tourist season and getting worse with high density development.

JOBS
County unemployment rate: 5.0%. **Florida Jobs and Benefits:** In Naples, (941) 434-5006.

UTILITIES
Electricity: Lee County Co-op, (941) 394-5164. **Gas:** None. **Water & sewer:** Florida Water Service, (941) 394-3168. **Telephone:** Sprint, (800) 699-0728. **Cable TV:** Media One, (941) 793-3577.

PLACES OF WORSHIP
One Catholic and 10 Protestant churches, plus one Jewish synagogue.

THE ENVIRONMENT
There are no water quality index measurements of the waters of Marco Island, but professional assessments state that the waters meet their intended uses. They are affected by the rapid and high density development of the island.

On the Mainland, these nearby areas have the designation of Outstanding Florida Water: Big Cypress National Preserve, Cape Romano State Aquatic Preserve, Rookery Bay State Aquatic Preserve and National Estuarine Research Reserve, Everglades National Park and the Fakahatchee Strand State Preserve. Everglades National Park/Florida Bay also has been designated for improvement and management. Health advisories recommending no consumption and limited consumption of largemouth bass have been issued for portions of Everglades National Park due to high mercury content. The Gordon River has a fair water quality rating. Henderson Creek Canal and Golden Gate Canal have generally good water quality ratings. Naples Bay has fair water quality.

EVENTS AND FESTIVALS
Maritime and Seafood Festival - January. **Jaycees' Fourth of July Picnic** - July. **Marco Island Film Festival** - October. **Christmas Island-Style** - December.

WHERE TO EAT
Cafe de Marco, 244 Royal Palm Drive, seafood, moderate to expensive, (941) 394-6262. **Olde Marco Inn**, 100 Palm St., German, French, moderate to expensive, usually closed mid-August to mid-October, (941) 394-3131. **Snook Inn**, 1215 Bald Eagle Drive, seafood, moderate to expensive, (941) 394-3313.

WHERE TO STAY
Eagle's Nest Beach Resort, (941) 394-5167. **Marco Hilton Beach Resort**, (941) 394-5000 or (800) 445-8667. **Marriott's Marco Island Resort and Golf Club**, (941) 394-2511 or (800) 438-4373. **Radisson All-Suite Beach Resort**, (941) 394-4100 or (800) 333-3333.

ISSUES
The Deltona Corp., which originally developed the island, had a plan for growth, but the deed restrictions in that plan could not be enforced by the county. Incorporation should allow the island to better deal with growth, zoning, infrastructure needs and such things as beach access, public parking and water supply.

Marianna

Wendell Taylor, county administrator, retired army colonel and former executive director of the Marianna Chamber of Commerce, explained the town this way: "It is large enough for basic services and small enough to be unrushed."

Marianna is the seat of Jackson County, where living and housing costs rank among the lowest in the state. It is horse country, serving as the site of several regional horse shows. Its other claim to fame is the spelunking caverns at Florida Caverns State Park. Its location, between Tallahassee 60 miles east, Panama City and the Gulf beaches 60 miles south, and Dothan, AL, just 35 miles to the north, gives prospective residents another reason to stop and look.

Kevin C. White, a newcomer to Marianna, described his feelings about the town. "This area is overflowing with 'down-home' folks who still know the value of being a good neighbor and have a genuine concern for fellow man. It is a community filled with folks who have a high sense of morality and value the simple things in life," he said. "In a world where deadbolts, alarms and firearms have replaced honesty, trust and respect, it's good to find a place like Marianna to call home and raise a family."

Similar feelings about the area are expressed in promotional materials. We left Marianna with a postcard calling it a place "where young people want to raise a family and retired folk want to relax and watch."

These words epitomize the qualities of Marianna. If you expect a lot more than that, you're going to be disappointed. If you can't live without art and history museums, performing arts theaters, literary guilds and a country club society, don't come.

But, if you like warm and friendly people, a restful atmosphere and forested, rolling terrain where wildlife and nature trails can be enjoyed 365 days a year — all an hour's drive from the pretty Gulf beaches — then what are you waiting for?

WEATHER

	Winter	Spring	Summer	Fall
Normal daily high/low	65/41	84/61	90/69	71/46
Normal precipitation	16 in.	13 in.	17 in.	11 in.

Disaster watch: Northwest Florida has been hit by six major hurricanes since 1900.

TAXES

Sales tax: 7.5%. **Property tax:** $18.83 per $1,000 valuation. Sample tax calculations include a $25,000 homestead exemption.

Home value	Tax
$100,000	$1,412
$150,000	$2,354
$250,000	$4,237

REAL ESTATE

Median home value: $73,013 (Jackson County). **Median rent:** $505/month (Jackson County). **Communities popular with retirees:** Robby Roberts of Jim Roberts Realty, (800) 841-7621, suggested the following: Indian Springs, a lake-front golf-course community of single-family homes priced from $85,000 to $750,000; Camellia Acres, a low-maintenance retirement community with homes priced from $85,000 to $250,000; and The Oaks and Forest Park, with homes starting at $100,000 and $150,000 respectively. **Licensed continuing-care retirement communities:** None.

CRIME & SAFETY

Crimes per 1,000 population: 21. **Non-emergency police:** (850) 482-6446. **Non-emergency fire department:** (850) 526-4612. **Police, fire, ambulance emergencies:** 911.

HOMELESS & BLIGHT

Marianna's main street project has given downtown a nice face lift. We saw no severely blighted areas and no evidence of homeless persons. Jackson County's U.S. Census count of 41,375 residents identified no homeless persons.

HEALTH CARE

Hospitals: Jackson Hospital, 107 beds, acute care, 24-hour emergency, (850) 526-2200.
Physicians: 40. **Specialties:** 12.

GETTING SMART

Chipola Junior College, (850) 526-2761. **Offerings:** Two-year degrees in arts and sciences, transferable credits to a four-year university. They add continuing-education courses in response to the needs of local residents. **Jackson County School Board**, (850) 482-1200. **Offerings:** Extensive adult education program.

JUST FOR SENIORS

Jackson County Senior Citizens Center /Senior Citizens Organization, (850) 482-5028.

GETTING INVOLVED

There are four social service organizations and eight associations and fraternal groups listed in Marianna. **Habitat for Humanity**, (850) 482-7997. **American Red Cross**, (850) 482-4384. **RSVP**, (850) 921-5554.

RECREATION, ENTERTAINMENT & AMENITIES

Public golf: Caverns Golf Course, nine holes; Great Oaks Golf Course, nine holes; and Indian Springs Golf Course, 18 holes. **Private golf:** Dogwood Lakes Golf Course in Bonifay, 20 miles west. **Public tennis courts:** City parks. **Private tennis courts:** None. **Parks:** Florida Caverns State Park has swimming, canoeing and spelunking. Also, Three Rivers State Recreation Area and Blue Springs Recreation Area. **Public swimming pools:** Chipola Junior College, Three Rivers State Recreation Area and Blue Springs Recreation Area. **Water sports:** Canoeing, fishing, boating and swimming. **River/gulf/ocean:** The Chipola River flows under

Marianna. Lake Seminole is 15 miles east. Apalachicola River is navigable and flows into Apalachicola Bay on the Gulf. **Running/walking/biking:** City parks have nature trails. The county is so rural that it is easy to find an area to run, walk or cycle. **Horses/riding:** Florida Caverns State Park has an equestrian facility and miles of hiking and horseback riding trails. Jackson County has many ranches, stables and horse farms. Showing is especially popular in the Marianna area. **Hunting:** Fishing and hunting (deer, wild turkey and birds) abound in the county. Contact the tax collector's office for specifics and license information, (850) 482-9653. **Movie theaters:** Marianna Twin. **Art museums:** None. **History museums:** None. **Theaters:** Chipola Junior College Artist Series. **Library:** Jackson County Public and Chipola Junior College. **Attractions:** Florida Caverns State Park is the main geographical attraction. There also are some beautiful, old homes. **Necessities:** Four banks, one savings and loan association, a post office, numerous gas stations, restaurants, real estate agencies, county government offices, supermarkets, discount stores and one department store.

   Smart Shopper Tip: The VF Factory Outlet Mall in Graceville is 25 miles away. Serious shoppers probably will want to travel the one hour to Tallahassee.

WHO LIVES HERE
Population: 6,750 year-round residents, an increase of 458 since 1990. Greater Marianna accounts for a population of about 17,000. **Age 65+** = 13.9% in Jackson County. **Median household income:** $22,573 (Jackson County). **Per capita income:** $14,604 (Jackson County).

NUMBERS TO KNOW
Chamber of commerce: (850) 482-8061. **Voter registration:** (850) 482-9652. **Vehicle registration, tags & title:** (850) 482-9653. **Driver's license:** (850) 482-9602.

WHAT TO READ
Jackson County Floridian, daily newspaper, (850) 526-3614.

GETTING AROUND
Bus: No public intra-city transportation. **Taxi:** City Cab Co., (850) 482-5441. **Tours:** None. **Airport:** Tallahassee Regional is 50 miles east. **Traffic:** Light.

JOBS
County unemployment rate: 5.9%. **Florida Jobs and Benefits:** (850) 482-9500.

UTILITIES
Electricity: Florida Public Utilities, (850) 526-6800. **Gas:** City of Marianna, (850) 482-4353. **Water & sewer:** City of Marianna, (850) 482-4353. **Telephone:** Sprint-CENTEL, (800) 326-2731. **Cable TV:** ComCast Cable of Marianna, (850) 482-5371.

PLACES OF WORSHIP
One Catholic and 43 Protestant churches.

THE ENVIRONMENT
The Chipola River goes underground near Marianna, with several springs and drainage tributaries south of town. Much of the river basin has been rated as having exceptional water quality and a diverse habitat, supporting rich wildlife.

   There is one EPA-listed Superfund site in Jackson County, located in Alford.

EVENTS AND FESTIVALS
Cutting Horse Show - January. **Marianna Quarter Horse Association Supershow** - April. **Spring Jubilee** - May. **Rodeo** - June. **American Quarter Horse Show** - July. **Annual Art Auction/Jackson County Fair** - October. **Farm-City Day** - November.

WHERE TO EAT
Madison's Warehouse, 2881 Madison St., American, moderate, (850) 526-4000. **Red Canyon Grill**, 3297 Caverns Road, Southwestern, moderate, (850) 482-4256. **Tony's Restaurant**, 4133 W. Lafayette, Italian, inexpensive to moderate, (850) 482-2232.

WHERE TO STAY
Comfort Inn, (800) 228-5150 or (850) 526-5600. **Hampton Inn**, (800) 426-7866 or (850) 526-1006. **Best Western Marianna Inn**, (800) 528-1234 or (850) 526-5666.

ISSUES
The issue for this community is its ability to provide services to a growing population. We feel that this area of Florida has too much to offer to remain a sleepy, dominantly agricultural area. With its rolling hills, clear streams and rivers, hardwoods and pines, highways and interstates, it invites significant growth and a new generation of retirees who want the Florida climate without the congestion, pollution and crime of south Florida.

RELOCATION TIPS

Chambers of commerce are usually a good source of specific relocation information for a community, but they may not be the only source. If you're willing to sift through sales materials, you may be able to obtain helpful tips and advice from a large bank, real estate development or real estate agency simply by asking for relocation information.

Melbourne

HE SAID: ★ ★ ★

I don't have any strong feelings about retiring to Melbourne. However, I would be concerned about the rapid growth of the area and would certainly want to take a hard look before deciding. If I found the right house in the right setting, I could be persuaded to spend a few years here.

SHE SAID: ★ ★

They call it historic, but sometimes "historic" is just old. Nothing has been fixed up here in years. The town is run-down and looks forsaken, with no positive signs that I could see. Maybe I didn't visit the right parts of town, but I didn't see anything that would make me want to stay other than some pretty nice housing subdivisions.

Talking about Melbourne really means talking about Greater Melbourne, which encompasses a total of 16 communities in south Brevard County. Palm Bay is included in this area because, even though it is larger in population and square miles, it still relies heavily on Melbourne-proper for its entertainment, shopping, employment and even beach access.

Melbourne attracts a lot of retirees looking for low-cost housing and a place in the sun. Retirees can be seen around town, dining in Morrison's Cafeteria and shopping at the numerous strip shopping centers of the area. For many retirees here, the South Brevard Senior Center is the city's social hub, where its 3,000 members play bridge, poker and bingo and go dancing on Saturday nights.

Patrick Air Force Base, immediately north, figures prominently in city demographics. In addition to the substantial economic impact of active Air Force personnel and the base's civilian employees, there are more than 13,000 military retirees in the area — more than 20 percent of Melbourne's population.

Melbourne probably has greater socioeconomic diversity and more varieties of housing and neighborhoods than almost any other community in central Florida. The newest community, Viera, is billed as a "city within a city." Located between Melbourne and Rockledge, this master-planned neighborhood is designed for self-contained convenience. Parks, schools, playgrounds, lakes, bike trails, nature preserves, golf courses, shops and churches are all within an easy distance of the homes. At build-out, projected for the year 2002, Viera is scheduled to have about 15,000 residents. It already is home to the Brevard County Government Operations Center, School Board Services Facility, Devereux Hospital, Brevard Zoo and spring training camp for the Florida Marlins.

Melbourne's proximity to Cape Kennedy (shuttle launches are within view) and Disney World (an hour's drive along U.S. Highway 192) are other points in its favor. The chamber of commerce cites climate, affordability, medical care, recreation and housing as strong suits.

WEATHER

	Winter	Spring	Summer	Fall
Normal daily high/low	73/53	84/66	89/72	78/60
Normal precipitation	8 in.	12 in.	17 in.	9 in.

Disaster watch: Southeast Florida has been hit by nine major hurricanes since 1900.

TAXES

Sales tax: 6%. **Property tax:** $19.55 per $1,000 valuation. Sample tax calculations include a $25,000 homestead exemption.

Home value	Tax
$100,000	$1,466
$150,000	$2,444
$250,000	$4,399

REAL ESTATE

Median home value: $100,769 (Brevard County). **Median rent:** $548/month (Brevard County). **Communities popular with retirees:** Barefoot Bay is a manufactured-home community with a golf course and clubhouse; homes are priced from the high $50s, (561) 664-3141. Suntree features distinctive communities to suit anyone's needs. In Magnolia Pointe, a gated neighborhood of townhomes, prices run from $119,000 to $145,000. Waterford Pointe has low-maintenance, detached single-family homes for $146,000 and up. Forest Lake Village features custom homes with a 1,900-square-foot minimum starting at $175,000, (800) 283-9715 or (407) 782-1058. **Licensed continuing-care retirement communities:** Buena Vida Estates has 145 independent living units, (407) 724-0060. Continuing health-care services are contracted with West Melbourne Health Care Center, (407) 725-7360, located next door.

CRIME & SAFETY

Crimes per 1,000 population: 92. **Non-emergency police:** (407) 259-1211. **Non-emergency fire department:** (407) 255-4601. **Police, fire, ambulance emergencies:** 911.

HOMELESS & BLIGHT

Though nothing struck us as being truly blighted, there are some substandard residential and commercial areas.

The U.S. Census recorded 196 homeless persons in shelters and 18 visible on the streets in Brevard County, population 398,978.

HEALTH CARE

Hospitals: Holmes Regional Medical Center, 528 beds, full service, (407) 727-7000. **Circles of Care**, psychiatric hospital, (407) 722-5200. **Holmes Regional Rehabilitation Center**, (407) 434-7182. **Healthsouth Sea Pines Rehabilitation Hospital**, 80 beds, (407) 984-4600.
Physicians: 270+. **Specialties:** 46.

GETTING SMART

Florida Institute of Technology, (407) 768-8000. **Offerings:** Undergraduate and graduate degree programs and Ph.D. programs in teaching, research, science, engineering, management, psychology, communication and aerospace engineering. **Brevard Community College**, (407) 632-1111. **Offerings:** Two-year arts and sciences degree programs plus technical and vocational training, adult and continuing-education programs. **Florida Metropolitan University of Melbourne**, (407) 254-6459. **Offerings:** Two-year degree programs.

JUST FOR SENIORS

Ruth E. Henegar Senior Center, (407) 723-5983. **South Brevard Senior Center**, (407) 724-2233.

GETTING INVOLVED

There are 67 non-profit organizations in Melbourne. **RSVP**, (407) 984-0479. **SCORE**, (407) 254-2288. **Getting to Know You**, (800) 255-GTKY.

RECREATION, ENTERTAINMENT & AMENITIES

Public golf: Baytree National, 18 holes/par 72, Spessard Holland, 18 holes/par 67; Harbor City Golf Course, 18 holes/par 72; Melbourne Golf Course, 18 holes/par 72; and Palm Gardens Golf Course, nine-hole executive course. **Private golf:** Suntree has two 18-hole/par 72 courses. Also, Indian River Colony Club, 18 holes/par 72. **Public tennis courts:** Greater Melbourne has 63 public courts, including those at Ballard Park, Crane Park, Fee Avenue Park, Flutie Athletic Complex and the Jimmy Moore Memorial Park. **Private tennis courts:** There are about 60 in the area. **Parks:** Among the 40 parks in the area are Ballard, Brothers, Canova Beach, Carver, Crane, Eau Gallie Causeway, Fee Avenue, Erna Nixon Hammock Park, Max K. Rodes and Spessard Holland. **Public swimming pools:** Brothers Park, Crane Park, Sherwood Park and Fee Avenue Park. **Water sports:** Two yacht clubs and 15 marinas provide ample public access to water for scuba diving, water-skiing, jet-skiing and surfing here at the self-proclaimed "small-wave capital of the U.S." **River/gulf/ocean:** Eau Gallie River, Crane Creek and several canals flow through Melbourne into the Indian River Lagoon. Two causeways cross the Indian River and connect residents with miles of Atlantic beaches along a barrier island. The St. Johns River and a series of lakes west of the city provide additional boating and canoeing opportunities. **Running/walking/biking:** Erna Nixon Hammock Park, Wickham Park, Desoto Exercise Trail, Hoover Exercise Trail and Tallwood Park Exercise Trail, among others. **Horses/riding:** Wickham Park has equestrian trails. There are several stables and riding academies. **Hunting:** Licenses required for hunting and fishing. Call the tax collector's office, (407) 255-4453, or South Brevard Service Complex, (407) 633-2000. **Movie theaters:** Three theaters offer 20 screens. **Art museums:** Brevard Museum of Art and Science. **History museums:** Liberty Bell Museum. **Theaters:** Melbourne Civic Theater-Henegar Center and Maxwell C. King Center for the Performing Arts. Arts groups include the Phoenix Production Company, Brevard Symphony Orchestra, Melbourne Municipal Band and the Melbourne Chamber Music Society. **Library:** Melbourne, Meadowlane Community and Stone Community. **Attractions:** Florida Institute of Technology Botanical Gardens has more than 300 species of palms, ferns and tropical foliage. Other attractions include Brevard Zoo, Melbourne Greyhound Park and the Space Coast Science Center. **Necessities:** Everything is available.

Smart Shopper Tip: The Melbourne Square Mall is nearly 1 million square feet with 125 stores, including Burdines, Dillard's, Belk-Lindsey, J.C. Penney and Mervyn's. The area has numerous shopping centers, plazas and malls. Historic downtown Melbourne, along the banks of Crane Creek, is a place to browse antique shops.

WHO LIVES HERE

Population: 68,056 year-round residents, an increase of 8,022 since 1990. **Age 65+** = 18.3% in Brevard County. **Median household income:** $33,061 (Brevard County). **Per capita income:** $20,747 (Brevard County).

NUMBERS TO KNOW

Chamber of commerce: (407) 724-5400. **Voter registration:** (407) 255-4455. **Vehicle registration, tags & title:** (407) 255-4410. **Driver's license:** (407) 984-4930. **Visitors bureau:** (407) 724-5400. **Space Coast Office of Tourism:** (800) USA-1969 or (407) 868-1126.

WHAT TO READ

Florida Today, daily newspaper, (407) 242-3500. **The Times**, weekly newspaper, (407) 242-3801. **50 Plus**, monthly, (407) 978-2226.

GETTING AROUND

Bus: Space Coast Area Transit, (407) 633-1878. **Taxi:** Checker Taxi, (407) 728-1200. **Tours:** None. **Airport:** Melbourne International, (407) 723-6227. **Traffic:** Moderate.

JOBS

County unemployment rate: 4.8%. **Florida Jobs and Benefits:** (407) 984-4831.

UTILITIES

Electricity: Florida Power & Light, (407) 723-7795. **Gas:** City Gas Co. of Florida, (407) 636-4644. **Water & sewer:** Melbourne Utilities, (407) 953-6211. **Telephone:** Bell South, (800) 789-9025 in Florida, or (800) 753-0710 out-of-state. **Cable TV:** Time-Warner Cable, (407) 254-3300.

PLACES OF WORSHIP

Six Catholic and 150 Protestant churches, plus two Jewish synagogues.

THE ENVIRONMENT

Crane Creek, to the north, has been rated as having poor water quality but should improve now that discharging from local waste-water treatment plants has ceased.

There is one EPA-listed Superfund site in Brevard County. It is the Harris Corp. site in Palm Bay.

EVENTS AND FESTIVALS

Grant Seafood Festival - February. **Melbourne Art Festival** - April. **Founders Day Art & Craft Show** - May. **Aqua-fest** - June. **Bavarian Fest** - October. **Melbourne Harbor Festival** - November.

WHERE TO EAT

The Chart House, 2250 Front St., prime rib, steak, seafood, moderate to expensive, (407) 729-6558. **Conchy Joe's Seafood**, 1477 Pineapple Ave., seafood, steak, inexpensive to moderate, (407) 253-3131.

WHERE TO STAY

Hilton Oceanfront, (407) 777-5000. **Radisson Suite Oceanfront**, (407) 773-9260.

ISSUES

The Greater Melbourne area is growing rapidly, gaining discontented former residents of the Miami-Fort Lauderdale area and many Midwesterners, who historically have favored the Gulf Coast for relocation. Lagging infrastructure development, especially new roads and water-sewer systems, is a major source of concern and frustration for residents. Some aerospace-connected industries have been downsizing, but the U.S. space program appears to be on solid ground.

Miami Beach

Across the country, chambers of commerce are going head-to-head in their attempts to attract relocating retirees to their towns. Not so in Miami Beach. "Miami Beach is not a retirement community," were the first words we heard from Bruce Singer, president of the Miami Beach Chamber of Commerce. Forty-five minutes later we thanked him for his honesty. Here's why.

Miami Beach, specifically the central section, is re-emerging as a tourist mecca. The area is experiencing an influx of foreign visitors and investors unprecedented in its history.

Since its founding in 1915, Miami Beach has metamorphosed several times. During the 1950s and 1960s, Miami Beach was a fun in the sun spot for visitors — it was *the* place for the American dream vacation. In the 1960s and 1970s, retirees discovered Miami Beach and flocked to the quiet community. They bought up ocean-front and ocean-access condos and single-family homes as fast as they were built. Unfortunately, the retiree rush brought with it the problems of rapid growth — traffic congestion, overcrowding and exorbitant prices. With that, retirees in the 1980s began looking for — and finding — other more appealing Florida locations. Fort Lauderdale, Stuart, Palm Bay, Naples and Fort Myers, among others, became the waterfronts of choice. Miami Beach entered an era of decline.

Now, with the help of at least five incentive programs designed to foster long-term capital investment, a new Miami Beach is being shaped. Touted internationally as both a tourist and residential community, it's drawing visitors from Europe, Central America and South America in droves.

Dozens of high-rise hotels fronting the ocean are being completely renovated and converted to investment condos for the foreign market. Discos have replaced retiree housing, providing entertainment for the younger, upbeat generation now taking over the city.

There is still some subsidized public housing for seniors, and there are still many retirees here. Thousands of older seniors continue to live in Miami Beach, trapped by time and financial circumstance in a radically changed environment. The peaceful retirement mecca they found 15 to 30 years earlier is disappearing.

The city's pulse is fast—faster than most retirees want. Miami Beach is no longer a retirement community. New retirees are choosing other locales and many of the retirees who live here wish they could, too.

WEATHER

	Winter	Spring	Summer	Fall
Normal daily high/low	75/64	82/74	87/78	79/69
Normal precipitation	6 in.	15 in.	15 in.	9 in.

Disaster watch: Southeast Florida has been hit by nine major hurricanes since 1900.

TAXES
Sales tax: 6.5%. **Property tax:** $27.69 per $1,000 valuation. Sample tax calculations include a $25,000 homestead exemption.

Home value	Tax
$100,000	$2,077
$150,000	$3,461
$250,000	$6,230

REAL ESTATE
Median home value: $120,199 (Dade County). **Median rent:** $764/month (Dade County). **Communities popular with retirees:** More than $200 million has been invested by the city to foster a healthy economic environment. Numerous incentive programs are generating growth and renewal.

Most retirees will drop Miami Beach from consideration when they see that the cost of housing is firmly fixed in the six- and seven-digit range. Crescent Heights Investments,(305) 372-1155, is the largest and most successful developer of the new Miami Beach. Since 1988 they have sold more than 2,000 condos. Most of these sales are in what used to be ocean-front, high-rise hotels, now fully renovated as condominiums. Holly Brent with Crescent Heights says that many units are purchased as investments and some serve as second homes, but most are occupied year-round. Retirees are not concentrated in a particular area. Some still live in ocean-front condos, but many others are moving into adult congregate living facilities. **Licensed continuing-care retirement communities:** None.

CRIME & SAFETY
Crimes per 1,000 population: 183. **Non-emergency police:** (305) 673-7900. **Non-emergency fire department:** (305) 673-7120. **Police, fire, ambulance emergencies:** 911.

HOMELESS & BLIGHT
While much of Miami Beach is being renewed, there are still run-down sections graciously described as "primed for redevelopment." We saw several homeless persons. The U.S. Census counted 1,730 homeless, with 1,235 in shelters and 495 visible on the streets of Dade County, population 1.9 million.

HEALTH CARE
Hospitals: Miami Heart Institute, 258 beds, full service, (305) 672-1111. **Mount Sinai Medical Center**, 707 beds, full service, (305) 674-2121. **South Shore Hospital**, 178 beds, affiliated with the University of Miami School of Medicine, full service, (305) 672-2100.
Physicians: 329. **Specialties:** 36.

GETTING SMART
There are no general-studies colleges or universities in Miami Beach. **Nearby: Barry University**, (305) 899-3000, in Miami Springs, is a private Catholic university. **Offerings:** Undergraduate and graduate degree programs.

JUST FOR SENIORS
Miami Beach Senior Center, (305) 673-6060, offers services, an adult day-care program and a full schedule of classes and activities in its 3,000-square-foot multipurpose room.

GETTING INVOLVED
Due to the transition from tourist mecca to retirement community to investment resort, Miami Beach lacks the continuity and stability required to develop strong, active social service and fraternal organizations. There are some here, but not as many as you would expect. The emphasis is more on night clubs than civic clubs.

RECREATION, ENTERTAINMENT & AMENITIES

Public golf: Bayshore Country Club, 18 holes; Normandy Shores Golf Course, 18 holes; Haulover Park, nine holes/par 27; and Bayshore, par 3. **Private golf:** In Miami. **Public tennis courts:** Most of the city's public parks have tennis courts. Courts are also available at Bayshore, Normandy Shores and North Shore Center. **Private tennis courts:** In Miami. **Parks:** South Pointe Park, Lummus Park, North Shore State Recreation Area and numerous public beaches. **Public swimming pools:** Several. **Water sports:** Miami Beach Marina and Haulover Marine Center offer boating, sailing and fishing. **River/gulf/ocean:** Miami Beach is separated from the Mainland by the Intracoastal Waterway. Ten miles of sandy beaches, shady palms and blue-green water line Route A1A. **Running/walking/biking:** Many trails and paths wind through parks and along seaside boardwalks. Scenic routes take you through the Art Deco District and revitalized central district. Call the Dade County Bicycle and Pedestrian Program, (305) 375-4507. **Horses/riding:** None. **Hunting:** None. **Movie theaters:** Two theaters. **Art museums:** South Florida Arts Center and Bass Museum of Art. **History museums:** Holocaust Memorial. **Theaters:** Area Stage Company, Jackie Gleason Theater of the Performing Arts, Lincoln Theatre, Colony Theater and Hirschfield Theatre. **Library:** Three public libraries. **Attractions:** Night views on (and of) the eight causeways to the Mainland, Miami Seaquarium and the Art Deco District. **Necessities:** All available on the island.

Smart Shopper Tip: If you're looking for chic high fashion, visit the Bal Harbour shops directly across from the Sheraton Bal Harbour Hotel on Collins Avenue. At the other end of the spectrum, and the other end of the island, sample the eclectic Ocean Drive shops of the Art Deco district. In between, in Central Miami Beach, there's ample shopping variety on 41st Street, Washington Avenue and at Lincoln Road Mall.

WHO LIVES HERE

Population: 92,927 year-round residents, an increase of 288 people since 1990. **Age 65+** = 14.4% in Dade County. **Median household income:** $26,743 (Dade County). **Per capita income:** $21,058 (Dade County).

NUMBERS TO KNOW

Chamber of commerce: (305) 672-1270. **Voter registration:** (305) 375-4600. **Vehicle registration, tags, title & driver's license:** (305) 229-6333. **Visitors bureau:** (305) 539-3000. **Economic & Community Development Department:** (305) 673-7193.

WHAT TO READ

Miami Herald, daily newspaper, (305) 350-2111. **Miami Today,** weekly newspaper, (305) 358-1008.

GETTING AROUND

Bus: Miami-Dade Transit, (305) 770-3131. Maps-by-Mail from Miami-Dade Transit, (305) 654-6586, ask for "First Time Rider's Kit." **Taxi:** Yellow Cab, (305) 444-4444; Central Cab, (305) 532-5555; and Coach USA, (305) 944-4422. **Tours:** Miami Design and Preservation League, (305) 672-2014, for information, maps and walking tours of Art Deco District. Old Town Trolley Tours of Miami and Miami Beach, (305) 296-6688. **Airport:** Miami International. SuperShuttle provides service to and from the airport, (305) 871-2000. **Traffic:** Alton Road and Collins Avenue are the principal north-south arteries and are very congested. If you can avoid those two streets, traffic isn't too bad.

JOBS

County unemployment rate: 7.2%. **Florida Jobs and Benefits:** (305) 470-5620.

UTILITIES

Electricity: Florida Power & Light, (305) 442-8770. **Gas:** Peoples Gas, (305) 947-7537. **Water & sewer:** Miami-Dade Water & Sewer Authority, (305) 665-7488. **Telephone:** Bell South, (800) 789-9025 in Florida, or (800) 753-0710 out-of-state. **Cable TV:** Gold Coast Cablevision, (305) 861-1564.

PLACES OF WORSHIP

19 Jewish synagogues and congregations, three Catholic churches and 14 Protestant churches.

THE ENVIRONMENT

The public water systems of North Miami Beach and North Miami failed to conduct a second round of monitoring for lead levels in drinking water, required by the EPA.

On the Mainland, the Miami River and New River have poor water quality ratings as a result of urban and agricultural runoff, boat discharges and sewage overflows. Miami River has high levels of coliform bacteria. It also has high levels of metals contamination in its sediment. A plan for the U.S. Army Corps of Engineers to dredge the river to improve navigation has been halted due to controversy regarding an acceptable disposal site for the dredged sediment. This affects the Mainland more than Miami Beach, which benefits from the good water quality of protected Biscayne Bay.

There are 12 EPA-listed Superfund sites in Dade County, including the Anodyne Inc. site in north Miami Beach.

EVENTS AND FESTIVALS

Miami Summer Boat Show - July. **Fontainebleau Hilton Annual Chocolate Festival** - September. **Taste of the Beach** - October. **South Florida Auto Show** - October/November. **Baron's Antique Show** - November. **Art in the Heart of Miami Beach** - December.

WHERE TO EAT

The Forge, 432 Arthur Godfrey Road, elegant American fare, wine cellar, expensive, (305) 538-8533. **Rascal House,** 17190 Collins Ave., deli, inexpensive to moderate, (305) 947-4581.

WHERE TO STAY

The Alexander, (305) 865-6500. **Windham Beach Resort,** (305) 532-3600 or (800) 223-6725. **Fontainebleau Hilton Resort and Spa,** (305) 538-2000. **Sheraton Bal Harbour,** (305) 865-7511.

ISSUES

Miami Beach has changed — again. It has become a trendy hot spot for the young, wealthy, international set. Renovations are improving many areas while uprooting and displacing the city's most recent incarnation as a retirement haven. Drug trafficking and crime are issues that require ongoing attention.

Mount Dora

FLORIDA'S BEST RETIREMENT TOWNS

The average visitor doesn't fall in love with century-old Mount Dora until he or she has been here at least 30 minutes. That's about how long it takes to tour the entire downtown, spend a few quiet minutes in Donnelly Park and take a stroll down to Lake Dora.

On the way around town, you can exchange greetings with the nicest folks you'll ever meet. We spoke with several retirees, and without exception they mentioned the friendliness of the people as one of the town's strong attractions.

This small-town geniality expresses itself in enthusiastic participation in competitive games of shuffleboard, croquet and championship-level bocce ball or lawn bowling. Art exhibitions, concerts, Ice House Theater productions, antique shows, golf tournaments and sailing regattas attract large numbers of participants and spectators in this town, where people like nothing better than the opportunity to rub elbows with their neighbors.

Six-mile long Lake Dora plays a major role in the lives of many residents; it's a popular locale for homes, boating and recreation. When wanderlust strikes, the lake can serve as an avenue of escape as well. Connected by the Dora Canal to a chain of lakes leading to the St. Johns River and ultimately to the Atlantic Ocean, Lake Dora gives residents seagoing access to faraway places few inland towns can offer.

There's plenty to do — or not do — in Mount Dora. One fellow said he likes to sit on a five-gallon pail while gardening, listening to the church bells and exchanging pleasantries with passers-by. And so, Mount Dora seems to be a great place to just be. It gives Northerners a sense of looking back at the hometowns of their childhoods and lets others see what could possibly be the quintessential all-American small town.

WEATHER

	Winter	Spring	Summer	Fall
Normal daily high/low	71/48	86/64	90/71	76/55
Normal precipitation	10 in.	12 in.	17 in.	7 in.

Disaster watch: Northeast Florida has not been hit by a major hurricane since 1900.

TAXES

Sales tax: 7%. **Property tax:** $22.61 per $1,000 valuation. Sample tax calculations include a $25,000 homestead exemption.

Home value	Tax
$100,000	$1,696
$150,000	$2,826
$250,000	$5,087

REAL ESTATE

Median home value: $90,181 (Lake County). **Median rent:** $438/month (Lake County). **Communities popular with retirees:** Coun-

try Club of Mount Dora builds custom homes priced from the $120s to the $500s and up, (352) 735-0115 or (800) 213-6132. Lakeshore Drive offers custom-built, single-family homes, townhouses and condominiums priced from the mid-$80s to $500,000, (352) 383-6121. **Licensed continuing-care retirement communities:** Forester Haven Florida has 116 independent living units, with assisted living provided on the premises and off-site health care, (352) 383-6158.

CRIME & SAFETY

Crimes per 1,000 population: 87. **Non-emergency police:** (352) 735-7131. **Non-emergency fire department:** (352) 735-7140. **Police, fire, ambulance emergencies:** 911.

HOMELESS & BLIGHT

We saw no homeless persons and no blighted areas in Mount Dora. The U.S. Census reported 68 homeless persons in shelters and one visible on the streets of Lake County, population 152,104.

HEALTH CARE

Hospitals: Florida Hospital Waterman, minutes away in Eustis, 182 beds, full service, 24-hour emergency, (352) 589-3333. **Sandybrook Center of Rebound**, 36 beds, rehabilitation center specializing in the treatment of head injuries, (352) 383-6007. **Physicians:** 125. **Specialties:** 31.

GETTING SMART

There are no college or university campuses in Mount Dora. **Lake County Vo-Tech** in Eustis, (352) 742-6486. **Offerings:** Vocational training and a school of cosmetology. **Lake-Sumter Community College** in Leesburg, (352) 365-3573. **Offerings:** Two-year associate of arts and sciences degrees, plus many continuing-education/non-credit courses.

JUST FOR SENIORS

Mount Dora has an AARP chapter. Call the chamber for the name and phone number of the current president.

GETTING INVOLVED

There are 64 clubs and organizations in Mount Dora. For a complete list, contact the chamber of commerce. Of interest: Mount Dora Art League, (352) 383-5205, Mount Dora Historical Society, (352) 383-8546, Friends of the Library, (352) 735-7180, and Mount Dora Lawn Bowling Club, (352) 383-2294.

RECREATION, ENTERTAINMENT & AMENITIES

Golf: Country Club of Mount Dora, semiprivate, 18 holes, and Mount Dora Golf Association, semiprivate, 18 holes. **Public tennis courts:** In Donnelly Park and at Lincoln Avenue Recreation Complex. Semiprivate Mount Dora Golf Association has courts. **Private tennis courts:** Mission Inn Golf and Tennis Resort is 15 minutes west in Howey-in-the-Hills. **Parks:** Four city parks provide a boat dock and ramp, croquet, shuffleboard, lawn bowling, tennis and the longest lakeside boardwalk in Florida. Tree-shaded Donnelly Park, occupying a full block in the center of town, invites picnickers and tennis and shuffleboard players. **Public swimming pools:** Lincoln Avenue Recreation Complex and several at semiprivate clubs. **Water sports:**

Boating, canoeing, sailing, water-skiing and windsurfing. **River/gulf/ocean:** Lake Dora leads to the St. Johns River and the Atlantic via a chain of lakes. **Running/walking/biking:** Palm Island Park on the shores of Lake Dora is one of the most beautiful nature walks in the state. There are many good routes for cyclists. The parks and downtown streets are perfect for walkers as well as strollers. **Horses/riding:** There are several stables, riding academies and horse training centers in the area. **Hunting:** Hunting and fishing licenses and information, (352) 343-9622. **Movie theaters:** None. **Art museums:** Art & Antique Union, Mount Dora Art League and Mount Dora Center for the Arts. **History museums:** Royellou Museum. **Theaters:** Ice House Theater hosts the Ice House Players. The Boards is an open-air stage in Donnelly Park, where free outdoor concerts are presented. The Community Concert Association offers classical and popular music in the Mount Dora Community Building. **Library:** Mount Dora Public Library. **Attractions:** Donnelly House, Mount Dora Lighthouse, Old Mount Dora Depot (now houses the chamber of commerce), Palm Island Park, Port of Mount Dora and Royellou Museum (the old city jail). **Necessities:** All here.

   Smart Shopper Tip: Browsers must visit the shops, boutiques and galleries of downtown Mount Dora for the sheer pleasure of it. Serious shopping is available in a number of shopping centers along U.S. Highway 441 and in Lake Square Mall at Leesburg.

WHO LIVES HERE
Population: 8,628 year-round residents, an increase of 1,312 since 1990. **Age 65+** = 27.9% in Lake County. **Median household income:** $24,804 (Lake County). **Per capita income:** $19,459 (Lake County).

NUMBERS TO KNOW
Chamber of commerce: (352) 383-2165. **Voter registration:** (352) 343-9734. **Vehicle registration, tags & title:** (352) 343-9602. **Driver's license:** In Tavares, (352) 742-6167.

WHAT TO READ
Mount Dora Topic, weekly newspaper, (352) 357-3199. **Daily Commercial,** Leesburg daily newspaper, (352) 365-8226. **Orlando Sentinel,** daily newspaper, (800) 359-5353.

GETTING AROUND
Bus: No public intra-city transportation. **Taxi:** Central Taxi, (352) 383-7433. **Tours:** Take the 3-mile, self-guided walking tour of historic Mount Dora with maps from the chamber of commerce. Rusty Anchor offers lake and Dora Canal cruises, (352) 383-3933. **Airport:** Orlando International is 50 miles away. **Traffic:** U.S. 441 has heavy traffic, but because it is a safe distance from downtown it has no influence on the small-town ambiance. Major events such as the Mount Dora Art Festival clog the streets, but normally the roads are quiet.

JOBS
County unemployment rate: 3.8%. **Florida Jobs and Benefits:** (352) 360-6518. **Job Line:** For Lake County, (352) 343-5627 or (352) 735-7172.

UTILITIES
Electricity: Florida Power, (800) 700-8744, or City Utilities, (352) 735-7151. **Gas:** Peoples Gas, (352) 357-3154. **Water & sewer:** City Utilities, (352) 735-7105. **Telephone:** Sprint-United, (352) 326-3535. **Cable TV:** Comcast, (352) 787-7875.

PLACES OF WORSHIP
One Catholic and 27 Protestant churches.

THE ENVIRONMENT
The main bodies of water downstream from Lake Apopka, including Lake Dora, Lake Eustis, Lake Griffin and the Dora Canal, have been rated as having generally poor to fair water quality. They receive pollutants and runoff from Lake Apopka and in the past have received discharge from local waste-water treatment plants (WWTP). Lake County has eliminated the WWTP discharge to the lakes. The water district is working to reclaim land surrounding the lakes to serve as flood plain wetlands. This, combined with efforts to restore Lake Apopka, should lead to improvement in the years ahead. The Lake Apopka and upper Oklawaha River basins have been designated for improvement and management. The Clermont Chain of Lakes and the Lake Griffin State Recreation Area have protected status as Outstanding Florida Waters.

   There is one EPA-listed Superfund site in Lake County, the Tower Chemical Co. in Clermont.

EVENTS AND FESTIVALS
Mount Dora Art Festival - February. **Antique Boat Festival** - March. **Sailing Regatta** - April. **Antique & Classic Car Show** - October. **Bicycle Festival** - October. **Crafts Fair** - October. **Light Up Mount Dora** - November.

WHERE TO EAT
Beauclaire Restaurant at the Lakeside Inn, 100 N. Alexander St., continental, moderate to expensive, (352) 383-4101. **Eduardo's Station,** 100 E. Fourth Ave., Mexican, moderate, (352) 735-1711. **The Gables,** 322 Alexander St., continental, moderate, (352) 383-8993. **The Park Bench,** 116 E. Fifth Ave., seafood, continental, moderate to expensive, (352) 383-7004.

WHERE TO STAY
Comfort Inn, (352) 383-3400. **Lakeside Inn,** (352) 383-4101. **Mission Inn Golf and Tennis Resort,** located in Howey-in-the-Hills, (352) 324-3101 or (800) 874-9053. **Seabrook Bed & Breakfast,** (352) 383-4800.

ISSUES
The only issue Mount Dora faces is its ability to assimilate the growing number of in-migrants — white-collar Orlandians, professionals and retirees — without overtaxing the systems, infrastructure and natural resources of the town and area. One of its most valuable assets is the small-town ambiance that can be felt while strolling its quiet streets, almost in solitude at times. A massive influx of automobiles and people could destroy the qualities that make it so desirable.

Naples

While Naples may not be "God's waiting room" in the literal sense, it is soon apparent to the observant newcomer that it has an uncommon number of white-haired inhabitants. Dressed in casual clothes, unhurried, relaxed in demeanor, many in larger-than-needed white limousines, a few driving too slow in the left lane, they are stereotypical retirees.

This town was built for retirees, the way retirees like their towns. There are plenty of exciting neighborhoods offering carefree, maintenance-free lifestyles. There are more golf holes per capita than in any other city in the country. Dozens of shopping centers, malls, plazas and factory stores serve to ignite the local economy. Shopping combines with social encounters in several unique theme destinations. The Village on Venetian Bay, the Waterside Shops at Pelican Bay, the Old Marine Market Place at Tin City and Olde Naples, the restored downtown, bring people out to mix, mingle, linger and spend. Art galleries, jewelers and financial institutions complete the picture of the heart of Naples: upscale, safe, stroller-friendly, busy but not crowded.

As everyone knows, one of the favorite pastimes of retirees is dining out. Naples has the quantity and variety of restaurants to make this normally pleasurable event unforgettable; the annual visitor's guide calls dining out in Naples an "award-winning experience." What the guide does not mention, however, is the one- to two- hour waits at many restaurants, most evenings.

The elegance, beauty and sophistication of the Ritz-Carlton and other Gulf-front resorts stamp Naples as a highly-rated destination for domestic and international travelers. At the same time, events such as craft shows, seafood festivals, swamp buggy races and American Indian Pow-Wow Days provide the foil that creates the homey ambiance so appealing to retirees.

So whether it's boating, fishing, golfing, shopping, dining, beach-going, sunset-viewing, sightseeing or simply puttering around your own piece of real estate that makes you happy, you can pursue these joys in Naples.

WEATHER

	Winter	Spring	Summer	Fall
Normal daily high/low	78/55	88/66	91/72	83/61
Normal precipitation	6 in.	14 in.	24 in.	6 in.

Disaster watch: Southwest Florida has been hit by five major hurricanes since 1900.

TAXES

Sales tax: 6%. **Property tax:** Most rates in Naples range from $13.76 to $16.84 per $1,000 valuation, depending on location. Sample taxes are calculated at the average rate of $15.50 and include a $25,000 homestead exemption.

Home value	Tax
$100,000	$1,163
$150,000	$1,938
$250,000	$3,488

REAL ESTATE

Median home value: $149,100 (Collier County). **Median rent:** $644/month (Collier County). **Communities popular with retirees:** Falling Waters is a gated community offering condominiums priced from the low to high $100s, (941) 774-5457. Lakewood Country Club features golf villas, duplexes and condominiums priced from the $100s, (941) 774-4056. Vineyards Country Club has 13 neighborhoods (six more to open) with condominiums, villas, patio homes and custom estate homes priced from the $120s to more than $1,000,000, (800) 749-1501. **Licensed continuing-care retirement communities:** Bentley Village has 392 independent living units and 93 sheltered nursing beds, (941) 598-3153. Glenview at Pelican Bay has 140 independent living units and 35 sheltered nursing beds, (941) 591-0011. Moorings Park has 312 independent living units, 16 sheltered nursing beds and 60 community beds, (941) 261-1616.

CRIME & SAFETY

Crimes per 1,000 population: 68. **Non-emergency police:** (941) 434-4790. **Non-emergency fire department:** (941) 774-7111. **Police, fire, ambulance emergencies:** 911.

HOMELESS & BLIGHT

Naples is one of the prettiest towns on the west coast of Florida. Its restored downtown is a scenic wonderland of art galleries, small parks and upscale shops and restaurants. If there is a blighted area within the city limits, it is small and well-hidden.

The U.S. Census reported 137 homeless persons in shelters and 218 visible in street locations in Collier County, population 152,099.

HEALTH CARE

Hospitals: Naples Community Hospital, 376 beds, 24-hour emergency, intensive care unit, full service, (941) 436-5000. **North Collier Hospital**, 50 beds, acute care, 24-hour-emergency, (941) 597-1417. **Psychiatric Center of Florida**, (941) 939-2205. **Physicians:** 230. **Specialties:** 48.

GETTING SMART

Edison Community College, (941) 732-3700. **Offerings:** Two-year associate's degrees. **Florida Gulf Coast University**, (941) 590-1000. **Offerings:** Undergraduate and graduate degrees. **International College of Naples**, (941) 774-4700. **Offerings:** Two- and four-year degrees.

JUST FOR SENIORS

Collier County Services for Seniors, (941) 774-8443. **East Naples Seniors Club** meets at the East Naples Community Center, (941) 793-4414. **Our Place Senior Center**, (941) 455-4122. **Seniors Aid Line**, (941) 263-7777.

GETTING INVOLVED

Senior Employment, (941) 774-1441. **Collier County Seniors**, (941) 774-8443. **Meals on Wheels/Help on Wheels/Friendly Visitors**, (941) 775-0443. **RSVP**, (941) 774-8833. **SCORE**, (941) 417-1280. **Volunteer Center**, (941) 953-5965.

RECREATION, ENTERTAINMENT & AMENITIES

Public golf: Eight public and two semiprivate courses. **Private golf:** 30 private courses. **Public tennis courts:** Cambier Park, Collier County Racquet Club, Fleishman Park, Golden Gate, Naples Beach Hotel and Naples Racquet Club. **Private tennis courts:** Le Club at Imperial, Naples Bath & Tennis Club, Port Royal Club,

World Tennis Center and Beckler Tennis Center. **Parks:** Big Cypress Swamp, Audubon's Corkscrew Swamp Sanctuary, Briggs Nature Center, Collier-Seminole State Park, Delnor-Wiggins Pass State Recreation Area and Lovers Key State Recreation Area, plus 12 city parks and beaches. **Public swimming pools:** One. **Water sports:** Boating, canoeing, jet-skiing, kayaking, parasailing, scuba diving and windsurfing. **River/gulf/ocean:** Naples Bay and the Gulf of Mexico. **Running/walking/biking:** Bike lanes are a part of many main streets. Collier-Seminole State Park has a 6.5-mile nature trail. Mackle Community Park and Clam Pass Park have jogging and nature trails. Also, miles and miles of beaches and the Florida Trail in Big Cypress National Preserve. **Horses/riding:** Naples Riding Academy and other stables in the area offer a variety of services. **Hunting:** None. **Movie theaters:** 13 screens. **Art museums:** Naples Depot Civic & Cultural Center, Arsenault Gallery and Naples Art Association & Gallery, plus many others. **History museums:** Collier County Museum and Palm Cottage, where the Collier County Historical Society is located. **Theaters:** The Philharmonic Center for the Arts, Naples Dinner Theatre, Naples Playhouse and Norris Center in Cambier Park. Performing arts groups include the Naples Concert Band, Naples Players, Naples Repertory Theatre, Once-in-a-While Park Players and Pelican Players. **Library:** Collier County Public and three branches. **Attractions:** Collier Automotive Museum, Conservancy Nature Center, Sand Dollar Sandal Factory & Outlet Store, Teddy Bear Museum and Zoological Park at Caribbean Gardens. **Necessities:** All here.

Smart Shopper Tip: Coastland Center, already huge, is being doubled in size. For a different kind of shopping experience, stroll the red brick walkways of The Village on Venetian Bay or the Waterside Shops at Pelican Bay. To go upscale, visit the Third Street and Fifth Avenue shops in old downtown.

WHO LIVES HERE
Population: 21,202 year-round residents, an increase of 1,697 since 1990. Seasonal residents add another 14,000 to the population. **Age 65+** = 25.6% in Collier County. **Median household income:** $33,598 (Collier County). **Per capita income:** $32,878 (Collier County).

NUMBERS TO KNOW
Chamber of commerce: (941) 262-6141. **Collier County Information:** (941) 774-8999. **First Impressions of Naples:** (941) 566-1300. **Voter registration:** (941) 774-8450. **Vehicle registration, tags & title:** (941) 774-8177. **Driver's license:** (941) 417-6385.

WHAT TO READ
Naples Daily News, daily newspaper, (941) 263-4839. **Fort Myers News-Press,** Naples edition, daily newspaper, (941) 591-2606. **Gulfshore Life Magazine,** 10 issues annually, (941) 643-3933. **Senior Times of Collier County,** monthly newspaper, (941) 353-0444.

GETTING AROUND
Bus: No public intra-city transportation. **Taxi:** Yellow Cab, (941) 262-1312. **Tours:** Naples Trolley Tours, (941) 262-7300. Tiki Islander Boat Tours, (941) 455-9832. Wooten's Everglades Tours, (941) 695-2781. **Airport:** Southwest Florida International and Naples Municipal. **Traffic:** Congestion usually is avoidable if you know your way around the city and can choose your timing. U.S. Highway 41 and Davis Boulevard are almost always congested.

JOBS
County unemployment rate: 5.0%. **Florida Jobs and Benefits:** (941) 434-5006. **Job Line:** (941) 434-4679.

UTILITIES
Electricity: Florida Power & Light, (941) 262-1322. **Gas:** None. **Water & sewer:** City of Naples, Utilities Dept., (941) 434-4752. **Telephone:** Sprint-United, (941) 262-2161. **Cable TV:** Media One, (941) 793-3577.

PLACES OF WORSHIP
Six Catholic and 92 Protestant churches, plus one Jewish synagogue.

THE ENVIRONMENT
Areas with the designation of Outstanding Florida Waters are the Big Cypress National Preserve, Cape Romano State Aquatic Preserve, Rookery Bay State Aquatic Preserve and National Estuarine Research Reserve, Everglades National Park and the Fakahatchee Strand State Preserve. Everglades National Park/Florida Bay also has been designated for improvement and management.

Health advisories recommending no consumption and limited consumption of largemouth bass have been issued for portions of Everglades National Park due to high mercury content.

The Gordon River has been rated as having fair water quality. Henderson Creek Canal and Golden Gate Canal have generally good water quality ratings. Naples Bay water quality is rated fair.

EVENTS AND FESTIVALS
Events: Collier County Fair - January. **Spring Arts Festival** - February. **PGA Tour Golf Event** - February. **Swamp Buggy Races** - March. **Festival of the Arts** - March. **The Taste of Collier** - April. **Summer Jazz on the Gulf** - June. **Oktoberfest. Festival of Lights** - November. **American Indian Pow-Wow Days** - November. **Snow Fest** - December.

WHERE TO EAT
Terra Mediterranean Grill, 1300 Third St. S., American, continental, expensive to very expensive, (941) 262-5500. **Truffles,** a less formal and less expensive bistro, (941) 597-8119. **Savannah,** 5200 Tamiami, Southern menu, moderate to expensive, (941) 261-2555. **Villa Pescatore,** 8920 Tamiami Trail N., northern Italian, expensive, (941) 597-8119.

WHERE TO STAY
Edgewater Beach Hotel, (800) 821-0196 or (941) 262-6511. **Hampton Inn Hotel,** (800) 426-7866 or (941) 261-8000. **La Playa Beach & Racquet Inn,** (941) 597-3123. **Ritz-Carlton Naples,** (800) 241-3333. **Vanderbilt Inn,** (800) 643-8654 or (941) 597-3151.

ISSUES
There doesn't seem to be a major issue facing this community today. It has grown by leaps and bounds, but still has room for new growth. Prices are increasing steadily, making it difficult for lower-income retirees to find affordable housing. Tax millage rates are surprisingly low, but probably not so when you consider the enormous tax base resulting from valuation of Gulf-front resort properties, high-rise condominiums and upscale country club developments. This is a wealthy town.

New Port Richey

HE SAID: ✶ ✶ ✶
This place has a lot of appeal. It's the first real town on the Gulf coast south of Panama City. It still has a few good years left before being overtaken by Tampa's urban sprawl and its own internal growth.

SHE SAID: ✶ ✶ ✶
On the positive side, it has palm tree-lined residential areas, beautiful parks, a nice location near the beach, the arts, good health-care facilities and a large mall. On the negative side, it's busy, with lots of cars clogging the roads. The traffic would stop me from retiring here.

This view of New Port Richey covers the 15-mile stretch along U.S. Highway 19 between the towns of Hudson and Holiday. The area includes Bayonet Point, Port Richey and some smaller unincorporated areas with parks, golf courses, lakes, Gulf access and recreational grounds.

The Pithlachascotee River plays a big part in the lives of many residents as it meanders slowly through the town. It is the setting for hundreds of fine homes with private boat docks, palm trees and Spanish moss-draped oaks. On the Gulf side of U.S. 19, Sea Forest Drive, Flor-A-Mar Terrace and Gulf Harbors offer an array of housing, from $300,000 canal homes to small single-family villas and condos in the $60,000 to $150,000 price range. All come with a view of the Gulf.

Downtown, just one block off Main Street, lies a large, circular park with a three-acre lake and oak-shaded benches. Here, in contrast to the never ending hustle and bustle of U.S. 19 just a couple of blocks away, residents of all ages relax and reflect on life's mysteries.

Innumerable shopping centers, plazas and the Gulf View Square Mall (in an unincorporated area just north of Port Richey), provide all conceivable goods and services. But if that's not enough, you are only 33 miles from Tampa.

Other drawing cards include 25 golf courses within 25 miles, legendary fishing grounds and proximity to all the urban amenities of Tampa, St. Petersburg and Clearwater, where there's professional sporting events, the performing and visual arts and other entertainment. Construction of Suncoast Parkway will both alleviate traffic through New Port Richey and give quicker access to points north and south. It's scheduled for completion in 2001.

If you like being near the Gulf, relish the proximity of major city sports and entertainment, and yearn for the quiet and serenity of small-town living, come take a look at this area.

WEATHER

	Winter	Spring	Summer	Fall
Normal daily high/low	72/52	85/66	90/73	78/58
Normal precipitation	10 in.	10 in.	23 in.	8 in.

Disaster watch: Northwest Florida has been hit by six major hurricanes since 1900.

TAXES

Sales tax: 6%. **Property tax:** $25.27 per $1,000 valuation. Sample tax calculations include a $25,000 homestead exemption.

Home value	Tax
$100,000	$1,895
$150,000	$3,159
$250,000	$5,686

REAL ESTATE

Median home value: $86,119 (Pasco County). **Median rent:** $422/month (Pasco County). **Communities popular with retirees:** The entire Sea Forest Drive/Gulf Harbor area along the Gulf is outstanding, offering canal homes, single-family homes and condos ranging from the $80s to more than $300,000. There are also beautiful homes along the Pithlachascotee River, near downtown. Gulf Harbors has condominiums priced from the mid-$40s to the $90s, (727) 848-0198. **Licensed continuing-care retirement communities:** None.

CRIME & SAFETY

Crimes per 1,000 population: 83. **Non-emergency police:** (727) 841-4550. **Non-emergency fire department:** (727) 841-4529. **Police, fire, ambulance emergencies:** 911.

HOMELESS & BLIGHT

We saw pockets of small, run-down homes on the fringes of downtown and a run-down mobile home park on the Gulf side of U.S. 19. The entire stretch of U.S. 19 through the area is cluttered with signs, but for some reason they are not quite as objectionable as in other areas. New Port Richey Community Co-operative has been working since 1986, with revitalization of downtown as its primary objective. Progress is evident.

There were no homeless persons in sight, though the U.S. Census did record 43 homeless persons in shelters and nine visible in street locations for Pasco County, population 281,131.

HEALTH CARE

Hospitals: Columbia New Port Richey Hospital, 414 beds, full service, 24-hour emergency, (727) 848-1733. **North Bay Hospital,** 122 beds, full service, 24-hour emergency, (727) 842-8468. **Physicians:** 167. **Specialties:** 41.

GETTING SMART

Pasco-Hernando Community College, (727) 847-2727. **Offerings:** Two-year degree programs in arts and sciences. Non-credit courses are offered as demand requires.

JUST FOR SENIORS

CARES Community Center in Port Richey, (727) 862-9291. **Claude Pepper Senior Center,** (727) 844-3077. **Elfers Senior Center,** (727) 847-1290. **Hudson Senior Center,** (727) 863-6868.

GETTING INVOLVED

Jewish Community Center, (727) 847-3814 or (727) 848-7985. **Meals on Wheels,** (727) 834-3340. **SCORE,** (727) 842-4638.

RECREATION, ENTERTAINMENT & AMENITIES

Public golf: Forest Hills, nine holes/par 35; Gulf Harbors Golf Course, 18 holes/par 60; Magnolia Valley Golf & Country Club, 18 holes/par 72 plus a nine-hole executive course; Seven Springs Golf & Country Club, 36 holes; and Tall Pines, nine holes/par

31. **Private golf:** There are several private country clubs in the area. **Public tennis courts:** Holiday Recreation Complex, New Port Richey Recreation Center and River Crossing Country Club. **Private tennis courts:** Several at various country clubs. **Parks:** There are eight county parks in the area. Crews Lake Park, with 113 acres, has a nature trail. **Public swimming pools:** City Recreation Complex. **Water sports:** Boating, canoeing, freshwater and saltwater fishing, and sailing. **River/gulf/ocean:** The Pithlachascotee and Anclote rivers, several Gulf-front bayous, numerous small lakes and the Gulf of Mexico. **Running/walking/biking:** Sims Park has pathways along the Pithlachascotee River. There are nature trails at Crews Lake Park and Starkey Wilderness Park. **Horses/riding:** No stables or riding academies in town. The nearest are in Spring Hill and Tarpon Springs. Jay B. Starkey Wilderness Park has an equestrian trail through parts of its 8,300 acres. **Hunting:** None in the immediate area. Licenses and information, (727) 847-8165. **Movie theaters:** Six screens. **Art museums:** None. **History museums:** West Pasco Historical Museum. **Theaters:** Performing Arts Center at River Ridge, Richey Sun Coast Theatre, Richey Community Orchestra and the Gulf High School Drama Department. **Library:** Public library and Regency Park branch. **Attractions:** Pasco Hands On Museum. The chamber cites beaches, fishing, weather, affordable housing and reasonable cost of living as the chief attractions. Nearby are Weeki Wachee Springs and Buccaneer Bay to the north and Busch Gardens in Tampa to the south. **Necessities:** All are available.

Smart Shopper Tip: Gulf View Square Mall has five anchors, 100 specialty shops and 18 food outlets.

WHO LIVES HERE
Population: 14,622 year-round residents, an increase of 578 since 1990. **Age 65+** = 29.0% in Pasco County. **Median household income:** $22,071 (Pasco County). **Per capita income:** $18,808 (Pasco County).

NUMBERS TO KNOW
Chamber of commerce: (727) 842-7651. **Voter registration:** (727) 847-8162. **Vehicle registration, tags & title:** (727) 847-8165. **Driver's license:** (727) 861-4826.

WHAT TO READ
The Sun Coast News, biweekly newspaper, (727) 849-7500. **West Pasco Press,** weekly newspaper, (727) 849-7500. **Tampa Tribune,** daily newspaper, (800) 282-5588.

GETTING AROUND
Bus: Pasco County Public Transportation for handicapped and senior citizens, (727) 834-3322. **Taxi:** Pasco Yellow Cab, (727) 848-1707. **Tours:** None. **Airport:** Tampa International. **Traffic:** If you can stay off U.S. Highway 19, traffic is a breeze.

JOBS
County unemployment rate: 4.2%. **Florida Jobs and Benefits:** (813) 930-7400. **Pasco County Job Line:** (727) 847-8141. **Senior Community Employment Program:** (727) 848-6649.

UTILITIES
Electricity: Florida Power Corp., (727) 842-9591. **Gas:** Clearwater Gas, (727) 845-1334. **Water & sewer:** Public Works, (727) 841-4500. **Telephone:** GTE, (800) 483-3300 or (800) 483-4200. **Cable TV:** TCI Cablevision, (727) 856-3278.

PLACES OF WORSHIP
Three Catholic, one Greek Orthodox and 56 Protestant churches.

THE ENVIRONMENT
The EPA reported finding lead measuring 18 parts per billion (ppb) in the drinking water of the Port Richey Water Department, which serves a population of 8,000. The EPA action level is 15 ppb.

The Anclote River has been rated as having generally good water quality, except the south branch, which has poor water quality. The Pithlachascotee River has fair to good water quality, but is affected by excessive use of off-road vehicles in the area and urban runoff. There have been some swimming bans in the area, presumably due to high bacteria counts caused by septic tank drainage and urban runoff.

EVENTS AND FESTIVALS
March on Art - April. **Chasco Fiesta** - March. **Holiday Country Western Jubilee** - April. **Hudson SeaFest** - November. **Christmas in the Park** - December.

WHERE TO EAT
John's Steak, Seafood & Pasta, U.S. Highway 19 N., seafood and steaks, inexpensive to moderate, (727) 841-0323. **Leverocks Seafood House,** 4927 U.S. Highway 19 S., seafood, moderate, (727) 849-8000.

WHERE TO STAY
Comfort Inn Gateway, (727) 842-6800. **Holiday Inn Express,** (727) 869-9999. **Quality Inn & Suites ,** (727) 847-9005.

ISSUES
The *West Pasco Press* asks, "At what point does progress quit being a blessing and start being a curse?" Rising tax burdens and increased crime are the underlying concerns of many New Port Richey residents, as they are for most Americans these days.

Some retirees who had fled Pinellas County (*i.e.* Tampa-St. Pete) for Pasco County because of the heavy tax burden and rising costs now are threatening to move to Hernando and other rural counties to recapture a simpler lifestyle. Another impetus for this sentiment is the impact of superhighway construction on housing, recreation and landscape in the county.

New Smyrna Beach

HE SAID: ★ ★
Undistinguished seems to be the appropriate descriptive adjective. Despite some nice residential neighborhoods and recent revitalization efforts, it doesn't quite measure up to retirement community status.

SHE SAID: ★ ★
It's a small, not very attractive beach town with high-rise condo housing and manufactured-home neighborhoods. Unfortunately, the beautiful, wide beach allows car traffic. The entire beach area is too congested. I would not retire here.

It has some good qualities, including nine miles of beach and a central coast location with good access to major population centers. There is some first-class housing, such as Bouchelle Island, a condominium community; Edgewater Landing, an adult manufactured-housing community on the riverfront just south of town; and the Fairgreen Golf and Country Club.

Downtown is on its way back after a long period of decline. A Main Street City rehabilitation project took longer than expected, and the lengthy construction process drove customers away and contributed to business closings. Now, new businesses have moved in and commercial activity is regaining strength in the area.

With little industrial development to produce new jobs and attract young, working families, and a limited cultural infrastructure, New Smyrna Beach is promoted simply as a beach resort. As such, it notes the obvious: proximity to Canaveral National Seashore, John F. Kennedy Space Center, Walt Disney World and Daytona Beach. Not a bad selling strategy, but not enough to entice retirees looking for an active, fulfilling lifestyle. In fact, if not for the presence of some very nice residential communities, New Smyrna Beach would have very little to attract newcomers.

WEATHER

	Winter	Spring	Summer	Fall
Normal daily high/low	71/50	84/65	89/72	76/57
Normal precipitation	9 in.	12 in.	18 in.	10 in.

Disaster watch: Northeast Florida has not been hit by a major hurricane since 1900.

TAXES
Sales tax: 6%. **Property tax:** $25.19 per $1,000 valuation. Sample tax calculations include a $25,000 homestead exemption.

Home value	Tax
$100,000	$1,889
$150,000	$3,149
$250,000	$5,668

REAL ESTATE
Median home value: $93,463 (Volusia County). **Median rent:** $517/month (Volusia County). **Communities popular with retirees:** Bouchelle Island is a condominium community with homes from the $70s to $220s, (904) 427-1239. Sea Woods, a beachside community of detached homes and condos, mid-$70s to $140s. Fairgreen Golf and Country Club offers single-family and attached homes from the high $50s to $160s, (904) 427-2465.

Licensed continuing-care retirement communities: None.

CRIME & SAFETY
Crimes per 1,000 population: 52. **Non-emergency police:** (904) 424-2220. **Non-emergency fire department:** (904) 424-2162. **Police, fire, ambulance emergencies:** 911.

HOMELESS & BLIGHT
While not exactly blighted, New Smyrna Beach is not particularly attractive. Recent rehabilitation programs addressed some of the more seriously deteriorated areas, but there are other sections that need a face lift.

The U.S. Census shows the population of Volusia County as 370,712, which includes 187 homeless persons in shelters and 35 homeless persons visible in street locations.

HEALTH CARE
Hospitals: Bert Fish Medical Center, 116 beds, 24-hour emergency, intensive care, surgery, full service, (904) 427-3401. **Physicians:** 39. **Specialties:** 23.

GETTING SMART
Daytona Beach Community College, south campus, (904) 427-3472. **Offerings:** Two-year degrees and transfer programs, plus continuing-education courses.

JUST FOR SENIORS
County Council on Aging and **Meals on Wheels**, (904) 423-5316.

GETTING INVOLVED
RSVP, (904) 423-5316. **United Way**, (904) 428-1520.

RECREATION, ENTERTAINMENT & AMENITIES
Public golf: Hidden Lakes at Fairgreen, 18 holes; New Smyrna Beach Municipal Course, 18 holes; Sugar Mill Country Club, 27 holes; and Turnbull Bay Golf Course, 18 holes. **Private golf:** None. **Public tennis courts:** Nine in various parks operated by New Smyrna Beach Recreation Department. **Private tennis courts:** Inlet Tennis. **Parks:** There are 19 parks in the area, including Lighthouse Point State Park and Smyrna Dunes. **Public swimming pools:** Aqua Park Aquatic Center in Edgewater. **Water sports:** Boating, fishing, water-skiing, sailing. **River/gulf/ocean:** Nine miles of Atlantic beach. Indian River (Intracoastal Waterway) and numerous cuts, creeks, flats, bays, coves and inlets exist in the area. **Running/ walking/biking:** There's a 1.5-mile boardwalk loop around Ponce de Leon Inlet, plus the entire shoreline. **Horses/riding:** There is one riding club and stable, but no significant riding trails. **Hunting:** No hunting, but excellent saltwater and freshwater fishing. Licenses required for both, (904) 423-3322. **Movie theaters:** eight screens. **Art museums:** Artists Workshop Gallery and the Atlantic Center for the Arts. **History museums:** Connor Library Museum, Sugar Mill Ruins (the remains of a sugar mill built in 1830) and the Ponce

de Leon Lighthouse. **Theaters:** The Atlantic Center for the Arts holds performances; also, Little Theatre and the Indian River Community Concert Association. **Library:** Brannon Memorial. **Attractions:** The Atlantic Center for the Arts, Turtle Mound, Ponce de Leon Lighthouse and the Sugar Mill Ruins. The New Smyrna Stock Car Races are held every Saturday night. **Necessities:** All within easy access.

   Smart Shopper Tip: The New Smyrna Beach Regional Shopping Center and Florida Shores Plaza in Edgewater are no match for the malls in Daytona Beach, 45 miles north.

WHO LIVES HERE
Population: 18,425 year-round residents, an increase of 1,876 since 1990. **Age 65+** = 22.6% in Volusia County. **Median household income:** $26,071 (Volusia County). **Per capita income:** $18,951 (Volusia County).

NUMBERS TO KNOW
Chamber of commerce: (904) 428-2449. **Voter registration:** (904) 423-3311. **Vehicle registration, tags & title:** (904) 423-3323. **Driver's license:** (904) 424-2010.

WHAT TO READ
Daytona Beach News-Journal, daily newspaper, (904) 428-9068. **The Observer**, daily newspaper, (904) 427-1000.

GETTING AROUND
Bus: Votran, (904) 424-6800. **Taxi:** Yellow Cab, (904) 252-5536. **Tours:** None. **Airport:** Daytona Beach International is 20 miles away. **Traffic:** Traffic is light downtown, moderately heavy on U.S. Highway 1 and Route A1A.

JOBS
County unemployment rate: 3.7%. **Florida Jobs and Benefits:** (904) 424-2085.

UTILITIES
Electricity: City Utilities Commission, (904) 427-1361. **Gas:** South Florida Natural Gas Co., (904) 428-5721. **Water & sewer:** City Utilities Commission, (904) 427-1361. **Telephone:** Bell South, (800) 789-9025 in Florida, or (800) 753-0710 out-of-state. **Cable TV:** Time Warner Communications, (904) 423-1151.

PLACES OF WORSHIP
Two Catholic and 36 Protestant churches.

THE ENVIRONMENT
Mosquito Lagoon has been rated as having fair water quality. Shellfish harvesting has been reclassified from "approved" to "conditionally approved." Shellfishing closures have occurred after heavy rains.

   The EPA reported finding lead measuring 19 parts per billion (ppb) in the public water system of New Smyrna Beach. The EPA action level is 15 ppb.

   Volusia County has one EPA-listed Superfund site, Sherwood Medical, located three miles north of DeLand.

EVENTS AND FESTIVALS
Arts Fiesta - February. **Black Heritage Festival** - February. **Images — Festival of the Arts** - March. **Seaside Fiesta** - June. **Flamingo Follies** - November.

WHERE TO EAT
Franco's, 1518 S. Dixie Freeway, Italian, inexpensive, (904) 423-3600. **Riverview Charlie's**, 101 Flagler Ave., seafood, moderate, (904) 428-1865. **The Skyline**, 2004 N. Dixie Freeway, steak and seafood, moderate, (904) 427-2652.

WHERE TO STAY
Coastal Waters Inn, (904) 428-3800. **Ocean Air Motel**, (904) 428-5748. **Riverview Hotel**, (904) 428-5858.

ISSUES
Canal Street (downtown), Riverside Park and Flagler Avenue (beachside), have recently undergone major revitalization efforts. The North Causeway bridge has been completed, improving traffic flow from the mainland to the beaches. New housing developments and shopping centers have opened. Despite progress, problems remain.

   Many residents feel that crime is on the rise; they are placing renewed emphasis on neighborhood watch programs and better personal security habits.

   This town, like many others, relies heavily on resort revenues, particularly from snowbirds. Without this income, the town could have serious economic problems.

RELOCATION TIPS

When moving from an urban environment to a small town or rural area, be prepared to make some adjustments. People, and the pace of life in general, are slower. You will be frustrated if you attempt to speed things up. Relocated retirees say a *mañana* attitude often prevails among service providers. This means that getting a plumber out on the weekend is unheard of, and that retail businesses may close down and lock up when the fish are biting. Remember, it's up to you, not the natives, to adapt.

North Fort Myers

HE SAID: ★ ★ ★

I love Greater Fort Myers, but the northern sector lacks the history and beauty of its southern neighbor.

SHE SAID: ★ ★ ★

Separated from Fort Myers by the Caloosahatchee River, North Fort Myers is known for its numerous manufactured-home developments and nice residential areas. There's also heavy traffic. I would not retire here.

This is unincorporated Fort Myers. Located north of the Caloosahatchee River, its housing and recreational opportunities have brought thousands of retirees streaming to its doors during the past ten years. All locations and styles of housing are available at affordable prices here. Manufactured and site-built homes, townhomes, condos and patio homes are found in a variety of neighborhood settings — on a golf course, by a river or lake, or in a forested area.

But when you get past the subjects of housing and recreation, there's not much left on the agenda. Residents rely on Fort Myers for health care, cultural outings, entertainment, upscale shopping and dining. In essence, it even relies on its neighbor for government services. Without its own municipal bureaucracy, North Fort Myers' slice of the revenue pie is determined by the Lee County commissioners — seated in Fort Myers.

These shortcomings are of little consequence to two retired couples we interviewed. Both couples chose North Fort Myers for one reason — the particular community in which they live. Sabal Springs Golf and Racquet Club, an affordable and first-class country club community of custom-built homes, lured one couple. The second couple has a home that fulfills their retirement dreams in Riverbend, a 212-acre country club on the banks of the Caloosahatchee offering condominiums and waterfront and golf course patio homes.

This once sleepy, recreation-oriented outpost of tall pines and oak hammocks, creeks, canals, wetlands, and horse and cattle ranches is undergoing rapid transformation. Due to the heavy influx of new arrivals, it will never be the same. This meteoric growth along the north shore and the U.S. Highway 41 corridor has pushed to the limit the ability of the roads to carry the traffic volume. Numerous road-widening projects are underway.

Perhaps that is one reason why representatives of five mobile home parks recently prevailed upon Lee County commissioners to build an eight-foot-wide bicycle path measuring six-tenths of a mile and linking the parks and the new Merchants Crossing Shopping Center. The 555,000-square-foot, still-expanding center accommodates almost all of their shopping needs. Once the bike path is completed, residents can reduce their roadway excursions.

This is a place in accelerated transition. Some of the rural areas and atmosphere still exist. But if you were here ten years ago and still dream of returning to the quiet corner you found back then, you better come back for a second look before signing any contracts.

WEATHER

	Winter	Spring	Summer	Fall
Normal daily high/low	76/55	88/68	91/75	81/62
Normal precipitation	7 in.	14 in.	26 in.	6 in.

Disaster watch: Southwest Florida has been hit by five major hurricanes since 1900.

TAXES

Sales tax: 6%. **Property tax:** $19.77 per $1,000 valuation. Sample tax calculations include a $25,000 homestead exemption.

Home value	Tax
$100,000	$1,483
$150,000	$2,471
$250,000	$4,448

REAL ESTATE

Median home value: $107,660 (Lee County). **Median rent:** $641/month (Lee County). **Communities popular with retirees:** Riverbend features waterfront and golf-course condominiums priced from the mid-$70s, patio homes priced from the low $100s, lots for single-family homes priced from the mid-$30s and single-family homes priced from the $140s to $500s, (941) 543-2200. Sabal Springs Golf and Racquet Club offers single-family homes priced from the low $100s to low $200s, (941) 731-3200. Tara Woods has manufactured homes priced from the mid-$50s to upper $70s, excluding the cost of the land lease, (800) 824-6284. **Licensed continuing-care retirement communities:** None.

CRIME & SAFETY

Crimes per 1,000 population: 36 (Lee County sheriff's jurisdiction). **Non-emergency police:** (941) 768-4361. **Non-emergency fire department:** (941) 997-8654. **Police, fire, ambulance emergencies:** 911.

HOMELESS & BLIGHT

North Fort Myers is a clean, open area. There is no downtown, and there are no old, run-down neighborhoods. Much of its growth has occurred in the last 10 years and seems to be good quality construction.

The U.S. Census reported 97 homeless persons in shelters and 203 visible in street locations in Lee County, population 335,113.

HEALTH CARE

Hospitals: There are no hospitals in North Fort Myers. The closest is **Cape Coral Hospital**, 202 beds (a 107-bed addition is under construction), acute care, 24-hour emergency, full service, (941) 574-2323. **Lee Memorial Hospital** in Fort Myers, 407 beds, full service, (941) 332-1111. **Southwest Florida Regional Medical Center** in Fort Myers, 400 beds, full service, (941) 939-1147.
Physicians: 10. **Specialties:** 4.

GETTING SMART

There are no college or university campuses in North Fort Myers. The following are in Fort Myers. **Adult and Community Education** is operated by the Lee County School District, (941) 334-7172. **Offerings:** Courses are designed to broaden general knowledge and introduce new subjects. **Barry University**, (941) 278-3041. **Offerings:** Adult and continuing education. **Edison Community College**, (941) 489-9300; continuing education, (941) 489-9235. **Offerings:** Two-year degrees and continuing-education programs. **Florida Gulf Coast Univer-**

sity, (941) 590-1001. **Offerings:** Four-year degrees, graduate degrees.

JUST FOR SENIORS
North Fort Myers Senior Center, (941) 939-8373.

GETTING INVOLVED
Lee County Community Improvement, (941) 656-7930. **RSVP**, (941) 688-2501. **Volunteer Center**, (941) 997-5288.

RECREATION, ENTERTAINMENT & AMENITIES
Public golf: Del Tura Country Club, 27 holes/par 90; El Rio Golf Club, 18 holes/par 60; Riverbend Golf Club, 18 holes/par 60; and Six Lakes Country Club, 18 holes/par 60. **Semiprivate golf:** Del Vera Country Club, 18 holes/par72; Lochmoor Country Club, 18 holes/par 72; Pine Lakes Country Club, 18 holes/par 61; and Sabal Springs Golf and Racquet Club, 18 holes/par 60. **Public tennis courts:** Colin Elementary School, Judd Park, North Fort Myers Senior Center, Suncoast Elementary School and Waterway Estates Park. **Private tennis courts:** Sabal Springs Golf and Racquet Club. **Parks:** Hancock Park, Judd Park, North Shore Park and Waterway Estates Park. **Public swimming pools:** None. **Water sports:** Boating, sailing, scuba diving, water-skiing and windsurfing. **River/gulf/ocean:** Caloosahatchee River. **Running/walking/biking:** The local redevelopment planning committee has approved construction of a bicycle path that will measure six-tenths of a mile long. There are numerous other paths and walkways. **Horses/riding:** There are several horse farms in the area. **Hunting:** Information and licenses, (941) 339-6000. **Movie theaters:** One screen. **Art museums:** None. **History museums:** None. **Theaters:** Lee Civic Center. **Library:** Lee County. **Attractions:** Babcock Wilderness Adventures offers a swamp-buggy trek through the Telegraph Creek Swamp. ECHO is a demonstration farm and training facility for missionaries and Peace Corps workers. Octagon Wildlife Sanctuary is home to more than 200 exotic animals. **Necessities:** All are available.

    Smart Shopper Tip: Merchants Crossing has a good variety of shops. If you can't find what you're looking for, Edison Mall is just across the river, off U.S. 41. The Shell Factory is a widely known shell shop, in case you can't find enough on your own.

WHO LIVES HERE
Population: 36,871 year-round residents in the unincorporated area known as North Fort Myers. **Age 65+** = 25.7% in Lee County. **Median household income:** $29,174 (Lee County). **Per capita income:** $23,664 (Lee County).

NUMBERS TO KNOW
Chamber of commerce: (941) 997-9111. **Voter registration:** (941) 339-6000. **Vehicle registration, tags & title:** (941) 339-6000. **Driver's license:** (941) 255-7408.

WHAT TO READ
Fort Myers News-Press, daily newspaper, (941) 335-0200.

GETTING AROUND
Bus: Lee TRAN, (941) 275-8726. **Taxi:** Yellow Cab, (941) 332-

1055. **Tours:** None. **Airport:** Southwest Florida International. **Traffic:** If you can avoid U.S. 41, traffic isn't too bad. But U.S. 41 is the principal, non-interstate, north-south artery and is hard to avoid.

JOBS
County unemployment rate: 3.3%. **Florida Jobs and Benefits:** In Fort Myers, (941) 278-7140.

UTILITIES
Electricity: Lee County Co-op, (941) 656-2300. **Gas:** None. **Water & sewer:** Florida Cities Water Co., (941) 936-0247. **Telephone:** Sprint, (941) 335-3111. **Cable TV:** Media One, (941) 793-3433.

PLACES OF WORSHIP
One Catholic and 15 Protestant churches.

THE ENVIRONMENT
The EPA reported that the Fort Myers Water District, serving a population of 52,500, had lead levels of 43 parts per billion (ppb) in its drinking water. The EPA action level for lead is 15 ppb.

    The Caloosahatchee River State Recreation Area has protected status as an Outstanding Florida Waterbody.

    The Caloosahatchee Estuary has been rated as having fair to poor water quality. It is affected by channelization and urban and agricultural runoff. Polluted tributaries flow into the Caloosahatchee. The river's quality ranges from good at and above Orange River, to fair in the Fort Myers area, to poor just upstream.

EVENTS AND FESTIVALS
Taste of North Fort Myers - February. **Hispanic Festival** - October. **RiverFest at Riverbend** - November.

WHERE TO EAT
Captain Fishbones, 2787 N. Tamiami Trail, seafood, moderate, (941) 995-2655. **Cottage Cafe**, 17251 N. Tamiami Trail, family style, moderate, (941) 995-3080.

WHERE TO STAY
Hampton Inn, (941) 656-4000. **Robert E. Lee Best Western**, (941) 997-5511. **Amtel Marina**, (941) 337-0300. **Sonesta Sanibel Harbour Resort**, (941) 466-4000.

ISSUES
The biggest issue seems to be whether or not new road construction and road widening projects can stay ahead of the area's rapid growth. When we were here the roads seemed to be losing the race.

    New residential and commercial developments are springing up everywhere, especially in the more rural areas along U.S. 41 and Pine Island Road. The absence of strict city zoning laws could result in a hodgepodge of construction and economic damage to residential areas. Zoning and deed restrictions seem worth further investigation for prospective residents.

Ocala

HE SAID: ★ ★ ★ ★

Ocala lives up to its claims. This is a land of lakes, streams, springs and rivers — the perfect setting for exploration, recreation and regeneration of mind and body. Finding nine golf courses in the county and many more within a 25-mile radius was the icing on the cake. I'm on my way.

SHE SAID: ★ ★ ★ ★

Beautiful, clean and uncongested, it seems to be a great place to live. There are well-manicured residential areas, planned retirement communities and a restored historic section, all right here in the center of the state. I would certainly look here for a place to retire.

One of the phrases coined to help sell Ocala, "Ocala is it," sums up the opinions of so many retirees here that this small town is gaining a real reputation among retirement meccas. While a chamber of commerce publication lists "horses, springs and historical things" as the three main attractions, other qualities have significantly greater import for retirees.

Good climate, affordable housing, low cost of living, excellent location, quality health care and plentiful recreational opportunities — terms used by many Florida towns to attract newcomers — are among Ocala's attributes, backed by cold, hard facts and realities.

Its location, within an hour of both Florida coasts and many major population centers, allows residents to take maximum advantage of all Florida has to offer. Much closer at hand is the Ocala National Forest, with a 67-mile segment of the Florida Trail crossing its 366,000 acres. There's also the surrounding countryside, with more than 500 horse farms and miles of riding, jogging and hiking trails.

The city proper is the jeweled centerpiece of this vast, underdeveloped playground. Thanks to the cooperative efforts of several restoration programs, downtown has a turn-of-the-century look. Numerous homes and businesses are on the National Register of Historic Places. Government buildings are dispersed throughout the city, many situated in parklike settings. Ocala proudly cares for its natural environment as well, enforcing a tree ordinance. There are beautiful and diversified residential neighborhoods and a myriad of organizations, programs, facilities and amenities for seniors. It is a place that appears comfortable, friendly, interesting and attractive.

It used to be that this area's claim to fame was the invention in nearby Silver Springs of the glass-bottom boat, drawing millions of vacationing Americans through town. But now, the look, the land, the location and the lifestyle of Ocala are the qualities attracting retirees to the area.

WEATHER

	Winter	Spring	Summer	Fall
Normal daily high/low	74/48	88/63	91/70	78/54
Normal precipitation	10 in.	14 in.	20 in.	7 in.

Disaster watch: North-central Florida is primarily affected by tropical storms and thunderstorms. Northwest Florida has been hit by six major hurricanes since 1990.

TAXES

Sales tax: 6%. **Property tax:** $22.00 per $1,000 valuation. Sample taxes include a $25,000 homestead exemption.

Home value	Tax
$100,000	$1,650
$150,000	$2,750
$250,000	$4,950

REAL ESTATE

Median home value: $76,737 (Marion County). **Median rent:** $544/month (Marion County). **Communities popular with retirees:** There are many, including On Top of the World Ocala, a 13,000-acre retirement community with its own orchestra, ballroom and shopping center. It offers villas from the $70s to the upper $90s and single-family homes from the high $60s to $130s, (352) 854-0805. Oak Run Country Club offers single-family homes on the golf course starting in the $130s. Off the course, homes start in the $70s, (800) 874-0898, or in Florida, (800) 342-9626. Ocala Palms, a gated, golf country club, has single-family and patio homes priced from the $80s to $130s, (800) 872-7256. **Licensed continuing-care retirement communities:** None.

CRIME & SAFETY

Crimes per 1,000 population: 139. **Non-emergency police:** (352) 629-8508. **Non-emergency fire department:** (352) 629-8385. **Police, fire, ambulance emergencies:** 911.

HOMELESS & BLIGHT

We saw no evidence of homeless persons nor blighted areas. On the contrary, maintenance and restoration of downtown seem to be a top priority, with at least three groups — Main Street Ocala, the Downtown Development Commission and Downtown Ocala — working on it.

The U.S. Census reported 51 homeless persons in shelters and none visible on the streets of Marion County, population 194,833.

HEALTH CARE

Hospitals: Ocala Regional Medical Center, 190 beds, five specialty pavilions, full service, (352) 732-2700. **Munroe Regional Medical Center**, 323 beds, full service, (352) 351-7200. **Physicians:** 299. **Specialties:** 33.

GETTING SMART

Central Florida Community College, (352) 854-2322. **Offerings:** The Continuing Education Department (ext. 468) operates the Senior Institute Program (ext. 605) through which seniors can enroll in up to 10 classes per term (three terms per year) and attend all events, socials and field trips. Class examples: world religions, oils and paintings, computers, Florida plants and creative writing.

JUST FOR SENIORS

Access of Marion County, (352) 867-0807. **Marion County Senior Services**, (352) 629-8661. Municipal centers: **8th Avenue Senior Center**, (352) 629-8545, and **Multipurpose Senior Center**, (352) 629-8351.

GETTING INVOLVED

Ocala has all the clubs, associations and organizations commonly found in large towns. **RSVP**, (352) 622-5444. **Volunteer Service Bureau**, (352) 732-4771.

RECREATION, ENTERTAINMENT & AMENITIES

Public golf: Baseline Golf Course, Golden Ocala Golf & Country Club, Huntington Golf Club, Marion Oaks Golf & Country Club and Ocala Municipal Golf Course. **Private golf:** Country Club of Ocala, Golden Hills Golf & Turf Club and Oak Run Country Club. **Public tennis courts:** Clyatt Park, three courts; Fort King Municipal Tennis Center, 12 courts; and Tuscawilla Park, six courts. **Private tennis courts:** Racquet Club of Ocala. **Parks:** 25 county parks, plus Ocala National Forest with 3,000 campsites. **Public swimming pools:** Hampton Memorial Pool and War Memorial Pool. **Water sports:** Canoeing, kayaking, tubing, sailing and boating. **River/gulf/ocean:** Silver Springs, Oklawaha and Withlacoochee rivers are nearby. Atlantic Ocean is 70 miles east, and the Gulf of Mexico is 40 miles west. **Running/walking/biking:** Trails are abundant throughout the county. **Horses/riding:** This is horse country. There are numerous stables, riding academies and riding trails, especially in the national forest. Darby Oaks Stable is a popular riding stable, (352) 568-2001. **Hunting:** Hunting and fishing licenses, (352) 368-8220. Quail, duck, dove and deer are abundant. Hunting is permitted in designated areas of Ocala National Forest. **Movie theaters:** 17 screens. **Art museums:** Appleton Museum of Art. **History museums:** East Hall Historical Museum, Historic Ocala Preservation Society and Silver River Museum. **Theaters:** Ocala Civic Theater, Central Florida Community College and Marion Actors Theatre. Performing arts groups include Marion Performing Ballet, Ocala Dance Theatre, Marion Chamber Music Society, Marion Civic Chorale, Community Concert Association and Ocala Festival Orchestra. **Library:** City Library. **Attractions:** Ocala National Forest, Silver Springs, Florida Motorsports Complex, Oakview Stable, Appleton Museum Complex and WMOP Museum of Sound. **Necessities:** All the amenities and necessities you would expect to find are here.

Smart Shopper Tip: In addition to the downtown shopping district, major shopping areas include two malls and four shopping centers. Paddock Mall is the largest and best in Ocala. For a change, drive down to Belleview to the 700-vendor outdoor market.

WHO LIVES HERE

Population: 43,630 year-round residents, an increase of 1,585 since 1990. **Age 65+** = 24.6% in Marion County. **Median household income:** $23,200 (Marion County). **Per capita income:** $18,130 (Marion County).

NUMBERS TO KNOW

Chamber of commerce: (352) 629-8051. **Voter registration:** (352) 620-3290. **Vehicle registration, tags & title:** (352) 368-8230 or (352) 245-3395. **Driver's license:** (352) 732-1251. **Florida Greeting Service:** (352) 873-2601.

WHAT TO READ

Star-Banner, daily newspaper, (352) 867-4010. **Ocala Today**, monthly magazine, (352) 622-2995. **Senior Floridian**, biweekly, free to seniors, (352) 629-1312.

GETTING AROUND

Bus: Senior Services Transportation, (352) 622-2450. **Taxi:** AAA Cab Co., (352) 629-6222. **Tours:** None. **Airport:** Gainesville Regional is 40 miles away. **Train:** Amtrak, (352) 629-9863. **Traffic:** Light to moderate except where highways 27, 301 and 441 converge. This area can be avoided easily.

JOBS

County unemployment rate: 4.8%. **Florida Jobs and Benefits:** (352) 955-2245.

UTILITIES

Electricity: City of Ocala, (352) 629-8411. For residences outside Ocala city limits, Florida Power Corp., (800) 700-8744. **Gas:** People's Gas, (352) 622-0111. **Water & sewer:** City of Ocala, (352) 629-8411. **Telephone:** Sprint-United, (352) 629-8114. **Cable TV:** Time Warner Communications, (352) 625-4944.

PLACES OF WORSHIP

Five Catholic and more than 100 Protestant churches, plus three Jewish synagogues.

THE ENVIRONMENT

Ocala is situated over Florida's largest aquifer. The area has some of the most pristine rivers and lakes in the state: Palatlakaha Chain of Lakes, Silver Springs Run, Orange and Lochloosa lakes, plus the Oklawaha River, downstream of Silver Springs. One problem area is Lake Weir; tests show good water quality, but it has had a persistent problem with diseased fish populations.

EVENTS AND FESTIVALS

Parade of Senior Services - February. **Golden Hills International Horse Show** - March. **All-Breed Extravaganza & Citrus Cup All-Morgan Horse Show** - May. **African-American Arts Festival** - June. **Arabian State Champion Show** - November.

WHERE TO EAT

Contact the chamber of commerce for suggestions.

WHERE TO STAY

Ocala Hilton, (352) 854-1400. **Hampton Inn**, (352) 854-3200. **Seven Sisters Inn**, (352) 867-1170.

ISSUES

Despite its pastoral setting, Ocala has a high per capita crime rate. This appears to be a major concern of residents at this time.

Orlando

HE SAID: ★ ★ ★
> *It is a booming, bustling place, good for the couple seeking a busy lifestyle, but not for those who want a quiet, out-of-the-way place to spend their after-work years. It's not what I'm looking for.*

SHE SAID: ★ ★ ★
> *This is another large, expensive city. It's a place to visit, but not to stay. Disney World, Epcot, Universal Studios, lots of toll roads and bumper-to-bumper traffic characterize Orlando for me. I would not retire here.*

It is natural to equate Orlando with Walt Disney World. Certainly, many of the 20 million annual visitors to the world's largest entertainment complex find their way into downtown Orlando at one point or another. But it is a credit to long-term growth management planning that you can drive through the city's business district on a typical day and remark that the least busy place in Orange County seems to be downtown Orlando. This is despite the fact that every week the Orlando Metropolitan Statistical Area produces almost $200 million in retail sales.

Skyscrapers aside, the inner city retains a small-town charm and atmosphere. There are trees and flowers along the sidewalks and an unhurried and peaceful ambiance at downtown's Lake Eola. The thoughtful placement of municipal and county administrative buildings grants an open, spacious quality to the town center. Importantly, comprehensive growth planning has dispersed new construction, highways and infrastructure support to natural activity centers throughout the metro area. This planning may help Orlando avoid the problems encountered by many older, deteriorating urban centers that bustle with enterprise during the day but are abandoned each evening. And it may be the single most important factor in making Orlando an attractive urban retirement area into the next century.

Orlando has all of the wonderful amenities that retirees cherish: cultural organizations, recreational facilities, good health-care facilities, educational institutions, entertainment, restaurants, shopping, proximity to the Atlantic Ocean and Gulf of Mexico, and some truly outstanding residential neighborhoods.

Retirees should not dismiss Orlando. Come and spend a few days just visiting. See how the natives live. Then decide if you and the fast pace set by tourists and working-age people can coexist.

WEATHER

	Winter	Spring	Summer	Fall
Normal daily high/low	74/51	87/66	91/73	79/58
Normal precipitation	9 in.	13 in.	20 in.	7 in.

Disaster watch: Northeast Florida has not been hit by a major hurricane since 1900.

TAXES

Sales tax: 6%. **Property tax:** There are many rates, depending on the property location. Most are between $21.36 and $23.22 per $1,000 valuation. Sample taxes are calculated at the rate of $23.22 and include a $25,000 homestead exemption.

Home value	Tax
$100,000	$1,742
$150,000	$2,903
$250,000	$5,225

REAL ESTATE

Median home value: $94,147 (Orange County). **Median rent:** $637/month (Orange County). **Communities popular with retirees:** Homes in historic areas such as Delaney Park and Eola Heights are available in a wide price range depending on condition. Dover Shores has homes built in the 1950s selling in the low $100s. Heritage Bay has homes from the $200s with gated entry, tennis courts and lakeside park, (407) 370-4771. Palma Vista has large custom homes starting at $250,000, (407) 292-2225. **Licensed continuing-care retirement communities:** Orlando Lutheran Towers has 245 independent living units, 24 rental units and 60 community beds, (407) 425-1033. Westminster Towers has 277 independent living units, 59 sheltered nursing beds and 61 community beds (407) 841-1310.

CRIME & SAFETY

Crimes per 1,000 population: 139. **Non-emergency police:** (407) 246-2470. **Non-emergency fire department:** (407) 246-2141. **Police, fire, ambulance emergencies:** 911.

HOMELESS & BLIGHT

The general impression of Orlando is of a clean, safe, open-spaced, attractive city.

The U.S. Census reported 798 homeless persons in shelters and 271 visible in street locations in Orange County, population 677,491.

HEALTH CARE

Hospitals: Florida Hospital, 897 beds, full service, (407) 896-6611. **Orlando Regional Medical Center**, 670 beds, full service, (407) 841-5111. There are nine other smaller hospitals in the area. **Physicians:** 1,000+. **Specialties:** 48.

GETTING SMART

Elderhostel operates several programs at various sites in the area. **Florida Southern College**, (407) 855-1302. **Offerings:** Four-year degrees. **Florida Institute of Technology**, (407) 894-9961. **Offerings:** Graduate degrees. **Orlando College**, (407) 628-5870. **Offerings:** Undergraduate and graduate degrees. **Southern College**, (407) 273-1000. **Offerings:** Two-year degrees. **University of Central Florida**, (407) 823-2000. **Offerings:** Undergraduate, graduate and professional degrees. **Valencia Community College**, (407) 299-5000. **Offerings:** Two-year degrees.

JUST FOR SENIORS

Orange County Seniors First, (407) 292-0177. **L. Claudia Allen Senior Center**, (407) 295-5722. **Marks Street Senior Center**, (407) 245-0921. **Senior Help Line**, (407) 631-2747. **William Beardall Senior Center**, (407) 246-2637.

GETTING INVOLVED

United Arts of Central Florida, (407) 425-0277. **Meals on Wheels**, (407) 292-0177. **RSVP**, (407) 422-1535. **Volunteer Center**, (407) 896-0945.

RECREATION, ENTERTAINMENT & AMENITIES

Public golf: 20-plus courses. **Private golf:** 44 private and semiprivate. **Public tennis courts:** Tennis Center, (407) 246-2161. **Private tennis courts:** 800-plus courts, public and private, at various locations. **Parks:** Numerous municipal and county facilities.

Tosohatchee State Reserve has 28,800 acres in eastern Orange County. **Public swimming pools:** Wadeview Pool & Community Center, (407) 246-2883. **Water sports:** Boating, canoeing, sailing, scuba diving and water-skiing. **River/gulf/ocean:** Most prominent among numerous small lakes is Lake Eola, downtown. The Atlantic Ocean is 50 miles away. **Running/walking/biking:** Turkey Lake City Park and Tosohatchee State Reserve have trails. **Horses/riding:** There are stables and academies. **Hunting:** Fishing and hunting licenses, (407) 836-4100. **Movie theaters:** 58 screens. **Art museums:** Several, including Pine Castle Folk Art Center and Orlando Museum of Art. **History museums:** Orange County Historical Museum. **Theaters:** Dr. Phillips Center for the Performing Arts, home of the Orlando Opera Company, Southern Ballet Theater, the Orlando Theater Project and the Central Florida Community Jazz Center. Also, the Carr Performing Arts Center, Civic Theatre of Central Florida, Theatre Downtown, University of Central Florida Theatre and Valencia Community College Performing Arts Center & Black Fox Theater, plus more than two dozen arts and cultural organizations. **Library:** Orange County Public has several branches, (407) 425-4694. **Attractions:** Cartoon Museum, Church Street Station, Leu Botanical Gardens, Orlando Centroplex, Orlando Magic basketball, Orlando Science Center and John Young Planetarium, Sea World, Walt Disney World and Universal Studios. **Necessities:** All here.

Smart Shopper Tip: There are more than 25 shopping centers and malls in Greater Orlando. A favorite is the Florida Mall, connected to the Sheraton Plaza Hotel. It has five major department stores and more than 200 specialty shops.

WHO LIVES HERE
Population: 176,373 year-round residents, an increase of 11,699 since 1990. **Age 65+ =** 11.0% in Orange County. **Median household income:** $31,649 (Orange County). **Per capita income:** $21,868 (Orange County).

NUMBERS TO KNOW
Chamber of commerce: (407) 425-1234. **Voter registration:** (407) 836-2070. **Vehicle registration, tags & title:** (407) 836-4120. **Driver's license:** (407) 275-4058. **Visitors bureau:** (407) 363-5871.

WHAT TO READ
Orlando Sentinel, daily newspaper, (407) 420-5000. **Orlando Business Journal**, weekly newspaper, (407) 649-8470. **Living in Orlando**, the chamber's relocation guide, (407) 425-1234.

GETTING AROUND
Bus: LYNX Mass Transit, (407) 841-8240. **Taxi:** Yellow Cab, (407) 699-9999. **Tours:** Several helicopter trips and tours are available. **Airport:** Orlando International. **Train:** Amtrak passenger service, (407) 843-7611. **Traffic:** I-4 through the city almost invariably grinds to a halt at rush hour and causes delays of up to 30 minutes. Local streets generally are clear with traffic flowing smoothly. There is a lot of pedestrian traffic — much of it tourist — no matter what part of the city you're in, but especially around the farmers market and Church Street Station.

JOBS
County unemployment rate: 3.4%. **Florida Jobs and Benefits:** (407) 897-2880. **Job Line:** (407) 246-2178.

UTILITIES
Electricity, water & sewer: Orlando Utilities Commission, (407) 423-9018. **Gas:** Peoples Gas, (407) 425-4661. **Telephone:** Bell South, (800) 789-9025 in Florida, or (800) 753-0710 out-of-state. **Cable TV:** Time-Warner Cable, (407) 277-4782 or (407) 291-2500, depending on location of residence.

PLACES OF WORSHIP
There are 11 Catholic and several hundred Protestant churches, plus six Jewish synagogues.

THE ENVIRONMENT
The surface water quality in some of the large lakes nearest the city has been rated as poor, particularly that of lakes Jessup and Howell. Lake Jessup has shown an improving trend. The Little Econlockhatchee River has fair to poor water quality, though the Econlockhatchee River has fair to good quality. South of Orlando, East Lake Tohopekaliga and lakes Conway and Butler generally have good water quality. The Econlockhatchee River System has protected status, designated as an Outstanding Florida Water.

Orange County did not meet the EPA's air quality standard for ozone on one occasion during the 1992 12-month sampling period.

There are two EPA-listed Superfund sites in Orange County: City Industries in Winter Park and Zellwood Ground Water Contamination in Zellwood.

EVENTS AND FESTIVALS
Citrus Bowl Football Classic - January. **Central Florida Fair** - February. **Shakespeare Festival** - April. **Light Up Orlando** - November. **Citrus Bowl Music Festival** - December.

WHERE TO EAT
Le Coq au Vin, 4800 S. Orange Ave., French, moderate to expensive, (407) 851-6980. **Dux**, 9801 International Drive at The Peabody, American, very expensive, (407) 345-4550. **La Normandie**, 2021 E. Colonial Drive, continental, moderate, (407) 896-9976. **La Cantina**, 4721 E. Colonial Drive, steak, moderate, (407) 894-4491.

WHERE TO STAY
Courtyard Inn at Lake Lucerne, (407) 648-5188. **The Peabody**, (407) 352-4000. **Sheraton World Resort**, (407) 352-1100.

ISSUES
Two important features set Orlando apart from many cities. First, while there is a pronounced downtown, the planners have been careful not to build a city that requires all workers to commute to and from a central business-government complex. In so doing, they've avoided — to some extent — the usual rush-hour patterns of traffic. Good growth management planning and zoning and an effective land-use approval process have been the keys to success.

Second, impact fees have been imposed to make sure the city's infrastructure keeps up with its development. Fees on new construction offset the costs of added police and fire protection, water and sewer capacity and a road network that is adequate to handle increased traffic volume.

Continued foresight is needed in years ahead. Also, tourist and resident safety is always an issue in a resort environment.

Ormond Beach

HE SAID: ☆ ☆ ☆ ☆
> *It has all of the prerequisites of an ideal retirement community with none of the drawbacks of many Florida locations (drugs, high crime rate and traffic congestion). I would definitely take a serious look before passing it up as just another Florida beach resort.*

SHE SAID: ☆ ☆ ☆ ☆ ☆
> *Lots of trees, clean downtown, beautiful beach area and no neon signs taller than the trees — in fact, very few neon signs at all. Everything you would need in retirement can be found here or nearby, including lots of different types of residential neighborhoods. I could retire here.*

We dropped into the chamber of commerce quarters in downtown Ormond Beach and were warmly greeted by the staff and a contingent of retiree volunteers hard at work planning Jazz Matazz, the town's annual celebration of music, food and people. The retirees we met on this and a previous visit are proud of their festival, which they tell us attracts more than 50,000 celebrants from all over the state and beyond. They also are proud of their town and describe it in loving terms.

One retiree says it's "a marvelously convenient place to live."

Another explains, "The quality of sereneness one feels when returning to Ormond Beach from Daytona is akin to the peace and quiet in the house after sending the grandkids home."

The charm, cleanliness and spaciousness of downtown was enhanced by a recent project called Streetscape, which created two miles of attractive storefronts and landscaped sidewalks. The area encourages leisurely strolling and browsing. Crossing the Halifax River Causeway presents a striking scene: Dense, lush tropical vegetation rises to the rooftops of low-slung houses (kept low by strictly enforced zoning ordinances), with no commercial-industrial land use in sight. The whole beach-side community, particularly neighboring Ormond by the Sea, is one of the premier areas of the Florida coast. Inland residential developments such as Tomoka Oaks, The Arbor, Lakebridge, The Trails, Foxwood and The Falls at Ormond exhibit the characteristics of nature reflected in their names.

Ormond Beach Senior Center is a splendid facility with a main ballroom large enough to accommodate 200 dancers, a spacious dining room where more than 100 meals are served daily, a game room with three pool tables, card rooms and a popular, well-appointed lounge. The full daily schedule of activities includes exercise classes, self-defense training, beginning Spanish classes, free blood pressure testing, keyboard instruction, bingo, billiards, bridge, shuffleboard, art classes, theater and chorus, dance instruction and, of course, lots of dances.

Ormond Beach has well-maintained municipal and private-sector buildings, manicured grounds and common areas, a small but select group of museums, parks and cultural organizations, some outstanding golf courses and tennis courts and a matchless variety of residential neighborhoods. We found it to be an appealing, self-sufficient small town.

WEATHER

	Winter	Spring	Summer	Fall
Normal daily high/low	71/50	84/65	89/72	76/57
Normal precipitation	9 in.	12 in.	18 in.	10 in.

Disaster watch: Northeast Florida has not been hit by a major hurricane since 1900.

TAXES

Sales tax: 6%. **Property tax:** $23.55 per $1,000 valuation. Sample tax calculations include a $25,000 homestead exemption.

Home value	Tax
$100,000	$1,766
$150,000	$2,944
$250,000	$5,299

REAL ESTATE

Median home value: $93,463 (Volusia County). **Median rent:** $517/month (Volusia County). **Communities popular with retirees:** The Falls at Ormond is a manufactured-home community with prices from the mid-$50s to the upper $120s, (904) 673-2333. Tomoka Oaks, The Arbor, The Trails, Lakebridge and Foxwood are other inland developments. The waterfront is completely residential — mostly single-family homes. **Licensed continuing-care retirement communities:** None.

CRIME & SAFETY

Crimes per 1,000 population: 42. **Non-emergency police:** (904) 677-0731. **Non-emergency fire department:** (904) 423-3357. **Police, fire, ambulance emergencies:** 911.

HOMELESS & BLIGHT

There are no homeless persons evident in Ormond Beach and no blighted areas. Instead of letting its downtown disintegrate into an eyesore, Ormond Beach renovated and landscaped it, making it a desirable place to go.

The U.S. Census reported 187 homeless persons in shelters and 35 visible in street locations in Volusia County, population 370,712.

HEALTH CARE

Hospitals: Memorial Hospital, 205 beds, full service, acute care, 24-hour emergency, (904) 677-6900. **Columbia Medical Center**, 119 beds, acute care, 24-hour emergency, (904) 672-4161.

Physicians: 300+. **Specialties:** 34.

GETTING SMART

There are no colleges or universities in Ormond Beach but six in nearby Daytona Beach, including **Daytona Beach Community College**, (904) 255-8131, which offers the Elder Institute program for seniors. **Offerings:** The institute has classes in computers, painting, dancing and one called "Retirement— Learning to Love It," plus workshops and seminars. **Bethune-Cookman College**, (904) 255-1401. **Offerings:** Courses are for degree credit and are attended by all age levels. **University of Central Florida**, (904) 255-7423. **Offerings:** Bachelor's and master's degree programs.

JUST FOR SENIORS

The City of Ormond Beach Civic & Cultural Services sponsors the **Senior Games**, (904) 676-3292, and **Senior Travel**, (904)

676-3293. **Ormond Beach Senior Center**, (904) 676-3256. Contact **AARP** through the senior center, (904) 676-3256.

GETTING INVOLVED
Chamber of commerce, (904) 677-3454. **RSVP** in Daytona Beach, (904) 253-4700. **SCORE** in Daytona Beach, (904) 255-6889.

RECREATION, ENTERTAINMENT & AMENITIES
Public golf: Halifax Plantation, 18 holes; Tomoka Oaks Golf & Country Club, 18 holes; River Bend Golf Course, 18 holes; and Riviera Country Club, 18 holes. **Private golf:** Oceanside Country Club and Plantation Bay. **Public tennis courts:** Nova Road Tennis Center, six courts; Tomoka Oaks, four courts; and Trails Racquet Club, eight courts. **Private tennis courts:** Trails Tennis Club. **Parks:** Tomoka State Park contains 914 acres, located at the juncture of the Tomoka and Halifax rivers. Also, Nova Road Recreation Area, Bicentennial Park and Smyrna Dunes Park. **Public swimming pools:** None. **Water sports:** Canoeing, yachting, windsurfing, scuba diving and water-skiing on the Halifax River. There's surf, pier and deep-sea fishing. **River/gulf/ocean:** Atlantic Ocean, Halifax River (Intracoastal Waterway), Tomoka River and several lakes a few miles west of the city, including lakes George, Crescent and Woodruff. **Running/walking/biking:** Parks, recreation areas, beaches and back roads provide plenty of opportunities for all three activities. **Horses/riding:** One riding academy, Brass Head Farm, (904) 676-7363, and one stable, Country Meadow Boarding Stables, (904) 672-6001. **Hunting:** For information on freshwater fishing and hunting, Florida Game and Freshwater Fish Commission, (352) 732-1225. **Movie theaters:** None; the nearest is in Daytona Beach. **Art museums:** The Casements Cultural Center, located in the John D. Rockefeller home, and the Ormond Memorial Art Museum. **History museums:** None. **Theaters:** Performing Arts Center. **Library:** Ormond Beach. **Attractions:** Birthplace of Speed Museum, The Casements Cultural Center, Tomoka State Park and the Bulow Plantation Ruins. **Necessities:** All here.

Smart Shopper Tip: A half-dozen shopping centers in the Greater Ormond Beach area will take care of most shopping needs. Malls and outlet shops in Daytona Beach, a few minutes away, will meet the rest.

WHO LIVES HERE
Population: 34,038 year-round residents, an increase of 4,317 since 1990. **Age 65+** = 22.6% in Volusia County. **Median household income:** $26,071 (Volusia County). **Per capita income:** $18,951 (Volusia County).

NUMBERS TO KNOW
Chamber of commerce: (904) 677-3454. **Voter registration:** (904) 254-4690. **Vehicle registration, tags & title:** (904) 254-4610. **Driver's license:** (904) 238-3140.

WHAT TO READ
Daytona Beach News-Journal, daily newspaper, (904) 252-1511.

GETTING AROUND
Bus: VOTRAN, (904) 761-7700. **Taxi:** Yellow Cab, (904) 255-5555. **Tours:** None. **Airport:** Daytona Beach International. **Traffic:** Moderate to heavy during Daytona Speedway events.

JOBS
County unemployment rate: 3.7%. **Florida Jobs and Benefits:** (904) 254-3780. **Job Line:** For Volusia County, (904) 254-4607.

UTILITIES
Electricity: Florida Power & Light, (904) 252-1541. **Gas:** Peoples Gas, (904) 437-4404. **Water & sewer:** City of Ormond Beach, (904) 677-0311. **Telephone:** Bell South, (800) 789-9025 in Florida, or (800) 753-0710 out-of-state. **Cable TV:** Time-Warner Cable, (904) 677-1232.

PLACES OF WORSHIP
Three Catholic and 35 Protestant churches, plus three Jewish synagogues.

THE ENVIRONMENT
The Halifax River, between Ormond Beach and Daytona Beach, is rated as having poor water quality. Other sections of the Halifax have fair water quality. Tomoka Marsh State Aquatic Preserve/Tomoka River has protected status and is designated as an Outstanding Florida Water.

The EPA has reported finding lead measuring 24 parts per billion (ppb) in the drinking water of the City of Ormond Beach. The EPA action level for lead is 15 ppb.

Volusia County has one EPA-listed Superfund site, Sherwood Medical, located three miles north of DeLand.

EVENTS AND FESTIVALS
Ormond Art Show - Easter weekend. **Jazz Matazz** - July Fourth weekend. **Senior Games** - October. **Birthplace of Speed Antique Car Show** - Thanksgiving weekend. **Santa Land** - December.

WHERE TO EAT
Julian's, 88 S. Atlantic Ave., seafood, chicken, steak, lobster, moderate to expensive, (904) 677-6767. **Billy's Tap Room & Grill**, 58 E. Granada Blvd., steak and seafood, moderate, (904) 672-1910. **Mario's**, 521 S. Yonge St., veal, seafood, moderate, (904) 677-2711.

WHERE TO STAY
Casa Del Mar Beach Resort, (904) 672-4550. **Comfort Inn Beachside**, (904) 677-8550. **Mainsail Motel**, (904) 677-2131. **Quality Inn Oceanside**, (904) 672-8510.

ISSUES
If Ormond Beach has a main issue, it is how to retain its air of serenity, friendliness and small-town charm in the face of increasing growth pressures. With the contrasting pace between Daytona Beach and Ormond Beach and the minimal space between the two, it is increasingly difficult to prevent spillover of Daytona's excesses, especially during Speedway events and spring break.

Palm Bay

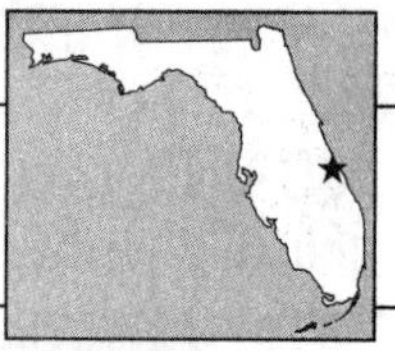

HE SAID: ✯ ✯

With a population growth of over 20% in seven years, it obviously appeals to a lot of people. I believe boredom would do me in long before old age if I lived in Palm Bay.

SHE SAID: ✯

Affordable housing is about all it has going for it. It's not for me.

This is essentially one huge residential neighborhood. There are houses, schools, roads — and little else. If ever the term "bedroom community" applied, it does here. Residents rely heavily on neighboring Melbourne and surrounding towns for shopping, restaurants, entertainment and cultural and social amenities. Access to Atlantic beaches is by car via the Melbourne Causeway to the north or by boat at Sebastian Inlet to the south.

There is no shortage of water for boating or fishing. The broad Indian River Lagoon and Turkey Creek form the eastern boundary of the city. For sports fishing, there are boats, bridges, beaches, canals, causeways, jetties and piers.

The Greater Palm Bay Senior Center has about 3,000 members. It is heavily used for arts and crafts, games, exercise classes and even wedding receptions. It *has* to be popular — there is nothing else to do here!

According to the chamber, housing is very reasonable, with new three-bedroom homes selling for as low as $50,000 to $60,000. Palm Bay was originally developed by General Development Corp. The company was largely responsible for Palm Bay's rapid growth, selling thousands of lots sight unseen to hungry buyers who just wanted to own a piece of land in Florida. It's not the proverbial Florida swamp — but it hasn't proved to be a great investment either.

Palm Bay has the basics that are typical of Florida's central east coast: nice climate, proximity to the water and low taxes. It's also close to the attractions of the Space Coast to the north and the Treasure Coast to the south. However, if judged strictly on its cultural and social amenities, Palm Bay wouldn't score very high. It all depends on your lifestyle needs.

WEATHER

	Winter	Spring	Summer	Fall
Normal daily high/low	73/53	84/66	89/72	78/60
Normal precipitation	8 in.	12 in.	17 in.	9 in.

Disaster watch: Southeast Florida has been hit by nine major hurricanes since 1900.

TAXES

Sales tax: 6%. **Property tax:** $22.97 per $1,000 valuation. Sample tax calculations include a $25,000 homestead exemption.

Home value	Tax
$100,000	$1,723
$150,000	$2,871
$250,000	$5,168

REAL ESTATE

Median home value: $90,929 (Brevard County). **Median rent:** $548/month (Brevard County). **Communities popular with retirees:** Holiday Park offers manufactured homes priced from $15,000 to $60,000. Lockmar has single-family homes priced from the mid-$80s to the $160s. Turkey Creek also offers single-family homes from the mid-$100s to $240s. Unit 50 a golf course community, has homes from the mid-$60s to mid-$140s. Monte Dean, Woodlake Realty, can provide information, (407) 724-5700 or (800) 723-8521. **Licensed continuing-care retirement communities:** None.

CRIME & SAFETY

Crimes per 1,000 population: 55. **Non-emergency police:** (407) 952-3456. **Non-emergency fire department:** (407) 952-3447. **Police, fire, ambulance emergencies:** 911.

HOMELESS & BLIGHT

We saw neither homeless persons nor blighted areas, but we did spot some unsightly areas along the Indian River. The city is essentially one huge single-family home neighborhood with some attractive and some not-so-attractive pockets scattered throughout.

According to the U.S. Census, Brevard County, with a population of 398,978, had 196 homeless persons in shelters and 18 visible on the streets.

HEALTH CARE

Hospitals: Palm Bay Community Hospital, 60 beds, 24-hour emergency, acute care, (407) 722-8000.
Physicians: 94. **Specialties:** 27.

GETTING SMART

Brevard Community College, (407) 632-1111. **Offerings:** Advanced technical curriculum, two-year degree programs, seminars, workshops and short courses.

JUST FOR SENIORS

Greater Palm Bay Senior Center, (407) 724-1338, has 3,000 members participating in arts and crafts, dancing, exercise, games and travel. **Area Agency on Aging**, (407) 228-1800. **Senior Helpline**, (407) 631-2747.

GETTING INVOLVED

RSVP, (407) 631-2749. **South Brevard Sharing Center**, (407) 676-2965.

RECREATION, ENTERTAINMENT & AMENITIES

Public golf: Palm Gardens, nine-hole executive course, and Summit View, 18-hole executive course. **Private golf:** Port Malibar Country Club. **Public tennis courts:** Driskell Park Court, Roach Park Court and Veteran's Memorial Park. **Parks:** Alex Goode Park, Fred Lee Park, Pollark Park, Veteran's Memorial Park, Community Center and Turkey Creek Sanctuary Park. Sebastian Inlet State Park, a few miles south, has more visitors than any other park in Florida. **Water sports:** Scuba diving, surfing, water-skiing and jet-skiing. **River/gulf/ocean:** Indian River, Palm Bay and Turkey Creek. The Atlantic is accessible via the Melbourne Causeway and Sebastian Inlet. **Running/walking/biking:** Tur-

COST OF LIVING
Florida Price Level Index: 97.65 (Brevard County). **Rank:** 16th most expensive county.

key Creek Sanctuary Trail is a one-mile nature trail and jogging/walking path. **Horses/riding:** There are several stables and riding academies in the area. **Hunting:** Rural areas of Brevard County have dove, duck, wild hogs, quail, turkey and woodcock. Contact the Game and Freshwater Fish Commission, (407) 752-3115. **Movie theaters:** Thirty screens at three theaters. **Theaters:** Spotlight Theatre. **Library:** Palm Bay. **Necessities:** Most are here or in Melbourne.

  Smart Shopper Tip: You can meet most of your shopping needs at the Palm Bay West Regional Shopping Center or Interchange Square Shopping Center in Palm Bay. But, if you want more, drive on up to Melbourne Square Mall, the Space Coast's largest.

WHO LIVES HERE
Population: 75,987 year-round residents, an increase of 13,444 since 1990. **Age 65+** = 18.3% in Brevard County. **Median household income:** $33,061 (Brevard County). **Per capita income:** $20,747 (Brevard County).

NUMBERS TO KNOW
Chamber of commerce: (407) 724-5400. **Voter registration:** (407) 952-6328. **Vehicle registration, tags & title:** (407) 952-4540. **Driver's license:** (407) 984-4931. **Visitors bureau:** (407) 633-2110.

WHAT TO READ
Florida Today, daily newspaper, (407) 259-5000. **The Bay Bulletin**, weekly newspaper, (407) 242-3801. **The Times**, weekly newspaper, (407) 242-3801.

GETTING AROUND
Bus: SCAT, (407) 633-1878. **Taxi:** Checker Taxi, (407) 724-2500. **Tours:** None. **Airport:** Melbourne International Airport. **Traffic:** Generally light.

JOBS
County unemployment rate: 4.8%. **Florida Jobs and Benefits:** (407) 725-8056.

UTILITIES
Electricity: Florida Power & Light, (407) 723-7795. **Gas:** City Gas Co. of Florida, (407) 632-1734. **Water & sewer:** Palm Bay Utilities, (407) 952-3420. **Telephone:** Bell South, (800) 789-9025 in Florida, or (800) 753-2909 out-of-state. **Cable TV:** Time Warner Communications, (407) 254-3300.

PLACES OF WORSHIP
Two Catholic and 52 Protestant churches, plus one Jewish synagogue.

THE ENVIRONMENT
Palm Bay has been rated as having mostly fair to good surface water quality, except for Crane Creek north of Melbourne, which has poor water quality. There is one EPA-listed Superfund site in Palm Bay, the Harris Corp. site.

EVENTS AND FESTIVALS
Events: Earth Day is Every Day - April. **Palm Bay Day** - May. **Palm Bay Holiday Season Tree Lighting** - December.

WHERE TO EAT
Rooney's, 2641 Palm Bay Road N.E., prime rib, beef, moderate to expensive, (407) 724-8520. **Stella's**, 5275 Babcock St. N.E., Italian, moderate, (407) 724-1209.

WHERE TO STAY
Days Inn, (407) 951-0350. **Ramada Inn**, (407) 723-8181. **Motel 6**, (407) 951-8222.

ISSUES
Inadequate groundwater drainage causes culverts to fill with water and overflow when it rains. The city is taking steps to correct this slight street flooding.

RELOCATION TIPS

When you find a neighborhood you really like, be sure to stop to talk to other residents. It's great to find out who your neighbors will be. But more than that, residents of the community can provide a wealth of information about issues and concerns within the area. Ask them about their satisfaction with the developer or property management. Ask about their satisfaction with their home and the warranty. Inquire about the local amenities, traffic congestion and safety.

Try to get involved in your new community before you unpack — maybe even before you move. If you've ever noticed that you begin a project or enterprise with boundless enthusiasm that gradually wanes, you'll know that an early effort to try new activities may be critical to your successful integration into your new town. Get involved at the earliest opportunity, before you develop the habit of keeping to yourself.

Visiting a place you may want to call home? Get a copy of the telephone directories including the yellow pages and business, government and resident white pages. It may seem like a burden to haul it all home, but if you do decide to move there, you'll find names and numbers and resources you need with half the effort.

Palm Coast

HE SAID: ✭ ✭ ✭ ✭
Great location, beautiful setting, outstanding amenities.
An almost perfect place to spend your retirement years.

SHE SAID: ✭ ✭ ✭ ✭
It has everything I would look for in a retirement locale.
I could retire here.

It is not often you have a choice of homesites overlooking the ocean, Intracoastal Waterway, a golf course or lake, all in the same development. This is one of the many unique features of Palm Coast — a quiet coastal village midway between historic St. Augustine and robust Daytona Beach — that have brought retirees in from around the country. It was the fastest growing county in the United States from 1980 to 1990.

Bisected by Interstate 95, with access to U.S. Highway 1 and A1A, its residents are just minutes from area malls, big city entertainment and cultural venues.

Six championship-caliber golf courses and The Players Club, an 18-court tennis complex, add to a myriad of water-related activities to provide opportunities for outdoor recreation. If you're into walking, there are miles of hiking-biking paths throughout the 42,000 acre community, including the 26-mile Coastal Greenway.

The best part of Palm Coast? It's all relatively new, spotlessly clean, beautifully landscaped and impeccably maintained.

WEATHER

	Winter	Spring	Summer	Fall
Normal daily high/low	71/50	84/65	89/72	75/57
Normal precipitation	9 in.	12 in.	18 in.	10 in.

Disaster watch: Northeast Florida has not been hit by a major hurricane since 1990.

TAXES
Sales tax: 7%. **Property tax:** $17.55 per $1,000 valuation. Sample tax calculations include a $25,000 homestead exemption.

Home value	Tax
$100,000	$1,316
$150,000	$2,194
$250,000	$3,949

REAL ESTATE
Median home value: $86,881 (Flagler County). **Median rent:** $435/month (Flagler County). **Communities popular with retirees:** Nick Sportini with Palm Coast Real Estate Co., (800) 441-3044, says retirees live in all of Palm Coast's neighborhoods. In Grand Haven, a gated community on the Intracoastal Waterway, patio homes start at $129,000 and single-family homes run from the $160s to $800s. Palm Harbor has canal-front homes from the mid-$120s to low $200s. Canal lots run from the $20s to $50s, and golf-course lots are available in the $30s and $40s. Ocean Hammock, an upscale golfing community under construction, has oceanfront lots from $400,000. **Licensed continuing-care retirement communities:** None.

CRIME & SAFETY
Crimes per 1,000 population: 34. **Non-emergency police:** (904) 437-4116. **Non-emergency fire department:** (904) 446-6750. **Police, fire, ambulance emergencies:** 911.

HOMELESS & BLIGHT
This is a clean, upscale community with no homeless persons. It is patrolled by the Flagler County Sheriff's Department.

HEALTH CARE
Hospitals: Memorial Hospital-Flagler, 81 beds, full service, 24-hour emergency department, (904) 437-2211. **Physicians:** 75. **Specialties:** 17.

GETTING SMART
Daytona Beach Community College, Flagler-Palm Coast Campus offers two-year associate degrees, (904) 445-4030.

JUST FOR SENIORS
Flagler County Council on Aging, (904) 437-7300.

GETTING INVOLVED
RSVP, (904) 437-7567.

RECREATION, ENTERTAINMENT & AMENITIES
Semiprivate golf: Matanzas Woods, Cypress Knoll, Palm Harbor, Pine Lakes, Grand Haven and Ocean Hammock. **Private golf:** Hammock Dunes. **Semiprivate tennis:** Belle Terre Swim & Racquet Club. The Players Club has 18 courts. **Parks:** Washington Oaks State Gardens (five miles north), Anastasia State Recreation Area (15 miles north). **Public swimming pool:** Frieda Zamba Aquatic Complex. **Semiprivate swimming pool:** Belle Terre Swim & Racquet Club. **Water sports:** 80-slip marina and private boat slips at hundreds of canal homes provide access to boating, sailing and other water-related recreational pursuits. **River/gulf/ocean:** Matanzas River and the Intracoastal Waterway. The newest development fronts the Atlantic. **Walking/biking/hiking/running:** Miles of hiking-biking paths wind through

the natural wetlands; 26 miles of uncrowded county beaches invite exploration. **Horses/riding:** None. **Hunting:** Fishing/hunting licenses: (904) 437-7424. **Movie theaters:** 33 screens. **Art museums:** None. Flagler County Art Society has moving exhibits throughout the county. **History museums:** None. **Theaters:** Palm Coast Little Theatre. Flagler Auditorium in Bunnell is a premier performing arts center. Tom Gabrielle Amphitheater. **Library:** Flagler County Library. **Attractions:** Marineland (seven miles north). **Necessities:** All available in the Village Square, or within a 20-minute drive.

   Smart Shopper Tip: Volusia Mall with five anchors is just a short drive down I-95 in Daytona Beach. Palm Harbor Shopping Village has over 50 shops.

WHO LIVES HERE
Population: 28,630. **Age 65+** = 30.0% in Flagler County. **Median household income:** $28,109 (Flagler County). **Per capita income:** $17,195 (Flagler County).

NUMBERS TO KNOW
Chamber of commerce: (904) 437-0106. **Voter registration:** (904) 437-7447. **Vehicle registration, tags & title:** (904) 437-7424. **Driver's license:** (904) 517-2080

WHAT TO READ
Daytona Beach News-Journal, daily newspaper, (904) 252-1511. **News Tribune**, biweekly, (904) 437-2491.

GETTING AROUND
Bus: Flagler County Transit provides on-call transportation in cooperation with the Council on Aging, (904) 437-7276. **Tours:** None. **Airport:** Daytona Beach International is 30 minutes south on the Interstate. **Traffic:** Moderate to light within the development. Always heavy on I-95.

JOBS
County unemployment rate: 3.5%. **Florida Jobs and Benefits:** (904) 437-7581.

UTILITIES
Electricity: Florida Power & Light, distributed by Palm Coast Utilities, (904) 445-3311. **Gas:** People's Gas (propane), (904) 446-0480. **Water & sewer:** Palm Coast Utilities, (904) 445-3311. **Telephone:** Bell South, (800) 789-9025 out-of-state, (904) 780-2355 in Florida. **Cable TV:** Palm Coast Cablevision, (904) 445-5464.

PLACES OF WORSHIP
Nine Protestant and one Catholic church, plus one Jewish synagogue.

THE ENVIRONMENT
The Matanzas River generally has been rated as having fair water quality. There are no EPA-listed Superfund sites in Flagler County.

EVENTS & FESTIVALS
Home Show/Service Fair - February. **A Taste of Flagler** - April. **Christmas at the Beach** - December.

WHERE TO EAT
Oak Tree by the Sea, 5949 Highway A1A, seafood, poultry, beef, expensive, (904) 446-1727. **Flagler's**, 300 Clubhouse Dr., American, moderate, (904) 445-6357. **Raymond's Restaurant**, 242 Palm Coast Parkway, continental, moderate, (904) 446-2433.

WHERE TO STAY
Harborside Inn at Palm Coast Resort, (904) 445-3000. **Hampton Inn**, (904) 446-4457.

ISSUES
Palm Coast lost 51 homes in windswept fires that ravaged Northeast Florida last year. Like hurricanes, they are totally unpredictable, but something to consider.

RELOCATION TIPS
When you've made the decision to relocate, start planning your move early so you aren't rushed into hasty decisions about what to move or where to buy. Make lists of things that need to be done and set a timetable for action. If you start early, you can do a little each week and still carry on some or all of your normal activities. Throughout the process, stay flexible and remain prepared to switch to an alternate plan if your original plan is foiled.

Palm Harbor

HE SAID: ★ ★ ★
It offers big-city amenities within a short drive, and water-related activities and golf courses are abundant. Even so, it has no strong attraction for me. I may go back for a second look, but I doubt it.

SHE SAID: ★ ★ ★
The town's name certainly sounds inviting, and it has its attractions, but it doesn't appeal to me. I would not retire here.

Palm Harbor has the advantages of a major, neighboring metropolis, Tampa-St. Petersburg. It has some peaceful corners, but with bustling U.S. Highway 19 bisecting the area, "quiet" and "suburban" are not adjectives that readily come to mind. It is a "near-to" community. No hospitals of its own, but near to three. No art museums, but near to many.

West of U.S. 19A, along Orange Street, there are vestiges of a quaint village with moss-draped oaks shading Key West-style homes. There is even a six- to eight-block area of old Palm Harbor that achieves a small-town ambiance, with a few shops, restaurants and a post office. But in recent years, all of the town's growth has been along the U.S. 19 corridor and east to the shores of Lake Tarpon.

Residents can choose from a variety of home sites: on the Gulf front, along a saltwater bayou or cove, on the hillside in downtown Palm Harbor overlooking the Gulf, in one of the lake-area communities east of U.S. 19, or in one of the lake-shore developments between Lake Tarpon and Safety Harbor. Any mention of Palm Harbor housing would not be complete without a comment on Highland Lakes, a lake-area adult community where a $50 monthly fee covers golf privileges and entertainment brought in by the Highland Lakes Activities Council. Each year, that entertainment includes 12 dinner-dances, six Las Vegas-style shows and a New Year's Eve party attended by as many as 5,000 people. There are now more than 65 social and special interest clubs spawned by the inhabitants of Highland Lakes, including an 800-member organ club, which attracts internationally known artists to its eight annual concerts, and an 80-member theater group, which produces an original musical each year.

The big drawback to living in this area is having to cross busy U.S. 19 to get to the Gulf. But with Lake Tarpon, Safety Harbor, the connecting Lake Tarpon Canal and dozens of smaller lakes in the area offering fishing, boating and sporting opportunities, who needs the Gulf?

Pinellas Trail, designed for hikers, bikers and roller skaters, stretches from Tarpon Springs to St. Petersburg and is a prominent feature of old Palm Harbor. It is prized by local residents, who join the more than 100,000 people using the trail each month.

Like so much of Florida developed in the last 25 years, Palm Harbor is neither a small town nor a major city. Many retirees have found their niche in this section of northern Pinellas County. It's a place you may want to look at to judge for yourself.

WEATHER

	Winter	Spring	Summer	Fall
Normal daily high/low	72/52	85/66	90/73	78/58
Normal precipitation	10 in.	10 in.	23 in.	8 in.

Disaster watch: Northwest Florida has been hit by six major hurricanes since 1900.

TAXES
Sales tax: 7%. **Property tax:** $21.66 per $1,000 valuation. Sample tax calculations include a $25,000 homestead exemption.

Home value	Tax
$100,000	$1,625
$150,000	$2,708
$250,000	$4,874

REAL ESTATE
Median home value: $105,258 (Pinellas County). **Median rent:** $614/month (Pinellas County). **Communities popular with retirees:** Agents with Century 21 West Bay Properties, (727) 586-3514, suggest looking at Highland Lakes, the largest and best development in the area, offering condominiums priced from the $70s and single-family homes priced up to the $150s. Two popular manufactured-home communities are Gull Aire Village and Blue Jay Estates. Pine Ridge has condominiums from the mid-$40s to $60s. **Licensed continuing-care retirement communities:** St. Mark Village has 361 independent living units, 20 sheltered nursing beds and 60 community beds, (813) 785-2577.

CRIME & SAFETY
Crimes per 1,000 population: 46 (Pinellas County sheriff's jurisdiction). **Non-emergency police:** (813) 582-6200. **Non-emergency fire department:** (813) 784-0454. **Police, fire, ambulance emergencies:** 911.

HOMELESS & BLIGHT
We saw no homeless persons. The area has a heavy concentration of manufactured housing and crowded RV rental parks with few apparent amenities. Many of the houses in the old downtown are not particularly attractive, reminiscent of old neighborhoods in many small towns. All new development is east of U.S. 19 — much of it very upscale.

According to the U.S. Census, Pinellas County's population of 851,659 included 1,105 homeless persons in shelters and 75 visible in street locations.

HEALTH CARE
Hospitals: There are no hospitals in Palm Harbor. **Helen Ellis Memorial Hospital** in Tarpon Springs, 150 beds, full service, (813) 942-5000. **Mease Hospital** in Dunedin, 300-plus beds, full service, (813) 733-1111. **Mease Hospital** in Countryside, 100 beds, full service, (813) 725-6111.
Physicians: 300-plus in upper Pinellas County. **Specialties:** 25.

GETTING SMART
St. Petersburg Junior College, (727) 341-3239. **Offerings:** Two-year degrees. **Eckerd College,** Palm Harbor campus, (813) 784-7566; **Tampa College** in Clearwater, (813) 530-9495. **Palm Harbor University High School,** (813) 669-1140, a new state-of-the-art facility, offers a regular high school curriculum, classes for students enrolled in the University of South Florida, and a broad selection of adult-education programs and classes. It is very popular with seniors. **University of Tampa,** (813) 253-3333.

JUST FOR SENIORS
AARP, St. Petersburg chapter, (813) 576-1155. **Palm Harbor Adult Day Care Center**, (813) 784-0680. **Palm Harbor Senior Center**, (813) 785-1936.

GETTING INVOLVED
Historical Society, (813) 786-5689. **Palm Harbor Civic Club**, (813) 784-8908. **Palm Harbor Newcomers Club**, (813) 785-9577. **SCORE**, Largo chapter, (813) 532-6800.

RECREATION, ENTERTAINMENT & AMENITIES
Public golf: Lansbrook Golf Club, 18 holes/par 72, and Tarpon Woods Golf & Tennis Club, 18 holes/par 72. **Private golf:** East Lake Woodlands Country Club and Highland Lakes Golf Course, two courses, nine holes/par 30 and 18 holes/par 60. **Public tennis courts:** Countryside High School. **Private tennis courts:** Several at area country clubs. **Parks:** Honeymoon Island State Park, "Pop" Stansell Park and John Chestnut Park, which has nature trails and a lengthy boardwalk. **Public swimming pools:** None. **Water sports:** Boating, fishing, sailing and water-skiing. **River/gulf/ocean:** Lake Tarpon and numerous smaller lakes, the Gulf of Mexico, St. Joseph Sound and several saltwater coves and bayous. **Running/walking/biking:** Pinellas Trail, a countywide, linear park running from Tarpon Springs to St. Petersburg, passes through Palm Harbor. It was designed exclusively for walkers, skaters and bicyclists. **Horses/riding:** No stables in the immediate area, but plenty of trails in the undeveloped eastern areas. **Hunting:** Fishing and hunting licenses and information, (813) 464-8721. **Movie theaters:** 10 screens. The Countryside Mall area has approximately 20 screens. **Art museums:** None. **History museums:** Historical Society museums. **Theaters:** Highland Lakes Auditorium, plus Ruth Eckerd Hall in Clearwater. **Library:** Palm Harbor. **Attractions:** Innisbrook Resort in Tarpon Springs. Also, the Toronto Blue Jays hold spring training in Dunedin, which is 10 minutes south, and the Tampa Bay Buccaneers play 15 miles away. **Necessities:** Most necessities are available within a five-mile radius. There is a Wal-Mart and a Publix.

Smart Shopper Tip: There are several shopping centers in the immediate area, but Countryside Mall is only 10 minutes south on U.S. 19 and offers excellent shopping.

WHO LIVES HERE
Population: 70,000 year-round residents in Greater Palm Harbor, according to the chamber of commerce. There were 270,524 people in 1995 in the unincorporated areas of Pinellas County. **Age 65+** = 24.6% in Pinellas County. **Median household income:** $29,009 (Pinellas County). **Per capita income:** $25,765 (Pinellas County).

NUMBERS TO KNOW
Chamber of commerce: (813) 784-4287. **Voter registration:** (813) 464-3551. **Vehicle registration, tags & title:** (813) 464-5560. **Driver's license:** (813) 757-9052.

WHAT TO READ
St. Petersburg Times, North Pinellas edition, daily newspaper, (813) 445-4205. **Tampa Tribune**, daily newspaper, (813) 799-7413. **Sun Coast News**, biweekly newspaper, (813) 849-7500.

GETTING AROUND
Bus: Pinellas Transit, (813) 530-9911. **Taxi:** Yellow Cab, (813) 799-2222. **Tours:** None. **Airport:** St. Petersburg-Clearwater International. Tampa International is 30 minutes away. **Traffic:** U.S. 19A through old Palm Harbor is a cakewalk, but U.S. 19, bisecting new Palm Harbor, is a nightmare.

JOBS
County unemployment rate: 3.4%. **Florida Jobs and Benefits:** (813) 725-7920.

UTILITIES
Electricity: Florida Power, (813) 443-2641. **Gas:** Clearwater Gas, (813) 462-6340. **Water & sewer:** Pinellas County Water Utility, (813) 464-4714. **Telephone:** GTE, within 813 area code, (800) 483-7762; outside 813 area code, (800) 483-4200. **Cable TV:** Time Warner Cable, (813) 797-1818.

PLACES OF WORSHIP
One Catholic and 22 Protestant churches, plus one Jewish synagogue.

THE ENVIRONMENT
Lake Tarpon and Lake Tarpon Canal have been rated as having good water quality. The Florida Department of Environmental Regulation states that the biological and water quality degradation of the Tampa Bay system is a major focus of local, regional and state actions to reverse the negative trends. Tampa Bay and Lake Tarpon have been designated as SWIM water bodies (Surface Water Improvement and Management). The worst water quality problems are found in Hillsborough and McKay Bays, though recent trends in Hillsborough Bay show improvement.

There is one EPA-listed Superfund site in Pinellas County. It is the Stauffer Chemical Co. plant in Tarpon Springs.

EVENTS AND FESTIVALS
Palm Harbor Day - May. **The Palm Harbor Arts, Crafts & Music Festival** - December.

WHERE TO EAT
Palm Harbor Restaurant, 2901 U.S. Highway 19A, seafood, moderate to very expensive, (813) 789-9383. **Olde Schoolhouse Restaurant**, 3419 U.S. Highway 19A N., American, moderate, (813) 784-2585. **Sutherland Cafe & Coffee Company**, 1026 Florida Ave., American, moderate, (727) 787-7734.

WHERE TO STAY
Red Roof Inn, (813) 786-2529. **Knights Inn**, (813) 789-2002. For a deluxe experience, there's the **Westin Innisbrook Resort** between Palm Harbor and Tarpon Springs, (800) 456-2000 or (813) 942-2000.

ISSUES
So far, Palm Harbor seems to be doing all the right things — except controlling growth. From what we've seen, most places need zoning or a planning board to manage new development.

Panama City

HE SAID: ✮ ✮ ✮
Those retirees who love boating and can afford homes on the bays and bayous near the city will find plenty of beautiful residences in quiet neighborhoods, some with golf and tennis country clubs. They can shop, dine and be entertained in a restored downtown.

SHE SAID: ✮ ✮
The beach offers everything you would want — for a vacation. I saw few residential areas that looked inviting. There's very little activity in Panama City — not even enough traffic downtown on Monday morning to activate the traffic signals. I would not look for a retirement home here. Possibly in the outlying areas.

Our initial plan was to profile Panama City Beach and Panama City separately. But after spending several days in the two communities, we were convinced that Panama City Beach itself has very little to offer retirees looking for a year-round home. It is essentially a resort town with beaches, sun, boats, fishing, motels, seafood and fast-food restaurants, cars and people, people, people.

While in Panama City Beach, we drove down the side streets — both of them — looking for residential neighborhoods. We found only two developments, both with homes priced from $150,000 to $400,000. The chamber of commerce said that the area attracts military retirees from nearby Tyndall Air Force Base and the Navy's coastal systems station, but enlisted personnel don't live in *these* pricey barracks.

This is a great little beach town. However, the hectic pace, lack of affordable housing and dearth of social and cultural amenities disqualify Panama City Beach from serious consideration as a retirement site.

Downtown Panama City has been given a much-needed restorative boost through the efforts of the Downtown Improvement Board and Community Redevelopment Agency. This group has parlayed a $37,500 annual allocation from the city into more than $5,000,000 of value-added projects in recent years, transforming a sleepy, unattractive downtown into a vibrant, popular cultural and entertainment center. Free public parking lots, a new Visual Arts Center, Martin Theatre, a multipurpose performing-arts venue and the renovated downtown McKenzie Park were all accomplished through the work of this agency.

Community redevelopment advocates now need to turn their attentions to renovation efforts in a wide belt of substandard housing around the city's restored center, in hopes of bringing retirees and others with above-average financial resources back from Lynn Haven and other bay-area communities to a closer relationship with the city.

WEATHER

	Winter	Spring	Summer	Fall
Normal daily high/low	66/43	84/62	89/70	73/49
Normal precipitation	16 in.	14 in.	23 in.	12 in.

Disaster watch: Northwest Florida has been hit by six major hurricanes since 1900.

TAXES
Sales tax: 6%. **Property tax:** $20.19 per $1,000 valuation. Sample tax calculations include a $25,000 homestead exemption.

Home value	Tax
$100,000	$1,514
$150,000	$2,524
$250,000	$4,543

REAL ESTATE
Median home value: $81,343 (Bay County). **Median rent:** $565/month (Bay County). **Communities popular with retirees:** Cherry Creekmore with Coldwell Banker, (850) 233-8664, identified these developments. The Glades at Hombre Golf Course has garden homes priced from the $140s to $175s and single-family homes on a golf course from the $175s to the $350s. Carillon, fronting on the Gulf, has homes from the $440s to $1.5 million. Southfield, within walking distance of the beach, has single-family homes from the $115s to $150s. Summer Winds offers two- and three-bedroom Gulf-front condos priced from $259,000 to $500,000. **Licensed continuing-care retirement communities:** None.

CRIME & SAFETY
Crimes per 1,000 population: 89 (Panama City); 324 (Panama City Beach). **Non-emergency police:** (850) 872-3100. **Non-emergency fire department:** (850) 872-3068. **Police, fire, ambulance emergencies:** 911.

HOMELESS & BLIGHT
Large areas of run-down residential housing ring the city. According to the U.S. Census, Bay County had 52 homeless persons in shelters and 24 visible on the streets in its population of 126,994.

HEALTH CARE
Hospitals: Bay Medical Center, 302 beds, full service, (850) 769-1511. **Columbia Gulf Coast Hospital**, 176 beds, full service, (850) 769-8341. **U.S. Air Force Hospital** at Tyndall AFB for active and retired military personnel, 71 beds, (850) 283-7515. **Physicians:** 300+. **Specialties:** 37.

GETTING SMART
Florida State University, Panama City campus, (850) 872-4750. **Offerings:** Undergraduate and graduate degree programs. **Gulf Coast Community College**, (850) 769-1551. **Offerings:** Two-year arts and sciences degrees. **Troy State University** at Tyndall AFB, (850) 283-4449. **Offerings:** Undergraduate degrees in business administration and management. Graduate degrees in counseling and human development, international relations and management.

JUST FOR SENIORS
AARP, (850) 222-7344. **Bay County Council on Aging** offers the Better Living for Seniors program, (850) 769-3468. **Bay County Senior Center**, (850) 769-3468, has more than 6,500 patrons at its seven Bay County centers. Services include meals served at the centers, meals delivered to the homebound, transportation, adult day care, arts and crafts, exercise, trips and tours.

GETTING INVOLVED
Bay Arts Alliance, (850) 769-1217. **Bay County Newcomers Club**, (850) 271-5042 or (850) 233-5375. **Bay County Homeless & Hunger Coalition**, (850) 769-2738. **RSVP**, (850) 769-3468 ext. 119. **United Way**, (850) 785-7521.

RECREATION, ENTERTAINMENT & AMENITIES
Public golf: Bay Dunes, 18 holes, par 71; Bay Point Country Club has two 18-hole/par-72 courses; Holiday Golf & Tennis

Club, 18 holes; Hombre Golf Course, 18 holes; and Signal Hill Golf Course, 18 holes. **Private golf:** Edgewater Golf Course, nine holes; Panama Country Club, 18 holes; and Tyndall/Pelican Point Golf Course, 18 holes/par 72. **Public tennis courts:** Daffin Park, Oakland Terrace Park and Truesdell Park. **Private tennis courts:** Bay Point Country Club, Edgewater Beach Resort and Panama City Swim & Tennis Club. **Parks:** St. Andrews State Park has more than 1,000 acres. There are nine community parks, nine nature parks and 11 neighborhood parks in the area. **Public swimming pools:** Carl Gray Park. **Water sports:** Windsurfing, boating, sailing, jet-skiing, shelling, snorkeling and scuba diving. **River/gulf/ocean:** West Bay, North Bay, St. Andrews Bay, East Bay and a multitude of bayous wrap around the city. St. Andrews Bay opens into the Gulf. **Running/walking/biking:** Bay Memorial Park has a 13-acre nature park, walking trail and 10 fitness stations. Harvey Demathis Park has an exercise trail and a 2.75-acre nature park. There are nature trails at St. Andrews State Recreation Area. **Horses/riding:** Several stables in unincorporated areas, none in the city. **Hunting:** Saltwater and freshwater fishing and game licenses, (850) 784-4090. **Movie theaters:** 20 screens. **Art museums:** Visual Arts Center. **History museums:** Junior Museum of Bay County and the Museum of Man in the Sea. **Theaters:** Gulf Coast Community College Fine Arts Auditorium, Marina Civic Center, Martin Theatre for Performing Arts and Panama City Music Association. **Library:** Panama City Public Library and Panama City Beach Public Library. **Attractions:** Eden State Gardens and Shell Island. **Necessities:** All here.

Smart Shopper Tip: Panama City is the retail center for an eight-county area. All major supermarkets and chain department stores are here. Panama City Mall has 100 stores. Specialty stores and antique shops are prevalent in downtown Panama City, along 23rd Street and among the shops of Panama City Beach.

WHO LIVES HERE
Population: In Panama City, 37,347 year-round residents, an increase of 2,951 since 1990. In Panama City Beach, 4,710 year-round residents, an increase of 659 since 1990. **Age 65+ =** 12.9% in Bay County. **Median household income:** $26,927 (Bay County). **Per capita income:** $18,229 (Bay County).

NUMBERS TO KNOW
Panama City Chamber of Commerce: (850) 785-5206. **Panama City Beach Chamber of Commerce:** (850) 235-1159. **Voter registration:** (850) 784-6100. **Vehicle registration, tags & title:** (850) 784-4090. **Driver's license:** (850) 872-4488. **Visitors bureau:** (850) 233-6503.

WHAT TO READ
The News Herald, daily newspaper, (850) 747-5000. **Bay Biz**, quarterly, (850) 785-5206.

GETTING AROUND
Bus: Baytown Trolley, (850) 769-0557. **Taxi:** AAA Taxi, (850) 785-0533. **Tours:** Shell Island Shuttle Boat, (850) 233-0504. **Airport:** Panama City International Airport. **Traffic:** Heavy in Panama City Beach. Practically none in Panama City.

JOBS
County unemployment rate: 5.3%. **Florida Jobs and Benefits:** (850) 872-4340.

UTILITIES
Electricity: Gulf Power Co., (850) 872-3200. **Gas:** Peoples Gas, (850) 872-6100. **Water & sewer:** Panama City Utility Dept., (850) 872-3166. **Telephone:** Bell South, (800) 789-9025 in Florida, or (800) 753-0710 out-of-state. **Cable TV:** ComCast Cablevision, (850) 769-0392.

PLACES OF WORSHIP
Four Catholic and 138 Protestant churches, one Jewish synagogue and one Islamic mosque.

THE ENVIRONMENT
The EPA reported finding lead in the water of the Panama City Beach system measuring 23 parts per billion (ppb) and in the Lynn Haven system measuring 32 ppb. The EPA action level is 15 ppb. The Panama City Beach water system serves 14,000 people, while the Lynn Haven water system serves 9,695.

Surface water quality in the area generally has been rated as fair; some parts are rated good, while the waters of Econfina Creek are nearly pristine. Deer Point Lake is the source of drinking water for Panama City. It is fed by Econfina Creek and other tributaries.

North Bay and Watson Bayou have poor to fair water quality ratings.

EVENTS AND FESTIVALS
Annual Watercolor Show - March to April. **Gulf Coast Triathlon** - May. **Spring Festival of the Arts** - May. **Indian Summer Seafood Festival** - October. **Boat Parade of Lights** - November.

WHERE TO EAT
Boar's Head Restaurant, 17290 Front Beach Road, American, moderate to expensive, (850) 234-6628. **Captain Anderson's**, 5551 N. Lagoon Drive, seafood, moderate to very expensive, (850) 234-2225. **Bay View**, 100 Delwood Beach Road at the Marriott's Bay Point Resort, nouvelle cuisine, steaks, lamb, seafood, expensive, (850) 234-3307.

WHERE TO STAY
Edgewater Beach Resort, (850) 235-4044. **Best Western Bayside Inn**, (850) 763-4622. **Marriott's Bay Point Resort**, (850) 234-3307.

ISSUES
Panama City Beach is essentially a 10-mile strip of motels, restaurants and beach boutiques. There are some very nice residential neighborhoods along the waterways of neighboring towns, but very few in these two communities. The whole area has enormous potential due to location, beaches, bays and the port. Through the efforts of the Downtown Improvement Board and the Main Street America program, some initiative is being taken to give downtown a face lift and to entice new businesses to the area. At this point, it appears to be working.

Pensacola

HE SAID: ✫ ✫ ✫ ✫ ✫
*After spending just two days here I was hooked.
A few more days, and the post office might be forwarding
my mail to Florida.*

SHE SAID: ✫ ✫ ✫ ✫
*It's large enough to offer all the cultural arts — but
not too large. The streets are lined with crape myrtles and
magnolias. There are three seasons — spring, summer and
fall — and the trees even change colors. Quoting one
retiree: "If you enjoy great weather, good seafood, boating,
fishing, golf, low-cost living and friendly people, this is the
place to be." I could retire here.*

Immediate impressions of Pensacola are not necessarily favorable, but don't let that deter you. One should drive around the area, walk its streets and gaze out across its snow-white beaches and blue-green Gulf waters to really begin to sense the essence of this place. It has so much. And, it is Pensacola's diversity that attracts retirees from many different backgrounds.

Thousands of naval personnel have returned to Pensacola for retirement, drawn by happy memories of their residencies at the U.S. Naval Air Station during the 1950s, '60s and '70s. Here they have ready access to the naval hospital, commissary and comrades in arms.

History buffs are attracted by the town's storied past under five different flags: Spanish, French, British, Confederate and American. Relics and artifacts of earlier settlements dating back to 1559, six years before the founding of St. Augustine, still are being uncovered today. Archaeological digs dot the city and county.

What else is there to make this town so inviting? Six hospitals, five universities and colleges, a strong cadre of cultural organizations, numerous golf courses, parks, recreation centers and no less than six distinct bodies of water are the lures drawing retirees to the area.

To its credit, the municipal government is both receptive and proactive in its search for ways to draw more retirees to its shores. It has created the Mayor's Committee on Retirement Opportunities to aggressively solicit retirees as newcomers. The low cost of living is described by retirees as a significant factor in their decision to relocate here. Of course, the wonderful climate is another incentive cited by retirees.

Anyone considering Pensacola as a possible retirement site should spend some time here. Enjoy local recreational, cultural and geographical attractions. Then, prepare to make a move — Pensacola's magnetism may snag you, too.

WEATHER

	Winter	Spring	Summer	Fall
Normal daily high/low	64/46	83/65	89/73	71/52
Normal precipitation	16 in.	14 in.	20 in.	12 in.

Disaster watch: Northwest Florida has been hit by six major hurricanes since 1900.

TAXES
Sales tax: 7%. **Property tax:** $22.93 per $1,000 valuation. Sample taxes include a $25,000 homestead exemption.

Home value	Tax
$100,000	$1,720
$150,000	$2,866
$250,000	$5,159

REAL ESTATE
Median home value: $80,395 (Escambia County). **Median rent:** $531/month (Escambia County). **Communities popular with retirees:** Marcus Pointe Country Club has single-family and patio homes priced from the $130s to $500s, and Tiger Point at Gulf Breeze has single-family homes priced from the $140s to $300s; contact Irma Short with Montgomery Realtors, (800) 445-2507. **Licensed continuing-care retirement communities:** Azalea Trace has 283 independent living units, 46 sheltered nursing beds and 60 community beds, (850) 478-5200.

CRIME & SAFETY
Crimes per 1,000 population: 68. **Non-emergency police:** (850) 435-1900. **Non-emergency fire department:** (850) 595-1213. **Police, fire, ambulance emergencies:** 911.

HOMELESS & BLIGHT
We saw no evidence of homeless persons, but did see some run-down residential areas, particularly driving into the city from the west on Gulf Beach Highway.

According to the U.S. Census, Escambia County's population of 262,798 includes 53 homeless persons in shelters and 22 visible on the streets.

HEALTH CARE
Hospitals: Baptist Hospital, 521 beds, full service, (850) 434-4011. **Columbia West Florida Regional Medical Center**, 547 beds, full service, (850) 494-4000. **Sacred Heart Hospital**, 431 beds, full service, plus a 50-bed children's hospital, (850) 416-7000. **Navy Hospital**, 138 beds, (850) 505-6413.
Physicians: Nearly 500. **Specialties:** 65+.

GETTING SMART
Pensacola Christian College, (850) 478-8496. **Offerings:** Four-year degrees emphasizing religious and academic courses. **Pensacola Junior College**, (850) 484-1000. **Offerings:** Two-year degree programs, job entry and retraining, GED and adult basic education plus a seniors club. **Elderhostel** conducts eight sessions here each year, (850) 484-1797. **Troy State University**, (850) 452-3491. **Offerings:** Four-year undergraduate programs in international relations, psychology, business and criminal justice. Master's programs in management, public administration and counseling. **University of West Florida**, (850) 474-3000, offers the **Center for Lifelong Learning**, (850) 474-3384, for people 55 and over. **Offerings:** Undergraduate and graduate programs in more than 100 disciplines. Lifelong Learning program features life enrichment classes. **Elderhostel** conducts eight sessions annually, (850) 474-2786. **George Stone Center**, (850) 944-1424. **Offerings:** Vocational training.

JUST FOR SENIORS
AARP, (850) 432-3898. **Bayview Senior Center**, (850) 435-1790. **Escambia County Council on Aging**, (850) 432-1475. **Senior Health Services**, (850) 494-4885. **Senior Resource Center**, (850) 494-4872. **West Escambia County Senior Center**, (850) 453-0288.

GETTING INVOLVED
Arts Council of Northwest Florida, an umbrella agency for 90 cultural groups, (850) 432-9906. **Habitat for Humanity**, (850) 434-5456. **Newcomer's Club**, (850) 458-6107.

RECREATION, ENTERTAINMENT & AMENITIES
Public golf: Creekside Golf Club, Green Meadows, Marcus

Pointe Golf Course, Osceola Municipal Golf Course, Perdido Bay Golf Club and Scenic Hills Golf & Country Club, semiprivate. **Private golf:** Pensacola Country Club. **Public tennis courts:** Roger Scott Tennis Center, Bayview Park, 1-110 Park and Sanders Beach Park. **Private tennis courts:** PensaCourt and Pensacola Racquet Club. **Parks:** Blackwater River State Park, Gulf Islands National Seashore and Big Lagoon State Recreation Area, plus 90 parks and eight community centers. **Public swimming pools:** Municipal. **Water sports:** Surfing, water-skiing, scuba diving, snorkeling, sailing and powerboating. **River/gulf/ocean:** Pensacola Bay, Escambia Bay, Perdido Bay, Big Lagoon, Santa Rosa Sound and the Gulf of Mexico. **Running/walking/biking:** Gulf Islands National Seashore at the Naval Live Oaks area, Big Lagoon State Recreation Area, Edward Ball Nature Walk at the University of West Florida and Bay Bluffs Park. **Horses/riding:** Several stables and riding academies. **Hunting:** Duck, deer and wild turkey. Florida Game and Freshwater Fish Commission, (850) 438-6500. **Movie theaters:** 21 screens. **Art museums:** Pensacola Museum of Art and Quayside Art Gallery. **History museums:** National Museum of Naval Aviation, Fort Pickens Museum and the Pensacola Historical Museum. **Theaters:** Bayfront Auditorium, Pensacola Civic Center, Pensacola Cultural Center, Saenger Theatre and University of West Florida Fine Arts Center. Performing arts groups: Pensacola Little Theater, Pensacola Jazz Society and Pensacola Symphony Orchestra. **Library:** West Florida Regional Library has five branches and a mobile unit. Also, libraries at college campuses. **Attractions:** Seville Square and Historic Pensacola Village have several museums, historic houses and the Colonial Archaeological Trail. National Museum of Naval Aviation and The Zoo. **Necessities:** All are available.

Smart Shopper Tip: Of the 38 malls, shopping centers and plazas, Cordova Mall and University Mall offer the best choices for concentrated shopping. Seville Square in the heart of the historic district is great for casual browsing and sightseeing.

WHO LIVES HERE
Population: 60,591 year-round residents, an increase of 1,393 since 1990. **Age 65+** = 13.2% in Escambia County. **Median household income:** $27,738 (Escambia County). **Per capita income:** $18,089 (Escambia County).

NUMBERS TO KNOW
Chamber of commerce: (850) 438-4081 or (800) 608-3479. **Voter registration:** (850) 595-3900. **Vehicle registration, tags, title & driver's license:** (850) 438-6500. **Visitors bureau:** (850) 434-1234.

WHAT TO READ
Pensacola News Journal, daily newspaper, (850) 435-8500. **Escambia Sun Press**, weekly newspaper, (850) 456-3121. **Pensacola Voice**, weekly newspaper, (850) 434-6963. **The New American Press**, weekly newspaper, (850) 432-8410. **Pensacola Today**, bimonthly magazine, (850) 433-1166.

GETTING AROUND
Bus and trolley: Escambia County Area Transit, (850) 595-3228. **Taxi:** ABC Taxi, (850) 456-8294. **Tours:** None. **Airport:** Pensacola Regional. **Train:** Amtrak's Sunset Limited runs from Los Angeles to Miami, stopping in Pensacola, (800) 872-7245. **Traffic:** Light to moderate.

JOBS
County unemployment rate: 4.5%. **Florida Jobs and Benefits:** (850) 595-5236.

UTILITIES
Electricity: Gulf Power Co., (850) 444-6111. **Gas:** Energy Services of Pensacola, (850) 435-1800. **Water & sewer:** Escambia County Utilities Authority, (850) 476-5110. **Telephone:** Bell South, (800) 789-9025 in Florida or (800) 754-1070 out-of-state. **Cable TV:** Cox Cable, (850) 478-0200.

PLACES OF WORSHIP
Fifteen Catholic and 368 Protestant churches, plus two Jewish synagogues.

THE ENVIRONMENT
Pensacola has a materials recovery facility where recyclables are separated from waste prior to disposal so separate pick-up is not required.

Santa Rosa Sound and Pensacola Bay have been rated as having generally good water quality. Escambia Bay and Bayou Texar have fair water quality. Bayou Chico has very poor water quality.

Escambia County has six EPA-listed Superfund sites: Agrico Chemical Co., two miles southwest of Pensacola Municipal Airport; American Creosote Works in the city proper; Beulah Landfill, within the city limits; Dubose Oil Products Co. in Cantonment; and the Pensacola Naval Air Station. Clean up activities at the Pioneer Sand Co., five miles west of Pensacola, have been completed, according to the EPA. The site is scheduled for review for possible deletion from the Superfund list.

Pensacola did not meet the air quality standard for ozone and sulfur dioxide once during 1992.

EVENTS AND FESTIVALS
Mardi Gras Festival - February. **Spring Fest** - May. **Fiesta of Five Flags** - June. **Fiesta Senior Citizen Celebration** - June. **Pensacola Seafood Festival** - September. **The Great Gulfcoast Arts Festival** - November.

WHERE TO EAT
Jamie's, 424 E. Zaragoza St., French, expensive, (850) 434-2911. **Jubilee**, 400 Quietwater Beach Road, seafood, chicken, steak, new menu weekly, moderate to expensive, (850) 934-3108. **New World Landing Restaurant**, 600 S. Palafox St., continental, moderate, (850) 434-7736.

WHERE TO STAY
The Dunes, (850) 932-3536. **Hampton Inn Pensacola Beach**, (850) 932-6800. **New World Inn**, (850) 432-4111. **Pensacola Grand Hotel**, (850) 433-3336.

ISSUES
There aren't too many issues facing this community, and when one arises, someone jumps on it to get it straightened out.

The decommissioning of the aircraft carrier Forrestal took some money out of the local economy, but the U.S. Naval Air Station was spared during the most recent round of cutbacks.

The future looks bright for this city. The retirees we talked with had nothing but positive remarks about their town. The city is actively and aggressively seeking new retiree in-migration.

Perry

HE SAID: ★ ★ ★
They lost me when I found out they only had one nine-hole golf course. But that aside, I would want to pay a long visit to test my aptitude for living in these particular circumstances before making a commitment.

SHE SAID: ★
This is a small, clean town with friendly people. But, it's too remote for me. I would not retire here.

A nice, friendly little town sitting squarely in the middle of Taylor County, Perry houses almost half of the county's residents. It offers the usual mixed bag of small-town pros and cons and fulfills most of the day-to-day needs of its inhabitants. But excursions into Tallahassee or other cities more than an hour's distance are required for advanced medical care, cultural happenings, institutions of higher learning and serious shopping.

Perry lies just 17 miles from the gentle breezes and recreational possibilities of the Gulf Coast. Keaton Beach, the point of easiest access, has a flat shoreline with shallow, marshy water, no waves and a small, man-made beach. It has a deep-water channel with some of the best fishing along the entire Gulf shore.

Three rivers flow past Perry, two of which are very popular for fishing, hiking, camping and observing wildlife. The third, the Fenholloway, was classified as an industrial river by the state in 1946, and neither fishing nor swimming is permitted. There is an effort underway to return the Fenholloway to a less polluted, more recreational state.

The Main Street Perry rehabilitation and restoration project, started in 1992, aims to return the downtown area to its turn-of-the-century appearance. The project is beginning to pick up steam and show noticeable results. There appears to be a dedicated effort on the part of property owners, community leaders and volunteers to transform downtown into an attractive center of commerce and a destination of choice for residents.

Another attraction is Steinhatchee, a scenic, unincorporated coastal town of about 1,500 people. About 40 miles south of Perry, Steinhatchee attracts Perry residents as well as tourists to its fish camps, lodges and seafood restaurants. It has enough retirees to start its own chapter of AARP.

On balance, Perry deserves consideration by retirees who prize small-town living, seek an outdoor-oriented lifestyle, are not culture-vultures, and don't object to the 101 little inconveniences associated with living in an isolated, rural environment. Steinhatchee's motto, "The way it was is the way it is," pretty much applies to the whole county.

WEATHER

	Winter	Spring	Summer	Fall
Normal daily high/low	70/44	87/61	91/70	76/50
Normal precipitation	13 in.	14 in.	23 in.	9 in.

Disaster watch: Northwest Florida has been hit by six major hurricanes since 1900.

TAXES

Sales tax: 7%. **Property tax:** $22.28 per $1,000 valuation. Sample tax calculations include a $25,000 homestead exemption.

Home value	Tax
$100,000	$1,671
$150,000	$2,785
$250,000	$5,013

REAL ESTATE

Median home value: $70,592 (Taylor County). **Median rent:** $464/month (Taylor County). **Communities popular with retirees:** Retirees live throughout the area in established neighborhoods. There are no subdivisions or country club communities. Keaton Beach, 17 miles south of Perry, and Steinhatchee, 40 miles south on the southern tip of Taylor County, attract retirees. **Licensed continuing-care retirement communities:** None.

CRIME & SAFETY

Crimes per 1,000 population: 114. **Non-emergency police:** (850) 584-5121. **Non-emergency fire department:** (850) 584-3311. **Police, fire, ambulance emergencies:** 911.

HOMELESS & BLIGHT

Perry's Main Street program is working to restore downtown, so what might have been blighted is getting the attention it deserves.

We saw no homeless persons or seriously blighted areas in the town. The U.S. Census reported Taylor County's population as 17,111 and counted no homeless persons in shelters or on the streets.

HEALTH CARE

Hospitals: Doctors Memorial Hospital, 50 beds, full service, (850) 584-0800.
Physicians: 26. **Specialties:** 14.

GETTING SMART

Taylor Technical Institute, (850) 838-2545. **Offerings:** Automotive, business and carpentry training.

JUST FOR SENIORS

Taylor Adult Meals Program and **Better Living for Seniors**, (850) 584-4924.

GETTING INVOLVED

Several organizations offer volunteering opportunities, including the Art Guild, Cancer Crusade and the Historical Society. Contact the chamber of commerce, (850) 584-5366.

RECREATION, ENTERTAINMENT & AMENITIES

Public golf: Perry Golf & Country Club, nine holes. **Private golf:** None. **Public tennis courts:** None. **Private tennis courts:** None. **Parks:** Pace Field and Festival Park. **Public swimming pools:** Perry Golf & Country Club and Pace Field Complex. **Water sports:** Airboating, canoeing, sailing and water-skiing. **River/gulf/ocean:** The Aucilla River and Econfina River west of town are popular for canoeing, boating and fishing. Keaton Beach, on the Gulf, is a developed community popular with boaters, beach-goers and fishermen. **Running/walking/biking:** Opportunities abound. **Horses/riding:** Pastures and wooded lands in the county make it horse country; the cattle industry also thrives here. **Hunting:** Some of the most rewarding hunting opportunities in Florida can be had in Taylor County; game includes wild hogs along the Econfina River, turkey, rabbit, squirrels and duck in the coastal marshes and Aucilla Wildlife Management Area. Florida Game and Freshwater Fish Commission, (850) 838-1306. **Movie theaters:** three screens. **Art museums:** None. **History museums:** Taylor County Historical Society and Forest Capital State Park Museum. **Theaters:** None. **Library:** Taylor County Public. **Attractions:** The pristine grass flats of the Econfina River, Keaton Beach for Gulf recreation and the picturesque fishing village of Steinhatchee. **Necessities:** Most are available, including a post office, banks, savings and loan associations, supermarkets, hardware store, discount stores, electronics store, home furnishings store, shopping centers, real estate agencies, credit unions, funeral homes, insurance companies, schools and pharmacies.

Smart Shopper Tip: Taylor Square Shopping Center, Perry Square and downtown Perry can't satisfy all of your shopping needs. Plan to drive to Tallahassee.

WHO LIVES HERE
Population: 7,210 year-round residents, an increase of 59 people since 1990. **Age 65+ =** 14.5% in Taylor County. **Median household income:** $23,304 (Taylor County). **Per capita income:** $15,722 (Taylor County).

NUMBERS TO KNOW
Chamber of commerce: (850) 584-5366. **Voter registration:** (850) 838-3515. **Vehicle registration, tags & title:** (850) 838-3517. **Driver's license:** (850) 584-2089.

WHAT TO READ
Perry News-Herald, biweekly newspaper, (850) 584-5513. **Taco Times,** weekly newspaper, (850) 584-5513.

GETTING AROUND
Bus: No intra-city public transportation. Big Bend Transit provides charters and rentals, (850) 584-5566. **Taxi:** Frankie's Taxi, (850) 584-6144. **Tours:** None. **Airport:** Tallahassee Regional is 60 miles northwest. **Traffic:** Light.

JOBS
County unemployment rate: 7.9%. **Florida Jobs and Benefits:** (850) 584-7604.

UTILITIES
Electricity: Florida Power Corp., (800) 700-8744. **Gas:** Perry Utilities, (850) 584-7940. **Water & sewer:** Perry Utility Dept., (850) 584-2721. **Telephone:** Gulf Telephone Co., (850) 584-2211. **Cable TV:** ComCast Cablevision, (850) 584-4249.

PLACES OF WORSHIP
One Catholic and 47 Protestant churches.

THE ENVIRONMENT
The pulp mill waste discharged from the Buckeye Cellulose Mill has degraded the Fenholloway River. The river, classified as an industrial waterway, has a poor water quality rating. Attempts are underway to reclassify the stream's usage, which would apply more stringent standards for release of waste from the mill. Residents near the Fenholloway have been given bottled water because of possible well contamination from the river.

Other streams and rivers in the area have fair to good water quality ratings.

EVENTS AND FESTIVALS
Arts & Antiques on Main Street - May. **Florida Forest Festival** - October. **Old Fashioned Christmas and Festival of Lights** - December.

WHERE TO EAT
Chaparral Steak House, 2135 S. Byron Butler Parkway, steak, chicken, buffet, moderate, (850) 584-3431. **Goodman's Barbecue,** 2429 S. Byron Butler Parkway, chicken, barbecued ribs, beef and pork, inexpensive to moderate, (850) 584-3751. **Pouncey's,** 2186 S. Byron Butler Parkway, American, homemade pies, inexpensive, (850) 584-9942.

WHERE TO STAY
Best Budget Inn, (800) 458-7215 or (850) 584-6231. **Days Inn,** (800) 325-2525 or (850) 584-5311. **Villager Lodge,** (850) 584-4221.

ISSUES
Perry is the seat and center of Taylor County. While almost 50 percent of the county's population resides in Perry, it serves more as a launching pad for those who enjoy outdoor activities and recreation than as a primary residential community. People come here on their way to enjoy hunting, fishing, water sports and wildlife viewing in the many woodlands, preserves and uncrowded coastal regions nearby.

The Fenholloway River, which flows south of town, is a dead river. It is the recipient of more than one million pounds of ammonia annually (as well as other chemicals) from the Buckeye Cellulose Mill. Because the river is classified as industrial, these discharges are within the legal limits.

A class action suit brought by property owners against the plant claims the groundwater aquifer that supplies well water is contaminated. Some residents now receive bottled water. Watch for other changes as efforts are made to reclassify the river.

The plant is the town's largest employer and the chief support of the town's hospital. One side of the issue was summed up when a resident said, "If Buckeye closes, Perry closes."

Mike Evans, executive director of the Development Authority of Taylor County, scoffs at this suggestion and says the town is moving forward.

Pine Island

HE SAID: ✮ ✮ ✮
What would you do here? Fish, golf, lie in the sun, take nature walks or go crazy. Take your pick.

SHE SAID: ✮
A fisherman's paradise is not what I'm after. If you don't fish or play golf, you could get plenty bored here. All types of housing are available, from trailer parks to single-family houses. But I would not be happy retiring here.

Variously tagged by its boosters as the "world's greatest fishing spot," "tropical jewel in the sun," "Sanibel as it used to be" and other equally exotic sobriquets, Pine Island is a wonderful, end-of-the-road, pine-covered island. Its residents have a surprising combination of interests, priorities and agendas, but none as focused as the preservation of their unencumbered lifestyle.

County, state and federal governments have a lot of local support in efforts to preserve the island's history and abundant wildlife. The Calusa Indian culture, dating back to 800 A.D., is zealously guarded. Much of the early Calusa Indian Village is listed on the National Register of Historic Places. Relics and artifacts of pirates and Spanish settlers who arrived here later lend more historical drama and mystique to the island. It is rumored that Ponce de Leon landed here in 1513.

Fishermen, preservationists and conservationists constitute a large percentage of the present population. Bird-watching, wildlife nurturing and environmental issues occupy the lives and attention of many residents. According to some, half the population is trying to keep the other half from ruining the environment.

An example of this protectiveness was evident in the remarks of one retired couple. While she bemoans the fact that she cannot go outdoors during summer without being eaten alive by biting insects called no-see-ums, he likes the bugs because they keep the tourists away.

The thing that really keeps the tourists away is the absence of a large beach area. For this, both residents and non-residents should be thankful because the roads are inadequate for any influx of traffic. With just one two-lane road leading on and off the island and a single two-lane road moving traffic north and south between two of the three major population centers, a seasonal heavy influx of tourists would tax this island beyond endurance. It would destroy the very qualities — peace, serenity and simple way of life — that bring retirees to the area.

Pine Island has a surprising diversity of housing choices. Inland canal sites are popular with manufactured home owners in St. James City. Others prefer golf-course villas, single-family homes, condos or townhomes overlooking Charlotte Harbor and Pine Island Sound.

As the natives say, if you come to Pine Island looking for a retirement home, come quietly, assimilate with the community and don't try to change things.

WEATHER

	Winter	Spring	Summer	Fall
Normal daily high/low	76/55	88/68	91/75	81/62
Normal precipitation	7 in.	14 in.	26 in	6 in.

Disaster watch: Southwest Florida has been hit by five major hurricanes since 1900.

TAXES
Sales tax: 6%. **Property tax:** $20.00 per $1,000 valuation. Sample tax calculations include a $25,000 homestead exemption.

Home value	Tax
$'00,000	$1,500
$150,000	$2,500
$250,000	$4,500

REAL ESTATE
Median home value: $101,528 (Lee County). **Median rent:** $641/month (Lee County). **Communities popular with retirees:** Relocation resource Jerry Myers, Greider Realty, (800) 476-2423 or (941) 283-7644, provided price information on popular retiree housing locations. In Bokeelia Village, at the northern end of the island and separated from the main island by a creek, bay-front homes range from the $300s to $750,000. At the southern end in St. James City, homes are priced from the $50s to $750,000, condos range from the $90s to $270s and canal-front manufactured homes in Cherry Estates range from the mid-$50s to more than $100,000. Waterfront lots start in the $40s in St. James City, while others are available for as high as $330,000 on 38-acre Galt Island, an exclusive, gated private island. In Matlacha Isles, canal homes are priced from the $80s to $250s. **Licensed continuing-care retirement communities:** None.

CRIME & SAFETY
Lee County Sheriff's Office has two cars on patrol on the island. Neighborhood security patrols in St. James City and Matlacha are in direct radio contact with the sheriff's department. **Crimes per 1,000 population:** 36 (Lee County sheriff's jurisdiction). **Non-emergency police:** (941) 768-4385. **Non-emergency fire department:** (941) 283-0030. **Police, fire, ambulance emergencies:** 911.

HOMELESS & BLIGHT
"Filltown," a collection of fishermen's and squatters' huts, is an eyesore that greets you as you cross over from Matlacha to Pine Island.

The U.S. Census reported 97 homeless persons in shelters and 203 visible in street locations in Lee County, population 335,113.

HEALTH CARE
Hospitals: There are no hospitals on the island. The nearest is **Cape Coral Hospital**, 309 beds, acute care, 24-hour emergency, full service, (941) 574-2323.
Physicians: 5. **Specialties:** 4.

GETTING SMART
There are no college or university campuses on Pine Island. The following are in Fort Myers. **Adult and Community Education**, Lee County School District, (941) 334-7172. **Offerings:** Courses are designed to broaden general knowledge and introduce new subjects. **Barry University**, (941) 278-3041. **Offerings:** Adult and continuing education. **Edison Community College**, (941) 489-9300; continuing education, (941) 489-9235. **Offerings:** Two-year degrees and continuing-education programs. **Florida Gulf Coast University**, (941) 590-1000. **Offerings:** Undergraduate and graduate degrees.

JUST FOR SENIORS
We found no services or centers for seniors.

GETTING INVOLVED
F.I.S.H. (Fellow Islanders Sending Help), (941) 283-4442. **Matlacha Community Center**, (941) 283-4110. Call the chamber for information and phone numbers for the **Greater Pine Island Civic Association**, **Matlacha Civic Association** and **St. James City Civic Association**.

RECREATION, ENTERTAINMENT & AMENITIES
Semiprivate golf: Alden Pines Country Club, 18 holes/par 71. **Public tennis courts:** Alden Pines Country Club and Phillips Park. **Private tennis courts:** Bocilla Island Club. **Parks:** Charlotte Harbor State Reserve & Aquatic Preserve, Matlacha Park & Community Center and Pine Island Sound & Estero Bay Aquatic Preserve. **Public swimming pools:** Pine Island Public. **Water sports:** Boating and sailing. **River/gulf/ocean:** Charlotte Harbor, Matlacha Pass, Pine Island Sound and San Carlos Bay. **Running/walking/biking:** Except for three developed areas, the entire island is ideal for recreational activities. A six-foot-wide bike lane runs the length of the island on Pine Island Boulevard/Stringfellow Road. **Horses/riding:** Pine Needles Stables and plenty of rural areas are perfect for riding. Quail Lodge Stables provides boarding, riding lessons and miles of beautiful trails. **Hunting:** None permitted on this island; much of the land is part of a protected wildlife preserve. The bald eagle nests here. **Movie theaters:** None. **Art museums:** Pine Island Art Association. **History museums:** Museum of the Islands. **Theaters:** Matlacha Community Association Building is where the Pine Island Players perform. **Library:** Pine Island Public. **Attractions:** Most people come for the quiet and for nature preserves such as Cayo Costa Island and Preserve on Cabbage Key, accessible from Pine Island by boat. **Necessities:** A post office, banks, pharmacy, service stations, hardware store, barber and beautician, restaurants, general store, grocery store and one supermarket.

Smart Shopper Tip: There are 44 merchants and professional offices in Pine Island Center, but not a department store among them. Plan regular trips to Cape Coral or North Fort Myers.

WHO LIVES HERE
Population: 8,500 year-round residents and about 16,000 during the winter. **Age 65+ =** 25.7% in Lee County. **Median household income:** $29,174 (Lee County). **Per capita income:** $23,664 (Lee County).

NUMBERS TO KNOW
Chamber of commerce: (941) 283-0888. **Voter registration:** In Cape Coral, (941) 458-7020. **Vehicle registration, tags & title:** In Cape Coral, (941) 458-7000. **Driver's license:** In Cape Coral, (941) 574-1991.

WHAT TO READ
Pine Island Eagle, weekly newspaper, (941) 283-2022. **Fort Myers News-Press**, daily newspaper, (941) 335-0233.

GETTING AROUND
Bus: No public intra-island transportation. **Taxi:** Pine Island Taxi, (941) 283-7777. **Tours:** Tropic Star Cruises to Cabbage Key, (941) 283-0015. Sunburst Tropical Fruit Co. gives tours of Florida's oldest mango groves, (941) 283-1200. **Airport:** Southwest Florida International is 30 miles away. **Traffic:** It's a breeze, since there is little to attract tourists and no through-traffic.

JOBS
County unemployment rate: 3.3%. **Florida Jobs and Benefits:** In Cape Coral, (941) 462-5350. **Job Line:** (941) 574-0535.

UTILITIES
Electricity: Lee County Electric Co-op, (941) 549-1131. **Gas:** None. **Water & sewer:** Pine Island Water Association, (941) 283-1071. **Telephone:** Sprint-United, (941) 335-3111. **Cable TV:** Continental Cablevision, (941) 432-9277.

PLACES OF WORSHIP
One Catholic, one metaphysical and eight Protestant churches.

THE ENVIRONMENT
Water quality throughout the Charlotte Harbor basin has been rated as generally good. Pine Island Sound has the best water quality. It is designated as an Outstanding Florida Water (OFW). Other OFWs in the area are Matlacha Pass State Aquatic Preserve, Gasparilla Sound/Charlotte Harbor State Aquatic Preserve and Cape Haze State Aquatic Preserve.

EVENTS AND FESTIVALS
Art Show and Sale - February. **Spring Festival** - March. **Mangomania** - July.

WHERE TO EAT
The Dock, 9706 Stringfellow Road, seafood and prime rib, moderate, (941) 283-0005. **Matlacha Oyster House**, 3930 Pine Island Road, seafood, moderate, (941) 283-2544.

WHERE TO STAY
Cabbage Key Inn, (941) 283-2278. **Beachhouse Motel**, (800) 348-6306.

ISSUES
The chamber's description of Pine Island as "our tropical jewel in the sun" is an affectionate misnomer. It is a precious treasure, but still in a raw, unpolished state. Residents hope it will stay this way, but worry. Will the developers permit Pine Island to retain its small-town, rural environment? Or will big-money interests turn it into another Coney Island? Today, the preservationists seem to be winning the battle, aided by historians, archaeologists and conservationists.

Pompano Beach

In some respects, Pompano Beach fits the bill as a traditional coastal Florida resort and retirement town. With nice beaches, it serves as a sun and fun playground for snowbirds escaping dark, damp winter weather. It has many types of housing to suit just about all tastes: high-rise condos and apartments on the ocean, canal-front villas, single-family homes and planned adult communities. There's an outstanding network of medical facilities and doctors. There's golf, tennis and water sports to keep outdoors enthusiasts busy. And while Pompano Beach lacks the arts and entertainment of a major city, both Fort Lauderdale and Boca Raton are close enough to provide broader cultural exposure.

But, there are some troubling aspects to retirement life in Pompano Beach — congestion, taxes and growth. Major traffic arteries already are afflicted with the same congestion found in other south Florida cities, and experts predict that Pompano's boom won't abate anytime soon. Pompano Beach is hemmed in on the west by Florida's Turnpike and the municipalities of Coconut Creek, Margate and Coral Springs. The area just within that border is reserved for industrial development, leaving no room within the city to expand its residential boundaries. Citizens hoping to escape congestion by moving west will find themselves in another city, which may not be a bad idea since Pompano Beach has one of the highest property tax rates in Broward County.

The city is pro-business and that's good — to a point. The chamber's literature has all the catch phrases that should warn retirees of this penchant for commerce first, residents later, claiming Pompano Beach is "south Florida's newest business capital."

With few cultural activities, severe traffic congestion and unabashed catering to business and industry, the leaders of Pompano Beach have neglected those things that make a good hometown. The retired couple with an eye for aesthetics and a concern about inflationary pricing may pass right through Pompano Beach on their way to a better, more appealing spot.

WEATHER

	Winter	Spring	Summer	Fall
Normal daily high/low	77/59	86/69	91/74	82/65
Normal precipitation	8 in.	18 in.	20 in.	13 in.

Disaster watch: Southeast Florida has been hit by nine major hurricanes since 1900.

TAXES
Sales tax: 6%. **Property tax:** $26.95 per $1,000 valuation. Sample taxes include a $25,000 homestead exemption.

Home value	Tax
$100,000	$2,021
$150,000	$3,369
$250,000	$6,064

REAL ESTATE
Median home value: $109,359 (Broward County). **Median rent:** $809/month (Broward County). **Communities popular with retirees:** No particular area. **Licensed continuing-care retirement communities:** John Knox Village has 692 independent living units and 107 sheltered nursing beds and 70 community beds (954) 783-4045. The Court at Palm-Aire has 231 independent living units and 60 community nursing beds, (954) 975-8900. Adult congregate living facilities include Seasons Retirement Center, (954) 943-1155, and Abbe Manor, (954) 942-3388.

CRIME & SAFETY
Crimes per 1,000 population: 128. **Non-emergency police:** (954) 786-4200. **Non-emergency fire department:** (954) 786-4510. **Police, fire, ambulance emergencies:** 911.

HOMELESS & BLIGHT
The Pompano Beach Community Redevelopment Agency was formed to rehabilitate or redevelop 22 blighted areas. The CRA is addressing these areas on a priority basis, working to relocate people in substandard housing to new homes. We saw no evidence of homeless persons.

According to the U.S. Census, there were 642 homeless persons counted on the streets and 381 in shelters in Broward County, population 1.25 million.

HEALTH CARE
Hospitals: Columbia Pompano Beach Medical Center, 273 beds, full service, (954) 782-2000. **North Broward Medical Center**, 419 beds, full service, (954) 786-6400. **Imperial Point Medical Center**, 204 beds, full service, (954) 776-8500.
Physicians: 1,000+ (North Broward). **Specialties:** 37.

GETTING SMART
Broward Community College, north campus, (954) 973-2240. **Offerings:** Two-year degree programs in English, math, foreign languages, science, business, computer science, humanities and other fields. **Florida Atlantic University**, (561) 297-3000, 10 miles north in Boca Raton, offers the Lifelong Learning Society, (561) 297-3171. **Offerings:** The University has nine colleges with programs in more than 61 four-year degree fields, as well as advanced degrees. Lifelong Learning Society members can enroll in regular course offerings or special LIFEcourse programs for degree credit, non-credit or audit.

JUST FOR SENIORS
Area Agency on Aging, (954) 714-3456. **RSVP**, (954) 563-8991. **Senior Connection**, information and referrals, (954) 714-3464. **Humana Seniors Association** in Pembroke, (954) 963-8030.

GETTING INVOLVED
Seniors Foundation of Northwest Broward, (954) 977-9505. **Volunteer Broward**, (954) 522-6761.

RECREATION, ENTERTAINMENT & AMENITIES
Public golf: Crystal Lake Country Club, 18 holes, and Pompano Beach Golf Course, two 18-hole courses. **Private golf:** Palm

Aire Country Club, five par-72 courses; Tam O'Shanter, 18 holes/par 71; and Wynmoor Village, 18 holes/par 60. **Public tennis courts:** Pompano Beach Tennis Center has 16 lighted clay courts. Crystal Lake Tennis Club has three lighted clay courts. Sea Garden Tennis Club has four hard and three clay courts, lighted. World of Palm-Aire Tennis has 37 hard courts. **Private tennis courts:** Numerous private courts, including those at Crystal Lake Tennis Club, Hillsboro Club and Silver Thatch Country Club. **Parks:** Loxahatchee Recreation Area is 14 miles west and offers fishing, airboats, hiking and picnicking in 200,000 acres of the Everglades. Closer in are North Broward Park, Quiet Waters Park and Tradewinds Park. **Public swimming pools:** Several. **Water sports:** Scuba diving, snorkeling, boating, sailing, water-skiing, windsurfing and fishing. Known as the swordfish capital of the world. **River/gulf/ocean:** Three miles of beach, plus miles of water access along canals and the Intracoastal Waterway. Many yacht clubs, marinas, piers, wharves and landings are open to the public. Pompano Canal and Cypress Creek provide access to the Intracoastal. **Running/ walking/biking:** Many parks feature trails and camping facilities. Notable are Tradewinds Park and Fern Forest Nature Center. **Horses/riding:** Tradewinds Park has horse rentals and trails. Pompano Park has harness racing every day except Sunday, October through April. Quarter horse races run May through August. **Hunting:** None. Information about fishing licenses, (561) 391-6409. **Movie theaters:** At last count, 14 screens at three theaters. **Art museums:** None. **History museums:** Pompano Beach Historical Museum at Founders Park. **Theaters:** Pompano Beach Amphitheater, Community Theater, Pompano Players Theater. **Library:** Main Public Library and two branches. **Attractions:** Goodyear Blimp Base, free tours, (954) 946-8300; Hillsboro Inlet Light Station; Ski Rixen Waterski Cableway, where skiers are pulled by cables, rather than behind boats. **Necessities:** All of the necessities and conveniences are readily accessible in Pompano Beach.

Smart Shopper Tip: The shopping is good here. Pompano Beach has everything from modern malls to sophisticated boutiques and specialty shops. Merchandise near the beach is priced for tourists; better buys are often just a few miles inland.

WHO LIVES HERE
Population: 74,245 year-round residents, an increase of 1,834 since 1990. **Age 65+** = 19.3% in Broward County. **Median household income:** $31,289 (Broward County). **Per capita income:** $26,192 (Broward County).

NUMBERS TO KNOW
Chamber of commerce: (954) 941-2940. **Voter registration:** (954) 831-1225. **Vehicle registration, tags & title:** (954) 765-5050. **Driver's license:** (954) 327-6333.

WHAT TO READ
Sun-Sentinel, daily newspaper, (954) 356-4000. **Miami Herald,** Broward edition, daily newspaper, (954) 462-3000. **The Pompano Ledger,** weekly newspaper, (954) 946-7277.

GETTING AROUND
Bus: Broward County Mass Transit, (954) 357-8400. **Taxi:** Yellow Cab, (954) 565-5400. **Tours:** Water Taxi, from Pompano Beach to Deerfield Beach, (954) 467-6677. **Airport:** Fort Lauderdale International is 10 miles away. Service to the airport by taxi, Shared Ride Limo Service or bus. **Traffic:** Can be heavy; major traffic arteries get backed up.

JOBS
County unemployment rate: 5.0%. **Florida Jobs and Benefits:** (954) 969-3541.

UTILITIES
Electricity: Florida Power & Light, (954) 797-5000. **Gas:** Peoples Gas, (954) 763-8900. **Water & sewer:** City of Pompano Beach or Broward Utilities, depending on residence location, (954) 786-4637. **Telephone:** Bell South, (800) 789-9025 in Florida, or (800) 753-0710 out-of-state. **Cable TV:** Media One, (954) 946-7011.

PLACES OF WORSHIP
Seven Catholic and 57 Protestant churches, plus one Jewish synagogue and one Islamic Center.

THE ENVIRONMENT
Like other urban areas in southeast Florida, surface water quality in canals and marinas has been rated fair to poor. This entire southeastern area will undergo gradual but vast changes to restore a more natural balance to the Everglades National Park and Water Conservation Area.

There are seven EPA-listed Superfund sites in Broward County, two in the Pompano Beach industrial area. Wilson Concepts of Florida is a two-acre site, and Chemform is a four-acre site.

EVENTS AND FESTIVALS
Pompano Beach Seafood Festival - April. **Fine Food and Wine Festival and Auction** - September. **Pompano Beach Holiday Boat Parade** - December.

WHERE TO EAT
Cafe Maxx, 2601 E. Atlantic Blvd., creative cuisine, known for fresh ingredients and open cooking area, expensive, (954) 782-0606. **Frank's,** 3428 E. Atlantic Blvd., Italian, moderate, (954) 785-1480. **Cafe Arugula,** 3150 N. Federal Hwy., snapper, crab cakes, venison, moderate to expensive, (954) 785-7732.

WHERE TO STAY
Best Western Beachcomber, (954) 941-7830. **Holiday Inn,** (954) 941-7300. **Palm-Aire Resort Spa,** (954) 972-3300.

ISSUES
We spoke with several couples who had retired to Pompano Beach. They had no major axes to grind, although one couple said they didn't go out at night for fear of being mugged, and another thought the traffic was terrible at times. But all enjoyed life in Pompano Beach, spending time visiting with friends, eating out, playing bridge and participating in community activities. Pompano Beach is lacking in the social amenities of bigger cities like Fort Lauderdale and Boca Raton, but one retiree notes, "The people are the nicest on the east coast."

Port Charlotte

This unincorporated, large non-city is strung out along U.S.
Highway 41 — the boon and curse of all west coast Florida
communities. It is home to more than 60,000 people. Yet Port
Charlotte has no municipal bureaucracy, police department or other
societal regulators layered over its county government to drive up
tax rates and duplicate services. Somehow its residents seem to fare
as well as taxpayers in cities where the property tax rates are 30
percent to 60 percent higher. The unincorporated status is just fine
with retirees.

Port Charlotte lacks the diverse cultural infrastructure found in
some cities. But a short drive across the Peace River into Punta
Gorda yields the offerings of The Museum of Charlotte County, the
Visual Arts Center and Charlotte County Memorial Auditorium and
Civic Center. Port Charlotte has the Port Charlotte Cultural Center,
which is the focal point for educational, cultural, recreational and
social activities for a large segment of the older retiree population.
It also attracts many younger retirees who volunteer to teach,
counsel, organize and transport many of the older members.

Probably the most important thing Port Charlotte has going for it
is 38 miles of waterfront on Charlotte Harbor and the Myakka and
Peace rivers. Man-made waterways crisscross 165 miles of the area.
Two out of three residents say they moved to Port Charlotte for the
water. It's the principal attraction for boaters, fishermen and other
water sports enthusiasts, and the freshwater and saltwater canals,
creeks, rivers and bays make nice settings for waterfront housing.

The U.S. Census Bureau says Charlotte County is among the
fastest growing counties in the country. When asked what they like
least about Port Charlotte, retirees unanimously respond with "fast
growth and traffic." One couple we spoke with said these factors
may eventually cause them to seek a quieter place.

WEATHER

	Winter	Spring	Summer	Fall
Normal daily high/low	77/54	88/66	92/73	81/59
Normal precipitation	7 in.	13 in.	22 in.	6 in.

Disaster watch: Southwest Florida has been hit by five major
hurricanes since 1900.

TAXES

Sales tax: 6%. **Property tax:** $16.53 per $1,000 valuation. Sample
tax calculations include a $25,000 homestead exemption.

Home value	Tax
$100,000	$1,240
$150,000	$2,066
$250,000	$3,719

REAL ESTATE

Median home value: $85,413 (Charlotte County). **Median**

rent: $329/month (Charlotte County). **Communities popular
with retirees:** Port Charlotte Village is an adult mobile home
park, with resales only, (941) 625-4105. Waterfront homes
generally start in the low $100s. Port Charlotte Country Club
offers homes priced from the low $120s. **Licensed continuing-
care retirement communities:** South Port Square has 440
independent living units, 140 rental units and 120 community
beds, (941) 625-1100.

CRIME & SAFETY

The Charlotte County Sheriff's Department serves Port Charlotte
with a substation and assigns deputies to a regular patrol. **Crimes
per 1,000 population:** 31 (Charlotte County sheriff's jurisdiction).
Non-emergency police: (941) 639-2101. **Non-emergency fire
department:** (941) 743-1367. **Police, fire, ambulance emergencies:** 911.

HOMELESS & BLIGHT

If your definition of blighted includes the presence of an uninter-
rupted strip of commercial activity, running the entire length of the
community, then this is blighted. If this is not your idea of blighted,
then consider this preplanned, unincorporated portion of Charlotte
County to be blessed with an abundance of purveyors of goods and
services. We saw no homeless persons.

The U.S. Census reported eight homeless persons visible in street
locations of Charlotte County, population 110,975.

HEALTH CARE

Hospitals: Bon Secours-St. Joseph Hospital, 212 beds, 24-hour
emergency, full service, (941) 625-4122. **Columbia Fawcett Memorial Hospital**, 254 beds, acute care, 24-hour emergency, full
service, (941) 629-1181. **Wellness Health & Fitness Center**, (941)
637-2450.
Physicians: 218. **Specialties:** 45.

GETTING SMART

Adult and Community Education Center, (941) 625-6155. **Offerings:** A variety of courses — more than 140 — includes everything from GED equivalency to recreational pursuits.

JUST FOR SENIORS

Port Charlotte Cultural Center, (941) 625-4175. **Senior Services**, (941) 637-2288.

GETTING INVOLVED

Arts & Humanities Council, (941) 764-8100. **Meals on Wheels**,
(941) 625-4343. **SCORE**, (941) 575-1818. **AARP** and **Community Greetings** also are active. Call the chamber of commerce for a
contact name and phone number.

RECREATION, ENTERTAINMENT & AMENITIES

Semiprivate golf: Eagle Pointe Golf Club, 18 holes/par 62;

Maple Leaf Country Club, 18 holes/par 60; Port Charlotte Golf and Tennis Club, 18 holes/par 72; Riverwood Golf Club, 18 holes/par 72; and Victoria Estates, nine holes/par 30. **Public tennis courts:** Harbor Heights Park, McGuire Park, Midway Courts and Port Charlotte Beach Complex. **Private tennis courts:** Port Charlotte Tennis Club. **Parks:** There are 40 parks in the county, including Harbor Heights Park and the Port Charlotte Beach Complex. **Public swimming pools:** Harbor Heights Park, Port Charlotte Beach Complex and West Charlotte Community Pool. **Water sports:** Boating, canoeing, fishing, sailing and water-skiing. **River/gulf/ocean:** Alligator Bay, Charlotte Harbor, Myakka River and Peace River. **Running/walking/biking:** Kiwanis Park has a jogging/fitness trail. Port Charlotte Beach Complex and Salyers Park have nature trails. **Horses/riding:** Horsemen's Association, Charlotte County, (941) 639-0233. **Hunting:** The Babcock-Webb Wildlife Management Area is a hunters' park with 65,373 acres famous for dove, quail, deer and wild hogs, (941) 637-2150. **Movie theaters:** 11 screens. **Art museums:** None. **History museums:** None. **Theaters:** Port Charlotte Cultural Center. **Library:** Port Charlotte Public. **Attractions:** Babcock-Webb Wildlife Management Area covers one-seventh of the county. Charlotte County Stadium is spring training base for the Texas Rangers. Ponce de Leon Park is a historical landmark. **Necessities:** All here.

Smart Shopper Tip: The Town Center Mall should fill the bill with its five anchors and 100 stores.

WHO LIVES HERE
Population: 60,000-plus year-round residents. **Age 65+ =** 34.3% in Charlotte County. **Median household income:** $26,094 (Charlotte County). **Per capita income:** $20,539 (Charlotte County).

NUMBERS TO KNOW
Chamber of commerce: (941) 627-2222. **Voter registration:** (941) 637-2232. **Vehicle registration, tags & title:** (941) 743-1337. **Driver's license:** (941) 255-7408.

WHAT TO READ
Charlotte Sun Herald-News, daily newspaper, (941) 629-7695. **Charlotte AM**, daily newspaper, (941) 627-7537. **Sarasota Herald-Tribune**, daily newspaper, (941) 365-6060.

GETTING AROUND
Bus: No public intra-city transportation. Charlotte County commissioners are discussing a countywide transit system. **Taxi:** Express Cab, (941) 624-4311. **Tours:** None. **Airport:** Southwest Florida International or Sarasota/Bradenton International. **Traffic:** Heavily traveled U.S. 41 is the only north-south thoroughfare. Fortunately, residents can avoid it in most of their local travels.

JOBS
County unemployment rate: 3.4%. **Florida Jobs and Benefits:** (941) 575-5770.

UTILITIES
Electricity: Florida Power & Light, (941) 639-1106. **Gas:** None. **Water & sewer:** County Water System, (941) 625-4164. **Telephone:** Sprint, (941) 637-5222. **Cable TV:** ComCast Cable, (941) 625-6000.

PLACES OF WORSHIP
Two Catholic and 38 Protestant churches, plus one Jewish synagogue.

THE ENVIRONMENT
Water quality throughout the Charlotte Harbor basin has been rated as generally good. Locally, Pine Island Sound has the best water quality. It is designated as an Outstanding Florida Water (OFW). Other OFWs in the area are Matlacha Pass State Aquatic Preserve, Gasparilla Sound/Charlotte Harbor State Aquatic Preserve and Cape Haze State Aquatic Preserve. The Charlotte/Placida Harbor has been designated for improvement and management. Charlotte Harbor's water quality varies. Above the Peace River and Myakka River it is generally good. In other locations it shows generally fair quality. There have been periodic bans on shellfishing. The north prong of Alligator Creek has good water quality, but the south prong has fair to poor quality. Historically, the most serious water quality problem in the basin has been the Sanibel River located on Sanibel Island at the southern end of the Charlotte Harbor basin.

EVENTS AND FESTIVALS
Peace River Seafood Fest and Boat Show - February. **Charlotte County Senior Olympics** - February. **Texas Rangers Spring Training Games** - March. **Sunshine State Bluegrass Festival** - March. **Waterfront Food-Arts-Jazz Festival** - October.

WHERE TO EAT
Johnny's Diner, 1951 Tamiami Trail, seafood, steaks and ribs, inexpensive, (941) 255-0994. **King's Gate Restaurant**, 24000 Rampart Blvd., steaks, seafood, chicken, moderate to expensive, (941) 629-0099.

WHERE TO STAY
Days Inn, (941) 627-8900. **Hampton Inn**, (941) 627-5600. **Quality Inn**, (941) 625-4181.

ISSUES
An area so dependent upon water as its primary attraction naturally is concerned about environmental protection of the Charlotte Harbor watershed. At issue is the impact of phosphate mining and oil pipeline construction. Traffic congestion is another problem — road widening to alleviate this is underway.

Port St. Lucie

HE SAID: ★ ★ ★ ★
*I like the orderliness, openness and common-sense develop-
ment of the city. It's short on cultural amenities, but nearby
towns fill in the gaps.*

SHE SAID: ★ ★ ★ ★
*I was almost immediately attracted to Port St. Lucie. Golf
courses, tennis courts, marinas and housing of all price
categories will fit many lifestyles. What made me take notice
was the absence of high-rise buildings and tall signs. Stop
here when looking for a place to retire.*

Several characteristics distinguish Port St. Lucie from other
coastal Florida towns. For one thing, it has no beach front. But that
is not to say that residents lack access to Atlantic beaches. They just
travel to neighboring Fort Pierce and Jensen Beach.

Port St. Lucie isn't a tourist stop; you won't find it listed in most
of the well-known vacation guides. With no beach front and limited
accommodations, Port St. Lucie is spared the snowbirds and summer vacationers that crowd the highways, golf courses and restaurants of resort towns.

General Development Co. designed Port St. Lucie in 1961 as a
master-planned community, a plan that continues to work. With 77
square miles, it is the second-largest city in Florida. Rapid population growth has been sustained for the last decade, yet due to its size
and the nature of its development, the city is not crowded. There are
canals, lakes and golf courses as well as a myriad of retail facilities
that put recreation, entertainment, education and shopping at your
fingertips.

Port St. Lucie's growth follows the lines of the developer's
initial dispersed-living concept. The city was not built in the
typical urban-suburban layout. It's made up of several residential neighborhoods or villages, each with its own shopping
centers, schools and parks blended into the community for
convenience and efficiency.

WEATHER

	Winter	Spring	Summer	Fall
Normal daily high/low	75/54	85/67	90/73	80/61
Normal precipitation	8 in.	12 in.	19 in.	11 in.

Disaster watch: Southeast Florida has been hit by nine major
hurricanes since 1900.

TAXES
Sales tax: 6%. **Property tax:** $25.28 per $1,000 valuation. Sample
tax calculations include a $25,000 homestead exemption.

Home value	Tax
$100,000	$1,896
$150,000	$3,160
$250,000	$5,688

REAL ESTATE
Median home value: $92,437 (St. Lucie County). **Median rent:**
$549/month (St. Lucie County). **Communities popular with retir-
ees:** Savanna Club has manufactured homes from the high $40s to
the $110s, (561) 879-3883 or (800) 967-3883. The Reserve offers
patio homes from the upper $130s to $160s, (561) 465-2000. Bonnie
East of St. Lucie West Realty, (800) 785-8243, provided information on the communities of St. Lucie West: Country Club Estates,

single-family homes from the $130s; Heatherwood, single-family
homes from the mid-$150s to mid-$200s; The Lakes at St. Lucie
West, patio homes from the upper $80s to mid-$120s; Westbrook
Isles, lake-front condominiums from the mid-$50s to mid-$90s;
Kings Isle, patio and single-family homes from the high $80s; and
Sun Terrace, patio homes from the $70s to $90s. **Licensed continu-
ing-care retirement communities:** None.

CRIME & SAFETY
Crimes per 1,000 population: 37. **Non-emergency police:** (561)
871-5000. **Non-emergency fire department:** (561) 462-2300.
Police, fire, ambulance emergencies: 911.

HOMELESS & BLIGHT
There are no blighted areas. The city was just created in 1961 and
looks fresh and new. Manicured lawns, clean streets, spacious
parks, outstanding residential developments — it's quiet and unhurried here.

According to the U.S. Census, St. Lucie County, population
150,171, had 309 homeless persons in shelters and 27 homeless
persons visible on the streets.

HEALTH CARE
Hospitals: Columbia Medical Center, 150 beds, full service,
(561) 335-4000. **Savannas Hospital,** 70 beds, psychiatry, (561)
335-0400. Physician referral service, (561) 466-6574. **Martin
Memorial Surgi-Center,** outpatient surgery, (561) 785-5577.
Physicians: 158. **Specialties:** 36.

GETTING SMART
Indian River Community College, (561) 879-4199. **Offerings:**
About 85 two-year degree programs, vocational certificate programs and continuing-education courses. **Barry University,** (561)
871-8000. **Offerings:** A new program for seniors is in development.
Call (800) 756-6000 for information. Other offerings include graduate and undergraduate degree programs and continuing-education
courses. **Florida Atlantic University,** (561) 785-9970. **Offerings:**
Undergraduate and graduate degrees.

JUST FOR SENIORS
Locals boast that the Port St. Lucie **AARP** chapter is one of the
biggest on the East Coast. They have more than 500 active
members, (561) 878-7465. **Better Living for Seniors Help Line**
provides transportation, (561) 465-5593. **Council on Aging,** (561)
465-5220. **Senior Social,** (561) 878-2277, meets Wednesdays 1-3
p.m. at Port St. Lucie Recreation Center. There is talk of building a
senior center.

GETTING INVOLVED
Port St. Lucie has the usual assortment of civic and social service
organizations. The nearest chapters of SCORE and RSVP are in Fort
Pierce. **Port St. Lucie Welcome Committee,** (561) 336-4795.

RECREATION, ENTERTAINMENT & AMENITIES
Public golf: Club Med, 36 holes; PGA golf Club, 18 holes; and

Savanna Club, 18 holes. **Private golf:** Country Club of St. Lucie West, 18 holes; Legacy Golf & Tennis Club, 18 holes; and Spanish Lakes Country Club, nine holes. **Public tennis courts:** Sportsman's Park and Lyngate Park. **Private tennis courts:** The Reserve. **Parks:** Numerous small parks dot the city, including Sportsman Park, Lyngate Park, Veterans Memorial Park and nine others with walking trails, ball fields and boat ramps. **Public swimming pools:** Several are operated by the Parks & Recreation Department, (561) 871-2277. **Water sports:** Sailing, boating, skiing, scuba diving, windsurfing. **River/gulf/ocean:** Easy access to the beach. Some frontage on the Indian River (Intracoastal Waterway). The north fork of St. Lucie River bisects the city. Savannas State Preserve provides freshwater recreation and fishing. **Running/walking/biking:** Jaycee Park has a walking/fitness trail; Indian River Lagoon Sport Cycling Group has weekend road and mountain bike rides through St. Lucie and Martin counties, (561) 334-4343. **Horses/riding:** No stables or academies. **Hunting:** Information on hunting and freshwater fishing, (561) 778-5094; saltwater fishing, (561) 624-6935. **Movie theaters:** Twelve screens at two theaters. **Art museums:** None. **History museums:** St. Lucie County Historical Museum in Fort Pierce. **Theaters:** St. Lucie Community Theatre, Treasure Coast Concert Association. **Library:** St. Lucie County branch. **Attractions:** Thomas J. White Stadium, better known as the Mets Stadium, is a smaller-scale replica of New York's Shea Stadium. It is the spring training site of the Mets. **Necessities:** The city's master-plan layout keeps all necessities conveniently placed near residential neighborhoods.

Smart Shopper Tip: Treasure Coast Square, the region's major shopping mall, is located on U.S. Highway 1 between Port St. Lucie and Stuart. It's anchored by Dillard's, Burdine's, Sears, J.C. Penney and Mervyns with 120 other stores. Look to U.S. 1, running north-south through Port St. Lucie, or Port St. Lucie Boulevard, running east-west through town, as the principal commercial areas, with no less than 20 plazas, shopping centers and malls.

WHO LIVES HERE
Population: 77,985 year-round residents, an increase of 22,224 since 1990. **Age 65+ =** 22.7% in St. Lucie County. **Median household income:** $26,387 (St. Lucie County). **Per capita income:** $17,747 (St. Lucie County).

NUMBERS TO KNOW
Chamber of commerce: (561) 595-9999. **Voter registration:** (561) 871-5410. **Vehicle registration, tags & title:** (561) 337-5600. **Driver's license:** (561) 398-1304.

WHAT TO READ
Port St. Lucie News, daily newspaper, (561) 221-4160. **Port St. Lucie Tribune,** daily newspaper, (561) 335-3804.

GETTING AROUND
Bus: No public intra-city transportation. **Taxi:** St. Lucie Checker, (561) 878-1234. **Tours:** None. **Airport:** Palm Beach International, 30 miles away, is the nearest served by major air carriers. St. Lucie International in Fort Pierce has commuter and private aircraft service. **Traffic:** Very light.

JOBS
County unemployment rate: 12.6%. **Florida Jobs and Benefits:** (561) 335-0603.

UTILITIES
Electricity: Florida Power & Light, (561) 287-5400. **Gas:** City Gas, (561) 871-5330. **Water & sewer:** St. Lucie County Utilities, (561) 871-5330. **Telephone:** Bell South, (800) 789-9025 in Florida, or (800) 753-0710 out-of-state. **Cable TV:** Adelphia, (561) 692-9010.

PLACES OF WORSHIP
One Catholic and 28 Protestant churches, plus one Jewish synagogue.

THE ENVIRONMENT
In 1993 the EPA reported finding lead measuring 41 parts per billion (ppb) in the water of St. Lucie County Utilities, which serves a population of approximately 40,750. The EPA's action level is 15 ppb.

A 1992 air quality report indicated that Port St. Lucie did not meet the standard for particulate matter in the air on at least one test date.

Fivemile and Tenmile creeks have been found to contain high levels of pesticides from runoff from citrus groves. The main stem of the St. Lucie River still receives runoff from construction sites and urban development, resulting in poor surface water quality ratings.

The Hutchinson Island Nuclear Power Plant is less than 10 miles from central Port St. Lucie.

EVENTS AND FESTIVALS
Rainbow Festival - January. **New York Mets Spring Training** - March/April. **Freedom Fest** - July 4.

WHERE TO EAT
Ole Zapatas, 8573 S. Federal Highway, Mexican, moderate, (561) 340-7288. **Smokey's,** 1002 S.E. Port St. Lucie Blvd., barbeque, inexpensive to moderate, (561) 337-6365. **Ruffino's,** 1145 S.E. Port St. Lucie Blvd., Italian, moderate to expensive, (561) 335-2988.

WHERE TO STAY
Best Western, (561) 878-7600. **Club Med-Sandpiper,** (561) 335-4400. **Holiday Inn,** (561) 337-2200.

ISSUES
We learned of no significant long-term issues facing the residents of Port St. Lucie. Upcoming New York Mets spring training seemed to be the primary topic of conversation at the time of our last visit.

Punta Gorda

HE SAID: ★ ★ ★ ★
Despite the fact that I am not a boater, I could live contentedly in Punta Gorda Isles, watching sunsets over Charlotte Harbor, playing a daily round at St. Andrews South Golf Club, lunching at Fishermen's Village and perhaps catching my dinner off a fishing pier somewhere along west Retta Esplanade or Jamaica Way.

SHE SAID: ★ ★ ★ ★
This is a pretty, clean and historic town located at the mouth of the Peace River on Charlotte Harbor. Look at the beautiful residential area on Mangrove Point. I would.

Going south over the Charlotte Harbor Bridge between Port Charlotte and Punta Gorda brings to mind the title of Ernest Hemingway's novel "Across the River and Into the Trees." Narrow, tree-lined streets and Key West-style, tin-roofed houses lend an Old Florida aura to a town undertaking significant revitalization.

It recently acquired status as a State Historic District and launched a Streetscape renovation program. Old-style street lamps, brick lanes, benches and other revered relics of a bygone age coupled with extensive planting of shade trees and careful restoration of old homes and commercial buildings are adding layers of charm and historic authenticity to a town steeped in tradition.

Going a step further, a proposed ordinance says that "the exterior of every structure... shall be maintained free from mold, dirt, water stains, debris or scaling paint." It is clear that these city officials are serious about putting an exceptionally fine face on this increasingly popular retirement haven.

A slow drive west on Marion Avenue provides a good look at some of the best of Punta Gorda. You will first pass through a historic residential neighborhood. Continue on to the quaint, popular Fishermen's Village. Be sure to stop for lunch at one of its over-the-water restaurants or just to stroll among the shops with other retirees enjoying the sea breeze and seaside atmosphere.

Farther down Marion Avenue you'll see the Charlotte County Visual Arts Center. The large, white stucco, Spanish tile-roofed structure makes quite an impression. You may be tempted to stop and view the offerings or at least make plans to return. Finally, continue on to Punta Gorda Isles, where canal-front homes are inhabited by hundreds of retirees. Both this tour and Marion Avenue end at Mangrove Point, where you can pause to consider your own move to Punta Gorda.

WEATHER

	Winter	Spring	Summer	Fall
Normal daily high/low	77/54	88/66	92/73	81/60
Normal precipitation	7 in.	13 in.	22 in.	6 in.

Disaster watch: Southwest Florida has been hit by five major hurricanes since 1900.

TAXES
Sales tax: 6%. **Property tax:** $18.60 per $1,000 valuation. Sample tax calculations include a $25,000 homestead exemption.

Home value	Tax
$100,000	$1,395
$150,000	$2,325
$250,000	$4,185

REAL ESTATE
Median home value: $91,147 (Charlotte County). **Median rent:** $329/month (Charlotte County). **Communities popular with retirees:** Punta Gorda Isles features canal homes, townhomes and condominiums priced from the mid-$150s to $500s and up, (800) 445-6560 or (941) 639-8500. Rivers Edge is an adult waterfront community with manufactured homes priced from the mid-$40s, (800) 322-5960 or (941) 637-5757. Seminole Lakes is a golf course community with single-family homes priced from the high $90s, (800) 273-5253 or (941) 639-0400. **Licensed continuing-care retirement communities:** None.

CRIME & SAFETY
Crimes per 1,000 population: 35. **Non-emergency police:** (941) 639-4111. **Non-emergency fire department:** (941) 575-5529. **Police, fire, ambulance emergencies:** 911.

HOMELESS & BLIGHT
This is a clean, orderly town. There was no evidence of homeless persons during our stay. The U.S. Census reported eight homeless persons visible in street locations in Charlotte County, population 110,975.

HEALTH CARE
Hospitals: Charlotte Regional Medical Center, 208 beds, free health management program for those age 55 and over, 24-hour emergency, full service, (941) 639-3131. **Wellness Health and Fitness Center**, (941) 637-2450.
Physicians: 48+. **Specialties:** 22.

GETTING SMART
Edison Community College, (941) 637-5605. **Offerings:** Two-year associate's degrees in liberal arts, technical and professional subjects. Mini-semester courses are offered in some areas of study.

JUST FOR SENIORS
Charlotte County Senior Services, (941) 637-2288.

GETTING INVOLVED
Arts and Humanities Council coordinates, supports and promotes the arts, (941) 764-8100. **Peace River Wildlife Center** is organized, operated and supported by volunteers, (941) 637-3830. **United Way of Charlotte County**, (941) 627-3539.

RECREATION, ENTERTAINMENT & AMENITIES
Public golf: Burnt Store Marina Golf Course, 27 holes/par 108; Chipshot Golf Course, nine holes/par 27; Deep Creek Golf Club, 18 holes/par 70; Emu Lakes, nine holes/par 27;

Sunnybreeze Palms, 27 holes; and Seminole Lakes Country Club, semiprivate, 18 holes/par 54. **Private golf:** Punta Gorda Country Club, 18 holes/par 68, and St. Andrews South Golf Club, 18 holes/par 72. **Public tennis courts:** Bissett Park, Gilchrist Park and South County Park. **Private tennis courts:** Emerald Pointe Racquet Club and Rio Paz Tennis Club. **Parks:** 34 county parks. **Public swimming pools:** Carmalita Pool. **Water sports:** Boating, canoeing, fishing, sailing and water-skiing. **River/gulf/ocean:** Peace River and Charlotte Harbor. **Running/walking/biking:** Punta Gorda Athletic Complex and Charlotte Harbor Environmental Center provide opportunities. Ponce de Leon Park has a quarter-mile nature trail. **Horses/riding:** There are several ranches south and east of town. Interested riders can join the Horsemen's Association, (941) 639-4402. **Hunting:** Cecil M. Webb Wildlife Management Area is a hunters' park with 65,373 acres for dove, quail, deer and wild hogs. Licenses and information, (941) 637-2150. **Movie theaters:** None. **Art museums:** Visual Arts Center. **History museums:** None. **Theaters:** Charlotte County Memorial Auditorium and Civic Center. **Library:** Punta Gorda Public. **Attractions:** Charlotte Harbor Environmental Center is a 3,000-acre upland/wetland ecosystem with a natural history museum and educational study lab. The Museum of Charlotte County focuses on natural history. Also, Fishermen's Village and Peace River Wildlife Center. **Necessities:** All are available in the county.

Smart Shopper Tip: Fishermen's Village is for those who enjoy the pleasure of shopping or browsing. Port Charlotte's Town Center Mall and Promenades Mall are for buying.

WHO LIVES HERE
Population: 12,531 year-round residents, an increase of 1,894 since 1990. **Age 65+** = 34.3% in Charlotte County. **Median household income:** $26,094 (Charlotte County). **Per capita income:** $20,539 (Charlotte County).

NUMBERS TO KNOW
Chamber of commerce: (941) 639-2222. **Voter registration:** (941) 637-2232. **Vehicle registration, tags & title:** (941) 637-2141. **Driver's license:** In Port Charlotte, (941) 255-7408.

WHAT TO READ
Charlotte A.M., daily newspaper, (941) 629-2010. **Charlotte Sun Herald-News**, daily newspaper, (941) 629-2855. **Charlotte Newcomer's Guide**, (941) 639-2222.

GETTING AROUND
Bus: Charlotte County commissioners are discussing a countywide transit system; there is no public intra-city transportation. **Taxi:** Brothers Taxi, (941) 639-0957. **Tours:** King Fisher Cruise Lines, (941) 639-0969. **Airport:** Southwest Florida International. **Traffic:** Two east-west arteries easily carry local traffic through the city, while I-75, only two miles east of downtown, accommodates passers-by.

JOBS
County unemployment rate: 3.4%. **Florida Jobs and Benefits:** (941) 637-6981. **Job Line:** (941) 575-3367.

UTILITIES
Electricity: Florida Power & Light, (941) 639-1106. **Gas:** None. **Water & sewer:** Charlotte Harbor Water Association, (941) 625-2288. **Telephone:** Sprint, (941) 639-1111 or (800) 339-1881. **Cable TV:** ComCast Cable, (941) 625-6000, or Time-Warner Cable, (941) 639-1562, depending on location of residence.

PLACES OF WORSHIP
One Catholic and 35 Protestant churches.

THE ENVIRONMENT
Water quality throughout the Charlotte Harbor basin has been rated as generally good. Pine Island Sound has the best water quality rating. It is designated as an Outstanding Florida Water (OFW). Other OFWs in the area are Matlacha Pass State Aquatic Preserve, Gasparilla Sound/Charlotte Harbor State Aquatic Preserve and Cape Haze State Aquatic Preserve. The Charlotte/Placida Harbor has been designated for improvement and management. Charlotte Harbor's water quality varies. Above the Peace River and Myakka River it is generally good. In other locations it shows generally fair quality. There have been periodic bans on shellfishing. The north prong of Alligator Creek has good water quality, but the south prong has fair to poor quality. Historically, the most serious water quality problem in the basin was the Sanibel River located on Sanibel Island at the southern end of the Charlotte Harbor basin. No samples have been taken for assessment since the 1970s.

WHEN TO VISIT
Events: Southwest Florida Quilt Festival - February. **Charlotte County Senior Olympics** - Spring. **Punta Gorda Days Celebration** - April. **Salute to the Arts** - October. **Oktoberfest. Holiday Arts and Crafts Festival** - November. **Christmas Light Canal Tours** - December.

WHERE TO EAT
Mama Nunzia, 1975 Tamiami Trail, Italian, moderate, (941) 575-7575. **Salty's Harborside**, 3150 Matecumbe Key Road at Burnt Store Marina, seafood, moderate, (941) 639-4151. Or, try any of the Fishermen's Village restaurants.

WHERE TO STAY
Burnt Store Marina, (941) 639-4151. **Best Western,** (941) 639-1165. **The Villas at Fishermen's Village,** (941) 639-8721.

ISSUES
Rapid growth in Charlotte County is prompting some concern about the area becoming another Miami. City, county and industrial leaders should be exploring all possible preventive measures.

St. Augustine

HE SAID: ★ ★ ★

I liked visiting St. Augustine. We strolled the narrow, interesting streets past fascinating antique shops, historic houses and museums, took the sightseeing tours and walked the beaches. It appeals to me as a nice place to visit, but after a few days I was ready to leave and continue my search for the ultimate retirement home.

SHE SAID: ★ ★ ★

This beautiful, historic town is overpopulated and overrun by tourists. The beach area, which is not very attractive, is difficult to access. The outlying areas are prettier, but the limited shopping bothers me. Besides, the fountain of youth, a big attraction here, does not work. I would not retire here.

First and foremost, St. Augustine is a major tourist destination. Fact and fiction have merged to bring a million curiosity-seekers annually to its Spanish towers, cathedrals, red-roofed architecture and archaeological ruins. Its claim as the oldest city in the United States is disputed by Pensacola, and it is unquestionably fiction that Ponce de Leon discovered the fountain of youth here. Yet, these two historical footnotes are the principal drawing cards for visitors from around the globe.

History aside, St. Augustine has other unique features that bring visitors back to the area as retirees. Water lovers will find a large assortment of housing along its beaches, canals, rivers and bays. Anastasia Island has several beach communities, such as St. Augustine Shores, that offer attractive and affordable housing. A number of country clubs with golf and tennis facilities beckon. Avid golf fans already know that the PGA Tournament Players Championship is played on the Sawgrass course in nearby Ponte Vedra Beach.

Much of the social and cultural pomp and pageantry in the city is staged around historical happenings, such as Florida's official state play "Cross and Sword," a symphonic drama depicting the settlement of St. Augustine. It attracts tens of thousands of spectators each summer.

The city is well-served by educational institutions, health-care facilities and shopping centers, and it goes without saying that recreational resources abound. Most retirees cite its location — less than an hour's drive from Daytona Beach and Jacksonville — as an important factor in their decision to make St. Augustine their home.

A bit of advice from a retired couple who moved here nearly a decade ago seems appropriate to mention. Choose the site of your home with care, they say. Don't be misled by the permanent population figure of about 12,000 and think that you will be able to get around this small city with ease. You can't. It's important to select a home in close proximity to your church, shopping and the activities you enjoy.

Their comments sum up the real disadvantage: St. Augustine is a small city so often packed with tourists that residents can completely miss its charms and the reasons they chose to live here.

WEATHER

	Winter	Spring	Summer	Fall
Normal daily high/low	69/48	84/64	88/72	75/56
Normal precipitation	10 in.	11 in.	18 in.	9 in.

Disaster watch: Northeast Florida has not been hit by a major hurricane since 1900.

TAXES

Sales tax: 6%. **Property tax:** $19.62 per $1,000 valuation in St. Augustine Beach and $25.12 in St. Augustine. Sample taxes are calculated at the rate of $25.12 and include a $25,000 homestead exemption.

Home value	Tax
$100,000	$1,884
$150,000	$3,140
$250,000	$5,652

REAL ESTATE

Median home value: $94,315 (St. Johns County). **Median rent:** $720/month (St. Johns County). **Communities popular with retirees:** St. Johns is a new commercial, residential and recreational development on 6,300 acres off I-95. Turnberry at Saint Johns offers homesites from the $50s and single-family homes starting in the $180s, (904) 940-4444. Pinehurst Pointe at Saint Johns has lakefront homesites from the $70s, (904) 940-5000. St. Andrews Place at Saint Johns has maintenance-free single-family homes including homesites, from the mid-$220s, (904) 940-3000. The Residence at World Golf Village offers 1,900- to 3,000-square-foot luxury condominiums in the mid-$200s, (904) 940-5500. Marsh Creek Country Club has patio homes priced from the $160s to $190s, single-family homes priced from the $200s to more than $500,000 and lots from the mid-$40s to mid-$90s, (904) 471-4343. Moultrie Oaks offers manufactured homes from the high $20s to the mid-$60s, excluding the cost of the lot lease, (904) 797-7493. John Long with Century 21 Sea Crest Realty, (904) 797-4814, also suggests St. Augustine Shores, a planned development with condos from the high $40s to $100s and single-family homes from the high $40s to $120s, and Beachwalk, with single-family homes from the $110s to $150s. **Licensed continuing-care retirement communities:** Glenmoor at Saint Johns, (904) 940-4800 or (800) 471-2335.

CRIME & SAFETY

Crimes per 1,000 population: 119 (St. Augustine); 60 (St. Augustine Beach). **Non-emergency police:** (904) 825-1070. **Non-emergency fire department:** (904) 825-1098. **Police, fire, ambulance emergencies:** 911.

HOMELESS & BLIGHT

Areas visited by tourists are neat and tidy, but St. Augustine has some older urban residential neighborhoods on the fringe of the historic district that need rehabilitation. Under consideration is a project along the San Sebastian Riverfront, which would involve a new development akin to Mystic Seaport in Connecticut. Also under consideration by city officials are some rehabilitation grants to low income families in adjoining neighborhoods.

The U.S. Census lists the population of St. Johns County as 83,829, which includes 37 homeless persons visible in street locations.

HEALTH CARE

Hospitals: Flagler Hospital, 245 beds, full service, (904) 829-5155. **St. Augustine Psychiatric Center**, 50 beds, (904) 824-9800. **Physicians:** 100. **Specialties:** 34.

GETTING SMART

Flagler College, (904) 829-6481. **Offerings:** Four-year liberal arts college. Continuing-education department offers a variety of courses. **St. Johns River Community College**, (904) 808-7400. **Offerings:** Two-year degree programs in arts and sciences. Seniors may audit courses or attend for credit. **St. Augustine Technical Center**, (904)

824-4401. **Offerings:** Adult vocational, basic education and community education classes. Community interest classes include art, beginning Spanish and gourmet cooking.

JUST FOR SENIORS
Senior Citizens Transportation, (904) 824-2000. **St. Johns Senior Center and Council on Aging,** (904) 824-1646. There are **AARP** chapters in both St. Augustine and St. Augustine Beach.

GETTING INVOLVED
There are 13 social service organizations and seven fraternal organizations. **RSVP,** (904) 826-4993. **United Way of St. Johns County,** (904) 829-9721.

RECREATION, ENTERTAINMENT & AMENITIES
Public golf: Radisson Ponce de Leon Golf & Conference Resort, St. Augustine Shores Country Club and St. Johns County Golf Course. **Private golf:** Cimarrone Golf & Country Club and Marsh Creek Country Club. **Public tennis courts:** Three major public facilities with 28 lighted courts. **Private tennis courts:** Marsh Creek Country Club, St. Augustine Beach & Tennis Club and St. Augustine Ocean & Racquet Resort. **Parks:** There are no less than 17 county recreation areas in Greater St. Augustine. Also, Anastasia State Recreation Area, Faver Dykes State Park and Guana River State Park. **Public swimming pools:** Willie Galimore Community Center. **Water sports:** Sailing, water-skiing, windsurfing, scuba diving, boating, canoeing and bass fishing. **River/gulf/ocean:** Atlantic Ocean, Matanzas Bay and River, Salt Run, San Sebastian River, Intracoastal Waterway/Tolomato River and Anastasia Island are important components of the St. Augustine metro area. **Running/walking/biking:** Anastasia State Recreation Area and Guana River State Park have good nature trails. St. Johns County has 43 miles of beach for serious walkers and runners. **Horses/riding:** Two stables provide boarding, training and riding lessons. **Hunting:** Licenses required for hunting and fishing, (904) 823-2250. **Movie theaters:** 14 screens. **Art museums:** St. Augustine Art Center. **History museums:** Government House Museum, Lighthouse Museum, Lightner Museum, Oldest Store Museum and Potter's Wax Museum. **Theaters:** Anastasia Dance Theatre, Bayfront Dinner Theatre and the Museum-Theater. **Library:** St. Augustine Historical Society and St. Johns County Public. **Attractions:** Castillo de San Marco, a 17th-century Spanish fort; the "Cross and Sword" production; fountain of youth; Lightner Museum; the Spanish Quarter; and World Golf Hall of Fame. **Necessities:** There's a little bit of everything here.

Smart Shopper Tip: There are more than 40 antique shops. Don't miss Heritage Walk Shopping Village on St. George Street, a walking mall that's closed to traffic, and the shops of San Marco Avenue. Traditional mall shoppers will enjoy Ponce de Leon Mall.

WHO LIVES HERE
Population: 12,342 year-round residents in St. Augustine, an increase of 647 since 1990. The population for St. Augustine Beach was 4,108, an increase of 451 since 1990. **Age 65+ =** 17.3% in St. Johns County. **Median household income:** $32,974 (St. Johns County). **Per capita income:** $28,140 (St. Johns County).

NUMBERS TO KNOW
Chamber of commerce: (904) 829-5681. **Voter registration:**

(904) 823-2238. **Vehicle registration, tags & title:** (904) 823-2270. **Driver's license:** (904) 825-5066. **Visitors bureau:** (800) 653-2489.

WHAT TO READ
St. Augustine Record, daily newspaper, (904) 829-6562. **Florida Times-Union,** regional daily newspaper, (904) 829-6203.

GETTING AROUND
Bus: No public intra-city transportation. **Taxi:** Ace Taxi, (904) 824-6888. **Tours:** Colee's Carriage Tours, (904) 829-2818. St. Augustine Historical Trolley Tours, (904) 829-3800. St. Augustine Sightseeing Trains, (904) 829-6545. Sightseeing Cruise, (904) 824-1806. **Airport:** Jacksonville International is 58 miles away. **Traffic:** Congested during tourist season.

JOBS
County unemployment rate: 2.9%. **Florida Jobs and Benefits:** (904) 825-5042.

UTILITIES
Electricity: Florida Power & Light, (800) 226-6543. **Gas:** None. **Water & sewer:** City Utilities Dept., (904) 825-1037. **Telephone:** Bell South, (800) 789-9025 in Florida, or (800) 753-0710 out-of-state. **Cable TV:** Time-Warner Cable, (904) 824-2813.

PLACES OF WORSHIP
Seven Catholic and 50 Protestant churches, plus one Jewish synagogue.

THE ENVIRONMENT
Pellicer Creek State Aquatic Preserve is designated as an Outstanding Florida Water. The Matanzas River generally has been rated as having fair water quality. Waters surrounding Anastasia Island are generally fair quality but have declined in recent years. Moultrie Creek has good water quality but has been threatened by contamination from septic tanks, a sludge disposal site and a toxic chemical spill.

EVENTS AND FESTIVALS
Events: St. Augustine Passion Play - March or April. **Arts & Crafts Spring Festival** - April. "Cross and Sword" - June through August. **Spanish Night Watch** - June. **Founders Day/Fiesta España** - September. **St. Augustine Maritime Festival** - October. **St. Augustine Folk Festival** - October. **Lincolnville Festival** - November.

WHERE TO EAT
The Columbia, 98 St. George St., Spanish, moderate, (904) 824-3341. **Le Pavillon,** 45 San Marco Ave., hearty European, moderate, (904) 824-6202. **Raintree,** 102 San Marco Ave., continental, moderate to expensive, (904) 824-7211.

WHERE TO STAY
The Augustin Inn, (904) 823-9559. **Casa de Solana,** (904) 824-3555. **Comfort Inn Downtown,** (904) 824-5554, **Radisson Ponce de Leon Golf & Conference Resort,** (904) 824-2821. **St. Francis Inn,** (904) 824-6068.

ISSUES
Retirees cite summer heat and humidity and heavy traffic during tourist season. They also worry about rising crime. However, none of these issues is serious enough to compel them to consider moving.

St. Petersburg

St. Petersburg is a complete city in more ways than one. It is complete — literally — in that there is no room for expansion of the city limits. New development requires razing old development. According to chamber officials, the city's large retiree population is distributed fairly evenly throughout the city.

To its credit, St. Petersburg is also complete in what it offers its residents. It takes maximum advantage of its peninsular characteristics, providing the trappings for a water-oriented society. Cradled on three sides by the waters of Tampa and Boca Ciega bays, the city is skirted by yacht clubs, marinas, docks, boat ramps, private boat slips, waterfront homes and a dozen public beaches.

The most prominent municipal buildings, public buildings and attractions are situated on the bay. There you'll find museums, performing arts centers, medical centers, Al Lang Stadium and a campus of the University of South Florida. The Pier, an upside-down pyramid-shaped building filled with shops, restaurants, entertainment and an aquarium, is the most popular visitor attraction in Pinellas County. It is located at the end of a quarter-mile pier.

For those seriously considering residency in St. Petersburg, there is a brief but helpful housing brochure available from the city. It identifies 90 neighborhoods with home prices ranging from the $70s to well over $1 million. There are luxury golf course communities, waterfront properties, townhomes, historical homes dating from the 1920s, bay-view condominiums and inland neighborhoods.

The booklet highlights the better neighborhoods. An excursion around St. Pete reveals many modest homes selling for well under the prices noted above. There also are areas of substandard housing.

Still, the pros outweigh the cons by a long shot. It's worth spending some time in this city to see if it has what you want.

WEATHER

	Winter	Spring	Summer	Fall
Normal daily high/low	71/56	85/70	89/76	77/62
Normal precipitation	9 in.	11 in.	22 in.	7 in.

Disaster watch: Since 1900, northwest Florida has been hit by six major hurricanes and southwest Florida has been hit by five.

TAXES

Sales tax: 7%. **Property tax:** $25.64 per $1,000 valuation. Sample tax calculations include a $25,000 homestead exemption.

Home value	Tax
$100,000	$1,923
$150,000	$3,205
$250,000	$5,769

REAL ESTATE

Median home value: $105,780 (Pinellas County). **Median rent:** $614/month (Pinellas County). **Communities popular with retirees:** Relocation resource Century 21 Mills First, (813) 398-7771, provided the following information. Barcley Estates has homes priced from the $150s to $300s. Dolphin Cay has condominiums and single-family homes priced from the low $130s to $500s. Isla Del Sol features waterfront condos priced from the high $90s and golf-course condos priced from the $80s. Mainlands & The Lakes offers single-family homes priced from the high $50s to the high $90s. **Licensed continuing-care retirement communities:** College Harbor, 102 independent living units, 63 rental units, 18 sheltered nursing beds, 42 community beds, (813) 866-3124. The Fountains, 92 CCRC units (units no longer being sold), 504 rental units, 53 sheltered nursing beds, 97 community beds, (813) 381-1482. Masonic Homes of Florida, 102 independent living units, 85 sheltered nursing beds, (813) 822-3499. Palm Shores, 189 independent living units, 42 community beds, (813) 894-2102. Suncoast Manor, 241 independent living units, 114 community beds, (813) 867-1131. Westminster Shores, 237 independent living units, 48 sheltered nursing beds, 72 community beds, (727) 867-2131.

CRIME & SAFETY

Crimes per 1,000 population: 100. **Non-emergency police:** (813) 893-7780. **Non-emergency fire department:** (813) 893-7694. **Police, fire, ambulance emergencies:** 911.

HOMELESS & BLIGHT

Residents and civic leaders participate in several community improvement programs including Adopt A Park, aimed at keeping parks clean and safe from vandalism; Save Our Shores, which sponsors coastal clean-up and environmental awareness; and the Memorial Tree Program, through which individuals may purchase a tree in a public area to commemorate a special day, event or individual.

Downtown St. Petersburg is clean, spacious and attractive, but there are some residential and small business areas on the perimeter that are substandard. We saw several homeless persons.

The U.S. Census reported 1,105 homeless persons in shelters and 75 visible in street locations in Pinellas County, population 851,659.

HEALTH CARE

Hospitals: There are eight hospitals in Greater St. Petersburg. **Bayfront Medical Center**, 502 beds, 24-hour emergency, full service, (813) 823-1234. **St. Anthony's Hospital**, 434 beds, full service, (813) 825-1100. **Columbia Edward White Hospital**, 167 beds, 24-hour emergency, (813) 323-1111. **Physicians:** 700. **Specialties:** All.

GETTING SMART

Eckerd College, (813) 867-1166. **Offerings:** In addition to bachelor's degrees, it offers the Academy of Senior Professionals, (813) 864-8834, with classes in life enrichment and liberal arts subjects as well as intergenerational, mentoring and community service programs. **St. Petersburg Junior College**, (813) 341-3600. **Offerings:** Two-year degrees. **University of South Florida at St. Petersburg**, (727) 553-1536. **Offerings:** 26 undergraduate and four master's degrees plus a doctorate in marine biology.

JUST FOR SENIORS
AARP, (813) 576-1155. Enoch Davis Senior Center, (813) 893-7134. Sunshine Center for Older Adults, (813) 893-7101.

GETTING INVOLVED
AARP, (727) 576-1155. Neighborly Senior Services, (727) 527-5212. RSVP, (727) 549-8050. United Way, (813) 822-4183.

RECREATION, ENTERTAINMENT & AMENITIES
Public golf: Mangrove Bay Municipal Golf Course and Twin Brooks Golf Course. Private golf: Isla Del Sol Yacht and Country Club, Lakewood Country Club, Pasadena Yacht and Country Club, and Stouffer Vinoy Golf Club. Public tennis courts: 64 courts including 15 at St. Petersburg Tennis Center. Private tennis courts: Bardmoor Tennis and Fitness Club, Dolphin Cay, Vinoy Club and Women's Tennis Association. Parks: 28 parks with 2,400 acres. Public swimming pools: Eight. Water sports: Boating, jet-skiing, parasailing, sailing, scuba diving and water-skiing. There are 610 municipal boat slips. River/gulf/ocean: Tampa Bay, Boca Ciega Bay, numerous harbors, small bays, bayous and Lake Maggiore. Running/walking/biking: Pinellas Trail, a railroad right-of-way converted to a linear park, extends 47 miles from St. Petersburg to Dunedin. Also, five exercise trails. Horses/riding: Several stables. Hunting: None. Movie theaters: 16 screens. Art museums: Museum of Fine Arts and Salvador Dali Museum. History museums: St. Petersburg Historical Museum. Theaters: Bayfront Center/Mahaffey Theater, American Stage, The Coliseum, Demens Landing and St. Petersburg Little Theatre. Library: Six public. Attractions: Al Lang Stadium (spring training camp of Baltimore Orioles and St. Louis Cardinals), Science Center, Great Explorations (a hands-on museum), Planetarium, Florida Thunderdome, Sunshine Skyway Bridge, The Pier, Florida Sunken Gardens. Necessities: All.

Smart Shopper Tip: Here's a quick summary. Beach Drive — upscale shopping. Gateway Mall — air-conditioned comfort. The Pier — shopping and dining on Tampa Bay. Tyrone Square Mall — four anchors and more than 140 stores.

WHO LIVES HERE
Population: 241,413 year-round residents, an increase of 1,095 since 1990. Age 65+ = 24.6% in Pinellas County. Median household income: $29,009 (Pinellas County). Per capita income: $25,765 (Pinellas County).

NUMBERS TO KNOW
Chamber of commerce: (813) 821-4069. Voter registration: (813) 582-7851. Vehicle registration, tags & title: (813) 464-5560. Driver's license: (813) 893-2747 or (813) 893-2583.

WHAT TO READ
St. Petersburg Times, daily newspaper, (813) 893-8111. Tampa Tribune, daily newspaper, (813) 823-7732. Neighborhoods of St. Petersburg, Department of Housing & Economic Development housing brochure, (813) 893-7788.

GETTING AROUND
Bus: Pinellas Suncoast Transit Authority, (813) 530-9911. Dial A Ride Transit (DART) offers half-price senior fares, (813) 531-0415. Taxi: Yellow Cab, (813) 821-7777. Tours: Europa Jet offers daily cruises from The Pier, (813) 393-2885. Airport: St. Petersburg/Clearwater International or Tampa International. Traffic: It's heavy, but not a problem if you know your way around. U.S. Highway 19 usually is the slowest. I-275 moves along well.

JOBS
County unemployment rate: 3.4%. Florida Jobs and Benefits: (813) 893-2255.

UTILITIES
Electricity: Florida Power Corp., (727) 895-8711. Gas: Peoples Gas, (813) 826-3300. Water & sewer: City Utility, (813) 893-7341. Telephone: GTE Florida, (800) 483-4200. Cable TV: Time Warner, (813) 562-5025.

PLACES OF WORSHIP
17 Catholic and 120 Protestant churches, two Jewish synagogues and three other faiths.

THE ENVIRONMENT
Water quality throughout the area has been rated as generally poor to fair. The best water quality is in lower Tampa Bay. The worst water quality in the area is in Hillsborough and McKay bays, though the Hillsborough Bay has shown some recovery.

A report by the Florida Department of Environmental Regulation states, "Due to the ecological, economic and aesthetic importance of this water body, Tampa Bay has become a major focus of local, regional and state actions to reverse the negative trends." The bay has been designated as a priority SWIM (Surface Water Improvement and Management) water body.

There is one EPA-listed Superfund site in Pinellas County. It is the Stauffer Chemical Co. plant in Tarpon Springs.

EVENTS AND FESTIVALS
International Folk Fair - March. Festival of States - March or April. Suncoast Sailing Regattas - April. Mainsail Arts Festival - May. Suncoast Home, Garden & Craft Show - September. Holiday Lights - November. Good Life Celebration (Events for ages 55 and up) - November. Lighted Boat Parades - December.

WHERE TO EAT
Basta's, 1625 Fourth St. S., northern Italian, continental, expensive, (813) 894-7880. Heritage Grille, 256 Second St. N., American, seafood, expensive, (813) 823-6382. Leverock's, 4801 37th St. S., seafood, moderate to expensive, (813) 864-3883.

WHERE TO STAY
Bayboro House Bed & Breakfast, (813) 823-4955. Hilton Towers, (813) 894-5000. Renaissance Vinoy Resort, (813) 894-1000. Heritage Holiday Inn, (813) 822-4814.

ISSUES
It has most of the problems associated with large cities today and appears to be working on solutions.

St. Petersburg Beach

HE SAID: ✮ ✮
It has the attributes of a desirable vacation spot. Since I'm looking for a place to spend the rest of my life and not a vacation home, I wouldn't want to take up residence here.

SHE SAID: ✮ ✮ ✮
A retiree would have to be a real beach lover to live here. There are people and traffic galore. The beach is the only appealing offering. I would not retire here.

St. Petersburg Beach is the southernmost town in a string of keys that stretches from Clearwater to a point just beyond the southern tip of St. Petersburg. If not for a series of bridges and causeways that connect these keys to the Mainland, it would be accessible only by boat.

Route 699 links the islands and leads to St. Petersburg Beach. You'll travel through a series of small beach towns, each very much alike and each very much like St. Petersburg Beach. Each town has its own city hall, post office, public beaches, piers, marinas, boat launching facilities, shopping villages, community centers, canal homes, high-rise condominiums and resort motels. Crime rates throughout the island towns are relatively low and per capita income is relatively high.

It's possible to retire and live happily ever after in St. Petersburg Beach, but it helps to be hooked on water sports or addicted to television. There's not a golf course on the island, and those nearest are all private. St. Petersburg Beach and the other towns lack most cultural, educational and social amenities, as well as hospitals and malls. Beach residents do benefit from convenient access to the goods, services and amenities of the Mainland coupled with the ability to escape to the tranquillity of a home on the keys.

Peace and quiet is not a permanent feature of the beaches, however. As a general rule, the population doubles during peak tourist season, when vacationers add to the traffic, noticeably slowing the flow.

Scenic sunsets, lush tropical vegetation and wide sandy beaches along a 7.5-mile shoreline are the most alluring qualities of St. Petersburg Beach. The inviting Gulf waters offer swimming, fishing, boating and a myriad of water sports. There are wonderfully convenient canal homes here, too. For those who cherish the beach and the water, St. Petersburg Beach may be the spot.

WEATHER

	Winter	Spring	Summer	Fall
Normal daily high/low	71/56	85/70	89/76	77/62
Normal precipitation	9 in.	11 in.	22 in.	7 in.

Disaster watch: Since 1900 northwest Florida has been hit by six major hurricanes and southwest Florida has been hit by five major hurricanes.

TAXES
Sales tax: 7%. **Property tax:** $20.00 per $1,000 valuation. Sample tax calculations include a $25,000 homestead exemption.

Home value	Tax
$100,000	$1,500
$150,000	$2,500
$250,000	$4,500

REAL ESTATE
Median home value: $105,780 (Pinellas County). **Median rent:** $614/month (Pinellas County). **Communities popular with retirees:** Key Van Kohan with Coldwell Banker, (800) 697-2330, provided these price ranges on real estate in the area: Dolphin Cay has condos and single-family homes from the $160s to the $500s. Madeira Cove has condos from the $140s to the $180s. Harbour Side offers high-rise condos from the $70s to mid-$200s. St. Petersburg Beach Tennis & Yacht Club has condos from the mid-$90s to the $300s. **Licensed continuing-care retirement communities:** None.

CRIME & SAFETY
Crimes per 1,000 population: 65. **Non-emergency police:** (813) 367-2735. **Non-emergency fire department:** (813) 363-9208. **Police, fire, ambulance emergencies:** 911.

HOMELESS & BLIGHT
We found no evidence of homeless persons and saw no blighted areas. The U.S. Census reported 1,105 homeless persons in shelters and 75 visible in street locations in Pinellas County, population 851,659.

HEALTH CARE
Hospitals: Palms of Pasadena Hospital is within a mile, 310 beds, 24-hour emergency, full service, (813) 381-1000.
Physicians: 349 on hospital staff, but only two or three with offices in St. Petersburg Beach. **Specialties:** 41 covered by hospital staff.

GETTING SMART
There are no college or university campuses in St. Petersburg Beach though there are several nearby. **Eckerd College** in St. Petersburg, (813) 867-1166. **Offerings:** In addition to bachelor's degrees, it offers the Academy of Senior Professionals, (813) 864-8834, with classes in life enrichment and liberal arts as well as intergenerational, mentoring and community service programs. **St. Petersburg Junior College**, (813) 341-3600. **Offerings:** Two-year degrees. **University of South Florida at St. Petersburg**, (727) 553-1536. **Offerings:** 26 undergraduate and four master's programs, plus a doctorate in marine biology.

JUST FOR SENIORS
Warren Webster Hall provides free bus transportation and lunch for seniors, (813) 367-2735.

GETTING INVOLVED
AARP, (727) 576-1155.

RECREATION, ENTERTAINMENT & AMENITIES
Public golf: None. **Private golf:** Isla del Sol Golf & Country Club, 18 holes/par 72. **Public tennis courts:** Egan Park, Hurley Park, Lazarillo Park and Vina del Mar Park. **Private tennis**

courts: Isla del Sol has nine championship courts, semiprivate. **Parks:** Fort de Soto is a 900-acre park composed of five islands with seven miles of waterfront and three miles of beaches. **Public swimming pools:** None. **Water sports:** Boating, jet-skiing, parasailing, sailing, scuba diving and water-skiing. **River/gulf/ocean:** Boca Ciega Bay and the Gulf of Mexico. **Running/walking/biking:** Streets, parks and beaches. Suncoast Runners Club sponsors monthly events. **Horses/riding:** None. **Hunting:** None. **Movie theaters:** One screen. **Art museums:** Suntan Art Center and Sanders & Markoe Gallery. **History museums:** Gulf Beaches Historical Museum and Port Royal Sunken Treasure Museum. **Theaters:** Tierra Verde Dinner Theatre. The performing arts are well represented on the Mainland. **Library:** St. Petersburg Beach Public. **Attractions:** John's Pass Village and Boardwalk at the north end of Treasure Island. **Necessities:** Five banks, a credit union, two post offices, a pharmacy and a supermarket.

 Smart Shopper Tip: Dolphin Village Shopping Center, Village Plaza Shopping Center on the Causeway and Treasure Island Shopping Center will supply the basics. Five miles inland, Tyrone Square Mall's 150 stores can satisfy your shopping needs.

WHO LIVES HERE
Population: 9,597 year-round residents, an increase of 397 people since 1990. **Age 65+** = 24.6% in Pinellas County. **Median household income:** $29,009 (Pinellas County). **Per capita income:** $25,765 (Pinellas County).

NUMBERS TO KNOW
Chamber of commerce: (813) 360-6957. **Voter registration:** (813) 464-3551. **Vehicle registration, tags & title:** (813) 975-6565. **Driver's license:** (813) 893-2746.

WHAT TO READ
St. Petersburg Times, daily newspaper, (813) 893-8111. **Tampa Tribune**, daily newspaper, (813) 823-7732.

GETTING AROUND
Bus: BATS City Transit, (813) 367-3086. **Taxi:** BATS Taxi, (813) 367-3702. **Tours:** Capt. Anderson Cruise Boat, (813) 367-7804. **Airport:** St. Petersburg/Clearwater International and Tampa International. **Traffic:** It can be hectic on Route 699 (Gulf Boulevard) because it is the only through-artery. But it's not as bad here as elsewhere on the islands since St. Petersburg Beach is the end of the road. Traffic gets worse during peak tourist season.

JOBS
County unemployment rate: 3.4%. **Florida Jobs and Benefits:** (813) 893-2255.

UTILITIES
Electricity: Florida Power Corp., (813) 893-9379. **Gas:** Peoples Gas, (813) 895-3621. **Water & sewer:** Pinellas County Utilities, (813) 464-4714. **Telephone:** GTE Florida, (800) 483-4200. **Cable TV:** Time Warner Communications, (813) 684-6400.

PLACES OF WORSHIP
One Catholic and three Protestant churches, plus one Jewish synagogue.

THE ENVIRONMENT
Water quality throughout the area generally has been rated as poor to fair. The best water quality is in lower Tampa Bay. The worst water quality in the area is in Hillsborough and McKay bays, though the Hillsborough Bay has shown some recovery.

 A report by the Florida Department of Environmental Regulation states, "Due to the ecological, economic and aesthetic importance of this water body, Tampa Bay has become a major focus of local, regional and state actions to reverse the negative trends." The bay has been designated as a priority SWIM (Surface Water Improvement and Management) water body.

 There is one EPA-listed Superfund site in Pinellas County. It is the Stauffer Chemical Co. plant in Tarpon Springs.

EVENTS AND FESTIVALS
Corey Avenue Art Show - March. **Taste of the Beaches** - May. **John's Pass Seafood Festival** - October. **Lighted Boat Parade** - December.

WHERE TO EAT
Hurricane, 807 Gulf Way, seafood, moderate, (813) 360-9558. **Maritana Grille**, 3400 Gulf Blvd., at the Don CeSar Beach Resort, American, expensive, (813) 360-1884. **Pelican Diner**, 7501 Gulf Blvd., home-style meals, inexpensive, (727) 363-9873. **Silas' Steakhouse**, 5501 Gulf Blvd., steak, seafood, moderate to expensive, (813) 360-6961.

WHERE TO STAY
Don CeSar Beach Resort, (813) 360-1881. **Radisson Sandpiper Beach Resort**, (813) 360-5551. **Trade Winds Resort**, (813) 562-1212.

ISSUES
"Water, water everywhere and not a drop to drink" is the way one retiree expressed the area's chronic water shortage. The problem has been alleviated somewhat by a pipeline from St. Petersburg carrying recycled water for outdoor use only.

 Beach erosion along the northern end of the key continues to be a matter of concern, putting a damper on the volume of vacationers coming to the area. Ways to correct the problem are being sought.

Sanford

HE SAID: ☆

Northern Seminole County has made significant strides in recent years in terms of access, shopping and economic growth. Sanford hasn't kept pace. It prides itself on being part of the Greater Orlando area but relies heavily on surrounding communities to provide the amenities.

SHE SAID: ☆ ☆

The clean downtown has a historic area. There are nice outlying residential areas and a large marina. The new mall is a real blessing, but not enough to overcome the town's shortfalls. I would not retire here.

It describes itself as "the heart of Florida, close to everything you want." Good thing it has proximity in its favor, because it has little else. With the exception of Lake Monroe and a fairly nice historic downtown, there's not much to brag about.

To see the best the town can offer, enter from I-4 along Seminole Boulevard and the shore of Lake Monroe. To see the worst, approach Sanford from the south on U.S. Highway 17/92. This section is lined with strip shopping centers, many with vacant, boarded-up buildings. Seminole Towne Center, a 1.25 million-square-foot mall which recently opened in nearby Lake Mary, is likely to put further pressure on Sanford's shopping outlets.

Sanford has Lake Monroe, which is scenically beautiful and enjoyed for fishing, water sports and dinner cruises. The Central Florida Zoo is certainly worth a stop. Another plus is the town's abundance of municipal parks. There are 23, and though many of them are small, they make a contribution to the environment.

The Auto Train from Washington, DC, terminates here and brings in a lot of visitors to this so-called "gateway to south Florida." A new $5 billion superhighway, the Central Florida Greeneway, connects the new mall and Walt Disney World via I-4 interchanges.

There are some attractive residential developments west of U.S. 17/92 in the Hidden Lakes area, and along Route 46A. Looking at a map, it seems that their inclusion as part of Sanford was probably gerrymandered based on an exchange of municipal services for property tax revenue. Judging by the run-down and unattractive condition of the older commercial, industrial and residential districts, the city needs this influx of taxable properties.

Opportunities for dining out are very limited, and you can forget about nightlife, unless dog racing is your cup of tea. Even then, the Sanford-Orlando Kennel Club is really in Longwood, some 15 miles south.

Sanford has some positives for retirees intrigued by lakes and rivers, who want a quiet, small-town atmosphere and a low cost of living. For those desiring more out of life — keep looking.

WEATHER

	Winter	Spring	Summer	Fall
Normal daily high/low	72/49	86/64	91/71	77/57
Normal precipitation	10 in.	12 in.	19 in.	8 in.

Disaster watch: Northeast Florida has not been hit by a major hurricane since 1900.

TAXES

Sales tax: 7%. **Property tax:** $23.05 per $1,000 valuation. Sample tax calculations include a $25,000 homestead exemption.

Home value	Tax
$100,000	$1,729
$150,000	$2,881
$250,000	$5,186

REAL ESTATE

Median home value: $92,108 (Seminole County). **Median rent:** $661/month (Seminole County). **Communities popular with retirees:** River Oaks, a gated community with a 52-slip marina on the St. Johns River, offers single-family homes priced from the mid-$150s to $300s, (407) 668-0000. There also are several nice residential developments in the extreme western areas of Sanford, adjoining Lake Mary, where homes range from the $80s to $200s. **Licensed continuing-care retirement communities:** None.

CRIME & SAFETY

Crimes per 1,000 population: 108. **Non-emergency police:** (407) 323-3030. **Non-emergency fire department:** (407) 302-1099. **Police, fire, ambulance emergencies:** 911.

HOMELESS & BLIGHT

Sanford has a nice, historic downtown with at least 22 buildings listed on the National Register of Historic Places. Seminole Boulevard, along Lake Monroe in the harbor marina area, is also very pretty. After that, it's all downhill. The town, settled in 1837, has many old commercial and residential buildings that have not been restored. Some should be razed and rebuilt. The homeless were evident in the parks during our visit.

The U.S. Census reported 53 homeless persons in shelters and 17 visible in street locations in Seminole County, population 287,529.

HEALTH CARE

Hospitals: Central Florida Regional Hospital, offers open-heart surgery, (407) 321-4500. **Orlando Regional South Seminole Hospital**, 226 beds, full service, 24-hour emergency, (407) 767-1200.

Physicians: 159. **Specialties:** 33.

GETTING SMART

Seminole Community College, (407) 786-7999 or (407) 328-4722. **Offerings:** Two-year degrees in arts and sciences, plus vocational and continuing-education classes.

JUST FOR SENIORS

Council on Aging's **Better Living for Seniors Help Line**, (407)

847-4357. **Senior Center**, (407) 302-1010.

GETTING INVOLVED
RSVP, (407) 323-4440. **United Way** in Orlando, (407) 897-6677. **Volunteer Center of Central Florida** in Orlando, (407) 896-0945.

RECREATION, ENTERTAINMENT & AMENITIES
Public golf: Cypress Point Golf Club & RV Retreat, nine holes, and Mayfair Country Club. **Private golf:** None. **Public tennis courts:** Coast Line Park, Fort Mellon Park, Jinkins Circle Park, Pinecrest Park and Randall Chase Park. **Private tennis courts:** Bayhead Racquet Club and Heathrow. **Parks:** Wekiva River State Preserve. Sanford has 23 municipal parks with a variety of facilities, and Seminole County has 18 parks. **Public swimming pools:** None. **Water sports:** Boating, canoeing, sailing and water-skiing. **River/gulf/ocean:** Lake Monroe on the St. Johns River forms the northern city limit. It's 25 miles to the Atlantic. **Running/walking/biking:** George Starke Park has a fitness trail; there's also Memorial Park Fitness Trail. **Horses/riding:** There are several riding academies and stables in the area. **Hunting:** Fishing and hunting licenses and information, (407) 330-4600. **Movie theaters:** One drive-in. There are 10 screens in Lake Mary. **Art museums:** Cultural Arts Building. **History museums:** Museum of Seminole County History and Sanford Museum. **Theaters:** Seminole Community College. **Library:** Seminole County branch. **Attractions:** Central Florida Zoo. **Necessities:** Most are available downtown or along U.S. 17/92.

Smart Shopper Tip: Seminole Towne Center, a five-anchor, two-level, regional mall, opened in fall 1995. Altamonte Mall and Winter Park Mall are both within 30 minutes.

WHO LIVES HERE
Population: 35,529 year-round residents, an increase of 3,142 since 1990. **Age 65+** = 11.0% in Seminole County. **Median household income:** $37,495 (Seminole County). **Per capita income:** $23,400 (Seminole County).

NUMBERS TO KNOW
Chamber of commerce: (407) 322-2212. **Voter registration:** (407) 321-1130 ext. 7709. **Vehicle registration, tags & title:** (407) 330-4600. **Driver's license:** (407) 330-6723.

WHAT TO READ
Seminole Herald, daily (except Saturday) newspaper, (407) 322-2611. **Orlando Sentinel**, daily newspaper, (407) 322-3513.

GETTING AROUND
Bus: No public intra-city transportation. **Taxi:** A-1 Taxi, (407) 328-4555. **Tours:** Rivership Romance offers dinner cruises on the St. Johns River, (407) 321-5091. **Airport:** Orlando Sanford Airport has both international and domestic flights. Orlando International is 45 minutes away via the Greeneway. **Train:**

Amtrak passenger service and Auto Train station. **Traffic:** Generally light. There is no major east-west highway through town, and even north-south U.S. 17/92 is relatively light, with most traffic detouring around town.

JOBS
County unemployment rate: 3.0%. **Florida Jobs and Benefits:** (407) 330-6700. **Job Line:** (407) 330-5676.

UTILITIES
Electricity: Florida Power & Light, (800) 226-6543, or Florida Power Corp., (407) 629-1010, depending on location of residence. **Gas, water & sewer:** City Public Utilities, (407) 330-5630. **Telephone:** Bell South, (407) 780-2355 in Florida, or (800) 753-0710 out-of-state. **Cable TV:** Time-Warner Cable, (407) 645-4701.

PLACES OF WORSHIP
One Catholic and 63 Protestant churches.

THE ENVIRONMENT
Lake Monroe has been rated as having poor water quality. The Sanford waste-water treatment plant discharges to the lake. It also receives untreated urban storm-water runoff and other pollution from upstream sources. The water quality has shown some improvement in recent years. Lake Jessup has poor water quality, but also has shown some improvement. The Wekiva River has good water quality. St. Johns River shows fair to good water quality and is improving. Both river systems have protected status as Outstanding Florida Waters.

EVENTS AND FESTIVALS
St. Johns River Festival - March. **Golden Age Games** - November. **Fall Festival of Arts, Crafts and Antiques** - November. **Sanford Historic Trust Holiday Tour of Homes** - December.

WHERE TO EAT
The Colonial Room, 115 E. First St., Southern-style home cooking, inexpensive to moderate, (407) 323-2999.

WHERE TO STAY
The Marina Hotel, (407) 323-1910.

ISSUES
The overall appearance of Sanford raises the issue of demolishing or restoring much of the residential and commercial area surrounding downtown. Is there the civic will — and are there the resources — to get it done?

Sanibel-Captiva Islands

HE SAID: ★ ★ ★ ★ ★
There is no spot more beautiful in Florida than the Sanibel-Captiva Islands. Even with high-season traffic, this is one of the most appealing retirement sites to me.

SHE SAID: ★ ★ ★
A great place for nature lovers, it is a nice place to visit — but not to stay. While there are nice, quiet residential areas away from the tourist crowds, you still must beware of the traffic getting on and off the islands. I would not retire here.

A $3 toll to get on the causeway to the islands is the only charge for a trip to paradise. The toll is enough to let you know you're on the road to someplace special. But the presence of colorfully uniformed policemen directing traffic on and off the islands tells you $3 isn't enough to deter vacationers and sightseers. They come for the seasonal ritual of exploring the most beautiful, tropical Garden of Eden in Florida.

The islands' hallmark is lush tropical foliage — so dense that many man-made structures are invisible from the two main thoroughfares of the islands. A heavily used, masterfully landscaped bike path paralleling the main road is symbolic of a resident-friendly local government.

Officials focus on two all-important principles. The first is controlling growth. Development is limited to roughly half the islands' total acreage. It is carefully managed to assure that it does not disturb the quality of life and aesthetic value of the surroundings. The second, closely related principle is the careful preservation and maintenance of the area's natural attributes. More than 40 percent of total acreage is preserved as wildlife sanctuaries. The goal, of course, is to keep the islands clean, unpolluted and unspoiled by those who would sacrifice beauty for profit. The remarkable extent to which this mission has been accomplished is a testament to the determination of both local government and active citizens.

Numerous public beaches, golf and tennis facilities, 22 miles of bike paths and the 5,030-acre J.N. "Ding" Darling National Wildlife Refuge provide recreational resources. Museums, 20-plus art galleries, theaters, two libraries and 54 shopping locations complete the offerings for a well-rounded lifestyle that both residents and visitors enjoy here.

Housing locales are diverse. Water lovers can settle by a canal, bay, harbor or the Gulf; others might opt for a home in a forested setting or on a fairway. Homes come in all sizes, shapes and colors — but all with a very expensive price tag. The Sanctuary, Sanibel's "first — and last — private golf community," advertises home sites priced from more than $300,000 and residences from $475,000. Duplex villas are available in The Dunes from just under $200,000. There are condominiums and townhomes throughout the islands in the $200,000 to $500,000 range. Really fabulous single-family estates climb into the millions.

WEATHER

	Winter	Spring	Summer	Fall
Normal daily high/low	76/55	88/68	91/75	81/62
Normal precipitation	7 in.	14 in.	26 in.	6 in.

Disaster watch: Southwest Florida has been hit by five major hurricanes since 1900.

TAXES

Sales tax: 6%. **Property tax:** $19.54 per $1,000 valuation. Sample taxes include a $25,000 homestead exemption.

Home value	Tax
$100,000	$1,465
$150,000	$2,442
$250,000	$4,396

REAL ESTATE

Median home value: $96,397 (Lee County). **Median rent:** $641/month (Lee County). **Communities popular with retirees:** The Sanctuary offers home sites priced from the $300s and luxury condominiums priced from the mid-$470s, (941) 472-4222. The Dunes Golf & Tennis Club offers both ground level and piling homes, as well as duplex villas priced from the mid-$190s to $500,000, (941) 472-2535. **Licensed continuing-care retirement communities:** None.

CRIME & SAFETY

Crimes per 1,000 population: 43. **Non-emergency police:** (941) 472-3111. **Non-emergency fire department:** (941) 472-5525. **Police, fire, ambulance emergencies:** 911.

HOMELESS & BLIGHT

This is one of the prettiest tropical settings in the state of Florida. We saw no homeless persons and no blighted areas.

The U.S. Census reported 97 homeless persons in shelters and 203 visible in street locations in Lee County, population 335,113.

HEALTH CARE

Hospitals: There are no hospitals on the islands. The following hospitals are in Fort Myers. **Gulf Coast Hospital**, 120 beds, full service, (941) 768-5000. **Lee Memorial Hospital**, 407 beds, full service, (941) 332-1111. **Lee Memorial Health Park Medical Center**, 220 beds, full service, (941) 433-7799. **Southwest Florida Regional Medical Center**, 400 beds, full service, (941) 939-1147. **Physicians:** 5. **Specialties:** 2.

GETTING SMART

There are no college or university campuses on the islands; however, there are several in Fort Myers. **Adult and Community Education**, Lee County School District, (941) 334-7172. **Offerings:** Popular courses are designed to broaden general knowledge and introduce new subjects. **Barry University**, (941) 278-3041. **Offerings:** Adult and continuing education. **Edison Community College**, (941) 489-9300; continuing education, (941) 489-9235. **Offerings:** Two-year degrees and continuing-education programs. **Florida Gulf Coast University**, (941) 590-1001. **Offerings:** Undergraduate and graduate degrees.

JUST FOR SENIORS

Sanibel Senior Center, (941) 472-5743.

GETTING INVOLVED

There are 25 clubs and organizations on the islands. **Captiva Civic Association**, (941) 472-2111. **Sanibel Community Association**, (941) 472-2155. **Sanibel-Captiva Conservation Foundation**, (941) 472-2329. Call the chamber of commerce for information about **Newcomers/Oldtimers**, a monthly luncheon group, and the **Sanibel-Captiva Art League**.

RECREATION, ENTERTAINMENT & AMENITIES

Public golf: Beachview Golf Club, semiprivate, 18 holes/par 71, and The Dunes Golf & Tennis Club, semiprivate, 18 holes/par 70. **Private golf:** South Seas Plantation Golf Course on Captiva and The Sanctuary on Sanibel. **Public tennis courts:** Dixie Beach Park and Sanibel Recreation Complex. **Private tennis courts:** South Seas Plantation, Sundial Beach and Tennis Resort, and The Dunes. **Parks:** Bowman's Beach, Causeway Park, J. N. "Ding" Darling National Wildlife Refuge and Lighthouse Point. **Public swimming pools:** Sanibel Recreation Complex. **Water sports:** Boating, parasailing, sailing, scuba diving, shelling and snorkeling. Sanibel-Captiva is considered one of the best shelling areas in the world. **River/gulf/ocean:** The Sanibel River runs through the heart of Sanibel Island. Also, Gulf of Mexico, Pine Island Sound, San Carlos Bay and Tarpon Bay. **Running/walking/biking:** There are 22 miles of bike paths on Sanibel, but none on Captiva. The Sanibel-Captiva Conservation Foundation has four miles of trails through native island vegetation. **Horses/riding:** None. **Hunting:** None. **Movie theaters:** One screen. **Art museums:** Barrier Island Group of the Arts (BIG Arts) and 20 art galleries. **History museums:** Sanibel Island Historical Museum. **Theaters:** Captiva Civic Association Center, Sanibel Community Center, Pirate Playhouse and The Old Schoolhouse Theater. **Library:** Two. **Attractions:** Bailey-Matthews Shell Museum, Cabbage Key, J.N. "Ding" Darling National Wildlife Refuge, five public beaches and the Sealife Learning Center. **Necessities:** Four banks, 13 shopping centers, 63 restaurants, two supermarkets and three service stations.

Smart Shopper Tip: Tahitian Gardens, Periwinkle Place, Chadwick's Square and Jerry's Shopping Center are tops for browsing. Serious shopping is only minutes away at Sanibel Factory Stores or 10 minutes farther at Fort Myers' Metro Mall.

WHO LIVES HERE

Population: 5,884 year-round residents, an increase of 416 since 1990. During the winter, the population rises to about 22,000. **Age 65+** = 25.7% in Lee County. **Median household income:** $29,174 (Lee County). **Per capita income:** $23,664 (Lee County).

NUMBERS TO KNOW

Chamber of commerce: (941) 472-1080. **Voter registration:** (941) 339-6300. **Vehicle registration, tags & title:** (941) 339-6000. **Driver's license:** In Fort Myers, (941) 278-7194.

WHAT TO READ

Captiva Current, weekly newspaper, (941) 472-1580. **Islander,** weekly newspaper, (941) 472-5185. **Island Reporter,** weekly newspaper, (941) 472-1580. **The Captiva Chronicle,** biweekly newspaper, (941) 395-2661.

GETTING AROUND

Bus: FISH (Friends in Service Here) provides transportation for seniors, (941) 472-0404. **Taxi:** Sanibel Island Taxi, (941) 472-4160. **Tours:** Captiva Cruises, (941) 472-7549. Canoe Adventures tours the J.N. "Ding" Darling National Wildlife Refuge, (941) 472-1100. Sanibel Historical Trolley Tours, (941) 472-4648. **Airport:** Southwest Florida International is 20 miles away. **Traffic:** Try to maintain a relaxed attitude. Traffic moves slowly even with uniformed police at the busiest intersections. Sanibel is linked to the Mainland by a causeway and to Captiva by a bridge.

JOBS

County unemployment rate: 3.3%. **Florida Jobs and Benefits:** In Fort Myers, (941) 278-7140.

UTILITIES

Electricity: Lee County Electric Co-op, (941) 656-2300. **Gas:** None. **Water & sewer:** Island Water Association, (941) 472-1502. **Telephone:** Sprint-United Telephone, (941) 335-3111. **Cable TV:** Media One Cablevision, (941) 432-9277.

PLACES OF WORSHIP

One Catholic and six Protestant churches.

THE ENVIRONMENT

Water quality throughout the Charlotte Harbor basin has been rated as generally good. Pine Island Sound has the best water quality. It is designated as an Outstanding Florida Water (OFW). The Caloosahatchee River State Recreation Area also has protected status as an OFW. Other OFWs in the area are Matlacha Pass State Aquatic Preserve, Gasparilla Sound/Charlotte Harbor State Aquatic Preserve and Cape Haze State Aquatic Preserve. Historically, the most serious water quality problem in the basin has been the Sanibel River on Sanibel Island. Its water quality is fair.

EVENTS AND FESTIVALS

Sanibel-Captiva Rotary Club Arts and Crafts Fair - February. **Sanibel Shell Fair** - March. **Sanibel Music Festival** - March. **Taste of the Islands** - May. **The International Hemingway Festival** - June. **Big Arts Fair** - November.

WHERE TO EAT

McT's Shrimphouse and Tavern, 1523 Periwinkle Way, dinner only, seafood, beef, chicken, moderate, (941) 472-3161. **The Bubble Room,** 15001 Captiva Drive, American, continental, expensive, (941) 472-5558. **The Jacaranda,** 1223 Periwinkle Way, seafood, expensive, (941) 472-1771.

WHERE TO STAY

Casa Ybel Resort, (800) 276-4753. **Kona Kai Motel,** (941) 472-1001. **Sanibel's Song of the Sea,** (941) 472-2220. **South Seas Plantation Resort and Yacht Harbour,** (800) 554-5454. **Sundial Beach and Tennis Resort,** (941) 472-4151. Call Reservation Central, (800) 290-6920.

ISSUES

Projects designed to clear up Sanibel's murky canal waters, restore lost sea grasses and improve drainage systems are all underway. There seems to be a continuing discussion of the problem of clogged island roads caused by cruisers and other visitors who spend time just driving around the islands.

Sarasota

HE SAID: ★ ★ ★ ★ ★

One retiree who had lived everywhere said, "I've never been to a city with so many diverse and interesting people." There's also lots to see and do here. As its publicists say, "It's one of a kind."

SHE SAID: ★ ★ ★ ★ ★

One of the prettiest places in Florida. Unique shopping areas, lots of cultural opportunities, many different types of residential areas and, on top of all that, it's a college town. Retirees seeking the city life should look here; I would.

Sarasota is unquestionably the most beautiful and resource-complete city on the Florida Gulf coast, and arguably in the state of Florida. John Ringling chose Sarasota as the winter home for his circus; he played a major part in shaping the city's arts scene. Books have been written about its cultural facilities, organizations and amenities. It's celebrated for the golden splendor of its waterfront as the sun sets over Sarasota Bay and for the wonders of the Marie Selby Botanical Gardens, with 6,000 species of orchids and bromeliads.

U.S. Highway 41 (Tamiami Trail) takes a prominent route through Sarasota from north to south. It brings visitors to the John and Mable Ringling Museum of Art and to the world-renowned Asolo Center for the Performing Arts. U.S. 41 delivers patrons of the arts to the Van Wezel Performing Arts Hall and Florida West Coast Symphony Music Center. At one point, U.S. 41 becomes Bay Front Drive before coursing due south as the main artery through the busiest retail-commercial district in the city.

This city is a place to see and be seen and hosts just the right spots to do so. Be sure to take a stroll through Sarasota Quay where you can dine, dance, shop and be entertained. A visit to Sarasota also must include a drive across the John Ringling Causeway to St. Armands Key and the shops and restaurants of St. Armands Circle. This unique tourist destination was conceived by Ringling and draws thousands of visitors.

Back in your automobile, head seaward for a brief drive to Lido Key Beach. It's a wonderful place to settle in for a short vacation — or a lifetime.

Recreational facilities abound in Sarasota, where the first golfing links in America were built in 1886. Today it has some of the most beautiful courses in the country — more than two dozen, including the 45-hole Bobby Jones Municipal Golf Complex.

The city, the keys and the suburbs are dotted with housing developments perfect for retirees. There also are a few manufactured-home developments in the outer reaches. If you haven't been to Sarasota, pack a large suitcase before you leave home because you just might decide to stay.

WEATHER

	Winter	Spring	Summer	Fall
Normal daily high/low	74/52	86/64	90/72	79/58
Normal precipitation	9 in.	12 in.	26 in.	7 in.

Disaster watch: Southwest Florida has been hit by five major hurricanes since 1900.

TAXES

Sales tax: 7%. **Property tax:** $18.10 per $1,000 valuation. Sample tax calculations include a $25,000 homestead exemption.

Home value	Tax
$100,000	$1,358
$150,000	$2,263
$250,000	$4,073

REAL ESTATE

Median home value: $107,053 (Sarasota County). **Median rent:** $714/month (Sarasota County). **Communities popular with retirees:** McIntosh Park Apartments has one- and two-bedroom apartments for $645-$905/month, (941) 377-7161. Eagles Point at the Landings has two-, three- and four-bedroom condominiums starting at $219,900, (941) 925-2299. Laurel Oak Estates and Country Club has homes from $235,000-$1,000,000, (941) 378-3608. Savannah at Turtle Rock has maintenance-free single-family homes from the $160s, (941) 925-0972. **Licensed continuing-care retirement communities:** Bay Village of Sarasota, 328 independent living units and 107 community beds, (941) 966-5611. Waterside Retirement Estates, 164 independent living units, (941) 377-0102. Lakehouse West, 157 independent living units, (941) 923-7525. Lake Pointe Woods, 188 independent living units, (941) 923-4944. Plymouth Harbor, 244 independent living units and 60 sheltered nursing beds, (941) 365-2600.

CRIME & SAFETY

Crimes per 1,000 population: 112. **Non-emergency police:** (941) 954-7025. **Non-emergency fire department:** (941) 951-4211. **Police, fire, ambulance emergencies:** 911.

HOMELESS & BLIGHT

One of the most beautiful cities in Florida, Sarasota has a restored downtown, a superb waterfront, strict sign ordinances and strong enforcement of zoning and housing codes. We did not see any homeless persons.

The U.S. Census reported 84 homeless persons in shelters and 11 visible in street locations in Sarasota County, population 277,776.

HEALTH CARE

Hospitals: Sarasota Memorial Hospital, 988 beds, plus 32 beds in intensive care, numerous specialties, acute care, full service, (941) 917-9000. **Columbia Doctors Hospital,** 168 beds, acute care, general care, 24-hour emergency, (941) 342-1100. **Sarasota Memorial Hospital,** mental health division, (941) 917-7760. **Healthsouth Rehabilitation Hospital of Sarasota,** 60 beds, inpatient and outpatient care for disabilities due to illness or injury, (941) 921-8600.

Physicians: 526. **Specialties:** 55.

GETTING SMART

University of South Florida/New College, (941) 359-4200. **Offerings:** Four-year liberal arts, honors programs (New College) and graduate degrees. **University of Sarasota,** (941) 379-0404. **Offerings:** MBA and doctoral programs in business and education for employed professionals. **Ringling School of Art and Design,** (941) 351-5100. **Offerings:** Four-year degrees in six arts disciplines.

JUST FOR SENIORS

First Call For Help, (941) 366-5025. **Multipurpose Senior Friendship Center/Elder Help Line,** (941) 955-2122. **Senior Community Service Employment Program,** (941) 366-9039.

GETTING INVOLVED

SCORE, (941) 955-1029. **Volunteer Center of Sarasota,** (941) 953-5965. **United Way of Sarasota County,** (941) 366-2686.

RECREATION, ENTERTAINMENT & AMENITIES

Public golf: There are 45 courses in the greater Sarasota area. Bobby Jones Municipal Golf Complex, 45 holes/par 71, par 72 and par 30; Rolling Green Golf Club, 18 holes/par 70; and Sarasota Golf Club, 18 holes/par 72. **Private golf:** Five semiprivate courses are Forest Lakes, 18 holes/par 71; Foxfire, three courses with nine holes each; Gulf Gate, 27 holes; Oakford, 27 holes; and Serenoa, 18 holes/par 72. 14 private. **Public tennis courts:** Payne Park Tennis Center, Siesta Racquet and Swim Club, and courts at six municipal parks. **Private tennis courts:** Ball and Racquet Club, Forest Lakes Tennis Club, Longwood Tennis and Health Club, Palm-Aire Racquet Club and the YMCA. **Parks:** Nine county parks and recreation centers offer a variety of outdoor activities. Myakka River State Park, with 28,875 acres, is the largest state park in Florida. **Public swimming pools:** Arlington Park Pool and Lido Beach Aquatic Complex. **Water sports:** Boating, canoeing, jet-skiing, parasailing, sailboarding, sailing, surfing and water-skiing. **River/gulf/ocean:** Sarasota Bay and the Gulf of Mexico. **Running/walking/biking:** Nature and bicycle trails wind throughout Myakka River State Park. Downtown shops and galleries invite walkers and strollers. **Horses/riding:** There are several stables and ranches in nearby Fruitville and areas east and south of the city. **Hunting:** Licenses and information, (941) 362-9898. **Movie theaters:** 45 screens. **Art museums:** There are 49 art galleries in a one-square-mile area downtown. John and Mable Ringling Museum of Art and the Ringling School of Art and Design. **History museums:** County Historical Archives. **Theaters:** A.B. Edwards Theatre, Asolo Center for the Performing Arts, Cabaret Club, Children's Theatre, Florida West Coast Symphony Music Center, Florida Studio Theater, Players Theater, Theatre Works and Van Wezel Performing Arts Hall. Performing arts and other groups include Conservatory for Actors Training, Conservatory of Film, Television and Recording Arts, Florida Symphonic Band, Florida West Coast Symphony, Jazz Club of Sarasota, Sarasota Ballet of Florida, Sarasota Music Festival, Sarasota Opera and The Players of Sarasota. **Library:** Gulf Gate, Selby Public and the Environmental libraries. **Attractions:** Bellm's Cars and Music of Yesterday, Mote Marine Laboratory, Pelican Man's Bird Sanctuary, Ringling Museums Complex, Marie Selby Botanical Gardens and Sarasota Jungle Gardens. **Necessities:** All here.

Smart Shopper Tip: Sarasota has an array of fine shopping centers (15) and malls (three), but for sheer shopping pleasure and elegant dining, visit legendary St. Armands Circle.

WHO LIVES HERE

Population: 51,315 year-round residents, an increase of 418 since 1990. **Age 65+ =** 32.6% in Sarasota County. **Median household income:** $30,662 (Sarasota County). **Per capita income:** $33,445 (Sarasota County).

NUMBERS TO KNOW

Chamber of commerce: (941) 955-8187. **Voter registration:** (941) 951-5307. **Vehicle registration, tags & title:** (941) 362-9898. **Driver's license:** (941) 361-6222 or (941) 361-6569. **Visitors bureau:** (941) 957-1877.

WHAT TO READ

Sarasota Herald-Tribune, daily newspaper, (941) 365-6060. **Sarasota Visitor's Guide**, monthly magazine, (941) 481-0266.

GETTING AROUND

Bus: SCAT Bus and Trolley System, (941) 316-1234. **Taxi:** Yellow Cab, (941) 955-3341. **Tours:** A self-guided walking tour of historic downtown Sarasota. Myakka Wildlife Tours, (941) 365-0100. **Airport:** Sarasota/Bradenton International. **Traffic:** Plenty. Traffic on U.S. 41 is always heavy. U.S. 301 is a little better. East-west routes are much better.

JOBS

County unemployment rate: 2.6%. **Florida Jobs and Benefits:** (941) 361-6100. **Job Line:** For Sarasota County, (941) 951-5495.

UTILITIES

Electricity: Florida Power & Light, (941) 917-0708. **Gas:** Peoples Gas, (941) 366-4277. **Water & sewer:** City of Sarasota, Water Dept., (941) 954-4196. **Telephone:** GTE, (800) 483-4200. **Cable TV:** ComCast Cable, (941) 371-6700.

PLACES OF WORSHIP

Six Catholic and 157 Protestant churches, one Islamic mosque and four Jewish synagogues.

THE ENVIRONMENT

Sarasota Bay is designated as an Outstanding Florida Water and is part of the EPA's National Estuary Program. Sarasota Bay, between Bradenton and Sarasota, and Longboat Key Estuary have been rated as having generally fair water quality. Anna Maria Key Estuary and the St. Armands Key Estuary have generally good water quality. Whitaker Bayou has poor water quality; there have been occasional closings of the shellfish harvesting areas. Siesta Key Estuary has fair to good water quality and is showing an improving trend. Phillippi Creek has poor but improving water quality. Matheny Creek has fair water quality; it is affected by urban runoff. Catfish Creek, south of Matheny, has poor water quality affected by urban runoff and a closed landfill in close proximity. Little Sarasota Bay near Catfish Creek has fair water quality.

EVENTS AND FESTIVALS

Sarasota Bay Arts & Crafts Festival - January. **Medieval Fair** - March. **Sarasota Jazz Festival** - April. **Selby Gardens Orchid Festival** - April. **Sarasota Festival of New Plays** - May. **Classical Music Festival** - June. **Suncoast Offshore Grand Prix** - July. **St. Armands Circle Arts Festival** - October. **A Taste of Sarasota** - October. **International Circus Festival** - December.

WHERE TO EAT

Bijou Cafe, 1287 First St., continental, moderate, (941) 366-8111. **Cafe L'Europe**, 431 St. Armands Circle, continental, expensive, (941) 388-4415. **Carmichael's**, 1213 N. Palm Ave., game dishes, expensive, (941) 596-3727. **Ristorante Bellini**, 1551 Main St., northern Italian, moderate to expensive, (941) 365-7380.

WHERE TO STAY

Hampton Inn, (941) 351-7734. **Half Moon Beach Club**, (941) 388-3694. **Hyatt Sarasota**, (941) 953-1234.

ISSUES

Population growth in unincorporated areas outpaced countywide infrastructure development. The county is playing catch-up. A rising crime rate, especially in an area north of downtown, has been somewhat ameliorated by the addition of more police officers.

Sebring

HE SAID: ✮ ✮ ✮
> *With 17 golf courses in the area and about the same number of lakes, Sebring has what it takes to make me give it a second hard look.*

SHE SAID: ✮ ✮
> *This small, rural town on the shores of Lake Jackson was founded in 1911 and has had few changes downtown since then. There are lots of RV parks, manufactured homes, golf courses and citrus groves. It is more rural than I like; I would not retire here.*

This heartland of south-central Florida has a number of attributes attractive to retirees, not the least of which is its secluded, yet convenient, location. Four excellent Florida cities — Fort Myers, Vero Beach, Orlando and Sarasota — are 85 to 90 miles away. Another, Lakeland, is only 60 miles north.

Its position in the rural environment of Highlands County, amid miles of citrus groves and grazing lands, provides another set of ingredients that attracts retirees: recreational opportunities and a peaceful, slow pace.

Surprisingly, Sebring has more social and cultural amenities than you would expect for a town of its size and rural nature. It also has a substantial number of natural and man-made resources that help elevate the quality of life for its residents. High on the list is Highlands Hammock State Park. Only minutes away, it offers 3,800 acres with 1,000-year-old trees, a large assortment of birds and other wildlife, hiking trails, boating and camping facilities. Lake Jackson, with an 11-mile circumference, and many smaller lakes are home to a variety of wildlife and are ideal for boating, fishing and swimming. The Allen Altvater Cultural Center is a hub of activity, housing the public library, Lakeside Playhouse, Highlands Museum of the Arts, Civic Center and City Pier. Circle Park is the popular, restored focal point of the city and is listed on the National Register of Historic Places. The Sebring International Raceway brings race fans and residents out for entertainment.

Sebring has many attractive housing communities with golf, tennis and clubhouse facilities. One really outstanding manufactured housing community in a country club setting is Highlands Ridge. For those in the market, there is a considerable amount of manufactured housing along the Lake Placid-Sebring-Avon Park corridor of central Florida.

Sebring is not a cultural mecca, shopper's paradise, major tourist attraction, recreational magnet, nor celebrated destination (except perhaps for Grand Prix Race fans). But it does have a lot of good qualities. In addition to those above, it has an affordable cost of living and some of the friendliest, most helpful people you'll find anywhere. So don't automatically exclude it from your itinerary just because it doesn't have saltwater lapping up on its city limits signs.

WEATHER

	Winter	Spring	Summer	Fall
Normal daily high/low	76/50	88/65	92/71	80/57
Normal precipitation	8 in.	14 in.	21 in.	7 in.

Disaster watch: Southeast Florida has been hit by nine major hurricanes since 1900. Southwest Florida has been hit by five major hurricanes since 1900.

TAXES
Sales tax: 7%. **Property tax:** $25.85 per $1,000 valuation. Sample tax calculations include a $25,000 homestead exemption.

Home value	Tax
$100,000	$1,939
$150,000	$3,231
$250,000	$5,816

REAL ESTATE
Median home value: $84,516 (Highlands County). **Median rent:** $357/month (Highlands County). **Communities popular with retirees:** The Country Club of Sebring offers golf-course homes priced from the $150s and homes not on the golf course from $105,000, (941) 382-6575. Golf Hammock Country Club has single-family homes priced from the $90s to $350s and from the mid-$60s to the $100s in Cormorant Point, (941) 382-3887. Highlands Ridge features manufactured homes in a country-club setting priced from the high $40s to mid-$70s, (800) 922-8099. Sun 'N' Lake Estates Golf and Country Club offers villas, townhomes, condominiums and single-family homes with prices starting in the mid-$60s and going to $125,000-plus for exclusive, larger homes in the Manor Hill section, (941) 385-9400. **Licensed continuing-care retirement communities:** The Palms of Sebring has 179 independent-living units, 33 sheltered nursing beds and 87 community beds, (941) 385-0161.

CRIME & SAFETY
Crimes per 1,000 population: 135. **Non-emergency police:** (941) 471-5107. **Non-emergency fire department:** (941) 471-5105. **Police, fire, ambulance emergencies:** 911.

HOMELESS & BLIGHT
Our first impressions of Sebring were not particularly good coming up U.S. Highway 27 but improved as we proceeded north around Lake Jackson to the historic circle — the showpiece heart of this 1986 Florida Main Street City. There are some outstanding residential neighborhoods north and west of the lake. There are some old, unattractive neighborhoods in Sebring, but the downtown restoration, construction of the Lakeshore Mall in 1992, and development of several upscale residential communities have combined to create a solid, upbeat town.

The U.S. Census reported no homeless persons in Highlands County, population 68,432.

HEALTH CARE
Hospitals: Highlands Regional Medical Center, 126 beds, 24-hour emergency, full service, (941) 385-6101. **Surgical Center of Central Florida**, non-emergency surgery, (941) 382-7500. **Florida Hospital**, 101 beds, 24-hour emergency, full service, (941) 453-7511. **Physicians:** 150. **Specialties:** 37.

GETTING SMART
South Florida Community College, (941) 382-6900. **Offerings:** Two-year degrees in liberal arts, adult and community education with a wide diversity of programs.

JUST FOR SENIORS
Sun Room Senior Center, (941) 382-8188.

GETTING INVOLVED

Children's Museum of the Highlands, (941) 385-5437. **Friends of the Library**, (941) 683-9760. **Meals on Wheels** can be contacted through the Sebring Care Center, (941) 382-2153. **RSVP**, (941) 382-2134. **United Way of Central Florida**, (941) 453-3401.

RECREATION, ENTERTAINMENT & AMENITIES

Public golf: Country Club of Sebring, 18 holes/par 72; Golf Hammock Country Club, semiprivate, 18 holes/par 72; Harder Hall Country Club, 18 holes/par 72 and nine holes/par 33; Sebring Municipal Golf Course, 18 holes/par 72; Sebring Shores Golf Club, nine holes/par 27; Spring Lake Golf and Tennis Resort, 18 holes/par 72; and Sun 'N' Lake Country Club, 18 holes/par 72. **Private golf:** Highlands Ridge Country Club, 18 holes/par 72. **Public tennis courts:** Golf and Racquet Club. **Private tennis courts:** Spring Lake Golf and Tennis Resort. **Parks:** Highlands Hammock State Park is one of the oldest state parks in Florida and has a 3,800-acre wildlife sanctuary. **Public swimming pools:** None. **Water sports:** Boating, sailing and water-skiing. **River/gulf/ocean:** Lake Jackson and several smaller lakes. **Running/walking/biking:** There are eight nature trails for hikers in Highlands Hammock State Park. **Horses/riding:** There are several horse farms and stables in the surrounding area and lots of rural areas to ride. **Hunting:** Small game and deer in season. **Movie theaters:** 14 screens. **Art museums:** Highlands Museum of the Arts. **History museums:** Lakeside Archives and Sebring Historical Society. **Theaters:** College Cultural Series, Lakeside Playhouse Theatre and Sebring Civic Center. **Library:** Sebring Public and the South Florida Community College library. **Attractions:** Children's Museum of the Highlands, Sebring Circle and the Sebring International Raceway. **Necessities:** All.

Smart Shopper Tip: Lakeshore Regional Mall has four major anchor stores and a host of smaller shops. Major shopping facilities also are located in five cities within 90 miles.

WHO LIVES HERE

Population: 8,774 year-round residents, a decrease of 67 people since 1990. **Age 65+** = 35.9% in Highlands County. **Median household income:** $21,514 (Highlands County). **Per capita income:** $19,124 (Highlands County).

NUMBERS TO KNOW

Chamber of commerce: (941) 385-8448. **Voter registration:** (941) 386-6655. **Vehicle registration, tags & title:** (941) 386-6685. **Driver's license:** (941) 386-6053.

WHAT TO READ

The News-Sun, semiweekly, (941) 385-6155. **Tampa Tribune**, Heartland insert, daily newspaper, (941) 382-1163.

GETTING AROUND

Bus: No public intra-city transportation. **Taxi:** Highlands Yellow Cab, (941) 382-6119. **Tours:** None. **Airport:** Orlando International is 90 miles away. **Train:** Amtrak Passenger Service, (800) 872-7245. **Traffic:** With a somewhat dispersed commercial and government district, traffic is light throughout the town. U.S. 98/27 through-traffic sometimes is heavy around the west side of Lake Jackson.

JOBS

County unemployment rate: 8.6%. **Florida Jobs and Benefits:** (941) 386-6060.

UTILITIES

Electricity: Florida Power Corp., (800) 700-8744. **Gas:** Sebring Gas System, (941) 385-0194. **Water & sewer:** Sebring Water & Sewer, (941) 471-5141, or Heartland Utilities, (941) 655-4300, depending on location of residence. **Telephone:** Sprint, (800) 699-0728. **Cable TV:** ComCast Cable, (941) 385-2578.

PLACES OF WORSHIP

One Catholic and 34 Protestant churches, plus one Jewish synagogue.

THE ENVIRONMENT

Lake Jackson has been rated as having mostly good water quality. The primary source of pollutants is storm-water runoff from Sebring. Nearby lakes Josephine and Istokpoga also have generally good water quality ratings. Health advisories recommending limited consumption of largemouth bass due to mercury content have been issued for Lake Istokpoga.

EVENTS AND FESTIVALS

Antiques Fair - January. **Roaring Twenties Arts & Crafts Festival** - February. **Grand Prix Endurance Race** - March. **Highlands Arts & Crafts Festival** - November. **Central Florida Pig Festival** - December.

WHERE TO EAT

Chicanes, 3100 Golfview Road, steaks, prime rib, moderate, (941) 314-0348.

WHERE TO STAY

Holiday Inn, (941) 385-4500. **Inn on the Lakes**, (941) 471-9400 or (800) 531-5253.

ISSUES

Change is coming to central Florida, and the issue is whether or not the growth will be adequately managed and controlled to protect the environment and natural resources of the area. Right now, Sebring is involved in a tug of war between those who want to recruit more industry to enlarge the tax base and create job opportunities for young workers and those whose main interest is protection of the rural environment. Based on relocation inquiries received by the chamber of commerce, 65 percent of potential new residents will come from coastal towns and cities in Florida — refugees from congestion and crime. But, congestion is coming here, too. U.S. 27, the principal north-south artery, already is heavily congested and will be widened — or a bypass will be constructed — within the next few years.

Siesta Key

Siesta Key is first and foremost a resort community, and a very expensive one at that. For boating or beach fanatics, it's possible to really enjoy living on the key while taking advantage of the amenities of Sarasota. Personally, I'd rather live on a Sarasota golf course and visit the key — off-season.

The name itself could make you stop and check it out, but there is nothing sleepy about Siesta Key. Water-people will love it. It has lots of nearby golf courses, tennis, a bike trail that runs the length of the island and lots more. It's beautiful and definitely a cut above. I could retire here.

It might be said that the Siesta Key Chamber of Commerce is getting down to the nitty-gritty when it publishes a 750-word dissertation on the quality and origin of the island's beach sand. They even sent us home with a tiny plastic bag full of the 99 percent pure, powdery quartz — judged to be the "finest, whitest sand in the world" during the Great International White Sand Beach Challenge of 1987.

Now, with all of that beautiful sand around there must be some water, right? In addition to the fact that Siesta Key is surrounded by water, there are almost 50 miles of canals and inland waterways where homes with boat docks are the residences of choice. That's not the only housing option, though. Midnight Pass Road, which runs the length of the key, is lined with condominiums, apartment buildings and resort motels.

Unlike nearby Longboat Key where zoning laws are designed to limit the number of persons occupying the island at any given time, Siesta Key actively recruits vacationers at the rate of 300,000 annually — many times the number that visit Longboat.

Aside from housing units, boats, docks, marinas, people, cars and fine, white sand, there really isn't much more than the basics on Siesta Key. A rough tally finds health-care professionals, five banks, four service stations, three churches, a book shop, hardware store, several recreation equipment rental locations, a handful of markets, boutiques, restaurants and realtors. But it must be enough because retirees we spoke with said they don't have to leave the island for anything. (Clearly not a golfer among them!)

Retirees cite peak season traffic as the part of island life that they least like. Most residents solve this problem by avoiding their cars as much as possible. Instead, they walk or ride bicycles to markets, pharmacies and other requisite destinations.

Siesta Key is ultimately a resort island that counts in its favor its proximity to Sarasota's social, cultural and recreational amenities.

WEATHER

	Winter	Spring	Summer	Fall
Normal daily high/low	74/52	86/64	90/72	79/58
Normal precipitation	9 in.	12 in.	26 in.	7 in.

Disaster watch: Southwest Florida has been hit by five major hurricanes since 1900.

TAXES
Sales tax: 7%. **Property tax:** $13.88 per $1,000 valuation. Sample tax calculations include a $25,000 homestead exemption.

Home value	Tax
$100,000	$1,041
$150,000	$1,735
$250,000	$3,123

REAL ESTATE
Median home value: $101,372 (Sarasota County). **Median rent:** $714/month (Sarasota County). **Communities popular with retirees:** Darla Furst with Coldwell Banker, (941) 349-4411, provided the following information: Single-family homes on the waterfront range from $185,000 to $2,500,000, with an average price of $500,000. Non-waterfront homes range from $125,000 to $990,000, with an average of $250,000. Condominiums on the waterfront are priced from $80,500 to $650,000, with an average of $232,000. Non-waterfront condos run from $76,000 to $550,000, with an average of $200,000. **Licensed continuing-care retirement communities:** None.

CRIME & SAFETY
Crimes per 1,000 population: 45 (Sarasota County sheriff's jurisdiction). **Non-emergency police:** (941) 951-5800. **Non-emergency fire department:** (941) 951-4211. **Police, fire, ambulance emergencies:** 911.

HOMELESS & BLIGHT
There are no blighted areas on the key; it is beautiful from end to end. The U.S. Census reported 84 homeless persons in shelters and 11 visible in street locations in Sarasota County, population 277,776.

HEALTH CARE
Hospitals: There are no hospitals on Siesta Key. **Sarasota Memorial Hospital** is 20 minutes north, 988 beds plus 32 beds in intensive care, acute care, full service, (941) 917-9000. **Physicians:** 5. **Specialties:** 4.

GETTING SMART
There are no college or university campuses on Siesta Key. There are several in Sarasota, including the **University of South Florida/New College**, (941) 359-4200. **Offerings:** Four-year liberal arts, honors programs (New College) and graduate degrees.

JUST FOR SENIORS
The word "senior" is not mentioned in the telephone book. We found no local entities dedicated to the elder citizen.

GETTING INVOLVED
The only club or organization listed in the local directory is the Single Gourmet. The chamber of commerce offers a social membership which allows the opportunity to attend chamber functions, (941) 349-3800.

RECREATION, ENTERTAINMENT & AMENITIES
Public golf: None on the key. **Private golf:** None on the key. **Public tennis courts:** None. **Private tennis courts:** Siesta Racquet and Swim Club. **Parks:** Glebe Park, Palmer Point Park North, Siesta Beach and Turtle Beach Park. **Public swimming pools:** Siesta Beach is public. **Water sports:** Jet skiing, parasailing, scuba diving, snorkeling, swimming, water-skiing and windsurfing. **River/gulf/ocean:** Sarasota Bay, Roberts Bay, Little Sarasota Bay, the Intracoastal Waterway, 50 miles of canals and the Gulf of Mexico. **Running/walking/biking:** Mopeds and bikes are the preferred method of transportation along most streets and paths. **Horses/riding:** None. **Hunting:** None. Fishing licenses, (941) 362-9898.

Movie theaters: None. **Art museums:** None. **History museums:** None. **Theaters:** None. **Library:** None. **Attractions:** "Finest, whitest sand in the world." Siesta Key Marina and Midnight Pass Marina are both full service, with 210 boat slips. **Necessities:** Three grocers, no supermarkets, several small boutiques, five banks, four service stations and a hardware store.

Smart Shopper Tip: Siesta Key Village is quaint, but drive across the causeway — north or south — for shopping at Southgate Mall or Gulf Gate Mall, just minutes away.

WHO LIVES HERE
Population: 12,000 year-round residents and about 12,000 snowbirds, plus around 300,000 tourists each year. **Age 65+** = 32.6% in Sarasota County. **Median household income:** $30,662 (Sarasota County). **Per capita income:** $33,445 (Sarasota County).

NUMBERS TO KNOW
Chamber of commerce: (941) 349-3800. **Voter registration:** (941) 951-5307. **Vehicle registration, tags & title:** (941) 362-9898. **Driver's license:** In Sarasota, (941) 361-6217.

WHAT TO READ
Pelican Press, weekly newspaper, (941) 349-4949. **Sarasota Herald-Tribune**, daily newspaper, (941) 365-6060.

GETTING AROUND
Bus: Siesta Key Trolley, (941) 346-3115. **Taxi:** Green Cab, (941) 922-6666. **Tours:** None. **Airport:** Sarasota/Bradenton International. **Traffic:** With only one two-lane road traversing the length of the key, traffic is a problem during peak tourist season. Residents walk or ride bicycles as much as possible.

JOBS
County unemployment rate: 2.6%. **Florida Jobs and Benefits:** In Sarasota, (941) 361-6100.

UTILITIES
Electricity: Florida Power & Light, (941) 917-0708. **Gas:** Propane only. **Water & sewer:** Siesta Key Utilities Authority, (941) 349-0202. **Telephone:** GTE, (800) 483-4200. **Cable TV:** ComCast Cable, (941) 371-4444.

PLACES OF WORSHIP
Three churches: one Catholic, one Presbyterian and one Episcopal.

THE ENVIRONMENT
Sarasota Bay is designated as an Outstanding Florida Water and is part of the EPA's National Estuary Program. Sarasota Bay, between Bradenton and Sarasota, and Longboat Key Estuary have been rated as having generally fair water quality. They are negatively affected by urban runoff and discharge from the Sarasota Wastewater Treatment Plant (WWTP). Anna Maria Key Estuary and the St. Armands Key Estuary have generally good water quality. Whitaker Bayou has poor water quality. It receives effluent from the Sarasota WWTP. There have been occasional closings of shellfish harvesting areas in Whitaker Bayou. Siesta Key Estuary has fair to good water quality and shows an improving trend. Phillippi Creek has poor but improv-

ing water quality. Matheny Creek has fair water quality; it is affected by urban runoff. Catfish Creek, south of Matheny, has poor water quality and is affected by urban runoff and a closed landfill in close proximity. Its water quality is declining. Little Sarasota Bay near Catfish Creek has fair water quality.

EVENTS AND FESTIVALS
Siesta Fiesta - April. **Siesta Key Sand Fest** - October. **Taste of the Holidays** - November.

WHERE TO EAT
Ophelia's on the Bay, 9105 Midnight Pass Road, seafood, moderate to expensive, (941) 349-2212. **Turtle's**, 8875 Midnight Pass Road, American, inexpensive to moderate, (941) 346-2207.

WHERE TO STAY
Best Western Siesta Beach Resort, (941) 349-3211. **Crescent View Beach Club**, (941) 349-2000. **Tropical Shores Inn**, (941) 349-3330.

ISSUES
Peace and tranquillity prevail. The last significant battle — a Save Our Sand campaign several years ago — was fought to prevent dredging of sand off the coast of Siesta Key for a Venice Beach renourishment project. The issue was resolved without a grain lost!

RELOCATION TIPS

Moving to a new town requires you to find new doctors, lawyers and CPAs. Before you move, ask your current professionals to recommend a colleague in your new community. Or, start your search with the local office of the appropriate professional association. While such associations do not give recommendations, they usually will make referrals based on convenience of location and area of expertise or specialty.

Doctors: Call the local chapter of the American Medical Association and any other state or local medical societies listed in the telephone book for referrals.

Lawyers: Call the local chapter of the American Bar Association or the state bar association. If you need a lawyer with a specific area of expertise, be sure to ask for a referral to someone practicing that kind of law.

CPAs: Call a local chapter of the state society of CPAs.

Ask your new friends and neighbors for referrals as well.

Stuart

HE SAID: ★ ★ ★ ★
It has a small-town atmosphere that made me feel right at home and enough diversity to make me wish I was.

SHE SAID: ★ ★ ★ ★
In the heart of Stuart lies a unique community — safe, spacious, clean and with many types of neighborhoods. I would definitely consider this area for retirement. A final plus: The people are very friendly.

Ten years ago, a half million-dollar Main Street grant was the catalyst for a renovated and revitalized downtown Stuart that brought new businesses and shoppers back to the city center. Today, you can explore one facet of this fishing-village-turned-retirement-mecca by visiting the historic downtown. Here, you can stop at the sidewalk cafes, browse the antique shops and take a stroll along the river walk.

To find another side of Stuart, leave downtown and head in any direction. You'll find spectacular retirement communities built within the last 20 years and populated to a large extent by refugees from Dade, Broward and Palm Beach counties. Residents here have found a more-peaceful, less-crowded place in the sun than their neighbors to the south. Housing is not inexpensive, but with the choices available, most can find just the right neighborhood.

Water probably plays a larger role in the lives of Stuart's residents than in almost any other town in Florida. There is so much waterfront property that almost everyone lives on or in sight of water. Fishermen love it. After all, Stuart is the "Sailfish Capital of the World" and home to blue marlin, cobia, king, bluefish and Spanish mackerel. If you're a boater, you can travel down the south fork of the St. Lucie River, through the Okeechobee Waterway to Lake Okeechobee and continue west on the Caloosahatchee River to Fort Myers and the Gulf of Mexico — about a 135-mile trip, and delightfully scenic.

There are no high-rise structures. A Martin County ordinance limits building heights to four stories, lending an openness to even the busiest parts of the city. Golf courses abound, and more are planned.

Stuart is not a magnet for cultural activities, but its populace is socially active. Elected officials are voter-oriented and focused on holding down costs and building densities while bringing up the quality of life. They have been successful in creating one of the finest retirement towns in Florida, and from all indications, they intend to keep it that way.

WEATHER

	Winter	Spring	Summer	Fall
Normal daily high/low	77/56	85/68	90/74	81/63
Normal precipitation	9 in.	14 in.	20 in.	11 in.

Disaster watch: Southeast Florida has been hit by nine major hurricanes since 1900.

TAXES
Sales tax: 6%. **Property tax:** $20.15 per $1,000 valuation. Sample tax calculations include a $25,000 homestead exemption.

Home value	Tax
$100,000	$1,511
$150,000	$2,519
$250,000	$4,534

REAL ESTATE
Median home value: $95,671 (Martin County). **Median rent:** $560/month (Martin County). **Communities popular with retirees:** Hidden Harbour has double-wide manufactured homes with marina boat slips; prices start in the $60s, (561) 287-6387. Hansons Landing, on the Intracoastal Waterway, has three-bedroom condos starting at $102,900, (561) 220-5865. Parkside is a development of lakes, parks and nature preserves with two-bedroom, two-bath patio homes starting in the $120s, (561) 391-9377. Harbour Island at Cutter Sound has three-bedroom luxury townhouses with private pools from $225,000, (561) 221-1822. Monarch Country Club has single-family homes from the $140s to the $400s, (561) 286-6800. Sailfish Point, a golf-course community on a peninsula north of St. Lucie Inlet at the juncture of the Indian River and the Atlantic Ocean, has condominiums for $375,000-$550,000 and homes for $500,000-$1,500,000, (561) 225-1000. **Licensed continuing-care retirement communities:** None.

CRIME & SAFETY
Crimes per 1,000 population: 86. **Non-emergency police:** (561) 287-1122. **Non-emergency fire department:** (561) 288-5360. **Police, fire, ambulance emergencies:** 911.

HOMELESS & BLIGHT
We saw no homeless people in Stuart. It does have some neighborhoods of substandard housing. Downtown has been renovated and rejuvenated and is very popular for shopping and dining.

The U.S. Census reported 26 homeless persons in shelters and 17 visible on the streets of Martin County, population 100,900.

HEALTH CARE
Hospitals: Martin Memorial Medical Center, 336 beds, full service, (561) 287-5200. **Martin Memorial Hospital South**, 100 beds, full service, (561) 223-2300. **Martin Memorial SurgiCenter**, outpatient surgery, (561) 223-5920. **Physicians:** 200. **Specialties:** 43.

GETTING SMART
Indian River Community College, Chastain Center, (561) 283-6550. **Offerings:** Two-year degrees in arts and sciences, a women's program and continuing-education courses for personal development. **Florida Institute of Technology**, (561) 234-4096. **Offerings:** Graduate degrees in business education.

JUST FOR SENIORS
Martin County Council on Aging, (561) 283-2242. **Transportation services**, (561) 283-1814. **Meals on Wheels** and adult day care, (561) 283-8384. **Log Cabin Senior Center**, Jensen Beach, (561) 334-2926, offers meals, crafts, exercise and other activities.

GETTING INVOLVED
There are almost 200 clubs and organizations in the Stuart area. **Martin County Council for the Arts**, (561) 287-6676.

RECREATION, ENTERTAINMENT & AMENITIES
Public golf: The Champion Club at Summerfield, 18 holes/par 72; 76 Golfworld, nine holes/par 27; Martin County Golf & Country Club, 36 holes/par 144; and Pine Lakes Golf Course, 18 holes/par 66. **Semi-private golf:** Florida Club at Martin County, 18 holes/par 72. **Private golf:** Indian River Plantation, 18 holes/par 61; Mariner Sands Country Club, 36 holes/par 144; Martin Downs Country

Club, 36 holes/par 144; Miles Grant Country Club, 18 holes/par 64; Monterey Yacht & Country Club, 18 holes/par 58; Sailfish Point Golf & Country Club, 18 holes/par 72; and Willoughby Golf Club, 18 holes/par 72. **Public tennis courts:** Memorial Park, East 10th Street Park and City Tennis Courts. **Private tennis courts:** Indian River Plantation, Falkenburg Tennis Club and North River Shores Tennis Club. **Parks:** Bathtub Reef Park has fishing, surfing, swimming, snorkeling, windsurfing, diving, a boat dock, boardwalk and nature center. St. Lucie Inlet State Park has a nature center, fishing, boating, snorkeling and diving. Hobe Sound National Wildlife Refuge offers fishing, swimming, shelling, diving and boating. **Public swimming pools:** Community swimming pool at Martin County High School. **Water sports:** St. Lucie River wraps around the west, north and east sides of Stuart. It provides boating, fishing, swimming, water-skiing and other recreational opportunities. There's also snorkeling and scuba diving. **River/gulf/ocean:** The St. Lucie River, Indian River (Intracoastal Waterway) and Atlantic Ocean. Stuart public beaches are the community's most popular attractions. **Running/walking/biking:** Martin County's Parks and Recreation Department provides bicycle paths that connect certain areas of the county. Hobe Sound Wildlife Refuge is good for self-guided walking tours. **Horses/riding:** Several stables in the area offer boarding and training. **Hunting:** Hunting and fishing licenses available through the Martin County Tax Collector's Office, (561) 288-5595. **Movie theaters:** 15 screens at three theaters. **Art museums:** Art Associates of Martin County, the Center for the Arts and the Courthouse Cultural Center. **History museums:** Elliott Museum and Gilbert's Bar House of Refuge Museum, which was built in the late 1800s as a haven for shipwrecked sailors. **Theaters:** Barn Theatre, Lyric Theatre and the Performing Arts Society of Stuart. **Library:** Martin County Public Library. **Attractions:** Coastal Science Center, Hutchinson Island and downtown Stuart, designated a Florida Main Street City by the State Bureau of Historic Preservation. The Environmental Studies Center in nearby Jensen Beach provides environmental instruction for schoolchildren as well as an environmental lecture series for adults, (561) 334-1262. **Necessities:** Stuart has it all.

Smart Shopper Tip: There are a half dozen major malls and several outlet centers within 30 minutes of downtown. Treasure Coast Square in Stuart and the Indian River Mall near Vero Beach offer traditional shopping amenities. The Gardens, to the south in Palm Beach Gardens, has Macy's, Burdines, Bloomingdale's, Saks Fifth Avenue and Sears.

WHO LIVES HERE
Population: 13,801 year-round residents, an increase of 1,865 since 1990. **Age 65+** = 29.3% in Martin County. **Median household income:** $32,358 (Martin County). **Per capita income:** $34,529 (Martin County).

NUMBERS TO KNOW
Chamber of commerce: (561) 287-1088. **Voter registration:** (561) 288-5637. **Vehicle registration, tags & title:** (561) 288-5600. **Driver's license:** (561) 398-1306.

WHAT TO READ
Stuart News, daily newspaper, (561) 287-1550. **Palm Beach Post**, daily newspaper, (800) 432-7595. **Indiantown News**, weekly newspaper, (561) 597-4243.

GETTING AROUND
Bus: Community Coach, (561) 283-1814. **Taxi:** Yellow Cab, (561) 334-1606. **Tours:** Island Princess offers cruises of area waterways, (561) 225-2100. **Airport:** Palm Beach International is 40 miles away. **Traffic:** No real problem areas.

JOBS
County unemployment rate: 5.9%. **Florida Jobs and Benefits:** (561) 221-4020.

UTILITIES
Electricity: Florida Power & Light, (561) 287-5400. **Gas:** None. **Water & sewer:** City of Stuart Water Dept., (561) 288-5322. **Telephone:** Southern Bell, (561) 780-2355 in Florida, or (800) 753-0710 out-of-state. **Cable TV:** Adelphia, (561) 692-1400.

PLACES OF WORSHIP
There are 83 Protestant and five Catholic Churches, and two Jewish synagogues in the greater Stuart area.

THE ENVIRONMENT
Surface water quality has been rated as good in the south fork of the St. Lucie River, fair in the main section of the St. Lucie River and poor in Manatee Creek at Manatee Pocket. The 15-mile-long Savannas between Fort Pierce and Stuart has fairly good water quality, but concentrations of mercury in fish warranted a no-consumption advisory for largemouth bass.

The Martin County/North County water system had lead in its drinking water measuring 84 parts per billion (ppb). The EPA action level is 15 ppb.

There is one EPA-listed Superfund site in Martin County, the Florida Steel Corp. site, located two miles northwest of Indiantown, quite a distance from Stuart.

EVENTS AND FESTIVALS
Sheriff's Barbecue - January. **Annual Arts Fest** - February. **Martin County Fair** - March. **Dancin' in the Streets** - August. **Christmas Boat Parade** - December.

WHERE TO EAT
The Jolly Sailor Pub & Restaurant, 1 S.W. Osceola St., British & American, moderate, (561) 221-1111. **Plaza Cafe**, 3168 S.E. Dixie Hwy., gourmet, moderate to expensive, (561) 286-9030. **Luna Italian Cuisine**, 49 Flagler Ave., pasta & pizza, moderate, (561) 288-0550.

WHERE TO STAY
Holiday Inn-Downtown, (561) 287-6200. **Indian River Plantation**, (561) 225-3700.

ISSUES
An expanded river walkway, the new Roosevelt Bridge spanning the St. Lucie River, a $10 million Martin County beach renourishment project, the new Indian River Mall and the redevelopment of Stuart's commercial downtown all appear to be moves in the right direction. Are they compatable with environmentalists goals of keeping Martin County green?

Sun City Center

HE SAID: ★ ★ ★ ★ ☆
From the time we turned off the interstate and began the short drive into Sun City Center, we felt this was a special place that might live up to its self-styled billing as America's premier retirement town. When we left, we were convinced of it.

SHE SAID: ★ ★ ★ ★ ☆
This is a true retirement setting: lots of activities, entertainment, neighborhoods in different price ranges, golf-cart transportation and gated areas. Look here for a place to retire — I would.

What is it about Sun City Center that is so appealing? The 5,000-acre, self-contained, planned adult community is pleasing to the eye, easy on the wallet and just what the doctor ordered for your mental and physical well-being. More than 13,000 people have chosen modest-to-fabulous new homes in a variety of styles and scenic locations here.

When you move in, you can sell the old jalopy and forget about auto insurance, registration, licenses, tags and the price of gasoline. Golf carts are the recognized and preferred means of transportation here. More than 2,700 privately owned carts transport residents to shopping centers, churches and doctors' offices. No driver's license is required to operate the carts, though there is a small annual trail fee to drive private carts on Sun City Center golf courses. When you leave the community, HARTline and resident-owned buses make scheduled trips to regional attractions and shopping facilities.

There's more than adequate incentive to buy into the amenities package, starting with 126 holes of golf. That doesn't begin to reveal the extent of the facilities available for recreation, hobbies, exercise and social enjoyment. During our visit, at least 500 residents and guests were participating in a hotly contested lawn bowling championship. At the same time, arts and crafts classes were filled with senior students of lapidary, ceramics, woodworking and a myriad of other activities.

One of the best examples of volunteerism is the 1,500-member Sun City Center Resident Volunteer Security Patrol. They provide 24-hour peace of mind to the community. In more than 200 clubs and organizations, volunteers manage, schedule and conduct the activities that help create an unbeatable retirement lifestyle.

Sun City Center has location, atmosphere, climate, cultural and recreational activities, community services, affordable housing and golf, golf, golf. Who could ask for anything more?

WEATHER

	Winter	Spring	Summer	Fall
Normal daily high/low	73/53	86/67	90/74	78/58
Normal precipitation	8 in.	10 in.	20 in.	6 in.

Disaster watch: Southwest Florida has been hit by five major hurricanes since 1900.

TAXES
Sales tax: 7.0%. **Property tax:** $25.26 per $1,000 valuation. Sample taxes include a $25,000 homestead exemption.

Home value	Tax
$100,000	$1,895
$150,000	$3,158
$250,000	$5,684

REAL ESTATE
Median home value: $100,951 (Hillsborough County). **Median rent:** $607/month (Hillsborough County). **Communities popular with retirees:** There are single-family homes, duplex homes and duplex villa condominiums. New two-bedroom condo villas are priced from the $70s. New single-family homes range from the $90s to $300s. Resales are priced from the $50s. Sun City Center Realty, (813) 634-5588. **Licensed continuing-care retirement communities:** Freedom Plaza, 388 independent living units, 42 sheltered nursing beds, (813) 633-1992. Lake Towers Retirement Center, 230 independent living units, 11 sheltered nursing beds, 109 community beds, (813) 634-3347.

CRIME & SAFETY
Crimes per 1,000 population: 66 (Hillsborough County sheriff's jurisdiction). **Non-emergency police:** Hillsborough Sheriff's Dept., (813) 247-8000. Sun City Center Security Patrol, (813) 634-6324. **Non-emergency fire department:** Hillsborough County Fire Department, (813) 272-6600, or Ed Powers Fire Department on the premises, (813) 671-7712. **Medical emergency:** (813) 634-3800. **Police, fire, ambulance emergencies:** 911.

HOMELESS & BLIGHT
There are no blighted areas or homeless persons in Sun City Center. This is one of the cleanest and best-organized communities we visited in all of Florida.

The U.S. Census reported 434 homeless persons in shelters and 327 visible in street locations in Hillsborough County, population 834,054.

HEALTH CARE
Hospitals: South Bay Hospital, 112 beds, 24-hour emergency, full service, (813) 634-3301.
Physicians: 82. **Specialties:** 30.

GETTING SMART
SCC Community Association, (813) 633-3500. **Offerings:** Lecture-discussion courses sponsored by the community association meet once a week for six weeks. A contribution of $1 per class session is requested. Sample subjects: personal finance, holistic medicine, five scrolls of the Bible, astronomy and the "Ocean and Florida."

JUST FOR SENIORS
Everything in Sun City Center is just for seniors. One person in each household must be at least 55. No permanent residents under 18. Young children are welcome to visit, with length-of-stay restrictions.

GETTING INVOLVED
There are more than 200 special interest organizations devoted to hobbies, crafts, social events and volunteerism. Examples: Samaritan Services, Security Patrol, Meals on Wheels.

RECREATION, ENTERTAINMENT & AMENITIES
Resident golf: Caloosa Greens Executive Course, 18 holes/par 54; Cypress Greens Country Club, 27 holes/par 108; Kings Point Executive Golf Course, 18 holes/par 54; North Course, 18 holes/par 72; and South Course, 27 holes/par 108. **Private equity golf:** Caloosa Golf and Country Club, 18 holes/par 72. **Resident tennis courts:** Seven courts. **Private tennis courts:** Golf & Racquet Club. **Parks:** Two indoor recreation facilities cover 36 acres, containing hobby centers, meeting rooms, exercise facilities, game rooms, a social club and auditorium. **Public swimming pools:** Five. **Water sports:** Paddle boats, canoes and pontoon boats are used by residents living on the waterfront. Bahia Beach Marina, eight miles away, provides boat access to Gulf waters. **River/gulf/ocean:** Numerous small lakes, including three large enough for boat traffic. **Running/walking/biking:** No trails specifically designed for these activities. Many people use the sidewalks and golf cart paths that run parallel to main roads. Rural areas to the east are excellent for hiking and biking. **Horses/riding:** No facilities in Sun City Center, but there are farms and stables in adjoining areas. **Hunting:** None. **Movie theaters:** Kings Point Auditorium shows first-run movies, free. **Art museums:** None. **History museums:** None. **Theaters:** Kings Point Auditorium. **Library:** Two. **Attractions:** Recreational facilities and the many opportunities to get involved. **Necessities:** Banks, attorneys, accountants, stockbrokers, financial planning services, travel agencies, several shopping plazas, supermarkets, pharmacies, restaurants, hair salons and a post office.

Smart Shopper Tip: Sun City Center Plaza and Rickenbacker Plaza are within walking distance. Resident-owned buses are available for extended shopping trips.

WHO LIVES HERE
Population: 14,000 year-round residents. **Age 65+** = 12.9% in Hillsborough County. **Median household income:** $30,296 (Hillsborough County). **Per capita income:** $21,509 (Hillsborough County).

NUMBERS TO KNOW
Chamber of commerce: (813) 634-8437 or (813) 634-5111. The staff of Florida Design Communities, which owns and operates the amenities serving the community, assists new and potential residents with information regarding vehicle registration, licenses and other residency requirements, (813) 634-3311.

WHAT TO READ
The Sun, weekly newspaper, (813) 634-9258. **The Shopper Observer News,** weekly newspaper, (813) 645-3111.

GETTING AROUND
Bus: Hillsborough Rapid Transit (HARTline), (813) 254-4278. Resident-owned buses make scheduled trips to attractions and shopping. **Taxi:** None. **Tours:** None. **Airport:** Tampa International is 37 miles away. Sarasota/Bradenton is 30 miles away. **Traffic:** Get a golf cart and put away your memories of rush hour madness.

JOBS
County unemployment rate: 3.1%. **Florida Jobs and Benefits:** In Tampa, (727) 861-4800.

UTILITIES
Electricity: Tampa Electric, (813) 876-3566. **Gas:** None. **Water & sewer:** Hillsborough County Public Utilities, (813) 272-6680. **Telephone:** GTE, (800) 483-4200. **Cable TV:** Interactive Cable, (813) 978-8000, or Time Warner Communications, (813) 684-6400, depending on location of residence.

PLACES OF WORSHIP
One Catholic and six Protestant churches, plus one Jewish synagogue.

THE ENVIRONMENT
Water quality throughout Tampa Bay generally has been rated as poor to fair. The best water quality is in lower Tampa Bay. The worst water quality is in Hillsborough and McKay bays. Hillsborough Bay has shown some recovery recently.

A report by the Florida Department of Environmental Regulation states, "Due to the ecological, economic and aesthetic importance of this water body, Tampa Bay has become a major focus of local, regional and state actions to reverse the negative trends." The bay has been designated as a priority SWIM (Surface Water Improvement and Management) water body.

There are nine EPA-listed Superfund sites in Hillsborough County. None are in Sun City Center.

EVENTS AND FESTIVALS
Art Club Show - February. **Strawberry Festival** in Plant City - March. **Florida Orchestra Concert** - April.

WHERE TO EAT
Sunsations Restaurant, 1335 Rickenbacker Drive, moderate, (813) 634-3331.

WHERE TO STAY
Comfort Inn, (813) 633-3318. **Sun City Center Hotel,** (813) 634-3331.

ISSUES
When we visited, two issues were being intensely debated by the leaders of the community association, and to a lesser extent by the resident members at-large. One issue was the cost of maintaining the plants and landscaping along the median of Route 674. The other involved a two-day referendum to change the community association's articles of incorporation.

Tallahassee

Tallahassee is a first-rate capital city. Clean, well-structured and easy to navigate, it gives off an aura of sophistication and competence. Whether those qualities are because of — or in spite of — the 44,000 politicos and bureaucrats living in the city is a matter of opinion. The ratio of one government employee to every two persons privately employed in Tallahassee's labor force has undoubtedly had an impact.

Whatever the cause, the results are clear. Tallahassee has excellent streets and highways, beautifully landscaped parks and grounds, impressive buildings with porticos and colonnades endemic to seats of government, and many museums, galleries, centers and auditoriums. Places to see and be seen.

Lest you begin to think Tallahassee is too stuffy and straight-laced for your taste, there are also 700 McDonald's employees, no less than 16 organizations devoted to providing services to senior citizens and 11 groups dedicated to preserving the natural resources and quality of life in north Florida.

Tallahassee offers a pleasant mix of elements — some with a southern accent and others strictly Floridian. It has history and tradition, government buildings and monuments, and, importantly, a sense of place that merits exploring.

WEATHER

	Winter	Spring	Summer	Fall
Normal daily high/low	68/42	86/61	90/70	73/48
Normal precipitation	17 in.	15 in.	22 in.	12 in.

Disaster watch: Northwest Florida has been hit by six major hurricanes since 1900.

TAXES

Sales tax: 7%. **Property tax:** $22.44 per $1,000 valuation. Sample tax calculations include a $25,000 homestead exemption.

Home value	Tax
$100,000	$1,683
$150,000	$2,805
$250,000	$5,049

REAL ESTATE

Median home value: $81,981 (Leon County). **Median rent:** $567/month (Leon County). **Communities popular with retirees:** Linda Rose with Fezler and Russell, (850) 545-8053, says there are no retirement communities, but plenty of retirees live in neighborhoods throughout the city. **Licensed continuing-care retirement communities:** Westminister Oaks has 258 independent living units, 30 sheltered nursing beds and 30 community beds, (850) 878-1136.

CRIME & SAFETY

Crimes per 1,000 population: 100. **Non-emergency police:** (850) 891-4200. **Non-emergency fire department:** (850) 891-6600. **Police, fire, ambulance emergencies:** 911.

HOMELESS & BLIGHT

We saw a few homeless persons and somewhat blighted neighborhoods, but the dominant features of the city are stately buildings, clean streets, pretty gardens and manicured lawns and grounds.

The U.S. Census reported 148 homeless persons in shelters and 30 homeless persons visible on the streets in Leon County, population 192,493.

HEALTH CARE

Hospitals: Tallahassee Community Hospital, 180 beds, full service, (850) 656-5000. **Tallahassee Memorial Regional Medical Center**, 771 beds, full service, (850) 681-1155. **Healthsouth Hospital**, 40 beds, (850) 656-4800. **Eastside Psychiatric Hospital**, (850) 487-0300.

Physicians: 540. **Specialties:** 47.

GETTING SMART

Florida State University, (850) 644-2525. **Offerings:** Colleges of arts and sciences, education, business, engineering, communication and law, as well as schools of nursing, music, social work, criminology, visual arts, etc. **Florida A&M University**, (850) 599-3000. **Offerings:** Undergraduate, graduate and doctoral degrees. Courses of study include business, pharmacy, architecture, journalism, arts and sciences, engineering and more. **Tallahassee Community College**, (850) 488-9200. **Offerings:** Two-year associate's degree program.

JUST FOR SENIORS

Area Agency on Aging of North Florida, (850) 488-0055. **AARP**, (850) 222-7344. **Elder Care Services**, (850) 921-5554. **Senior Citizens Center**, (850) 891-4000.

GETTING INVOLVED

RSVP, (850) 222-2253.

RECREATION, ENTERTAINMENT & AMENITIES

Public golf: Hilaman Park Municipal Golf Course, Jake Gaither Golf Course and Seminole Golf Course. **Private golf:** Capital City Country Club, Gadsden Golf & Country Club, Golden Eagle Country Club, and Killearn Country Club and Inn. **Public tennis courts:** 123 courts, mostly municipal. **Private tennis courts:** Capital City Country Club. **Parks:** 48 city, state and county parks and recreation areas. Apalachicola National Forest forms the southwest border of the city. **Public swimming pools:** 14, mostly municipal. **Water sports:** Boating, water-skiing and canoeing. **River/gulf/ocean:** The Ochlockonee and Little rivers flow west of the city. St. Marks and Aucilla rivers are to the east. Lakes Talquin, Jackson, Iamonia and Miccosukee provide fishing and water sports. Apalachee Bay is 25 miles south on the Gulf. **Running/walking/biking:** Numerous trails. Apalachicola National Forest offers hiking, horseback riding, boating, canoeing, bicycling, bird-watching and wildlife viewing. The 16.5-mile St. Marks Trail follows an abandoned railroad bed. **Horses/riding:** Several riding academies, stables, breeders and trainers and many riding trails. **Hunting:** Florida Game and Freshwater Fish Commission, (850) 488-4676, for licenses and

194

information. **Movie theaters:** 43 screens. **Art museums:** Foster Tanner Fine Arts Gallery, LeMoyne Art Foundation and University Gallery & Museum. **History museums:** Knott House Museum, Museum of Florida History, San Luis Archaeological & Historic Site, State Archives & History Building, and Tallahassee Museum of History and Natural Science. **Theaters:** Tallahassee Little Theatre, Ruby Diamond Auditorium at FSU, Leon County Civic Center, FSU School of Theater, Young Actor's Theater and Monticello Opera House. Performing arts groups include Tallahassee Ballet, Dance Arts Guild, FSU Dance Repertory and Tallahassee Symphony. **Library:** Main Library and three branches, State Library, plus libraries at FSU, FSU Law, Community College and Florida A&M. **Attractions:** Florida A&M University, (850) 599-3000; FSU, (850) 644-3246; FSU football, (850) 644-1830, and basketball, (850) 644-1461; Florida Capitol Complex; Florida Governor's Mansion; Maclay State Gardens; and Adams Street Commons. Don't miss the roads canopied by moss-draped oaks: Old St. Augustine Road, Centerville Road (Route 151) and Miccosukee Road (Route 146). **Necessities:** Yes! Just ask, it's here.

Smart Shopper Tip: Tallahassee is a shopper's paradise. You don't have to go any farther than the Governor's Square Mall with its more than 140 shops including Burdine's, J.C. Penney, Sears and Dillards. If that's not enough, the Tallahassee Mall with 165 stores is only minutes away.

WHO LIVES HERE
Population: 140,643 year-round residents, an increase of 15,870 since 1990. **Age 65+** = 8.7% in Leon County. **Median household income:** $32,005 (Leon County). **Per capita income:** $20,875 (Leon County).

NUMBERS TO KNOW
Chamber of commerce: (850) 224-8116. **Voter registration:** (850) 488-1350. **Vehicle registration, tags, title & driver's license:** (850) 488-7856. **Visitors bureau:** (850) 413-9200.

WHAT TO READ
Tallahassee Democrat, daily newspaper, (850) 599-2191. **Capital Outlook**, weekly newspaper, (850) 681-1852. **Tallahassean**, weekly newspaper, (850) 224-3806. **The Florida Flambeau**, FSU student newspaper, (850) 561-6653. **Tallahassee Magazine**, bimonthly, (850) 878-0554.

GETTING AROUND
Bus: TalTran, (850) 891-5200. Old Town Trolley operates downtown on weekdays, (850) 891-5200. **Taxi:** City Taxi, (850) 562-4222. Yellow Cab, (850) 580-8080. **Tours:** None. **Airport:** Tallahassee Regional is seven miles from downtown. **Traffic:** Surprisingly light for a city of this size.

JOBS
County unemployment rate: 3.5%. **Florida Jobs and Benefits:** (850) 488-8701. **Job Line:** (850) 891-8219. **Senior Community Service Employment Program:** (850) 224-0220.

UTILITIES
Electricity: City of Tallahassee, (850) 891-8120. **Gas, water & sewer:** City Utilities Dept., (850) 891-8120. **Telephone:** Sprint-CENTEL, (850) 599-1073. **Cable TV:** ComCast Cablevision, (850) 574-4000.

PLACES OF WORSHIP
Churches: 293 Protestant representing 54 denominations plus 12 non-denominational, seven Catholic and one Greek Orthodox. Temples: one Buddhist, one Hindu and one Taoist. Also, three Jewish synagogues.

THE ENVIRONMENT
The water quality rating of Lake Jackson is still good. Recent acquisitions around Lake Jackson have relieved the pressure of suburban development, with much of the land managed as a passive park-greenway system.

The Megginnis arm restoration project results have been positive and monitoring is ongoing. Health advisories have been issued advising limited consumption of largemouth bass taken from Lake Talquin, Lake Iamonia and Ochlockonee River due to mercury content.

Much of the St. Marks and Wakulla Rivers have excellent water quality ratings. Portions of St. Marks have been troubled by oil spills. Lake Munson and Munson Slough have poor water quality caused by urban runoff.

EVENTS AND FESTIVALS
Natural Bridge Battlefield Historic Site Re-enactment - March. **Springtime Tallahassee Festival** - March/April. **Native American Heritage Festival** - September. **Market Days** - November/December. **Celebration of Lights** - December.

WHERE TO EAT
There are 549 restaurants in the area. Among those often recommended: **Andrew's Second Act**, 228 S. Adams St., continental, expensive to very expensive, (850) 222-3444. **Anthony's**, 1950-G Thomasville Road, Italian, moderate, (850) 224-1447. **Chez Pierre**, 115 N. Adams St., French, moderate, (850) 222-0936.

WHERE TO STAY
There are 54 hotels and motels in Leon County. Among the notables: **Governors Inn**, (850) 681-6855. **Tallahassee Motor Hotel**, (800) 251-1962. **Doubletree Tallahassee**, (800) 325-3535 or (850) 224-5000.

ISSUES
As the state's capital, Tallahassee has a large role to play in the future of tourism and retiree migration to Florida with regard to crimes against tourists and overall violence. But as a city, Tallahassee has much less to worry about than the state's southern sectors.

With a very low unemployment rate, a strong support system of service organizations for seniors and youths, two major universities, strong law enforcement and the headquarters of city, county and state governments, Tallahassee is about as rock solid as a city can be.

Its primary concern over the next decade should be the development and maintenance of roads and infrastructure to handle the population growth of the city and surrounding area.

Tampa

It's a city that offers tourist attractions, entertainment, shopping and more. It boasts two major theme parks, Adventure Island and Busch Gardens. There's also the Lowry Park Zoo, Ybor City, Tampa Stadium, the Tampa Bay Buccaneers, Old Hyde Park Village, The Shops on Harbour Island and the Tampa Bay Performing Arts Center, to name just a few of its amenities. Serving the city are four colleges and universities, 10 hospitals with 3,728 beds, numerous golf courses, 87 parks, Tampa International Airport and the Port of Tampa. Bayshore Boulevard's 6.5-mile sidewalk is the longest waterfront promenade in the world. The list goes on and on.

But these multiple attractions are the very features that diminish Tampa's attractiveness as a retirement community. Even when you're not using one of these resources, it is virtually impossible to avoid being caught in the maelstrom caused by too many people occupying too little space. With 10 million people using Tampa International Airport each year, there are too many comings and goings.

Tampa has so much to offer that it seems best to sample it on an occasional basis. Living in a quiet haven in the southwest Florida countryside would allow plenty of opportunity to enjoy this busy city's output. Two or three times each year you could go to the Performing Arts Center for cultural experiences or to Tampa Stadium to watch the Buccaneers get beat. These excursions could involve an hour's drive from Dade City, Dunedin or Brandon, dinner at one of the 980 restaurants in the area and, after the evening's main event, a night at one of the 200 or so lodging establishments.

Tampa's attractions can be a real asset for retirees looking for a well-rounded active lifestyle, as long as you can make a fast retreat to a quieter haven at bedtime.

WEATHER

	Winter	Spring	Summer	Fall
Normal daily high/low	73/53	86/67	90/74	78/58
Normal precipitation	8 in.	10 in.	20 in.	6 in.

Disaster watch: Since 1900, northwest Florida has been hit by six major hurricanes and southwest Florida has been hit by five.

TAXES
Sales tax: 6.5%. **Property tax:** Rates range from $24.00 to $29.00 per $1,000 valuation. Sample taxes are calculated at the rate of $29.00 and include a $25,000 homestead exemption.

Home value	Tax
$100,000	$2,175
$150,000	$3,625
$250,000	$6,525

REAL ESTATE
Median home value: $100,951 (Hillsborough County). **Median rent:** $607/month (Hillsborough County). **Communities**

popular with retirees: Heritage Greens is a golf-course retirement community with homes from the $70s, (813) 948-6610. Westchase is a master-planned community with homes priced from the $120s to $500s, (800) 833-2494. Cory Lake Isles is a gated, waterfront community with single-family homes from the $200s, (813) 986-2679. **Licensed continuing-care retirement communities:** Canterbury Towers, 125 independent living units, 40 community beds and 20 sheltered nursing beds, (813) 837-1083. The Home Association, 30 independent living units, 60 community beds, (813) 229-6901. John Knox Village, 512 independent living units, 103 sheltered nursing beds, 60 community beds, (813) 977-4950. University Village Retirement Center, 520 independent living units, 120 sheltered nursing beds and 120 community beds, (813) 975-5000.

CRIME & SAFETY
Crimes per 1,000 population: 148. **Non-emergency police:** (813) 276-3200. **Non-emergency fire department:** (813) 227-7015. **Police, fire, ambulance emergencies:** 911.

HOMELESS & BLIGHT
Tampa has a modern, clean and exciting downtown and many points of interest. To bring people downtown, there are street markets and renovated historic buildings alongside the corporate towers. It has some run-down houses and commercial buildings. We saw some homeless persons.

The U.S. Census reported 434 homeless persons in shelters and 327 visible in street locations in Hillsborough County, population 834,054.

HEALTH CARE
Hospitals: Tampa General Hospital, 1,000 beds, full service, (813) 251-7000. **St. Joseph's Hospital**, 650 beds, and **Women's Hospital**, 219 beds, (813) 870-4000. **James A. Haley Veterans Administration Hospital**, 697 beds, (813) 972-2000. **University Community Hospital**, 404 beds, 24-hour emergency, (813) 971-6000. **Memorial Hospital of Tampa**, 174 beds, 24-hour emergency, (813) 873-6400. **Town & Country Hospital**, 201 beds, 24-hour emergency, (813) 885-6666.
Physicians: 2,546 (Hillsborough County). **Specialties:** All.

GETTING SMART
Hillsborough Community College, (813) 253-7802. **Offerings:** Two-year degrees and continuing-education courses. **Tampa College**, (813) 879-6000. **Offerings:** Four-year degrees, graduate degrees and diplomas. **University of South Florida**, (813) 974-2011. **Offerings:** More than 200 undergraduate and graduate degrees in 13 schools and colleges. **University of Tampa**, (813) 253-3333. **Offerings:** Four-year liberal arts and science degrees and an MBA program.

JUST FOR SENIORS
Bethune Senior Center, (813) 273-3695. **Senior Friends**, (727) 844-7856. **Jewish Community Center**, (813) 264-9000. **Life Enrichment Multi-Purpose Senior Center**, (813) 932-0241. **Senior Care** at University Community Hospital, (813) 972-7887. **Senior Citizens Information**, (813) 273-3779.

GETTING INVOLVED
Meals on Wheels of Tampa, (813) 238-8410. **SCORE,** (727) 532-6800. **Volunteers of America,** (813) 282-1525.

RECREATION, ENTERTAINMENT & AMENITIES
Public golf: Eight courses including Babe Zaharias Golf Course. **Private golf:** Avila Golf and Country Club, Cheval Country Club, Hunter's Green Country Club, Tampa Palms Golf and Country Club, Tournament Players Club and Palma Ceia Golf and Country Club. **Public tennis courts:** 98 courts. **Private tennis courts:** Avila Golf, Bahia Beach Island Resort Tennis Club, Hunter's Green Tennis and Athletic Center, Northdale Tennis Club and Saddlebrook Club. **Parks:** 87 in the city. **Public swimming pools:** 10. **Water sports:** Boating, parasailing, sailing, swimming, windsurfing and water-skiing. **River/gulf/ocean:** Hillsborough River, Hillsborough Bay, McKay Bay, Old Tampa Bay and Tampa Bay. **Running/walking/biking:** Bayshore Boulevard, parks and beaches are very popular with joggers and walkers. Malls also are popular with walkers. **Horses/riding:** Tampa Bay Downs. **Hunting:** None. **Movie theaters:** 75 screens. **Art museums:** Tampa Museum of Art. **History museums:** Henry B. Plant Museum and Ybor City State Museum. **Theaters:** Tampa Theatre, David Falk Theatre and the University of South Florida Fine Arts Theatre. **Library:** Main library and 11 branches. **Attractions:** Adventure Island, Busch Gardens, Children's Museum, Courtney Campbell Causeway, Florida Aquarium, the Jose Gasparilla pirate ship, Lowry Park and Zoo, Museum of Science and Industry, The Shops on Harbour Island, Tampa Bay Buccaneers, Tampa Dog Track, Tampa Bay Lightning hockey and Ybor City. **Necessities:** All.

Smart Shopper Tip: A shopper's paradise! There are five major enclosed malls, a great factory outlet mall and dozens of fine shopping centers and plazas. Old Hyde Park Village and The Shops of Harbour Island are musts.

WHO LIVES HERE
Population: 290,886 year-round residents, an increase of 10,871 since 1990. **Age 65+** = 12.9% in Hillsborough County. **Median household income:** $30,296 (Hillsborough County). **Per capita income:** $21,509 (Hillsborough County).

NUMBERS TO KNOW
Chamber of commerce: (813) 228-7777. **Voter registration:** (813) 272-5850. **Vehicle registration, tags & title:** (813) 272-6020. **Driver's license:** (813) 272-6020. **Visitors bureau:** (813) 223-1111, ext. 44.

WHAT TO READ
Tampa Tribune, daily newspaper, (813) 259-7711. **St. Petersburg Times,** daily newspaper, (813) 273-4414.

GETTING AROUND
Bus: Hillsborough Regional Transit, (813) 623-5835. Downtown, try the PeopleMover monorail. **Taxi:** Yellow Cab, (813) 253-0121. **Tours:** Too many to list. **Airport:** Tampa International. **Traffic:** The interstates, highways and thoroughfares are jammed with traffic at all hours.

JOBS
County unemployment rate: 3.1%. **Job Service of Florida:** (813) 930-7400. **Job and Career Assessment:** For senior citizens, (813) 272-5321.

UTILITIES
Electricity: Florida Power Corp., (813) 229-2981, or Tampa Electric Co., (813) 223-0800, depending on location of residence. **Gas:** Peoples Gas, (813) 275-3700. **Water & sewer:** Tampa Utilities, (813) 274-8811. **Telephone:** GTE Florida, (813) 229-2105. **Cable TV:** Several serve the area, including TCI Cablevision, (813) 736-1436, and Time Warner Cable, (727) 562-5025.

PLACES OF WORSHIP
52 Catholic and 444 Protestant churches, eight Jewish synagogues and 36 other faiths.

THE ENVIRONMENT
Water quality throughout the area generally has been rated as fair to poor. The best water quality is in lower Tampa Bay. The worst water quality in the area is in Hillsborough and McKay bays, though the Hillsborough Bay has shown some recovery. Tampa Bay has been designated as a priority SWIM (Surface Water Improvement and Management) water body and is a major focus of governmental actions to reverse negative trends.

Hillsborough County has nine EPA-listed Superfund sites. Those in Tampa are the Helena Chemical Plant, Kassouf-Kimerling Battery Disposal, Peak Oil Co./Bay Drum Co., Sixty-Second Street Dump and Stauffer Chemical Co. Tampa plant.

EVENTS AND FESTIVALS
First Night Tampa Bay - January. **College Football Hall of Fame Bowl** - January. **Gasparilla Festival** - February. **Florida State Fair** - February. **GTE Suncoast Golf Classic** - February. **Presidents Cup Regatta** - March. **Winter Equestrian Festival** - March. **Senior Life Festival** - April. **Florida Dance Festival** - June. **Summer Arts & Crafts Festival** - July. **Labor Day Festival** - September. **A Taste of Florida** - October.

WHERE TO EAT
Bern's Steak House, 1208 S. Howard Ave., steak, expensive, (813) 251-2421. **Crawdaddy's Restaurant & Lounge,** 2500 Rocky Point Road, seafood, moderate, (813) 281-0407. **Selena's,** 1623 Snow Ave., Creole, southern Italian, moderate to expensive, (727) 937-0076. **Silver Ring Cafe,** 1831 E. Seventh Ave., Cuban, inexpensive, (813) 677-1487.

WHERE TO STAY
Embassy Suites, (800) 362-2779. **Hyatt Regency Westshore,** (813) 874-1234. **Residence Inn by Marriott,** (813) 281-5677. **Wyndham Harbour Island,** (813) 229-5000 or (800) 996-3426.

ISSUES
Drugs, gangs and violence are major themes in Tampa, as they are in most cities. During our most recent visit, two armed teenagers threatened and robbed 10 people during a two-hour spree in the middle of the day. This is not typical, but underscores one concern retirees may have about living in an urban setting.

Tarpon Springs

HE SAID: ★ ★

*I feel a little like the early tourists must have felt
about Tarpon Springs: It's an interesting place to visit, but
I wouldn't want to take up permanent residency.
There just isn't enough to see or do.*

SHE SAID: ★ ★

*It has a historic area downtown and lots of different types
of residential neighborhoods. But it's small and so laid back
that there is very little going on. It's not busy enough for me.
I would not retire here.*

In the 1880s and 1890s, Tarpon Springs developed a considerable reputation as a winter resort. Thousands came from as far away as New York City — 36 hours by train — to bask in its splendor.

In the early 20th century, as many as 1,500 Greek immigrants harvested sponges in the shallow Gulf waters off Tarpon. Today, the industry remains important to the local economy, generating revenues of more than $7 million. The famous Sponge Docks are still a highlight of tours and the focal point of local celebrations and festivals.

The Greek influence continues as strong as ever today in food, dance and cultural activities. The Epiphany Celebration each January attracts more than 40,000 visitors and participants. St. Nicholas Greek Orthodox Cathedral and Community Center is by far the most striking edifice in the city.

The waterfront areas have some very nice residential neighborhoods of single-family homes, condos and villas. Many of the spring-fed lakes and bayous off the Anclote River are surrounded by houses in varying price ranges.

One unique and popular feature is the Pinellas Trail (formerly the Atlantic Coast Line Railroad tracks), winding north and south through the town and beyond, all the way to St. Petersburg. It offers open space for bicyclists, joggers, walkers and roller skaters.

The town scores high in location, being only 15 to 20 minutes away from New Port Richey and Clearwater and 30 minutes from parts of Tampa and St. Petersburg. Because it sits on U.S. 19A, rather than heavily commercialized U.S. 19, it is relatively easy to maneuver around by car.

Downtown Tarpon Springs is on the National Register of Historic Places, and the Tarpon Springs Main Street Association has accomplished some admirable restoration projects. But to an outsider visiting the town for the first time, the comeback is not as "astonishing" as the official chamber of commerce publication describes it. There are still plenty of shabby, run-down buildings, vacant storefronts and unattractive mobile home parks that need serious attention by demolitionists or restorers.

On paper, it comes across as a quaint, picturesque haven, but in reality it doesn't quite measure up to that billing.

WEATHER

	Winter	Spring	Summer	Fall
Normal daily high/low	72/52	85/66	90/73	78/58
Normal precipitation	10 in.	10 in.	23 in.	8 in.

Disaster watch: Northwest Florida has been hit by six major hurricanes since 1900.

TAXES

Sales tax: 7%. **Property tax:** $23.16 per $1,000 valuation. Sample tax calculations include a $25,000 homestead exemption.

Home value	Tax
$100,000	$1,737
$150,000	$2,895
$250,000	$5,211

REAL ESTATE

Median home value: $105,258 (Pinellas County). **Median rent:** $614/month (Pinellas County). **Communities popular with retirees:** Karol Thornburg with Century 21 West Bay Properties provided the following information: Green Dolphin has condominiums and villas priced from the $50s to mid-$70s. Windrush Bay condominiums are priced from the $50s to low $100s. Whitcomb Place has single-family homes from the $130s to 240s. Pointe Alexis has villas and single-family homes from the $80s to $200s, (813) 937-9047.The Meadows, (813) 938-3788, and Stonehedge, (813) 934-7917 are manufactured-home communities. **Licensed continuing-care retirement communities:** None.

CRIME & SAFETY

Crimes per 1,000 population: 50. **Non-emergency police:** (813) 938-2840. **Non-emergency fire department:** (813) 938-3737. **Police, fire, ambulance emergencies:** 911.

HOMELESS & BLIGHT

We saw no homeless persons. There are pockets of dilapidated houses and commercial buildings on the fringes of downtown.

According to the U.S. Census, Pinellas County, population 851,659, had 1,105 homeless persons in shelters and 75 visible in street locations.

HEALTH CARE

Hospitals: Helen Ellis Memorial Hospital, 150 beds, 24-hour emergency, full service, (813) 942-5000. **Physicians:** 32. **Specialties:** 17.

GETTING SMART

There are no college or university campuses in Tarpon Springs, though **St. Petersburg Junior College** has a campus five miles away in Palm Harbor, (813) 791-2400, and a campus in Clearwater, less than 25 miles away, (813) 791-2464.

JUST FOR SENIORS

The **Tarpon Springs Community Center**, (813) 938-3711, is the focal point for numerous programs for seniors including AARP meetings, a senior employment program, noon meals and other services.

GETTING INVOLVED

Citizens Alliance for Progress aids disadvantaged children, (813)

934-5881. **Meals on Wheels** is operated from the community center, (813) 446-3504.

RECREATION, ENTERTAINMENT & AMENITIES
Public golf: Tarpon Springs Golf Club. **Private golf:** Crescent Oaks Country Club; Cypress Run Country Club; Innisbrook Resort, 63 holes; and Wentworth Golf Club. **Public tennis courts:** Craig Park, two courts; Riverside Park, two courts; and Dorsett Park. **Private tennis courts:** Innisbrook Resort has 15 courts. **Parks:** There are eight city and county parks in Tarpon Springs. Fred Howard Park & Beach is 150 acres with a mile-long causeway connecting an offshore swimming area with the Mainland. Anderson Park has 128 acres along Lake Tarpon. **Public swimming pools:** None. **Water sports:** Boating, canoeing and sailing. **River/gulf/ocean:** Lake Tarpon, Anclote River, Gulf of Mexico and numerous saltwater bayous. **Running/walking/biking:** A.L. Anderson Park Nature Trail, Highland Nature Park and the Pinellas Trail. **Horses/riding:** There are plenty of trails and a riding academy. **Hunting:** Fishing and hunting licenses and information, (813) 934-0841. **Movie theaters:** Three screens. **Art museums:** No museums. The Inness Paintings, 11 works by early 20th-century artist George Inness Jr., are at the Universalist Church. **History museums:** The Atlantic Coastline Railroad Depot is now the Historical Society Museum. **Theaters:** Tarpon Springs Cultural Center, Flamingo Dinner Theatre and The Patchwork Players. **Library:** Tarpon Springs Public. **Attractions:** Sponge Docks and Spongeorama. **Necessities:** Local shopping centers and grocers supply basic necessities. There are plenty of banks and service companies.

Smart Shopper Tip: Take your pick of two malls: Countryside, the larger of the two, is 15 minutes south near Clearwater, and Gulf View Square is 30 minutes north in Port Richey.

WHO LIVES HERE
Population: 19,827 year-round residents, an increase of 1,953 since 1990. **Age 65+** = 24.6% in Pinellas County. **Median household income:** $29,009 (Pinellas County). **Per capita income:** $25,765 (Pinellas County).

NUMBERS TO KNOW
Chamber of commerce: (813) 937-6109. **Voter registration:** (813) 942-5614. **Vehicle registration, tags & title:** (813) 464-5560. **Driver's license:** (813) 942-5436.

WHAT TO READ
The Suncoast News, biweekly newspaper, (813) 595-0608. **St. Petersburg Times,** daily newspaper, (813) 895-1181. **Tampa Tribune,** daily newspaper, (813) 799-7400.

GETTING AROUND
Bus: Pinellas Suncoast Transit Authority, (813) 530-9911. **Taxi:** Tarpon Springs Yellow Cab, (813) 799-2222. **Tours:** St. Nicholas Boatline offers half-hour cruises around the historic Sponge Docks, (813) 942-6425. **Airport:** Tampa International. **Traffic:** Through-traffic stays on U.S. 19 so it's easy to get around the village itself.

JOBS
County unemployment rate: 3.4%. **Florida Jobs and Benefits:** (813) 942-5438.

UTILITIES
Electricity: Florida Power Corp., (813) 443-2641. **Gas:** Clearwater Gas, (813) 462-6340. **Water & sewer:** City of Tarpon Springs, (813) 942-5609. **Telephone:** GTE, (800) 483-4200. **Cable TV:** TCI of Pinellas County, (813) 736-1436.

PLACES OF WORSHIP
Two Catholic and 36 Protestant churches, plus two Jewish synagogues.

THE ENVIRONMENT
The Anclote River generally has been rated as having good water quality except for the south branch, which has poor water quality. The waters of the Gulf of Mexico are generally fair to good. Lake Tarpon, which has received the Surface Water Improvement and Management designation, has good water quality, though the canals to the south have only fair to poor quality.

There is one EPA-listed Superfund site in Pinellas County. It is the Stauffer Chemical Co. plant in Tarpon Springs.

EVENTS AND FESTIVALS
Epiphany Celebration - January. **Fine Arts & Crafts Festival** - April. **Taste of Tarpon Springs** - May. **Tarpon Springs Seafest/Boat Show** - September. **Christmas Parade** - December.

WHERE TO EAT
Costa's Restaurant, 521 Athens St., Greek, inexpensive to moderate, (813) 938-6890. **Louis Pappas' Riverside Restaurant,** 10 W. Dodecanese Blvd., Greek, moderate, (813) 937-5101.

WHERE TO STAY
Westin Innisbrook Resort, (813) 942-2000. **Spring Bayou Inn,** (813) 938-9333. **Tarpon Shores Inn,** (813) 938-2483

ISSUES
Downtown renovations, historic district improvements and the Pinellas Trail bode well for the town's future. It needs to maintain this momentum and eliminate or upgrade its neighborhoods of substandard housing to enhance its status.

Titusville

HE SAID: ✶
Titusville is not one of my favorite cities on the Space Coast in spite of its excellent location, abundant water resources and proximity to Merritt Island's attractions. I just can't get excited about the prospect of retirement here.

SHE SAID: ✶ ✶
Small, quiet town with little to do. I might stop here to watch a space launch, but I wouldn't launch my retirement here.

It has the best seats in the house for viewing launches from the John F. Kennedy Space Center. It's only 40 miles due east of Orlando, almost dead center on the east coast, and seems to have at least one of everything.

It has the low-income, substandard housing often found in older cities, mixed with the first-rate housing developments expected in a community with a large high-tech, scientific and engineering population. But, in contrast with nearby Melbourne, Cocoa Beach and the other Space Coast communities, there is very little waterfront housing in Titusville. Throughout the town, there are only a few streets along the riverside, and none with canal or boat access. The Florida East Coast Railroad owns all the riverfront north of town. The south end of town is bordered by U.S. Highway 1. The Canaveral National Seashore, Merritt Island National Wildlife Refuge and Kennedy Space Center have appropriated all of Merritt Island's shore on the Indian River as it flows past Titusville. The town has attempted to compensate for the lack of private boat slips with a large municipal marina. But, boat owners know it's not the same as having your own backdoor tie-up.

On the positive side, because development has been kept at bay, wildlife has been preserved. More than 300 species of birds have been counted in the Merritt Island National Wildlife Refuge. Alligators, armadillos, bobcats, wild pigs and raccoons inhabit the area as well.

As tourist attractions go, Kennedy Space Center is in the big leagues. Attendance at the Space Center totaled almost 3 million in 1996. Many of those visitors dined, slept and probably shopped in Titusville; the city plays up its Space Center connection whenever possible to attract tourists, residents and industry. Therefore, it's likely that any decisions out of Washington that impact space launch routines will have an economic impact on Titusville.

A Florida Main Street project and Waterfront Revitalization District program are responsible for preservation and restoration efforts that have cured some of the blighted areas and brought renewed pedestrian traffic downtown.

WEATHER

	Winter	Spring	Summer	Fall
Normal daily high/low	73/50	86/64	90/71	78/57
Normal precipitation	9 in.	13 in.	23 in.	10 in.

Disaster watch: Southeast Florida has been hit by nine major hurricanes since 1900. Northeast Florida has not been hit by a major hurricane since 1990.

TAXES
Sales tax: 6%. **Property tax:** $22.43 per $1,000 valuation. Sample tax calculations include a $25,000 homestead exemption.

Home value	Tax
$100,000	$1,682
$150,000	$2,804
$250,000	$5,047

REAL ESTATE
Median home value: $84,370 (Brevard County). **Median rent:** $548/month (Brevard County). **Communities popular with retirees:** La Cita Country Club offers three-bedroom/two-bath patio homes from the high $90s and two-bedroom/two-bath golf villas from the low $70s. Royal Oak Country Club has an 18-hole golf course and single-family homes priced from $80,000 to $100,000; Pat Seifreit, ERA Realty, (800) 268-0868. Swan Lake, an adult manufactured-home community, has units priced from $45,000 to $65,000, (800) 647-4310. **Licensed continuing-care retirement communities:** None.

CRIME & SAFETY
Crimes per 1,000 population: 67. **Non-emergency police:** (407) 264-7800. **Non-emergency fire department:** (407) 269-4400. **Police, fire, ambulance emergencies:** 911.

HOMELESS & BLIGHT
We did not see any homeless persons, but there are blighted neighborhoods that are run-down, littered and in need of rehabilitation.

In Brevard County, population 398,978, the U.S. Census counted 196 homeless persons in shelters and 18 visible on the streets.

HEALTH CARE
Hospitals: Parrish Medical Center, 210 beds, full service, (407) 268-6111. Affiliated health facilities include Parrish Same-Day Surgery Center, Parrish Diagnostic Center and Parrish Medical Offices.
Physicians: 105. **Specialties:** 31.

GETTING SMART
Brevard Community College, Titusville campus, (407) 632-1111. **Offerings:** Two-year programs, technical and vocational education and adult continuing-education courses.

JUST FOR SENIORS
Senior Resource Alliance, (407) 228-1800. **AARP**, (407) 267-6190. **North Brevard Senior Center**, (407) 268-2333.

GETTING INVOLVED
Titusville has a dozen social service organizations and two dozen associations, clubs and fraternal organizations. **Habitat for Humanity**, (407) 264-1549. **Meals on Wheels**, (407) 639-8770, offered through the North Brevard Senior Center. **RSVP**, (407) 383-5609.

RECREATION, ENTERTAINMENT & AMENITIES
Public golf: Bent Oak Golf Course, 18 holes/par 71; Royal Oak Golf Course, 18 holes; The Great Outdoors, 18 holes/par 72; and

Vacation Villas Golf Course. **Private golf:** La Cita Country Club. **Public tennis courts:** Cuyler Park, Fay Boulevard Park, Singleton Courts Complex, Sylvan Park and Titusville High School. **Private tennis courts:** The Great Outdoors. **Parks:** Canaveral National Seashore / Merritt Island National Wildlife Refuge is a 57,000-acre wilderness with 25 miles of beach. Fox Lake Park is one of the most popular recreational areas and the site of many special events. There are 20 county and city parks and recreation complexes. **Public swimming pools:** Madison Pool and Jackson Middle School. **Water sports:** Sailing, jet-skiing, windsurfing, airboat rides, scuba diving, parasailing, canoeing, rafting, swimming and fishing. Playalinda Beach on the Canaveral National Seashore is popular with swimmers, sunbathers and fishermen. **River/gulf/ocean:** The Indian River is seven miles wide between Titusville and the Kennedy Space Center. There's also Mosquito Lagoon, Banana Creek and River, Atlantic Ocean, Fox Lake, South Lake and a string of lakes along St. Johns River. **Running/walking/biking:** Many trails within the Merritt Island Refuge, including the Oak Hammock Hiking Trail. There's also an exercise trail at Fox Lake Park. **Horses/riding:** Several stables for boarding, training and trail rides. **Hunting:** In Melbourne, information and licenses for freshwater fishing and hunting, Florida Game and Freshwater Fish Commission, (407) 752-3115. **Movie theaters:** Three theaters with multiple screens. **Art museums:** Art Center of Titusville offers classes, lectures and demonstrations for children, adults and seniors. **History museums:** North Brevard Historical Museum and the Valiant Air Command Warbird Museum. **Theaters:** Titusville Playhouse and Emma Parrish Theater. **Library:** North Brevard Library and the Titusville branch of the county law library. **Attractions:** Astronaut Hall of Fame, Kennedy Space Center/Spaceport USA. At U.S. Space Camp, youngsters in fourth through seventh grades build and launch model rockets, eat an astronaut meal, see a simulated space shuttle mission and tour Kennedy Space Center. **Necessities:** All available.

Smart Shopper Tip: Stay on U.S. 1 — it will take you to Miracle City Mall and Searstown Mall. Main Street is a national historic district with a nice section of antique shops, restaurants and specialty stores.

WHO LIVES HERE
Population: 41,376 year-round residents, an increase of 1,982 since 1990. **Age 65+ =** 18.3% in Brevard County. **Median household income:** $33,061 (Brevard County). **Per capita income:** $20,747 (Brevard County).

NUMBERS TO KNOW
Chamber of commerce: (407) 267-3036. **Voter registration:** (407) 264-6740. **Vehicle registration, tags & title:** (407) 264-5224. **Driver's license:** (407) 383-2763. **Visitors bureau:** (407) 267-3036.

WHAT TO READ
Orlando Sentinel, daily newspaper, (407) 639-1605. **Star-Advocate**, weekly newspaper, (407) 267-4711. **News Observer**, weekly newspaper, (407) 267-0287.

GETTING AROUND
Bus: Space Coast Area Transit, (407) 633-1878. **Taxi:** AAA Yellow Cab, (407) 268-1208. **Tours:** Spaceport Shuttle, (407) 383-

0374. **Airport:** Orlando International is 40 miles west; Melbourne International is 40 miles south. **Traffic:** Light.

JOBS
County unemployment rate: 4.8%. **Florida Jobs and Benefits:** (407) 383-2735. **Senior Employment Program:** (407) 636-9632.

UTILITIES
Electricity: Florida Power & Light, (407) 723-7795. **Gas:** City Gas of Florida, (407) 636-4644. **Water & sewer:** City Utilities Dept., (407) 269-4400. **Telephone:** Bell South, (800) 789-9025 in Florida, or (800) 753-0710 out-of-state. **Cable TV:** Time-Warner Cable, (407) 631-3770.

PLACES OF WORSHIP
Two Catholic and 60 Protestant churches. The nearest synagogue is in south Merritt Island.

THE ENVIRONMENT
There is extensive curbside recycling of aluminum, glass, plastic and newspapers.

The middle portion of the Indian River, along the developed, western side from Titusville to Cocoa, has a poor water quality rating due to effluents from Titusville's two waste-water treatment plants, urban runoff and several causeway bridges that limit water circulation. Water quality north of Titusville, where there is little development, is good to excellent. Water quality of Mosquito Lagoon is fair.

There is one EPA-listed Superfund site in Brevard County, located in Palm Bay.

EVENTS AND FESTIVALS
Indian River Festival - April. **Warbird Airshow** - March. **Octoberfest.**

WHERE TO EAT
Dixie Crossroads, 1475 Garden St., local seafood, family-style, moderate, (407) 268-5000.

WHERE TO STAY
Motor hotels dominate the lodgings of Titusville. **Comfort Inn-Kennedy Space Center**, (407) 783-2221. **Ramada Inn-Kennedy Space Center**, (407) 269-5510.

ISSUES
As in the Cocoa Beach area, the biggest issue for Titusville is the future of the U.S. space program. Tourists will continue to come even if launch schedules are pared back, but any major reduction of space program jobs would have a strongly negative impact on the economy here.

Venice

HE SAID: ★ ★ ★ ★
Take a casual stroll, drive or bicycle ride along Venice Avenue from downtown to the Gulf beaches, and you are struck with the charm, grace and beauty of Venice. Draped in tropical vegetation, shaded by huge oaks, Florida pines and palms, and crafted in the architectural style of the canal city of northern Italy, this picturesque little village exudes the trappings of a retiree's paradise.

SHE SAID: ★ ★ ★ ★
A beautiful town, it is well-planned for retirees. It offers a choice of just about any style neighborhood you could want. There's golf, tennis, surf and pier fishing and trails for walking and biking. It's clean and feels safe. There are lots of retirees, but not a lot of traffic. I would have no problem retiring here.

Venice has a large retirement population, 54 percent over age 65, and for good reason. It has all of the qualities retirees look for in a retirement community. The chamber of commerce lists location, beautiful beaches, quiet neighborhoods, a quaint downtown, excellent health facilities, a wide range of cultural activities and nice people. Based on personal observations and talks with retirees who have relocated here, we concur with the entire list.

If you haven't been to Venice recently, a sand replenishment project completed in 1996 widened a three-mile stretch along the beach up to 300 feet deep, correcting an erosion problem and providing acres of additional space for beachfront activities.

Small parks with tennis courts, lawn bowling greens and shuffleboard lanes are within walking distance of downtown retiree housing, restaurants and boutiques. One gets the impression that seniors in Venice are active, health-conscious and happily engaged in walking, jogging, bicycling and playing.

Another pleasing feature of the town is the paucity of vehicular traffic through downtown and residential areas. The U.S. 41 bypass handles most of the through-traffic. Beach-going traffic is limited by a scarcity of resort accommodations. Resident-owned condominiums, yacht clubs and marinas occupy much of the waterfront property. It would be difficult to imagine a finer combination of housing opportunities, styles, locations and price ranges than exists in Venice.

Venice seems to be a community where retirees have a considerable impact on — and input into — planning for the present and future. An excellent job has been done.

WEATHER

	Winter	Spring	Summer	Fall
Normal daily high/low	74/54	85/67	90/73	80/60
Normal precipitation	8 in.	11 in.	22 in.	7 in.

Disaster watch: Southwest Florida has been hit by five major hurricanes since 1900.

TAXES

Sales tax: 7%. **Property tax:** $17.49 per $1,000 valuation. Sample tax calculations include a $25,000 homestead exemption.

Home value	Tax
$100,000	$1,312
$150,000	$2,186
$250,000	$3,935

REAL ESTATE

Median home value: $101,531 (Sarasota County). **Median rent:** $458/month (Sarasota County). **Communities popular with retirees:** Bay Indies, a manufactured-home community with excellent amenities, has resales only from $20,000 to $60,000, (941) 485-5441. Janice Holloway of Bradway, Moore & Associates has Gulf-view condominiums listed from $114,900 to $200,000. Gulf- and bay-front offerings run up to $750,000, (941) 484-9715. Pelican Pointe Golf & Country Club, a gated community, has homes from the $130s to $300s, (941) 496-4663. Calusa Lakes has lake-front and golf-course locations. Homesites run from $49,900 to $89,000, maintenance-free homes from $156,500 to $225,000 and custom homes from the $190s to $300s , (941) 484-6004. The Venice Golf and Country Club has detached maintenance-free patio and custom single-family homes from the $180s, (941) 493-3100. The Eagle Point Club, a gated community on Roberts Bay, with a historic clubhouse and deepwater boat docks, has homesites from $135,000 to $575,000, (941) 484-9995. **Licensed continuing-care retirement communities:** Village on the Isle has 280 independent living units and 60 community beds, (941) 484-9753.

CRIME & SAFETY

Crimes per 1,000 population: 31. **Non-emergency police:** (941) 488-6711. **Non-emergency fire department:** (941) 492-3196. **Police, fire, ambulance emergencies:** 911.

HOMELESS & BLIGHT

Venice is a beautiful, clean city with a small, historic downtown, wide, tree-lined medians, a beautiful waterfront and the usual excessive commercialization along U.S. 41.

The U.S. Census reported 84 homeless persons in shelters and 11 visible in street locations in Sarasota County, population 277,776.

HEALTH CARE

Hospitals: Bon Secours-Venice Hospital, 342 beds, full service, 24-hour emergency, (941) 485-7711. **Physicians:** 176. **Specialties:** 40.

GETTING SMART

Applied Technology and Adult Education Center, (941) 927-9000. **Offerings:** Adult basic education and enrichment classes. **Manatee Community College**, (941) 493-3504. **Offerings:** Two-year associate's degrees in more than 90 fields of study.

JUST FOR SENIORS

Senior Friendship Center, (941) 493-3065. **Senior Street Dances at the Venice Community Center**, (941) 486-2311.

GETTING INVOLVED

Meals on Wheels, (941) 488-1889. **Volunteer Center South**, (941) 488-5683.

RECREATION, ENTERTAINMENT & AMENITIES

Public golf: Lake Venice Golf Club, 27 holes/par 108; Calusa Lakes Golf Club, semiprivate, 18 holes/par 72; Pelican Pointe Golf and Country Club, semiprivate, 18 holes/par 72; Venice East Golf Club, 18 holes/par 54; Bird Bay Golf Club, semiprivate, 18 holes/par 56; Capri Isles Golf Club, semiprivate, 18 holes/par 70; Country Club at Jacaranda West, semiprivate, 18 holes/par 70; and Waterford Golf Club, semiprivate, 18 holes/par 71. **Private golf:** Plantation Golf and Country Club, 36 holes/par 141, and Venice Golf and Country Club, 18 holes/par 72. **Public tennis courts:** Hecksher Park, Shamrock Park and Pinebrook Recreation Area. **Private tennis courts:** Plantation Golf and Country Club and Courtside Tennis Club. **Parks:** Myakka River State Park has 28,000-plus acres of wetlands, woodlands and prairies. Oscar Scherer State Park has 462 acres. **Public swimming pools:** Wellfield Recreation Area. **Water sports:** Boating, canoeing, jet-skiing, sailing, scuba diving, snorkeling and windsurfing. **River/gulf/ocean:** Roberts Bay, Myakka River and the Gulf of Mexico. **Running/walking/ biking:** New Shamrock Park and Nature Center has 82 acres of nature trails. Pinebrook Recreation Area has a fitness/nature trail. Oscar Scherer State Park has paths. City sidewalks and many medians are popular with walkers and bicyclists. **Horses/ riding:** There are stables and ranches in the area and plenty of room to ride east of town. **Hunting:** Cecil M. Webb Wildlife Management Area in Charlotte County allows hunting. Seniors are eligible for complimentary fishing licenses after six months residency. Call (941) 362-9898 for information. **Movie theaters:** Six screens. **Art museums:** Venice Art Center. **History museums:** None. **Theaters:** Venice Little Theatre, Venice Community Center and Palm Tree Playhouse. Performing arts groups include Venice Symphony and Theatre Works. **Library:** Venice Public. **Attractions:** Venice Beach and Nokomis Beach, Venice Avenue, Historic Spanish Point and Warm Mineral Springs Resort and Spa. **Necessities:** All here.

Smart Shopper Tip: The Tamiami Trail (U.S. 41) from Osprey to South Venice is lined with shopping centers anchored by major department stores.

WHO LIVES HERE

Population: 18,886 year-round residents, an increase of 1,834 since 1990. **Age 65+** = 32.6% in Sarasota County. **Median household income:** $30,662 (Sarasota County). **Per capita income:** $33,445 (Sarasota County).

NUMBERS TO KNOW

Chamber of commerce: (941) 488-2236. **Voter registration:** (941) 492-3060. **Vehicle registration, tags & title:** (941) 362-9898. **Driver's license:** (941) 483-5999.

WHAT TO READ

Venice Gondolier, semiweekly newspaper, (941) 484-2611. **Sarasota Herald-Tribune**, daily newspaper, (941) 488-6767. **The Weekly,** newspaper, (941) 485-5425.

GETTING AROUND

Bus: SCAT, Sarasota County Area Transit, (941) 316-1234. **Taxi:** Yellow Cab, (941) 488-0822. **Tours:** None. **Airport:** Sarasota/ Bradenton International is 25 miles north. **Traffic:** The U.S. 41 bypass carries most of the through-traffic east of the residential neighborhoods and away from the beaches. Downtown traffic is light.

JOBS

County unemployment rate: 2.6%. **Florida Jobs and Benefits:** In Sarasota, (941) 361-6100.

UTILITIES

Electricity: Florida Power & Light, (800) 700-8744. **Gas:** Peoples Gas, (941) 366-4277. **Water & sewer:** Venice Utility Dept., (941) 486-2626. **Telephone:** GTE, (800) 483-4200. **Cable TV:** ComCast Cable, (941) 484-0602.

PLACES OF WORSHIP

Two Catholic and 38 Protestant churches, plus one Jewish synagogue.

THE ENVIRONMENT

Sarasota Bay is designated as an Outstanding Florida Water and is part of the EPA's National Estuary Program. Catfish Creek, south of Matheny Creek, has been rated as having poor water quality; it is affected by urban runoff and a closed landfill in close proximity. Little Sarasota Bay near Catfish Creek has fair water quality. Hatchett Creek also has fair water quality. Alligator Creek and Forked Creek have fair water quality index ratings but both show generally good quality overall.

EVENTS AND FESTIVALS

Rotary Club Annual Arts & Crafts Festival - January. **St. Patrick's Day Parade** - March. **Sharks Tooth & Seafood Festival** - August. **Sun Fiesta** - October. **Art Fest** - November. **Christmas Boat Parade** - December.

WHERE TO EAT

Sharky's Crab & Oyster Bar, 1600 S. Harbor Drive on the pier, seafood, pasta, steaks, moderate to expensive, (941) 488-1456. **The Expedition Co. Bar and Grill**, 997 Tamiami Trail N., seafood, moderate, (941) 485-6393.

WHERE TO STAY

Holiday Inn-Venice, (941) 485-5411. **Days Inn**, (941) 493-4558. **Veranda Inn-Venice**, (941) 484-9559. **Quarterdeck Resort Condominiums**, (941) 488-0449.

ISSUES

If there are any unresolved issues, the retirees we met don't know about them.

Vero Beach

HE SAID: ★ ★ ★ ★ ★
*While it may not be my favorite Florida city,
its overall attractiveness would definitely place
it near the top of my list.*

SHE SAID: ★ ★ ★ ★
*If you are looking for a place to stay busy after
retirement, Vero Beach certainly has something to offer.
It seems to be a place where retirees can easily become
involved in politics, arts or education. The beaches
are beautiful but narrow.*

We were not immediately stricken by the charms of Vero Beach. As one retired couple said, "It took us about 20 minutes to decide to move here."

That's about the amount of time it takes to drive through downtown, across the Indian River (Barber) Bridge to Orchid Island, past Riverside Park and the Center for the Arts, and through some of the beautiful residential neighborhoods along the river and seashore.

This is a year-round tourist resort. One retired couple said they keep their new car garaged when the snowbirds are in town. But traffic and crowds don't really seem to be a major problem.

At first, Vero Beach is a little surprising. One does not expect to find so much. It is surprisingly small, but has the upscale cultural and recreational attractions of a much larger city. It also has the high pricing structure of a larger city — especially in real estate.

Vero Beach offers Dodgertown, where baseball fans can follow the Los Angeles Dodgers in spring training. It also has the Riverside Theatre, the Center for the Arts and the Theatre Guild, which bring exceptional entertainment to this arts-oriented society. Leisure Square, dozens of parks and the Environmental Learning Center combine with the land's natural attributes to offer residents unparalleled opportunities.

WEATHER

	Winter	Spring	Summer	Fall
Normal daily high/low	75/53	85/66	90/72	79/60
Normal precipitation	8 in.	13 in.	19 in.	11 in.

Disaster watch: Southeast Florida has been hit by nine major hurricanes since 1900.

TAXES

Sales tax: 7%. **Property tax:** $20.55 per $1,000 valuation. Sample tax calculations include a $25,000 homestead exemption.

Home value	Tax
$100,000	$1,541
$150,000	$2,569
$250,000	$4,624

REAL ESTATE

Median home value: $94,085 (Indian River County). **Median rent:** $440/month (Indian River County). **Communities popular with retirees:** Grand Harbor, homes from the $170s to more than $1 million, (800) 275-4537, Grove Isle, condos priced from the $90s, (561) 569-8011. Heron Cay, manufactured homes priced from the high $40s to the $70s, not including land lease, (800) 367-6715. Indian River Club, fairway homes from the $190s to $400s, (800) 575-0005. Village Green, manufactured homes from the $30s to $80s, not including land lease, (561) 567-5796. Condos and villas at Villas at Lexington, priced from the mid-$60s to high $100s, (561) 778-1601. **Licensed continuing-care retirement communities:** Indian River Estates has 541 independent living units and 60 community beds, (561) 562-7400.

CRIME & SAFETY

Crimes per 1,000 population: 83. **Non-emergency police:** (561) 978-4600. **Non-emergency fire department:** (561) 562-2028. **Police, fire, ambulance emergencies:** 911.

HOMELESS & BLIGHT

We saw no homeless persons nor blighted areas in Vero Beach. Vero Beach appears to have a strong economy, fueled by tourism, agriculture and light industry. Its residents and government seem to have made a commitment to downtown revitalization.

The U.S. Census reported no homeless persons in shelters and 11 visible on the streets of Indian River County, population 90,208.

HEALTH CARE

Hospitals: Indian River Memorial Hospital, 293 beds, full-service, (561) 567-4311. **Treasure Coast Rehabilitation Hospital**, 70 beds, inpatient/outpatient rehabilitation programs, (561) 778-2100.

Physicians: 200+. **Specialties:** 39.

GETTING SMART

Indian River Community College, (561) 569-0333. **Offerings:** Approximately 100 two-year degree programs, plus vocational courses and continuing-education classes for personal and professional enrichment.

JUST FOR SENIORS

Area Agency on Aging, (561) 569-0760. **Indian River Senior Center**, (561) 569-0760. **AARP**, (561) 231-5350.

GETTING INVOLVED

Meals on Wheels and **RSVP** are offered through the Agency on Aging, (561) 569-0760. **SCORE**, (561) 567-3491. **Vero Beach Theatre Guild**, (561) 562-8300.

RECREATION, ENTERTAINMENT & AMENITIES

Public golf: Dodgertown Golf Course, 18 holes; Dodger Pines Country Club, 27 holes; Sandridge Golf Course, 18 holes; and Whisper Lakes Golf Course, 18 holes/par 55. **Private golf:** Moorings Club; Bent Pine Golf Course, 18 holes; and Vero Beach Country Club, 18 holes/par 72. **Public tennis courts:** Pocahontas Park, Charles Park, Riverside Park, Leisure Square, Easy Street Park, Gifford Park and Twin Oaks Tennis Club. **Private tennis courts:** Timber Ridge Tennis & Fitness Ranch and Westside Racquet Club. **Parks:** City parks include

Pocahontas, Troy Moody, Humiston, Charles, South Beach, Jaycee, MacWilliam, Riverside and the Municipal Athletic Complex. County parks include the 70-acre South County Regional Park. Also, the 576-acre Sebastian Inlet State Park. **Public swimming pools:** Leisure Square is a multipurpose athletic complex run by the city recreation department. **Water sports:** Boating, surfing, scuba diving, water-skiing, freshwater and saltwater fishing. **River/gulf/ocean:** The Atlantic, Sebastian Inlet, Indian River (Intracoastal Waterway) and 200-acre Blue Cypress Lake are the most popular for boating and fishing. **Running/walking/biking:** Troy Moody Park has the Serpentine Jogging Path. Charles Park has two half-mile walking/running trails. Riverside Park has a one-mile trail. Easy Street Park has a jogging trail and seven-mile Jungle Trail, a dirt road bordering some of the most pristine shoreline of the Indian River. It's popular with bikers and walkers. **Horses/riding:** None. **Hunting:** Licenses are required for fishing and hunting, (561) 567-8180. **Movie theaters:** Six screens at one theater. **Art museums:** Center for the Arts and Museum, and Vero Beach Art Club Gallery. **History museums:** Indian River Historical Society portrays the county's history in a restored turn-of-the-century railroad station. McLarty State Museum and Visitors Center features Indian artifacts and sunken treasures rescued from 18th-century ships wrecked off the coast. **Theaters:** Riverside Children's Theatre, Riverside Theatre, Theatre Guild and Mashed Potato Players. **Library:** Indian River County Main Library is downtown. The North Indian River County Library opened in 1990. **Attractions:** The Environmental Learning Center, (561) 589-5050, offers adults and children a unique opportunity to learn about ecology and conservation through interpretive nature trails, indoor and outdoor labs and classrooms. Dodgertown is a 450-acre complex and the site of L.A. Dodgers spring training. Windsor Polo Club presents exhibition matches. **Necessities:** Everything is on hand or nearby.

Smart Shopper Tip: Try Indian River Mall or the Miracle Mile of shops downtown. For specialty stores, seek out Ocean Drive and the Village Shops on the beach side at Indian River Shores.

WHO LIVES HERE
Population: 17,787 year-round residents, an increase of 437 since 1990. **Age 65+ =** 29.9% in Indian River County. **Median household income:** $29,518 (Indian River County). **Per capita income:** $31,845 (Indian River County).

NUMBERS TO KNOW
Chamber of commerce: (561) 567-3491. **Voter registration:** (561) 567-8187. **Vehicle registration, tags & title:** (561) 567-8180. **Driver's license:** (561) 778-5090. **Visitors bureau:** (561) 567-3491.

WHAT TO READ
The Press Journal, daily newspaper, (561) 569-7100. **Florida Today**, daily newspaper, (561) 562-1771. **50 Plus**, monthly newspaper, (561) 778-9800.

GETTING AROUND
Bus: Minibus service for seniors, (561) 569-0760. **Taxi:** City Cab,

(561) 562-3022. **Tours:** None. **Airport:** Vero Beach Municipal Airport has commuter service to Orlando and Miami. Melbourne Regional is 35 miles north and offers commercial jet service. **Traffic:** Light.

JOBS
County unemployment rate: 10.8%. **Florida Jobs and Benefits:** (561) 778-5072.

UTILITIES
Electricity, water & sewer: Vero Beach Utilities Dept., electricity – (561) 978-5151, water & sewer – (561) 978-5220. **Gas:** None. **Telephone:** Bell South, (800) 789-9025 in Florida, or (800) 753-0710 out-of-state. **Cable TV:** TCI Cablevision, (561) 567-3444.

PLACES OF WORSHIP
Four Catholic and 73 Protestant and non-denominational churches, plus one Jewish synagogue.

THE ENVIRONMENT
Surface water quality in the area has been rated as mostly fair. The Indian River does receive urban runoff. The Outstanding Florida Water designation has been given to a portion of the Indian River, from Vero Beach to the Pierce Aquatic Preserve. The Indian River Lagoon system has been designated for improvement and management.

There is one EPA-listed Superfund site in Vero Beach, the Piper Aircraft/Vero Beach Water & Sewer Department site.

EVENTS AND FESTIVALS
The Citrus Celebration - March. **Under the Oaks** - March. **Summer Fest** - August. **Autumn in the Park** - October

WHERE TO EAT
Black Pearl, 1409 Route A1A, haute continental, moderate to expensive, (561) 234-4426. **Ocean Grill**, 1050 Sexton Plaza, American, moderate to expensive, (561) 231-5409. **Beachside**, 3125 Ocean Drive, Italian, American, inexpensive to moderate, (561) 234-4477.

WHERE TO STAY
Doubletree Guest Suite , (561) 231-5666. **Islander Resort**, (561) 231-4431. **Holiday Inn Oceanfront**, (561) 231-2300.

ISSUES
One retired couple, when summing up what makes Vero Beach stand above other towns, says it's "fairly close to its pioneer days, has a can-do spirit and is not waiting for big government." As long as this attitude prevails, it seems Vero Beach will have a bright future.

The Villages

HE SAID: ★ ★ ★ ★
*If you're looking for a turn-key retirement spot —
active, secure, convenient and planned — take a look at
The Villages. If you like to make your own way,
look elsewhere.*

SHE SAID: ★ ★ ★ ★
*A well-planned community. It's all here.
Charming, organized and lots of people. I might
consider retirement here.*

The Villages are on a course to become megalopolises at the rate they are presently growing. Since acquiring a 400-mobile-home park in 1983, The Villages has grown to a 10,000-home, 20,000-resident community. Its 1997 sales totaled 1,075 new homes, making it the largest single-site real estate developer in the country.

But don't be concerned that it will sell out before you retire. The projected build-out date is some 25 years away, with an expected 25,000 homes and 50,000 inhabitants.

In this self-contained community, all one needs is a golf cart to enjoy a host of recreational activities as well as access to banking, medical care, hair salons, supermarkets and specialty shops.

Golf, tennis, swimming and other recreational pursuits are covered by a monthly amenities fee, currently $99 per housing unit. Liz Clayton, a resident since 1994, rates the amenities second to none. "We have so many nice, planned activities, we almost need a private social director to keep up with our schedule," she says.

"If we ever move, we won't move out of The Villages," Liz declares. "Even if we won the lottery," husband Charles adds.

WEATHER

	Winter	Spring	Summer	Fall
Normal daily high/low	71/48	86/64	90/71	76/55
Normal precipitation	10 in.	12 in.	17 in.	7 in.

Disaster watch: Northeast Florida has not been hit by a major hurricane since 1900.

TAXES
Sales tax: 6%. **Property tax:** $20.36 per $1,000 valuation. Sample tax calculations include a $25,000 homestead exemption.

Home value	Tax
$100,000	$1,527
$150,000	$2,545
$250,000	$4,581

REAL ESTATE
Median home value: $180,000 (Lake County). **Median rent:** No rentals in The Villages. **Communities popular with retirees:** The 18 villages feature a variety of styles, from 1,262-square-foot patio villas starting at about $60,000 to 3,200-square-foot luxury homes ranging as high as $400,000. The average price of new homes is about $125,000. **Licensed continuing-care retirement communities:** None.

CRIME & SAFETY
Crimes per 1,000 population: 18. **Non-emergency police:** (352) 753-3810. **Non-emergency fire department:** (352) 383-1200. **Police, fire, ambulance emergencies:** 911.

HOMELESS & BLIGHT
This is a clean, neat and tidy community with no homeless persons. It is patrolled by the Lake County Sheriff's Department, and a 24-hour neighborhood watch program provides additional security and controlled access to each village neighborhood.

HEALTH CARE
Hospitals: Hometown Health Care Clinic has X-ray and laboratory facilities and three on-site physicians. **Leesburg Regional Medical Center**, a 414-bed facility, is only seven miles away, (352) 365-4545. **Physicians:** 3. **Specialties:** 13.

GETTING SMART
Lake-Sumter Community College, Leesburg, (352) 787-3747. **Offerings:** Associate degrees in arts and science. Continuing- and adult-education classes.

JUST FOR SENIORS
Most of The Villages residents are retired, so most recreational activities, events, trips and outings are designed for seniors.

GETTING INVOLVED
There are approximately 300 resident-sponsored organizations and an equal number of weekly scheduled events by The Villages Recreation Department. The Drama/Music/Dance Group, Creative Writing Club and Haven of Lake/Sumter are very popular.

RECREATION, ENTERTAINMENT & AMENITIES
Public golf: None. **Private golf:** 108 holes of golf are available for owners and registered visitors. **Public tennis:** None. **Private tennis:** 18 courts. There also are 22 bocce ball courts. **Parks:** Ocala National Forest and Lake Griffin State Recreation Area are close by. **Public swimming pools:** Nine heated pools, including a Junior Olympic-sized pool. **Water sports:** Boating, canoeing, sailing and water-skiing

are all available in the county. **River/gulf/ocean:** 20 fishing lakes on the premises. Fifty miles to the Gulf of Mexico. **Walking/biking/hiking/running:** six miles of recreational trails and 11 wildlife preserves. **Horses/riding:** Numerous stables and riding trails in the horse country surrounding Ocala, a few miles north. **Hunting:** None. **Movie theaters:** Eight screens. **Art museums:** Appleton Museum in Ocala. **History museums:** None. **Theaters:** Paradise Center and La Hacienda Center. **Library:** Lady Lake Library. **Attractions:** The old-fashioned downtown district known as the Village of Spanish Springs. Katie Belle's Dining and Music Hall. **Necessities:** 612,000 square feet of retail, commercial and office space in the downtown district provides most necessities.

   Smart Shopper Tip: The Villages Town Square District is a convenient collection of shops, offices and restaurants.

WHO LIVES HERE
Population: 17,417. **Age 65+** = 27.9% in Lake County. **Median household income:** $24,804 (Lake County). **Per capita income:** $19,459 (Lake County).

NUMBERS TO KNOW
The Villages: 1-800-346-4556. **Voter registration:** (352) 343-9734. **Vehicle registration, tags & title:** (352) 343-9602. **Driver's license:** (352) 742-6165.

WHAT TO READ
Daily Sun, newspaper, (352) 753-1119. **Tri-County Sun**, twice-weekly newspaper, (352) 753-9652.

GETTING AROUND
The Villages is a self-contained golf-cart community with super-markets, shops, restaurants and professional services available just a short cart drive from home. **Taxi:** None. **Tours:** The Village Recreation Department regularly organizes day trips, longer excursions and cruises. **Airport:** Orlando International is 70 miles away. **Traffic:** Light, mostly golf-cart traffic inside the development.

JOBS
County unemployment rate: 3.8% **Florida Jobs and Benefits:** (352) 360-6518.

UTILITIES
Electricity: Sumter Electric Co-op, (352) 793-3801. **Gas:** Amerigas, (352) 821-3721. **Water & sewer:** Village Center Department of Public Works, (352) 750-0000. **Telephone:** Sprint, (800) 339-1811. **Cable TV:** Comcast, (352) 787-7875.

PLACES OF WORSHIP
Church on the Square (non-denominational), St. Timothy Catholic, All Faiths Chapel and North Lake Presbyterian.

THE ENVIRONMENT
Lake Harris has been rated as having fair water quality. Lake Griffin is negatively affected by upstream pollution for Lake Apopka and waste-water treatment plants (WWTP). Lake County has eliminated further WWTP discharge to its lakes. The water district is working to acquire farms along the chain of lakes and Oklawaha River to restore the flood-plain wetlands. Lake Griffin State Recreation Area and the Clermont Chain of Lakes have protected status as Outstanding Florida Waters.

   There is one EPA-listed Superfund site in Lake County: Tower Chemical in Clermont.

EVENTS & FESTIVALS
Easter Arts & Crafts Festival. Octoberfest. Winter Wonderland - December.

WHERE TO EAT
There are 16 restaurants at The Villages. **Hacienda Hills Restaurant**, prime rib, lamb, veal, moderate to expensive, (352) 753-0100.

WHERE TO STAY
La Hacienda Hotel. The Retirement Preview Plan offers on-site lodging at the hotel or in a private villa, (800) 346-4556.

ISSUES
Can infrastructure needs for utilities and recreational facilities keep pace with new-home construction and sales? From all indications, so far they are right on target.

RELOCATION TIPS
If you're not intimately familiar with your new town, lease a home before you buy. *Where to Retire* magazine reports that the most common complaint of relocated retirees concerns neighborhood selection. Leasing gives you a trial period to find the part of town you like best as well as the neighborhood and home that are just right for your new lifestyle.

West Palm Beach

A county with more than 1,100 tennis courts and 200-plus golf courses can't be too bad. West Palm Beach claims its fair share of the county's bounty and has a host of other facilities that provide a broad spectrum of recreational fare for its active, outdoor-oriented populace. The theaters, museums and performing arts groups here are legendary. Health-care facilities are more than adequate. The town boasts an array of boutiques, shopping centers and malls — not to mention Palm Beach's Worth Avenue, which charges $4 just for a map of its shops — that would delight the most inveterate shopper.

While Palm Beach, block for block, is undeniably one of the prettiest towns in America, West Palm Beach is a mosaic, some parts pretty, some not so pretty. Originally inhabited by domestics and service providers who worked for the residents of Palm Beach, West Palm Beach now is home to an eclectic mix of Fortune 500 companies, elegant waterfront residential neighborhoods, middle-class communities of small homes and apartments and World War II-era hotels and motels that house transients, prostitutes and drug dealers.

During the 1980s, West Palm Beach was one of the principal destinations for retirees seeking an alternative to the urban sprawl of Dade and Broward counties. Now it would behoove retirees to avoid West Palm Beach as well, looking to northern and southern parts of Palm Beach County for a comfortable residential environment.

WEATHER

	Winter	Spring	Summer	Fall
Normal daily high/low	76/58	85/69	90/75	80/65
Normal precipitation	9 in.	17 in.	21 in.	14 in.

Disaster watch: Southeast Florida has been hit by nine major hurricanes since 1900.

TAXES
Sales tax: 6%. **Property tax:** Rates range from $25.93 to $27.93 per $1,000 valuation, depending upon location. Sample taxes are calculated at rate of $27.93 and include a $25,000 homestead exemption.

Home value	Tax
$100,000	$2,095
$150,000	$3,491
$250,000	$6,284

REAL ESTATE
Median home value: $104,167 (Palm Beach County). **Median rent:** $773/month (Palm Beach County). **Communities popular with retirees:** Wellington has condominiums from the $60s and single-family homes from the $100s to $2 million. Greenway is an adult condominium community with prices from the upper $40s to low $80s. Housing information provided by relocation resource John Reed, Ablaze Realty, (561) 793-7207. **Licensed continuing-care retirement communities:** None.

CRIME & SAFETY
Crimes per 1,000 population: 157. **Non-emergency police:** (561) 837-4000. **Non-emergency fire department:** (561) 835-2900. **Police, fire, ambulance emergencies:** 911.

HOMELESS & BLIGHT
We saw homeless persons and blighted areas while driving through the city. According to the U.S. Census, Palm Beach County, population 863,518, had 219 homeless persons living in shelters and 197 visible on the streets.

HEALTH CARE
Hospitals: Good Samaritan Medical Center, 341 beds, full service, (561) 655-5511. **Columbia Hospital**, 250 beds (acute care), 88 beds (psychiatric), (561) 842-6141. **St. Mary's Hospital**, 430 beds, acute care, (561) 844-6300. **Wellington Regional Medical Center**, 120 beds, acute care, (561) 798-8500. **Physicians:** 450+. **Specialties:** 29+.

GETTING SMART
Palm Beach Community College, (561) 967-7222. **Offerings:** The Institute of New Dimensions is a membership program for retired persons offering life enrichment, liberal arts and wellness classes during eight-week terms. Other offerings include non-credit, continuing-education courses. **Palm Beach Atlantic College**, (561) 803-2000. **Offerings:** Four-year liberal arts degrees, MBA program, continuing-education, credit and non-credit courses. **Northwood University**, (561) 478-5500. **Offerings:** Associate's and bachelor's degrees in accounting, advertising, banking and finance, business management, computer science management, hotel and restaurant management.

JUST FOR SENIORS
JCC Community Center, (561) 689-7700. **Howard Park Senior Center**, (561) 835-7055. **Widowed Person's Service**, sponsored by AARP and the Mental Health Association, (561) 832-3755.

GETTING INVOLVED
Ambassadors, a chamber of commerce committee, (561) 833-3711. **RSVP Mid-County**, (561) 732-1674. **The Historical Society**, (561) 832-4164

RECREATION, ENTERTAINMENT & AMENITIES
Public golf: Emerald Dunes, 18 holes/par 72; PGA National Resort & Spa, five tournament courses; and Golf & Sports Center. **Private golf:** Everglades, Ibis, Ironhorse and Mayacoo Lakes. **Public tennis courts:** PGA National Resort & Spa has 19 courts. There are more than 1,100 public and private courts in the county. **Parks:** Over 300 acres in 35 city parks, plus county and state parks. Phipps Ocean Park and Palm Beach Municipal Beach are in nearby Palm Beach. **Public swimming pools:** Gaines Park and Howard Park. **Water sports:** Boating,

sailing, scuba diving, snorkeling, windsurfing and jet-skiing are available in the waters off Palm Beach, including Lake Worth Cove in the Singer Island resort area. **River/gulf/ocean:** The city's only beach is a sliver of sand along the Intracoastal Waterway, but water lovers have unlimited access to the Intracoastal, Lake Okeechobee, a 170-acre lake in Okeeheelee County Park, the Loxahatchee National Wildlife Refuge and numerous smaller lakes. Visit the John D. MacArthur Beach State Park for snorkeling. **Running/walking/biking:** Dreher Park Heart Trail, Loxahatchee walking trails and the Lake Trail Bike Path, known for its scenic beauty. **Horses/riding:** Several riding academies and stables offer a full range of boarding, training, lessons and trail rides. **Hunting:** Call the Florida Game and Freshwater Fish Commission, (561) 625-5122, for information and licensing for hunting and fishing. **Movie theaters:** Four multi-screen theaters. **Art museums:** Armory Art Center, Norton Gallery of Art, Palm Beach Community College Museum of Art, Society of the Four Arts and Hibel Museum of Art. **History museums:** The Henry M. Flagler Museum, also known as Whitehall. **Theaters:** Raymond F. Kravis Center for the Performing Arts offers ballet, the symphony, musicals and the Palm Beach Opera. The Royal Poinciana Playhouse features Broadway productions. Coral Sky Amphitheatre. Performing arts organizations include Ballet Florida, Palm Beach Symphony, Theatre Club of the Palm Beaches and Masterworks Chorus. **Library:** West Palm Beach Public Library and several county library branches. **Attractions:** Spring training grounds for the Montreal Expos and St. Louis Cardinals, Palm Beach Kennel Club, Palm Beach Polo & Country Club Stadium, Palm Beach Jai Alai Fronton, Dreher Park Zoo, Cluett Gardens, Mounts Botanical Garden, South Florida Science Museum, Gibson Observatory, Aldrin Planetarium, Lion Country Safari, Chicago's First Lady dining yacht, plus hockey, horse racing and motor sports. **Necessities:** They're all here.

   Smart Shopper Tip: There are numerous malls, shopping centers and plazas in the area offering all the great names, chains and varieties. Browse Worth Avenue in Palm Beach and the Gardens Mall of the Palm Beaches, then make your purchases at the Palm Beach Outlet Center, a 127,000-square-foot enclosed mall in West Palm Beach. For fun, check out the Clematis Cultural, Retail & Entertainment District downtown.

WHO LIVES HERE
Population: 79,783 year-round residents, an increase of 12,019 since 1990. **Age 65+ = 25.0%** in Palm Beach County. **Median household income:** $33,094 (Palm Beach County). **Per capita income:** $36,057 (Palm Beach County).

NUMBERS TO KNOW
Chamber of commerce: (561) 833-3711. **Voter registration:** (561) 355-2650. **Vehicle registration, tags & title:** (561) 355-2622. **Driver's license:** (561) 681-6333. **Visitors bureau:** (561) 471-3995.

WHAT TO READ
Palm Beach Post, daily newspaper, (561) 820-4663. **Daily News**, daily newspaper, (561) 820-3800. **The Miami Herald**, Palm Beach edition, (561) 848-3155. **News & Sun Sentinel**, daily newspaper, (561) 243-6600. **Palm Beach Review**, daily newspaper, (561) 820-

2060. **Palm Beach Society**, weekly magazine, (561) 659-5555. **Palm Beach Today**, monthly magazine, (561) 655-8667. **50 Plus**, monthly, (561) 778-9800.

GETTING AROUND
Bus: CoTran, (561) 233-1111, offers several routes including the Saturday Shopper to area malls. **Taxi:** Palm Beach Transportation, (561) 689-4222. Yellow Cab, (561) 689-2222. **Tours:** Palm Beach Cruise Line, (800) 841-7447. Old Northwood Historic District Tours, (561) 863-5633. **Airport:** Palm Beach International is two miles from the city. **Traffic:** Heavy, but arteries carry it swiftly.

JOBS
County unemployment rate: 6.4%. **Florida Jobs and Benefits:** (561) 616-5200.

UTILITIES
Electricity: Florida Power & Light, (561) 697-8000. **Gas:** Florida Public Utilities, (561) 278-2636. **Water & sewer:** City of West Palm Beach, Utilities Dept., (561) 641-3400. **Telephone:** Bell South, (800) 789-9025 in Florida, or (800) 753-0710 out-of-state. **Cable TV:** ComCast Cable, (561) 478-8300.

PLACES OF WORSHIP
More than 100 Protestant churches representing 48 denominations, plus 10 Catholic churches, one Greek Orthodox church and 12 Jewish synagogues.

THE ENVIRONMENT
The Loxahatchee National Wildlife Refuge and Loxahatchee River State Aquatic Preserve to the south and west of town are designated as protected water bodies. To the far west, the West Palm Beach canal from Lake Okeechobee has been rated as having poor water quality with periodic fish kills that occur after heavy rains drain from the Chemair Spray hazardous waste site. Otherwise, most surface water quality is fair.

   There is one EPA-listed Superfund site in Palm Beach County, BMI-Textron in Lake Park.

EVENTS AND FESTIVALS
South Florida Fair - January. **Seafood Festival** - February. **PGA Seniors Golf Championship** - April. **SunFest** - April/May.

WHERE TO EAT
Chuck & Harold's, 207 Royal Poinciana Way, seafood, continental, expensive, (561) 659-1440. **Taboo**, 221 Worth Ave., continental, expensive, (561) 835-3500.

WHERE TO STAY
Hampton Inn, (561) 471-8700. **Hibiscus House**, (561) 863-5633. **Palm Beach Polo and Country Club**, (561) 798-7000. **Sheraton Hotel**, (561) 833-1234.

ISSUES
According to the *Palm Beach Post*, there is a significant base of transients, immigrants, prostitutes and drug dealers in the older hotels and motels. Hopefully, city officials will not allow this situation to continue.

Winter Garden

The town is gaining visual appeal, modern housing, cultural and social infrastructure, upscale shopping and just about everything else needed to attract retirees. Its strongest attribute is location. Its strongest hope — a restored Lake Apopka.

It's getting better, but not yet there. I would not retire here.

One of four communities in west Orange County, Winter Garden is often grouped with tiny Oakland, which measures its geographic area in acres and its population in hundreds; Ocoee, a town comparable to Winter Garden in size and whose longtime claim to fame is the Florida Auto Auction; and Windermere, whose sparkling lakes and canals provide much of the fishing and recreational activity for area residents.

A stable employment base, anchored by the Winter Garden Citrus Products Cooperative, and the new Health Central hospital in Ocoee are among the area's strong points. In times past, Lake Apopka, the largest freshwater lake in central Florida and fourth largest in the state, was a magnificent recreational resource. Once a haven for swimming, fishing and other water sports, it now is so polluted that it is often referred to as a dead lake. But, the Lake Apopka Restoration Act of 1996 has set remedial actions in motion that show promise of significant improvement in seven to 10 years.

The town's newer attractions, such as the West Orange Trail and Main Street Winter Garden, show that civic leaders are working to improve their city. Running through the heart of town, the West Orange Trail is a new 17-mile linear park for joggers, bicyclists, skaters, and in some sections, equestrians. It is part of the Rails-to-Trails program that converts railroad rights-of-way to natural park trails. The Main Street Winter Garden program was formed in 1991, with a mission to "restore, promote and maintain the historic character of downtown." While there is still much to be done, it is encouraging to see that residents and city officials are focusing their efforts and attention on the city's problems and potential.

The restoration of Lake Apopka, the building of a new north-south beltway, and the potential of Horizons West, a Disney-sponsored development plan for 30,000 acres of land south of Winter Garden, may make this one of the most coveted areas of Florida in coming years.

WEATHER

	Winter	Spring	Summer	Fall
Normal daily high/low	74/51	88/65	91/72	77/58
Normal precipitation	9 in.	13 in.	21 in.	7 in.

Disaster watch: Northeast Florida has not been hit by a major hurricane since 1900.

TAXES

Sales tax: 6%. **Property tax:** $19.94 per $1,000 valuation. Sample tax calculations include a $25,000 homestead exemption.

Home value	Tax
$100,000	$1,496
$150,000	$2,493
$250,000	$4,487

REAL ESTATE

Median home value: $96,065 (Orange County). **Median rent:** $637/month (Orange County). **Communities popular with retirees:** Courtlea Oaks offers custom-built homes from the $180s, (407) 656-6397. Hyde Park offers manufactured homes starting at $33,600, excluding cost of the land lease, (407) 656-9712. **Licensed continuing-care retirement communities:** None.

CRIME & SAFETY

Crimes per 1,000 population: 71. **Non-emergency police:** (407) 656-3636. **Non-emergency fire department:** (407) 656-1111. **Police, fire, ambulance emergencies:** 911.

HOMELESS & BLIGHT

In 1991, Winter Garden initiated a Main Street program to revitalize its downtown. The old downtown shows promise as restorations, historic walking tours and a new farmers market attract visitors. A new commercial center stretches along Route 50 in the southern part of the town.

The U.S. Census reported 798 homeless persons in shelters and 271 visible in street locations in Orange County, population 677,491.

HEALTH CARE

There are no hospitals in Winter Garden. **Hospitals: Health Central**, four miles east in Ocoee, 141 beds, full service, (407) 296-1000. **Central Florida Surgical Center**, (407) 656-2700. **Physicians:** 225. **Specialties:** 35.

GETTING SMART

No college or university campuses in Winter Garden, though there are many in the Orlando area, including the **University of Central Florida**, (407) 823-2000; **Orlando College**, (407) 628-5870; and **Rollins College**, (407) 646-2000.

JUST FOR SENIORS

RSVP, (407) 422-1535.

GETTING INVOLVED

There are 40 organizations in the west Orange County area, all within a few minutes drive. They include: **Friends of Lake Apopka (FOLA)**, (407) 656-1304, **Main Street Winter Garden**, (407) 656-6363, and **Winter Garden Historical Association**, (407) 656-5544.

RECREATION, ENTERTAINMENT & AMENITIES

Public golf: Windermere Country Club. **Private golf:** West Orange Country Club. **Public tennis courts:** Three recreational complexes with tennis courts, sports fields and pools. **Private tennis courts:** None. **Parks:** Three parks, one on Lake Apopka with a public boat ramp. **Public swimming pools:** Municipal recreation complex at Garden Avenue. **Water sports:** Boating, sailing and water-skiing. **River/gulf/ocean:** Lake Apopka. **Running/walking/biking:** The new West Orange Trail is a 17-mile Rails-to-Trails project through Winter Garden that offers recreation for joggers, bicyclists, walkers and equestrians. **Horses/**

riding: Along certain sections of the West Orange Trail. **Hunting:** Hunting and fishing licenses, (407) 836-4100. **Movie theaters:** 17 screens. **Art museums:** None. **History museums:** None. **Theaters:** Tanner Auditorium. **Library:** West Orange Public. **Attractions:** Universal Studios is nine miles away; Citrus Tower is 13 miles away. **Necessities:** Five banks, a post office, five shopping centers and two new-car dealerships.

Smart Shopper Tip: New West Oaks Mall in nearby Ocoee has it all.

WHO LIVES HERE
Population: 12,738 year-round residents, an increase of 2,875 since 1990. **Age 65+** = 11.0% in Orange County. **Median household income:** $31,649 (Orange County). **Per capita income:** $21,868 (Orange County).

NUMBERS TO KNOW
Chamber of commerce: (407) 656-1304. **Voter registration:** In Orlando, (407) 836-2070. **Vehicle registration, tags & title:** In Ocoee, (407) 656-2425. **Driver's license:** In Ocoee, (407) 656-2393.

WHAT TO READ
Orlando Sentinel, daily newspaper, (407) 420-5353. **The West Orange Times**, weekly newspaper, (407) 656-2121.

GETTING AROUND
Bus: LYNX, (407) 841-8240. **Taxi:** Moore's Taxi, (407) 656-4194. **Tours:** None. **Airport:** Orlando International is 20 miles southeast. **Traffic:** Florida's Turnpike, minutes from Winter Garden, can put you in Orlando in 15 minutes.

JOBS
County unemployment rate: 3.4%. **Florida Jobs and Benefits:** In Orlando, (407) 897-2880. **Job Line:** For Orange County, (407) 246-2178.

UTILITIES
Electricity: Florida Power Corp., (407) 629-1010. **Gas:** Lake Apopka Natural Gas District, (407) 656-2734. **Water & sewer:** Winter Garden Water Dept., (407) 656-4100. **Telephone:** Sprint United, (407) 656-7538. **Cable TV:** Time Warner Communications, (407) 656-3327.

PLACES OF WORSHIP
One Catholic and 23 Protestant churches.

THE ENVIRONMENT
Lake Apopka has the worst pollution problem in the region. It has been designated as a SWIM water body for surface water improvement and management. To date, many pollution point sources have been eliminated or reduced. The long-term plan calls for converting a total of 14,000 acres from farmland to treatment wetlands.

Lake Butler, near Windermere, has been rated as having good water quality, but authorities say its status is threatened by the massive development of the area.

There are two EPA-listed Superfund sites in Orange County, one in Winter Park and one in Zellwood.

EVENTS AND FESTIVALS
Art Auction - August. **West Orange Weekend** - November.

WHERE TO EAT
The Country House Restaurant, 13394 W. Colonial Drive, Southern, inexpensive, (407) 656-1421.

WHERE TO STAY
Best Western Winter Garden, (407) 654-1188. **Holiday Inn Orlando West**, (407) 656-5050. **Colony Plaza Hotel**, (407) 656-3333.

ISSUES
Issues affecting Winter Garden's future are being addressed in a positive fashion. Horizons West, the development plan for 30,000 acres south of Winter Garden, will bring untold economic opportunities to this area — and hordes of people.

RELOCATION TIPS

Before you buy a vacation home with an eye to making it your future retirement home, consider how the home will suit you, your furniture and your lifestyle when you spend years rather than weeks there. A typical vacation home may be just 600 to 900 square feet — much smaller than most year-round residences — and could leave you with no room for retirement hobbies. Living areas may be too small to accommodate large furniture such as china cabinets or pianos. Check the home's storage areas too, since pantries, garages, closets and attics are often small or non-existent in a vacation home. Make sure the kitchen is large enough for meal preparation when friends or relatives come to visit. Finally, remember that your neighbors may be vacationers and may not be present for months at a time, or could rent out their property to a constant stream of newcomers.

Winter Haven

HE SAID: ★ ★ ★ ★
It's a nice town. A little too touristy and resort-oriented, but it's complete, with all the necessary services. The lakes are great for boating and fishing and for those who just want to lounge by the water and soak in the beauty and tranquillity of the surroundings.

SHE SAID: ★ ★ ★ ★
This is a clean, medium-sized town with lots of lakes, nice residential areas, nice golf courses and good medical facilities. I would consider Winter Haven for retirement.

Best known as the home of Cypress Gardens, it has several times the number of lakes of its better-known sister city, Lakeland. A series of canals connects the chain of lakes, allowing fishermen and sightseers to move through the city from neighborhood to neighborhood without interference from vehicular traffic — a luxury few cities can provide.

As you might expect, lake shores are the most popular places for homes. Residents who don't live on the water with a dock and boathouse live close enough to enjoy a good lake vista.

For those who don't elect to live on a lake, there are plenty of inland neighborhoods — both near the downtown and in the suburbs — that count retirees among their residents. Golfers can choose from half a dozen places, including Cypresswood Golf & Country Club, a master-planned private community that's off the beaten path in eastern Winter Haven. Farther east, in the lush, heavily wooded country just south of Haines City, is Grenelefe Golf & Tennis Resort, a 1,000-acre development with three par-72 courses.

Chain O'Lakes Convention Center and Recreation Complex is the site of most art and cultural activities in the community; it's also spring-training grounds for the Cleveland Indians. Six of the lakes in the chain form the venue for the annual Christmas Boat Parade.

Major league baseball, Cypress Gardens and a striking landscape highlighted by gardens, parks and lakes bring many visitors back to Winter Haven to stay. Add to this the good shopping, excellent health care and low-key, relaxed lifestyle, and you have all the ingredients for a quality retirement town.

WEATHER

	Winter	Spring	Summer	Fall
Normal daily high/low	76/51	88/64	92/71	80/58
Normal precipitation	8 in.	13 in.	21 in.	6 in.

Disaster watch: Southwest Florida has been hit by five major hurricanes since 1900. Northwest Florida has been hit by six major hurricanes since 1900.

TAXES
Sales tax: 6%. **Property tax:** Rates range from $24.05 to $24.88 per $1,000 valuation, depending on location. Sample taxes are calculated at the rate of $24.88 and include a $25,000 homestead exemption.

Home value	Tax
$100,000	$1,866
$150,000	$3,110
$250,000	$5,598

REAL ESTATE
Median home value: $89,362 (Polk County). **Median rent:** $542/ month (Polk County). **Communities popular with retirees:** Cypresswood Golf & Country Club offers estate homes, patio homes and golf villas priced from the high $60s to $400s, (800) 248-2491. Towerwood has manufactured homes priced from the $50s to the $80s, adults only, (800) 262-4576. Winter Ridge Condominiums are priced in the mid-$50s, (800) 682-6636. **Licensed continuing-care retirement communities:** None.

CRIME & SAFETY
Crimes per 1,000 population: 104. **Traffic accidents:** 672. **Fatal crashes:** 5. **Police employees:** 65 officers. **Fire department employees:** 33 firefighters. **Non-emergency police:** (941) 291-5858. **Non-emergency fire department:** (941) 291-5677. **Police, fire, ambulance emergencies:** 911.

HOMELESS & BLIGHT
The town is clean and open. Downtown is encircled by lakes, many of them connected by canals. Cypress Gardens Boulevard and U.S. Highway 17 through the city are both heavily commercialized and could benefit from a more stringent sign ordinance. We did not see any homeless persons.

The U.S. Census recorded 172 homeless persons in shelters and 33 visible in street locations in Polk County, population 405,382.

HEALTH CARE
Hospitals: Winter Haven Hospital, 579 beds, full service, 24-hour emergency, (941) 293-1121. **Center for Psychiatry**, (941) 297-1744. **Regency Medical Center**, 50 beds, women's health services, (941) 294-7010.
Physicians: 200+. **Specialties:** 37.

GETTING SMART
Polk Community College, (941) 297-1000. **Offerings:** Two-year degrees in arts and sciences, plus non-credit courses.

JUST FOR SENIORS
Senior Adult Center sponsors movies, dances, concerts, shopping excursions, games, trips and tours, (941) 291-5870.

GETTING INVOLVED
There are more than 40 clubs and organizations. **Habitat for Humanity**, (941) 318-1902. **Meals on Wheels**, (941) 299-1616.

RECREATION, ENTERTAINMENT & AMENITIES
Public golf: Baytree Golf Club, Lucerne Park Par Three and Willowbrook Golf Course. **Private golf:** Cypresswood Golf & Country Club, Grenelefe Golf & Tennis Resort and Lake Region Yacht & Country Club. **Public tennis courts:** City Tennis Center has 12 lighted courts. **Private tennis courts:** Grenelefe Golf & Tennis Resort has 18 courts. **Parks:** There are seven municipal parks with more than 90 acres. Lake Shipp Park is an 18-acre county park. The 40-acre Audubon Nature Center has a nature trail. **Public**

swimming pools: Chain O'Lakes Recreation Complex and Winter Haven Northeast Recreation Center. **Water sports:** Boating, sailing, scuba diving, snorkeling and water-skiing. **River/gulf/ocean:** There are more than 100 lakes in the Greater Winter Haven area, including Lake Eloise at the famed Cypress Gardens, where the longest-running water-skiing show in the world takes place. Fourteen lakes are connected. **Running/walking/biking:** Audubon Nature Center and Saddlecreek Park have trails. Many of the lakes have walking/jogging trails. **Horses/riding:** One boarding stable in the area. **Hunting:** No local hunting. There are plenty of good places to fish, but a license is required. Information, (941) 534-4700. **Movie theaters:** 18 screens. **Art museums:** Ridge Art Association at the Chain O'Lakes Recreation Complex and Polk Community College Art Gallery. **History museums:** None. **Theaters:** Polk Community College Fine Arts Complex hosts the College Players. Chain O'Lakes Convention Center has a 350-seat auditorium. Theatre Winter Haven is a community theater company. **Library:** One public library. **Attractions:** Bok Tower Gardens in Lake Wales, Cypress Gardens and the Water Ski Museum and Hall of Fame. **Necessities:** All here.

 Smart Shopper Tip: There are several shopping centers and the Winter Haven Mall, but none are of the caliber of Lakeland Square Mall just 30 minutes away.

WHO LIVES HERE
Population: 25,638 year-round residents, an increase of 913 since 1990. **Age 65+** = 19.6% in Polk County. **Median household income:** $26,191 (Polk County). **Per capita income:** $19,126 (Polk County).

NUMBERS TO KNOW
Chamber of commerce: (941) 293-2138. **Voter registration:** (941) 534-7380. **Vehicle registration, tags & title:** (941) 298-7576. **Driver's license:** (941) 421-3201.

WHAT TO READ
Winter Haven News Chief, daily newspaper, (941) 294-7731. **Tampa Tribune**, daily newspaper, (941) 683-6531. **The Ledger**, daily newspaper, (941) 293-9982.

GETTING AROUND
Bus: No public intra-city transportation. **Taxi:** Winter Haven Taxi, (941) 324-9166. **Tours:** Chain O'Lakes Boat Tours features pontoon trips through Winter Haven, (941) 294-8181. **Train:** Amtrak has daily passenger service, (941) 294-9203. **Airport:** Tampa International is an hour away. Orlando International is a little farther. **Traffic:** If you can avoid U.S. 17 and Cypress Gardens Boulevard, you will have little trouble navigating Winter Haven.

JOBS
County unemployment rate: 6.6%. **Florida Jobs and Benefits:** (941) 291-5292.

UTILITIES
Electricity: Tampa Electric Co., (888) 223-0800. Florida Power Corp. serves nearby Haines City, (800) 700-8744. **Gas:** Central Florida Gas Co., (941) 293-2125. **Water & sewer:** Winter Haven Utilities, (941) 291-5678. **Telephone:** GTE, (800) 483-4200. **Cable TV:** Time-Warner Cable, (941) 965-7766.

PLACES OF WORSHIP
Three Catholic and more than 80 Protestant churches, plus one Jewish synagogue.

THE ENVIRONMENT
The Lakeland/Winter Haven region is in the upper portion of the Peace River Basin, which has been rated as having some of the worst water quality problems in the state. Lakes Hancock, Hamilton, Lena and Banana have poor water quality. Peace Creek has poor water quality and Saddle Creek has fair to poor quality. The Banana-Hancock Canal also has poor water quality. The Winter Haven Chain of Lakes is located between lakes Hancock and Hamilton. During the 1980s, Polk County received federal grants to clean up some of the pollution problems in several of these lakes; results show significant improvement. The chain of lakes and Banana Lake also have been designated as SWIM (Surface Water Improvement and Management) water bodies, but they continue to show poor water quality.

 There is one EPA-listed Superfund site in the county, Alpha Chemical Corp. in Kathleen.

EVENTS AND FESTIVALS
Poinsettia Festival - January. **Florida Citrus and Polk County Festival** - February. **Bach Festival** - March. **Spring Floral Festival** - March to May. **Polk County Senior Artist's Show** - April. **Chrysanthemum Festival** - November. **WinterFest** - Last week of November and first two weeks of December.

WHERE TO EAT
Christy's Sundown, U.S. 17 S., seafood and steak, moderate, (941) 293-0069.

WHERE TO STAY
Best Western Admiral's Inn, (800) 247-2799 or (941) 324-5950. **Chain of Lakes Beach Resort**, (941) 324-6320. **Quality Inn Townhouse**, (941) 294-4104.

ISSUES
Winter Haven continues to improve and renovate its infrastructure. Recognized as a Main Street City in 1995, its downtown is undergoing extensive rehabilitation, including restoration of the old Ritz Theatre. There have been improvements to the Chain O'Lakes Convention Center and Recreation Complex, enhancements of the Boat Tours program, widening of heavily traveled U. S. 17 and the opening of several new restaurants. These are signs of a vital city, getting better with age.

Winter Park

HE SAID: ★ ★ ★
> *It has many attractive, desirable attributes.*
> *Unfortunately, it got caught up in the urban sprawl and*
> *spillover of Orlando. If Winter Park was ten miles farther*
> *north and I was ten times wealthier, it definitely*
> *would be on my short list.*

SHE SAID: ★ ★ ★ ★
> *This quaint, busy college town is surrounded*
> *by lakes and filled with upscale homes, plenty of golf*
> *courses, excellent shopping, flowering gardens and all the*
> *other things anyone would want in a nice place to live.*
> *I could retire here.*

One of the most telling bits of information about Winter Park is that there are no mobile home parks within the city limits. It is a place where the real estate agents add "Winter Park address" to a listing as a status symbol — and as an explanation for the relatively high asking price. Winter Park has one of the lowest residential property tax millage rates in Florida, but don't let that fool you. Property appraisals are sky high, so what the city loses in its tax rate it makes up for in taxable value.

The heart of the city is a ten-square-block area bordered by lakes Killarney, Osceola and Virginia. It holds the historic and cultural essence of old Winter Park, where in times past the ultra-wealthy chose to winter, enjoying the tree-lined streets, shaded benches and charming views. Remnants of the beauty and charm that originally brought those snowbirds still remain for the pleasure of a much wider audience.

It has its own Park Avenue, though not as long and extravagant as the more famous one in New York City. A walking tour reveals an assortment of churches, galleries, museums and theaters that would be the envy of almost any city. Rollins College, known for its Mediterranean architecture, serves as the cultural center of the city. Many social and recreational activities revolve around the college as well.

Winter Park is a place where lawn bowling and shuffleboard are popular pastimes. For many, dining out entails only a short stroll to a quiet, elegant downtown restaurant or sidewalk cafe.

Big-city amenities are only minutes away in Orlando. Transportation facilities are excellent: Orlando International Airport is 18 miles away, an Amtrak passenger station is within blocks of many residences, and the interstate and Florida's Turnpike are just beyond earshot.

When asked what they like most about Winter Park, one retired couple cites the quality of life, accessibility to cultural and social opportunities, trees, lakes, concerned citizens and health-care services. They also like the fact that residents are able to make an impact on local government policy.

These are just a few of Winter Park's outstanding qualities.

WEATHER

	Winter	Spring	Summer	Fall
Normal daily high/low	74/51	87/66	91/73	79/58
Normal precipitation	9 in.	13 in.	20 in.	7 in.

Disaster watch: Northeast Florida has not been hit by a major hurricane since 1900.

TAXES
Sales tax: 6%. **Property tax:** $18.70 per $1,000 valuation. Sample tax calculations include a $25,000 homestead exemption.

Home value	Tax
$100,000	$1,403
$150,000	$2,338
$250,000	$4,208

REAL ESTATE
Median home value: $94,147 (Orange County). **Median rent:** $637/month (Orange County). **Communities popular with retirees:** Homes on — or with views of — a lake generally are priced from the $200s to $250s; others start in the mid-$70s and range up to the $200s. Homes around Lake Virginia, by Rollins College, range from the $100s to $500s. **Licensed continuing-care retirement communities:** The Mayflower has 240 independent living units, 36 sheltered nursing beds and 24 community beds, (407) 672-1620. Winter Park Towers has 376 independent living units, 29 sheltered nursing beds and 92 community beds, (407) 647-4083.

CRIME & SAFETY
Crimes per 1,000 population: 76. **Non-emergency police:** (407) 599-3455. **Non-emergency fire department:** (407) 623-3288. **Police, fire, ambulance emergencies:** 911.

HOMELESS & BLIGHT
It's like a pearl in an oyster shell. The inner town is beautiful and charming, but the periphery has the usual assortment of highway businesses and signs proclaiming their presence.

The U.S. Census counted 798 homeless persons living in shelters and 271 visible on the streets of Orange County, population 677,491.

HEALTH CARE
Hospitals: Winter Park Memorial Hospital, 301 beds, full service, 24-hour emergency, specialties, (407) 646-7075. **Physicians:** 229. **Specialties:** 38.

GETTING SMART
Elderhostel offers a program at San Pedro Catholic Retreat and Conference Center on Lake Howell. **Rollins College**, (407) 646-2000. **Offerings:** Four-year undergraduate and graduate degrees. **Warner Southern College**, (407) 629-2322. **Offerings:** One-year program in organizational management. It requires 60 undergraduate hours prerequisite to a bachelor's degree. **Winter Park Adult and Community Education Center**, (407) 647-6366. **Offerings:** Life enrichment and basic education courses.

JUST FOR SENIORS
Adult Day Care Center, (407) 629-5771. **Area Agency on Aging**, (407) 228-1800.

GETTING INVOLVED
United Way, (407) 644-2005. **Volunteer Center of Central Flor-**

ida in Orlando, (407) 896-0945.

RECREATION, ENTERTAINMENT & AMENITIES

Public golf: Winter Park Country Club, nine holes/par 35, and Winter Pines Golf Club, 18 holes/par 63. **Private golf:** Dubsdread Golf Course. **Public tennis courts:** Azalea Lane Recreation Center. **Private tennis courts:** Rollins College and Winter Park Racquet Club. **Parks:** Central Park, a large and popular downtown village green, and Azalea Lane Recreation Center. **Public swimming pools:** Cady Way and Westside Municipal. **Water sports:** Boating, sailing and water-skiing. **River/gulf/ocean:** There are more than 30 named lakes within a four-mile radius. **Running/walking/biking:** Central Park and quiet side streets are good venues. **Horses/riding:** None in the city. **Hunting:** None. **Movie theaters:** 21 screens. **Art museums:** Albin Polasek Foundation, Cornell Fine Arts Center Museum at Rollins College and Loch Haven Art Center. **History museums:** Morse Museum of American Art features turn-of-the-century functional and decorative arts, including a noted collection of stained-glass items by Tiffany. **Theaters:** Anne Russell Theatre at Rollins College and Mead Gardens Amphitheatre. **Library:** Winter Park. **Attractions:** Kraft Azalea Gardens on Lake Maitland, Mead Botanical Gardens, Scenic Boat Tours and Winter Park Civic Center. **Necessities:** All here, including two municipal farmers markets.

Smart Shopper Tip: Famed Park Avenue shops are a must for boutique browsing. Serious shoppers should try the 57 stores in Winter Park Mall.

WHO LIVES HERE

Population: 24,855 year-round residents, an increase of 595 since 1990. **Age 65+** = 11.0% in Orange County. **Median household income:** $31,649 (Orange County). **Per capita income:** $21,868 (Orange County).

NUMBERS TO KNOW

Chamber of commerce: (407) 644-8281. **Voter registration:** (407) 836-2070. **Vehicle registration, tags & title:** (407) 647-0022. **Driver's license:** (407) 623-1148.

WHAT TO READ

Orlando Sentinel, daily newspaper, (407) 420-5000. **Winter Park-Maitland Observer**, weekly newspaper, (407) 628-8500.

GETTING AROUND

Bus: The city operates a minibus that serves many parts of town, LYNX, (407) 841-8240. **Taxi:** Yellow Cab, (407) 425-3111. **Tours:** Scenic Boat Tours offers a 12-mile cruise through the Winter Park Chain of Lakes, (407) 644-4056. **Airport:** Orlando International is 18 miles away. **Train:** Amtrak passenger station, (407) 645-5055. **Traffic:** Avoid Fairbanks Avenue and U.S. Highway 17/92, and you'll get around fairly well.

JOBS

County unemployment rate: 3.4%. **Florida Jobs and Benefits:** In Orlando, (407) 897-2880.

UTILITIES

Electricity: Florida Power, (407) 629-1010. **Gas:** Peoples Gas, (407) 425-4661. **Water & sewer:** Winter Park Utilities, (407) 599-3220. **Telephone:** Sprint-United Telephone, (407) 339-1811. **Cable TV:** Time-Warner Cable, (407) 578-2777.

PLACES OF WORSHIP

Three Catholic and 37 Protestant churches, plus one Jewish synagogue.

THE ENVIRONMENT

Sinkholes in the city have claimed a number of buildings; the latest was in the 1980s.

Several of the large lakes near the city have been rated as having poor water quality, particularly lakes Jessup and Howell; however, Lake Jessup has shown an improving trend. The Little Econlockhatchee River has fair to poor water quality, though the Econlockhatchee River itself has fair to good quality. To the south, East Lake Tohopekaliga, as well as lakes Conway and Butler, generally have good water quality. The Econlockhatchee River System has protected status, designated as an Outstanding Florida Water.

There is one EPA-listed Superfund site in Winter Park. City Industries, also known as City Chemical, is about a mile from the nearest residence. There is one other EPA-listed Superfund site in the county, in the town of Zellwood.

EVENTS AND FESTIVALS

Winter Park Sidewalk Art Festival - March. **Fall Orchid Show & Sale** - November.

WHERE TO EAT

La Venezia, 142 Park Ave. S, Mediterranean, very expensive, (407) 647-7557. **Park Avenue Grille**, 358 N. Park Ave., seafood, veal, moderate, (407) 647-4556. **Park Plaza Gardens**, 319 Park Ave. S., continental, expensive to very expensive, (407) 645-2475.

WHERE TO STAY

Langford Hotel, (407) 644-3400. **Park Plaza Hotel**, (407) 647-1072.

ISSUES

The ugly side of commercialism and the sprawl of Orlando are threatening the beauty and tranquillity of this one-time favorite. Efforts are underway to upgrade the west side, which has been most heavily impacted.

Winter Springs

HE SAID: ☆
I was disappointed in the town itself. With two of the magic Florida words in its name, "winter" and "springs," it should be more attractive. It needs to raise the millage rate a few pennies and get to work on beautification. Until Winter Springs' leadership demonstrates a higher vision, I would not commit my retirement years to this town.

SHE SAID: ☆ ☆ ☆
Beautiful planned residential areas offer all types of housing, but you would have to travel to nearby Orlando for shopping. The business district of Winter Springs is minute — so small it hardly exists. I would not retire here.

It was incorporated in 1959 as the Village of North Orlando and became Winter Springs in 1972 when it annexed the Tuscawilla Planned Urban Development. Just 15 minutes north of Orlando — but worlds apart — Winter Springs has little going for it except a low property tax rate, a quiet and rural environment, Lake Jessup and the sizeable Tuscawilla community.

Since there are no significant employers in the immediate area, residents are either retired or commute to jobs in Orlando. This is changing as current and planned road construction opens the area to commercial and industrial development.

Tuscawilla, the established country-club community of Winter Springs, is virtually self-contained. Made up of 11 neighborhoods, it offers just about the only amenities of the entire town and has its own elementary school, church, golf course and club. Its Towne Center supplies most of the basic goods and services needed by residents.

Tuscawilla has a broad spectrum of housing in a picture-perfect setting. Residents enjoy forests, lakes, wildlife and the natural splendor of central Florida, yet have almost immediate access to the entertainment, restaurants and cultural offerings of Orlando.

There are other, almost-as-beautiful residential developments in Florida. None have Tuscawilla's winning combination of a lush tropical setting, exquisitely manicured lawns and commons, masterfully designed homes and strategic location.

But this is only true of Tuscawilla, and not at all reflective of the town of Winter Springs. Like the luminaria display that's set up each winter in Tuscawilla, Winter Springs needs to light up its dark corners.

WEATHER

	Winter	Spring	Summer	Fall
Normal daily high/low	72/49	86/64	91/71	77/57
Normal precipitation	10 in.	12 in.	19 in.	8 in.

Disaster watch: Northeast Florida has not been hit by a major hurricane since 1900.

TAXES
Sales tax: 7%. **Property tax:** $19.48 per $1,000 valuation. Sample tax calculations include a $25,000 homestead exemption.

Home value	Tax
$100,000	$1,461
$150,000	$2,435
$250,000	$4,383

REAL ESTATE
Median home value: $91,695 (Seminole County). **Median rent:** $661/month (Seminole County). **Communities popular with retirees:** Hacienda Village is an adult manufactured-home community where resale prices range from $7,000 to $40,000. There are 447 units, an exercise room, shuffleboard courts, tennis courts and park, (407) 327-0051. Tuscawilla offers villas priced from the $80s to $220s and single-family homes from the $120s to $600s, (407) 366-3600. Tuskawilla Trails has manufactured homes starting at $49,900. **Licensed continuing-care retirement communities:** None.

CRIME & SAFETY
Crimes per 1,000 population: 34. **Non-emergency police:** (407) 327-1000. **Non-emergency fire department:** (407) 327-2332. **Police, fire, ambulance emergencies:** 911.

HOMELESS & BLIGHT
We saw no homeless persons or blighted areas, but Winter Springs — with the exception of Tuscawilla — is not an attractive town. Inexpensive housing and no-frills public facilities are standard fare.

The U.S. Census reported 53 homeless persons in shelters and 18 visible in street locations in Seminole County, population 287,529.

HEALTH CARE
Hospitals: South Seminole Hospital is the closest hospital, five miles away in Longwood, 206 beds, full service, 24-hour emergency, (407) 767-1200.
Physicians: 3. **Specialties:** In Winter Springs there are family-practice physicians only.

GETTING SMART
There are no college or university campuses in Winter Springs, though there are many in and around Greater Orlando, including the **University of Central Florida**, (407) 823-2000; **Orlando College**, (407) 628-5870; and **Rollins College**, (407) 646-2000.

JUST FOR SENIORS
Better Living for Seniors, Help Line, (407) 333-8877. **Winter Springs Senior Center** offers dances, card games, crafts, lunches, potluck dinners and holiday parties, (407) 327-4031.

GETTING INVOLVED
United Way in Orlando, (407) 897-6677. **Volunteer Center of**

Central Florida in Orlando, (407) 896-0945. **Winter Springs Civic Association** meets once a month and publishes the *Winter Springs Bulletin Quarterly*. Call the chamber for more information.

RECREATION, ENTERTAINMENT & AMENITIES
Public golf: Winter Springs Golf Club. **Private golf:** Tuscawilla Country Club. **Public tennis courts:** Sunshine Park and South Moss Road Park. **Private tennis courts:** Tuscawilla Country Club has eight courts. **Parks:** Central Winds Park is a delightful 58-acre park. Sunshine and South Moss Road parks have the usual recreational facilities. The town also has set aside land for several parks where residents can go for quiet reflection. **Public swimming pools:** None. **Water sports:** Boating, canoeing, sailing and water- skiing. **River/gulf/ocean:** Lake Jessup and the St. Johns River. **Running/walking/biking:** Winter Springs fronts on Lake Jessup, an area that affords ample opportunity for outdoor activities. **Horses/riding:** Some areas in Tuscawilla offer lots up to 1.5 acres where residents can keep horses. **Hunting:** None in the immediate area. **Movie theaters:** None. **Art museums:** None. **History museums:** None. **Theaters:** Theater for Children. **Library:** None. **Attractions:** Tuscawilla Country Club. **Necessities:** Most necessities are available in one of the local shopping centers or in neighboring Longwood.

Smart Shopper Tip: Try Longwood Village at I-4 and Route 434 or Seminole Towne Center Mall. Orange Blossom Trail Mall on U.S. Highway 17/92 at Sand Lake Road is an all-time Florida favorite.

WHO LIVES HERE
Population: 27,466 year-round residents, an increase of 5,315 since 1990. **Age 65+** = 11.0% in Seminole County. **Median household income:** $37,495 (Seminole County). **Per capita income:** $23,400 (Seminole County).

NUMBERS TO KNOW
Chamber of commerce: (407) 425-1234. **Voter registration:** (407) 321-1130 ext. 7709. **Vehicle registration, tags & title:** (407) 321-1130. **Driver's license:** (407) 856-6500.

WHAT TO READ
Orlando Sentinel, daily newspaper, (407) 420-5000. **Sanford Herald**, daily newspaper, (407) 322-2611.

GETTING AROUND
Bus: No public intra-city transportation. **Taxi:** None. **Tours:** None. **Airport:** Orlando International and Orlando Sanford. **Traffic:** Very light. The new Central Florida Greeneway has greatly improved access to the area. No significant traffic is generated in this out-of-the-way location.

JOBS
County unemployment rate: 3.0%. **Florida Jobs and Benefits:** In Sanford, (407) 330-6700.

UTILITIES
Electricity: Florida Power, (407) 629-1010. **Gas:** Some sections are served by Florida Public Utilities, (407) 322-5733. **Water & sewer:** City Utility Dept., (407) 327-1641. **Telephone:** Sprint-United Telephone, (800) 877-7746. **Cable TV:** Time-Warner Cable, (407) 321-0431.

PLACES OF WORSHIP
One Catholic and 14 Protestant churches.

THE ENVIRONMENT
Lakes Jessup and Howell and the Little Econlockhatchee River have been rated as having the worst water quality in the area. The Econlockhatchee River System has been designated as an Outstanding Florida Water (OFW) and should in time show improvement. Water quality of Lake Jessup is poor, lakes Kathryn and Harney are good to fair, and the St. Johns River is mostly good to fair. Both Lake Harney and the St. Johns River show improving trends. The St. Johns River National Wildlife Refuge has protected status as an OFW. Health advisories recommending limited consumption of largemouth bass due to mercury content have been issued for Lake Sawgrass, Puzzle Lake, Lake Hellen Blazes and the St. Johns River at the Econlockhatchee River.

EVENTS AND FESTIVALS
Winter Springs Parade - November. **Luminaria—Light Up Tuscawilla** - December.

WHERE TO EAT/WHERE TO STAY
Winter Springs is not on the tourist trail and does not offer much in the way of restaurants or hotel accomodations. Residents say they travel the short distance to Orlando or Altamonte Springs for dining out.

ISSUES
Its current status as a so-called bedroom community for Orlando has changed significantly in the past few years. The suburban development that encircles urban Orlando got a shot in the arm from new roads and road improvements. These roads brought both commercial and industrial development to Winter Springs. The issue is whether the added convenience of quick access to larger metropolitan areas will be offset by heavier volumes of traffic, people and general activity.

Zephyrhills

HE SAID: ★ ★

In my mind, nothing we saw can account for its popularity with the thousands of snowbirds who keep coming back year after year. If it has anything going for it, it is proximity to Tampa Bay and Lakeland.

SHE SAID: ★

Just another small town in Florida that has little to offer except the climate. It's a poor town with few redeeming features. I wouldn't retire here.

Located in the hilly terrain of rural Pasco County northeast of Tampa, Zephyrhills has three traits that distinguish it from other towns in central Florida but fail to lend distinction to its character.

First is the vast proliferation of mobile homes and travel trailers stretching in every direction from the town center. A map of Zephyrhills produced for the chamber of commerce lists more than 140 mobile home and RV parks that provide housing for some 80,000 snowbirds who winter here each year, almost 10 times the year-round population.

Second, while significant principally to those who profit from it, Zephyrhills has a widespread reputation for its pure drinking water, which the Zephyrhills Bottled Water Co. pumps, bottles and distributes throughout the state.

Third, Zephyrhills has an international reputation for its skydiving facilities and terrain, which brings enthusiasts from around the world to its parachute centers to train and compete in year-round parachuting meets.

In addition to these traits, the chamber of commerce cites "location central to all attractions, economical living and friendliness" as the motivating forces at work.

The town itself lacks character, style and quaintness, which are the hallmarks of most popular small towns. It most assuredly is absent the amenities that draw people to larger population centers. While receptiveness to mobile home parks has apparently been the linchpin of growth in years past, several new upscale golf and country club-type communities, most notably The Links and others near Lake Bernadette, are attracting new retirees. New developments featuring site-built homes in the $150,000 to $300,000 price range dot the landscape along Route 54 between Zephyrhills and I-75. But a beautiful new home is not enough incentive to pull up established roots and migrate to this part of Florida.

WEATHER

	Winter	Spring	Summer	Fall
Normal daily high/low	75/51	88/65	92/71	79/57
Normal precipitation	11 in.	14 in.	22 in.	7 in.

Disaster watch: Northwest Florida has been hit by six major hurricanes since 1900.

TAXES

Sales tax: 6%. **Property tax:** $26.49 per $1,000 valuation. Sample tax calculations include a $25,000 homestead exemption.

Home value	Tax
$100,000	$1,987
$150,000	$3,311
$250,000	$5,960

REAL ESTATE

Median home value: $79,923 (Pasco County). **Median rent:** $422/month (Pasco County). **Communities popular with retirees:** The chamber of commerce lists 149 mobile home and RV parks, condominium complexes and small, single-family home developments. Crystal Lake is a 128-acre manufactured-home community with a lake for fishing and boating. Homes range from $35,000 to $100,000, excluding the cost of the land lease, (800) 541-4362 or (813) 782-2826. Forest Lake Estates is a 210-acre manufactured-home development, also with a lake for fishing. Homes are priced from $32,900 to $75,000 or more, excluding the cost of the land lease, (800) 468-7979 or (813) 783-7979. **Licensed continuing-care retirement communities:** None.

CRIME & SAFETY

Crimes per 1,000 population: 81. **Non-emergency police:** (813) 782-1551. **Non-emergency fire department:** (813) 782-8184. **Police, fire, ambulance emergencies:** 911.

HOMELESS & BLIGHT

No homeless persons noted, but there's plenty of sub-par housing — mobile, manufactured and site built. Despite efforts being made to revitalize downtown and build new parks and recreation facilities, it has very little to attract residents to the town center.

The U.S. Census reported 43 homeless persons in shelters and nine visible on the streets of Pasco County, population 281,131.

HEALTH CARE

Hospitals: East Pasco Medical Center, a member of the Seventh-Day Adventist Health System, 85 beds, full service, 24-hour emergency, (813) 788-0411.

Physicians: 120 on staff at East Pasco Medical Center. **Specialties:** 34.

GETTING SMART

There are no college or university campuses in Zephyrhills, but six within driving distance. **Pasco-Hernando Community College**, (352) 567-6701. **St. Leo College**, (813) 840-0259. **University of South Florida**, (813) 974-2011. **University of Tampa**, (813) 253-3333. **Stetson School of Law**, (727) 562-7800. **Eckerd College**, (813) 867-1166.

JUST FOR SENIORS

Zephyrhills Senior Center, (813) 788-0471.

GETTING INVOLVED

East Pasco Meals on Wheels, (813) 782-2793.

RECREATION, ENTERTAINMENT & AMENITIES

Public golf: Betmar Golf Course and Zephyrhills Municipal Golf Course. **Private golf:** Silver Oaks Golf Course & Country Club, The Links at Lake Bernadette and Zephyr Springs Golf &

Country Club. **Public tennis courts:** There are at least 10 municipal courts. **Private tennis courts:** Several country clubs and housing developments offer tennis memberships. **Parks:** There are at least eight municipal, county and state parks in Greater Zephyrhills. **Public swimming pools:** Hercules Aquatic Center. **Water sports:** None in the immediate area, except on private property. There is canoeing on rivers north and south, and the usual Gulf Coast activities 25 miles away. **River/gulf/ocean:** The Hillsborough River originates within the southern city limits, the Withlacoochee River is northeast, and the Gulf of Mexico is about 25 miles west. **Running/walking/biking:** Hillsborough River State Park has 3,000 acres available with paths and trails. The rural nature of the area provides plenty of opportunities. **Horses/riding:** There are farms and stables throughout eastern Pasco County. **Hunting:** Licenses and permits, (813) 847-8165. **Movie theaters:** Eight screens. **Art museums:** Art Club of Zephyrhills. **History museums:** Zephyrhills Historical Association. **Theaters:** The Alice Hall Community Center and Zephyrhills Festival Park are the focal points for civic activities and events. **Library:** New River branch and Zephyrhills Public. **Attractions:** Zephyrhills Parachute Center. **Necessities:** Seven banks, nine shopping centers, new-car dealerships, plus the usual general merchandise stores and service providers.

Smart Shopper Tip: We noted that the army-navy surplus store is about the finest-looking facility downtown. There are nine squares, plazas and shopping centers in town, but a 30-minute run to Lakeland Square Mall puts you in shopper's paradise.

WHO LIVES HERE
Population: 8,913 year-round residents, an increase of 693 since 1990. During winter there are about 80,000 people, including snowbirds, in Greater Zephyrhills. **Age 65+ =** 29.0% in Pasco County. **Median household income:** $22,071 (Pasco County). **Per capita income:** $18,808 (Pasco County).

NUMBERS TO KNOW
Chamber of commerce: (813) 782-1913. **Voter registration:** In Dade City, (352) 521-4302. **Vehicle registration, tags & title:** In Dade City, (352) 521-4368. **Driver's license:** In Dade City, (352) 521-1441.

WHAT TO READ
Zephyrhills News, weekly newspaper, (813) 782-1558. **St. Petersburg Times**, daily newspaper, (352) 521-5757 ext. 2100. **Tampa Tribune**, daily newspaper, (813) 788-5541.

GETTING AROUND
Bus: Pasco County Star, (813) 834-3322. **Taxi:** Pasco Yellow Cab, (813) 949-1077. **Tours:** None. **Airport:** Tampa International is 35 miles away. **Traffic:** Not a problem. U.S. 301 is more than adequate to carry traffic north of town. Traffic is dispersed over three highways to the south. The Zephyrhills West Bypass gives north-south travelers an easy way around town.

JOBS
County unemployment rate: 4.2%. **Florida Jobs and Benefits:** In Dade City, (352) 521-1485.

UTILITIES
Electricity: Florida Power, (800) 700-8744, or Withlacoochee Electric Co-op for rural areas, (352) 567-5133. **Gas:** None. **Water & sewer:** Zephyrhills Utilities, (813) 782-1526. **Telephone:** GTE, within 813 area code, (800) 483-4200; outside 813 area code, (800) 483-1000. **Cable TV:** Florida Satellite Network, (813) 788-7634.

PLACES OF WORSHIP
One Catholic and 53 Protestant churches.

THE ENVIRONMENT
The upper Hillsborough River has been affected by rapid development and construction and currently is assessed as having fair water quality. The Hillsborough River at Hillsborough River State Park is designated as an Outstanding Florida Water and has good water quality. Big Ditch historically has had poor water quality, but current information is not available.

EVENTS AND FESTIVALS
Senior Citizens Day Festival & Parade - January. **Winter Fest** - February. **Founder's Day Celebration** - March. **Annual Fish Fry** - March. **Auto & Antique Fall Festival** - November. **Holiday Festival** - November.

WHERE TO EAT
Friendly Folks, 4447 Gall Blvd., home-style breakfast, lunch and dinner, inexpensive, (813) 788-2686. **Village Inn Restaurant & Bakery**, 5214 Gall Blvd., sandwiches, salads, moderate, (813) 782-9556.

WHERE TO STAY
Best Western, (813) 782-5527. **Saddlebrook Golf & Tennis Resort** in nearby Wesley Chapel, (813) 973-1111.

ISSUES
Zephyrhills has been hugely successful in attracting retirees, mostly snowbirds with modest incomes, with almost nothing to offer except a warm climate and inexpensive housing. Can it successfully diversify? It is attempting to improve its tax base by attracting more prosperous taxpayers to the new, upscale housing developments and expanded golfing facilities. If it can do this, will it become an aesthetically and culturally attractive place through wise allotment of the new revenues?

FOR FURTHER INFORMATION

Bureau of Economic & Business Research
University of Florida
University Press of Florida
15 N.W. 15th St.
Gainesville, FL 32611
(800) 226-3822

Department of Highway Safety and Motor Vehicles
Neil Kirkman Building
Tallahassee, FL 32399
(850) 922-9000

Florida Association of Realtors
7025 Augusta National Drive
Orlando, FL 32822-5017
(407) 438-1400

Florida Department of Environmental Protection
3900 Commonwealth Blvd.
Tallahassee, FL 32399
(850) 488-1554

Florida Department of Health and Rehabilitative Services
Program Office of Aging and Adult Services
1317 Winewood Blvd.
Building 8, Room 311
Tallahassee, FL 32399-0700
(850) 488-8922

Florida Department of Insurance
Bureau of Consumer Outreach & Education
200 E. Gaines St.
Tallahassee, FL 32399
(800) 342-2762 (in Florida)
(850) 922-3133

Florida Department of Law Enforcement
Uniform Crime Reports Section
Special Services Bureau
P.O. Box 1489
Tallahassee, FL 32302-1489
(850) 410-7980

National Climatic Data Center
151 Patton Ave., Room 120
Asheville, NC 28801-5001
(704) 271-4800

National Flood Insurance Program
P.O. Box 6468
Rockville, MD 20849-6468
(800) 427-5583

National Technical Information Service
Technology Administration
U.S. Department of Commerce
Springfield, VA 22161
(703) 605-6000

Office of Education Budget and Management
Florida Department of Education
PL-08
The Capitol Building
Tallahassee, FL 32399-0400
(850) 487-1785

Standards and Monitoring Section
Bureau of Surface Water Management
Division of Water Facilities
Department of Environmental Protection
2600 Blair Stone Road, M.S. 3570
Tallahassee, FL 32399
(904) 487-1855

United States Environmental Protection Agency
Office of Emergency & Remedial Response
Office of Program Management
401 M St. SW, M.S. 5201G
Washington, DC 20460
(703) 603-8960

ALSO AVAILABLE FROM VACATION PUBLICATIONS

RETIREMENT RELOCATION MAGAZINE   **PRINT COST HERE**

❏ *Where to Retire*, one-year subscription, $10.95   _____

RETIREMENT RELOCATION BOOKS

❏ *America's Best Places to Retire* (Includes Undiscovered Havens and Low-Cost Edens), Richard Fox, $14.95   _____

❏ *Choose the Southwest* (Retirement Discoveries for Every Budget), John Howells, $12.95   _____

❏ *Choose Mexico* (Live Well on $600 a Month), John Howells, $12.95   _____

❏ *Choose Costa Rica* (A Guide to Retirement and Investment), John Howells, $13.95   _____

❏ *Choose the Northwest* (Includes Washington, Oregon and British Columbia), John Howells, $12.95   _____

❏ *Where to Retire House Plans* (200 Beautiful and Efficient Designs for Retirement Lifestyles), $5.95   _____

RETIREMENT RELOCATION SPECIAL REPORTS

❏ SR1   How to Plan and Execute a Successful Retirement Relocation, 48 pages, $3.95   _____

❏ SR2   America's Best Neighborhoods for Active Retirees, 64 pages, $3.95   _____

❏ SR4   Should You Retire to a Manufactured Home? 32 pages, $3.95   _____

❏ SR5   Retiring Outside the United States, 48 pages, $3.95   _____

❏ SR8   America's Most Affordable Retirement Towns, 48 pages, $3.95   _____

❏ SR18   Intangibles Taxes, 5 pages, $3.95   _____

❏ MSS   How to Get the Most Out of Your Social Security, 32 pages, $3.95   _____

	Subtotal	_____

Texas residents only add 8.25% sales tax   **Tax**   _____

Add $2.50 postage and handling per book. Add $2.50 total postage and handling
  for any number of Special Reports. Postage included in magazine subscription price.   **Postage**   _____

Total Due   _____

Name_____

Address_____

City, State, Zip_____

Check the appropriate boxes and fill in the price for each title ordered. Total at the bottom. Include your payment and return this order form or a copy to: Vacation Publications, 1502 Augusta Drive, Suite 415, Houston, TX 77057. **For faster service call (800) 338-4962 and order by credit card.**

NOTES